✳ *Highlights* ✳
of this
Study Guide

 Each Chapter of this **Study Guide** includes—

✳ List of **Key Points** & Learning Objectives

✳ Chapter **Introduction**

✳ Easy to Read & Understand, Comprehensive **Outline**

✳ **True-False** Questions

✳ **Fill-In** Questions

✳ **Multiple-Choice** Questions

✳ **Short Essay** Questions

✳ **Issue Spotters**—hypothetical fact problems & black letter law questions on key issues

✳ **Special Information for CPA Candidates**

✳ Most Chapters of this **Study Guide** include one or more questions based on past **CPA Exam Questions**

✳ Each Unit of this **Study Guide** ends with a **Cumulative Hypothetical** and corresponding **Multiple-Choice** Questions

✳ This **Study Guide** also contains an **Answer Appendix** with answers to all of the Questions & explanations of the Answers

Study Guide

to Accompany
West's Business Law

Text
Cases
Legal, Ethical, International, and
E-Commerce Environment

EIGHTH EDITION

Guide prepared by

William Eric Hollowell
Member of
   U.S. Supreme Court Bar
   Minnesota State Bar
   Florida State Bar

Roger LeRoy Miller
Institute for University Studies
Arlington, Texas

WEST
THOMSON LEARNING

Australia · Canada · Mexico · Singapore · Spain · United Kingdom · United States

WEST

THOMSON LEARNING

STUDY GUIDE TO ACCOMPANY WEST'S BUSINESS LAW:
TEXT, CASES, LEGAL, ETHICAL, INTERNATIONAL, AND E-COMMERCE ENVIRONMENT
by Kenneth W. Clarkson, Roger LeRoy Miller, Gaylord A. Jentz and Frank B. Cross

Vice President/Team Director
Jack Calhoun

Senior Acquisitions Editor
Rob Dewey

Senior Developmental Editor
Jan Lamar

Marketing Manager
Mike Worls

Production Editor
Bill Stryker

Manufacturing Coordinator
Charlene Taylor

Printer
Globus Printing Company

Table of Contents

Preface

To the Student

This *Study Guide* is designed to help you read and understand *West's Business Law*, **Eighth Edition**.

How this Study Guide Can Help You

This study guide can help you maximize your learning, subject to the constraints and the amount of time you can allot to this course. There are at least six specific ways in which you can benefit from using this guide.

1. This study guide can help you concentrate on the *crucial topics* in each chapter.

2. If you are forced to miss a class, you can use this study guide to help you learn the material discussed in your absence.

3. There is a possibility that the questions that you are required to answer in this study guide are representative of the types of questions that you will be asked during examinations.

4. You can use this study guide to help you review for examinations.

5. This study guide can help you decide whether you really understand the material. Don't wait until examination time to find out!

6. Finally, the questions in this study guide will help you develop critical thinking skills that you can use in other classes and throughout your career.

The Contents of this *Study Guide*

Business law sometimes is considered a difficult subject because it uses a specialized vocabulary and also takes most people much time and effort to learn. Those who work with and teach business law believe that the subject matter is exciting and definitely worthy of your efforts. Your text, *West's Business Law*, **Eighth Edition**, and this student learning guide have been written for the precise purpose of helping you learn the most important aspects of business law. We always try to keep you, the student, in mind.

Every chapter includes the following sections:

1. **Key Points:** From five "key points" are presented to you. By the time you finish studying each chapter you should be able to "pass" each checkpoint.

2.   Introduction: You are introduced to the main subject matter of each chapter in this section titled: What this Chapter Is About.

3.   Chapter Outline: Using an outline format, the salient points in each chapter are presented.

4.   True-False Questions: Ten true-false questions are included for each chapter. Generally, these questions test knowledge of terminology and principles. The answers are given at the back of the book. Whenever an answer is false, the reasons why it is false are presented at the back of the book also.

5.   Fill-in Questions: Here you are asked to choose between two alternatives for each space that needs to be filled in. Answers are included at the back of the book.

6.   Multiple-Choice Questions: Multiple-choice questions are given for each chapter. The answers, along with an explanation, are included at the back of this book.

7.   Short Essay Questions: Two essay questions are presented for each chapter.

8.   Issue Spotters: These questions alert you to certain principles within the chapter. Brief answers to these questions are included at the end of this text.

9.   Special Information for CPA Candidates: This section alerts CPA candidates to principles within the chapter that are of special importance for the CPA exam and includes study tips of particular utility to these students.

How to Use This Study Guide

What follows is a recommended strategy for improving your grade in your business law class. It may seem like a lot of work, but the payoffs will be high. Try the entire program for the first three or four chapters. If you then feel you can skip some steps safely, try doing so and see what happens.

For each chapter we recommend you follow the sequence of steps below:

1.   Read the Key Points, Introduction, Chapter Outline, and Issue Spotters.

**2.   Read about half the textbook chapter (unless it is very long), being sure to underline only the most important topics (which you should be able to recognize after having read no more than two chapter outlines in this study guide). Put a check mark by the material that you do not understand.

**3.   If you find the textbook's chapter easy to understand, you might want to finish reading it. Otherwise, rest for a sufficient period before you read the second half of the chapter. Again, be sure to underline only the most important points and to put a check mark by the material you find difficult to understand.

**4.   After you have completed the entire textbook chapter, take a break. Then read only what you have underlined throughout the entire chapter.

**5.   Now concentrate on the difficult material, for which you have left check marks. Reread this material and *think about it*; you will find that it is very exciting to figure out difficult material on your own.

6.   Now reread the Issue Spotters. Answer them in the book and compare your answers with those at the back of this book. Next, do the True-False Questions, Fill-In Questions, and Multiple-Choice Questions. Compare your answers with those at the back of this book. Make a note of the questions you have missed and find the pages in your textbook upon which these questions are based. If you still don't understand, ask your instructor.

Now reread the Key Points and see if you have mastered all of the points.

7.   If you still have time, do one or both of the essay questions.

8.   Before your examination, study your class notes. Then review the chapter outline in the text and write out your answers to the Issue Spotters in the study guide again. Reread the Key Points and Chapter Outline in this study guide, then redo all of the questions within each chapter. Compare your answers with the answers at the back of this study guide. Identify your problem areas and reread the relevant pages in *West's Business Law*, **Eighth Edition**. Think through the answers on your own.

If you have followed the strategy outlined above, you should feel sufficiently confident and be relaxed enough to do well on your exam.

Study Skills for *West's Business Law*, Eighth Edition

Every student has a different way to study. We give several study hints below that we think will help any student to better master the textbook *West's Business Law*, **Eighth Edition**. These skills involve outlining, marking, taking notes, and summarizing. You may not need to use all these skills. Nonetheless, if you do improve your ability to use them, you will be able to understand more easily the information in *West's Business Law*, **Eighth Edition**.

MAKING AN OUTLINE

An outline is simply a method for organizing information. The reason an outline can be helpful is that it shows how concepts relate to each other. Outlining can be done as part of your reading or at the end of your reading, or as a rereading of each section within a chapter before you go on to the next section. Even if you do not believe that you need to outline, our experience has been that the act of *physically* writing an outline for a chapter helps most students to improve greatly their ability to retain the material in *West's Business Law*, **Eighth Edition**, and master it, thereby obtaining a higher grade in the class, with less effort.

To make an effective outline you have to be selective. Outlines that contain all the information in the text are not very useful. Your objective in outlining is to identify main concepts and to subordinate details to those main concepts. Therefore, your first goal is to *identify the main concepts in each section*. Often the large first-level headings within your textbook are sufficient as identifiers of the major concepts within each section. You may decide, however, that you want to phrase an identifier in a way that is more meaningful to you. In any event, your outline should consist of several levels written in a standard outline format. The most important concepts are assigned a roman numeral; the second most important a capital letter; the third most important, numbers; and the fourth most important, lower-case letters. Even if you make an outline that is no more than the headings in the text, you will be studying more efficiently than you would be otherwise. As we stated above, the process of physically writing the words will help you master the material.

MARKING A TEXT

From kindergarten through high school you typically did not own your own textbooks. They were made available by the school system. You were told not to mark in them. Now that you own your own text for a course, your learning can be greatly improved by marking your text. There is a trade-off here. The more you mark up your textbook, the less you will receive from your bookstore when you sell it back at the end of the semester. The benefit is a better understanding of the subject matter, and the cost is the reduction in the price you receive for the resale of the text. Additionally, if you want a text that you can mark with your own notations, you necessarily have to buy a new one or a used one that has no markings. Both carry a higher price tag than a used textbook with markings. Again there is a trade-off.

Different Ways of Marking The most commonly used form of marking is to underline important points. The second most commonly used method is to use a felt-tipped highlighter, or marker, in yellow or some other transparent color. Marking also includes circling, numbering, using arrows, brief notes, or any other method that allows you to remember things when you go back to skim the pages in your textbook prior to an exam.

Why Marking is Important Marking is important for the same reason that outlining is—it helps you to organize better the information in the text. It allows you to become an *active* participant in the mastery of the material. Researchers have shown that the physical act of marking, just like the physical act of outlining, helps you better retain the material. The better the material is organized in your mind, the more you will remember. There are two types of readers—passive and active. The active reader outlines and/or marks. Active readers typically do better on exams. Perhaps one of the reasons that active readers retain more is because the physical act of outlining and/or marking requires greater concentration. It is through greater concentration that more is remembered.

Points to Remember When Marking

1. Read one section at a time before you do any extensive marking. You can't mark a section until you know what is important and you can't know what is important until you read the whole section.

2. Don't over mark. Just as an outline cannot contain everything that is in a text (or in a lecture), marking can't be of the whole book. Don't fool yourself into thinking you've done a good job just because each page is filled up with arrows, asterisks, circles, and underlines. When you go back to review the material you won't remember what was important. The key is *selective* activity. Mark each page in a way that allows you to see the most important points at a glance. You can follow up your marking by writing out more in your subject outline.

SUMMARIZING THE MATERIAL

Even if each chapter has a chapter summary, it is still worthwhile for you to make your own summary points. The reason is that the more active you are as a reader, the better you will understand the material.

Summarization helps you in your reading comprehension. It is the final step in reviewing the book. There is probably nothing else you can do that works as well to help you remember what your textbook has to say.

The importance of summarization is that the notes you make are in your own words, not in the words of the author. Writing down a summary in your own words is the most effective use of your time. This allows you to process the information into your own memory by being required to think about it. You also have to make it part of your vocabulary. Whenever you cannot state important legal concepts in your own words, you probably haven't understood the concepts necessary to master the material. Indeed, summary notes are a good way to determine whether you have actually understood something. Don't simply make a mechanical listing of quotes taken right out of the textbook. Rather, you should make summary notes using complete sentences with correct grammar. This forces you to develop your ideas logically and clearly. Also, summary notes written in this matter can be more easily remembered.

Be Brief. Your notes should condense the information in the text into statements that summarize the concepts. It is when you force yourself to make the statements brief that you best learn the material. By making only brief summary notes, you have to think about the essence of each concept and present it in a form that is compact enough to remember. You should typically have no more than a one-paragraph summary for each important topic in the chapter.

What Format to Use? The authors find that using 5" x 8" cards is the best way to take summary notes. Don't fill up each note card. You need to leave room to make additional notes later on when you are reviewing for the final exam. That is to say, leave margins for further notes and study markings. Additionally, if you leave enough room, you can integrate the notes that you take during lectures on to these summary note cards.

Another reason to place your summary notes on 5" x 8" cards is because in so doing you have a set of flash cards that you can use in studying for a final exam.

HOW TO STUDY AND TAKE EXAMS

There is basically one reason why you have purchased this *Study Guide*—to improve your exam grade. By using this study guide assiduously, you will have the confidence to take your mid-terms and final examinations and to do well. The study guide, however, should not just be used a day before each exam. Rather, the guide is most helpful if you use it at the time that you read the chapter. That is to say, after you read a chapter in *West's Business Law,* **Eighth Edition,** you should directly go to the appropriate chapter in the study guide. This systematic review technique is the most effective study technique you can use.

Besides learning the concepts in each chapter as well as possible, there are additional strategies for taking exams. You need to know in advance what type of exam you are going to take—essay or objective or both. You need to know which reading materials and lectures will be covered. For both objective and essay exams (but more importantly for the former) you need to know if there is a penalty for guessing incorrectly. If there is, your strategy will be different: you will usually only mark what you are certain of. Finally, you need to know how much time will be allowed for the exam.

FOLLOWING DIRECTIONS

Students are often in a hurry to start an exam so they take little time to read the instructions. The instructions can be critical, however. In a multiple-choice exam, for example, if there is no indication that there is a penalty for guessing, then you should never leave a question unanswered. Even if there only remains a few minutes at the end of the exam, you should guess for those questions about which you are uncertain.

Additionally, you need to know the weight given to each section of an exam. In a typical multiple-choice exam, all questions have equal weight. In some exams, particularly those involving essay questions, different parts of the exam carry different weights. You should use these weights to apportion your time accordingly. If an essay part of an exam accounts for only 20 percent of the total points on the exam, you should not spend 60 percent of your time on the essay.

You need to make sure you are answering the question correctly. Some exams require a No. 2 lead pencil to fill in the dots on a machine-graded answer sheet. Other exams require underlining or circling. In short, you have to look at the instructions carefully.

Lastly, check to make sure that you have all the pages of the examination. If you are uncertain, ask the instructor or the exam proctor. It is hard to justify not having done your exam correctly because you failed to answer all the questions. Simply stating that you did not have them will pose a problem for both you and your instructor. Don't take a chance. Double check to make sure.

TAKING OBJECTIVE EXAMINATIONS

The most important point to discover initially with any objective test is if there is a penalty for guessing. If there is none, you have nothing to lose by guessing. In contrast, if a half-point is subtracted for each incorrect answer, then you probably should not answer any question for which you are purely guessing.

Students usually commit one of two errors when they read objective-exam questions: (1) they read into the questions things that don't exist, or (2) they skip over words or phrases.

Most test questions include key words such as:

- all
- always
- never
- only

If you miss these key words you will be missing the "trick" part of the question. Also, you must look for questions that are only *partly* correct, particularly if you are answering true/false questions.

Never answer a question without reading all of the alternatives. More than one of them may be correct. If more than one of them seems correct, make sure you select the answer that seems the most correct.

Whenever the answer to an objective question is not obvious, start with the process of elimination. Throw out the answers that are clearly incorrect. Even with objective exams in which there is a penalty for guessing, if you can throw out several obviously incorrect answers, then you may wish to guess among the remaining ones because your probability of choosing the correct answer is high.

Typically, the easiest way to eliminate incorrect answers is to look for those that are meaningless, illogical, or inconsistent. Often test authors put in choices that make perfect sense and are indeed true, but they are not the answer to the question under study.

WRITING ESSAY EXAMS

To write an essay exam, you should be prepared. One way of being prepared is to practice writing timed essays. In other words, find out in advance how much time you will have for each essay question, say 15 minutes, and then practice writing an answer to a sample essay question during a 15-minute time period. This is the only way you will develop the skills needed to pace yourself for an essay exam. Do your timed essay practice without using the book, since most essay exams are closed book.

Usually you can anticipate certain essay exam questions. You do this by going over the major concept headings, either in your lecture notes or in your text; search for the themes that tie the materials together and then think about questions that your instructor might ask you. You might even list possible essay questions as a review device; then write a short outline for each of those most likely questions.

As with objective exams, you need to read the directions to the essay questions carefully. It's best to write out a brief outline *before* you start writing. The outline should present your conclusion in one or two sentences, then your supporting argument. It is important to stay on the subject. We can tell you from first hand experience that no instructor likes to read answers to unasked questions.

Finally, make a strong attempt to write legibly. Again speaking from experience, we can tell you that it's easier to be favorably inclined to a student's essay if we don't have to reread it five times to decipher the handwriting.

xiv PREFACE

Acknowledgments

We wish to thank Suzanne Jasin of K & M Consulting for her expert design and composition of this guide.

We welcome comments and criticisms to help us make this guide even more useful. All errors are our sole responsibility.

W. E. H.
R. L. M.

Chapter 1
Introduction to Law and Legal Reasoning

WHAT THIS CHAPTER IS ABOUT

The first chapters in Unit 1 provide the background for the entire course. Chapter 1 sets the stage. From this chapter, you must understand that (1) the law is a set of general rules, (2) in applying these general rules, a judge cannot fit a case to suit a rule, but must fit (or find) a rule to suit the case, and (3) in fitting (or finding) a rule, a judge must also supply reasons for the decision.

CHAPTER OUTLINE

I. **WHAT IS LAW?**
Law consists of enforceable rules governing relationships among individuals and between individuals and their society.

A. **THE NATURAL LAW SCHOOL**
Natural law is a system of moral and ethical principles that are believed to be inherent in human nature and discoverable by humans through the use of their natural intelligence.

B. **THE POSITIVIST SCHOOL**
Legal positivists believe that there is no higher law than a nation's positive law (the law created by a particular society at a particular point in time). The law is the law and must be obeyed.

C. **THE HISTORICAL SCHOOL**
Followers of this school focus on legal principles that have been applied in past cases, emphasizing that those principles should be applied strictly in present cases.

D. LEGAL REALISM

Legal realists believe that in making decisions, judges are influenced by their own beliefs, the application of principles should be tempered by each case's circumstances, and extra-legal sources should be consulted.

E. JUDICIAL INTERPRETATION OF THE LAW

Judges interpret and apply the law. When the law is expressed in general terms, there is some flexibility in interpreting it. This interpretation can be influenced by a judge's personal philosophy.

II. THE COMMON LAW TRADITION

The American legal system, based on the decisions judges make in cases, is a **common law** system, which involves the application of principles applied in earlier cases with similar facts. This system comes from early English courts, which made a distinction between remedies at law and remedies in equity.

A. REMEDIES AT LAW AND REMEDIES IN EQUITY

As a rule, courts grant an equitable remedy only if the remedy at law is inadequate.

1. Remedies at Law

Remedies at law include awards of land, money, and items of value. A jury trial is available only in an action at law.

2. Remedies in Equity

Remedies in equity include decrees of specific performance, injunctions, and rescission. Decisions to award equitable remedies are guided by equitable maxims.

B. THE DOCTRINE OF *STARE DECISIS*

The use of precedent in a common law system is the doctrine of ***stare decisis***. *Stare decisis* makes the legal system more efficient, just, uniform, stable, and predictable.

1. When There Is No Precedent

When there is no precedent, a court may look at other legal principles and policies, social values, or scientific data.

2. When a Precedent Is Incorrect

A judge may decide that a precedent is incorrect if there have been changes in technology, business practices, or society's attitudes.

C. LEGAL REASONING

1. Issue-Rule-Application-Conclusion (IRAC)

Legal reasoning requires learning the facts of a case, identifying the issues and the relevant legal rules, applying the rules to the facts, and coming to a conclusion.

2. Forms of Legal Reasoning

In applying an old precedent or establishing a new one, judges use many forms of reasoning—**deductive reasoning, linear reasoning,** reasoning by **analogy,** and others—to harmonize theirs decisions with earlier cases.

III.　SOURCES OF AMERICAN LAW

A.　CONSTITUTIONAL LAW
The U.S. Constitution distributes power among the branches of government. It is the supreme law of the land. Any law that conflicts with it is invalid. The states also have constitutions, but the federal constitution prevails.

B.　STATUTORY LAW
Statutes and ordinances are enacted by Congress and by state and local legislative bodies. Uniform laws (such as the Uniform Commercial Code) and model codes are created by panels of experts and scholars and adopted at the option of each state's legislature.

C.　ADMINISTRATIVE LAW
Administrative law consists of the rules and regulations issued by administrative agencies, which derive their authority from the legislative and executive branches of government.

D.　CASE LAW
Case law includes courts' interpretations of constitutional provisions, statutes, and administrative rules. Because statutes often codify common law rules, courts often rely on the common law as a guide to the intent and purpose of a statute. Case law governs all areas not covered by statutes.

IV.　CLASSIFICATIONS OF LAW

A.　SUBSTANTIVE AND PROCEDURAL LAW
Substantive law includes laws that define, describe, regulate, and create rights and duties. *Procedural law* includes rules for enforcing those rights.

B.　CRIMINAL AND CIVIL LAW
Criminal law regulates relationships between individuals and society. *Civil law* regulates relationships between individuals.

C.　PRIVATE AND PUBLIC LAW
Private law concerns relationships between private entities. *Public law* addresses the relationship between persons and their government.

V.　HOW TO FIND PRIMARY SOURCES OF THE LAW

A.　FINDING STATUTORY LAW

1.　Publication of Statutes
Federal statutes are arranged by date of enactment in *United States Statutes at Large*. State statutes are collected in similar state publications. Statutes are also published in codified form (the form in which they appear in the federal and state codes) in other publications.

2.　Finding a Statute in a Publication
Statutes are usually referred to in their codified form. In the codes, laws are compiled by subject. For example, the *United States Code* (U.S.C.) arranges by subject most federal laws. Each subject is assigned a title number and each statute a section number within a title.

B.　FINDING ADMINISTRATIVE LAW

1. **Publication of Rules and Regulations**
   Rules and regulations adopted by federal administrative agencies are published initially in the *Federal Register*. They are also compiled by subject in the *Code of Federal Regulations* (C.F.R.).

2. **Finding a Rule or Regulation in a Publication**
   In the C.F.R., rules and regulations are arranged by subject. Each subject is assigned a title number and each rule or regulation a section number within a title.

C. **FINDING CASE LAW**

1. **Publication of Court Opinions**
   State appellate court opinions are often published by the state in consecutively numbered volumes. They may also be published in units of the *National Reporter System*, by West Publishing Company. Federal court opinions appear in other West publications.

2. **Finding a Court Opinion in a Publication**
   After a decision is published, it is usually referred to by the name of the case and the volume, name, and page number of one or more reporters (which are often, but not always, West reporters). This information is called the **citation**.

VI. HOW TO READ AND UNDERSTAND CASE LAW

A. **THE PARTIES**

1. **Plaintiff v. Defendant**
   In the title of a case (*Adams v. Jones*), the *v.* means versus (against). Adams is the plaintiff (the person who filed the suit) and Jones the defendant. Some appellate courts place the name of the party appealing a decision first, so that this case on appeal may be called *Jones v. Adams*.

2. **Appellant v. Appellee**
   The appellant is the party who appeals a case to another court or jurisdiction from the one in which the case was originally brought. An appellant may be referred to as a **petitioner**. The appellee is the party against whom an appeal is taken. An appellee may be referred to as a **respondent**.

B. **THE COURT'S OPINION**
   The opinion contains the court's reasons for its decision, the rules of law that apply, and the judgment.

1. **Unanimous Opinion**
   When more than one judge (or justice) decides a case, and they all agree, a unanimous opinion is written for the whole court.

2. **Majority Opinion**
   If a decision is not unanimous, a majority opinion outlines the views of the majority.

3. **Concurring Opinion**
   A concurring opinion is one in which a judge emphasizes a point that was not emphasized in the unanimous or majority opinion.

4. **Dissenting Opinion**

A dissenting opinion may be written by a judge who does not agree with the majority. A dissent may form the basis of arguments used years later in overruling the majority opinion.

VII. BUSINESSPERSONS AND THE LAW

Although the law is split into different topics to make it easier to study, more than one of those areas of the law can affect individual business decisions.

TRUE-FALSE QUESTIONS

(Answers at the Back of the Book)

____ 1. Law consists of enforceable rules governing relationships among individuals and between individuals and their society.

____ 2. Legal positivists believe that law should reflect universal moral and ethical principles that are part of human nature.

____ 3. *Stare decisis* refers to the practice of deciding new cases with reference to previous decisions.

____ 4. Common law is a term that normally refers to the body of law consisting of rules of law announced in court decisions.

____ 5. Statutes are a primary source of law.

____ 6. Each state's constitution is supreme within each state's borders even if it conflicts with the U.S. Constitution.

____ 7. The Uniform Commercial Code was enacted by Congress for adoption by the states.

____ 8. The civil law regulates relationships between individuals.

____ 9. In most states, the same courts can grant both legal and equitable remedies.

____ 10. A plaintiff is a party who files a suit.

FILL-IN QUESTIONS

(Answers at the Back of the Book)

The common law system, on which the American legal system is based, involves the application of principles applied in earlier cases _____ _____(with similar facts/whether or not the facts are similar). This use of previous case law, or _____ (precedent/preeminent), is known as the doctrine of *stare decisis*, and _____ _____ (emphasizes a flexible/permits a predictable) resolution of cases.

MULTIPLE-CHOICE QUESTIONS

(Answers at the Back of the Book)

____ 1. Adam and Bob are discussing various legal philosophies. Which of the following statements by Adam is FALSE?

a. According to the natural law tradition, the law should reflect universal moral and ethical principles that are part of human nature.
b. Legal positivists believe that there can be no higher law that a nation's positive law.
c. Legal realists believe that the law should be applied the same in all cases in all circumstances.
d. None of the above

____ 2. In a lawsuit between Best Products, Inc., and Computer Data Corporation, a court applies the doctrine of *stare decisis*. This doctrine performs many useful functions, including

a. efficiency, but not stability.
b. stability, but not efficiency.
c. stability and efficiency.
d. none of the above.

____ 3. To resolve a controversy between EZ Service Corporation and First State Bank, a court may consider, in addition to case law, other sources of law, including

a. the U.S. Constitution and state constitutions only.
b. administrative agency rules and regulations only.
c. the U.S. Constitution, state constitutions, and agency rules and regulations.
d. none of the above.

____ 4. In a suit between Mike and his employer, National Supply Company, to apply the doctrine of *stare decisis*, the judge compares the facts in the case to the facts in

a. another case.
b. a hypothetical.
c. the arguments of the parties involved in the case.
d. none of the above.

____ 5. Which of the following is a CORRECT statement about the distinction between law and equity?

a. Equity involves different remedies from those available at law.
b. Most states maintain separate courts of law and equity.
c. Damages may be awarded only in actions in equity.
d. None of the above

____ 6. Kim wants to learn about the coverage of a statute and how the statute is applied. To do so, Kim must

a. only read the statute.
b. only see how courts in his or her jurisdiction have interpreted the statute.
c. read the statute and see how courts in his or her jurisdiction have interpreted it.
d. none of the above.

____ 7. Our common law system involves the application of legal principles applied in earlier cases

    a. with different facts.
    b. with similar facts.
    c. whether or not the facts are similar.
    d. none of the above.

____ 8. The statutory law of the United States includes

    a. the statutes enacted by Congress and state legislatures.
    b. the rules, orders, and decisions of administrative agencies.
    c. both the statutes enacted by Congress and state legislatures and the rules, orders, and decisions of administrative agencies.
    d. none of the above.

____ 9. Matt is a judge. To reason by analogy, Matt compares the facts in one case to

    a. the facts in another case.
    b. the defendant's arguments.
    c. the plaintiff's hypothetical.
    d. none of the above.

____ 10. A common law system is one in which the primary source of law is

    a. case law.
    b. a statutory code.
    c. principles of civility.
    d. principles of equity.

SHORT ESSAY QUESTIONS

1. What is the primary function of law and how does the law accomplish it?

2. What is *stare decisis*? Why is it important?

ISSUE SPOTTERS

(Answers at the Back of the Book)

1. Under what circumstance might a judge rely on case law to determine the intent and purpose of a statute?

2. The First Amendment of the U.S. Constitution protects the free exercise of religion. A state legislature enacts a law that outlaws all religions that do not derive from the Judeo-Christian tradition. Is this state law valid? Why or why not?

3. Where would you find the case that is referred to as "*Hoffman v. Red Owl Stores, Inc.,* 26 Wis.2d 683, 133 N.W.2d 267 (1965)"?

4. In the title of a case (*Jones v. Smith*, for example), is the name on the right (Smith) always the name of the party against whom the suit was brought?

5. What are the different types of opinions that might be issued by a court with more than one judge or justice?

SPECIAL INFORMATION FOR CPA CANDIDATES

Those students planning to sit for the CPA examination will find it most helpful to learn, from the introductory material in this chapter, the terms that designate the different parties to a lawsuit. The general background provided in this chapter is, of course, helpful in understanding the specific concepts and principles set out in subsequent chapters. For that reason—and because much of that material includes information that a successful CPA candidate is expected to know—the background in this chapter is important.

Regarding general preparation for the examination—or for any exam, including ones in this course—CPA candidates and other students may find it helpful to review the significant material weekly. For concepts and principles that will be tested, some students find it helpful to make flashcards. Those cards can be reviewed weekly, together with whatever notes have been taken, and the relevant sections of this study guide.

Chapter 2
Courts and Alternative Dispute Resolution

WHAT THIS CHAPTER IS ABOUT

This chapter explains which courts have power to hear what disputes and when. The chapter also covers alternative dispute resolution—alternatives to litigation that can be as binding to the parties as a court decree.

CHAPTER OUTLINE

I. **THE JUDICIARY'S ROLE IN AMERICAN GOVERNMENT**
The power of **judicial review**: the courts can decide whether the laws or actions of the executive branch and the legislative branch are constitutional.

II. **BASIC JUDICIAL REQUIREMENTS**

A. **JURISDICTION**
To hear a case, a court must have jurisdiction over (1) the defendant or the property involved and (2) the subject matter.

1. **Jurisdiction over Persons or Property**
A court has *in personam* (personal) jurisdiction over state residents. Long arm statutes permit courts to exercise jurisdiction over nonresidents who have *minimum contacts* with the state (e.g., do business there). A court has *in rem* jurisdiction over property within its borders.

2. **Jurisdiction over Subject Matter**
A court of **general jurisdiction** can decide virtually any type of case. A court's jurisdiction may be **limited** by the subject of a suit, the amount of money in controversy, or whether a proceeding is a trial or appeal.

3. **Jurisdiction of the Federal Courts**

a. **Federal Questions**

Any suit based on the Constitution, a treaty, or a federal law can originate in a federal court.

b. **Diversity of Citizenship**

Federal jurisdiction covers cases involving (1) citizens of different states, (2) a foreign government and citizens of a state or of different states, or (3) citizens of a state and citizens or subjects of a foreign government. The amount in controversy must be more than $75,000.

4. **Exclusive v. Concurrent Jurisdiction**

Exclusive: when cases can be tried only in federal courts or only in state courts. Concurrent: When both federal and state courts can hear a case.

B. **VENUE**

Venue is concerned with the most appropriate location for a trial.

C. **STANDING TO SUE**

Standing is the interest (injury or threat) that a plaintiff has in a case. A plaintiff must have standing to bring a suit, and the controversy must be **justiciable** (real, as opposed to hypothetical or purely academic).

III. THE STATE AND FEDERAL COURT SYSTEMS

A. **STATE COURT SYSTEMS**

1. **Trial Courts**

Trial courts are courts in which trials are held and testimony is taken.

2. **Courts of Appeals**

Courts that hear appeals from trial courts look at *questions of law* (what law governs a dispute) but not *questions of fact* (what occurred in the dispute), unless a trial court's finding of fact is clearly contrary to the evidence. Decision of a state's highest court on state law is final.

B. **THE FEDERAL COURT SYSTEM**

1. **U.S. District Courts**

The federal equivalent of a state trial court of general jurisdiction. There is at least one federal district court in every state. Other federal trial courts include the U.S. Tax Court and the U.S. Bankruptcy Court.

2. **U.S. Courts of Appeals**

The U.S. (circuit) courts of appeals for twelve of the circuits hear appeals from the federal district courts located within their respective circuits. The court of appeals for the thirteenth circuit (the federal circuit) has national jurisdiction over certain cases.

3. **United States Supreme Court**

The highest level of the federal court system. The Supreme Court can review any case decided by any of the federal courts of appeals, and it has authority over some cases decided in state courts.

4. **How Cases Reach the Supreme Court**

To appeal a case to the Supreme Court, a party asks for a writ of *certiorari*. Whether the Court issues the writ is within its discretion.

IV. ALTERNATIVE DISPUTE RESOLUTION (ADR)

A. NEGOTIATION

Parties come together informally, with or without attorneys, to try to settle or resolve their differences without involving independent third parties. Forms of ADR associated with negotiation include—

1. Mini-trial

A private proceeding in which attorneys briefly argue each party's case. A third party indicates how a court would likely decide the issue.

2. Early Neutral Case Evaluation

Parties select a neutral third party (generally an expert) to evaluate their positions, with no hearing and no discovery. The evaluation is a basis for negotiating a settlement.

3. Summary Jury Trial (SJT)

Like a mini-trial, but a jury renders a nonbinding verdict. Negotiations follow. If no settlement is reached, either side can seek a full trial.

4. Conciliation

A conciliator assists disputing parties in negotiating, communicating offers, etc. Conciliators sometimes recommend solutions.

B. MEDIATION

Parties come together informally with a mediator, who is expected to propose solutions. A mediator is often an expert in a particular field.

C. ARBITRATION

An arbitrator—the third party hearing the dispute—decides the dispute. If the parties agree, the decision may be legally binding.

1. Arbitration and the Courts

Many courts require parties to try to settle their differences through arbitration before going to trial. The arbitrator's decision is not binding—if either party rejects the award, the case goes to trial.

2. The Arbitration Process

At an arbitration hearing, the parties make their arguments, present evidence, and call and examine witnesses, and the arbitrator makes a decision. The decision is called an **award**, even if no money is involved.

3. Arbitration Clauses

Disputes are often arbitrated because of an arbitration clause in a contract entered into before the dispute. Courts enforce such clauses.

4. Arbitration Statutes

Most states have statutes under which arbitration clauses are enforced. The Federal Arbitration Act (FAA) enforces arbitration clauses in contracts involving interstate commerce.

D. PROVIDERS OF ADR SERVICES

ADR services are provided by government agencies and private organizations, such as the American Arbitration Association and JAMS/Endispute.

TRUE-FALSE QUESTIONS

(Answers at the Back of the Book)

____ 1. Under a long arm statute, a state court can compel someone outside the state to appear in the court.

____ 2. A court that has jurisdiction always has venue.

____ 3. The decisions of a state's highest court on all questions of state law are final.

____ 4. Federal district courts have original jurisdiction in federal matters.

____ 5. A federal court may refuse to enforce a state statute that violates the U.S. Constitution.

____ 6. The U.S. Constitution set the basis for the jurisdiction of the federal courts.

____ 7. The United States Supreme Court has only original (not appellate) jurisdiction.

____ 8. The jury verdict, in a summary jury trial, is binding.

____ 9. A major similarity between negotiation and mediation is that no third parties are involved.

____ 10. In binding arbitration, an arbitrator's decision is usually the final word.

FILL-IN QUESTIONS

(Answers at the Back of the Book)

Courts of original jurisdiction are _____ (trial/reviewing) courts. Courts of appellate jurisdiction are _____ (trial/reviewing) courts. Trial courts resolve disputes through determining _____ (factual issues/the law) and applying _____ (the facts to the law/ the law to the facts). Reviewing courts most commonly reverse cases on the basis of errors _____ (of law but not of fact/of fact and of law) committed by lower courts within the same system.

MULTIPLE-CHOICE QUESTIONS

(Answers at the Back of the Book)

____ 1. National Computers, Inc., was incorporated in Delaware, has its main office in California, and does business in New York. National is subject to the jurisdiction of

a. Delaware, California, or New York.
b. Delaware or California, but not New York.
c. Delaware or New York, but not California.
d. California or New York, but not Delaware.

____ 2. In a suit filed by General Distributors, Inc., against First National Bank, the defendant seeks a change of venue. Venue concerns

a. the appropriate location for bringing a case.
b. *in personam* jurisdiction.
c. standing.
d. subject-matter jurisdiction.

____ 3. Alpha, Inc., sued Beta, Inc., in state court. Alpha loses and files an appeal with the state appeals court. The appeals court will

a. not retry the case, because the appropriate place for the retrial of a state case is a federal court.
b. not retry the case, because an appeals court examines the record of a case, looking at questions of law and procedure for errors by the trial court.
c. retry the case, because after a case is tried a party has a right to an appeal.
d. retry the case, because Alpha and Beta disagree on the result of the trial.

____ 4. Randy wants to file a suit against Standard Products Corporation in a federal court. A suit can be brought in a federal court if it involves

a. a question under the Constitution, a treaty, or a federal law.
b. citizens of different states, a foreign country and an American citizen, or a foreign citizen and an American citizen, and the amount in controversy is more than $75,000.
c. either a or b.
d. none of the above.

____ 5. Concurrent jurisdiction exists when the power to hear a case is in

a. a state court only.
b. a federal court only.
c. both a state court and a federal court.
d. none of the above.

____ 6. Best Tools, Inc., manufactures a defective tool. Carl, a consumer, can sue Best

a. if Carl suffers an injury because of the defect.
b. solely on the ground that the tool is defective.
c. solely on the ground that the tool is defective or if Carl suffers an injury because of the defect.
d. none of the above.

____ 7. Ann sues Carla in a state trial court. Ann loses the suit. If Ann wants to appeal, the most appropriate court in which to file the appeal is

a. the state appellate court.
b. the nearest federal district court.
c. the nearest federal court of appeals.
d. the United States Supreme Court.

____   **8.**   Paul and Diane submit their dispute to binding arbitration.   A court can set aside the arbitrator's award if

   a.   the award involves at least $75,000.
   b.   the award violates public policy.
   c.   Paul is not satisfied with the award.
   d.   Diane is not satisfied with the award.

____   **9.**   Red Ball Shoes, Inc., and International Exporting Corporation submit their dispute to arbitration. Arbitration is the settling of a dispute

   a.   by an impartial third party.
   b.   that must involve less than $75,000.
   c.   that arises only from a contract in writing.
   d.   none of the above.

____   **10.**   Regional Transport Company and Midwest Trucking, Inc., submit their dispute to mediation. Mediation is the settling of a dispute

   a.   by an impartial third party.
   b.   that must involve less than $75,000.
   c.   that arises only from a contract in writing.
   d.   none of the above.

SHORT ESSAY QUESTIONS

1.   What is jurisdiction? How does jurisdiction over a person or property differ from subject matter jurisdiction?

2.   What does a long arm statute do?

ISSUE SPOTTERS

(Answers at the Back of the Book)

1.   Ron wants to sue Art's Supply Company for Art's failure to deliver supplies that Ron needed to prepare his work for an appearance at a local Artists Fair. What must Ron establish before a court will hear the suit?

2.   Carlos, a citizen of California, is injured in an automobile accident in Arizona. Alex, the driver of the other car, is a citizen of New Mexico. Carlos wants Alex to pay Carlos's $125,000 in medical expenses and car repairs. Can Carlos sue in federal court?

3.   Jay is fired from his job and sues his employer. Jay loses the trial, and he appeals. The reviewing court affirms the decision of the trial court. Jay wants to appeal to the United States Supreme Court. Can the Supreme Court refuse to hear the case?

4.   What are the advantages of resolving disputes outside the courts?

5.   Beth rents an apartment from Jane. When they dispute the payment of $200 in back rent, they get together, discuss the matter, and compromise with a payment of $100. What is the basic difference between their negotiation and litigation?

SPECIAL INFORMATION FOR CPA CANDIDATES

The procedural steps in a civil trial in an American court are not specifically tested on the CPA examination. A general understanding of the legal system will prove helpful, however, to comprehending other materials that are tested on the exam. In particular, understanding the procedural course of a trial will help in reading the case excerpts in this textbook and in understanding the course of trials and judgments in general.

Chapter 3
Court Procedures

WHAT THIS CHAPTER IS ABOUT

After the decision to take a dispute to court, one of the most important parts of the judicial process is the application of procedural rules in the case. The goal of this chapter is to outline what happens before, during, and after a civil trial.

CHAPTER OUTLINE

I. PROCEDURAL RULES
The Federal Rules of Civil Procedure govern trials in federal district court. Each state has its own rules of procedure that apply in its courts, as well as to the federal courts within the state.

II. CONSULTING WITH AN ATTORNEY
The time and expense of litigation are important considerations when deciding what legal course to pursue. Attorney fees can be fixed, may accrue on an hourly or a contingency basis, or may be set by a judge.

III. PRETRIAL PROCEDURES

A. THE PLEADINGS
The pleadings inform each party of the claims of the other and specify the issues in the case. They include the complaint and answer (and counterclaim and reply).

1. **The Plaintiff's Complaint**
   Filed by the plaintiff with the clerk of the trial court (with the proper venue). The complaint contains (1) a statement alleging the facts necessary for the court to take jurisdiction, (2) a short statement of the facts necessary to show that the plaintiff is entitled to a remedy, and (3) a statement of the remedy the plaintiff is seeking.

2. **Service of Process**
   The complaint is delivered to the defendant, with a summons. The summons tells the defendant to answer the complaint and file a copy of

the answer with the court and the plaintiff within a specified time (usually twenty to thirty days). Corporations receive service through their officers or registered agents.

3. **The Defendant's Response**

   a. **Answer**
      An answer admits the allegations in the complaint or denies them and sets out any defenses.

      1) **Affirmative Defense**
         Exists when the defendant admits the truth of the complaint but raises new facts to dismiss the action (for example, the time period for raising the claim has passed).

      2) **Counterclaim**
         The defendant's claim against the plaintiff, who will have to answer it with a **reply**, which has the same characteristics as an answer.

   b. **Motion to Dismiss**
      This motion alleges that even if the facts in the complaint are true, their legal consequences are such that there is no reason to go on with the suit and no need for the defendant to present an answer.

      1) **Denial of the Motion**
         If the court denies the motion, and the defendant does not file a further pleading, a judgment will be entered for the plaintiff.

      2) **Grant of the Motion**
         If the court grants the motion, the defendant is not required to answer the complaint. If the plaintiff does not file an amended complaint, a judgment will be entered for the defendant.

   c. **No Response**
      Results in a default judgment for the plaintiff (who is awarded the relief sought in the complaint).

B. **DISMISSALS AND JUDGMENTS BEFORE TRIAL**

   1. **Motion to Dismiss**
      (See above.) Either party may file a motion to dismiss if they have agreed to settle the case. A court may file such a motion on its own.

   2. **Motion for Judgment on the Pleadings**
      Any party can file this motion (after the complaint, answer, and any counterclaim and reply have been filed), when no facts are disputed and only questions of law are at issue. A court may consider only those facts stated in the pleadings.

   3. **Motion for Summary Judgment**
      Any party can file this motion, if there is no disagreement about the facts and the only question is which laws apply to those facts. A court can consider evidence outside the pleadings (for example, sworn statements by witnesses).

C. DISCOVERY

1. What Discovery Is

The process of obtaining information from the opposing party or from witnesses. Privileged material is safeguarded and only relevant matters are discoverable.

a. Depositions

Sworn testimony, recorded by a court official. Can be used as testimony, if a witness is unavailable, or to impeach (challenge the credibility of) a party or witness who testifies differently at trial.

b. Interrogatories

A series of written questions for which written answers are prepared and signed under oath. Interrogatories are directed to the plaintiff or the defendant.

c. Request for Admissions

A written request to a party for an admission of the truth of matters relating to the trial. Any matter admitted is considered to be true.

d. Request for Documents, Objects, and Entry on Land

A written request to examine documents and other items not in the party's possession.

e. Request for Examinations

Granted when a party's physical or mental condition is in question.

2. What Discovery Does

Allows both parties to learn as much as they can about what to expect at a trial and helps to narrow the issues so that trial time is spent on the main questions.

D. PRETRIAL CONFERENCE

After discovery, the attorneys may meet with the judge to discuss resolving the case or at least to clarify the issues and agree on such things as the number of expert witnesses or the admissibility of certain types of evidence.

E. JURIES

1. Right to a Jury Trial

The Seventh Amendment to the U.S. Constitution guarantees the right to a jury trial for cases at law in federal courts when the amount in controversy exceeds $20. Most states have similar guarantees in their own constitutions (with a higher dollar-amount). The right to a trial by jury does not have to be exercised.

2. Jury Selection

Most civil matters can be heard by six-person juries. Some trials must be heard by twelve persons.

a. *Voir Dire*

The process by which a jury is selected. The parties' attorneys ask prospective jurors questions to determine whether any are biased or have a connection with a party or a witness.

b. Challenges

1) Peremptory Challenge
Asking, without providing a reason, that an individual not be sworn in as a juror.

2) Challenge for Cause
Asking, for a specific reason, that an individual not be sworn in as a juror.

IV. THE TRIAL

A. OPENING STATEMENTS
Each side sets out briefly his or her version of the facts and outlines the evidence that will be presented. The plaintiff goes first.

B. PRESENTATION OF EVIDENCE

1. Burden of Proof
In a civil case, a plaintiff must prove his or her case by a **preponderance of the evidence** (the claim is more likely to be true than the defendant's). Some claims (such as fraud) must be proved by **clear and convincing evidence** (the truth of the claim is highly probable). Evidence includes the testimony of witnesses.

2. Admissible Evidence
Evidence that is relevant to the matter in question (tends to prove or disprove a fact in question or to establish that a fact or action is more probable or less probable than it would be without the evidence).

3. Inadmissible Evidence
Relevant evidence whose probative value is substantially outweighed by other considerations (the issue has been proved or disproved, or the evidence would mislead the jury, or cause the jury to decide the issue on an emotional basis). Hearsay is not admissible.

4. Examination of Witnesses

a. Plaintiff's Side of the Case
After the opening statements, the plaintiff calls and questions the first witness (direct examination); the defendant questions the witness (cross-examination); the plaintiff questions the witness again (redirect examination); the defendant follows (recross-examination). The plaintiff's other witnesses are then called.

b. Defendant's Side of the Case

1) Motion for a Directed Verdict
At the conclusion of the plaintiff's case, the defendant can ask the judge to direct a verdict for the defendant on the ground that the plaintiff presented no evidence that would justify granting the plaintiff relief. The judge grants the motion if there is insufficient evidence to raise an issue of fact.

2) Defendant's Witnesses
If the motion is denied, the defendant calls the witnesses for his or her side of the case (and there is direct, cross-, redirect, and recross-examination). At the end of the defendant's case, either side can move for a directed verdict.

  c.   Rebuttal
  At the conclusion of the defendant's case, the plaintiff can present a rebuttal (additional evidence to refute the defendant's case).

  d.   Rejoinder
  The defendant can refute the plaintiff's rebuttal in a rejoinder.

C.   CLOSING ARGUMENTS

Each side summarizes briefly his or her version of the facts, outlines the evidence that supports his or her case, and reveals the shortcomings of the points made by the other party. The plaintiff goes first.

D.   JURY TRIALS

  1.   Jury Instructions
  In a jury trial, the judge instructs (charges) the jury in the law that applies to the case. The jurors may disregard the facts as stated in the charge, but they are not free to ignore the statements of law. (A reviewing court ordinarily remands a case for a new trial if a judge misstates the law in the jury instructions.)

  2.   Jury Verdict
  In a jury trial, the jury specifies the factual findings and the amount of damages to be paid by the losing party. This is the verdict. After it is announced, the trial is ended, and the jurors are discharged.

V.   POSTTRIAL MOTIONS

A.   MOTION FOR A JUDGMENT IN ACCORDANCE WITH THE VERDICT
The prevailing party usually files this motion.

B.   MOTION FOR A NEW TRIAL
This motion is granted if the judge believes that the jury erred but that it is not appropriate to grant a judgment for the other side (for example, the jury verdict resulted from a misapplication of the law or misunderstanding of the evidence, or there is newly discovered evidence, misconduct by the parties, or error by the judge).

C.   MOTION FOR JUDGMENT N.O.V.
The defendant can file this motion, if he or she previously moved for a directed verdict (*n.o.v.* is from the Latin *non obstante veredicto,* "notwithstanding the verdict;" federal courts use "motion for judgment as a matter of law"). The standards for granting this motion are the same as those for granting a motion to dismiss or a motion for a directed verdict.

VI.   THE APPEAL

A.   FILING THE APPEAL
The papers to be filed include—

  1.   Notice of Appeal
  The appellant (the losing party—or the winning party, if that party is dissatisfied with the relief obtained) must file a notice of appeal with the clerk of the trial court within a certain period of time.

  2.   Record on Appeal
  The appellant files in the reviewing court: (1) the pleadings, (2) a transcript of the trial and copies of the exhibits, (3) the judge's rulings on

the parties' motions, (4) the arguments of counsel, (5) the jury instructions, (6) the verdict, (7) the posttrial motions, and (8) the judgment order from which the appeal is taken.

3. Brief
The appellant files with the abstract a brief, which contains (1) a short statement of the facts; (2) a statement of the issues; (3) the rulings by the trial court that the appellant contends are erroneous and prejudicial; (4) the grounds for reversal of the judgment; (5) a statement of the applicable law; and (6) arguments on the appellant's behalf, citing applicable statutes and relevant cases.

4. Reply
The appellee (respondent) may file an answering brief.

B. APPELLATE REVIEW
Appellate courts do not usually reverse findings of fact unless they are contradicted by evidence at the trial. An appellate court can **affirm**, **reverse**, or **modify** a trial court's decision, or **remand** the case to the trial court for further proceedings consistent with the appellate court's opinion.

C. FURTHER APPEALS
If the reviewing court is an intermediate appellate court, the case may be appealed to the state supreme court. The state supreme court can affirm, reverse, or remand. If a federal question is involved, the case may be appealed to the United States Supreme Court, which may agree to hear it. Otherwise, the case is ended.

VII. ENFORCING THE JUDGMENT
The court can order a sheriff to seize property owned by the defendant and hold it until the defendant pays the judgment owed to the plaintiff. If the defendant fails to pay, the property can be sold at an auction and the proceeds given to the plaintiff, or the property can be transferred to the plaintiff in lieu of payment.

TRUE-FALSE QUESTIONS

(Answers at the Back of the Book)

_____ 1. Pleadings consist of a complaint, an answer, and a motion to dismiss.

_____ 2. In ruling on a motion for summary judgment, a court cannot consider evidence outside the pleadings.

_____ 3. At a pretrial conference, the parties and the judge may set ground rules for the trial.

_____ 4. If a party does not deny the truth of a complaint, he or she is in default.

_____ 5. To obtain documents in the hands of an opposing party in anticipation of a trial, a party uses the appeal process.

_____ 6. In a jury trial, the parties have a right to conduct _voir dire_.

_____ 7. In a civil case, a plaintiff must establish his or her case beyond a reasonable doubt.

_____ 8. A motion for a new trial will be granted if a jury verdict is the obvious result of a misapplication of the law.

___ **9.** The standards for granting a motion for a judgment *n.o.v.* are the same as those for granting a motion to dismiss.

___ **10.** Either party may appeal any pretrial or posttrial motion.

FILL-IN QUESTIONS

(Answers at the Back of the Book)

A motion _____ (to dismiss/for summary judgment) alleges that even if the facts in the complaint are true, their legal consequences are such that there is no reason to go on with the suit and no need for the defendant to present an answer. A motion _____ (to dismiss/for judgment on the pleadings) is properly filed after the complaint, answer, and any counterclaim and reply have been filed, when no facts are disputed and only questions of law are at issue. A motion for _____ (summary judgment/a new trial) is proper if there is no disagreement about the facts and the only question is which laws apply to those facts.

MULTIPLE-CHOICE QUESTIONS

(Answers at the Back of the Book)

___ **1.** Consolidated Industries, Inc., is considering filing a suit against First City Bank. In deciding whether to sue, the considerations include

a. the cost of going to court.
b. the patience to follow a case through the judicial system.
c. alternatives to settling the dispute without going to court.
d. all of the above.

___ **2.** Digital Computer Corporation initiates a lawsuit against Eagle Distribution Company. Digital's complaint should contain

a. a statement alleging jurisdictional facts.
b. a statement of facts entitling the complainant to relief.
c. a statement asking for a specific remedy.
d. all of the above.

___ **3.** American Delivery Systems is involved in litigation with Best Products Corporation. The parties may use discovery to

a. narrow the issues, but not prevent surprises at trial.
b. prevent surprises at trial, but not narrow the issues.
c. narrow the issues and prevent surprises at trial.
d. none of the above.

___ **4.** In Doug's suit against Erin, Erin would like to file a motion to dismiss. This motion may be filed

a. only if the court lacks jurisdiction.
b. only if the complaint does not state a claim for which relief can be granted.
c. if the court lacks jurisdiction or if the complaint does not state a claim for which relief can be granted.
d. none of the above.

_____ 5. Grant serves a complaint on Lee. Lee files a motion to dismiss. Lee will also need to file an answer to the complaint if

   a. the motion to dismiss is granted.
   b. the motion to dismiss is denied.
   c. Grant files a motion for judgment on the pleadings.
   d. none of the above.

_____ 6. Jim and Bill are involved in an automobile accident. Sue is a passenger in Bill's car. Jim wants to ask Sue, as a witness, some questions concerning the accident. Sue's answers to the questions are given in

   a. a deposition.
   b. a response to interrogatories.
   c. a response to a judge's request at a pretrial conference.
   d. none of the above.

_____ 7. In National Computer Corporation's suit against Owen, each party makes an opening statement. The order in which the next steps in the trial will proceed is

   a. each party's case and each party's rebuttal.
   b. the plaintiff's case and the defendant's rebuttal.
   c. the plaintiff's case and rebuttal; the defendant's case and rebuttal.
   d. the defendant's case and rebuttal; the plaintiff's case and rebuttal.

_____ 8. Todd files a suit against Denny. At the trial, Todd calls and questions Wendy. What happens next?

   a. Denny questions Wendy.
   b. Todd questions Wendy again.
   c. Todd calls his second witness.
   d. Denny calls his first witness.

_____ 9. The jury returns a verdict against Internet Services Corporation, in its suit against International Equipment, Inc. Internet Services can file a motion for

   a. a directed verdict.
   b. a judgment on the pleadings.
   c. a new trial or for a judgment notwithstanding the verdict.
   d. summary judgment.

_____ 10. ABC Computers Company wins its suit against Digital Products, Inc. After the entry of a judgment, who can appeal?

   a. ABC only
   b. Digital only
   c. Either ABC or Digital
   d. None of the above

SHORT ESSAY QUESTIONS

1. What is the primary consideration in deciding whether to settle a dispute or take the dispute to court?

2. What evidence is, and what evidence is not, admissible in a trial?

ISSUE SPOTTERS

(Answers at the Back of the Book)

Jan contracted with Dean to deliver a quantity of computers to Jan's Computer Store. They disagree over the amount, the delivery date, the price, and the quality.

1.   Jan wants to sue Dean. What are the first steps Jan must take?

2.   As Jan prepares her suit against Dean, Jan wants to see copies of Dean's paperwork relating to the deal—Dean's copy of the original order, any notes of later telephone conversations, and so on. Jan also wants Dean to answer some questions relating to their dispute. What means should Jan use to see the papers and get Dean's answers?

3.   At the trial, after Jan calls her witnesses, offers her evidence, and otherwise presents her side of the case, Dean has at least two choices between courses of actions. Dean can call his first witness. What else might Dean do?

4.   After the trial, the judge issues a judgment that includes a grant of relief for Jan, but the relief is not as much as Jan wanted. Neither Jan nor Dean are satisfied with this result. Can either party—or both—appeal to a higher court?

5.   The appellate court upholds the lower court's judgment and rules against Dean, who decides not to appeal further. How can Jan enforce the judgment?

SPECIAL INFORMATION FOR CPA CANDIDATES

The procedural steps in a civil trial in an American court is not specifically tested on the CPA examination. A general understanding of the legal system will prove helpful, however, to comprehending other materials that are tested on the exam. In particular, understanding the procedural course of a trial will help in reading the case excerpts in this textbook and in understanding the course of trials and judgments in general.

Chapter 4

Constitutional Authority to Regulate Business

WHAT THIS CHAPTER IS ABOUT

This chapter emphasizes that the Constitution is the supreme law in this country and discusses some of the constitutional limits on the law. Neither Congress nor any state may pass a law that conflicts with the Constitution. To sustain a federal law or action, a specific federal power must be found in the Constitution. A state has inherent power to enact laws that have a reasonable relationship to the welfare of its citizens.

CHAPTER OUTLINE

I. **THE CONSTITUTIONAL POWERS OF GOVERNMENT**

A. **FEDERAL FORM OF GOVERNMENT**
In a federal form of government (the United States), the states form a union and sovereign power is divided between a central authority and the states.

B. **CHECKS AND BALANCES**
Under the Constitution, the legislative branch makes the laws; the executive branch enforces the laws; and the judicial branch interprets the laws. Each branch has some power to limit the actions of the other two.

C. **THE COMMERCE CLAUSE**
The Constitution (Article I, Section 8) gives Congress the power to regulate commerce among the states.

1. **The Breadth of the Commerce Clause**
The national government can regulate every commercial enterprise in the United States. This power means that Congress can legislate in areas in which it has no explicit grant of power. Only rarely has the United States Supreme Court limited the reach of this power.

2. **The Regulatory Powers of the States**
States possess police powers (the right to regulate private activities to protect or promote the public order, health, safety, morals, and general welfare). Statutes covering almost every aspect of life have been enacted under the police powers.

3. **When State Laws Impinge on Interstate Commerce**
Courts balance the state's interest in the merit and purpose of the law against the burden on interstate commerce. State laws that *substantially* interfere with interstate commerce violate the commerce clause.

D. **THE SUPREMACY CLAUSE AND FEDERAL PREEMPTION**
The Constitution (Article IV) provides that the Constitution, laws, and treaties of the United States are the supreme law of the land.

1. **When Federal and State Laws Are in Direct Conflict**
The state law is rendered invalid.

2. **Preemption**
If Congress chooses to act exclusively in an area in which states have concurrent power, Congress preempts the area (the federal law takes precedence over a state law on the same subject). It can be difficult to predict how a court will interpret congressional intent, however.

E. **THE TAXING AND SPENDING POWERS**

1. **The Taxing Power**
The Constitution (Article I, Section 8) gives Congress the power to levy taxes, but Congress may not tax some states and exempt others. Any tax that is a valid revenue-raising measure will be upheld.

2. **The Spending Power**
The Constitution (Article I, Section 8) gives Congress the power to spend the money it raises with its taxing power. This involves policy choices, with which taxpayers may disagree. Congress can spend funds to promote any objective, so long as it does not violate the Bill of Rights.

II.   BUSINESS AND THE BILL OF RIGHTS
The first ten amendments to the Constitution protect individuals and businesses against some interference by the federal government. Under the due process clause of the Fourteenth Amendment, many rights also apply to the states.

A. **FREEDOM OF SPEECH**
The First Amendment guaranty of freedom of speech applies to the federal and state governments.

1. **Protected Speech**
Includes symbolic speech—nonverbal expressions, such as gestures, articles of clothing, some acts and so on. Governments can regulate the time, place, and manner of speech.

2. **Speech with Limited Protection**

a. **Commercial Speech**
A state restriction on commercial speech, such as advertising, is valid as long as it (1) seeks to implement a substantial government

interest, (2) directly advances that interest, and (3) goes no further than necessary to accomplish its objective.

b. Corporate Political Speech

States can prohibit corporations from using corporate funds for independent expressions of opinion about political candidates.

3. Unprotected Speech

a. Defamatory Speech

Speech that harms the good reputation of another. Such speech can take the form of libel (if it is in writing) or slander (if it is oral).

b. Lewd and Obscene Speech

States can ban child pornography. One court has banned lewd speech and pornographic pinups in the workplace.

c. "Fighting Words"

Words that are likely to incite others to violence.

B. FREEDOM OF RELIGION

Under the First Amendment, the government may not establish a religion (the establishment clause) nor prohibit the exercise of religion (the free exercise clause).

1. The Establishment Clause

The government cannot show a preference for one religion over another, but must accommodate all religions. Sunday "closing laws" (restrictions on commercial acts on Sunday) have been upheld on the ground it is a legitimate government function to provide a day of rest.

2. The Free Exercise Clause

A law that infringes on the free exercise of religion in public places must be justified by a compelling state interest. Employers must reasonably accommodate the religious practices of their employees.

C. SELF-INCRIMINATION

Under the Fifth Amendment, no person can be compelled to give testimony that might subject him or her to a criminal prosecution.

1. Sole Proprietors

Individuals who own their own businesses and have not incorporated cannot be compelled to produce their business records.

2. Partnerships and Corporations

Partnerships and corporations *can* be compelled to produce their business records, even if the records incriminate the persons who constitute the business entity.

D. SEARCHES AND SEIZURES

Under the Fourth Amendment, law enforcement and other government officers cannot conduct unreasonable searches or seizures.

1. Search Warrant

An officer must obtain a search warrant before searching or seizing private property. It must describe what is to be searched or seized.

a. Probable Cause
To obtain a warrant, the officer must convince a judge that there is **probable cause** (evidence that would convince a reasonable person a search or seizure is justified).

b. General and Neutral Enforcement Plan
To obtain a warrant to inspect business premises, government inspectors must have probable cause, but the standard is different: a general and neutral enforcement plan is enough.

2. No Search Warrant
No warrant is required for seizures of spoiled or contaminated food or searches of businesses in highly regulated industries. General manufacturing is not considered a highly regulated industry.

III. OTHER CONSTITUTIONAL PROTECTIONS

A. THE PRIVILEGES AND IMMUNITIES CLAUSE

1. State Citizens
The Constitution (Article IV, Section 2) requires each state to provide the citizens of other states with the same privileges and immunities it provides its own citizens. A state cannot treat nonresidents engaged in basic, essential activities differently without substantial justification.

2. U.S. Citizens
The Fourteenth Amendment prohibits a state from infringing on the privileges or immunities (such as the right to travel) of U.S. citizens.

B. THE FULL FAITH AND CREDIT CLAUSE
The Constitution (Article IV, Section 1) requires that property and contract rights established by the law in one state be honored by other states.

C. DUE PROCESS
Both the Fifth and the Fourteenth Amendments provide that no person shall be deprived "of life, liberty, or property, without due process of law."

1. Procedural Due Process
Any government decision to take away the life, liberty, or property of an individual must include procedural safeguards to ensure fairness.

2. Substantive Due Process
Substantive due process focuses on the content (substance) of legislation.

a. Compelling Interest Test
A statute can restrict an individual's fundamental right (such as all First Amendment rights) only if the statute promotes a compelling or overriding governmental interest.

b. Rational Basis Test
Restrictions on business activities must relate rationally to a legitimate government purpose. Most business regulations qualify.

D. EQUAL PROTECTION
The Fourteenth Amendment prohibits a state from denying any person "the equal protection of the laws." The due process clause of the Fifth Amendment applies the equal protection clause to the federal government.

1. **What Equal Protection Means**
   Equal protection means that the government must treat similarly situated individuals in a similar manner. If a law distinguishes among individuals, the basis for the distinction (classification) is examined.

   a. **Strict Scrutiny**
      A law that inhibits some persons' exercise of a fundamental right or a classification based on a suspect trait must be necessary to promote a compelling state interest.

   b. **Intermediate Scrutiny**
      Laws using classifications based on gender or legitimacy must be substantially related to important government objectives.

   c. **The "Rational Basis" Test**
      In matters of economic or social welfare, the classification will be considered valid if there is any conceivable rational basis on which it might relate to any legitimate government interest.

2. **The Difference between Substantive Due Process and Equal Protection**
   A law that limits the liberty of *all* persons to do something may violate substantive due process. A law that limits the liberty of only *some* persons may violate equal protection.

E. **PRIVACY RIGHTS**
   There is no specific guarantee of this right, but it is derived from guarantees in the First, Third, Fourth, Fifth, and Ninth Amendments.

TRUE-FALSE QUESTIONS

(Answers at the Back of the Book)

____ 1. A federal form of government is one in which all of the power is held by a central authority.

____ 2. The judicial branch of the federal government enforces the law.

____ 3. Each of the executive, legislative, and judicial branches of the federal government has some power to limit the actions of the other branches.

____ 4. Under the commerce clause, Congress can regulate every commercial enterprise in the United States.

____ 5. State laws that *substantially* interfere with interstate commerce violate the commerce clause.

____ 6. When there is a direct conflict between a federal law and a state law, the state law is valid and the federal law is invalid.

____ 7. If a tax is a valid revenue-producing measure, it is within the federal taxing power and will be upheld as constitutional.

____ 8. Because of the First Amendment protections, a state cannot restrict advertising.

____ 9. A right to privacy is derived from various amendments to the U.S. Constitution.

____ 10. Due process and equal protection are different terms for the same thing.

FILL-IN QUESTIONS

(Answers at the Back of the Book)

Police power is possessed by the _____ (federal government/states). Police power refers to the right of the _____ (federal government/states) to regulate private activities to protect or promote the public order, health, safety, morals, and general welfare. Building codes, licensing requirements, and many other _____ (federal/state) statutes have been enacted under the police power. It is difficult to predict the outcome in a particular case, but _____ (federal/state) laws enacted pursuant to police powers carry a strong presumption of _____ (validity/invalidity).

MULTIPLE-CHOICE QUESTIONS

(Answers at the Back of the Book)

____   1.   Of the branches of the federal government provided by the Constitution, which branch makes the laws?

a. Executive branch
b. Legislative branch
c. Judicial branch
d. Administrative branch

____   2.   The Bill of Rights provides protections against various types of interference by

a. state governments.
b. the federal government.
c. private corporations.
d. both a and b.

____   3.   A state enacts a law that impinges on Brad's business and the business of his competitors. Brad challenges the law in court, claiming that it unlawfully interferes with interstate commerce. The court will consider

a. the state's interest in the merit and purpose of the law.
b. the burden that the law places on interstate commerce.
c. both a and b.
d. none of the above.

____   4.   As part of a tax audit, the Internal Revenue Service asks to see the business records of Syncom Corporation. The records incriminate Syncom executives. The corporation

a. can refuse to provide the records.
b. can agree to provide only those records that are not incriminating.
c. either a or b.
d. none of the above.

_____ **5.** A state law prohibits pharmacists from advertising the prices of prescription drugs. Ted, a pharmacist, challenges the law, claiming that it is unconstitutional. Under the First Amendment, advertising is

    a. protected unless it concerns an unlawful activity or is misleading.
    b. protected to the same extent as "fighting words."
    c. protected to the same extent as defamatory words.
    d. not protected.

_____ **6.** Under the First Amendment

    a. a law that does not promote or significantly burden a religion is constitutional.
    b. the government must generally accommodate all religions.
    c. the government must be neutral toward religion.
    d. all of the above.

_____ **7.** If a law limits the liberty of _all_ persons in a way that is unconstitutional, it is a violation of

    a. substantive due process.
    b. the right to privacy.
    c. equal protection.
    d. none of the above.

_____ **8.** If a law limits the liberty of _some_ persons in a way that is unconstitutional, it is a violation of

    a. substantive due process.
    b. the right to privacy.
    c. equal protection.
    d. none of the above.

_____ **9.** Congress enacts a comprehensive and detailed series of regulations covering airports. If a state enacts a law regulating airports

    a. the federal law always takes precedence.
    b. the state law always takes precedence.
    c. the state law takes precedence if the laws do not conflict.
    d. none of the above.

_____ **10.** To obtain a search warrant, in most cases, including the inspection of business premises, a government officer must have

    a. possible cause.
    b. probable cause.
    c. precedential cause.
    d. none of the above.

SHORT ESSAY QUESTIONS

1. What does the supremacy clause provide? How does it affect state law?

2. What is the commerce clause? What is its significance?

ISSUE SPOTTERS

(Answers at the Back of the Book)

1. If a farmer grows wheat wholly for consumption by her family on her farm, under what clause of the Constitution can Congress regulate that activity? Why?

2. Can a state, in the interest of energy conservation, ban all advertising by electric utilities if conservation could be accomplished by less restrictive means? Why or why not?

3. An employee is discharged for using drugs for "sacramental purposes" during a religious ceremony. There is a statute disqualifying, for unemployment compensation, employees who are discharged for misconduct. Would it violate the First Amendment's freedom of religion to deny unemployment compensation to this individual?

4. Would a state law imposing a fifteen-year term of imprisonment without allowing a trial on all businesspersons who appear in their own television commercials be a violation of substantive due process? Would it violate procedural due process?

5. Would it be a violation of equal protection for a state to impose a higher tax on out-of-state companies doing business in the state than it imposes on in-state companies if the only reason for the tax is to protect the local firms from out-of-state competition?

SPECIAL INFORMATION FOR CPA CANDIDATES

In the past, most of the information covered in this chapter has not been included in the CPA examination. Those who sit for the exam are expected to know, however, that states base their regulation of professional licensing on their police powers. Test-takers will also be expected to know that the Securities Exchange Commission bases its regulation of securities on the Constitution's commerce clause.

When confronted with a multiple-choice question on the exam that covers these areas of the law, it is important to attempt to answer the question, even if it is not clear what the answer is. This is because in grading the multiple-choice portion of the exam, there is no deduction for wrong answers. Scores are based only on the total number of correct answers.

Chapter 5
Torts

WHAT THIS CHAPTER IS ABOUT

The law of **torts** is concerned with wrongful conduct by one person that causes injury to another. *Tort* is French for "wrong." For acts that cause physical injury or that interfere with physical security and freedom of movement, tort law provides remedies, typically damages (money).

This chapter outlines intentional torts, including torts that are more specifically related to business, and negligence. Strict liability, another part of tort law, is outlined in Chapter 6.

CHAPTER OUTLINE

I. THE BASIS OF TORT LAW
Tort law recognizes that some acts are wrong because they cause physical injuries to persons or property, interfere with others' security or freedom, or harm certain intangible interests, such as privacy or reputation.

II. INTENTIONAL TORTS AGAINST PERSONS AND BUSINESS RELATIONSHIPS
Intentional torts involve acts that were intended or could be expected to bring about consequences that are the basis of the tort. A **tortfeasor** (one committing a tort) must intend to commit an act, the consequences of which interfere with the personal or business interests of another in a way not permitted by law.

A. ASSAULT AND BATTERY

1. Assault
An intentional act that creates in another person a reasonable apprehension or fear of immediate harmful or offensive contact.

2. **Battery**
An intentional and harmful or offensive physical contact. Physical injury need not occur. Whether the contact is offensive is determined by the reasonable person standard.

3. **Compensation**
A plaintiff may be compensated for emotional harm or loss of reputation resulting from a battery, as well as for physical harm.

4. **Defenses to Assault and Battery**

   a. **Consent**
   When a person consents to an act that damages him or her, there is generally no liability for the damage.

   b. **Self-Defense**
   An individual who is defending his or her life or physical well-being can claim self-defense.

   c. **Defense of Others**
   An individual can act in a reasonable manner to protect others who are in real or apparent danger.

   d. **Defense of Property**
   Reasonable force may be used in attempting to remove intruders from one's home, although force that is likely to cause death or great bodily injury can never be used just to protect property.

B. **FALSE IMPRISONMENT**

1. **What False Imprisonment Is**
The intentional confinement or restraint of another person without justification. The confinement can be accomplished through the use of physical barriers, physical restraint, or threats of physical force.

2. **The Defense of Probable Cause**
In some states, a merchant is justified in delaying a suspected shoplifter if the merchant has probable cause. The detention must be conducted in a reasonable manner and for only a reasonable length of time.

C. **INTENTIONAL INFLICTION OF EMOTIONAL DISTRESS**
Infliction of emotional distress is an intentional act that amounts to extreme and outrageous conduct resulting in severe emotional distress to another (a few states require physical symptoms). Repeated annoyance, with threats (such as extreme methods of debt collection), is one way to commit this tort.

D. **DEFAMATION**
Defamation is wrongfully hurting another's good reputation through false statements. Doing it orally is **slander**; doing it in writing is **libel**.

1. **The Publication Requirement**
The statement must be published (communicated to a third party). Anyone who republishes or repeats a defamatory statement is liable.

2. **Types of False Utterances That Are Torts *Per Se***
Proof of injury is not required when one falsely states that another has a loathsome communicable disease, has committed improprieties while engaging in a profession or trade, or has committed or been imprisoned for a serious crime, or that an unmarried woman is unchaste.

3. **Defenses to Defamation**

    a. **Truth**
        The statement is true. It must be true in whole, not in part.

    b. **Privileged Speech**
        The statement is privileged: absolute (made in a judicial or legislative proceeding) or qualified (for example, made by one corporate director to another and was about corporate business).

    c. **Public Figures**
        The statement is about a public figure, made in a public medium, and related to a matter of general public interest. To recover damages, a public figure must prove a statement was made with **actual malice** (knowledge of its falsity or reckless disregard for the truth).

E. **INVASION OF PRIVACY**
    Four acts qualify as invasions of privacy:

    1. The use of a person's name, picture, or other likeness for commercial purposes without permission. (This is **appropriation**—see below.)

    2. Intrusion on an individual's affairs or seclusion.

    3. Publication of information that places a person in a false light.

    4. Public disclosure of private facts about an individual that an ordinary person would find objectionable.

F. **APPROPRIATION**
    The use of one person's name or likeness by another, without permission and for the benefit of the user, is **appropriation**. An individual's right to privacy includes the right to the exclusive use of his or her identity.

G. **FRAUDULENT MISREPRESENTATION**
    Fraud is the use of misrepresentation and deceit for personal gain. Puffery (seller's talk) is not fraud. The elements of fraudulent misrepresentation—

    1. **Misrepresentation** of material facts or conditions with knowledge that they are false or with reckless disregard for the truth.

    2. **Intent** to induce another to rely on the misrepresentation.

    3. **Justifiable reliance** by the deceived party.

    4. **Damages** suffered as a result of reliance.

    5. **Causal connection** between the misrepresentation and the injury.

H. **WRONGFUL INTERFERENCE**
    Torts involving wrongful interference with another's business rights generally fall into the two categories outlined here.

    1. **Wrongful Interference with a Contractual Relationship**
        This occurs when one party induces another to break a contract. Simply reaping the benefits of a broken contract is not enough. Elements include:

        a. A **contract** between two parties.

        b. A third party's **knowledge** of the contract.

        c. The third party's intentionally causing either of the two parties to **break the contract**. The third party's bad faith or harmful intent is immaterial, but the purpose of the interference must be to advance the third party's economic interest.

      2. **Wrongful Interference with a Business Relationship**
If there are two shoe stores in a mall, placing an employee of Store A in front of Store B to divert customers to Store A is the tort of wrongful interference with a business relationship (an unfair trade practice).

      3. **Defenses to Wrongful Interference**
A person is not liable if the interference is justified or permissible (such as bona fide competitive behavior).

III. INTENTIONAL TORTS AGAINST PROPERTY

A. TRESPASS TO LAND

Trespass to land occurs if a person, without permission, enters onto, above, or below the surface of land owned by another; causes anything to enter onto the land; or remains on the land or permits anything to remain on it.

      1. **Trespass Criteria, Rights, and Duties**
Posted signs *expressly* establish trespass. Entering onto property to commit an illegal act *impliedly* does so. Trespassers are liable for any property damage. Owners may have a duty to post notice of any danger.

      2. **Defenses against Trespass to Land**
Defenses against trespass include that the trespass was warranted or that the purported owner had no right to possess the land in question.

B. TRESPASS TO PERSONAL PROPERTY

Occurs when an individual unlawfully harms the personal property of another or interferes with an owner's right to exclusive possession and enjoyment. Defenses include that the interference was warranted.

C. CONVERSION

      1. **What Conversion Is**
An act depriving an owner of personal property without the owner's permission and without just cause. Conversion is the civil side of crimes related to theft. Buying stolen goods is conversion.

      2. **Defenses**
Defenses to conversion include that the purported owner does not own the property or does not have a right to possess it that is superior to the right of the holder. Necessity is also a defense.

D. DISPARAGEMENT OF PROPERTY

Disparagement of property occurs when economically injurious falsehoods are made about another's product or ownership of property. It is a general term for torts that can be specifically referred to as **slander of quality** (product) or **slander of title** (ownership of property).

IV. NEGLIGENCE

A. THE ELEMENTS OF NEGLIGENCE

1. **What Negligence Is**
    Someone's failure to live up to a required duty of care, causing another to suffer injury. The breach of the duty must create a risk of certain harmful consequences, whether or not that was the intent.

2. **The Elements of Negligence**
    (1) A duty of care, (2) breach of the duty of care, (3) damage or injury as a result of the breach, and (4) the breach causes the damage or injury.

B. **THE DUTY OF CARE AND ITS BREACH**

1. **The Reasonable Person Standard**
    The duty of care is measured by the **reasonable person standard** (how a reasonable person would have acted in the same circumstances).

2. **Duty of Landowners**
    Owners are expected to use reasonable care (guard against some risks and warn of others) to protect persons coming onto their property.

3. **Duty of Professionals**
    A professional's duty is consistent with his or her knowledge, skill, and intelligence, including what is reasonable for that professional.

4. **Factors for Determining a Breach of the Duty of Care**
    The nature of the act (whether it is outrageous or commonplace), the manner in which the act is performed (cautiously versus heedlessly), and the nature of the injury (whether it is serious or slight). Note: Failing to rescue a stranger in peril is *not* a breach of a duty of care.

C. **THE INJURY REQUIREMENT AND DAMAGES**
    To recover damages (receive compensation), the plaintiff must have suffered some loss, harm, wrong, or invasion of a protected interest. Punitive damages (to punish the wrongdoer and deter others) may also be awarded.

D. **CAUSATION**

1. **Causation in Fact**
    The breach of the duty of care must cause the injury—that is, "but for" the wrongful act, the injury would not have occurred.

2. **Proximate Cause**
    There must be a connection between the act and the injury strong enough to justify imposing liability. Generally, the harm or the victim of the harm must have been foreseeable in light of all of the circumstances.

E. **DEFENSES TO NEGLIGENCE**

1. **Assumption of Risk**
    A plaintiff who voluntarily enters into a risky situation, knowing the risk, cannot recover. This does not include a risk different from or greater than the risk normally involved in the situation.

2. **Superseding Cause**
    A superseding intervening force breaks the connection between the breach of the duty of care and the injury or damage. Taking a defensive action (such as swerving to avoid an oncoming car) does not break the connection. Nor does someone else's attempt to rescue the injured party.

3. **Contributory Negligence**

    In some states, a plaintiff cannot recover for an injury if he or she was negligent. The **last-clear-chance doctrine** allows a negligent plaintiff to recover if the defendant had the last chance to avoid the damage.

4. **Comparative Negligence**

    In most states, the plaintiff's and the defendant's negligence is compared and liability prorated. Some states allow a plaintiff to recover even if his or her fault is greater than the defendant's. In many states, the plaintiff gets nothing if he or she is more than 50 percent at fault.

F. **SPECIAL NEGLIGENCE DOCTRINES AND STATUTES**

1. *Res Ipsa Loquitur*

    If negligence is very difficult to prove, a court may infer it, and the defendant must prove he or she was *not* negligent. This is only if the event causing the harm is one that normally does not occur in the absence of negligence and is caused by something within the defendant's control.

2. **Negligence *Per Se***

    A person who violates a statute providing for a criminal penalty is liable when the violation causes another to be injured, if (1) the statute sets out a standard of conduct, and when, where, and of whom it is expected; (2) the injured person is in the class protected by the statute; and (3) the statute was designed to prevent the type of injury suffered.

3. **"Danger Invites Rescue" Doctrine**

    A person who endangers another is liable for injuries to third persons who attempt to rescue the endangered party.

4. **Special Negligence Statutes**

    Good Samaritan statutes protect those who aid others from being sued for negligence. Dram shop acts impose liability on bar owners for injuries caused by intoxicated persons who are served by those owners. A statute may impose liability on social hosts for acts of their guests.

TRUE-FALSE QUESTIONS

(Answers at the Back of the Book)

____ 1. To commit an intentional tort, a person must intend the consequences of his or her act or know with substantial certainty that certain consequences will result.

____ 2. Immediate harmful or offensive contact is an element of assault.

____ 3. Defamation does not occur unless a defamatory statement is made in writing.

____ 4. Bona fide competitive behavior does not constitute wrongful interference with a contractual relationship.

____ 5. There are no legitimate defenses to wrongful interference torts.

____ 6. An individual's right to privacy normally includes the right to the exclusive use of his or her identity.

____ 7. Disparagement of property is another term for appropriation.

___ 8. Ed tells customers that he is "the best plumber in town." This is fraudulent misrepresentation, unless Ed actually believes that he is the best.

___ 9. A person who borrows a friend's car and fails to return it at the friend's request is guilty of conversion.

___ 10. To avoid liability for negligence, the same duty of care must be exercised by all individuals, regardless of their knowledge, skill, or intelligence.

FILL-IN QUESTIONS

(Answers at the Back of the Book)

1. Basic defenses to _____ (negligence/intentional torts) include comparative negligence, contributory negligence, and assumption of risk.

2. One who voluntarily and knowingly enters into a risky situation normally cannot recover damages. This is the _____ (defense of contributory negligence/defense of assumption of risk).

3. When both parties' failure to use reasonable care combines to cause injury, in some states the injured party's recovery is precluded by his or her own negligence. This is the _____ (comparative/contributory) negligence doctrine.

4. When both parties' failure to use reasonable care combines to cause injury, in most states damages are reduced by a percentage that represents the degree of the plaintiff's negligence. This is the _____ (comparative/contributory) negligence doctrine.

MULTIPLE-CHOICE QUESTIONS

(Answers at the Back of the Book)

___ 1. Driving his car negligently, Paul crashes into a telephone pole. The pole falls, smashing through the roof of a house onto Karl, who is sitting inside. Karl dies. But for Paul's negligence, Karl would not have died. Regarding Karl's death, Paul's crash is the

   a. cause in fact.
   b. proximate cause.
   c. intervening cause.
   d. superseding cause.

___ 2. Tom owns Tom's Computer Store. Tom sees Nan, a customer, pick software from a shelf and put it in her bag. As Nan is about to leave, Tom tells her that she can't leave until he checks her bag. If Nan sues Tom for false imprisonment, Nan will

   a. win, because a merchant cannot delay a customer on a mere suspicion.
   b. win, because Nan did not first commit a tort.
   c. lose, because a merchant may delay a suspected shoplifter for a reasonable time based on probable cause.
   d. lose, because Tom did not intend to commit the tort of false imprisonment.

____   **3.**   During a trial, a judge calls an attorney unethical. If the attorney sues the judge for defamation, the attorney will

a. win, because the attorney is a public figure.
b. win, if the attorney can prove the statement was made with actual malice.
c. lose, because the judge's statement was privileged.
d. lose, because the judge is a public figure.

____   **4.**   Al, a landlord, installs two-way mirrors in his tenants' bedrooms through which he watches them without their knowledge. Al is guilty of

a. using another's likeness for commercial purposes without permission.
b. public disclosure of private facts about another.
c. publication of information that places another in false lights.
d. intrusion into another's affairs or seclusion.

____   **5.**   Fred returns home from work to find Barney camped in Fred's backyard. Fred says, "Get off my property." Barney says, "I'm not leaving." Fred forcibly drags Barney off the property. If Barney sues Fred, Barney will

a. win, because Fred used too much force.
b. win, because Barney told Fred that he was not leaving.
c. lose, because Fred did not use deadly force.
d. lose, because Barney is a trespasser.

____   **6.**   Gus sends a letter to Jose in which he accuses Jose of embezzling. Jose's secretary Tina reads the letter. If Jose sues Gus for defamation, Jose will

a. win, because Tina's reading of the letter satisfies the publication element.
b. win, because Gus's writing of the letter satisfies the publication element.
c. lose, because the letter is not proof that Jose is an embezzler.
d. lose, because the publication element is not satisfied.

____   **7.**   Wandering in Don's air-conditioned market on a hot day with her sisters, four-year-old Silvia drops her ice cream on the floor. Two hours later, Jan stops to buy milk, slips on the ice cream puddle, and breaks her arm. Don is

a. liable, because a merchant is always liable for customers' actions.
b. liable, if Don failed to take all reasonable precautions against Jan's injury.
c. not liable, because Jan's injury was her own fault.
d. not liable, because Jan's injury was the fault of Silvia's sisters.

____   **8.**   Joe, a 99-pound weakling, clenches his fist, stands as if ready to throw a punch, and orally threatens to hit a 360-pound lineman for the Chicago Bears. Joe is

a. not guilty of assault, because words alone are not enough.
b. not guilty of assault, because it is unlikely that the lineman is afraid of Joe.
c. guilty of assault, because the words are accompanied by a threatening act.
d. guilty of assault, because a professional football player is a public figure.

____   **9.**   A salesperson for Woodco tells the owner of Pat's Lumber that Timber, Inc., does not sell mahogany. The salesperson knows that the statement is false. Pat had intended to buy mahogany from Timber, but instead buys it from Woodco. If Timber sues Woodco for slander of quality, Woodco will be held

a. liable, if Timber proves that it suffered damages from Pat's decision.
b. liable, if Timber proves that Pat did not see Timber's salesperson.
c. not liable, if Woodco proves that its prices are competitive.
d. not liable, if Woodco proves that it made no profit on the deal.

____ **10.** Bio Box Company advertises so effectively that Product Packaging, Inc., stops doing business with Styro Cartons, Inc. Bio is

a. liable to Styro for wrongful interference with a contractual relationship.
b. liable to Styro for wrongful interference with a business relationship.
c. liable to Styro for disparagement of property.
d. not liable.

SHORT ESSAY QUESTIONS

1. What is a *tort*?

2. Identify and describe the elements of a cause of action based on negligence.

ISSUE SPOTTERS

(Answers at the Back of the Book)

1. Adam kisses the sleeve of Eve's blouse, to which she did not consent. Is Adam guilty of a tort?

2. If a student takes another student's business law textbook as a practical joke and hides it for several days before the final examination, has a tort been committed?

3. Standing next to a gasoline truck, Joe lights a cigarette and carelessly tosses the match into the truck's storage tank. The ensuing explosion and fire ends in the evacuation and destruction of downtown Richmond. During the evacuation, eleven-year-old Mandy is trampled by a fleeing mob. Is Joe liable for Mandy's injuries?

4. Sam is a programmer for Data, Inc. Web International, Inc., offers Sam a higher salary, adding that it will pay any costs for Sam's breach of his employment contract with Data. If Sam goes to work for Web, does Data have a cause of action against Web?

5. Mike applies for credit with First National Bank, but Ace Credit Agency reports that Mike has not paid several previous debts. Mike claims that this is not true and offers proof, but the bank denies Mike credit. Does Mike have any recourse against Ace?

SPECIAL INFORMATION FOR CPA CANDIDATES

Usually, the CPA examination tests your knowledge of torts in such situations as the following:

- Liability for damages and injuries caused by defective products (see Chapter 6).
- Employers' liability for the torts of their employees (see Chapter 32).
- Liability for the torts of corporate officers and directors committed in the course of their corporate duties (see Chapter 35).
- Liability of auditors, accountants, and other professionals (see Chapter 51).

Chapter 6
Strict Liability and Product Liability

WHAT THIS CHAPTER IS ABOUT

Strict liability is liability for injury imposed for reasons other than fault. Manufacturers, processors, and sellers may be liable to consumers, users, and bystanders for physical harm or property damage caused by defective goods. This is **product liability**.

CHAPTER OUTLINE

I. STRICT LIABILITY

A. ABNORMALLY DANGEROUS ACTIVITIES
The basis for imposing strict liability on an abnormally dangerous activity is that the activity creates an extreme risk. Balancing the risk against the potential for harm, it is fair to ask the person engaged in the activity to pay for injury caused by that activity.

B. OTHER APPLICATIONS OF STRICT LIABILITY
A person who keeps a dangerous animal is strictly liable for any harm inflicted by the animal. A significant application of strict liability is in the area of product liability (discussed below).

II. PRODUCT LIABILITY
Product liability may be based on negligence, misrepresentation, or strict liability. It may also be based on warranty law (see Chapter 23).

A. PRODUCT LIABILITY BASED ON NEGLIGENCE
If the failure to exercise reasonable care in the making or marketing of a product causes an injury, the basis of liability is negligence.

1. Manufacturer's Duty of Care
Due care must be exercised in designing, assembling, and testing a product; selecting materials; inspecting and testing products bought for

use in the final product; and placing warnings on the label to inform users of dangers of which an ordinary person might not be aware.

2. Privity of Contract between Plaintiff and Defendant Is Not Required

3. Violation of Statutory Duty
Manufacturers have statutory duties, such as those relating to labeling. Violation of a statutory duty may be negligence *per se* (see Chapter 5).

B. PRODUCT LIABILITY BASED ON MISREPRESENTATION
If misrepresentation causes injury, there may liability if it (1) is of a material fact, (2) is intended to induce a buyer's reliance, and (3) the buyer relies on it.

1. Proof of Defects Not Required
Plaintiff does not have to show product was defective or malfunctioned.

2. Fraudulent Misrepresentation
Occurs when misrepresentation is done knowingly or with reckless disregard for the facts (such as intentionally concealing defects).

3. Nonfraudulent Misrepresentation
Occurs when a merchant innocently misrepresents the character or quality of goods (the misrepresentation need not be done knowingly).

III. STRICT PRODUCT LIABILITY
A defendant may be held liable for the result of his or her act regardless of intention or exercise of reasonable care (see Chapter 5).

A. PUBLIC POLICY
Public policy assumes that (1) consumers should be protected from unsafe products, (2) manufacturers and distributors should not escape liability solely for lack of privity, and (3) sellers and lessors are in a better position to bear the cost of injuries caused by their products.

B. REQUIREMENTS FOR STRICT PRODUCT LIABILITY
Under the *Restatement (Second) of Torts*, Section 402A—

1. Product Is in a Defective Condition When the Defendant Sells It

2. Defendant Is Normally in the Business of Selling the Product

3. Defect Makes the Product Unreasonably Dangerous
A product may be so defective if either—

a. Product Is Dangerous beyond the Ordinary Consumer's Expectation
There may have been a flaw in the manufacturing process that led to some defective products being marketed, or a perfectly made product may not have had adequate warning on the label.

b. There Is a Less Dangerous, Economically Feasible Alternative that the Manufacturer Failed to Use
A manufacturer may have failed to design a safe product.

4. Plaintiff Incurs Harm to Self or Property by Use of the Product

5. Defect Is the Proximate Cause of the Harm

6. Product Was Not Substantially Changed After It Was Sold
Between the time the product was sold and the time of the injury.

C. MARKET-SHARE LIABILITY
Some courts hold that all firms that manufactured and distributed DES (diethylstilbestrol) during a certain period are liable for injuries in proportion to the firms' respective shares of the market.

D. OTHER APPLICATIONS OF STRICT PRODUCT LIABILITY

1. Who May Be Liable
Sellers of goods, including manufacturers, processors, assemblers, packagers, bottlers, wholesalers, distributors, and retailers. Suppliers of component parts and lessors may be liable for injuries caused by defective products.

2. Strict Liability Extends to Bystanders
All courts extend strict liability to cover injured bystanders (limited in some cases to those whose injuries are reasonably foreseeable).

IV. THE *RESTATEMENT (THIRD) OF TORTS*
The *Restatement (Third) of Torts: Products Liability* categorizes defects as—

A. MANUFACTURING DEFECT
When a product departs from its intended design even though all possible care was taken (strict liability).

B. DESIGN DEFECT
When a foreseeable risk of harm posed by a product could have been reduced by use of a reasonable alternative design and the omission makes the product unreasonably unsafe. A court would consider such factors as consumer expectations and warnings.

C. WARNING DEFECT
When a foreseeable risk of harm posed by a product could have been reduced by providing a reasonable warning and the omission makes the product unreasonably unsafe. Factors include the content and comprehensibility of a warning, and the expected users.

V. DEFENSES TO PRODUCT LIABILITY

A. ASSUMPTION OF RISK
In some states, this is a defense if (1) plaintiff knew and appreciated the risk created by the defect and (2) plaintiff voluntarily engaged in the risk, event though it was unreasonable to do so.

B. PRODUCT MISUSE
The use must not be the one for which the product was designed, and the misuse must not be reasonably foreseeable.

C. COMPARATIVE NEGLIGENCE
Most states consider a plaintiff's actions in apportioning liability.

D. COMMONLY KNOWN DANGERS
Failing to warn against such a danger is not ground for liability.

E. **STATUTES OF LIMITATIONS**
    A statute of limitations provides that an action must be brought within a specified period of time after the cause of action accrues (after some damage occurs or after a harmed party discovers the damage).

F. **STATUTES OF REPOSE**
    A statute of repose limits the time in which a suit can be filed. It runs from an earlier date and for a longer time than a statute of limitations.

G. **TYPE OF INJURY OR LOSS**
    Some courts limit recovery to personal injuries. Recovery for economic loss is rarely available.

H. **TYPE OF GOODS OR LACK OF RECOGNITION**
    Some states limit the application of strict liability to new goods. Some states refuse to recognize the doctrine of strict liability.

TRUE-FALSE QUESTIONS

(Answers at the Back of the Book)

____ 1. Strict liability is imposed for reasons other than fault.

____ 2. In a product liability action based on strict liability, a plaintiff must prove that there was a failure to exercise due care.

____ 3. In a defense of comparative negligence, an injured party's failure to take care against a known product defect will be considered in apportioning liability.

____ 4. Under the doctrine of strict liability, a defendant is liable for the results of his or her acts only if he or she intended those results.

____ 5. Failure to comply with a statute may constitute negligence *per se*.

____ 6. Product liability is imposed only if a defect in the design or construction of a product causes an injury.

____ 7. Strict product liability does not apply to lessors of goods.

____ 8. Suppliers are generally required to design products that are safe when misused or that include some protective device.

____ 9. In a product liability suit based on fraudulent misrepresentation, the plaintiff does not have to show that the product was defective.

____ 10. If a defective product causes only property damage, the seller may not be liable under a theory of strict product liability.

FILL-IN QUESTIONS

(Answers at the Back of the Book)

Statutes of limitations and statutes of repose restrict the time within which an action may be brought. A statute of _____ (limitations/repose) typically provides a specified period after a cause of action accrues within which an action must be brought. Sometimes the running of this period _____
_____ (does not begin until/ends when) the injured party discovers, or should have

discovered, the injury. A statute of _____ (limitations/repose) provides a time limit on filing a claim, whether or not a cause of action has accrued, so that a defendant will not be vulnerable to a lawsuit indefinitely. Usually, a statute of _____ (limitations/repose) begins to run at an earlier date and runs for a longer time than a statute of _____ (limitations/repose).

MULTIPLE-CHOICE QUESTIONS

(Answers at the Back of the Book)

____   1. Sam is injured in an accident involving a defective tractor. Sam sues the maker of the tractor. To successfully claim assumption of risk as a defense, the defendant must show

a. Sam voluntarily engaged in the risk while realizing the potential danger.
b. Sam knew and appreciated the risk created by the defect.
c. Sam's decision to undertake the known risk was unreasonable.
d. all of the above.

____   2. Kate is standing in line at a convenience store. A bottle of Bolt Cola is on the floor about six inches from where she is standing. The bottle explodes, and Kate's legs are severely injured. If Kate sues Bolt Cola Company on the ground of strict liability, Bolt will likely be held

a. liable, because it was reasonably foreseeable that a bystander would be injured by the defective bottle of Bolt.
b. liable, if Kate can prove that the company failed to exercise due care.
c. not liable, because Kate assumed the risk that the Bolt might explode—she was voluntarily standing in line.
d. not liable, because there was no privity between Kate and Bolt.

____   3. Sport Supplies sells a treadmill to John without warning him of the fact, known to Sport, that the safety shut-off device does not work. In using the treadmill, John discovers the defect. Later, while running on the treadmill, John's shoelace is caught in the gears, which do not shut off, and his foot is injured. If John sues Sport on the ground of strict liability in a jurisdiction that recognizes comparative negligence, Sport may be

a. entirely liable, because Sport was comparatively negligent.
b. partially liable, because Sport was comparatively negligent.
c. entirely liable, because John was comparatively negligent.
d. not liable, because John was comparatively negligent.

____   4. Laura tells the pharmacist at Green's Pharmacy that Laura needs something to cure her cough. In reaching for a bottle of cough medicine, the pharmacist unintentionally selects a bottle of poison, which Laura buys and uses. Laura is seriously injured. If Laura sues Green's, it will be held

a. liable, because the pharmacist's selection of the poison was an intervening cause.
b. liable, because the pharmacist misrepresented the contents of the bottle.
c. not liable, because Laura voluntarily assumed the risk of the harm when she asked the pharmacist for advice.
d. not liable, because the pharmacist unintentionally selected the poison.

_____ 5. Strict liability is imposed as a matter of public policy. This public policy rests on the assumption that

   a. consumers should be protected against unsafe products.
   b. manufacturers and distributors should not escape liability for faulty products simply because they are not in privity of contract with the ultimate users of those products.
   c. manufacturers and sellers of products are in a better position to bear the costs associated with injuries caused by their products.
   d. all of the above.

_____ 6. T&T, Inc., designs a product that is safe when used properly. Bob uses the product for an unforeseeable, improper use. If Bob sues T&T, the manufacturer will likely be held

   a. liable for negligence or misrepresentation only.
   b. strictly liable only.
   c. liable for negligence or misrepresentation or strictly liable.
   d. none of the above.

_____ 7. While using a grain auger made by Silo Implements, Bob fell into an opening on the top of the machine, injuring his legs. At the opening were several warning labels. Jane, Bob's employer, later welded a grid over the top to prevent future similar events. The grid did not interfere with the auger. If Bob sues Silo, on the ground of strict liability, Silo will likely be

   a. liable, because Silo did not disclaim its warranties.
   b. liable, because a less dangerous alternative (than the unguarded opening) was economically feasible, but Silo failed to use it.
   c. not liable, because warning labels were around the opening.
   d. not liable, because a less dangerous alternative (than the unguarded opening) was economically feasible, but Bob and Jane failed to use it.

_____ 8. Jane buys a defective product from Valu-Mart and is injured as a result of using the product. If Jane sues Valu-Mart based on strict liability, to recover damages she must prove that Valu-Mart

   a. defectively designed the product.
   b. failed to exercise due care.
   c. was engaged in the business of selling the product.
   d. was in privity of contract with Jane.

_____ 9. SmithCo supplies Jones, Inc., with components for its products. Jones assembles the components and sells the assembled products to consumers. Lee buys and uses one of the products and is injured due to a defective component. In a suit based on strict liability, Lee may recover damages from

   a. SmithCo only.
   b. Jones only.
   c. either SmithCo or Jones.
   d. none of the above.

____ **10.** Medco, Inc., manufactures a drug that it unknowingly misrepresents to physicians as nonaddictive. Dr. Ira prescribes the drug for Ben, who becomes addicted and dies. In a suit based on misrepresentation, Medco will likely

a. not be liable, because the physician prescribed the drug.
b. not be liable, because the misrepresentation was innocent.
c. be liable, even though the misrepresentation was innocent.
d. be liable, even though the patient assumed the risk.

SHORT ESSAY QUESTIONS

1. What distinguishes strict liability as a theory for recovery in a product liability case from other bases for recovery?

2. What sort of product defect will support a cause of action in strict liability?

ISSUE SPOTTERS

(Answers at the Back of the Book)

1. RollCo makes automobile wheels, which it sells to Mac Motor Corporation to put on its cars. One set of wheels is made of defective materials, which an inspection, before putting them on a car, would reveal. Mac does not inspect the wheels. The car is sold to Used Auto Sales. Keith buys the car. The wheels collapse while he is driving the car, causing an accident in which he and his passengers are injured. Is Mac liable?

2. Powell Candies manufactures a box of candy, which it sells to Jingle Concessions, a distributor of candy to theaters. Jingle sells it to Sky Cinemas. Judy buys the candy from Sky and gives it to Marie. Eating the candy, Marie breaks a tooth on a stone that is the same size, shape, and color of a piece of the candy. If they were not negligent, can Powell, Jingle, or Sky be held liable for the injury?

3. Edison, Inc., manufactures furniture polish. Edison does not intend that children drink the polish, but it does not include warnings to that effect on the label, and it does not sell the polish with a child-proof cap. Mary uses the polish and leaves it capped on a table near her baby's crib. The baby drinks it and dies. Can Edison be held liable for failing to guard against a reasonably foreseeable "misuse" of its product?

4. Anchor, Inc., makes prewrapped mattress springs. Through an employee's carelessness, an improperly wrapped spring is sold to Bloom Company, which uses it in the manufacture of a mattress. Bloom sells the mattress to Beds Unlimited, which sells it to Kay. While sleeping on the mattress, Kay is stabbed in the back by the spring. The wound becomes infected, and Kay becomes seriously ill. Can Anchor be held liable?

5. Good Lock Company makes automobile door locks. Premier Motors Corporation installs the locks on Premier cars. Doug buys a Premier car. While driving home, Doug does not wear a seat belt. In a one-car accident, he is thrown from the car when the door flies open and is killed. In a suit based on strict liability, could Good and Premier claim that Doug's failure to wear a seat belt contributed to his death?

SPECIAL INFORMATION FOR CPA CANDIDATES

The CPA examination has traditionally tested on three kinds of product liability actions: (1) UCC warranties (see Chapter 23), (2) negligence, and (3) strict liability.

In particular, in a negligence or strict liability action, remember that no privity of contract is required. Keep in mind that the negligence may occur at any stage in a product's development, manufacture, and sale. Review the elements for an action in strict product liability. Also, don't forget relevant defenses, including assumption of risk and foreseeable misuse.

Chapter 7
Intellectual Property

WHAT THIS CHAPTER IS ABOUT

Intellectual property consists of the products of intellectual, creative processes. Many of these products (such as inventions, books, software, movies, and songs) are protected by the law of trademarks, patents, copyrights, and related concepts. The first parts of this chapter outlines the laws that protect these products. The last part of this chapter covers the protection of intellectual property in cyberspace.

CHAPTER OUTLINE

I. TRADEMARKS AND RELATED PROPERTY

A. TRADEMARKS
Trademarks are protected at the federal level by the Lanham Act. Many states also have statutes that protect trademarks.

1. **What a Trademark Is**
   A distinctive mark, motto, device, or emblem that a manufacturer stamps, prints, or otherwise affixes to the goods it produces to distinguish them from the goods of other manufacturers.

2. **The Federal Trademark Dilution Act of 1995**
   Prohibits **dilution** (unauthorized use of marks on goods or services, even if they do not compete directly with products whose marks are copied).

3. **Trademark Registration**
   A trademark may be registered with a state or the federal government. Trademarks do not need to be registered to be protected.

   a. **Requirements for Federal Registration**
      A trademark may be filed with the U.S. Patent and Trademark Office on the basis of (1) use or (2) the intent to use the mark within six months (which may be extended to thirty months).

       b. **Renewal of Federal Registration**
       Between the fifth and sixth years and then every ten years (twenty years for marks registered before 1990).

    4. **Requirements for Trademark Protection**
    The extent to which the law protects a trademark is normally determined by how **distinctive** the mark is.

       a. **Fanciful, Arbitrary, or Suggestive Trademarks**
       Generally considered the most distinctive trademarks.

       b. **Descriptive Terms, Geographic Terms, and Personal Names**
       Not inherently distinctive and not protected until they acquire a **secondary meaning** (which means that customers associate the mark with the source of a product)

       c. **Generic Terms**
       Terms such as *bicycle* or *computer* receive no protection, even if they acquire secondary meaning.

    5. **Trademark Infringement**
    When a trademark is copied to a substantial degree or used in its entirety by another, the trademark is infringed.

B. **TRADE DRESS**
Trade dress is the image and appearance of a product, and is subject to the same protection as trademarks.

C. **SERVICE, CERTIFICATION, AND COLLECTIVE MARKS**
The same policies and restrictions that apply to trademarks normally apply to service, certification, and collective marks.

    1. **Service Marks**
    Used to distinguish the services of one person or company from those of another. Registered in the same manner as trademarks.

    2. **Certification Marks**
    Used by one or more persons, other than the owner, to certify the region, materials, mode of manufacture, quality, or accuracy of the owner's goods or services.

    3. **Collective Marks**
    Certification marks used by members of a cooperative, association, or other organization.

D. **TRADE NAMES**
Used to indicate part or all of a business's name. Trade names cannot be registered with the federal government but may be protected under the common law if they are used as trademarks or service marks.

II. PATENTS

A. **WHAT A PATENT IS**
A grant from the federal government that conveys and secures to an inventor the exclusive right to make, use, and sell an invention for a period of twenty years (fourteen years for a design).

B. REQUIREMENTS FOR A PATENT
An invention, discovery, or design must be genuine, novel, useful, and not obvious in light of the technology of the time. A patent is given to the first person to invent a product, not to the first person to file for a patent.

C. PATENT INFRINGEMENT
Making, using, or selling another's patented design, product, or process without the patent owner's permission. The owner may obtain an injunction, damages, destruction of all infringing copies, attorneys' fees, and court costs.

D. PATENTS FOR SOFTWARE
The basis for software is often a mathematical equation or formula, which is not patentable, but a patent can be obtained for a process that incorporates a computer program.

III.   COPYRIGHTS

A. WHAT A COPYRIGHT IS
An intangible right granted by statute to the author or originator of certain literary or artistic productions. Protection is automatic; registration is not required.

B. COPYRIGHT PROTECTION
Automatic for the life of the author plus fifty years. Copyrights owned by publishing houses expire seventy-five years from the date of publication or a hundred years from the date of creation, whichever is first. For works by more than one author, copyright expires fifty years after the death of the last surviving author.

C. WHAT IS PROTECTED EXPRESSION?
To be protected, a work must meet these requirements—

1. Fit a Certain Category
It must be a (1) literary work; (2) musical work; (3) dramatic work; (4) pantomime or choreographic work; (5) pictorial, graphic, or sculptural work; (6) film or other audiovisual work; or (7) a sound recording. The Copyright Act also protects computer software and architectural plans.

2. Be Fixed in a Durable Medium
From which it can be perceived, reproduced, or communicated.

3. Be Original
A compilation of facts (formed by the collection and assembling of preexisting materials of data) is copyrightable if it is original.

D. WHAT IS NOT PROTECTED
Ideas, facts, and related concepts. If an idea and an expression cannot be separated, the expression cannot be copyrighted.

E. COPYRIGHT INFRINGEMENT
A copyright is infringed if a work is copied without the copyright holder's permission. A copy does not have to be exactly the same as the original—copying a substantial part of the original is enough.

1. Penalties
Actual damages (based on the harm to the copyright holder); damages under the Copyright Act, not to exceed $150,000; and criminal proceedings (which may result in fines or imprisonment).

   2. **Exception—Fair Use Doctrine**
   The Copyright Act permits the fair use of a work for purposes such as criticism, comment, news reporting, teaching (including multiple copies for classroom use), scholarship, or research.

F. **COPYRIGHT PROTECTION FOR SOFTWARE**
The Computer Software Copyright Act of 1980 provides protection.

   1. **What Is Protected**
   The binary object code (the part of a software program readable only by computer); the source code (the part of a program readable by people); and the program structure, sequence, and organization.

   2. **What May or May Not Be Protected**
   The "look and feel"—the general appearance, command structure, video images, menus, windows, and other displays—of a program.

IV.   TRADE SECRETS

A. **WHAT A TRADE SECRET IS**
Customer lists, formulas, plans, research and development, pricing information, marketing techniques, production techniques, and generally anything that provides an opportunity to obtain an advantage over competitors who do not know or use it.

B. **TRADE SECRET PROTECTION**
Protection of trade secrets extends both to ideas and their expression. Liability extends to those who misappropriate trade secrets by any means. Trade secret theft is also a federal crime.

V.   INTERNATIONAL PROTECTION

A. **THE BERNE CONVENTION**
The Berne Convention is an international copyright treaty.

   1. **For Citizens of Countries That Have Signed the Berne Convention**
   If, for example, an American writes a book, the copyright in the book is recognized by every country that has signed the convention.

   2. **For Citizens of Other Countries**
   If a citizen of a country that has not signed the convention publishes a book first in a country that has signed, all other countries that have signed the convention recognize that author's copyright.

B. **THE TRIPS AGREEMENT**
Trade-Related Aspects of Intellectual Property Rights (TRIPS) Agreement is part of the agreement creating the World Trade Organization (WTO). Each member nation must not discriminate (in administration, regulation, or adjudication of intellectual property rights) against owners of such rights.

TRUE-FALSE QUESTIONS

(Answers at the Back of the Book)

_____   1.   To obtain a patent, an inventor must prove to the patent office that his or her invention is genuine, novel, useful, and not obvious in light of contemporary technology.

____ 2. To obtain a copyright, an author must prove to the copyright office that a work is genuine, novel, useful, and not a copy of another copyrighted work.

____ 3. Copyright infringement occurs if a computer program's structure, sequence, and organization is copied.

____ 4. A personal name can be trademarked if it has acquired a secondary meaning.

____ 5. Service, certification, and collective marks are covered by the same policies and restrictions that apply to copyrights.

____ 6. Protection of trade secrets extends only to the expression of ideas, not to the ideas themselves.

____ 7. Theft of trade secrets can be both a violation of common law and a crime.

____ 8. Common law protection of trademarks does not extend to trade names.

____ 9. A compilation of facts can be copyrighted if it is original.

____ 10. A copyright is infringed only if a work is copied in its entirety.

FILL-IN QUESTIONS

(Answers at the Back of the Book)

Copyright protection is automatic for the life of the author of a work plus _____ (70/95/120) years. Copyrights owned by publishing houses expire _____ (70/95/120) years from the date of the publication of a work or _____ (70/95/120) years from the date of its creation, whichever is first. For works by more than one author, a copyright expires _____ (70/95/120) years after the death of the last surviving author.

MULTIPLE-CHOICE QUESTIONS

(Answers at the Back of the Book)

____ 1. Without Tom's permission, Mary makes and sells computer monitors identical to Tom's patented monitor, except for slight differences in the controls. Tom's monitor is not trademarked. He sues Mary for patent infringement. Mary is

a. liable, because she is making and selling Tom's monitor without permission.
b. not liable, because Tom does not also have a trademark.
c. not liable, because of the differences between the monitors' controls.
d. not liable, because she is not stealing actual monitors that Tom made.

____ 2. Mark Corporation uses a monkey symbol in marketing its Monkey brand jeans but has not registered the symbol with a government office. Quick, Inc., imports jeans made abroad and sells them with the monkey symbol, which it also has not registered. Mark sues Quick. Quick is

a. liable, because it had no right to trade on Mark's goodwill.
b. not liable, because Mark did not register the symbol with the government.
c. not liable, because it did not manufacture the jeans, it only imported them.
d. not liable, because a monkey symbol cannot be a trademark.

___ **3.** To compile a directory of all persons living in Chicago organized by the name of the street on which they live, A&B Directories, Inc., uses, without permission, information in a telephone directory published by National Pages, Inc. A&B has probably NOT violated copyright law because

   a. an alphabetical list of persons is not original.
   b. facts are protected by federal trademark law.
   c. only literary works are protected by copyright law.
   d. the two directories are not directly competitive.

___ **4.** Betty develops accounting software for Worldwide Corporation. The Computer Software Copyright Act of 1980 extends copyright protection to the software's

   a. source code and binary code only.
   b. structure, sequence, and organization only.
   c. source code, binary code, structure, sequence, and organization.
   d. none of the above.

___ **5.** Univision Products develops new desktop publishing software. The software may NOT be patentable if it

   a. simply automates procedures that can be performed manually.
   b. has a mathematical equation or formula as its basis.
   c. either a and b.
   d. none of the above.

___ **6.** Ken invents a light bulb that lasts longer than ordinary bulbs. To prevent others from making, using, or selling the bulb or its design, he should obtain

   a. a copyright.
   b. a patent.
   c. a trademark.
   d. none of the above.

___ **7.** Standard Products, Inc., obtains a patent on a laser printer. This patent is violated if the printer is copied

   a. in its entirety only.
   b. in part.
   c. not at all.
   d. none of the above.

___ **8.** Bob works for Eagle Manufacturing Company, under a contract in which he agrees not to disclose any process he uses while in Eagle's employ. When Bob goes into business for himself, he copies some of Eagle's unique production techniques. Bob has committed

   a. copyright infringement.
   b. patent infringement.
   c. theft of a trade secret.
   d. trademark infringement.

____ 9. To identify its goods, Nationwide Products use a red, white, and blue symbol that combines the letter N and a map of the United States. This symbol is protected by

a. copyright law.
b. patent law.
c. trademark law.
d. all of the above.

____ 10. Clothes made by members of the Union of Clothing Workers are sold with tags that identify this fact. This tag is a

a. certification mark.
b. collective mark.
c. service mark.
d. trade name.

SHORT ESSAY QUESTIONS

1. What does a copyright protect?

2. What is a trade secret and how is it protected?

ISSUE SPOTTERS

(Answers at the Back of the Book)

1. A video game manufacturer develops a gladiator video game with distinctive graphics. Can the developer prevent a competitor from producing another game based on gladiators? Can the developer prevent competitors from copying the graphics?

2. Maldo writes, copyrights, and publishes in the United States a book in Spanish titled *En la Casa del Tigre*. What copyright protection does Maldo have in other countries?

3. Crabb's Apple Ball Company makes and sells "Crabb's Apple Balls," a distinctively flavored candy. Green Candy Corporation begins making and marketing "Green's Apple Balls." Can Crabb prevent Green from using the words "Apple Balls" for its candy?

4. Burley Seed Company discovers that it can extract data from the computer of North King Hybrids, Inc., its major competitor, by making a series of telephone calls over a high-speed modem. When Burley uses its discovery to extract North King's customer lists, without North King's permission, what recourse does North King have?

5. Global Products develops, patents, and markets software. World Copies, Inc., sells Global's software without the maker's permission. Is this patent infringement? If so, how might Global save the cost of suing World for infringement and at the same time profit from World's sales?

SPECIAL INFORMATION FOR CPA CANDIDATES

The material in this chapter has not traditionally been part of the CPA examination.

When studying for the CPA exam, many students integrate their review of business law topics with their review of other topics that make up distinct subject matter on the exam.   For example, when reviewing the law behind business organizations, it can be most helpful to review the accounting and reporting details behind businesses' financial statements. Which topics to integrate and how much time to spend on each depends in part on each student's knowledge and understanding of the individual topics, as well as the emphasis that should be placed on a topic because of its importance for the exam.

Chapter 8:
Criminal Law and Procedures

WHAT THIS CHAPTER IS ABOUT

This chapter defines what makes an act a crime, describes crimes, lists defenses to crimes, and outlines criminal procedure. Sanctions for crimes are different from those for torts or breaches of contract. Another difference between civil and criminal law is that individuals can bring civil suits but only the government can prosecute criminals.

CHAPTER OUTLINE

I. CIVIL LAW AND CRIMINAL LAW

A. CIVIL LAW
Civil law consists of the duties that exist between persons or between citizens and their governments, excluding the duty not to commit crimes.

B. CRIMINAL LAW
A **crime** is a wrong against society proclaimed in a statute and, if committed, punishable by society through fines, imprisonment, or death. Crimes are offenses against society as a whole (some torts are also crimes) and are prosecuted by public officials, not victims. In a criminal trial, the state must prove its case beyond a reasonable doubt.

II. CLASSIFICATION OF CRIMES
Felonies are serious crimes punishable by death or by imprisonment in a federal or state penitentiary for more than a year. A crime that is not a felony is a **misdemeanor**—punishable by a fine or by confinement (in a local jail) for up to a year. Petty offenses are minor misdemeanors.

III. THE ESSENTIALS OF CRIMINAL LIABILITY
Two elements must exist for a person to be convicted of a crime:

A. THE CRIMINAL ACT (*ACTUS REUS*)
A criminal statute prohibits certain behavior—an act of commission (doing something) or an act of omission (not doing something that is a legal duty).

B. STATE OF MIND (INTENT TO COMMIT A CRIME, OR *MENS REA*)
The mental state required to establish criminal guilt depends on the crime.

IV. CORPORATE CRIMINAL LIABILITY

Corporations are liable for (1) crimes committed by their agents and employees within the course and scope of employment, (2) failing to perform a specific affirmative duty imposed by law, or (3) crimes authorized, commanded, committed, or recklessly tolerated by a firm's high managerial agents. Directors and officers are personally liable for crimes they commit and may be liable for the actions of employees under their supervision.

V. TYPES OF CRIMES

A. VIOLENT CRIME
These include murder, rape, assault and battery (see Chapter 5), and *robbery* (forcefully and unlawfully taking personal property from another). Classified by degree, depending on intent, weapon, and victim's suffering.

B. PROPERTY CRIME
Robbery could also be in this category.

  1. Burglary
  Unlawful entry into a building with the intent to commit a felony.

  2. Larceny
  Wrongfully taking and carrying away another's personal property with the intent of depriving the owner permanently of the property (without force or intimidation, which are elements of robbery).

   a. Property
   Property includes computer programs, computer time, trade secrets, cellular phone numbers, long-distance phone time, and natural gas.

   b. Grand Larceny and Petit Larceny
   In some states, grand larceny is a felony and petit larceny a misdemeanor. The difference depends on the value of the property taken.

  3. Arson
  The willful and malicious burning, by fire or explosion, of a building (and in some states, personal property) owned by another. Every state has a statute that covers burning a building to collect insurance.

  4. Receiving Stolen Goods
  The recipient need not know the identity of the true owner of the goods.

  5. Forgery
  Fraudulently making or altering any writing in a way that changes the legal rights and liabilities of another.

  6. Obtaining Goods by False Pretenses
  Obtaining goods through fraud or deceit.

C. PUBLIC ORDER CRIME
Examples: public drunkenness, prostitution, gambling, and illegal drug use.

D. WHITE-COLLAR CRIME

1. **Embezzlement**
   Fraudulently appropriating another's property or money by one who has been entrusted with it (without force or intimidation).

2. **Mail and Wire Fraud**

   a. **The Crime**
      It is a federal crime to (1) mail or cause someone else to mail something written, printed, or photocopied for the purpose of executing (2) a scheme to defraud (even if no one is defrauded). Also a crime to use wire, radio, or television transmissions to defraud.

   b. **The Punishment**
      Fine of up to $1,000, imprisonment for up to five years, or both. If the violation affects a financial institution, the fine may be up to $1 million, the imprisonment up to thirty years, or both.

3. **Bribery**

   a. **Bribery of Public Officials**
      Attempting to influence a public official to act in a way that serves a private interest by offering the official a bribe. Committed when the bribe (anything the recipient considers valuable) is offered.

   b. **Commercial Bribery**
      Attempting, by a bribe, to obtain proprietary information, cover up an inferior product, or secure new business.

   c. **Bribery of Foreign Officials**
      Attempting, by bribing foreign officials, to obtain business contracts. Banned by Foreign Corrupt Practices Act of 1977 (see Chapter 52).

4. **Bankruptcy Fraud**
   Filing a false claim against a debtor; fraudulently transferring assets to favored parties; or fraudulently concealing property before or after a petition for bankruptcy is filed.

5. **Insider Trading**
   Using inside information (information not available to the general public) about a publicly traded corporation to profit from the purchase or sale of the corporation's securities (see Chapter 37).

6. **Theft of Trade Secrets**
   Under the Economic Espionage Act of 1996, it is a federal crime to steal trade secrets, or to knowingly buy or possess another's stolen secrets. Penalties include up to ten years' imprisonment, fines up to $500,000 (individual) or $5 million (corporation), and forfeiture of property.

E. **ORGANIZED CRIME**

   1. **Money Laundering**
      Transferring the proceeds of crime through legitimate businesses. Financial institutions must report transactions of more than $10,000.

   2. **RICO**
      Two offenses under the Racketeer Influenced and Corrupt Organizations Act (RICO) of 1970 constitutes "racketeering activity."

a. Activities Prohibited by RICO

(1) Use income from racketeering to buy an interest in an enterprise, (2) acquire or maintain such an interest through racketeering activity' (3) conduct or participate in an enterprise through racketeering activity, or 4) conspire to do any of the above.

b. Civil Liability

Civil penalties include divestiture of a defendant's interest in a business or dissolution of the business. Private individuals can recover treble damages, plus attorneys' fees, for business injuries.

c. Criminal Liability

RICO can be used to attack white-collar crime. Penalties include fines of up to $25,000 per violation, imprisonment for up to 20 years, or both.

F. COMPUTER CRIME

Computer crime is any act that is directed against computers or computer parts, that uses computers as instruments of crime, or that involves computers and constitutes abuse.

1. Financial Crimes

Unauthorized transfer of monies among accounts; unauthorized alteration of computer records.

2. Property Crimes

Theft of computer equipment (hardware) or of goods controlled or accounted for by means of a computer is subject to the same criminal and tort laws as thefts of other property. Using another's computer, computer information system, or data without authorization is larceny. Destructive programming is a crime.

VI. DEFENSES TO CRIMINAL LIABILITY

A. INFANCY

In some states, children up to age seven are considered not to understand they are committing a crime. Children between seven and fourteen may be presumed incapable of committing a crime, but this can be rebutted.

B. INTOXICATION

Involuntary intoxication is a defense to a crime if it makes a person incapable of understanding that the act committed was wrong or incapable of obeying the law. *Voluntary* intoxication may be a defense if the person was so intoxicated as to lack the required state of mind.

C. INSANITY

1. The *M'Naughten* Test

Some states use this test: a person is not responsible if at the time of the offense, he or she did not know the nature and quality of the act or did not know that the act was wrong.

2. The Irresistible Impulse Test

Some states use this test: a person operating under an irresistible impulse may know an act is wrong but cannot refrain from doing it.

3. **The Model Penal Code Test**

Most federal courts and some states use this test: a person is not responsible for criminal conduct if at the time, as a result of mental disease or defect, the person lacks substantial capacity either to appreciate the wrongfulness of the conduct or to conform his or her conduct to the law.

D. MISTAKE

1. **Mistake of Fact**

Defense if it negates the mental state necessary to commit a crime.

2. **Mistake of Law**

A person not knowing a law was broken may have a defense if (1) the law was not published or reasonably made known to the public or (2) the person relied on an official statement of the law that was wrong.

E. CONSENT

Defense if it cancels the harm that the law is designed to prevent, unless the law forbids an act without regard to the victim's consent.

F. DURESS

1. **What Duress Is**

When a person's threat induces another person to perform an act that he or she would not otherwise perform.

2. **When Duress Is a Defense**

(1) The threat is one of serious bodily harm, (2) the threat is immediate and inescapable, (3) the threatened harm is greater than the harm caused by the crime, (4) the defendant is involved through no fault of his or her own, and (5) the crime is not murder.

G. JUSTIFIABLE USE OF FORCE

1. **Nondeadly Force**

People can use as much nondeadly force as seems necessary to protect themselves, their dwellings, or other property or to prevent a crime.

2. **Deadly Force**

Can be used in self-defense if there is a reasonable belief that imminent death or serious bodily harm will otherwise result, if the attacker is using unlawful force, and if the defender did not provoke the attack.

H. NECESSITY

A defendant may be relieved of liability if his or her criminal act was necessary to prevent an even greater harm.

I. ENTRAPMENT

When a law enforcement agent suggests that a crime be committed, pressures or induces an individual to commit it, and arrests the individual for it.

J. STATUTE OF LIMITATIONS

Provides that the state has only a certain amount of time to prosecute a crime. Most statutes of limitations do not apply to murder.

K. IMMUNITY

A state can grant immunity from prosecution or agree to prosecute for a less serious offense in exchange for information. This is often part of a plea bargain between the defendant and the prosecutor.

VII.   CRIMINAL PROCEDURES

A. CONSTITUTIONAL SAFEGUARDS

Most of these safeguards apply not only in federal but also in state courts by virtue of the due process clause of the Fourteenth Amendment.

1. **Fourth Amendment**

   Protection from unreasonable searches and seizures. No warrants for a search or an arrest can be issued without probable cause.

2. **Fifth Amendment**

   No one can be deprived of "life, liberty, or property without due process of law." No one can be tried twice (double jeopardy) for the same offense. No one can be required to incriminate himself or herself.

3. **Sixth Amendment**

   Guarantees a speedy trial, trial by jury, a public trial, the right to confront witnesses, and the right to a lawyer in some proceedings.

4. **Eighth Amendment**

   Prohibits excessive bail and fines, and cruel and unusual punishment.

B. THE EXCLUSIONARY RULE

Evidence obtained in violation of the Fourth, Fifth, and Sixth Amendments, as well as all "fruit of the poisonous tree" (evidence derived from illegally obtained evidence), must be excluded.

C. THE *MIRANDA* RULE

A person in custody who is to be interrogated must be informed (1) he or she has the right to remain silent, (2) anything said can and will be used against him or her in court, (3) he or she has the right to consult with an attorney, and (4) if he or she is indigent, a lawyer will be appointed.

1. **Exceptions**

   Rights can be waived. "Public safety" (need to protect public may warrant admissibility). If other evidence justifies a conviction, it will not be overturned if confession was coerced. A suspect must assertively state that he or she wants a lawyer, to exercise the right.

2. **Section 3501 of the Omnibus Crime Control Act of 1968**

   Statements can be used against defendants as long as statements are voluntary. (This provision may be unconstitutional.)

D. CRIMINAL PROCESS

1. **Arrest**

   Requires a warrant based on probable cause (a substantial likelihood that the person has committed or is about to commit a crime). To make an arrest without a warrant, an officer must also have probable cause.

2. **Indictment or Information**

   A formal charge is called an **indictment** if issued by a grand jury and an **information** if issued by a public prosecutor.

3. **Trial**

   Criminal trial procedures are similar to those of a civil trial, but the standard of proof is higher: the prosecutor must establish guilt beyond a reasonable doubt.

4. **Federal Sentencing Guidelines**
   Possible penalties for federal crimes. Sentence is based on a defendant's criminal record, seriousness of the offense, and other factors.

TRUE-FALSE QUESTIONS

(Answers at the Back of the Book)

____ 1. A crime is a wrong against society proclaimed in a statute.

____ 2. A person can be convicted simply for intending to commit a crime.

____ 3. If a crime is punishable by death, it must be a felony.

____ 4. Children over age fourteen are presumed competent to stand trial.

____ 5. A person who has been granted immunity from prosecution cannot be compelled to answer any questions.

____ 6. Burglary is the taking of another's personal property, from his or her person or immediate presence.

____ 7. The willful and malicious burning of a building or some other structure owned by another is arson.

____ 8. Stealing a computer program is not a crime.

____ 9. Fraudulently altering a public document can be forgery.

____ 10. Persons suffering from mental illness are sometimes judged incapable of the state of mind required to commit a crime.

FILL-IN QUESTIONS

(Answers at the Back of the Book)

Specific constitutional safeguards for those accused of crimes apply in all federal courts, and most of them also apply in state courts under the due process clause of the Fourteenth Amendment. The safeguards include (1) the Fourth Amendment protection from _____ (unexpected/unreasonable) searches and seizures, (2) the Fourth Amendment requirement that no warrants for a search or an arrest can be issued without _____ (probable/possible) cause, (3) the Fifth Amendment requirement that no one can be deprived of "life, liberty, or property without _____ _____ (consent/due process of law)," (4) the Fifth Amendment prohibition against double _____ (immunity/jeopardy), (5) the Sixth Amendment guaranties of a speedy _____ (appeal/trial), _____ _____ (appeal to/trial by) a jury, a public trial, the right to confront _____ (counsel/witnesses), and the right to legal counsel, and (6) the Eighth Amendment prohibitions against excessive _____ (bail/bail and fines) and cruel and unusual punishment.

MULTIPLE-CHOICE QUESTIONS

(Answers at the Back of the Book)

1. Tom commits a crime. Regarding this situation, which of the following is TRUE?

    a. Tom may be prosecuted by the state.
    b. If Tom is prosecuted, he must prove his innocence.
    c. Prosecution of Tom would be intended to give the victims compensation.
    d. Tom's crime may be a violation of common law but never a statute.

2. For Beth to commit a crime, she must

    a. perform a prohibited act only.
    b. intend to commit a crime only.
    c. intend to commit a crime and perform a prohibited act.
    d. none of the above.

3. Helen, an undercover police officer, pressures Pete to buy stolen goods. When he does so, he is arrested and charged with dealing in stolen goods. Pete will likely be

    a. acquitted, because he was entrapped.
    b. acquitted, because Helen was entrapped.
    c. acquitted, because both parties were entrapped.
    d. convicted.

4. Police officer Carol arrests John on suspicion of burglary. Carol advises John of his *Miranda* rights. These rights include

    a. the right to remain silent and to consult with an attorney.
    b. being told that anything said can and will be used against John in court.
    c. both a and b.
    d. none of the above.

5. Sue is charged with car theft. Rob, the prosecutor, tells her that if she will inform on her criminal companions, he will grant her immunity. This is

    a. an inquisition.
    b. an indictment.
    c. a plea bargain.
    d. none of the above.

6. In a jewelry store, April takes a diamond ring from the counter and puts it in her pocket. She walks three steps toward the door before the manager stops her. April is arrested and charged with larceny. She will likely be

    a. acquitted, because she was entrapped.
    b. acquitted, because she only took three steps.
    c. acquitted, because she did not leave the store.
    d. convicted.

_____ 7. Kevin takes home the company-owned laptop computer that he uses in his office. He has no intention of returning it. Kevin has committed

   a. embezzlement.
   b. larceny.
   c. obtaining goods by false pretenses.
   d. none of the above.

_____ 8. Police detective Howard suspects Eva of a crime. Howard may be issued a warrant to search Eva's premises if he can show

   a. causation in fact.
   b. intent to search the premises.
   c. probable cause.
   d. proximate cause.

_____ 9. Greg is convicted of committing a crime. Trying Greg a second time for the same crime (double jeopardy) is

   a. permitted only if the verdict in the first trial was "guilty."
   b. permitted only if the verdict in the first trial was "not guilty."
   c. permitted regardless of the verdict in the first trial.
   d. prohibited.

_____ 10. Police officer Katy obtains a confession from criminal suspect Bart after an illegal arrest. At Bart's trial, the confession would likely be

   a. admitted as evidence of Bart's crime.
   b. admitted as proof of Bart's guilt.
   c. admitted as support for Katy's suspicions.
   d. excluded.

SHORT ESSAY QUESTIONS

1. What are some of the significant differences between criminal law and civil law?

2. What constitutes civil liability under the Racketeer Influenced and Corrupt Organizations Act (RICO) of 1968 and what are the penalties?

ISSUE SPOTTERS

(Answers at the Back of the Book)

1. Bob drives off in Fred's car mistakenly believing that it is his. Is this theft?

2. Holding Gail's child by the arm, Frank threatens to kill the child unless Gail takes part in a convenience store robbery. If Gail participates, and is subsequently arrested and charged, could she be acquitted on the basis of Frank's threat to her child?

3. With Jim's permission, Lee signs Jim's name to several traveler's checks that were issued to Jim and cashes them. Jim reports that the checks were stolen and receives replacements. Has Lee committed forgery?

4.   Jennifer takes her roommate's credit card, intending to charge expenses that she incurs on a vacation. Jennifer's first stop is a gas station, where she uses the card to pay for gas. With respect to the gas station, has Jennifer committed a crime? If so, what?

5.   Carl appears on television talk shows touting a cure for AIDS that he knows is fraudulent, because it has no medical validity. He frequently mentions that he needs funds to make the cure widely available, and donations pour into local television stations to be forwarded to Carl. Has Carl committed a crime? If so, what?

SPECIAL INFORMATION FOR CPA CANDIDATES

In the past, the CPA examination has not tested knowledge of specific crimes. Instead, the exam has asked for responses concerning liability in the context of corporate crime and in the area of accountants' liability. The first topic is covered in part in this chapter and in part in Chapter 35. Depending on the circumstances, corporate officers or directors may be liable for corporate crimes. An employer may also be liable for the crimes of his or her employees, although probably not in the absence of a specific statute setting out that liability. Accountants' criminal liability is covered in Chapter 51.

★ Key Points

The **key points** in this chapter include:

1. When a court can exercise jurisdiction over a party who does business over the Internet.

2. Limits on government restrictions of Web site access and content.

3. Laws that apply to crimes and torts in cyberspace.

4. The legal protection for intellectual property in digital form.

5. The legal framework for doing business in cyberspace.

Chapter 9
Cyberlaw and E-Commerce

WHAT THIS CHAPTER IS ABOUT

How the law deals with cyberspace, the Internet, and the World Wide Web is the focus of this chapter. The most distinguishing feature of the new technology is that geographical, physical, and political boundaries are not limiting factors. This affects how the law applies. Currently, there are more questions than answers.

CHAPTER OUTLINE

I. THE COURTS

A. CHANGES IN PRACTICES AND PROCEDURES
To save time, storage space, etc., courts are switching from paper to electronic document filing, using the Internet, electronic mail (e-mail) systems, and computer disks. The future may see the use of virtual courtrooms, in which proceedings take place only on the Internet.

B. JURISDICTION IN CYBERSPACE
Whether a court can compel the appearance of a party *outside* the physical limits of the court's jurisdiction depends on the amount of business the party transacts over the Internet with parties *within* the court's jurisdiction.

II. THE CONSTITUTION
Most tech-related constitutional issues involve regulations of speech. Challenges are often based on the commerce clause or the First Amendment (which limits the government's power to censor speech) (see Chapter 4).

A. ENCRYPTION CODES
Encryption code is used in software to scramble data so that it is virtually unreadable except to those with the decryption code. Regulations of the code have been challenged as violations of the First Amendment, but courts do not always consider encryption code to be "speech."

B. **THE CONTENTS OF WEB SITES**
Content restrictions are generally held to violate the First Amendment, but even legal restrictions are almost impossible to enforce in cyberspace (in part because the Internet crosses all jurisdictions).

C. **ACCESS TO WEB SITES**
The use of filters by government employers, public schools, and public libraries may be held to violate the First Amendment.

III. CYBER CRIMES
Investigation and prosecution of cyber crimes are sometimes hampered by jurisdictional issues and the anonymous nature of technology.

A. **CYBER STALKING**
Harassing a person in cyberspace (such as via e-mail). Prohibited by federal law and by about half the states. Some states require a "credible threat" that puts the person in reasonable fear for his or her safety or the safety of the person's family.

B. **CYBER THEFT**
Accessing a computer online, without authority, to obtain classified, restricted, or protected data, or attempting to do so. Prohibited by the National Information Infrastructure Protection Act of 1996. Penalties include fines and imprisonment for up to twenty years (and civil suits).

C. **CYBER TERRORISM**
Exploiting computers for such serious impacts as the exploding of a "bomb" to shut down a central computer. Federal Intrusion Detection Network (FIDNET) is intended to protect the nation's data system from terrorists through an extensive computer monitoring system

IV. CYBER TORTS

A. **DEFAMATION ONLINE**
Under the Communications Decency Act of 1996, Internet service providers (ISPs) are not liable for the defamatory remarks of those who use their services. (Defamation is discussed in Chapter 5.)

B. **SPAM**
Spam is junk e-mail. The First Amendment limits what the government can do to restrict it, but its sending may constitute trespass to personal property.

V. VIRTUAL PROPERTY
Too much legal protection of virtual property (intellectual property in cyberspace) impairs the fair use of data; too little reduces its availability.

A. **CYBER MARKS**
Some questions concerning cyber marks (trademarks in cyberspace) relate to Web site links and frames (see Chapter 7).

1. **Domain Names**
The Internet Corporation for Assigned Names and Numbers (ICANN) oversees the Internet domain name system. A Uniform Domain Name Dispute Resolution Policy sets out a procedure for a complaint about the impact of a domain name on a trademark.

2. **Meta Tags**
Words in a Web site's key-word field that determine the site's appearance in search engine results. Using others' marks as tags without permission may constitute infringement.

3. **Dilution**

Using a mark, without permission, in a way that diminishes its distinctive quality. Tech-related cases have concerned the use of marks as domain names and spamming under another's logo.

4. **Licensing**

Permitting the use of a mark for certain purposes. Use for other purposes is a breach of the license agreement.

B. PATENTS ONLINE

The number of software patents is increasing rapidly. (Patent data is available online.) Software developers should—

1. **Obtain Licenses for Products**

When using others' software to create new products.

2. **Issue Licenses for Products**

To prevent patent infringement.

3. **Reveal Products in Development**

To prevent others working on the same products from obtaining a patent.

C. COPYRIGHTS IN DIGITAL INFORMATION

Copyright law is important in cyberspace in part because the nature of the Internet means that data is "copied" before being transferred online.

1. **Copyright Act of 1976**

Copyright law requires the copyright holder's permission to sell a "copy" of a work. For these purposes, loading a file or program into a computer's random access memory (RAM) is the making of a "copy."

2. **World Intellectual Property Organization (WIPO) Copyright Treaty**

Enacted in 1996. Strengthens some rights for copyright owners in cyberspace, but does not make clear what, under international law, constitutes the making of a "copy" in electronic form.

3. **Digital Millennium Copyright Act of 1998**

Imposes penalties on anyone who circumvents encryption software or other technological anti-piracy protection. Also prohibits the manufacture, import, sale, or distribution of devices or services for circumvention. ISP s are not liable for their customers' violations.

D. TRADE SECRETS IN CYBERSPACE

The nature of technology (especially e-mail) undercuts a firm's ability to protect its confidential information, including trade secrets (see Chapter 7).

VI. E-COMMERCE

A. CONTRACTING IN CYBERSPACE

How should the law adapt to reflect practices regarding Web site click-on agreements, software licenses, e-data interchange, and online sales?

1. **Uniform Computer Information Transactions Act (UCITA)**

Our economy is centered on information products and services. UCITA provides uniform legal rules for this context. It parallels UCC Article 2, with additional provisions to cover new tech-related circumstances.

2. **Uniform Electronic Transactions Act**

Supports the enforcement of e-contracts and the validity of electronic signatures.

3. **International Steps**
The United Nations Commission on International Trade Law (UNCITRAL) issued a model law for e-contracts. The International Chamber of Commerce issued model e-commerce guidelines.

B. **E-MONEY**
Alternatives to traditional means of payment include prepaid funds recorded on a consumer's personal computer or on a card.

1. **Card-Based E-Money**
A balance of funds may be recorded on a magnetic stripe on a card, which is debited by a computer terminal with each use, or a microprocessor chip may be embedded on a "smart" card. A smart card may function as a credit card, a debit card, a stored value card, and a personal information card.

2. **Payment Information: Privacy and Security**
It is not clear what law applies. Federal law prohibiting unauthorized access to e-communications might apply. Financial institutions are being encouraged to create a plan of self-regulation.

C. **MARKETING ON THE INTERNET**
How can the law be applied against fraud, deception, and misleading information without stifling the potential of the Internet?

1. **Consumer Data**
Data about users can be gathered (and sold) without their permission or knowledge. Some see this as an invasion of privacy.

2. **Web Site Content**
To avoid possible penalties and suits, Web site content must be current.

3. **Cyber Fraud**
Most state and federal laws that apply to unfair and deceptive acts also apply to cyber fraud. Prosecution is complicated by the nature of technology, and questions of jurisdiction and other legal issues.

TRUE-FALSE QUESTIONS

(Answers at the Back of the Book)

____ 1. A court cannot compel the appearance of a party outside the physical limits of the court's jurisdiction.

____ 2. Courts always consider encryption code to be "speech."

____ 3. Courts generally hold that Web-site content restrictions violate the First Amendment.

____ 4. Cyber stalking is not a crime.

____ 5. Internet service providers are not normally liable for the defamatory remarks of those who use their services.

____ 6. There is no limit on what the government can do to restrict spam.

____ 7. Using another's trademark as a meta tag without permission may constitute trademark infringement.

____ 8. Loading a file or program into a computer's random access memory (RAM) is the making of a "copy" for purposes of international law.

___ **9.** Federal law specifically protects e-money payment information.

___ **10.** Most laws that apply to unfair and deceptive acts also apply to cyber fraud.

FILL-IN QUESTIONS

(Answers at the Back of the Book)

Using others' marks as meta tags, without permission, violates _____ (copyright/patent/trademark/no) law. Using a mark, without permission, in a way that diminishes its distinctive quality is a violation of _____ (copyright/patent/trademark/no) law. "Liberating" another's patented product by incorporating it, without permission, into a newer, better product is a violation of _____ (copyright/patent/trademark/no) law. Circumventing encryption software is, with some exceptions, a violation of _____ (copyright/patent/trademark/no) law.

MULTIPLE-CHOICE QUESTIONS

(Answers at the Back of the Book)

___ **1.** Bob, who lives in Texas, advertises his business on the Web. Bob's page receives hundreds of "hits" by residents of Ohio. If a resident of Ohio files a suit against Bob in an Ohio state court, the court can compel Bob to appear, under the "sliding scale" test, if

a. Bob conducted substantial business with Ohio residents at his Web site.
b. there was any interactivity with any Ohio resident at Bob's Web site.
c. Bob's Web site was only a passive ad.
d. any of the above.

___ **2.** Adams County Library wants to prevent children from viewing, on its public access computers, obscene materials available on the Internet. To reach this goal, under the First Amendment, Adams can use any means

a. available.
b. broadly capable of attaining the objective.
c. narrowly drawn to achieve the end.
d. specifically aimed at particular Web sites.

___ **3.** Internet Services, Inc. (ISI), is an Internet service provider. ISI does not create, but disseminates, a defamatory statement by Jill, its customer, about Ron. Liability for the remark may be imposed on

a. both ISI and Jill.
b. either ISI or Jill, but not both.
c. ISI only.
d. Jill only.

___ **4.** Online Services Company (OSC) is an Internet service provider. Ads Unlimited, Inc., transmits unsolicited e-mail (spam) to OSC's customers, some of whom then cancel OSC's services. Ads Unlimited is liable for

a. cyber fraud.
b. cyber terrorism.
c. trespass in a public forum.
d. trespass to personal property.

___ 5. Regional Sales, Inc., is named Small Business of the Year (SBY) by Business Enterprises, Inc. (BEI). SBY is a BEI trademark. Regional Sales uses SBY as a tag for its Web site. This is

a. cyber theft.
b. fair use of another's trademark.
c. trademark infringement.
d. trespass to personal property.

___ 6. Data View Corporation (DVC) licenses to Datavista Company the use of DVC's trademark for the sole purpose of including it in Datavista's domain name. Datavista redesigns its Web site to resemble DVC's site. This is

a. a legal, sincere form of flattery.
b. within the terms of the licensing agreement.
c. a violation of the licensing agreement.
d. none of the above.

___ 7. International Media, Inc. (IMI), publishes *U.S. Opinion* magazine, which contains an article by Carl. Without Carl's permission, IMI puts Carl's article into an online database. This is

a. copyright infringement.
b. patent infringement.
c. trademark infringement.
d. none of the above.

___ 8. One World, Inc., an ISP, collects data about its members and without their knowledge or consent sells it to advertisers. One World may be liable for

a. cyber theft.
b. misrepresentation.
c. trespass to personal property.
d. violation of a licensing agreement.

___ 9. Ace Manufacturing Corporation orders from E-One Products Company goods that E-One offers for sale on the Web. Ace pays for the goods, but E-One does not deliver. This is

a. cyber fraud.
b. trespass to personal property.
c. violation of a licensing agreement.
d. none of the above.

___ 10. John advertises his consulting service with false testimonials that purport to be from satisfied clients. These testimonials are sent to members of Internet newsgroups. This is

a. cyber fraud.
b. trespass to personal property.
c. violation of a licensing agreement.
d. none of the above.

SHORT ESSAY QUESTIONS

1. What permits a court to exercise jurisdiction based on contacts over the Internet?

2. Why is copyright the most important form of intellectual property protection on the Internet? What is the protection for copyrighted works online?

ISSUE SPOTTERS

(Answers at the Back of the Book)

1. Mary, who lives in Illinois, advertises her business on the Web. The Web page is a passive ad that includes a toll-free phone number. Nick, a resident of Utah, files a suit against Mary in a Utah state court. Can the court compel Mary to appear based on her ad on the Web?

2. Digital Products, Inc., markets encryption software in the United States. Can Digital Products sell this software in Europe? If not, why not?

3. Ben downloads consumer credit files over the Internet from a computer of Ace Credit Agency, without Ace's permission. Ben sells the data to Paula. Has Ben committed a crime? If so, what are the penalties?

4. Eagle Corporation begins marketing financial software in 1990 and owns the mark "Eagle." In 1992, Eagle.com, Inc., a different company selling different products, begins to use "eagle.com" as part of its URL and registers it as a domain name. Can Eagle block this use of "eagle"? If so, what must the company prove to do so?

5. Alpha Applications, Inc., develops software applications code. Under an agreement, Alpha gives the code to Beta Products, Inc., for the sole purpose of incorporating parts of it in Beta's new operating system (OS) software. Beta alters the code so that, as incorporated in Beta's OS, it will run only with Beta's software products. Is this a violation of the agreement between Alpha and Beta?

SPECIAL INFORMATION FOR CPA CANDIDATES

The material in this chapter has not traditionally been part of the CPA examination.

When studying for the CPA exam, many students integrate their review of business law topics with their review of other topics that make up distinct subject matter on the exam. For example, when reviewing the law behind business organizations, it can be most helpful to review the accounting and reporting details behind businesses' financial statements. Which topics to integrate and how much time to spend on each depends in part on each student's knowledge and understanding of the individual topics, as well as the emphasis that should be placed on a topic because of its importance for the exam.

CUMULATIVE HYPOTHETICAL PROBLEM FOR UNIT ONE—INCLUDING CHAPTERS 1–9

(Answers at the Back of the Book)

Computer Data, Inc. (CDI), incorporated and based in California, signs a contract with Digital Products Corporation (DPC), incorporated and based in Arizona, to make and sell customized software for DPC to, in turn, sell to its clients.

—— **1.** To protect the rights that CDI has in the software it produces, CDI's best protection is offered by

 a. constitutional law.
 b. criminal law.
 c. intellectual property law.
 d. tort law.

___ **2.** CDI ships defective software to DPC, which sells it to a customer, Eagle Distribution Corporation. The defective software causes losses that Eagle estimates at $100,000. With respect to Eagle, CDI has likely violated

    a. constitutional law.
    b. criminal law.
    c. intellectual property law.
    d. tort law.

___ **3.** In the previous question, DPC's customer Eagle is located in Tennessee. Eagle could file a suit against DPC in

    a. Arizona only.
    b. Tennessee only.
    c. a federal court only.
    d. Arizona, Tennessee, or a federal court.

___ **4.** DPC's officers order some employees to access CDI's computers online to obtain its data without CDI's permission. This is

    a. cyber fraud.
    b. cyber theft.
    c. cyber trespass.
    d. none of the above.

___ **5.** During an investigation into DPC's activities, some of its officers are suspected of having committed crimes. As a corporation, DPC can

    a. be fined or denied certain privileges if it is held criminally liable.
    b. be imprisoned if it is held criminally liable.
    c. be fined, denied privileges, or imprisoned if it is held criminally liable.
    d. not be found to be criminally liable.

Chapter 10
Nature and Terminology

WHAT THIS CHAPTER IS ABOUT

Contract law concerns the formation and keeping of promises, the excuses our society accepts for breaking such promises, and what promises are considered contrary to public policy and therefore legally void. This chapter introduces the basic terms and concepts of contract law, including the rules for interpreting contract language.

CHAPTER OUTLINE

I. THE FUNCTION OF CONTRACT LAW

A. ENFORCE PROMISES
Contract law assures the parties to private agreements that the promises they make will be enforceable. Without the framework that the law provides, businesspersons could rely only on the good faith of others to keep their promises.

B. AVOID PROBLEMS
The rules of contract law are often followed in business agreements to avoid potential problems.

C. SUPPORT THE EXISTENCE OF A MARKET ECONOMY
Businesspersons can usually rely on the good faith of others to keep their promises, but when price changes or adverse economic factors make it costly to comply with a promise, good faith may not be enough.

II. ELEMENTS OF A CONTRACT

A. REQUIREMENTS TO FORM A CONTRACT

1. Agreement
Includes an offer and an acceptance. One party must offer to enter into a legal agreement, and another party must accept the offer.

2. **Consideration**
   Promises must be supported by legally sufficient and bargained-for consideration.

3. **Contractual Capacity**
   Characteristics that qualify the parties to a contract as competent.

4. **Legality**
   A contract's purpose must be to accomplish a goal that is not against public policy.

B. **DEFENSES TO THE ENFORCEMENT OF A CONTRACT**

1. **Genuineness of Assent**
   The apparent consent of both parties must be genuine.

2. **Form**
   A contract must be in whatever form the law requires (some contracts must be in writing).

III.   THE OBJECTIVE THEORY OF CONTRACTS

Intention to enter into a contract is judged by objective (outward) facts as interpreted by a reasonable person, rather than by a party's subjective intention. Objective facts include (1) what the party said when entering into the contract, (2) how the party acted or appeared, and (3) the circumstances surrounding the transaction.

IV.   TYPES OF CONTRACTS

A. **BILATERAL VERSUS UNILATERAL CONTRACTS**

1. **Bilateral Contract**
   A promise for a promise—to accept the offer, the offeree need only promise to perform.

2. **Unilateral Contract**
   A promise for an act—the offeree can accept only by completing the contract performance. A problem arises when the promisor attempts to revoke the offer after the promisee has begun performance but before the act has been completed.

   a. **Revocation—Traditional View**
      The promisee can accept the offer only by performing fully. Offers are revocable until accepted.

   b. **Revocation—Modern View**
      The offer becomes irrevocable once performance begins. Thus, even though it has not yet been accepted, the offeror cannot revoke it.

B. **EXPRESS VERSUS IMPLIED CONTRACTS**

1. **Express Contract**
   The terms of the agreement are fully and explicitly stated in words (oral or written).

2. **Implied-in-Fact Contract**
   Implied from the conduct of the parties.

C. **QUASI CONTRACTS—CONTRACTS IMPLIED IN LAW**
In the absence of an actual contract, a quasi contract is imposed by a court to avoid the unjust enrichment of one party at the expense of another. Cannot be invoked if there is an actual contract that covers the area in controversy.

D. **FORMAL VERSUS INFORMAL CONTRACTS**

1. **Formal Contract**
Requires a special form or method of creation to be enforceable (such as a contract under seal, a formal writing with a special seal attached).

2. **Informal Contract**
All contracts that are not formal. Except for certain contracts that must be in writing, no special form is required.

E. **EXECUTED VERSUS EXECUTORY CONTRACTS**

1. **Executed Contract**
A contract that has been fully performed on both sides.

2. **Executory Contract**
A contract that has not been fully performed by one or more parties.

F. **VALID, VOID, VOIDABLE, AND UNENFORCEABLE CONTRACTS**

1. **Valid Contract**
Has all the elements necessary for contract formation.

2. **Void Contract**
Has no legal force or binding effect (for example, a contract is void if its purpose was illegal).

3. **Voidable Contract**
Valid contract that can be avoided by one or more parties (for example, contracts by minors are voidable at the minor's option).

4. **Unenforceable Contract**
Contract that cannot be enforced because of certain legal defenses (for example, if a contract that must be in writing is not in writing).

V. INTERPRETATION OF CONTRACTS
Rules of contract interpretation provide guidelines for determining the meaning of contracts. The primary purpose of these rules is to determine the parties' intent from the language of their agreement and to give effect to that intent.

A. **THE PLAIN MEANING RULE**
When the writing is clear and unequivocal, it will be enforced according to its plain terms. The meaning of the terms is determined from the written document alone.

B. **OTHER RULES OF INTERPRETATION**
When the writing contains unclear terms, courts use the following rules—

1. A reasonable, lawful, and effective meaning is given to all terms.

2. A contract is interpreted as a whole; individual, specific clauses are considered subordinate to the contract's general intent.   All writings that are part of the same transaction are interpreted together.

3. Terms that were negotiated separately are given greater consideration than standard terms and terms that were not negotiated separately.

4. A word is given its ordinary, common meaning, and a technical word its technical meaning, unless the parties clearly intended otherwise.

5. Specific, exact wording is given greater weight than general language.

6. Written or typewritten terms prevail over preprinted ones.

7. When the language has more than one meaning, it is interpreted against the party who drafted the contract.

8. Evidence of trade usage, prior dealing, and course of performance may be admitted to clarify meaning.

C. **PLAIN-LANGUAGE LAWS**
The federal government and most states require an agreement to be written clearly, coherently, and in words of common, everyday meaning.

TRUE-FALSE QUESTIONS

(Answers at the Back of the Book)

____ 1. All contracts involve promises, and every promise is a legal contract.

____ 2. An agreement includes an offer and an acceptance.

____ 3. Consideration, in contract terms, refers to the competency of a party to enter into a contract.

____ 4. A unilateral contract involves performance instead of promises.

____ 5. Formal contracts are contracts between parties who are in formal relationships—employer-employee relationships, for example.

____ 6. An unenforceable contract is a contract in which one or both of the parties has the option of avoiding his or her legal obligations.

____ 7. Under the plain meaning rule, a court will enforce a contract as it is written, regardless of any previous contracts between the parties.

____ 8. When the language in a contract has more than one meaning, it will be interpreted against the party who drafted the contract.

____ 9. If outside evidence is admissible to interpret an ambiguous contract, express terms are given the greatest weight.

____ 10. A quasi contract is imposed by a court to avoid the unjust enrichment of one party at the expense of another.

FILL-IN QUESTIONS

(Answers at the Back of the Book)

Whether or not a party intended to enter into a contract is determined by the _____ (objective/subjective) theory of contracts. The theory is that a party's intention to enter into a contract is judged by _____ (objective/subjective) facts as they would be interpreted by a reasonable person. Relevant facts include: (1) what the party said; (2) what the party _____ _____ (did/secretly believed); and (3) the _____ _____ (circumstances surrounding/party's personal thoughts concerning) the transaction. Generally, courts examine facts in _____ _____ (a particular transaction/similar transactions) to determine whether the parties made a contract and, if so, what its terms are.

MULTIPLE-CHOICE QUESTIONS

(Answers at the Back of the Book)

_____ 1. Rita calls Rick on the phone and agrees to buy his laptop computer for $200. This is

a. an express contract.
b. an implied-in-fact contract.
c. an implied-in-law contract.
d. no contract.

_____ 2. Don contracts with Jan to paint Jan's townhouse while she's on vacation. By mistake, Don paints Mick's townhouse. Mick sees Don painting but says nothing. Who can Don recover from?

a. Jan, because she was the party with whom Don contracted
b. Jan, under the theory of quasi contract
c. Mick, because his house was painted
d. Mick, under the theory of quasi contract

_____ 3. Brian offers to sell Ashley his CD-ROM collection, forgetting that he does not want to sell some of the disks. Unaware of Brian's forgetfulness, Ashley accepts. Is there a contract including all of Brian's disks?

a. Yes, according to the objective theory of contracts
b. Yes, according to the subjective theory of contracts
c. No, because Brian did not intend to sell his favorite disks
d. No, because Ashley had no reason to know of Brian's forgetfulness

_____ 4. Greg promises to imprint four thousand t-shirts with Rona's logo. Rona pays in advance. Before Greg delivers the shirts, the contract is classified as

a. executed, because it is executed on Greg's part.
b. executory, because it is executory on Greg's part.
c. executory, because it is executory on Rona's part.
d. none of the above.

_____ 5. Without agreeing on payment, Mary accepts the services of Lee, an accountant, and is pleased with the work. Between Mary and Lee

a. there is an express contract.
b. there is an implied-in-fact contract.
c. there is an implied-in-law contract.
d. there is no contract, because they made no agreement concerning payment.

    6. Alpha Computer Systems and Beta Products Corporation enter into a contract. The requirements of this contract, like other contracts, include

    a. agreement and consideration.
    b. formation and creation.
    c. both a and b.
    d. none of the above.

    7. When considering the rules that govern courts' interpretation of contracts, the most important principle to keep in mind is that

    a. if contract language is ambiguous, the law will void the contract.
    b. the law attempts to enforce the contract that the parties made.
    c. specific clauses are more important than the contract as a whole.
    d. when parties put their contract in writing, there is nothing to interpret.

    8. General Contractors, Inc., and United Suppliers, Inc., enter into a contract with standardized terms and terms that are the subject of separate negotiations. If there is a conflict between these types of terms

    a. a court will rewrite the terms to make them consistent.
    b. the standardized terms will prevail.
    c. the terms that were the subject of separate negotiations will prevail.
    d. none of the above.

    9. Sam contracts with Hugo's Sports Equipment to buy a jet ski and to pay for it in installments. Sam is a minor, and so he can choose to avoid his contractual obligations. The contract between Sam and Hugo is

    a. valid.
    b. void.
    c. voidable.
    d. both a and c.

    10. Best Products, Inc., enters into a contract with National Distribution Corporation. This contract may consist of promises between the parties to

    a. refrain from performing some act.
    b. perform some act in the future.
    c. perform some act now.
    d. any of the above.

SHORT ESSAY QUESTIONS

1. What are the basic elements of a contract?

2. What is the function of contract law?

ISSUE SPOTTERS

(Answers at the Back of the Book)

1. Jay signs and returns a letter from Bill referring to a certain saddle and its price. When Bill delivers the saddle, Jay sends it back, claiming that they have no contract. Bill claims that they do have a contract. Do they?

2. Alison receives from the local tax collector a notice of property taxes due. The notice is for tax on Jerry's property, but Alison believes that the tax is hers and pays it. Can Alison recover from Jerry the amount that she paid?

3. Dick tells Ben that he will pay Ben $1,500 to set fire to Dick's store, so that Dick can collect money under his fire insurance policy. Ben sets fire to the store, but Dick refuses to pay. Can Ben enforce this deal?

4. Henry and Rich negotiate an employment contract. The first draft is a standard printed contract. Clause 9 reads that no vacations can be taken in December. Beneath the clause in the final draft is written, in ink, "Only one-week vacations can be taken in December." If a dispute arises about December vacations, which term controls?

5. Lou applies for a credit card with the First National Bank under a contract specifying that the customer is liable for charges made on a lost or stolen card "until the card issuer is notified of the card's loss." Lou loses his card. When his bank statement shows purchases that he did not make, he tells the bank that he won't pay for any of those items. He contends that the contract means that once the bank is notified of a card's loss, a customer is no longer liable. Would a court agree with Lou?

SPECIAL INFORMATION FOR CPA CANDIDATES

Among the attributes for success on the CPA examination is a positive attitude. Preparation for the exam is a long process, and it can be difficult to keep one's mind focused on a successful conclusion. Because a positive attitude can make the difference between passing and failing, however, it is important that you stay refreshed, confident, and optimistic. To accomplish this, take time off from your studies once in a while. Spend an evening or an afternoon with friends; get some exercise; do some leisure reading; go to a movie—or do whatever else it takes, when your spirits sag, to regain a positive attitude.

Chapter 11
Agreement

WHAT THIS CHAPTER IS ABOUT

An agreement is the essence of every contract. The parties to a contract are the **offeror** (who makes an offer) and the **offeree** (to whom the offer is made). If, through the process of offer and acceptance, an agreement is reached, and the other elements are present (consideration, capacity, legality), a valid contract is formed.

A contract must contain reasonably definite terms. Generally, a contract must include, either expressed in the contract or capable of being reasonably inferred from it, the following terms: identification of the parties; identification of the contract's subject matter (also quantity); the consideration to be paid; and the time of performance.

CHAPTER OUTLINE

I. **REQUIREMENTS OF THE OFFER**
An offer is a promise or commitment to do or refrain from doing some specified thing in the future. An offer has three elements—

A. **INTENTION**
The offeror must intend to be bound by the offer.

1. **How to Determine the Offeror's Intent**
The offeror's intent is determined by what a reasonable person in the offeree's position would conclude the offeror's words and actions meant. Offers made in obvious anger, jest, or undue excitement do not qualify.

2. **Nonoffers**
What appears to be an offer may not be sufficient to form the basis of a contract. It is important to recognize what does not constitute an offer. Nonoffers include: (1) expressions of opinion, (2) statements of intention, (3) preliminary negotiations, and (4) advertisements, catalogues, price lists, and circulars. Auctions represent a special situation.

3. **Agreements to Agree**
Agreements to agree to a material term of a contract at some future date may be enforced if the parties clearly intended to be bound.

B. DEFINITENESS

1. Major Terms
All of the major terms must be stated with reasonable definiteness in the offer (or, if the offeror directs, in the offeree's acceptance).

2. Missing Terms
Courts are sometimes willing to supply a missing term when the parties have clearly manifested an intent to form a contract.

C. COMMUNICATION
The offer must be communicated to the offeree.

II. TERMINATION OF THE OFFER

A. TERMINATION BY ACTION OF THE PARTIES

1. Revocation of the Offer by the Offeror
The offeror usually can revoke the offer (even if he or she has promised to keep it open), by express repudiation or by performance of acts that are inconsistent with the offer and that are made known to the offeree.

a. Communicated to the Offeree
Revocation must be communicated to the offeree (or the offeree's agent) before the offeree accepts. A revocation becomes effective when the offeree or offeree's agent actually receives it.

b. Offers to the General Public
An offer made to the general public can be revoked in the same manner the offer was originally communicated.

2. Irrevocable Offers

a. Option Contract

1) What an Option Contract Is
A promise to hold an offer open for a specified period of time. A separate contract that takes away the offeror's power to revoke the offer for the period of time specified.

2) How Long an Offer Must Be Held Open
If no time is specified, a reasonable time is implied.

3) Death or Incompetence of a Party
Generally, the death or incompetence of a party does not terminate an option contract—unless the offeror's personal performance is essential to the fulfillment of the contract.

b. Detrimental Reliance

1) Promissory Estoppel
When the offeree justifiably relies on an offer to his or her detriment, this reliance may make the offer irrevocable.

2) Unilateral Contracts
Many courts will not allow the offeror to revoke the offer after the offeree has performed some substantial part of his or her duties under a unilateral contract. In effect, partial

performance renders the offer irrevocable, giving the original offeree reasonable time to complete performance.

3. **Rejection of the Offer by the Offeree**
The offer may be rejected by the offeree by words or conduct evidencing an intent not to accept the offer.

   a. **Subsequent Attempt by the Offeree to Accept**
   Construed as a new offer.

   b. **Communicated to the Offeror**
   Rejection of an offer is effective only when it is actually received by the offeror or the offeror's agent.

   c. **Inquiring about an Offer**
   Asking about an offer is not rejecting it.

4. **Counteroffer by the Offeree**
The offeree's attempt to include different terms is a rejection of the original offer and a simultaneous making of a new offer. The mirror image rule requires the acceptance to match the offer exactly.

B. TERMINATION BY OPERATION OF LAW

1. **Lapse of Time**
An offer terminates automatically by law when the period of time specified in the offer has passed.

   a. **When the Time Begins to Run**
   When the offer is received by the offeree, not when it is sent. If the offer is delayed, the period begins to run from the date the offeree would have received the offer (if the offeree knows or should know that the offer is delayed).

   b. **If No Time Is Specified**
   If no time is specified , then a reasonable time is implied.

2. **Destruction of the Subject Matter**
An offer is automatically terminated.

3. **Death or Incompetence of the Offeror or Offeree**
An offeree's power of acceptance is terminated. Exceptions include irrevocable offers (see above).

4. **Supervening Illegality of the Proposed Contract**
When a statute or court decision makes an offer illegal, the offer is automatically terminated.

III. ACCEPTANCE

A. UNEQUIVOCAL ACCEPTANCE
The offeree must accept the offer unequivocally. This is the mirror image rule (see above).

B. SILENCE AS ACCEPTANCE
Ordinarily, silence cannot operate as an acceptance. Silence or inaction can constitute acceptance under the following circumstances—

1. **Receipt of Offered Services**
   If an offeree receives the benefit of offered services even though he or she had an opportunity to reject them and knew that they were offered with the expectation of compensation.

2. **Prior Dealings**
   The offeree had prior dealings with the offeror that lead the offeror to understand that silence will constitute acceptance.

C. COMMUNICATION OF ACCEPTANCE

1. **Bilateral Contract**
   A contract is formed when acceptance is communicated. The offeree must use reasonable efforts to communicate the acceptance to the offeror.

2. **Unilateral Contract**
   Communication is unnecessary (because acceptance is by performance), unless the offeror requests notice or has no adequate means of determining if the act has been performed, or the law requires notice.

D. MODE AND TIMELINESS OF ACCEPTANCE IN BILATERAL CONTRACTS

1. **Mode**

   a. **Authorized Means of Acceptance**
      If an offeree uses a mode of communication expressly or impliedly authorized by the offeror, acceptance is effective when sent. This is the mailbox rule (deposited acceptance rule).

      1) **Express**
         When an offeror specifies how acceptance should be made, a contract is not formed unless the offeree uses that mode of acceptance. If the offeree uses that mode, the acceptance is effective even if the offeror never receives it.

      2) **Implied**
         When an offeror does not specify how acceptance should be made or specifies that the acceptance will be effective only when received, the offeree may use any medium that is reasonable under the circumstances (which include the means used by the offeror to make the offer).

      3) **Exception**
         If the acceptance is not properly dispatched (for example, it is not correctly addressed), in most states it will not be effective until received by the offeror or the offeror's agent. (If timely sent and timely received, however, it is considered to have been effective on dispatch.)

   b. **Unauthorized Means of Acceptance**

      1) **Effective When Received**
         If an offeree uses a mode of communication that was not authorized by the offeror, acceptance is effective when received.

2) Effective When Sent

If an acceptance is timely sent and timely received, however, despite the means by which it is sent, it is considered to have been effective when sent.

c. Rejection and Acceptance

Sometimes an offeree sends a rejection first, then later changes his or her mind and sends an acceptance. The first communication to be received by the offeror determines whether a contract is formed. If the rejection is received first, there is no contract.

2. Timeliness

Acceptance is timely if it is made before the offer is terminated.

TRUE-FALSE QUESTIONS

(Answers at the Back of the Book)

____ 1. The seriousness of an offeror's intent is determined by what a reasonable offeree would conclude the offeror's words and actions meant.

____ 2. A contract providing that Joe is to pay Bill "a fair share of the profits" will be enforced.

____ 3. A simple rejection of an offer will terminate it.

____ 4. Offers that must be kept open for a period of time include advertisements.

____ 5. The mirror image rule is an old common law rule that no longer applies.

____ 6. If an offeree is silent, he or she can never be considered to have accepted an offer.

____ 7. An offer terminates when the time specified in the offer has passed and the offeror has given one last chance to the offeree to accept.

____ 8. Anyone who is aware of an offer can accept it and create a binding contract.

____ 9. Acceptance is timely if it is made before an offer terminates.

____ 10. Acceptance is effective when sent if the offeree uses a mode of communication authorized by the offeror.

FILL-IN QUESTIONS

(Answers at the Back of the Book)

The elements of an effective offer are (1) a _____ (serious/subjective) intent by the _____ (offeror/offeree) to be bound by the offer; (2) _____ (detailed/reasonably definite) contractual terms; and (3) communication of the offer to the _____ (offeror/offeree).

MULTIPLE-CHOICE QUESTIONS
(Answers at the Back of the Book)

_____ 1. Owen mails to Pat an offer to sell his computer, stating that Pat has ten days to accept by e-mail. The next day, Pat e-mails a note of acceptance. The acceptance is effective when

a. received.
b. sent.
c. received or sent, depending on what Kelly decides later.
d. none of the above.

_____ 2. **Based on a Sample CPA Exam Question.** Before opening her new sports merchandise store, Kay places an ad in the newspaper showing cross-training shoes at certain prices. Within hours of opening for business, the store is sold out of some of the shoes. In this situation

a. Kay has made an offer to the people reading the ad.
b. Kay has made a contract with the people reading the ad.
c. Kay has made an invitation seeking offers.
d. Any customer who demands goods advertised and tenders the money is entitled to them.

_____ 3. Icon Properties, Inc., makes an offer in a letter to Bob to sell a certain lot for $30,000, with the offer to stay open for thirty days. Bob would prefer to pay $25,000, if Icon would sell at that price. What should Bob reply to Icon to leave room for negotiation without rejecting the offer?

a. "I will not pay $30,000."
b. "Will you take $25,000?"
c. "I will pay $25,000."
d. "I will pay $27,500."

_____ 4. Julio offers to sell Christine a certain piece of land. Which of the following replies would constitute an acceptance?

a. "I accept. Please send a written contract."
b. "I accept, if you send a written contract."
c. "I accept, if I can pay in monthly installments."
d. None of the above

_____ 5. Bill makes an offer to Ann. If Bill dies before Ann can reply, the offer

a. remains open.
b. remains open until Ann learns of Bill's death.
c. terminates immediately.
d. none of the above.

_____ 6. In a letter, Vern offers his services as an accountant to Lee, stating that the offer will stay open for thirty days. Vern

a. cannot revoke the offer for thirty days.
b. can revoke the offer only in another letter.
c. can revoke the offer any time before Lee accepts.
d. can revoke the offer any time within thirty days, even after Lee accepts.

____ 7. Digit Computers places an ad announcing a sale of its inventory at public auction. At the auction, Digit's auctioneer holds up a high-speed modem and asks, "What am I bid for this item?" Which of the following is TRUE?

   a. The first bid is an acceptance subject to no other bid being received.
   b. Each bid is an acceptance subject to no higher bid being received.
   c. Each bid is an offer that may be accepted or rejected.
   d. Each bid is an offer that must be accepted if no higher bid is received.

____ 8. Ed sends to Sounds, Inc. (SI), a written order for a sound system to be specially manufactured, offering a certain amount of money. If SI does not respond, it can be considered to have accepted the offer

   a. after a reasonable time has passed.
   b. if Ed knows that SI accepts all offers unless it sends notice to the contrary.
   c. only when SI begins the work.
   d. none of the above.

____ 9. Paul makes an offer to Lynn in a letter, saying nothing about how her acceptance should be sent. Lynn indicates her acceptance in a return letter. Lynn's acceptance is effective when

   a. Lynn decides to accept.
   b. Lynn sends the letter.
   c. Paul receives the letter.
   d. none of the above.

____ 10. Cindy makes an offer to Neal in a fax. Neal indicates his acceptance in a return fax. Neal's acceptance is effective when

   a. Neal decides to accept.
   b. Neal sends the fax.
   c. Cindy receives the fax.
   d. none of the above.

SHORT ESSAY QUESTIONS

1. What are the elements necessary for an effective offer?

2. What are the elements necessary for an effective acceptance?

ISSUE SPOTTERS

(Answers at the Back of the Book)

1. One morning, when Jane's new car—with an $18,000 market value—doesn't start, she yells in anger, "I'd sell this car to anyone for $500." If you drop $500 in her lap, is the car yours?

2. Joe advertises in the *New York Times* that he will pay $5,000 to anyone giving him information as to the whereabouts of Elaine. Max sees a copy of the ad in a Tokyo newspaper, in Japanese, and sends Joe the information. Does Max get the reward?

3. Fidelity Corporation offers to hire Ron to replace Monica, who has given Fidelity a month's notice of intent to quit. Fidelity gives Ron a week to decide whether to accept. Two days later, Monica signs an employment contract with Fidelity for another

year. The next day, Monica tells Ron of the new contract. Ron immediately sends a formal letter of acceptance to Fidelity. Do Fidelity and Ron have a contract?

4.   Jay offers to sell Guy his motorcycle for $1,000. Jay says that he needs an answer within a week. Two days later, Jay dies in an accident. Guy mourns the loss of his friend, but would like to buy the motorcycle for the price Jay quoted. Is the offer good?

5.   Mary offers to sell her farm to Don, adding, "If you want the farm, you must accept in person at my office at ten o'clock tomorrow morning." Don sends a fax to Mary's office at noon the next day, in which Don says, "I accept your offer." Do they have a contract?

SPECIAL INFORMATION FOR CPA CANDIDATES

One of the points covered in this chapter and often tested on the CPA examination is the mailbox rule. Sometimes, the examination has included a problem in which the offeror specifies that an acceptance must be received before it is effective. In that circumstance, of course, the mailbox rule does not apply. It might be helpful to remember, too, that the mailbox rule is the only exception to the rule that a communication is effective only on receipt—offers, revocations, rejections, counteroffers, and acceptances not subject to the mailbox rule must be received to be effective.

Chapter 12
Consideration

WHAT THIS CHAPTER IS ABOUT

Good reasons for enforcing promises have been held to include something given as an agreed exchange, a benefit that the promisor received, and a detriment that the promisee incurred. These are referred to as "consideration." No contract is enforceable without it.

Consideration is the value given in return for a promise. For example, the value can consist of money given in return for a promise to deliver certain goods. Thus, when Roy pays for a computer to be delivered by Sam, there is consideration. This chapter outlines the concepts and principles of consideration.

CHAPTER OUTLINE

I. ELEMENTS OF CONSIDERATION
Consideration has two elements: (1) there must be a bargained-for exchange between the parties (if a party intends to make a gift, he or she is not bargaining) and (2) what is bargained for must have legal value.

II. LEGAL SUFFICIENCY OF CONSIDERATION
Something of legal value must be given in exchange for a promise. It may be a return promise. If it is performance, that performance may be (1) an act (other than a promise); or (2) a forbearance (refraining from action). Whatever it is, it must be either—

A. LEGALLY DETRIMENTAL TO THE PROMISEE
Legal detriment is not always economic detriment. A person can incur legal detriment by (1) doing or promising to do something that he or she had no prior legal duty to do or (2) refraining from or promising to refrain from doing something that he or she had no prior legal duty to refrain from doing (that is, by forbearance).

B. LEGALLY BENEFICIAL TO THE PROMISOR

III. ADEQUACY OF CONSIDERATION

Adequacy of consideration refers to the fairness of a bargain. Normally, a court will not question the adequacy of consideration. Normally, a court will not question the adequacy of consideration unless it indicates fraud, duress, incapacity, undue influence, or a lack of bargained-for exchange.

IV. CONTRACTS THAT LACK CONSIDERATION

Situations in which promises or acts do not qualify as consideration include—

A. PREEXISTING DUTY

A promise to do what one already has a legal duty to do is not constitute legally sufficient consideration.

1. Example

If a merchant contracts to sell a computer to a consumer, that duty cannot serve as consideration for a second contract with the consumer to raise the price.

2. Exceptions

a. Unforeseen Difficulties

When a party runs into extraordinary difficulties that were unforeseen at the time the contract was formed, some courts will enforce an agreement to pay more.

1) Ordinary Business Risks Not Included

2) Typical Cases

Cases involving unforeseen difficulties frequently arise under construction contracts and relate to soil conditions.

b. Rescission and New Contract

Two parties can agree to rescind their contract to the extent that it is executory.

1) Preexisting Duties Discharged by Rescission

There are three separate agreements—the initial agreement, the rescission agreement, and the later agreement. Preexisting duties are discharged by the rescission.

2) When Rescission and New Contract Occur at the Same Time

Some courts hold that the new agreement is unenforceable, on the ground of insufficient consideration, unless both contracting parties' duties are changed. Other courts hold that the consideration for the original agreement carries over into the new agreement.

B. PAST CONSIDERATION

Promises made with respect to events that have already taken place are unenforceable.

V.   PROBLEM AREAS CONCERNING CONSIDERATION

A. UNCERTAIN PERFORMANCE

If the terms of a contract express such uncertainty of performance that the promisor has not definitely promised to do anything, the promise is illusory—without consideration and unenforceable.

1. Example

Tio's Restaurant promises to buy from Pizza King, Inc., "such pizza ingredients as we may wish to order from Pizza King." Tio's promise is illusory, because performance depends solely on the discretion of Tio's. There is no bargained-for consideration.

2. Option-to-Cancel Clauses

Reserving, in a contract, the right to cancel or withdraw at any time can be an illusory promise. If the right is at all restricted, however—such as by requiring thirty days' notice—there is consideration.

B. SETTLEMENT OF CLAIMS

1. Accord and Satisfaction

Accord and satisfaction deals with a debtor's offer of payment and a creditor's acceptance of a lesser amount than the creditor originally purported to be owed.

a. Accord

The agreement under which one of the parties undertakes to give or perform, and the other to accept, in satisfaction of a claim, something other than that which was originally agreed on.

b. Satisfaction

Satisfaction takes place when the accord is executed. There can be no satisfaction unless there is first an accord.

c. Amount of the Debt Must Be Unliquidated (in Dispute)

1) Unliquidated Debt—Consideration

When the amount of the debt is in dispute, acceptance of a lesser sum discharges the debt. Consideration is given by the parties' giving up a legal right to contest the amount of debt.

2) Liquidated Debt—No Consideration

Acceptance of less than the entire amount of a liquidated debt is not satisfaction, and the balance of the debt is still owed. No consideration is given by the debtor, because the debtor has a preexisting obligation to pay the entire debt.

2. Release

A release (a promise to refrain from suing on a valid claim) bars any further recovery beyond the terms stated in the release. Releases will generally be binding if they are (1) given in good faith, (2) stated in a signed writing, and (3) accompanied by consideration.

3. Covenant Not to Sue

The parties substitute a contractual obligation for some other type of legal action based on a valid claim (such as promising not to sue on a valid claim if the cost of all damage is paid). In this case, if all damage is not paid, an action can be brought for breach of contract.

C. PROMISES ENFORCEABLE WITHOUT CONSIDERATION

1. **Promises to Pay Debts Barred by a Statute of Limitations**
   Creditors must sue within a certain period to recover debts. If a debtor promises to pay a debt barred by a statute of limitations (promise can be implied if debtor acknowledges debt by making part payment), a creditor can sue to recover the entire debt, or at least the amount promised.

2. **Detrimental Reliance, or Promissory Estoppel**
   In some states, the doctrine of promissory estoppel prevents a promisor from asserting a lack of consideration as a defense. This occurs when—

   a. **Justifiable Reliance**
      A promise given by one party induces another party to rely (justifiably) on that promise to his or her detriment.

   b. **Foreseeability**
      The promisor must have known or had reason to believe that the promisee would likely be induced to change position. The change usually must be of substantial nature.

   c. **Fairness**
      If injustice cannot be avoided, the promise will be enforced.

3. **Charitable Subscriptions**
   Promises to make gifts to charitable institutions are unenforceable because they are not supported by legally sufficient consideration.

   a. **Specific Use**
      Consideration may be found if the promisor bargained for and received a promise that the gift would be used in a specific way.

   b. **Promissory Estoppel**
      Some courts enforce these promises under the doctrine of promissory estoppel if a charity changes its position in reliance on the promise.

TRUE-FALSE QUESTIONS

(Answers at the Back of the Book)

____   1. Ordinarily, courts evaluate the adequacy or fairness of consideration even if the consideration is legally sufficient.

____   2. A promise to do what one already has a legal duty to do is not legally sufficient consideration under most circumstances.

____   3. Promises made with consideration based on events that have already taken place are fully enforceable.

____   4. Rescission is the unmaking of a contract so as to return the parties to the positions they occupied before the contract was made.

____   5. A promise has no legal value as consideration.

___ 6. A covenant not to sue is an agreement to substitute a contractual obligation for some other type of action.

___ 7. A covenant not to sue always bars further recovery.

___ 8. Only a liquidated debt can serve as consideration for an accord and satisfaction.

___ 9. Consideration is the value given in return for a promise.

___ 10. Promissory estoppel may prevent a party from asserting a lack of consideration as a defense.

FILL-IN QUESTIONS

(Answers at the Back of the Book)

The doctrine of promissory estoppel, or detrimental reliance, involves a _____ (promise/performance) given by one party that induces another party to rely on it to his or her _____ (benefit/detriment). When the _____ (promisor/promisee) can reasonably have expected the reliance, and injustice cannot otherwise be avoided, the _____ (promise/benefit) will be _____ (enforced/awarded). In other words, the _____ (promisor/promisee) must have acted with justifiable reliance. Generally, the act must have been of a _____ (substantial/inconsequential) nature.

MULTIPLE-CHOICE QUESTIONS

(Answers at the Back of the Book)

___ 1. Eve questions whether there is consideration for her contract with Frank. Consideration has two elements—there must be a bargained-for exchange and the value of whatever is exchanged must be

a. legally sufficient.
b. economically sufficient.
c. both a and b.
d. none of the above.

___ 2. Dave offers to buy a book owned by Lee for $40. Lee accepts and hands the book to Dave. The transfer and delivery of the book constitute performance. Is this performance consideration for Dave's promise?

a. Yes, because performance always constitutes consideration.
b. Yes, because Dave sought it in exchange for his promise, and Lee gave it in exchange for that promise.
c. No, because performance never constitutes consideration.
d. No, because Lee already had a duty to hand the book to Dave.

____ 3. Max agrees to supervise a construction project for Al for a certain fee. In mid-project, without an excuse, Max removes the plans from the site and refuses to continue. Al promises to increase Max's fee. Max returns to work. Is going back to work consideration for the promise to increase the fee?

a. Yes, because performance always constitutes consideration.
b. Yes, because Al sought it in exchange for his promise.
c. No, because performance never constitutes consideration.
d. No, because Max already had a duty to supervise the project.

____ 4. **Based on a Sample CPA Exam Question.** Jay is seeking to avoid performing a promise to pay Karen $150. Jay is claiming a lack of consideration on Karen's part. Jay will win if he can show that

a. before Jay's promise, Karen had already performed the requested act.
b. Karen's only claim of consideration was the relinquishment of a legal right.
c. Karen's asserted consideration is only worth $50.
d. the consideration to be performed by Karen will be performed by a third party.

____ 5. Ed has a cause to sue Mary in a tort action, but agrees not to sue her if she will pay for the damage. If she fails to pay, Ed can bring an action against her for breach of contract. This is an example of

a. a covenant not to sue.
b. an accord and satisfaction.
c. a release.
d. an unenforceable contract.

____ 6. John's car is hit by Ben's truck. A doctor tells John that he will be disabled only temporarily. Ben's insurance company offers John $5,000 to settle his claim. John accepts and signs a release. Later, John learns that he is permanently disabled. John sues Ben and the insurance company. John will

a. win, because John did not know when he signed the release that the disability was permanent.
b. win, because Ben caused the accident.
c. lose, because John signed a release.
d. none of the above.

____ 7. Tom, a real estate broker, sells Glen's house. Tom believes that he is owed a commission of 8 percent. Glen claims in good faith that he owes only 5 percent. Glen offers to pay 6.5 percent. Tom accepts. Glen's payment is

a. consideration for Tom's promise to give up his claim.
b. not legally sufficient to constitute consideration.
c. not economically sufficient to constitute consideration.
d. both b and c.

____ 8. Gail takes out two student loans from a bank. After collection of the debts is barred by a statute of limitations, Gail promises to pay back one of the loans. Gail's promise is

a. binding as to that loan only.
b. binding and covers both loans.
c. binding and covers both loans and all of Gail's other debts.
d. not binding.

____   **9.**   Mike promises that next year he will sell Kim a certain house, allowing her to live in it until then. Kim puts a new roof on the house, repairs the heating system, and landscapes the property. The next year, Mike tells Kim he's decided to keep the house. The person entitled to the house is

    a. Kim, under the doctrine of promissory estoppel.
    b. Kim, because Mike's decision to keep the house is an unforeseen difficulty.
    c. Mike, because his promise to sell the house to Kim was illusory.
    d. Mike, because he initially stated only his intention to sell.

____   **10.**   Deb has a cause to sue Jim in a tort action. Jim offers Deb $5,000 not to sue, and she agrees. This an example of

    a. a covenant not to sue.
    b. an accord and satisfaction.
    c. a release.
    d. an unenforceable contract.

SHORT ESSAY QUESTIONS

1.   When is consideration legally sufficient?

2.   What are the circumstances in which a court will question whether consideration is adequate?

ISSUE SPOTTERS

(Answers at the Back of the Book)

1.   In September, Sharon agrees to work for Cole Productions, Inc., at $500 a week for a year beginning January 1. In October, Sharon is offered the same work at $600 a week by Quintero Shows, Ltd. When Sharon tells Cole about the other offer, they tear up their contract and agree that Sharon will be paid $575. Is the new contract binding?

2.   Rick, the president of Pye Corporation, announces to Pye employees that "if you work hard, and profits remain high, you'll get a bonus, if management thinks it's warranted." Profits remain high, but no bonus is paid. If the employees sue, would a court enforce the promise?

3.   Before Maria starts her first year of college, Fred promises to give her $5,000 when she graduates. She goes to college, borrowing and spending far more than $5,000. At the beginning of the spring semester of her senior year, she reminds Fred of the promise. Fred sends her a note that says, "I revoke the promise." Is Fred's promise binding?

4.   Gus promises Brad, his nephew who is sixteen years old, that Gus will pay Brad $5,000 when Brad turns twenty-one if Brad does not drink liquor before then. If Brad does not drink before he turns twenty-one, is he entitled to the $5,000?

5.   Don renders consulting services to Sue, without discussing the price. There is no standard price for the particular services. Don sends Sue a bill for $1,000. Sue believes this is too much. She sends Don a check for $750, with "payment in full for services rendered" written on the back. Don cashes the check. Does Sue owe Don $250?

SPECIAL INFORMATION FOR CPA CANDIDATES

On the CPA examination, questions concerning consideration have often concentrated on the modification of contracts. You might find it helpful to review those rules. In particular, remember that an agreement to pay less than the amount that is owed for an unliquidated debt is not binding without consideration. Under the UCC, however, consideration is not required to modify a contract (for a sale of goods). Other important points to keep in mind include that the consideration exchanged by the parties does not have to have equal value—it does not even have to be reasonable or fair.

Capacity and Legality

★ **Key Points**

The **key points** in this chapter include:

1. The contractual rights and obligations of minors.

2. How intoxication affects contractual liability.

3. The effects of mental incompetency on contractual liability.

4. Some contracts that are contrary to state or federal statutes.

5. The enforceability of contracts and clauses that are contrary to public policy.

WHAT THIS CHAPTER IS ABOUT

If a party to a contract lacks capacity, an essential element for a valid contract is missing, and the contract is void. Some persons have capacity to enter into a contract, but if they wish, they can avoid liability under the contract. Also, to be enforceable, a contract must not violate any statutes or public policy.

CHAPTER OUTLINE

I. **CONTRACTUAL CAPACITY**

A. **MINORS**
A minor can enter into any contract that an adult can enter into, as long as it is not prohibited by law (for example, the sale of alcoholic beverages).

1. **Age of Majority, Marriage, and Emancipation**
A person who reaches the age of majority (eighteen, in most states) is not a minor for contractual purposes. In some states, marriage terminates minority status. Minors, over whom parents have relinquished control, have full contractual capacity.

2. **Right to Disaffirm**
A minor can disaffirm a contract by manifesting an intent not to be bound. A contract can ordinarily be disaffirmed at any time during minority or for a reasonable time after a minor comes of age.

3. **Obligation on Disaffirmance**
A minor cannot disaffirm a fully executed contract without returning whatever goods have been received or paying their reasonable value.

a. **What the Adult Recovers**

1) **In Most States**
If the goods (or other consideration) are in the minor's control, the minor must return them (without added compensation).

    2) **In a Growing Number of States**
    If the goods have been used, damaged, or ruined, the adult must be restored to the position he or she held before the contract.

  b. **What the Minor Recovers**
  All property that a minor has transferred to an adult as consideration, even if it is in the hands of a third party. If the property cannot be returned, the adult must pay the minor its value.

4. **Exceptions to the Right to Disaffirm**

  a. **Misrepresentation of Age**

    1) **In Most States**
    A minor who misrepresents his or her age can still disaffirm a contract. In some states, he or she is not liable for fraud, because indirectly that might force the minor to perform the contract.

    2) **In Some States**
    Some states prohibit disaffirmance; some courts refuse to allow minors to disaffirm executed contracts unless they can return the consideration; some courts allow a minor to disaffirm but hold the minor liable for damages for fraud.

  b. **Contracts for Necessaries**
  Necessaries are food, clothing, shelter, medicine, and hospital care—whatever a court believes is necessary to maintain a person's status. A minor may disaffirm a contract for necessaries but will be liable for the reasonable value.

  c. **Insurance and Loans**
  Some jurisdictions prohibit a minor's right to disaffirm insurance contracts. If a loan is for the express purpose of enabling the minor to buy necessaries and the lender makes sure the money is so spent, then the minor must repay.

5. **Ratification**
Ratification is the act of accepting and thereby giving legal force to an obligation that was previously unenforceable.

  a. **Express Ratification**
  When a person, after reaching the age of majority, states orally or in writing that he or she intends to be bound by a contract.

  b. **Implied Ratification**
  When a minor performs acts inconsistent with disaffirmance or fails to disaffirm an executed contract within a reasonable time after reaching the age of majority.

6. **Parents' Liability**
Generally, parents are not liable for contracts made by their minor children acting on their own.

B. **INTOXICATED PERSONS**

1. **If a Person Is Sufficiently Intoxicated to Lack Mental Capacity**
Any contract he or she enters into is voidable at the option of the intoxicated person, even if the intoxication was voluntary.

2. **If a Person Understands the Legal Consequences of a Contract**
    Despite intoxication, the contract is usually enforceable.

C. **MENTALLY INCOMPETENT PERSONS**

1. **Persons Adjudged Mentally Incompetent by a Court**
    If a person has been adjudged mentally incompetent by a court of law
    and a guardian has been appointed, a contract by the person is void.

2. **Incompetent Persons Not So Adjudged by a Court**

    a. **Those Who Do Not Understand Their Contracts**
        A contract is voidable (at the option of the person) if a person does
        not know he or she is entering into the contract or lacks the capacity
        to comprehend its nature, purpose, and consequences.

    b. **Those Who Understand Their Contracts**
        If a mentally incompetent person understands the nature and effect
        of entering into a certain contract, the contract will be valid.

II.   LEGALITY

A. **CONTRACTS CONTRARY TO STATUTE**

1. **Usury**
    Every state sets rates of interest charged for loans (exceptions are made
    for certain business deals). Charging a higher rate is usury—some states
    allow recovery of the principal plus interest; other states allow recov-
    ery of the principal but no interest; a few states permit no recovery.

2. **Gambling**
    All states regulate gambling (any scheme that involves distribution of
    property by chance among persons who pay for the chance to receive the
    property). Some states do not enforce gambling debts.

3. **Sabbath (Sunday) Laws**

    a. **Prohibited Contracts**
        In some states, all contracts entered into on a Sunday are illegal.
        Other states prohibit only the sale of certain merchandise (such as
        alcoholic beverages) on a Sunday.

    b. **Exceptions**
        Contracts for necessities and works of charity; executed contracts.

4. **Licensing Statutes**

    a. **Professional Licenses**
        Members of certain professions (such as doctors) must be licensed.

    b. **Business Licenses**
        Business licenses provide a means of regulating and taxing certain
        businesses, and protecting the public. Lack of a business license can
        bar the enforcement of a work-related contract.

        1) **Illegal Contracts**
            If the statute's purpose is to protect the public, a contract with
            an unlicensed individual is illegal.

    2) Enforceable Contracts
    If the statute's purpose is to raise revenue, a contract with an unlicensed individual is enforceable.

5. Contracts to Commit a Crime
A contract to commit a crime is illegal. If the contract is rendered illegal by statute after it has been entered into, the contract is discharged.

B. CONTRACTS CONTRARY TO PUBLIC POLICY

1. Contracts in Restraint of Trade

    a. Prohibited Contracts
    Contracts that restrain trade, adversely affect the public, or violate an antitrust statute.

    b. Covenant Not to Compete
    Acceptable if reasonable, determined by the length of time and size of area in which the party agrees not to compete. (In the sale of a business, it must also be a separate agreement.)

2. Unconscionable Contracts or Clauses
A bargain that is unfairly one-sided is **unconscionable**.

    a. Procedural Unconscionability
    Relates to a party's lack of knowledge or understanding of contract terms because of small print, "legalese," etc. An adhesion contract (drafted by one party for his benefit) may be held unconscionable.

    b. Substantive Unconscionability
    Relates to the parts of a contract that are so unfairly one-sided they "shock the conscience" of the court.

3. Exculpatory Clauses

    a. What an Exculpatory Clause Is
    Contract that absolves a party of negligence or other wrong. Sometimes found in rental agreements and real property leases.

    b. Legality
    Often held to be unconscionable. In most real property leases, held to be contrary to public policy. Not enforced if the party seeking its enforcement is involved in a business important to the public as a matter of practical necessity (airlines, public utilities).

4. Other Contracts Contrary to Public Policy

    a. Discriminatory Contracts
    Contracts in which a party promises to discriminate in terms of color, race, religion, national origin, disability, or gender.

    b. Contracts for the Commission of a Tort

    c. Contracts Injuring Public Service
    Contracts that interfere with a public officer's duties or involve a conflict between duties and private interests.

    d. Agreements Obstructing the Legal Process

C. EFFECT OF ILLEGALITY

1. The General Rule
An illegal contract is void. No party can sue to enforce it and no party can recover for its breach.

2. Exceptions

a. Justifiable Ignorance of the Facts
A party who is innocent may recover benefits conferred in a partially executed contract or enforce a fully performed contract.

b. Members of Protected Classes
When a statute is designed to protect a certain class of people, a member of that class can enforce a contract in violation of the statute (the other party to the contract cannot enforce it).

c. Withdrawal from an Illegal Agreement
If the illegal part of an agreement has not been performed, the party rendering performance can withdraw and recover the performance or its value.

d. Fraud, Duress, or Undue Influence
A party induced to enter into an illegal bargain by fraud, duress, or undue influence can enforce the contract or recover for its value.

3. Severable, or Divisible, Contracts
A court may enforce the legal part of a contract, if the illegal part does not affect the essence of the bargain.

TRUE-FALSE QUESTIONS

(Answers at the Back of the Book)

_____ 1. A minor who enters into a contract may be able to avoid the contract.

_____ 2. When a minor disaffirms a contract, whatever the minor transferred as consideration (or its value) must be returned.

_____ 3. A person who is so intoxicated as to lack mental capacity when he or she enters into a contract must perform the contract even if the other party has reason to know of the intoxication.

_____ 4. Emancipation has no effect on a minor's contractual capacity.

_____ 5. If an individual who has not been judged mentally incompetent understands the nature and effect of entering into a certain contract, the contract is normally valid.

_____ 6. An exculpatory clause may not be enforced.

_____ 7. An adhesion contract will never be deemed unconscionable.

_____ 8. An illegal contract is valid unless it is executory.

_____ 9. If the purpose of a licensing statute is to protect the public from unlicensed practitioners, a contract entered into with an unlicensed practitioner is unenforceable.

_____ 10. Covenants not to compete are never enforceable.

FILL-IN QUESTIONS

(Answers at the Back of the Book)

The act of accepting and giving legal force to an obligation that previously was not enforceable is _____ (disaffirmance/ratification). In relation to contracts entered into by minors or persons who are intoxicated or mentally incompetent, this is an act or an expression in words by which the person, on or after reaching majority or regaining sobriety or mental competence, indicates intent to be bound by a contract.

Disaffirmance or ratification may be express or implied. For example, a person's continued use and payments on something bought when he or she was incompetent is inconsistent with a desire to _____ (disaffirm/ratify) and _____ (indicates/does not indicate) an intent to be bound by the contract. In general, any act or conduct showing an intent to affirm the contract will be deemed _____ (disaffirmance/ratification).

MULTIPLE-CHOICE QUESTIONS

(Answers at the Back of the Book)

_____ 1. **Based on a Sample CPA Exam Question.** Tom is minor who enters into a contract with Diane. All of the following are effective methods for Tom to ratify the contract EXCEPT

a. expressly ratifying the contract after Tom reaches the age of majority.
b. failing to disaffirm the contact within a reasonable time after Tom reaches the age of majority.
c. ratifying the contract before Tom reaches the age of majority.
d. impliedly ratifying the contract after Tom reaches the age of majority.

_____ 2. Doug has been drinking heavily. Joe offers to buy Doug's farm for a fair price. Believing the deal is a joke, Doug writes and signs an agreement to sell and gives it to Joe. Joe believes the deal is serious. The contract is

a. enforceable, if the circumstances indicate Doug understands what he did.
b. enforceable, because Joe believes that the transaction is serious.
c. unenforceable, because the intoxication permits Doug to avoid the contract.
d. unenforceable, because Doug thinks it is a joke.

_____ 3. Ed is adjudged mentally incompetent. Irwin is appointed to act as Ed's guardian. Irwin signs a contract to sell some of Ed's property to pay for Ed's care. On regaining competency, Ed can

a. disaffirm, because he was mentally incompetent.
b. disaffirm, because he is no longer mentally incompetent.
c. not disaffirm, because Irwin could enter into contracts on his behalf.
d. not disaffirm, because he may become mentally incompetent again.

____ **4.** Eve, a fifteen-year-old minor, buys a computer from EZ Computers. The contract is fully executed. Eve now wants to disaffirm it. To do so, she

a. must return the computer to EZ.
b. must return only the computer components that she does not want.
c. need not return anything to EZ.
d. none of the above.

____ **5.** At the start of the football season, Bob bets Murray about the results of the next SuperBowl. Adam holds their money. By the time of the divisional play-offs, Bob changes his mind and asks for his money back. Gambling on sports events is illegal in their state. Can Bob be held to the bet?

a. Yes. It would be unconscionable to let Bob to back out so late in the season.
b. Yes. No party to the contract is innocent, and thus, no party can withdraw.
c. No. If an illegal agreement is still executory, either party can withdraw.
d. No. The only party who can be held to the bet is Murray.

____ **6.** Al sells his business to Dan and as part of the agreement promises not to engage in a business of the same kind within thirty miles for three years. Competition within thirty miles would hurt Dan's business. Al's promise

a. violates public policy, because it is part of the sale of a business.
b. violates public policy, because it unreasonably restrains Al from competing.
c. does not violate public policy, because it is no broader than necessary.
d. none of the above.

____ **7.** Luke practices law without an attorney's license. The state requires a license to protect the public from unauthorized practitioners. Clark hires Luke to handle a legal matter. Luke cannot enforce their contract because

a. it is illegal.
b. Luke has no contractual capacity.
c. Luke did not give consideration.
d. none of the above.

____ **8.** Amy contracts to buy Kim's business. Kim agrees not to compete with Amy for one year in the same county. Six months later, Kim opens a competing business six blocks away. Amy

a. cannot enforce the contract because it is unconscionable.
b. cannot enforce the contract because it is a restraint of trade.
c. can enforce the contract because all covenants not to compete are valid.
d. can enforce the contract because it is reasonable in scope and duration.

____ **9.** Sam signs an employment contract that contains a clause absolving the employer of any liability if Sam is injured on the job. If Sam is injured on the job due to the employer's negligence, the clause will

a. protect the employer from liability.
b. likely not protect the employer from liability.
c. likely be held unconscionable.
d. both b and c.

_____   **10.**   Ann contracts with Bob, a financial planner who is required by the state to have a license. Bob does not have a license. Their contract is enforceable if

    a.   the purpose of the statute is to protect the public from unlicensed practitioners.

    b.   the purpose of the statute is to raise government revenue.

    c.   Bob does not know that he is required to have a license.

    d.   Ann does not know that Bob is required to have a license.

SHORT ESSAY QUESTIONS

1.   Who has protection under the law relating to contractual capacity and what protection do they have?

2.   What makes an agreement illegal? What is the effect of an illegal agreement?

ISSUE SPOTTERS

(Answers at the Back of the Book)

1.   Joan, who is sixteen years old, moves out of her parents' home and signs a one-year lease for an apartment at Kenwood Apartments. Joan's parents tell her that she can return to live with them at any time. Unable to pay the rent, Joan moves to her parents' home two months later. Can Kenwood enforce the lease against Joan?

2.   Nick buys a franchise from Dave for $24,000. Later, while extremely drunk, Nick sells the franchise back to Dave, at Dave's urging, for $10,000. On becoming sober, Nick cannot remember selling the franchise back to Dave. Can Nick cancel the sale?

3.   Pam is mentally incompetent. She signs a contract to sell land to Marion, who is unaware of the incompetency. Before the deal is completed, Pam regains her competency and decides not to go through with it. Can she disaffirm the contract?

4.   Diane bets Tex $1,000 that the Dallas Cowboys will win the SuperBowl. A state law prohibits gambling. Do Diane and Tex have an enforceable contract?

5.   Potomac Airlines prints on the backs of its tickets that it is not liable for any injury to a passenger caused by Potomac's negligence. Ron buys a ticket and boards the plane. On takeoff, the plane crashes, and Ron is injured. If the cause of the accident is found to be Potomac's negligence, can Potomac use the clause as defense to liability?

SPECIAL INFORMATION FOR CPA CANDIDATES

The CPA examination has not generally tested heavily on capacity. Those points that it may be important to keep in mind include that a minor can disaffirm a contract for a reasonable time after reaching majority. The CPA exam recognizes the rule that for a minor to disaffirm, he or she must return whatever the minor received under the contract. Also, on the CPA exam, intoxication qualifies as a defense only if it was involuntary.

The CPA exam has often asked questions relating to covenants not to compete and to contracts that violate licensing statutes. A covenant not to compete is usually legal if it is part of the sale of a business. A covenant not to compete between an employer and an employee is legal if it is reasonable in length of time and geographic scope.

If a contracting party failed to comply with a licensing statute that has as its purpose the raising of revenue, the contract will likely still be enforceable. If the purpose of the statute is to regulate members of the profession of which the noncomplying party claims to be a part, however, the contract is not enforceable.

Chapter 14
Genuineness of Assent

WHAT THIS CHAPTER IS ABOUT

A contract may be unenforceable if the parties have not genuinely assented to its terms. Assent may be lacking because of mistakes, misrepresentation, undue influence, or duress. A party who has not truly assented can choose to avoid the transaction. Lack of assent is both a defense to the enforcement of a contract and a ground for rescission (cancellation) of a contract.

CHAPTER OUTLINE

I. MISTAKES

It is important to distinguish between mistakes made in judgment as to value or quality and mistakes made as to facts. Only the latter have legal significance.

A. MISTAKES OF FACT

1. Unilateral Mistake
When *one* contracting party makes a mistake as to some material fact, he or she is *not* entitled to relief from the contract. Exceptions are—

a. Other Party's Knowledge
A contract may not be enforceable if the other party to the contract knows or should have known that a mistake was made.

b. Mathematical Mistakes
A contract may not be enforceable if a mistake in addition, subtraction, division, or multiplication was inadvertent.

2. Bilateral Mistake of Fact
If *both* parties are mistaken as to a *material fact*, the contract can be rescinded by either. This is also true if the parties attach different meanings to a term subject to more than one reasonable interpretation.

B. MISTAKES IN VALUE

When *one or both* parties make a mistake as to the *market value* or quality of the object of a contract, the contract can be *enforced* by either party.

II. FRAUDULENT MISREPRESENTATION

When an innocent party is fraudulently induced to enter into a contract, the contract normally can be avoided because that party has not voluntarily consented to its terms.

A. THE ELEMENTS OF FRAUD

(1) Misrepresentation of a material fact, (2) an intent to deceive, and (3) an innocent party's justifiable reliance on the misrepresentation.

1. Misrepresentation Has Occurred

Misrepresentation can be in words or actions.

a. Statements of Opinion

Statements of opinion are generally not subject to claims of fraud. But when a naïve purchaser relies on an expert's opinion, the innocent party may be entitled to rescission or reformation.

b. Misrepresentation by Conduct

Misrepresentation can occur by, for example, concealment, which prevents the other party from learning of a material fact.

c. Misrepresentation of Law

Misrepresentation of law does not entitle a party to relief, unless the misrepresenting party is in a profession that is known to require greater knowledge of the law than the average person has.

d. Misrepresentation by Silence

Generally, no party to a contract has a duty to disclose facts. Exceptions include—

1) Latent Defect

If a serious defect is known to the seller but could not reasonably be suspected by the buyer, the seller may have a duty to speak.

2) Fiduciary Relationship

In a fiduciary relationship, if one party knows facts that materially affect the other's interests, they must be disclosed.

3) Statutory Provisions

Some statutes (for example, the Truth-in-Lending Act) provide exceptions to the rule of nondisclosure.

2. Intent to Deceive (*Scienter*)

A misrepresenting party must know that facts are falsely represented.

a. When This Occurs

If a party (1) knows a fact is not as stated; (2) makes a statement he or she believes not to be true or makes it recklessly, without regard to the truth; or (3) says or implies that a statement is made on a basis such as personal knowledge when it is not.

b. When Proof of Fault Is Not Necessary

In many cases (often involving sales of land or stock), a buyer need prove only a seller's representation was false, without regard to the seller's state of mind.

3. **Reliance on the Misrepresentation**
The misrepresentation must be an important factor in inducing the party to contract. Reliance is not justified if the party knows the true facts or relies on obviously extravagant statements, or the defect is obvious.

B. **INJURY TO THE INNOCENT PARTY**
To rescind a contract, most courts do not require proof of injury. To recover damages, proof of injury is required. In actions based on fraud, punitive damages are often granted, on the public-policy ground of punishing the defendant or setting an example to deter similar wrongdoing by others.

III. NONFRAUDULENT MISREPRESENTATION

A. **INNOCENT MISREPRESENTATION**
This occurs when a person misrepresents a material fact without the intent to defraud (he or she believes the statement to be true). A party who relies on the statement to his or her detriment can rescind the contract.

B. **NEGLIGENT MISREPRESENTATION**
This occurs when a person misrepresents a material fact by failing to exercise reasonable care in uncovering or disclosing the facts, or not using the skill and competence that his or her business or profession requires. In effect, this is treated as fraudulent misrepresentation.

IV. UNDUE INFLUENCE
Undue influence occurs when a contract enriches a party at the expense of another who is dominated by the enriched party. Such a contract is voidable.

A. **LACK OF FREE WILL**
The essential feature is that the party taken advantage of does not exercise free will.

B. **CONFIDENTIAL OR FIDUCIARY RELATIONSHIPS**
Undue influence often occurs in relationships in which one party can greatly influence another (attorney-client, parent-child). The dominant party is held to extreme or utmost good faith in dealing with the subservient party.

1. **Presumption**
When a contract between the parties favors the dominant party, a court will often presume that it was made under undue influence.

2. **To Rebut the Presumption**
The dominant party has to show that full disclosure was made, that consideration was adequate, and that the subservient party received independent and competent advice before completing the transaction.

V. DURESS
Duress involves conduct of a coercive nature.

A. **WHAT DURESS IS**
Forcing a party to enter into a contract by threatening the party with a wrongful or illegal act—threatening blackmail or extortion, for example.

B. **WHAT DURESS IS NOT**
Threatening to exercise a legal right; economic need (unless the party exacting the price also creates the need).

VI. ADHESION CONTRACTS AND UNCONSCIONABILITY

A. WHAT AN ADHESION CONTRACT IS
A contract written exclusively by one party (the dominant party, usually a seller or creditor) and presented to the other (buyer or borrower) on a take-it-or-leave-it basis. Typically, a standard form contract.

B. TO AVOID ENFORCEMENT OF THE CONTRACT
The adhering party must show that the parties had substantially unequal bargaining positions and that enforcement would be unfair or oppressive.

1. Unconscionability
Unconscionability under UCC 2–302 applies only to contracts for sales of goods. Many courts, however, apply the concept to other contracts.

2. Fraud, Undue Influence, and Duress
In states that have not adopted UCC 2–302, the courts rely on traditional notions of fraud, undue influence, and duress.

TRUE-FALSE QUESTIONS

(Answers at the Back of the Book)

____ 1. Under a mistake of fact, a contract can sometimes be avoided.

____ 2. When parties to both sides of a contract are mistaken as to the same fact, the contract cannot be rescinded by either party.

____ 3. To commit fraudulent misrepresentation, one party must intend to mislead another.

____ 4. In an action to rescind a contract for fraudulent misrepresentation, proof of injury is required to collect damages.

____ 5. Threatening a civil suit does not normally constitute duress.

____ 6. The essential feature of undue influence is that the party taken advantage of does not exercise free will.

____ 7. Adhesion contracts are always enforced.

____ 8. If a person believes a statement to be true, he or she cannot be held liable for misrepresentation.

____ 9. A seller has no duty to disclose to a buyer a defect that is known to the seller but could not reasonably be suspected by a buyer.

____ 10. When both parties make a mistake as to the market value of the object of their contract, the contract can be rescinded by either party.

FILL-IN QUESTIONS

(Answers at the Back of the Book)

Believing something is worth more than it is a mistake of _____ (fact/value). When parties contract, their agreement establishes the worth of the object of their contract for the moment. The next moment, the worth may change. Either party may be mistaken as to what the change may be. This is a mistake of _____ (fact/value). Under such a mistake, a contract _____ (cannot/may) be avoided. Mistakes as to _____ (value/fact) will almost never justify voiding a contract.

MULTIPLE-CHOICE QUESTIONS

(Answers at the Back of the Book)

1. **Based on a Sample CPA Exam Question.** Metro Transport asks for bids on a construction project. Metro estimates that the cost will be $200,000. Most bids are about $200,000, but A&B Construction bids $150,000. In adding a column of figures, A&B mistakenly omitted a $50,000 item. Because Metro had reason to know of the mistake

   a. A&B can avoid the contract because Metro knew of the errors.
   b. A&B can avoid the contract because the errors were the result of negligence.
   c. Metro can enforce the contract because the errors were unilateral.
   d. Metro can enforce the contract because the errors were material.

2. To induce Sam to buy a lot in a Mel's development, Mel tells Sam that he intends to add a golf course. The terrain is suitable, and there is enough land, but Mel has no intention of adding a golf course. Sam is induced by the statement to buy a lot. Sam's reliance on Mel's statement is justified because

   a. Mel is the owner of the development.
   b. Sam does not know the truth and has no way of finding it out.
   c. Sam did not buy the golf course.
   d. the golf course had obviously not been built yet.

3. Bob agrees to sell to Pam ten shares of Mina Corporation stock. Neither party knows whether the stock will increase or decrease in value. Pam believes that it will increase in value. If she is mistaken, her mistake will

   a. justify voiding the contract.
   b. not justify voiding the contract.
   c. warrant a refund to her from Bob of the difference.
   d. warrant a payment from her to Bob of the difference.

4. Fran is an eighty-year-old widow with no business experience. Fran's nephew Mark urges her to sell some of her stock at a price below market value to Tim, Mark's "business" partner. Fran, relying on Mark, agrees to sell the stock to Tim. She may avoid the contract on the ground of

   a. duress.
   b. mistake.
   c. undue influence.
   d. any of the above.

____   5.   Dick offers to sell amplifiers to Gina for her theater. Intending to deceive her, he describes the 120-watt amplifiers as "210 watts per channel." The number of watts is a material fact. Gina relies on Dick's description. This is

   a.   duress.
   b.   fraudulent misrepresentation.
   c.   undue influence.
   d.   none of the above.

____   6.   Ken, who is not a real estate broker, sells Cathy some land. Which of the following statements by Ken, with the accompanying circumstance, would be a fraudulent misrepresentation in that sale?

   a.   "This acreage offers the most spectacular view of the valley." From higher up the mountain, more of the valley is visible.
   b.   "You can build an office building here." The county requires the property to be exclusively residential, but neither Ken nor Cathy know that.
   c.   "This property includes ninety acres." Ken knows it is only eighty acres.
   d.   "The value of this property will triple in five years." Ken does not know whether the value of the property will triple in five years.

____   7.   Energy Source, a chain of computer stores, presents its customer Joe with a form contract on a take-it-or-leave basis to finance his purchase. The contract is

   a.   not enforceable if enforcement would be unfair or oppressive.
   b.   not enforceable if the terms are fair but the customer does not want to pay.
   c.   not enforceable in states that have not adopted UCC 2–302.
   d.   enforceable under all circumstances.

____   8.   Ron contracts with Gail under what Ron later learns to have been misrepresented facts. Ron has not yet suffered an injury. He can

   a.   only obtain damages from Gail.
   b.   only rescind the contract.
   c.   either obtain damages or rescind the contract.
   d.   none of the above.

____   9.   To sell his house to Amy, Ray does not tell her that the foundation was built on unstable pilings. Amy may later avoid the contract on the ground of

   a.   duress.
   b.   fraudulent misrepresentation.
   c.   undue influence.
   d.   none of the above.

____   10.   Lou and Paula enter into a contract. Lou later tells Paula that if she does not perform her part of the deal, he will sue her. Paula can avoid the contract on the basis of

   a.   duress.
   b.   fraudulent misrepresentation.
   c.   undue influence.
   d.   none of the above.

SHORT ESSAY QUESTIONS

1.   Why are mistakes of value not accorded the same relief as mistakes of fact?

2.   What are the elements of fraudulent misrepresentation?

ISSUE SPOTTERS

(Answers at the Back of the Book)

1.   Michael, a famous and wealthy musician, dies. Michael's wife Jessy sells their farm to Carl, who asks what should be done with all the "junk" on the property. Jessy says that Carl can do whatever he wants with it. Unknown to Jessy or Carl, in a cabinet in the house are the master tapes for an unreleased album. Can Carl keep the tapes?

2.   Brad, an accountant, files Dina's tax returns. When the Internal Revenue Service assesses a large tax against Dina, she retains Brad to resist the assessment. The day before the deadline for replying to the IRS, Brad tells Dina that unless she pays a higher fee, he will withdraw. If Dina agrees to pay, is the contract enforceable?

3.   In selling a house, Matt tells Ann that the wiring, fixtures, and appliances are of a certain quality. Matt knows nothing about the quality, but it is not as specified. Ann buys the house. On learning the true quality, Ann confronts Matt, who says he wasn't trying to fool her, he was only trying to make a sale. Can she rescind the deal?

4.   Julie, an accountant, certifies several audit reports to Olive Corporation, Julie's client, knowing that Olive intends to use the reports to obtain loans from Ace Credit Company. Julie believes that the reports are true and does not intend to deceive Ace, but does not check the reports before certifying them. Can Julie be held liable to Ace?

5.   For years, Pat, who is not experienced in business, has relied in business matters on the advice of her attorney, Greg. Greg constantly urges Pat to sell to Dave a tract of land at a price well below its fair value. Pat finally agrees. Is the contract voidable?

SPECIAL INFORMATION FOR CPA CANDIDATES

The CPA examination has traditionally covered at least four of the types of conduct mentioned in this chapter—fraudulent misrepresentation, nonfraudulent misrepresentation, undue influence, and duress. You may want to review the elements of those types of conduct, keeping in mind that each of these is interpreted according to the person defrauded, unduly influenced, or under duress (they are not interpreted according to what a reasonable person in the position of the innocent party would have believed). Remember, too, that the conduct must relate to a material fact, or otherwise be material, and it must truly result in the innocent party's assent.

Chapter 15
The Statute of Frauds

WHAT THIS CHAPTER IS ABOUT

Under the Statute of Frauds, certain types of contracts must be in writing to be enforceable. If there is no written evidence of a contract that falls under this statute, i t is not void, but it may not be enforceable. This chapter covers contracts that fall under the Statute of Frauds and the parol evidence rule, which concerns the admissibility a t trial of evidence that is external to written contracts.

CHAPTER OUTLINE

I. ORIGIN OF THE STATUTE OF FRAUDS

The English passed the Statute of Frauds in 1677. Today, every state has a statute that stipulates what types of contracts must be in writing to be enforceable. If one of these contracts is not in writing, the contract is not void but the Statute of Frauds is a defense to its enforcement.

II. CONTRACTS FALLING WITHIN THE STATUTE OF FRAUDS

A. CONTRACTS INVOLVING INTERESTS IN LAND
Land includes all objects permanently attached, such as trees. Contracts to transfer interests in land (such as leases; see Chapter 48) must be in writing.

B. THE ONE-YEAR RULE

1. **Performance Objectively Impossible Must Be in Writing**
A contract must be in writing if performance is objectively impossible within a year of the date of the contract's formation.

2. **Possibility of Performance Need Not Be in Writing**
A contract need not be in writing if performance within one year is possible—even if it is improbable, unlikely, or takes longer.

C. COLLATERAL PROMISES

A promise ancillary to a principal transaction and made by a third party to assume the debts or obligations of the primary party (only if the primary party does not perform) must be in writing to be enforceable.

1. **Exception—"Main Purpose" Rule**

   An oral promise to answer for the debt of another is enforceable if the guarantor's main purpose is to secure a personal benefit.

2. **Estate Debts**

   Promises made by the administrator or executor of an estate to pay personally the estate debts must be in writing to be enforceable.

D. PROMISES MADE IN CONSIDERATION OF MARRIAGE

Prenuptial agreements must be in writing to be enforceable.

E. CONTRACTS FOR SALES OF GOODS

The Uniform Commercial Code (UCC) requires a writing for a sale of goods priced at $500 or more (see Chapter 19).

F. EXCEPTIONS TO THE STATUTE OF FRAUDS

1. **Partial Performance**

   a. **Contracts for the Transfer of Interests in Land**

      If a buyer pays part of the price, takes possession, and makes permanent improvements and the parties cannot be returned to their pre-contract status quo, a court may grant specific performance.

   b. **Contracts Covered by the UCC**

      Under the UCC, an oral contract is enforceable to the extent that a seller accepts payment or a buyer accepts delivery of the goods.

2. **Admissions**

   In some states, if a party admits in pleadings, testimony, or in court that a contract was made, the contract will be enforceable.

3. **Promissory Estoppel**

   An oral contract may be enforced if (1) a promisor makes a promise on which the promisee justifiably relies to his or her detriment, (2) the reliance was foreseeable to the promisor, and (3) injustice can be avoided only by enforcing the promise.

4. **Special Exceptions under the UCC**

   Oral contracts that may be enforceable under the UCC include those for customized goods and those between merchants that have been confirmed in writing (see Chapter 19).

III. SUFFICIENCY OF THE WRITING

No formal writing is required, but there must be at least a memo that includes the following.

A. SIGNATURE OF THE PARTY TO BE CHARGED

The writing must be signed (initialed) by the party against whom enforcement is sought (the party who refuses to perform). The signature can be anywhere in the writing.

B. ESSENTIAL TERMS

1. Contracts Covered by the UCC
The writing must include a quantity term. Other terms need not be stated exactly, if they adequately reflect the parties' intentions.

2. Other Contracts
The writing must include the identity of the parties, subject matter, consideration, and essential terms (in a sale of land these would include the price and a description of the property).

IV. THE PAROL EVIDENCE RULE

A. THE RULE
If a written contract is the final expression of the parties' agreement, evidence of prior negotiations, prior agreements, or contemporaneous oral agreements that contradicts or varies the terms is not admissible at trial.

B. EXCEPTIONS
Parol evidence is admissible to show—

1. Contract Subsequently Modified
Evidence of subsequent modification (oral or written) of a written contract is admissible (but oral modifications may not be enforceable if they bring the contract under the Statute of Frauds).

2. A Contract Is Voidable or Void

3. Meaning of Ambiguous Terms

4. Essential Term Lacking in an Incomplete Contract

5. Prior Dealing, Course of Performance, or Usage of Trade
Under the UCC, evidence can be introduced to explain or supplement a contract by showing a prior dealing, course of performance, or usage of trade (see Chapter 19).

6. Orally Agreed-on Condition
Proof of such a condition does not modify the written terms but involves the enforceability of the written contract.

7. An Obvious or Gross Clerical Error

TRUE-FALSE QUESTIONS

(Answers at the Back of the Book)

_____ 1. A contract must be in writing to be enforceable if performance is objectively impossible within a year of the date of the contract's formation.

_____ 2. A promise to answer for the debt of another must always be in writing to be enforceable.

_____ 3. A promise on which a promisee justifiably relies to his or her detriment will not be enforced unless it is in writing.

_____ 4. In some states, if a party admits in pleadings that a contract was made, even if the contract was oral, it will be enforceable.

____ 5. Oral contracts that are *not* enforceable under the UCC include those for customized goods.

____ 6. Contracts for transfers of interests in land need not be in writing to be enforceable under the Statute of Frauds.

____ 7. A contract for a sale of goods of under $100 must be in writing to be enforceable under the Statute of Frauds.

____ 8. An oral contract that should be in writing to be enforceable under the Statute of Frauds may be enforceable if it has been partially performed.

____ 9. The only writing sufficient to satisfy the Statute of Frauds is a printed form, with the heading "Contract," signed at the bottom by all parties.

____ 10. Under the parol evidence rule, virtually any evidence is admissible to prove or disprove the terms of a contract.

FILL-IN QUESTIONS

(Answers at the Back of the Book)

A collateral promise is a promise that is _____ (superior/ancillary) to a _____ (primary/secondary) contractual relationship.

A promise by one person to pay the debts or discharge the duties of another person if the other fails to perform _____ (must/need not) be in writing to be enforceable under the Statute of Frauds. If the main purpose of a promise to pay another's debts or perform another's duties is to benefit the promisor, however, the agreement _____ (must/need not) be in writing to be enforceable.

MULTIPLE-CHOICE QUESTIONS

(Answers at the Back of the Book)

____ 1. Jim orally promises to work for Pat, and Pat orally promises to employ Jim at a rate of $500 a week. This contract must be in writing to be enforceable if Jim promises to work for

   a. his entire life.
   b. at least five years.
   c. five years but either party can terminate the contract on two weeks' notice.
   d. both a and c.

____ 2. On March 1, the chief engineer for the software design division of Digital Products (DP) orally contracts to hire Lee for one year, beginning March 4. Lee works for DP for five months. When sales decline, Lee is discharged. Lee sues DP for reinstatement or seven months' salary. Lee will

   a. win, because the contract can be performed within one year.
   b. win, because employment contracts need not be in writing to be enforceable.
   c. lose, because the contract cannot be performed within one year.
   d. lose, because employment contracts must be in writing to be enforceable.

_____ 3. **Based on a Sample CPA Exam Question.** Under a written agreement, Adam sells a motel to Bill. When Adam removes the furniture, Bill sues. The court decides the written agreement includes everything the parties intended. Which of the following agreements about the furniture will be admissible?

   a. A prior written agreement only
   b. A subsequent oral agreement only
   c. Either a prior written agreement or a subsequent oral agreement
   d. None of the above

_____ 4. National Properties, Inc., orally contracts for a sale of its land to U.S. Merchants, Inc., then later decides not to go through with the sale. The contract is most likely enforceable against

   a. both National and U.S. Merchants.
   b. National only.
   c. U.S. Merchants only.
   d. neither National nor U.S. Merchants.

_____ 5. ABC Distribution, Inc., orally contracts for a lease of its storage facilities to Delta Manufacturing Company. Delta pays part of the price, takes possession, and makes permanent improvements to the property. The contract is most likely enforceable against

   a. ABC only.
   b. Delta only.
   c. ABC and Delta.
   d. none of the above.

_____ 6. Alpha Computers contracts with Engineers. Inc. (EI), to buy EI's circuit boards. The contract is most likely enforceable against EI if Alpha offers as proof of the agreement

   a. a sales slip signed by EI.
   b. a purchase order that sets out all the terms but is signed by neither party.
   c. the sales slip signed by EI or the unsigned work order.
   d. none of the above.

_____ 7. Investors, Inc., contracts with J&J Properties to buy J&J's warehouse. The contract is most likely enforceable against J&J if Investors offers as proof of the agreement

   a. a blank sheet of J&J's letterhead stationery only.
   b. J&J's business card only.
   c. a blank sheet of J&J's letterhead stationery or J&J's business card.
   d. none of the above.

_____ 8. Beta Products, Inc., orally promises to sell to Omega Processing, Inc., the software and equipment for Omega to network its computers. This contract must be in writing to be enforceable if the price is for

   a. any amount of money.
   b. $500 or less.
   c. $500 or more.
   d. none of the above.

___   9.   April owes Bell Credit Company $10,000. Chris orally promises Bell that he will pay April's debt if April does not. This promise is

   a. not enforceable because it is not in writing.
   b. enforceable under the "main purpose rule" exception.
   c. not enforceable because the debt is April's.
   d. enforceable under the part performance exception.

___   10.   Bob hires General Contractors (GC) to build an office building. GC owes Building Supplies, Inc. (BSI), $10,000. BSI will not sell GC more supplies without a guaranty that the debt will be paid. Bob orally promises BSI that he will pay GC's debt if GC does not. This promise is

   a. enforceable under the "main purpose rule" exception.
   b. enforceable under the part performance exception.
   c. not enforceable because it is not in writing.
   d. not enforceable because the debt is GC's.

SHORT ESSAY QUESTIONS

1.   What is required to satisfy the writing requirement of the Statute of Frauds?

2.   What is *not* admissible under the parol evidence rule?

ISSUE SPOTTERS

(Answers at the Back of the Book)

1.   In selling an office building, Jill tells Kyle that the filing cabinets are included. The sales agreement, which says that it "supercedes all oral promises relating to the sale," says nothing about the filing cabinets. Are the cabinets a part of the deal?

2.   American Goods, Inc. (AGI), and International Sales Corporation orally agree to a deal. AGI types up the essential terms on letterhead stationery and files it in AGI's office. If AGI later refuses to complete the transaction, is this memo a sufficient writing to enforce the contract against it?

3.   GamesCo orders $800 worth of game pieces from Midstate Plastic, Inc. Midstate delivers, and GamesCo pays for, $450 worth. GamesCo then says it wants no more pieces from Midstate. GamesCo and Midstate have never dealt with each other before and have nothing in writing. Can Midstate enforce a deal for $350 more?

4.   Paula orally agrees with Next Corporation to work in New York City for Next for two years. Paula moves her family to New York and begins work. Three months later, Paula is fired for no stated cause. She sues for reinstatement or pay. Next argues that there is no written contract between them. What will the court say?

5.   David orally agrees to sells his computer to Jan. Later, David refuses to go through with the transaction, and Jan sues. In court, David admits that he did agree to sell the computer. Is the contract now enforceable?

SPECIAL INFORMATION FOR CPA CANDIDATES

Among the details covered in this chapter, the CPA examination has asked questions about the types of contracts that fall within the Statute of Frauds, the enforceability of oral contracts that come under the Statute of Frauds, and the effect of an oral acceptance of a written offer. Sometimes, these details have been woven into questions are less direct. For example, a question might ask for a calculation of damages for the breach of an oral contract, which requires a consideration of the types of contracts subject to the Statute of Frauds.

Chapter 16
Third Party Rights

WHAT THIS CHAPTER IS ABOUT

A party to a contract can assign the rights arising from it to another or delegate the duties of the contract by having another perform them. A third party also acquires rights to enforce a contract when the contract parties intend the contract to benefit the third party (who is an intended beneficiary). When a contract only incidentally benefits a third party, he or she is an incidental beneficiary and cannot enforce it.

CHAPTER OUTLINE

I. ASSIGNMENTS AND DELEGATIONS

Assignment and delegation occur after the original contract is made, when one of the parties transfers to another party an interest or duty in the contract.

A. ASSIGNMENTS

1. What an Assignment Is

Parties to a contract have rights and duties. One party has a *right* to require the other to perform, and the other has a *duty* to perform. The transfer of the *right* to a third person is an assignment.

2. Effect of an Unconditional Assignment

(1) The rights of the assignor are extinguished; (2) the assignee has a right to demand performance from the obligor; and (3) the assignee's rights are subject to the defenses the obligor has against the assignor.

3. How Assignments Function

Assignments are involved in much business financing. The most common contractual right that is assigned is the right to the payment of money.

4. Form of an Assignment

An assignment can take any form, oral or written. Assignments covered by the Statute of Frauds must be in writing to be enforceable. Most states require contracts for the assignment of wages to be in writing.

5. Rights That Cannot Be Assigned

a. Statute Prohibits Assignment
(For example, assignment of future workers' compensation benefits.)

b. Contract Is Personal
The rights under the contract cannot be assigned unless all that remains is a money payment. (Personal services are unique to the person rendering them. Rights to receive personal services are likewise unique and cannot be assigned.)

c. Assignment Materially Increases or Alters Risk or Duties of Obligor

d. Contract Stipulates That It Cannot Be Assigned
Exceptions: a contract cannot prevent an assignment of—

1) A right to receive money.
2) Rights in real estate (restraint against alienation).
3) Rights in negotiable instruments (see Chapter 24).
4) A right to receive damages for breach of a sales contract or for payment of amount owed under it (even if contract prohibits it).

6. Notice of Assignment
An assignment is effective immediately, with or without notice.

a. Same Right Assigned to More Than One Party
If the assignor assigns the same right to different persons, in most states, the first assignment in time is the first in right. In some states, priority is given to the first assignee who gives notice.

b. Discharge before Notice
Until an obligor has notice, his or her obligation can be discharged by performance to the assignor. Once the obligor has notice, only performance to the assignee can act as a discharge.

B. DELEGATIONS
Duties are delegated. The party making the delegation is the delegator; the party to whom the duty is delegated is the delegatee.

1. Form of Delegation
No special form is required.

2. Duties That Cannot Be Delegated
Any duty can be delegated, unless (1) performance depends on the personal skill or talents of the obligor, (2) special trust has been placed in the obligor, (3) performance by a third party will vary materially from that expected by the obligee (the one to whom performance is owed) under the contract, or (4) the contract expressly prohibits it.

3. Effect of a Delegation
The obligee (the one to whom performance is owed) must accept performance from the delegatee, unless the duty is one that cannot be delegated. If the delegatee fails to perform, the delegator is still liable.

4. Liability of the Delegatee

If the delegatee makes a promise of performance that will directly benefit the obligee, there is an "assumption of duty." Breach of this duty makes the delegatee liable to the obligee, and the obligee can sue both the delegatee and the delegator.

C. ASSIGNMENT OF ALL RIGHTS

A contract that provides in general words for an assignment of all rights (for example, "I assign the contract" or "I assign all my rights under the contract") is both an assignment of rights and a delegation of duties.

II. THIRD PARTY BENEFICIARIES

Only intended beneficiaries acquire legal rights in a contract.

A. INTENDED BENEFICIARIES

An intended beneficiary is one for whose benefit a contract is made. If the contract is breached, he or she can sue the promisor.

1. Types of Intended Beneficiaries

a. Creditor Beneficiaries

A creditor beneficiary benefits from a contract in which a promisor promises to pay a debt that the promisee owes to him or her.

b. Donee Beneficiaries

A donee beneficiary benefits from a contract made for the express purpose of giving a gift to him or her.

2. Vesting of an Intended Beneficiary's Rights

To enforce a contract against the original parties, the rights of the third party must first vest (take effect). The rights vest when (1) the third party manifests assent to the contract or (2) the third party materially alters his or her position in detrimental reliance

3. Modification or Rescission of the Contract

Until the third party's rights vest, the others can modify or rescind the contract without the third party's consent. If the contract reserves the power to rescind or modify, vesting does not terminate the power.

B. INCIDENTAL BENEFICIARIES

The benefit that an incidental beneficiary receives from a contract between other parties is unintentional. An incidental beneficiary cannot enforce a contract to which he or she is not a party.

C. INTENDED OR INCIDENTAL BENEFICIARY?

1. Reasonable Person Test

A beneficiary is intended if a reasonable person in his or her position would believe that the promisee intended to confer on the beneficiary the right to sue to enforce the contract.

2. Other Factors Indicating an Intended Beneficiary

(1) Performance is rendered directly to the third party, (2) the third party has the right to control the performance, or (3) the third party is expressly designated as beneficiary in the contract.

TRUE-FALSE QUESTIONS

(Answers at the Back of the Book)

____   1.   Intended beneficiaries have no legal rights under a contract.

____   2.   A third party can enforce a contract against the original parties when the third party's rights in the contract vest.

____   3.   The party who makes an assignment is the obligor.

____   4.   All rights can be assigned.

____   5.   If a contract contains a clause that prohibits assignment of the contract, then ordinarily the contract cannot be assigned.

____   6.   A right to the payment of money may be assigned.

____   7.   An assignment is not effective without notice.

____   8.   No special form is required to create a valid delegation of duties.

____   9.   Only intended beneficiaries acquire legal rights in a contract.

____   10.   A contract cannot prevent an assignment of a right to receive money.

FILL-IN QUESTIONS

(Answers at the Back of the Book)

The transfer of rights to a third person is _____ (an assignment/a delegation) and the transfer of duties to a third person is _____ _____ (an assignment/a delegation). Probably the most common contractual right that is _____ (assigned/delegated) is the right to the payment of money. For instance, Digital Computer Corporation sells its computers on credit. Digital has the right to installment payments from its customers. To obtain funds to buy more inventory, Digital can _____ (assign/delegate) the right to the payments to a financing agency, which will pay Digital for the right.

MULTIPLE-CHOICE QUESTIONS

(Answers at the Back of the Book)

____   1.   Gary contracts with Dan to buy Dan a new car manufactured by General Motors Corporation (GMC). GMC is

  a.   an incidental beneficiary.
  b.   an intended beneficiary.
  c.   an obligee.
  d.   none of the above.

____   2.   Ben has a right to $100 against Carol. Ben assigns the right to Doug. Doug's rights against Carol

  a.   are subject to any defenses that Carol has against Ben.
  b.   do not vest until Carol assents to the assignment.
  c.   include the right to demand performance from Carol.
  d.   both a and c.

_____ 3. Frank owes Gail $100. Frank contracts with Hal to pay the $100 and notifies Gail of the contract by mail. Gail replies by mail that she agrees. After Frank receives Gail's reply, Frank and Hal send Gail a letter stating that they decided to rescind their contract. Gail's rights under the contract

    a. vested when Frank and Hal formed their contract.
    b. vested when Gail learned of the contract and manifested assent to it.
    c. will not vest because Frank and Hal rescinded their contract.
    d. will not vest because Gail is an incidental beneficiary.

_____ 4. Jenny sells her Value Auto Parts store to Burt and makes a valid contract not to compete. Burt wants to sell the store to Discount Auto Centers and assign to Discount the right to have Jenny not compete. Burt can

    a. sell the business and assign the right.
    b. sell the business but not assign the right.
    c. assign the right but not sell the business.
    d. neither assign the right nor sell the business.

_____ 5. Dick contracts with Jane to cut the grass on Jane's lawn. Dick delegates performance of the duty to Sally with Jane's assent. Who owes Jane a duty to cut her grass?

    a. Dick, but not Sally
    b. Sally, but not Dick
    c. Both Dick and Sally
    d. Neither Dick nor Sally

_____ 6. Nate and Owen sign a contract. Patty, a third party, is an intended beneficiary to the contract if

    a. Patty has rights to control the details of performance.
    b. performance is rendered directly to Patty.
    c. there is an express designation in the contract.
    d. any of the above.

_____ 7. **Based on a Sample CPA Exam Question.** Dan assigns to Evan a contract to buy a used car from Fran. To be valid, the assignment must

    a. be in writing and be signed by Dan.
    b. be supported by adequate consideration from Evan.
    c. not be revocable by Dan.
    d. not materially increase Fran's risk or duty.

_____ 8. A contract for a sale of goods between John and Mary provides that the right to receive damages for its breach cannot be assigned. This clause

    a. is not effective.
    b. is effective only before the contract is executed.
    c. is effective only after the contract is executed.
    d. is effective under all circumstances.

_____ 9. Fred unconditionally assigns to Ellen his rights under a contract with Paul. Fred's rights under the contract

    a. continue until the contract is fully executed.
    b. continue until Paul performs his obligations under the contract.
    c. continue until Ellen receives Paul's performance.
    d. are extinguished.

____ **10.** Ann has a right to receive payment under a contract with Bill. Without notice, Ann assigns the right first to Carl and then to Diane. In most states, the party with priority to the right would be

a. Ann.
b. Bill.
c. Carl.
d. Diane.

SHORT ESSAY QUESTIONS

1. What is a third party beneficiary contract? What are the circumstances under which a third party can bring an action to enforce it?

2. Who are the parties in an assignment? What are their rights and duties?

ISSUE SPOTTERS

(Answers at the Back of the Book)

1. Brian owes Jeff $100. Ed tells Brian to give him the money and he'll pay Jeff. Brian gives Ed the money. Ed never pays Jeff. Can Jeff successfully sue Ed for the money?

2. Abby owes Penny $100. Penny assigns her right to the money to Charlie. Can Charlie successfully sue Abby for the money?

3. Joe contracts to sell his car to Hal for $3,500. Hal gives Joe a worthless check for the price, which means that Joe has a right to refuse to deliver the car to Hal. Hal assigns his right to the car to Gina. If Joe refuses to deliver the car to Gina and Gina sues, can Joe raise Hal's fraud as a defense against delivery of the car to Gina?

4. A&B Construction Company contracts to build a house for Mike. The contract states that "any assignment of this contract renders the contract void." After A&B builds the house, but before Mike pays, A&B assigns its right to payment to Ace Credit Company. Can Ace enforce the contract against Mike?

5. Bo contracts with Cole to personally unload Cole's truck. Bo's friend Lee is competent to unload a truck. Can Bo delegate performance of the duty to Lee?

SPECIAL INFORMATION FOR CPA CANDIDATES

It is important to remember for the CPA examination that only a creditor or donee beneficiary may recover from a promisor who fails to perform according to the contract—an incidental beneficiary has no enforceable rights under the contract. It is also important to remember that generally any contract can be assigned (unless the contract expressly prohibits it). There are more restrictions on delegations of duties. The point to remember in regard to delegation of duties is that when a duty is personal, it cannot be assigned.

Finally, it should be remembered that unless there is a release or a novation, the assignor remains liable on the contract despite its assignment. A party who, without notice of an assignment, pays an assignor will not later be liable to the assignee: the assignee should notify the obligor of the assignment.

Chapter 17
Performance and Discharge

WHAT THIS CHAPTER IS ABOUT

This chapter discusses performance and discharge of contracts. Performance of a contract (when the parties do what they agreed to do) discharges it. Discharging a contract terminates it. Discharge usually results from performance but can occur in other ways: (1) the occurrence or failure of a condition on which a contract is based, (2) breach of the contract, (3) agreement of the parties, and (4) operation of law.

CHAPTER OUTLINE

I. CONDITIONS

A **condition** is a possible future event, occurrence or nonoccurrence of which triggers performance of an obligation or terminates an obligation. If performance is contingent on a condition that is not satisfied, neither party has to perform.

A. CONDITION PRECEDENT
A condition that must be fulfilled before a party's performance can be required. Such conditions are common. For example, a real estate contract is usually conditioned on the buyer's ability to get financing.

B. CONDITION SUBSEQUENT
A condition that operates to terminate an obligation to perform. The condition follows a duty to perform. Such conditions are rare.

C. CONCURRENT CONDITION
When each party's duty to perform is conditioned on the other party's duty to perform. Occurs only when the parties are to perform their duties simultaneously (for example, paying for goods on delivery). No party can recover for breach unless he or she first tenders performance.

D. EXPRESS AND IMPLIED CONDITIONS

1. Express Condition
Provided for by the parties' agreement. Usually prefaced by the word "if," "provided," "after," or "when."

2. Implied-in-Fact Condition
Understood to be part of the agreement but not found in the express language of the agreement. The court infers them from the promises (notice is an implied condition to correct a defect under warranty).

II. DISCHARGE BY PERFORMANCE
Most contracts are discharged by the parties' doing what they promised to do.

A. TENDER OF PERFORMANCE
Discharge can be accomplished by **tender** (an unconditional offer to perform by one who is ready, willing, and able to do so). If performance has been tendered and the other party refuses to perform, the party making the tender can sue for breach.

B. TYPES OF PERFORMANCE

1. Complete Performance
Express conditions fully satisfied in all aspects.

2. Substantial Performance
Performance that does not vary greatly from the performance promised in the contract. If one party fulfills the terms of the contract with substantial performance, the other party is obligated to perform (but may obtain damages for the deviations).

3. Performance to the Satisfaction of One of the Parties
When the subject matter of the contract is personal, performance must actually satisfy the party (a condition precedent). Contracts involving mechanical fitness, utility, or marketability need only be performed to the satisfaction of a reasonable person.

4. Performance to the Satisfaction of a Third Party
When the satisfaction of a third party is required, most courts require the work to be satisfactory to a reasonable person.

C. MATERIAL BREACH OF CONTRACT
A **breach of contract** is the nonperformance of a contractual duty. It is material when performance is not at least substantial; the nonbreaching party is excused from performing. If a breach is minor (not material), the nonbreaching party's duty to perform may be suspended until the breach is remedied.

D. ANTICIPATORY REPUDIATION
Before either party has a duty to perform, one party refuses to perform.

1. Damages and a Similar Contract
This can discharge the nonbreaching party, who can sue to recover damages immediately and can also seek a similar contract elsewhere.

2. Retraction
Until the nonbreaching party treats a repudiation as a breach, the repudiating party can retract his or her repudiation by proper notice.

E. TIME FOR PERFORMANCE
If a specific time is stated, the parties must usually perform by that time. If time is stated to be vital or construed to be "of the essence," it is a condition of the contract. If no time is stated, a reasonable time is implied, and a delay will not affect the performing party's right to payment.

III.   DISCHARGE BY AGREEMENT

A.   DISCHARGE BY RESCISSION

Rescission is the process by which a contract is canceled and the parties are returned to the positions they occupied prior to forming it.

1.   Executory Contracts

Contracts that are executory on both sides can be rescinded.

a.   Requirements

The parties must make another agreement, which must satisfy the legal requirements for a contract. Their promises not to perform are consideration for the second contract.

b.   Form

A rescission agreement is enforceable if oral (even if the original agreement was in writing), except an agreement must be in writing if it is subject to the UCC and the contract requires written rescission.

2.   Executed Contracts

Contracts that are executed on one side can be rescinded only if the party who has performed receives consideration to call off the deal.

B.   DISCHARGE BY NOVATION

Occurs when the parties to a contract and a new party get together and agree to substitute the new party for one of the original parties. Requirements are (1) a previous valid obligation, (2) an agreement of all the parties to a new contract, (3) the extinguishment of the old obligation (discharge of the prior party), and (4) a new, valid contract.

C.   DISCHARGE BY SUBSTITUTED AGREEMENT

Parties to a contract can execute a new agreement with different terms. The new agreement can either expressly or impliedly revoke and discharge the previous contract's obligations.

D.   DISCHARGE BY ACCORD AND SATISFACTION

To discharge by accord and satisfaction, the parties must agree to accept performance that is different from the performance originally promised.

1.   Accord

An accord is an executory contract to perform an act that will satisfy an existing duty. An accord suspends, but does not discharge, the duty.

2.   Satisfaction

Satisfaction is the performance of the accord, which discharges the original contractual obligation.

3.   If the Obligor Refuses to Perform

The obligee can sue on the original obligation or seek a decree for specific performance on the accord.

IV.   DISCHARGE BY OPERATION OF LAW

A.   ALTERATION OF THE CONTRACT

An innocent party can treat a contract as discharged if the other party materially alters a term (such as quantity or price) without consent.

B. STATUTES OF LIMITATIONS

Statutes of limitations limit the period during which a party can sue based on a breach of contract.

1. UCC 2–725

An action for the breach of a contract for a sale of goods must be commenced within four years after the breach occurs, whether the innocent party knows of the breach. The parties can shorten this period to one year but cannot extend it.

2. New Promise to Perform Starts the Period Again

If the party who owes the obligation makes a new promise to perform, the cause of action barred by the statute of limitations is revived.

C. BANKRUPTCY

A discharge in bankruptcy (see Chapter 32) will ordinarily bar enforcement of most of a debtor's contracts.

D. IMPOSSIBILITY OR IMPRACTICABILITY OF PERFORMANCE

1. Objective Impossibility of Performance

A contract may be discharged if, after it is made, performance becomes objectively impossible, as in the following: (1) death or incapacity of one of the parties, (2) specific subject matter of the contract is destroyed, or (3) change in the law that renders performance illegal.

2. Commercial Impracticability

Performance may be excused if it becomes much more difficult or expensive than contemplated when the contract was formed.

3. Frustration of Purpose

A contract will be discharged if supervening circumstances make it impossible to attain the purpose the parties had in mind.

4. Temporary Impossibility

An event that makes it temporarily impossible to perform will suspend performance until the impossibility ceases.

TRUE-FALSE QUESTIONS

(Answers at the Back of the Book)

____ 1. If performance of a contract is contingent on a condition and it is not satisfied, a party does not have to perform.

____ 2. Complete performance occurs when a contract's conditions are fully satisfied.

____ 3. A material breach of contract does not discharge the other party's duty to perform.

____ 4. An executory contract cannot be rescinded.

____ 5. Performance may be excused if it becomes much more difficult or expensive than contemplated when the contract was formed.

_____ 6. A condition can trigger the performance of a legal obligation.

_____ 7. If a contract does not require a certain time for performance, a reasonable time will be implied.

_____ 8. A party can treat a contract as discharged if the other party materially alters the quantity term without consent.

_____ 9. If, before either party to a contract has a duty to perform, one party refuses to do so, there is nothing the other party can do.

_____ 10. There is no limit to the time that a party can file a suit against another based on a breach of contract.

FILL-IN QUESTIONS

(Answers at the Back of the Book)

Most contracts are discharged by performance—by doing what was promised. Any contract can be discharged by agreement of the parties. _____ (Rescission/Novation) is the process by which a contract is canceled and the parties are returned to the positions they occupied before forming it. _____ (Rescission/Novation) substitutes a new party for an original party by agreement of all the parties. _____ (Substitution of a new contract/Accord and satisfaction) revokes and discharges a prior contract. _____ _____ (A substitution/An accord) suspends a contractual duty that has not been discharged. Once the _____ (substitution/accord) is performed, the original contractual obligation is discharged.

MULTIPLE-CHOICE QUESTIONS

(Answers at the Back of the Book)

_____ 1. Don contracts to build a store for Pat for $500,000, with payments to be in installments of $50,000 as building progresses. Don finishes the store except for a cover over a compressor on the roof. A cover can be installed for $500. Pat refuses to pay the last installment. If Don's breach is not material

a. Don has a claim against Pat for $50,000.
b. Pat has a claim against Don for damages for Don's breach of his duty to put a cover over the compressor.
c. both a and b.
d. none of the above.

_____ 2. Gil contracts to produce a movie for A&B Studios, Inc. A&B knows that Gil's only source of funds is a $500,000 deposit in First Bank. The bank fails. Gil loses the money. Gil's duty to produce the movie is

a. discharged on the ground of impossibility.
b. discharged on the ground of commercial impracticability.
c. suspended on the ground of temporary impossibility.
d. not discharged, and Gil is liable to Big for breach of contract.

_____ 3. Ron contracts to repair Joe's building for $30,000. Payment is to be made "on the satisfaction of Will, Joe's architect." To save money, Joe tells Will not to approve the repairs. If Ron sues Joe for $30,000, Ron will

a. win, because Will is Joe's architect.
b. win, because Joe is not acting reasonably.
c. lose, because Ron is not acting reasonably, honestly, and in good faith.
d. lose, because Will has not expressed satisfaction with the work.

_____ 4. Sam owes Lyle $10,000. Sam promises, in writing, to give Lyle a video-game machine in lieu of payment of the debt. Lyle agrees and Sam delivers the machine. Substituting and performing one duty for another is

a. an accord and satisfaction.
b. a novation.
c. a rescission.
d. none of the above.

_____ 5. On May 1, Val agrees to work for Babco, Inc., for four months beginning June 1. On May 15, Babco tells Val that it doesn't need her after all. Val's duty to work for Babco

a. was discharged on May 15.
b. was discharged on May 16.
c. will be discharged on June 1.
d. will be discharged on September 30.

_____ 6. Jim and Gail contract for the sale of one thousand computers. The agreement states that "the obligations of the parties are conditional on Gail obtaining financing from First Bank by August 1." This financing clause is

a. a condition precedent.
b. a condition subsequent.
c. a concurrent condition.
d. none of the above.

_____ 7. C&D Services contracts with Ace Concessions, Inc., to service Ace's vending machines. Later, C&D wants Dean Vending Services to assume the duties under a new contract. Ace consents. This is

a. an accord and satisfaction.
b. an alteration of contract.
c. a novation.
d. a rescission.

_____ 8. Kate contracts with Bob to transport Bob's goods to his stores. If this contract is discharged like most contracts, it will be discharged by

a. agreement.
b. operation of law.
c. performance.
d. none of the above.

____ **9. Based on a Sample CPA Exam Question.** Eve contracts with Frank to act as his personal financial planner. Eve's duties under this contract will be discharged if

a. Frank declares bankruptcy.
b. it becomes illegal for Eve to provide the service.
c. the cost of providing the service doubles.
d. none of the above.

____ **10.** Tony and Carol contract for the sale of Tony's business. Carol gives Tony a down payment, and Tony gives Carol the keys to one of his stores. Before the contract is fully performed, however, they agree to return the down payment and keys, and cancel the sale. This is

a. an accord and satisfaction.
b. an alteration of contract.
c. a novation.
d. a rescission.

SHORT ESSAY QUESTIONS

1. How are most contracts discharged?

2. What effect does a material breach have on the nonbreaching party? What is the effect of a nonmaterial breach?

ISSUE SPOTTERS

(Answers at the Back of the Book)

1. General Construction (GC) contracts with Federated Retail Corporation to build a store on Federated's lot. The work is to begin on May 1 and be completed by November 1, so that Federated can open for the Christmas buying season. GC does not finish until November 6. Federated opens, but due to the delay it loses some sales. Is Federated's duty to pay for the construction of the store discharged?

2. Red Tiger Foods contracts to buy from Bree Distributors two hundred carloads of frozen pizzas. Before Red Tiger or Bree start performing, can they call off the deal? What if Bree has already shipped the pizzas?

3. The Ramrods contract with Howard to perform the last concert of their current tour in Indianapolis. The night before the concert, the Ramrods are killed in a plane crash. How do their deaths affect the contract?

4. Remington and Brandt agree to go into the house painting business together as Rem, Brandt & Company. They agree that the business will begun when they raise $10,000 in capital to buy supplies. What happens if they can't raise the money?

5. Clark Stores contracts to buy from Bud Farms sixty crates of fresh peaches. Bud never delivers the peaches. Clark suffers a loss. Is there any limit to the time within which Clark can file a suit against Bud for breach of contract?

SPECIAL INFORMATION FOR CPA CANDIDATES

In the past, the CPA examination has tested heavily on discharge, agreements to discharge, and discharge by operation of law. For this reason, it would be good to review those topics. In particular, releases and novations are covered in connection with assignments (discussed in the previous chapter), and accord and satisfaction is tested. Discharge by operation of law should not be confused with termination of an offer by operation of law. For example, the death of an offeror will terminate an offer, but the death of a party to a contract will not necessarily discharge the contract. Other important points to remember, among those covered in this chapter, include what will discharge a party by frustration of purpose. Only something that was not expected will qualify (unusual weather, for example). A statute of limitations begins to run from the time of a breach, or when the breach should have been discovered.

Chapter 18
Breach of Contract and Remedies

WHAT THIS CHAPTER IS ABOUT

Breach of contract is the failure to perform what a party is under a duty to perform. When this happens, the nonbreaching party can choose one or more remedies. Unless damages would be inadequate, that is usually what a court will award.

CHAPTER OUTLINE

I. DAMAGES

Damages compensate a nonbreaching party for the loss of a bargain and, under special circumstances, for additional losses. Generally, the party is placed in the position he or she would have occupied if the contract been performed.

A. TYPES OF DAMAGES

1. Compensatory Damages
Damages compensating a party for the *loss* of a bargain—the difference between the promised performance and the actual performance.

a. Incidental Damages
Expenses that are caused directly by a breach of contract (such as those incurred to obtain performance from another source). Incidental damages are added to compensatory damages.

b. Measurement of Compensatory Damages

1) **Contract for a Sale of Goods**
The usual measure is the difference between the contract price and the market price. If the buyer breaches and the seller has not yet made the goods, the measure is lost profits on the sale.

2) **Contract for a Sale of Land**

a) Majority Rule

If specific performance (see below) is unavailable, or if the buyer breaches, the measure of damages is the difference between the land's contract price and its market price.

b) Minority Rule

If the seller breaches and the breach is not deliberate, the buyer recovers any down payment, plus expenses.

3) Construction Contracts

a) Owner's Breach Before, During, or After Construction

Contractor can recover (1) before construction: only profits (contract price, less cost of materials and labor); (2) during construction: profits, plus cost of partial construction; (3) after construction: the contract price, plus interest.

b) Contractor's Breach

Owner can recover for (1) stopping mid-project: cost of completion; (2) late completion: costs related to loss of use; (3) substantial performance: cost of completion, if there would be no substantial economic waste (if cost to complete does not exceed value that the extra work contributes.)

2. Consequential Damages

Damages giving an injured party the entire *benefit* of the bargain—foreseeable losses caused by special circumstances beyond the contract. The breaching party must know (or have reason to know) that special circumstances will cause the additional loss.

3. Punitive Damages

Damages punishing a guilty party and making an example to deter similar, future conduct. Awarded for a tort, but not for a contract breach.

4. Nominal Damages

Damages (such as $1) establishing, when no actual loss resulted, that a defendant acted wrongfully.

B. MITIGATION OF DAMAGES

An injured party has a duty to mitigate damages. For example, persons whose jobs have been wrongfully terminated have a duty to seek other jobs. The damages they receive are their salaries, less the income they received (or would have received) in similar jobs.

C. LIQUIDATED DAMAGES VERSUS PENALTIES

1. Liquidated Damages Provision

Specifies a certain amount to be paid in the event of a breach to the nonbreaching party for the loss. Such provisions are enforceable.

2. Penalty Provision

Specifies a certain amount to be paid in the event of a breach *to penalize the breaching party*. Such provisions are *not* enforceable.

3. How to Determine If a Provision Will Be Enforced

Ask: (1) When contract was made, was it clear damages would be difficult to estimate? (2) Was amount set as damages a reasonable estimate? If either answer is "no," provision will not be enforced.

II. RESCISSION AND RESTITUTION

A. RESCISSION
Rescission is an action to undo, or cancel, a contract—to return nonbreaching parties to the positions they occupied prior to the transaction. Rescission is available if fraud, mistake, duress, or failure of consideration is present. The rescinding party must give prompt notice to the breaching party.

B. RESTITUTION
To rescind a contract, the parties must make **restitution** by returning to each other goods, property, or money previously conveyed.

III. SPECIFIC PERFORMANCE
This remedy calls for the performance of the act promised in the contract.

A. WHEN SPECIFIC PERFORMANCE IS AVAILABLE
Damages must be an inadequate remedy. If goods are unique, a court will decree specific performance. Specific performance is granted to a buyer in a contract for the sale of land (every parcel of land is unique).

B. WHEN SPECIFIC PERFORMANCE IS NOT AVAILABLE
Contracts for sale of goods (other than unique goods) rarely qualify, because substantially identical goods can be bought or sold elsewhere. Courts normally refuse to grant specific performance of personal service contracts.

IV. REFORMATION
Used when the parties have imperfectly expressed their agreement in writing. Allows the contract to be rewritten to reflect the parties' true intentions.

A. WHEN REFORMATION IS AVAILABLE
(1) In cases of fraud or mutual mistake; (2) to prove the correct terms of an oral contract; (3) if a covenant not to compete is for a valid purpose (such as the sale of a business), but the area or time constraints are unreasonable, some courts will reform the restraints to make them reasonable.

B. WHEN REFORMATION IS NOT AVAILABLE
If the area or time constraints in a covenant not to compete are unreasonable, some courts will throw out the entire covenant.

V. RECOVERY BASED ON QUASI CONTRACT
When there is no enforceable contract, quasi contract prevents unjust enrichment. The law implies a promise to pay the reasonable value for benefits received.

A. WHEN QUASI-CONTRACTUAL RECOVERY IS USEFUL
A party has partially performed under a contract that is unenforceable. The party may recover the reasonable value (fair market value).

B. ELEMENTS TO RECOVER IN QUASI CONTRACT
The party seeking recovery must show (1) he or she conferred a benefit on the other party, (2) he or she had the reasonable expectation of being paid, (3) he or she did not act as a volunteer in conferring the benefit, and (4) the other party would be unjustly enriched by retaining it without paying.

VI. ELECTION OF REMEDIES
A nonbreaching party must choose which remedy to pursue. The purpose of the doctrine is to prevent double recovery. The doctrine has been eliminated in contracts for sales of goods—UCC remedies are cumulative [UCC 2–703, 2–711].

VII. WAIVER OF BREACH
Occurs when a nonbreaching party accepts defective performance.

A. EFFECT OF A WAIVER
A waiver keeps a contract going.

1. Past Breaches
A party waiving a breach cannot take later action based on the breach. In effect, the waiver erases the past breach.

2. Future Breaches
Normally, a waiver of one breach does not waive future breaches. It extends to future breaches, however, if a reasonable person would conclude that similar defective performance would be acceptable in the future.

B. LIABILITY FOR DAMAGES
A nonbreaching party can recover damages for defective performance.

VIII. CONTRACT PROVISIONS LIMITING REMEDIES

A. EXCULPATORY CLAUSES
A provision excluding liability for fraudulent or intentional injury or for illegal acts will not be enforced. An exculpatory clause for negligence contained in a contract made between parties who have roughly equal bargaining positions usually will be enforced.

B. LIMITATION-OF-LIABILITY CLAUSES
Provide that the only remedy for breach is replacement, repair, or refund of the purchase price (or some other limit). Such clauses may be enforced.

C. CONTRACTS FOR SALES OF GOODS
Remedies can be limited (see Chapter 22).

TRUE-FALSE QUESTIONS
(Answers at the Back of the Book)

_____   1. Normal damages compensate a nonbreaching party for the loss of the contract or give a nonbreaching party the benefit of the contract.

_____   2. Punitive damages are usually not awarded for a breach of contract.

_____   3. Nominal damages are awarded when it cannot be proved that a party actually breached a contract.

_____   4. Liquidated damages are uncertain in amount.

_____   5. Reformation allows a contract to be rewritten to reflect the contracting parties' true intention.

_____   6. Limitation-of-liability clauses are never enforced.

_____   7. A covenant not to compete that is for a valid purpose and has reasonable area and time constraints will usually be enforced by the courts.

_____   8. Quasi contract provides relief only when there is an enforceable contract.

____   9.   Consequential damages are awarded for foreseeable losses caused by special circumstances beyond the contract.

____   10.   Specific performance is available only when damages are also an adequate remedy.

FILL-IN QUESTIONS

(Answers at the Back of the Book)

The usual measure of compensatory damages under a contract for a sale of goods is the difference between _____ (the contract price and the market price/the market price and lost profits on the sale). The usual remedy for a seller's breach of a contract for a sale of real estate is _____ (specific performance/rescission and restitution). If this remedy is unavailable or if the buyer breaches, in most states the measure of damages is the difference between _____ (the contract price and the market price/the market price and lost profits on the sale).

MULTIPLE-CHOICE QUESTIONS

(Answers at the Back of the Book)

____   1.   Larry contracts to send his daughter Ann to Quality School for $10,000 tuition. After the school year begins, he withdraws Ann from Quality, refuses to pay, and enrolls Ann in ABC School for $5,000. Quality, which cannot find another student to replace Ann, has a right to damages equal to

    a. $15,000.
    b. $10,000.
    c. $5,000.
    d. $0.

____   2.   Sam contracts to sell several rendering tanks to Bob for $10,000, payable in advance. Bob pays the money, which Sam deposits in the First National Bank. The bank goes out of business. Sam refuses to perform. Bob can

    a.   rescind the contract.
    b.   get restitution of the $10,000 but may not rescind the contract.
    c.   rescind the contract and get restitution of the $10,000.
    d.   do nothing.

____   3.   BuildRite Construction contracts to build a store for Boutique Stores for $1 million. In mid-project, Boutique repudiates the contract, and BuildRite stops working. BuildRite, which incurred costs of $600,000 and would have made a profit of $100,000, has a right to damages equal to

    a. $1 million.
    b. $700,000.
    c. $100,000.
    d. $0.

____ 4. Mix Corporation contracts to sell to Frosty Malts, Inc., eight steel mixers. When Mix refuses to deliver, Frosty buys mixers from MaxCo, for 25 percent more than the contract price. Frosty is entitled to damages equal to

  a. what Mix's profits would have been.
  b. the price Frosty would have had to pay Mix.
  c. the difference between what Frosty would have had to pay Mix and what Frosty did pay MaxCo.
  d. what Frosty paid MaxCo.

____ 5. Dave contracts with Paul to buy six computers. Dave tells Paul that if the goods are not delivered on Monday, he will lose $12,000 in business. Paul does not deliver the goods on Monday. Dave is forced to rent computers on Tuesday. Paul delivers four computers on Friday. Dave is entitled to

  a. compensatory damages.
  b. consequential damages.
  c. incidental damages.
  d. all of the above.

____ 6. Jay agrees in writing to sell a warehouse and the land on which it is located to Nora. When Jay refuses to go through with the deal, Nora sues. Jay must transfer the land and warehouse to Nora if she is awarded

  a. quasi-contractual recovery.
  b. reformation.
  c. rescission and restitution.
  d. specific performance.

____ 7. Ken orally agrees to work for Jennifer for two years. He works for her for six months when, because she hasn't paid him, he quits and files a suit. He is entitled to the reasonable value of his services for the work if he obtains

  a. quasi-contractual recovery.
  b. reformation.
  c. rescission and restitution.
  d. specific performance.

____ 8. Joe signs a contract to work for NuCorp. The contract provides that if he quits, he cannot work in the same business anywhere in North America for ten years. Joe quits. NuCorp files a suit to enforce the clause. If the court decides that the clause is unreasonable, the clause may be subject to

  a. quasi-contractual recovery.
  b. reformation.
  c. rescission and restitution.
  d. specific performance.

____ 9. Brenda agrees to sell her house to Carl. Under the contract, he gives her a deposit, which she can keep if he breaches. Carl breaches. Brenda keeps the deposit and files a suit, asking the court for damages. If the court refuses to give Brenda damages, it may be because

  a. the election of remedies doctrine applies.
  b. the election of remedies doctrine does not apply.
  c. the appropriate remedy is quasi-contractual recovery.
  d. none of the above.

_____ 10. **Based on a Sample CPA Exam Question.** Eagle Manufacturing, Inc., contracted with Digital Repair Services to maintain Eagle's computers. A "Liquidated Damages Clause" provides that Digital will pay Eagle $500 for each day that Digital is late in responding to a service request. If Digital is three days late in responding, and Eagle sues to enforce this clause, Eagle will

    a. lose, because liquidated damages clauses violate public policy.
    b. lose, unless the liquidated damages clause is determined to be a penalty.
    c. win, because liquidated damages clauses are always enforceable.
    d. win, unless the liquidated damages clause is determined to be a penalty.

SHORT ESSAY QUESTIONS

1. What are damages designed to do in a breach of contract situation?

2. What must parties do to rescind a contract?

ISSUE SPOTTERS

(Answers at the Back of the Book)

1. George contracts to build a storage shed for Ron. Ron pays George in full, but George completes only half the work. Ron pays Paula $500 to finish the shed. If Ron sues George, what would be the measure of recovery?

2. Amy contracts to sell her ranch to Mark, who is to take possession on June 1. Amy delays the transfer until August 1. Mark incurs expenses in providing for cattle that he bought to stock the ranch. When they made the contract, Amy had no reason to know of the cattle. Is Amy liable for Mark's expenses in providing for the cattle?

3. Jack contracts to sell his art collection to Dean. The collection includes original works of art that cannot be obtained anywhere else at any price. When Jack refuses to go through with the deal, Dean sues. Can Dean be awarded the collection?

4. A doctor is passing the scene of a car accident when she notices that several people are unconscious and injured. She stops and renders assistance. Under what legal doctrine can the doctor recover for the medical services rendered?

5. MCT Engineering signs a contract to design a jet for the Clark Company. In the contract is a clause that excludes liability for errors in design and construction of the jet. An error in design causes the jet to crash, killing the pilot and the president of Clark. Is the clause that excluded liability enforceable?

SPECIAL INFORMATION FOR CPA CANDIDATES

One of the points in this chapter covered in the past on the CPA examination has been that if damages are appropriate, specific performance will not be granted. Specific performance is granted most typically in cases involving unique goods. Also remember that liquidated damages must be reasonable in light of what could have been expected when the contract was made.

CUMULATIVE HYPOTHETICAL PROBLEM FOR UNIT TWO—INCLUDING CHAPTERS 10–18

(Answers at the Back of the Book)

Doe & Roe is a small accounting firm that provides bookkeeping, payroll, and tax services for small businesses. Java, Inc., is a small manufacturing firm, making and selling commercial espresso machines.

_____ 1. Java sends e-mail to Doe & Roe, offering to contract for Doe & Roe's services for a certain price. The offer is sent on June 1 and is seen by Doe on June 2. The offer states that it will be open until July 1. This offer

a. cannot be revoked because it is a firm offer.
b. cannot be revoked because it is an option contract.
c. could have been revoked only before Doe saw it.
d. may be revoked any time before it is accepted.

_____ 2. Java and Doe & Roe discuss terms for a contract, but nothing is put in writing. If a dispute develops later, and one party files a suit against the other, alleging breach of contract, the court will determine whether or not there is a contract between the parties by looking at

a. the fairness of the circumstances.
b. the offeree's subjective intent.
c. the parties' objective intent.
d. the parties' subjective intent.

_____ 3. Java and Doe & Roe sign a written contract for Doe & Roe's services. The contract includes a large arithmetical error. Java later files a breach of contract suit against Doe & Roe, which asserts the mistake as a defense. Doe & Roe will win

a. if Java wrote the contract.
b. if the mistake was unilateral and Java knew it.
c. only if the mistake was due to Java's negligence.
d. only if the mistake was mutual.

_____ 4. Java and Doe & Roe sign a written contract for Doe & Roe's services. Java later files a breach of contract suit against Doe & Roe. Doe & Roe could avoid liability on the contract if

a. the contract has been assigned.
b. there is an unexecuted accord between the parties.
c. Java has been discharged by a novation.
d. none of the above.

_____ 5. Java and Doe & Roe sign a written contract for Doe & Roe's services. Java later files a suit against Doe & Roe. Doe & Roe is held to be in breach of contract. The court is most likely to grant relief to Java in the form of

a. damages.
b. specific performance.
c. damages and specific performance.
d. none of the above.

Chapter 19
The Formation of Sales and Lease Contracts

WHAT THIS CHAPTER IS ABOUT

This chapter introduces two parts of the Uniform Commercial Code: Article 2, which covers sales of goods, and Article 2A, which covers leases. The chapter also includes a section on contracts for an international sale of goods.

CHAPTER OUTLINE

I. THE UNIFORM COMMERCIAL CODE

The UCC provides rules to deal with all phases of a commercial sale: Articles 2 and 2A cover contracts for sales or leases of goods; Articles 3, 4, and 4A cover payments by checks, notes, and other means; Article 7 covers warehouse documents; and Article 9 covers transactions that involve collateral.

II. THE SCOPE OF ARTICLE 2—SALES

Article 2 governs contracts for sales of goods.

A. WHAT IS A SALE?

A **sale** is "the passing of title from the seller to the buyer for a price" [UCC 2–106(1)]. The price may be payable in money, goods, services, or land.

B. WHAT ARE GOODS?

Goods are tangible and movable. Legal disputes concern the following—

1. Goods Associated with Real Estate

Goods include minerals or the like and structures, if severance from the land is by the seller (but not if the buyer is to do it); growing crops or timber to be cut; and other "things attached" to realty but capable of severance without material harm to the land [UCC 2–107].

2. Goods and Services Combined

a. General Rule
Services are not included in the UCC. If a transaction involves both goods and services, a court determines which aspect is dominant.

b. Special Cases
Serving food or drink is a sale of goods [UCC 2–314(1)]. Other goods include unborn animals and rare coins.

C. WHO IS A MERCHANT?
UCC 2–104: Special rules apply to those who (1) deal in goods of the kind involved; (2) by occupation, hold themselves out as having knowledge and skill peculiar to the practices or goods involved in the transaction; (3) employ a merchant as a broker, agent, or other intermediary.

III. THE SCOPE OF ARTICLE 2A—LEASES
Article 2A governs contracts for leases of goods.

A. DEFINITION OF A LEASE
A **lease agreement** is the bargain of the lessor and lessee, in their words and deeds, including course of dealing, usage of trade, and course of performance [UCC 2A–103(k)].

B. CONSUMER LEASES
Special provisions apply to leases involving (1) a lessor who regularly leases or sells, (2) a lessee who leases for a personal, family, or household purpose, and (3) total payments of less than $25,000 [UCC 2A–103(1)(e)].

C. FINANCE LEASES
A finance lease involves a lessor (financier) who buys or leases goods from a supplier and leases or subleases them to a lessee [UCC 2A–103(g)]. The lessee must perform, whatever the financier does [UCC 2A–407].

IV. THE FORMATION OF SALES AND LEASE CONTRACTS
The following summarizes how the UCC *changes* the common law of contracts.

A. OFFER
An agreement sufficient to constitute a contract can exist even if verbal exchanges, correspondence, and conduct do not reveal exactly when it became binding [UCC 2–204(2), 2A–204(2)].

1. Open Terms
A sales or lease contract will not fail for indefiniteness even if one or more terms are left open, as long as (1) the parties intended to make a contract and (2) there is a reasonably certain basis for the court to grant an appropriate remedy [UCC 2–204(3), 2A–204(3)].

a. Open Price Term

1) If the parties have not agreed on a price, a court will determine "a reasonable price at the time for delivery" [UCC 2–305(1)].

2) If either the buyer or the seller is to determine the price, the price is to be fixed in good faith [UCC 2–305(2)].

3) If a price is not fixed through the fault of one party, the other can cancel the contract or fix a reasonable price [UCC 2–305(3)].

b. **Open Payment Term**
When parties do not specify payment terms—

1) Payment is due at the time and place at which the buyer is to receive the goods [UCC 2–310(a)].

2) The buyer can tender payment in cash or a commercially acceptable substitute (a check or credit card) [UCC 2–511(2)].

c. **Open Delivery Term**
When no delivery terms are specified—

1) The buyer normally takes delivery at the seller's place of business [UCC 2–308(a)]. If the seller has no place of business, the seller's residence is used. When goods are located in some other place and both parties know it, delivery is made there.

2) If the time for shipment or delivery is not clearly specified, a court will infer a "reasonable" time [UCC 2–309(1)].

d. **Duration of an Ongoing Contract**
A party who wishes to terminate an indefinite but ongoing contract must give reasonable notice to the other party [UCC 2–309(2), (3)].

e. **Options and Cooperation Regarding Performance**

1) When no specific shipping arrangements have been made but the contract contemplates shipment of the goods, the seller has the right to make arrangements [UCC 2–311].

2) When terms relating to an assortment of goods are omitted, the buyer can specify the assortment [UCC 2–311].

f. **Open Quantity Term**
If parties do not specify a quantity, there is no basis for a remedy. Exceptions include [UCC 2–306]—

1) **Requirements Contract**
The buyer agrees to buy and the seller agrees to sell all or up to a stated amount of what the buyer needs or requires. There is consideration: the buyer gives up the right to buy from others.

2) **Output Contract**
The seller agrees to sell and the buyer agrees to buy all or up to a stated amount of what the seller produces. Because the seller forfeits the right to sell goods to others, there is consideration.

3) **The UCC Imposes a Good Faith Limitation**
The quantity under these contracts is the amount of requirements or output that occurs during a normal production year.

2. **Merchant's Firm Offer**
If a merchant gives assurances in a signed writing that an offer will remain open, the offer is irrevocable, without consideration, for the stated period, or if no definite period is specified, for a reasonable period (neither to exceed three months) [UCC 2–205, 2A–205].

    a. The offer must be written and signed by the offeror. When a firm offer is contained in a form contract prepared by the offeree, a separate firm offer assurance must be signed as well.

    b. The other party need not be a merchant.

B. ACCEPTANCE

1. Methods of Acceptance
When an offeror does not specify a means of acceptance, acceptance can be by any reasonable means [UCC 2–206(1), 2A–206(1)].

2. Promise to Ship or Prompt Shipment

    a. Promise or Shipment of Conforming Goods
    An offer to buy goods for current or prompt shipment can be accepted by a promise to ship or by a prompt shipment [UCC 2–206(1)(b)].

    b. Shipment of Nonconforming Goods
    Prompt shipment of nonconforming goods is both an acceptance and a breach, unless the seller (1) seasonably notifies the buyer that it is offered only as an accommodation and (2) indicates clearly that it is not an acceptance.

3. Communication of Acceptance
To accept a unilateral offer, the offeree must notify the offeror of performance if the offeror would not otherwise know [UCC 2–206(2)].

4. Additional Terms
If the offeree's response indicates a definite acceptance of the offer, a contract is formed, even if the acceptance includes terms in addition to, or different from, the original offer [UCC 2–207(1)].

    a. Subject to the Offeror's Assent
    If the offeree's additional terms are conditioned on the offeror's assent, the offeree's response is not an acceptance.

    b. Not Subject to the Offeror's Assent—Battle of the Forms
    Does the contract include the additional terms?

        1) When One or Both Parties Are Nonmerchants
        Additional terms are considered proposals and not part of the contract. The contract is on the offeror's terms [UCC 2–207(2)].

        2) When Both Parties Are Merchants
        Additional terms are part of the contract unless (1) the offer expressly states no other terms; (2) they materially alter the original contract; or (3) the offeror objects to the modified terms in a timely fashion [UCC 2–207(2)].

        3) When the Parties Act As If They Have a Contract
        Regardless of what parties write down, they have a contract according to their conduct [UCC 2–207(3)]. If they do not act in accord with added terms, the terms are not part of a contract.

C. CONSIDERATION
An agreement modifying a sales or lease contract needs no consideration to be binding [UCC 2–209(1), 2A–208(1)].

1. **Modification Must Be Sought in Good Faith [UCC 1–203]**

2. **When Modification without Consideration Requires a Writing**

    a. Contract prohibits changes except by a signed writing.

    b. If a consumer (nonmerchant) is dealing with a merchant, and the merchant's form prohibits oral modification, the consumer must sign a separate acknowledgment [UCC 2–209(2), 2A–208(2)].

    c. Any modification that brings a *sales* contract under the Statute of Frauds must be in writing to be enforceable [UCC 2–209(3)].

D. THE STATUTE OF FRAUDS
To be enforceable, a sales contract must be in writing if the goods are $500 or more and a lease if the payments are $1,000 or more [UCC 2–201, 2A–201].

1. **Sufficiency of the Writing**
    A writing is sufficient if it indicates the parties intended to form a contract and is signed by the party against whom enforcement is sought. A sales contract is not enforceable beyond the quantity stated. A lease must identify and describe the goods and the lease term.

2. **Written Confirmation between Merchants**
    The requirement of a writing is satisfied if one merchant sends a signed written confirmation to the other.

    a. **Contents of the Confirmation**
        The confirmation must indicate the terms of the agreement, and the merchant receiving it must have reason to know of its contents.

    b. **Objection Within Ten Days**
        Unless the merchant who receives the confirmation objects in writing within ten days, the confirmation is enforceable [UCC 2–201(2)].

3. **Exceptions**
    An oral contract for a sale or lease that should otherwise be in writing will be enforceable in cases of [UCC 2–201(3), 2A–201(4)]—

    a. **Specially Manufactured Goods**
        The seller (or lessor) makes a substantial start on the manufacture of the goods, or makes commitments for it, and the goods are unsuitable for resale to others in the ordinary course of the business.

    b. **Admissions**
        The party against whom enforcement of a contract is sought admits in pleadings or court proceedings that a contract was made.

    c. **Partial Performance**
        Some payment has been made and accepted or some goods have been received and accepted (enforceable to that extent).

E. PAROL EVIDENCE

1. **The Rule**
    If the parties to a contract set forth its terms in a writing intended as their final expression, the terms cannot be contradicted by evidence of any prior agreements or contemporaneous oral agreements.

2. Exceptions [UCC 2–202, 2A–202]

A court may accept evidence of the following—

a. Consistent Additional Terms

Such terms clarify or remove ambiguities in a writing.

b. Course of Dealing and Usage of Trade

The meaning of an agreement is interpreted in light of commercial practices and other surrounding circumstances [UCC 1–205].

c. Course of Performance

Conduct that occurs under the agreement indicates what the parties meant by the words in their contract [UCC 2–208(1), 2A–207(1)].

3. Rules of Construction

Express terms, course of performance, course of dealing, and usage of trade are to be construed together when they do not contradict one another. If that is unreasonable, the priority is: (1) express terms, (2) course of performance, (3) course of dealing, and (4) usage of trade [UCC 1–205(4), 2–208(2), 2A–207(2)].

F. UNCONSCIONABILITY

An unconscionable contract is so one-sided and unfair (when it is made) that enforcing it is unreasonable. A court can (1) refuse to enforce the contract, (2) enforce it without the unconscionable clause, or (3) limit the clause to avoid an unconscionable result [UCC 2–302, 2A–108].

V. CONTRACTS FOR THE INTERNATIONAL SALE OF GOODS

Contracts for the international sale of goods are governed by the 1980 United Nations Convention on Contracts for the International Sale of Goods (CISG).

A. APPLICABILITY OF THE CISG

The CISG is to international sales contracts what UCC Article 2 is to domestic sales contracts (except the CISG does not apply to consumer sales). The CISG applies when the parties to an international sales contract do not specify in writing the precise terms of their contract.

B. COMPARISON OF CISG AND UCC PROVISIONS

1. Mirror Image Rule

The terms of the acceptance must mirror those of the offer [Art. 19].

2. Irrevocable Offers

An offer is irrevocable if the offeror states that it is or if the offeree reasonably relies on it as being irrevocable. The offer is irrevocable even without a writing and consideration [Art. 16(2)].

3. The Statute of Frauds

Article 11 does not include the requirements of the Statute of Frauds. (This accords with the law of most nations, in which contracts no longer need to meet formal requirements to be enforceable.)

4. Price Term

Must be specified or be determinable from the contract.

5. Time of Contract Formation

When an acceptance is sent, an offer becomes irrevocable, but the acceptance is not effective until it is received. Acceptance by performance does not require notice to the offeror.

C. SPECIAL PROVISIONS IN INTERNATIONAL CONTRACTS

1. **Choice of Language**
   Designates official language for interpreting contract in the event of disagreement. May indicate language for translations and arbitration.

2. **Choice of Forum**
   Designates forum, including specific court, for litigating a dispute. Clause is invalid if it denies one party an effective remedy, is the product of fraud or unconscionable conduct, causes substantial inconvenience to one party, or violates public policy.

3. **Choice of Law**
   Designates the applicable law. Under international law, there is no limit on parties' choice of law. If a choice is not specified, the governing law is that of the country of the seller's place of business.

4. *Force Majeure* ("Impossible or Irresistible Force")
   Stipulates that acts of God and other eventualities (government orders, regulations, embargoes, shortages of materials) may excuse a party from liability for nonperformance.

TRUE-FALSE QUESTIONS

(Answers at the Back of the Book)

____ 1. If the subject of a sale is goods, Article 2 of the UCC applies.

____ 2. A contract for a sale of goods is subject to the same traditional principles that apply to all contracts.

____ 3. If the subject of a transaction is a service, Article 2 of the UCC applies.

____ 4. The UCC requires that an agreement modifying a contract must be supported by new consideration to be binding.

____ 5. Under the UCC's Statute of Frauds, a writing must include all material terms except quantity.

____ 6. An unconscionable contract is a contract so one-sided and unfair, at the time it is made, that enforcing it would be unreasonable.

____ 7. Under the CISG, if the parties to a contract have not agreed on a price, a court will supply one.

____ 8. Under the CISG, a writing for a contract for a sale of goods is not required.

____ 9. A lease agreement is a bargain between a lessor and a lessee, as shown by their words and conduct.

____ 10. A consumer lease involves a lessee who leases for a personal, family, or household purpose.

FILL-IN QUESTIONS

(Answers at the Back of the Book)

_____ (Course of dealing/Usage of trade) is a sequence of conduct between the parties that occurred before their agreement

and establishes a common basis for their understanding. _____
_____ (Course of dealing/Usage of trade) is any practice or method of dealing
having regularity of observance in a place, vocation, or _____ (deal/trade)
so as to justify an expectation that it will be observed with respect to the transaction in
question. The express terms of an agreement, the course of dealing, and the usage of
trade will be construed to be _____(consistent/ inconsistent) with each
other whenever reasonable. When that is not possible, the _____
_____ (course of dealing/usage of trade/terms in the agreement) prevail.

MULTIPLE-CHOICE QUESTIONS

(Answers at the Back of the Book)

____   1. Digital Computer Corporation and Electronic Data Systems, Inc., enter into
            a contract for a sale of goods. Under UCC Article 2, the price of a sale may
            be payable in

   a. money only.
   b. goods only.
   c. money or goods only.
   d. money, goods, services, or real estate.

____   2. Morro Beverage Company has a surplus of carbon dioxide (which is what
            puts the bubbles in Morro beverages). Morro agrees to sell the surplus to
            Rock Ale Company. Morro is a merchant with respect to

   a. carbon dioxide but not Morro beverages.
   b. Morro beverages but not carbon dioxide.
   c. both Morro beverages and carbon dioxide.
   d. neither Morro beverages nor carbon dioxide.

____   3. Marina Shipyard agrees to build a barge for MaxCo Shipping. The contract
            includes an option for up to five more barges, but states that the prices of
            the other barges could be higher. Marina and MaxCo have

   a. a binding contract for at least one barge and up to six barges.
   b. a binding contract for one barge only.
   c. no contract, because the terms of the option are too indefinite.
   d. no contract, because both parties are merchants with respect to barges.

____   4. Gary leases a construction crane from Able Machinery and subleases it to
            Baker Contractors. This arrangement is

   a. a consumer lease.
   b. a finance lease.
   c. a sale of goods, not a lease.
   d. none of the above.

____   5. Mike and Rita orally agree to a sale of 100 pair of hiking boots at $50 each.
            Rita gives Mike a check for $500 as a down payment. Mike takes the check.
            At this point, the contract is enforceable

   a. to the full extent because it is for specially made goods.
   b. to the full extent because it is oral.
   c. to the extent of $500.
   d. none of the above.

_____ 6. Med Labs sends Kraft Instruments a purchase order for scalpels. The order states that Med will not be bound by any additional terms. Kraft ships the scalpels with an acknowledgment that includes an additional, materially different term. Med is

a. not bound by the term, because the offer expressly states that no other terms will be accepted.
b. not bound by the term, because the additional term constitutes a material alteration.
c. both a and b.
d. bound by the term.

_____ 7. Best Products, Inc., and Nationwide Transport Company are involved in a suit over a contract for a sale of goods. Under the parol evidence rule, evidence of contradictory prior agreements or contemporaneous oral agreements is inadmissible at trial EXCEPT

a. consistent terms can clarify or remove an ambiguity in the writing.
b. commercial practices can be used to interpret the contract.
c. both a and b.
d. none of the above.

_____ 8. **Based on a Sample CPA Exam Question.** Eagle Products, Inc., assures General Retail Corporation that its offer to sell its products at a certain price will remain open. This is a firm offer only if

a. General (the offeree) gives consideration for the offer.
b. General (the offeree) is a merchant.
c. the offer is made by Eagle (a merchant) in a signed writing.
d. the offer states the time period during which it will remain open.

_____ 9. Digital Computers agrees to buy and SmartCorp agrees to sell all of the microchips that Digital needs this year. The quantity of microchips that Digital must buy under this contract is the amount that

a. Digital would buy during a normal year.
b. SmartCorp would sell during a normal year.
c. SmartCorp would make this year.
d. none of the above.

_____ 10. Diana, in Great Britain, and Maria, in Mexico, orally agree to a sale of one hundred VCRs at $125 each. Both Britain and Mexico have adopted the CISG. The contract is

a. enforceable because the CISG does not require that a contract be in writing.
b. unenforceable because the CISG requires that a contract be in writing..
c. enforceable because the UCC does not require that a contract be in writing..
d. unenforceable because the UCC requires that a contract be in writing..

STARBUCKS COFFEE COMPANY
INTERNATIONAL SALES CONTRACT
APPLICATIONS

(Answers at the Back of the Book)

The following hypothetical situation and multiple-choice questions relate to your text's fold-out exhibit of the international sales contract used by Starbucks Coffee

Company. In that contract, Starbucks orders five hundred tons of coffee at $10 per pound from XYZ Co.

____   1. Starbucks and XYZ would have an enforceable contract even if they did *not* state in writing

    a. the amount of coffee ordered.
    b. the price of the coffee.
    c. both a and b.
    d. none of the above.

____   2. If Starbucks and XYZ did not include a "DESCRIPTION" of the coffee as "High grown Mexican Altura," then the delivered coffee must met

    a. Starbuck's subjective expectations of their quality.
    b. Starbuck's description of the goods in ads, on labels, and so on.
    c. XYZ's description of the goods in ads, on labels, and so on.
    d. XYZ's subjective belief in their quality.

____   3. Starbucks's incentive to pay on time, according to the terms of this contract, is the clause titled

    a. CLAIMS.
    b. GUARANTEE.
    c. PAYMENT.
    d. PRICE.

____   4. XYZ's incentive to deliver coffee that conforms to the contract is the clause titled

    a. CLAIMS.
    b. GUARANTEE.
    c. PAYMENT.
    d. PRICE.

____   5. Under this contract, until the coffee is delivered to its destination, the party who bears the risk of loss is

    a. Bonded Public Warehouse.
    b. Green Coffee Association
    c. Starbucks.
    d. XYZ.

SHORT ESSAY QUESTIONS

1. UCC Article 2 deals with sales of goods. What is a sale? What are goods?

2. In certain phases of sales transactions involving merchants, the UCC imposes special standards. For these purposes, who is a merchant?

ISSUE SPOTTERS

(Answers at the Back of the Book)

1. Chuck orally agrees to sell a tool shed to Ron for $450. Chuck removes the shed from his property and takes it to Ron's place. Ron does not pay, and Chuck sues. Ron

claims that the sale of the shed was an oral contract that is not enforceable under the Statute of Frauds. What will the court say?

2.   Lena, a car dealer, writes to Sam that "I have a 1992 Honda Civic that I will sell to you for $4,000. This offer will be kept open for one week." Six days later, Pam tells Sam that Lena sold the car that morning for $5,000. Did Lena breach any contract?

3.   Brad orders 150 computer desks. Fred ships 150 printer stands. Is this an acceptance of Brad's offer or a counteroffer? If it is an acceptance, is it a breach of the contract? What if Fred told Brad, "I'm sending printer stands as an accommodation"?

4.   Smith & Sons, Inc., sells truck supplies to J&B, which services trucks. Over the phone, J&B and Smith negotiate for the sale of eighty-four sets of tires. Smith sends a letter to J&B detailing the terms. Smith ships the tires two weeks later. J&B refuses to pay. Is there an enforceable contract between them?

5.   Under three contracts for the delivery of 23-inch steel, United Steel Company delivers, and City Construction accepts, 23-inch and 24-inch steel. Under a new contract for the delivery of 24-inch steel, City rejects United's tender of 23-inch steel. In light of their course of dealing under the other contracts, was City's rejection proper?

SPECIAL INFORMATION FOR CPA CANDIDATES

Concepts introduced in this chapter that are important to keep in mind for the CPA examination include the differences between common law and the UCC. The UCC rules that apply in transactions between merchants have also been on the exam in the past (questions covering firm offers, for instance), as have questions about which contracts must be in writing and what satisfies the writing requirement. Remember, too, that although the UCC applies to any sale of goods, regardless of the amount, an agreement for a sale of goods priced under $500 need not be in writing to be enforceable.

Chapter 20
Title, Risk, and Insurable Interest

WHAT THIS CHAPTER IS ABOUT

The UCC has special rules involving title, which may determine the rights and remedies of the parties to a sales contract. In most situations, however, issues concerning the rights and remedies of parties to sales or lease contracts are controlled by three other concepts: (1) identification, (2) risk of loss, and (3) insurable interest.

CHAPTER OUTLINE

I. **IDENTIFICATION**

For an interest in goods to pass from seller to buyer or lessor to lessee, the goods must (1) exist and (2) be identified as the goods subject to the contract. **Identification** is designation of the goods as the subject matter of the contract.

A. **SIGNIFICANCE OF IDENTIFICATION**

Identification gives the buyer (1) the right to obtain insurance and (2) the right to obtain the goods from the seller.

B. **WHEN IDENTIFICATION OCCURS**

According to the parties agreement [UCC 2–501, 2A–217]. If they do not specify a time and the goods are—

1. **Existing Goods**

Identification occurs when the contract is made.

2. **Future Goods**

If a sale involves unborn animals or crops to be harvested within twelve months of the contract (or, for crops, during the next harvest season, whichever is further in the future), identification occurs when the goods are conceived, planted, or begin to grow.

3. **Goods That Are Part of a Larger Mass**
Identification occurs when—

a. **Goods Are Marked, Shipped, or Otherwise Designated**

b. **Exception—Fungible Goods**
A buyer can acquire rights to goods that are alike by physical nature, agreement, or trade usage and that are held by owners in common by replacing the seller as owner [UCC 2–105(4)].

II.   WHEN TITLE PASSES

Parties can agree on when and under what conditions title will pass. If they do not specify a time, title passes on delivery [UCC 2–401(2)]. Delivery terms determine when this occurs.

A.   SHIPMENT CONTRACTS

If the seller is required or authorized to ship goods by carrier, title passes at time and place of shipment [UCC 2–401(2)(a)]. All contracts are shipment contracts unless they say otherwise.

B.   DESTINATION CONTRACTS

If the seller is required to deliver goods to a certain destination, title passes when the goods are tendered there [UCC 2–401(2)(b)].

C.   DELIVERY WITHOUT MOVEMENT OF THE GOODS

If a buyer is to pick up goods, passing title turns on whether a seller must give a document of title (bill of lading, warehouse receipt).

1. **When a Document of Title Is Required**
Title passes when and where the document is delivered. The goods do not need to move (for example, they can stay in a warehouse).

2. **When No Document of Title Is Required**
If the goods have been identified, title passes when and where the contract was made. If the goods have not been identified, title does not pass until identification [UCC 2–401(3)].

D.   SALES OR LEASES BY NONOWNERS

Generally, a buyer acquires whatever title the seller has to the goods sold [UCC 2–402, 2–403]. A lessee acquires whatever title a lessor could transfer, subject to the lease [UCC 2A–303, 2A–304, 2A–305].

1. **Void Title**
If the seller or lessor stole the goods, the buyer or lessee acquires nothing; the real owner can reclaim the goods.

2. **Voidable Title**
Seller has voidable title if goods obtained by fraud, paid for with check that is later dishonored, bought on credit from insolvent seller, or bought from a minor. Real owner can reclaim, except goods in possession of good faith purchaser for value [UCC 2–403(3)].

3. **Entrustment Rule**
Entrustment includes both delivering goods to a merchant and leaving goods with a merchant for later delivery or pickup [UCC 2–403(3)].

     a. Entrusting Goods to a Merchant Who Deals in Goods of the Kind
     The merchant can transfer all rights to a buyer or sublessee in the ordinary course of business [UCC 2–403(2), 2A–305(2)].

     b. What a Buyer or Sublessee in the Ordinary Course Gets
     Only those rights held by the person who entrusted the goods.

III. RISK OF LOSS

The question of who suffers a financial loss if goods are damaged, destroyed, or lost (who bears the *risk of loss*) is determined by the parties' contract. If the contract does not state who bears the risk, the UCC has rules to determine it.

A. DELIVERY WITH MOVEMENT OF THE GOODS—CARRIER CASES
When goods are to be delivered by truck or other paid transport—

     1. Shipment Contracts
     Risk passes to the buyer or lessee when the goods are delivered to a carrier [UCC 2–509(1)(a), 2A–219(2)(a)].

     2. Destination Contracts
     Risk passes to the buyer or lessee when the goods are tendered to the buyer at the destination [UCC 2–509(1)(b), 2A–219(2)(b)].

     3. Contract Terms

          a. F.O.B. (Free on board)—delivery is at seller's expense to a specific location. Risk passes at the location [UCC 2–319(1)].

          b. F.A.S. (Free alongside)—seller delivers goods next to the ship that will carry them, and risk passes to buyer [UCC 2–319(2)].

          c. C.I.F. or C.&F. (Cost, insurance, and freight)—seller puts goods in possession of a carrier before risk passes [UCC 2–320(2)].

          d. Delivery Ex-ship (From the carrying vessel)—risk passes to buyer when goods leave the ship or are unloaded [UCC 2–322].

B. DELIVERY WITHOUT MOVEMENT OF THE GOODS
When goods are to be picked up by the buyer or lessee—

     1. If the Seller or Lessor Is a Merchant
     Risk passes only on the buyer's or lessee's taking possession of the goods.

     2. If the Seller or Lessor Is Not a Merchant
     Risk passes on tender of delivery [UCC 2–509(3), 2A–219(c)].

     3. If a Bailee Holds the Goods
     Risk passes when (1) the buyer receives a negotiable document of title for the goods, (2) the bailee acknowledges the buyer's (or in the case of a lease, the lessee's) right to the goods, or (3) the buyer receives a nonnegotiable document of title, presents the document to the bailee, and demands the goods. If the bailee refuses to honor the document, the risk remains with the seller [UCC 2–503(4)(b), 2–509(2), 2A–219(2)(b)].

C. CONDITIONAL SALES

     1. Sale or Return (or Sale and Return)
     A seller delivers goods to a buyer who may retain any part and pay accordingly. The balance is returned or held by the buyer as a bailee.

a. Title and Risk Pass to the Buyer with Possession

Title and risk stay with the buyer until he or she returns the goods to the seller within the specified time. A sale is final if the buyer fails to return the goods in time. Goods in the buyer's possession are subject to the claims of the buyer's creditors.

b. Consignment

A consignment is a sale or return. Goods in the consignee's (buyer's) possession are subject to his or her creditors' claims [UCC 2–326(3)].

2. Sale on Approval

A seller offers to sell goods, and the buyer takes them on a trial basis. Title and risk remain with the seller until the buyer accepts the goods.

a. What Constitutes Acceptance

Any act inconsistent with the trial purpose or the seller's ownership; or by the buyer's choice not to return the goods on time.

b. Return

Return is at the seller's expense and risk [UCC 2–327(1)]. Goods are not subject to the claims of the buyer's creditors until acceptance.

D. RISK OF LOSS WHEN A SALES OR LEASE CONTRACT IS BREACHED

Generally, the party in breach bears the risk of loss.

1. When the Seller or Lessor Breaches

Risk passes to the buyer or lessee when the defects are cured or the buyer or lessee accepts the goods in spite of the defects. If, after acceptance, a buyer discovers a latent defect, acceptance can be revoked and the risk goes back to the seller [UCC 2–510(2), 2A–220(1)].

2. When the Buyer or Lessee Breaches

Risk shifts to the buyer or lessee (if the goods have been identified), where it stays for a commercially reasonable time after the seller or lessor learns of the breach. The buyer or lessee is liable to the extent of any deficiency in seller or lessor's insurance [UCC 2–510(3), 2A–220(2)].

IV. INSURABLE INTEREST

A party buying insurance must have a "sufficient interest" in the insured item. More than one party can have an interest at the same time.

A. INSURABLE INTEREST OF THE BUYER OR LESSEE

A buyer or lessee has an insurable interest in goods the moment they are identified, even before risk of loss passes [UCC 2–501(1), 2A–218(1)].

B. INSURABLE INTEREST OF THE SELLER OR LESSOR

A seller or lessor has an insurable interest in goods as long as he or she holds title or a security interest in the goods [UCC 2–501(2), 2A–218(3)].

V. BULK TRANSFERS

A *bulk transfer* is a transfer of more than half of a seller's inventory not made in the ordinary course of business [UCC 6–102(1)]. Subject to UCC Article 6, which, because of changes in the context in which bulk sales are made, has been repealed in most states.

TRUE-FALSE QUESTIONS

(Answers at the Back of the Book)

____   1. Identification occurs when a seller designates the goods to pass under a contract.

____   2. Unless the parties agree otherwise, title passes at the time and place that the buyer accepts the goods.

____   3. Unless a contract provides otherwise, it is normally assumed to be a shipment contract.

____   4. A sale on approval occurs when a coin dealer mails coins to a prospective buyer to examine for fourteen days to decide whether to buy or return them.

____   5. A buyer and a seller cannot both have an insurable interest in the same goods at the same time.

____   6. A bulk transfer is a transfer of a major part of the inventory not made in the ordinary course of the transferor's business.

____   7. In a sale on approval, the risk of loss passes to the buyer as soon as the buyer takes possession.

____   8. A buyer can acquire valid title to stolen goods if he or she does not know that the goods are stolen.

____   9. Under a destination contract, title passes at time and place of shipment.

____   10. If a seller is a merchant, the risk of loss passes when a buyer takes possession of the goods.

FILL-IN QUESTIONS

(Answers at the Back of the Book)

_____ (F.A.S./F.O.B.) means that delivery is at a seller's expense to a specific location—the place of shipment or a place of destination. When the term is _____ (F.A.S./F.O.B.) place of *shipment*, risk passes when the seller puts the goods into a carrier's possession. When the term is _____ (F.A.S./F.O.B.) place of *destination*, risk passes when the seller tenders delivery. _____ (F.A.S./ F.O.B.) requires a seller at his or her own expense and risk to deliver goods alongside the ship that will transport them at which point risk passes.

MULTIPLE-CHOICE QUESTIONS

(Answers at the Back of the Book)

____   1. Bob contracts to sell to the State University Bookstore 10,000 black felt-tipped pens. Bob identifies the pens by boxing the order, attaching labels with SU's address to the cartons, and leaving the boxes on the loading dock for shipping. Between Bob and SU,

a. the risk of loss has passed with respect to all of the pens.
b. the risk of loss has passed with respect to half of the pens.
c. the risk of loss has passed with respect to the pens with labels on the boxes.
d. none of the above.

____   2.   **Based on a Sample CPA Exam Question.** Best Products Corporation agrees to ship one hundred calculators to International Engineering, Inc. (IEI). Before the calculators arrive at IEI's offices, they are lost. The most important factor in determining who bears the risk of loss is

a. how the calculators were lost.
b. the contract's shipping terms.
c. the method by which the calculators were shipped.
d. title to the calculators.

____   3.   On Monday, Stan buys a mountain bike from Tom, his neighbor, who says, "Take the bike." Stan says, "I'll leave it in your garage until Friday." On Tuesday, Rosie steals the bike from Tom's garage. Who bore the risk?

a. Stan
b. Tom
c. Both a and b
d. None of the above.

____   4.   Pat's goods are in Andy's warehouse. Pat has a negotiable document of title for the goods. On Tuesday, she sells the goods to Nick and gives him the title document. On Friday, the warehouse collapses in an earthquake. The goods are destroyed. Who suffers the loss?

a. Pat
b. Andy
c. Nick
d. Both b and c

____   5.   Jay steals a car from Diamond Car Rental in Arizona. Jay leaves the car with Bull's Sales in North Carolina, for repairs. Bull's sells the car to Kim, who does not know that Bull's has no right to sell the car. Against whom does Kim have good title?

a. Jay
b. Diamond
c. Bull's
d. Both a and c

____   6.   Suzy buys a jeep from Sheridan Jeep Sales. Suzy says, "I'll pick up the jeep Monday." On Sunday, Sheridan sells the jeep to Pam, who does not know Sheridan has no right to sell it. Against whom does Pam have good title?

a. Suzy
b. Sheridan
c. Both a and b
d. None of the above

____   7.   On Monday, Craft Computers in Seattle delivers five hundred keyboards to Pac Transport to take to Portland under a destination contract with Comp Stores. The keyboards arrive in Portland on Tuesday, and Pac tells Comp they are at Pac's warehouse. On Thursday, the warehouse burns down. On Friday, Comp learns of the fire. The risk of loss passed to Comp on

a. Monday.
b. Tuesday.
c. Friday.
d. none of the above.

____ 8. Alpha Comm agrees to sell one hundred cellular phones to Beta Electronics. Alpha identifies the goods by marking the crates with red stripes. Title has not yet passed to Beta. Who has an insurable interest in the goods?

   a. Only Alpha
   b. Only Beta
   c. Both Alpha and Beta
   d. None of the above

____ 9. Under a contract with QT Corp., Gold Media ships sixty hard drives. When QT opens the crates, it discovers that the drives are the wrong model, but agrees to accept them anyway. The risk of loss passed to QT when

   a. Gold shipped the drives.
   b. QT opened the crates.
   c. QT discovered that the goods were the wrong model.
   d. QT accepted the drives.

____ 10. Apple Bike Makers agrees to sell forty mountain bikes to Orange Mountain Recreation, under a shipment contract. Apple delivers the goods to Sugar Trucking to take to Orange Mountain. Sugar delivers the goods. Title to the goods passed when

   a. Apple agreed to sell the goods.
   b. Apple delivered the goods to Sugar.
   c. Sugar delivered the goods to Orange Mountain.
   d. none of the above.

SHORT ESSAY QUESTIONS

1. What is "risk of loss" under the UCC?

2. When does risk pass (a) under a shipment contract? (b) under a destination contract? (c) when the buyer is to pick up the goods and the seller is a merchant? (d) when the buyer is to pick up the goods and the seller is not a merchant? (e) when a bailee holds the goods?

ISSUE SPOTTERS

(Answers at the Back of the Book)

1. Adams Textiles in Kansas City sells certain fabrics to Silk n' Satin Stores in Oklahoma City. Adams packs the fabric and ships it by rail to Silk. In transit across Kansas, a tornado derails the train and scatters and shreds the fabric across miles of cornfields. What are the consequences if Silk bore the risk? If Adams bore the risk?

2. Under a contract between a seller in New York and a buyer in Dallas, if delivery is "F.O.B. New York," the risk passes when the seller puts the goods in the carrier's hands. If delivery is "F.O.B. Dallas," the risk passes when the goods reach Dallas. What if the contract says only that the seller is "to ship goods at seller's expense"?

3. Butler Farms in Washington sells Astor Produce in Alaska a certain size of apples to be shipped "F.O.B. Seattle." The apples Butler delivers to the shipping company for transport are too small. The apples are lost in transit. Who suffers the loss?

4.   Paula boards her horse Blaze at Gold Spur Stables. She sells the horse to George and calls Gold Spur to say, "I sold Blaze to George." Gold Spur says, "Ok." That night, Blaze is kicked in the head by another horse and dies. Who pays for the loss?

5.   Chocolate, Inc., sells five hundred cases of cocoa mix to Dan's Food Company, which pays with a bad check. Chocolate does not discover that the check is bad until after Dan sells the cocoa to Chip's Food Stores, which suspects nothing. Can Chocolate recover the cocoa from Chip's?

SPECIAL INFORMATION FOR CPA CANDIDATES

The most important concept in this chapter to master for the CPA examination is passage of the risk of loss. In most of the problems on the CPA examination, the party who bears the loss has traditionally been the party who breached the contract. You should bear in mind, however, that who ultimately bears the risk of loss is not necessarily the same party who has title or an insurable interest, nor does it depend on whether the buyer has paid for the goods or on whether some action by a party outside the contract contributed to the loss of the goods.

Other concepts discussed in this chapter may occur on the CPA exam. The concept of title is often tested in a context involving stolen goods, voidable title, or entrustment. The passage of title and risk may be at issue in questions on sales on approval and sales or return. Questions are also sometimes asked about bulk sales.

Chapter 21
Performance of Sales and Lease Contracts

WHAT THIS CHAPTER IS ABOUT

This chapter examines the basic obligations of a seller and a buyer under a sales contract. A seller has the obligation to deliver conforming goods, and the buyer has the obligation to accept and pay for those goods [UCC 2–301]. When a contract is unclear or its terms are indefinite and disputes arise, courts look to the UCC.

CHAPTER OUTLINE

I. THE GOOD FAITH REQUIREMENT

The obligations of good faith and commercial reasonableness underlie every contract within the UCC [UCC 1–203]. There is a higher standard for merchants: Honesty in fact and the observance of reasonable commercial standards of fair dealing in the trade [UCC 2–103, 2A–516(1)].

II. OBLIGATIONS OF THE SELLER OR LESSOR

The seller or lessor must **tender** delivery (hold conforming goods at the disposal of the buyer or lessee and give whatever notice is reasonably necessary to enable the buyer or lessee to take delivery) [UCC 2–503(1), 2A–508(1)].

A. WHEN TENDER MUST OCCUR

At a reasonable hour, in a reasonable manner, and the goods must be kept available for a reasonable time [UCC 2–503(1)(a)]. Goods must be tendered in a single delivery unless parties agree otherwise [UCC 2–612, 2A–510] or, under the circumstances, a party can request delivery in lots [UCC 2–307].

B. PLACE OF DELIVERY

The parties may agree on a particular destination, or their contract or the circumstances may indicate a place.

1. Noncarrier Cases

a. Seller's Place of Business

If the contract does not designate a place of delivery, and the buyer is to pick up the goods, the place is the seller's place of business or if none, the seller's residence [UCC 2–308].

b.   Identified Goods That Are Not at the Seller's Place of Business
Wherever they are is the place of delivery [UCC 2–308].

2.   Carrier Cases

a.   Shipment Contract
The seller must [UCC 2–504]—

1)   Put the goods into the hands of a carrier.

2)   Make a contract for the transport of the goods that is reasonable according to their nature and value.

3)   Tender to the buyer any documents necessary to obtain possession of the goods from the carrier.

4)   Promptly notify the buyer that shipment has been made.

5)   If a seller fails to meet these requirements, and this causes a material loss or a delay, the buyer can reject the shipment.

b.   Destination Contract
The seller must give the buyer appropriate notice and any necessary documents of title [UCC 2–503].

C.   THE PERFECT TENDER RULE
A seller or lessor must deliver goods in conformity with every detail of the contract. If goods or tender fail in any respect, the buyer or lessee can accept the goods, reject them, or accept part and reject part [UCC 2–601, 2A–509].

D.   EXCEPTIONS TO THE PERFECT TENDER RULE

1.   Agreement of the Parties
Parties can agree in their contract that, for example, the seller can repair or replace any defective goods within a reasonable time.

2.   Cure

a.   Within the Contract Time for Performance
If nonconforming goods are rejected, the seller or lessor can notify the buyer or lessee of an intention to repair, adjust, or replace the goods and can then do so within the contract time for performance [UCC 2–508, 2A–513].

b.   After the Time for Performance Expires
The seller or lessor can cure if there were reasonable grounds to believe the nonconformance would be acceptable.

c.   Substantially Restricts the Buyer's Right to Reject
If the buyer or lessee refuses goods but does not disclose the nature of the defect, he or she cannot later assert the defect as a defense if it is one that could have been cured [UCC 2–605, 2A–514].

3.   Substitution of Carriers
If, through no fault of either party an agreed manner of delivery is not available, a substitute is sufficient [UCC 2–614(1)].

4.   Installment Contracts

    a. Substantial Nonconformity

       A buyer or lessee can reject an installment only if a nonconformity substantially impairs the value of the installment and cannot be cured [UCC 2–612(2), 2–307, 2A–510(1)].

    b. Breach of the Entire Contract

       A breach occurs if one or more nonconforming installments substantially impair the value of the whole contract. If the buyer or lessee accepts a nonconforming installment, the contract is reinstated [UCC 2–612(3), 2A–510(2)]

5. Commercial Impracticability

Delay or nondelivery is not a breach if performance is impracticable "by the occurrence of a contingency the nonoccurrence of which was a basic assumption on which the contract was made" [UCC 2–615(a)]. The seller must notify the buyer.

    a. Unforeseeability

       The unforeseen contingency (such as a sudden shortage of raw materials) must alter the essential nature of the performance.

    b. Partial Performance

       If a seller is able to fulfill a contract partially, the seller must allocate in a fair and reasonable manner deliveries among all contracted customers [UCC 2–615(b),(c)].

6. Destruction of Identified Goods

When goods are destroyed (through no fault of a party) before risk passes to the buyer, the parties are excused from performance [UCC 2–613(a)]. If goods are only partially destroyed, a buyer can treat a contract as void or accept damaged goods with a price allowance.

7. Assurance and Cooperation

    a. The Right of Assurance

       If a party has reasonable grounds to believe the other will not perform, he or she may "in writing demand adequate assurance."

       1) Suspension of Performance

          Until assurance is received, the party may "suspend" performance without liability.

       2) Between Merchants

          The grounds are determined by commercial standards [UCC 2–609, 2A–401]. If assurances are not provided within thirty days, this may be treated as a repudiation of the contract.

    b. The Duty of Cooperation

       When cooperation is not forthcoming, a party can suspend his or her performance and hold the uncooperative party in breach or perform in any reasonable manner [see UCC 2–311(3)(b)].

III. OBLIGATIONS OF THE BUYER OR LESSEE

The buyer or lessee must make payment at the time and place he or she receives the goods unless the parties have agreed otherwise [UCC 2–310(a), 2A–516(1)].

A. PAYMENT
Payment can be by any means agreed on between the parties [UCC 2–511].

B. RIGHT OF INSPECTION
The buyer or lessee can verify, before making payment, that the goods are what were contracted for. The buyer has no duty to pay if the goods are not what were ordered [UCC 2–513(1), 2A–515(1)].

1. Time, Place, and Manner
Inspection can be in any reasonable place, time and manner, determined by custom of the trade, practice of the parties, and so on [UCC 2–513(2)].

2. C.O.D. Shipments
If a buyer agrees to a C.O.D. shipment or to pay for goods on presentation of a bill of lading, no right of inspection exists [UCC 2–513(3)].

3. Payment Due—Documents of Title (C.I.F. and C.&F. Contracts)
Payment is required on receipt of documents of title, before inspection, and must be made unless the buyer knows the goods are nonconforming [UCC 2–310(b), 2–513(3)].

C. ACCEPTANCE
Acceptance is presumed if a buyer or lessee has a reasonable opportunity to inspect and fails to reject in a reasonable time [UCC 2–606, 2–602, 2A–515].

1. How a Buyer or Lessee Can Accept
A buyer or lessee can accept by words or conduct. Under a sales contract, a buyer can accept by any act (such as using or reselling the goods) inconsistent with the seller's ownership [UCC 2–606(1)(c)].

2. A Buyer or Lessee Can Accept Only Some of the Goods
But not less than a single commercial unit [UCC 2–601(c), 2A-509(1)].

IV.   ANTICIPATORY REPUDIATION
The nonbreaching party can (1) treat the repudiation as a final breach by pursuing a remedy or (2) wait, hoping that the repudiating party will decide to honor the contract [UCC 2–610, 2A–402]. If the party decides to wait, the breaching party can retract the repudiation [UCC 2–611, 2A–403].

V.   INTERNATIONAL CONTRACTS—LETTERS OF CREDIT

A. PRINCIPAL PARTIES
The issuer (a bank) agrees to issue a letter of credit and to ascertain whether the beneficiary (seller) performs certain acts. The account party (buyer) promises to reimburse the issuer for amounts paid to the beneficiary.

B. OTHER BANKS
There may be an advising bank that transmits information and a paying bank that expedites payment.

C. ISSUER'S OBLIGATION
The issuer is bound to pay the beneficiary when the beneficiary complies with the terms of the letter (by presenting the required documents—typically a bill of lading).

TRUE-FALSE QUESTIONS

(Answers at the Back of the Book)

____   1.   Performance of a sales contract is controlled by the agreement between the seller and the buyer.

____   2.   If a particular carrier is unavailable through no fault of either party, a commercially reasonable substitute may be used.

____   3.   If identified goods are destroyed through no fault of either party, and risk has not passed to the buyer, the parties are excused from performance.

____   4.   Payment is always due at the time of delivery.

____   5.   A buyer or lessee can always reject delivered goods on discovery of a defect, regardless of previous opportunities to inspect.

____   6.   Merchants are held to the same standard of good faith as nonmerchants.

____   7.   When one party's performance depends on the other's cooperation and it is not forthcoming, the first party can suspend performance.

____   8.   If a buyer has a reasonable opportunity to inspect goods and fails to reject them within a reasonable time, acceptance is presumed.

____   9.   A buyer's principal obligation is to tender delivery.

____   10.   In an installment contract, a buyer can reject any installment for any reason.

FILL-IN QUESTIONS

(Answers at the Back of the Book)

A seller's obligations include holding _____ (conforming/nonconforming) goods at a buyer's disposal _____ (and/or) giving notice reasonably necessary for the buyer to take delivery. The _____ (seller/buyer) must make payment at the time and place of _____ (delivery/receipt) of the goods _____ (even if/unless) the parties have agreed otherwise.

MULTIPLE-CHOICE QUESTIONS

(Answers at the Back of the Book)

____   1.   Silver Textiles, Inc., contracts to sell five hundred bolts of denim to Gold Clothing. Silver is to deliver the goods in Chicago. Gold is to specify the exact address before the delivery date. Gold fails to specify the address, causing Silver to fail to deliver on time. Which of the following is TRUE?

    a.   Gold can cancel the contract.
    b.   Silver is excused for the delay in delivery.
    c.   Gold is excused for failing to specify the address.
    d.   Silver is in breach of contract.

    2. Smith Company in San Diego agrees to ship 500,000 plastic silver dollars to the Zenith Casino in Las Vegas. The goods are in a warehouse in Barstow. The agreement says that Zenith will pick up the goods, but says nothing about the place. The place of delivery is

    a. San Diego.
    b. Las Vegas.
    c. Barstow.
    d. none of the above.

    3. Pep Paints agrees to sell to Monar Painters Grade A-1 latex outdoor paint to be delivered September 8. On September 7, Pep tenders Grade B-2 paint. Monar rejects the Grade B-2 paint. If, two days later, Pep tenders Grade C-3 paint with an offer of a price allowance, Pep will have

    a. one day to cure.
    b. a reasonable time to cure.
    c. additional, unlimited time to cure.
    d. none of the above.

    4. Roy's Game Town orders virtual reality helmets from VR, Inc. VR delivers, but Roy rejects the shipment without telling VR the reason. If VR had known the reason, it could have corrected the problem within hours. If Roy sues VR for damages, Roy will

    a. win, because VR's tender did not conform to the contract.
    b. win, because VR made no attempt to cure.
    c. lose, because Roy's rejection was unjustified—VR could have cured.
    d. lose, because a buyer cannot reject goods *and* sue for damages.

    5. Max Products agrees to sell sports equipment to Geo Sports. Before the time for performance, Max tells Geo that it will not deliver. Geo may

    a. treat this as a breach and pursue a remedy.
    b. wait to see whether Max will perform.
    c. either a or b.
    d. none of the above.

    6. Pete, a buyer in Hungary, and Fred, a seller in the United States, enter into a contract with a letter of credit. Fred delivers required documents to the issuing bank. The bank must

    a. pay Fred.
    b. pay Pete.
    c. do nothing until Pete certifies the documents.
    d. do nothing until Fred delivers the goods to Pete.

    7. **Based on a Sample CPA Exam Question.** Standard Office Products orders one hundred computers from National Suppliers. Unless the parties agree otherwise, National's obligation to Standard is to

    a. deliver the computers to a common carrier.
    b. deliver the computer's to Standard's place of business.
    c. hold conforming goods and give notice for Standard to take delivery.
    d. set aside conforming goods for Standard's inspection before delivery.

_____ 8. Bill delivers six satellite dishes to Tom, according to their contract. The contract says nothing about payment. Tom must pay for the goods

   a. within thirty days of the seller's request for payment.
   b. within ten days.
   c. within ten business days.
   d. on delivery.

_____ 9. Eagle Products ships ten computer monitors to Data Resources, Inc., as per Data's request. Data can accept the goods

   a. only be telling the seller, "We accept."
   b. only by unpacking the monitors and using them.
   c. either by notifying the seller or by using the goods.
   d. none of the above.

_____ 10. Neal contracts to sell five laser printers to Laura. Under either a shipment or a destination contract, Neal must give Laura

   a. the documents necessary to obtain the goods.
   b. appropriate notice regarding delivery.
   c. both a and b.
   d. none of the above.

SHORT ESSAY QUESTIONS

1. What is a seller's right to cure? How does it affect a buyer's right to reject?

2. What is a buyer's right to inspect? How does it affect a seller's right to payment?

ISSUE SPOTTERS

(Answers at the Back of the Book)

1. Mike agrees to sell 1,000 espresso makers to Jenny to be delivered on May 1. Due to a strike in the last week of April, there is a temporary shortage of delivery vehicles. Mike can deliver the espresso makers 200 at a time over a period of ten days, with the first delivery on May 1. Does Mike have the right to deliver the goods in five lots?

2. Country Fruit Stand orders eighty cases of peaches from Citrus Farms. For no good reason, Citrus delivers thirty cases instead of eighty, and the delivery is late. Does Country have the right to reject the shipment?

3. Parade Instruments agrees to sell to American Carnivals fifteen electronic calliopes, to be delivered in five installments. The first installment consists of two electronic calliopes and a manual one. Can American cancel the whole contract?

4. Pic Post-Stars agrees to sell Ace Novelty 5,000 posters of celebrities, to be delivered on April 1. On March 1, Pic tells Ace, "The deal's off." Ace says, "I expect you to deliver. I'll be waiting." Can Ace sue Pic without waiting until April 1?

5. Gina contracts to sell to Rick eighteen hot-dog carts to be delivered in three installments. After delivery of the first two installments, Gina hears a rumor that Rick is in financial trouble. Gina reasonably believes that the rumor may be true. Under these circumstances, what are Gina's rights?

SPECIAL INFORMATION FOR CPA CANDIDATES

A number of the concepts in this chapter often occur on the CPA examination, sometimes intertwined with the rules set out in other chapters covering Article 2 of the UCC. For example, a seller who does not tender delivery of conforming goods is in breach of the contract. Such a tender is also necessary for the risk of loss to pass.

It may be easiest to remember all of these rules by imagining a real sales contract situation and applying them to that situation. In particular, it can be helpful to sort out the rules in Article 2 that apply when one of the parties is a merchant and when both parties are merchants. The following topics (discussed in this chapter), as they relate to merchants, are often tested in the part of the CPA exam covering the UCC: risk of loss, the buyer's responsibility regarding rejected goods, the buyer's obligation to designate defects, sales on approval and sales or returns, and either party's right to assurance of performance.

Chapter 22
Remedies for Breach of Sales and Lease Contracts

WHAT THIS CHAPTER IS ABOUT

When a sales or lease contract is breached, the nonbreaching party has a number of remedies from which to choose. The general purpose is to put the party "in as good a position as if the other party had fully performed." This chapter sets out the remedies and the situations in which each is appropriate.

CHAPTER OUTLINE

I. **REMEDIES OF THE SELLER OR LESSOR**

A. **WHEN THE GOODS ARE IN POSSESSION OF THE SELLER OR LESSOR**

1. **The Right to Cancel the Contract**
    A seller or lessor can cancel a contract (with notice to the buyer or lessee) if the other party breaches it [UCC 2–703(f), 2A–523(1)(a)].

2. **The Right to Withhold Delivery**
    A seller or lessor can withhold delivery if a buyer or lessee wrongfully rejects or revokes acceptance, fails to pay, or repudiates [UCC 2–703(a), 2A–523(1)(c)]. If a buyer or lessee is insolvent, a seller or lessor can refuse to deliver unless a buyer pays cash [UCC 2–702(1), 2A–525(1)].

3. **The Right to Resell or Dispose of the Goods**

    a. **When a Seller or Lessor Can Resell or Lease to Another Party**
        A seller or lessor still has the goods and the buyer or lessee wrongfully rejects or revokes acceptance, fails to pay, or repudiates the contract [UCC 2–703(d), 2–706(1), 2A–523(1)(e), 2A–527(1)].

    b. **Unfinished Goods**
        A seller or lessor can (1) resell the goods as scrap or (2) finish and resell them (buyer or lessee is liable for any difference in price). The goal is to obtain maximum value [UCC 2–704(2), 2A–524(2)].

  c. **How to Conduct a Resale**

   In good faith and a commercially reasonable manner; give the original buyer notice, unless goods are perishable or will rapidly decline in value [UCC 2–706(2), (3)].

  d. **What the Seller or Lessor Can Recover**

   Any deficiency between the resale (or new lease) price and the contract price, plus incidental damages [UCC 2–706, 2–710, 2A–527].

4. **The Right to Recover the Purchase Price or Lease Payments Due**

 A seller or lessor can bring an action for the price if he or she is unable to resell [UCC 2–709(1), 2A–529(1)]. The buyer gets the goods, unless the seller or lessor disposes of them before collection of the judgment (with the proceeds credited to the buyer).

5. **The Right to Recover Damages**

 If a buyer or lessee repudiates a contract or wrongfully refuses to accept, the seller or lessor can recover the difference between the contract price and the market price (at the time and place of tender), plus incidental damages. If the market price is less than the contract price, the seller or lessor gets lost profits [UCC 2–708, 2A–528].

B. **WHEN THE GOODS ARE IN TRANSIT**

A seller or lessor can stop delivery of goods if (1) buyer or lessee is insolvent or (2) buyer or lessee is solvent but in breach (if the quantity shipped is a carload, a truckload, or larger) [UCC 2–705, 2A–526]. This right is lost if—

1. Buyer or lessee has possession of the goods.
2. The carrier acknowledges rights of buyer or lessee.
3. A bailee other than a carrier acknowledges that he or she is holding the goods for buyer or lessee.
4. A document of title covering the goods is negotiated to the buyer.

C. **WHEN THE GOODS ARE IN POSSESSION OF THE BUYER OR LESSEE**

1. **The Right to Recover the Purchase Price or Lease Payments Due**

 A seller or lessor can bring an action for the price if the buyer or lessee accepts the goods but refuses to pay [UCC 2–709(1), 2A–529(1)].

2. **The Right to Reclaim the Goods**

  a. **Sales Contracts—Buyer's Insolvency**

   If an insolvent buyer gets goods on credit, the seller can (within ten days) reclaim them. A seller can reclaim any time if a buyer misrepresents solvency in writing within three months before delivery [UCC 2–702(2)].

  b. **Sales Contracts—A Buyer in the Ordinary Course of Business**

   A seller cannot reclaim goods from such a buyer.

  c. **Sales Contracts—Bars the Pursuit of Other Remedies**

   A seller who reclaims gets preferential treatment over a buyer's other creditors (but cannot pursue other remedies) [UCC 2–702(3)].

  d. **Lease Contracts**

   A lessor can reclaim goods from a lessee in default [UCC 2A–525(2)].

II. REMEDIES OF THE BUYER OR LESSEE

A. WHEN THE SELLER OR LESSOR REFUSES TO DELIVER THE GOODS

When a seller or lessor fails to deliver or repudiates the contract, the buyer or lessee has the following rights.

1. **The Right to Cancel the Contract**

   The buyer or lessee can rescind (cancel) the contract. On notice to the seller, the buyer or lessee is discharged [UCC 2–711(1), 2A–508(1)(a).

2. **The Right to Recover the Goods**

   A buyer or lessee who paid for goods in the hands of the seller or lessor can recover them if the seller or lessor becomes insolvent within ten days of receiving payment and the goods are identified to the contract. Buyer or lessee must tender any unpaid balance [UCC 2–502, 2A–522].

3. **The Right to Obtain Specific Performance**

   A buyer or lessee can obtain specific performance if goods are unique or damages would be inadequate [UCC 2–716(1), 2A–521(1)].

4. **The Right of Cover**

   Buyer or lessee can obtain cover (substitute goods) and then sue for damages. The measure of damages is the difference between the cost of cover and the contract price, plus incidental and consequential damages, less expenses saved by the breach [UCC 2–712, 2–715, 2A–518, 2A–520].

5. **The Right to Replevy the Goods**

   A buyer or lessee can use, against the seller or lessor, replevin (an action to recover goods from a party wrongfully withholding them) if the buyer or lessee is unable to cover [UCC 2–716(3), 2A–521(3)].

6. **The Right to Recover Damages**

   The measure of damages is the difference between the contract price and, when the buyer or lessee learned of the breach, the market price (at the place of delivery), plus incidental and consequential damages, less expenses saved by the breach [UCC 2–713, 2A–519].

B. WHEN THE SELLER OR LESSOR DELIVERS NONCONFORMING GOODS

1. **The Right to Reject the Goods**

   A buyer or lessee can reject the part of goods that fails to conform to the contract (and rescind the contract or obtain cover) [UCC 2–601, 2A–509].

   a. **Notice Required**

   Notice must be **seasonable** (timely), and a buyer or lessee must tell the seller or lessor what the defect is [UCC 2–602(1), 2–605, 2A–509(2), 2A–514].

   b. **Duties of a Merchant Buyer or Lessee**

   Follow the seller or lessor's instructions about the goods [UCC 2–603, 2A–511]. Without instructions, perishable goods can be resold; otherwise they must be stored or returned. A buyer or lessee is entitled to reimbursement for the cost.

   c. **The Right to Retain and Enforce a Security Interest**

   Buyers who rightfully reject or who justifiably revoke acceptance of goods in their possession have a security interest in the goods. A buyer can recover payments made for the goods and expenses to inspect, transport, and hold the goods, or can resell, withhold delivery, or stop delivery [UCC 2–711, 2–706].

2. **The Right to Revoke Acceptance**

    a. **Substantial Impairment**
        Any nonconformity must substantially impair the value of the goods *and* either not be seasonably cured or be difficult to discover [UCC 2–608, 2A–517].

    b. **Notice of a Breach Must Be within a Reasonable Time**
        Before the goods have undergone substantial change (not caused by their own defects, such as spoilage) [UCC 2–608(2), 2A–517(4)].

3. **The Right to Recover Damages for Accepted Goods**
    Notice of a breach must be within a reasonable time [UCC 2–607, 2A–516]. The measure of damages is the difference between value of goods as accepted and value if they had been as promised [UCC 2–714(2), 2A–519(4)].

III. CONTRACTUAL PROVISIONS AFFECTING REMEDIES
Parties can provide for remedies in addition to or in lieu of those in the UCC, or they can change the measure of damages [UCC 2–719, 2A–503]. If a buyer or lessee is a consumer, limiting consequential damages for personal injuries on a breach of warranty is *prima facie* unconscionable.

IV. LEMON LAWS
If an automobile under warranty has a defect that significantly affects the vehicle's value or use, and the seller does not fix it within a specified number of opportunities, the buyer is entitled (after following certain procedures) to a new car, replacement of defective parts, or return of all consideration paid.

V. REMEDIES FOR INTERNATIONAL SALES CONTRACTS
The United Nations Convention on Contracts for the International Sale of Goods (CISG) provides remedies similar to those of the UCC, including, in the appropriate circumstances, damages (difference between contract and market prices), the right to avoid the contract, and the right to specific performance.

TRUE-FALSE QUESTIONS

(Answers at the Back of the Book)

____ 1. An award of damages is inappropriate if specific performance is possible.

____ 2. When a buyer accepts goods, if he or she fails to make proper and timely payment, the seller can sue to recover the price of the goods.

____ 3. When a seller discovers that a buyer has received goods on credit while insolvent, the seller can reclaim the goods.

____ 4. If a buyer or lessee is in breach, the seller or lessor can cancel the contract and sue for damages.

____ 5. If a seller or lessor cancels a contract without justification, he or she is in breach, and the buyer or lessee can sue for damages.

____ 6. A buyer cannot reject nonconforming goods once they have been delivered.

___ **7.** When a seller is in breach, the buyer can cancel the contract, but he or she then loses all rights to any other remedy.

___ **8.** A buyer can revoke acceptance for any reason.

___ **9.** If the seller has not yet delivered the goods, he or she can cancel the contract without liability.

___ **10.** Remedies for the breach of international contracts are different from those available under the UCC.

FILL-IN QUESTIONS

(Answers at the Back of the Book)

Most states have lemon laws, which provide that if _____
_____ (any automobile/an automobile under warranty) possesses
a defect that significantly affects the vehicle's _____
(value/use/value or use), and the defect is not remedied by the seller _____
_____ (by a certain date/within a certain number
of opportunities), the buyer is entitled to _____
_____ (replacement of defective
parts or return of all consideration paid/a new car, replacement of defective parts, or
return of all consideration paid).

MULTIPLE-CHOICE QUESTIONS

(Answers at the Back of the Book)

___ **1.** **Based on a Sample CPA Exam Question.** Digital Products Company agrees to sell to Eagle Manufacturing, Inc., a customized software system. If Eagle materially breaches the contract, the remedies available to Digital include the right

a. to cancel the contract only.
b. to recover damages only.
c. to cancel the contract and recover damages.
d. none of the above.

___ **2.** Alto Corporation agrees to buy one hundred harddrives from Gopher Equipment. When Gopher fails to deliver, Alto is forced to cover. Alto sues Gopher. Alto can recover from Gopher

a. the cover price, less the contract price.
b. incidental and consequential damages.
c. both a and b.
d. none of the above.

___ **3.** AdamCo agrees to sell the latest version of the Go! CD-ROMs to Cutter Computers. AdamCo delivers an outdated version of Go! (nonconforming goods). Cutter's possible remedies may include

a. recovering damages.
b. revoking acceptance.
c. rejecting part or all of the goods.
d. all of the above.

____   4.   Eagle Furniture, Inc., and Nationwide Stores contract for the sale of thirty bookcases. They can agree

a.   only to add to their UCC remedies.
b.   only to substitute for their UCC remedies.
c.   only to change the measure of damages under the UCC.
d.   to add to or substitute for their UCC remedies, or to change the measure of damages under the UCC.

____   5.   Phil Parts, Inc., agrees to sell clock parts to Time Clocks. Phil does not deliver. Time's normal remedies include

a.   damages.
b.   a forced discount.
c.   specific performance.
d.   all of the above.

____   6.   ABC Market orders a truckload of apples from Hill Orchards. Hill can stop delivery of these apples in transit

a.   only if ABC is insolvent.
b.   only if ABC breaches the contract.
c.   if ABC is insolvent or breaches the contract.
d.   under no circumstances.

____   7.   American Computers delivers sixty computers to QT Software, as per QT's order. QT does not reject nor pay for the goods. American can

a.   only bring an action to recover the price.
b.   only bring an action to reclaim the goods.
c.   bring an action to recover the price or reclaim the goods.
d.   none of the above.

____   8.   Gala Instruments, Inc., refuses to deliver a piano to City Orchestra Hall, as agreed. City, which has not yet paid for the piano, can cancel the contract

a.   with only notice to Gala.
b.   only on payment of Gala's incidental expenses.
c.   with notice to Gala and on payment of Gala's incidental expenses.
d.   none of the above.

____   9.   Commercial Builders orders forty window frames from J&J Windows. Only half of the frames that J&J delivers conform to the contract. Commercial can reject the frames that do not conform and

a.   cancel the contract, but not obtain cover.
b.   obtain cover, but not cancel the contract.
c.   cancel the contract or obtain cover.
d.   none of the above.

____   10.   Office Equip, Inc., agrees to lease fifty computers to Pine Company. When Office tries to deliver, Pine refuses to accept. There is nothing wrong with the computers. Office sues Pine, seeking damages. Office is entitled to the difference between

a.   the contract price and the market price.
b.   the market price and Office's lost profits.
c.   Office's lost profits and the contract price.
d.   none of the above.

SHORT ESSAY QUESTIONS

1.   What can a seller do to protect itself on hearing that a buyer is in financial trouble?

2.   What is the buyer's right of cover?

ISSUE SPOTTERS

(Answers at the Back of the Book)

1.   Plain Clothes, Inc., contracts to sell to Fashion Outlets six hundred pairs of jeans, to be delivered and paid for in six monthly installments. Plain tenders the first installment. For no good reason, Fashion sends the shipment back to Plain without payment. Can Plain withhold delivery of the next installment?

2.   American Gauge agrees to make thermoformers for P&G Manufacturing, Inc. There is no other potential buyer for the thermoformers. What recourse does American have if, on delivery, P&G refuses to pay? If P&G refuses to accept? If, the goods are delivered but before P&G pays, they are destroyed?

3.   Garth Masks, Ltd., contracts to sell to Ace Costumers, Inc., seven hundred plastic masks at $1 each to be delivered by October 1. Garth knows that Ace will use the masks to make Halloween costumes. Ace usually makes $7,000 profit from the costumes' sale. Garth fails to deliver on October 1. Ace attempts to buy substitute masks elsewhere, but must pay $1.20 each and take delivery on October 15, cutting Ace's sales in half. Ace sues Garth. What is Ace entitled to?

4.   Felix Distributors, contracts to sell to National Motor Company (NMC) 10,000 cogwheels at $1 each to be delivered to NMC's factory in Detroit on May 1. Felix knows that NMC will use the cogwheels to manufacture specialty motors and that NMC's operation will be at a standstill if it does not receive the goods. When Felix fails to deliver, the price of cogwheels in Detroit is $1.20 each. NMC's operation shuts down. NMC sues Felix. What is NMC entitled to?

5.   Pizza King agrees to buy tomatoes from Mac Farms. When Mac tenders the goods, the owner of Pizza King says, "I changed my mind. I don't want the tomatoes." Mac quickly sells the tomatoes to another buyer, for a lower price. Can Mac recover from Pizza King even though the tomatoes are sold? If so, what's the measure of recovery?

SPECIAL INFORMATION FOR CPA CANDIDATES

The topics and details set out in this chapter have not been as heavily tested on the CPA examination as the concepts covered in other chapters in this unit. Knowing which remedies are available in which situations may prove useful, however.

Chapter 23
Sales and Lease Warranties

WHAT THIS CHAPTER IS ABOUT

Most goods are covered by some type of warranty designed to protect consumers. A warranty imposes a duty on the seller; a breach of warranty is a breach of the seller's promise. If the parties have not agreed to limit the remedies available to the buyer, the buyer can sue to recover damages or, sometimes, rescind the contract.

CHAPTER OUTLINE

I. WARRANTIES OF TITLE

A. GOOD TITLE
Sellers warrant that they have good and valid title and that the transfer of title is rightful [UCC 2–312(1)(a)].

B. NO LIENS
Sellers warrant that goods are free of a security interest of which the buyer has no knowledge [UCC 2–312(1)(b)]. Lessors warrant no third party will interfere with the lessee's use of the goods [UCC 2A–211(1)].

C. NO INFRINGEMENTS
Sellers warrant that the goods are free of any third person's patent, trademark, or copyright claims [UCC 2–312(3), 2A–211(2)].

1. **Sales Contract—If the Warranty Is Breached and the Buyer Is Sued**
The buyer must notify the seller. If the seller agrees in writing to defend and bear all costs, the buyer must let the seller do it (or lose all rights against the seller) [UCC 2–607(3)(b), (5)(b)].

2. **Lease—If the Warranty Is Breached and the Lessee Is Sued**
Same as above, except that a consumer who fails to notify the lessor within a reasonable time does not lose any rights against the lessor [UCC 2A–516(3)(b), (4)(b)].

D. DISCLAIMER OF TITLE WARRANTY

In a sales contract, a disclaimer can be made only by specific contractual language [UCC 2–312(2)]). In a lease, the disclaimer must be specific, in writing, and conspicuous [UCC 2A–214(4)].

II. EXPRESS WARRANTIES

A. WHEN EXPRESS WARRANTIES ARISE

A seller or lessor warrants that goods will conform to affirmations or promises of fact, descriptions, samples or models [UCC 2–313, 2A–210].

B. BASIS OF THE BARGAIN

An affirmation, promise, description, or sample must be part of the basis of the bargain: it must come at such a time that the buyer could have relied on it when agreeing to the contract [UCC 2–313, 2A–210].

C. STATEMENTS OF OPINION AND VALUE

1. Opinions

A statement relating to the value of goods or a statement of opinion or recommendation about goods is not an express warranty [UCC 2–313(2), 2A–210(2)], unless the seller or lessor who makes it is an expert and gives an opinion as an expert.

2. Puffing

Whether a statement is an express warranty or puffing is not easy to determine. Factors include the reasonableness of the buyer's reliance on the statement and the specificity of the statement.

III. IMPLIED WARRANTIES

An **implied warranty** is derived by implication or inference from the nature of a transaction or the relative situations or circumstances of the parties.

A. IMPLIED WARRANTY OF MERCHANTABILITY

A warranty automatically arises in every sale or lease of goods by a merchant who deals in such goods that the goods are merchantable [UCC 2–314, 2A–212].

1. Merchantable Goods

a. Reasonably Fit for Ordinary Purposes

Goods that are merchantable are "reasonably fit for the ordinary purposes for which such goods are used" [UCC 2–314(2)].

b. Characteristics of Merchantable Goods

Average, fair, or medium-grade quality; pass without objection in the market for goods of the same description; adequate package and label, as provided by the agreement; and conform to the promises or affirmations of fact made on the container or label.

c. Merchant's Knowledge

It makes no difference whether the merchant knew of or could have discovered a defect that makes a product unsafe.

2. Merchantable Food

Merchantable food is food that is fit to eat.

B. IMPLIED WARRANTY OF FITNESS FOR A PARTICULAR PURPOSE

Arises when seller or lessor (merchant or nonmerchant) knows or has reason to know the purpose for which buyer or lessee will use goods and knows he or she is relying on seller to select suitable goods [UCC 2–315, 2A–213]. Goods can be merchantable but unfit for a particular purpose.

C. IMPLIED WARRANTY—DEALING, PERFORMANCE, OR TRADE USAGE

When the parties know a well-recognized trade custom, it is inferred that they intended it to apply to their contract [UCC 2–314, 2A–212].

IV. OVERLAPPING WARRANTIES

A. WHEN WARRANTIES ARE CONSISTENT

They are cumulative [UCC 2–317, 2A–215].

B. WHEN WARRANTIES ARE INCONSISTENT

1. Express warranties displace inconsistent implied warranties (except fitness for a particular purpose).

2. Samples take precedence over inconsistent general descriptions.

3. Technical specs displace inconsistent samples or general descriptions.

V. WARRANTIES AND THIRD PARTIES

A. THE COMMON LAW REQUIRES PRIVITY

At common law, privity of contract must exist between a plaintiff and a defendant to bring any action based on a contract.

B. THE UCC ELIMINATES PRIVITY

The UCC includes three optional, alternative provisions eliminating privity with respect to certain types of injuries for certain beneficiaries. Each state may adopt one of the alternatives [UCC 2–318, 2A–216].

VI. WARRANTY DISCLAIMERS

A. EXPRESS WARRANTIES

A seller can avoid making express warranties by not promising or affirming anything, describing the goods, or using of a sample or model [UCC 2–313].

1. **Oral Warranties**

   Oral warranties made during bargaining cannot be modified later.

2. **Negating or Limiting Express Warranties**

   A written disclaimer—clear and conspicuous—can negate all warranties not in the written contract [UCC 2–316(1), 2A–214(1)].

B. IMPLIED WARRANTIES

1. **General Language**

   Implied warranties can be disclaimed by the expression "as is" or a similar phrase [UCC 2–316(3)(a), 2A–214(3)(a)].

2. **Specific Language**

   Fitness for a particular purpose—disclaimer must be in writing and conspicuous (word *fitness* is not required). Merchantability—disclaimer must mention *merchantability*; if in writing, must be conspicuous.

3. What Is Conspicuous

A term or clause that a reasonable person against whom it is to operate would notice (such as larger or contrasting type) [UCC 1–201(10)].

C. BUYER'S OR LESSEE'S EXAMINATION OF THE GOODS

If a buyer examines the goods before entering a contract, there is no implied warranty with respect to defects that a reasonable examination would reveal [UCC 2–316(3)(b), 2A–214(2)(b)]. The same is true if the buyer refuses to examine over the seller's or lessor's demand.

D. UNCONSCIONABILITY

Courts view disclaimers with disfavor, especially when consumers are involved, and have sometimes held disclaimers unconscionable [UCC 2–302, 2A–108].

VII. STATUTE OF LIMITATIONS

An action for breach of contract under the UCC must be brought within four years after the cause of action accrues. In their contract, the parties can change the period to not less than one, and not more than four, years [UCC 2–725(1)].

A. WHEN A CAUSE OF ACTION FOR BREACH OF WARRANTY ACCRUES

When the seller tenders delivery, even if the nonbreaching party is unaware the cause has accrued [UCC 2–725(2)]. When a warranty extends to future performance, discovery of breach must await that time [UCC 2–725(2)], which is also when the statute of limitations begins to run.

B. WHEN THE LIMITATIONS PERIOD DOES NOT APPLY

When a buyer or seller brings suit on a legal theory unrelated to the UCC, the four-year period does not apply, even if the claim relates to the goods.

VIII. MAGNUSON–MOSS WARRANTY ACT

No seller is required to give a written warranty for consumer goods, but if a seller chooses to do so and the cost of the goods is more than—

A. $10

The warranty must be clearly labeled full or limited. A **full warranty** requires free repair or replacement of defective parts (there is no time limit). A **limited warranty** is any warranty that is not full.

B. $15

The seller must state (fully and conspicuously in a single document in "readily understood language") the seller's name and address, what is warranted, procedures for enforcing the warranty, any limitations on relief, and that the buyer has legal rights.

C. TIME LIMITS

Sellers can impose a time limit on the duration of an implied warranty, if it corresponds to the duration of the express warranty.

IX. WARRANTIES UNDER THE CISG

The United Nations Convention on Contracts for the International Sale of Goods (CISG) uses different language ("conformity of the goods" instead of "warranty"), but in effect provides for protection similar to the UCC's.

TRUE-FALSE QUESTIONS

(Answers at the Back of the Book)

_____ 1. If a seller makes a specific representation concerning the condition of a product, an express warranty arises.

_____ 2. A contract cannot involve both an implied warranty of merchantability and an implied warranty of fitness for a particular purpose.

_____ 3. A trade custom does not apply to a contract unless it is in writing.

_____ 4. A seller's best protection from being held accountable for promises is not to make them in the first place.

_____ 5. A clear, conspicuous, written statement brought to a buyer's attention when a contract is formed can disclaim all warranties not in a written contract.

_____ 6. No seller is required to give a written warranty for consumer goods.

_____ 7. Sellers warrant that they have good and valid title.

_____ 8. A seller's statement of opinion about goods is always an express warranty.

_____ 9. To disclaim the implied warranty of merchantability, a merchant must mention "merchantability."

_____ 10. Whether or not a buyer examines goods before entering into a contract, there is an implied warranty with respect to defects an examination would reveal.

FILL-IN QUESTIONS

(Answers at the Back of the Book)

An express warranty _____ (can/cannot) be disclaimed in writing i f it is called to the buyer's attention. An implied warranty of fitness for a particular purpose _____ (can/cannot) be disclaimed in writing. An implied warranty of merchantability _____ (can/cannot) be disclaimed in writing. A disclaimer of the implied warranty of fitness for a particular purpose _____ (must/need not) use the word "fitness." A disclaimer of the implied warranty of merchantability _____ (must/need not) include the word merchantability.

MULTIPLE-CHOICE QUESTIONS

(Answers at the Back of the Book)

_____ 1. Noel's Ski Shop sells a pair of skis to Fred. When he first uses the skis, they snap in two. The cause is something that Noel did not know about and could not have discovered. If Fred sues Noel, he will likely

a. win, because Noel breached the merchant's implied duty of inspection.
b. win, because Noel breached the implied warranty of merchantability.
c. lose, because Noel knew nothing about the defect that made the skis unsafe.
d. lose, because consumers should reasonably expect to find on occasion that a product will not work as warranted.

____ 2. As a hobby, Dick converts old Volkswagens into off-road vehicles and sells them. During one sale, the buyer tells Dick that she knows nothing about off-road vehicles and wants Dick to pick a "good one" for her. On her first off-road drive, she is injured when the car's front axle snaps in two and the car rolls over. The axle would not have broken in ordinary driving. Dick is

   a. liable, because he breached the implied warranty of fitness.
   b. liable, because he is not a merchant.
   c. not liable, because the axle would not have snapped in ordinary driving.
   d. not liable, because he is not a merchant.

____ 3. Tyler Desk Corporation writes in its contracts, in large red letters, "THERE ARE NO WARRANTIES THAT EXTEND BEYOND THE DESCRIPTION ON THE FACE HEREOF." The disclaimer negates the implied warranty of

   a. merchantability.
   b. fitness for a particular purpose.
   c. title.
   d. all of the above.

____ 4. Linn Manufacturing, Inc., sells a watch to Ted. Their contract states, "The manufacturer warrants that this watch will not lose more than one second for one year from the date of purchase." Under the Magnuson-Moss Warranty Act, making this express warranty means that Linn

   a. cannot disclaim or modify the implied warranty of merchantability or the implied warranty of fitness for a particular purpose.
   b. can impose a time limit of one year on any implied warranty.
   c. both a and b.
   d. none of the above.

____ 5. ABC Electronics sells electronic products. In sales to its customers, as a merchant ABC warrants that its title to the products is

   a. good.
   b. subject to the security interest of a third person.
   c. subject to a third person's patent, trademark, or copyright claim.
   d. the best that money can buy at the contract price.

____ 6. Eagle Equipment sells motor vehicle parts to dealers. In response to a dealer's order, Eagle ships a crate with a label that reads, "Crate contains one 150-horsepower diesel engine." This statement is

   a. an express warranty.
   b. an implied warranty of merchantability.
   c. an implied warranty of fitness for a particular purpose.
   d. none of the above.

____ 7. Adam buys one hundred computer monitors from Paula. There is no specific disclaimer of any title warranty. Regarding the transfer of title, Paula warrants

   a. that it is rightful.
   b. that it may be subject to the security interest of a third person.
   c. that the goods are the best that money can buy at that price.
   d. nothing.

____ 8. Smith Hardware sells tools. One of Smith's brochures states, "This drill bit will penetrate steel without dulling." This statement is

    a. an express warranty.
    b. an implied warranty of merchantability.
    c. an implied warranty of fitness for a particular purpose.
    d. none of the above.

____ 9. B&B Autos sells cars, trucks, and other motor vehicles. A B&B salesperson claims, "This is the finest car ever made." This statement is

    a. an express warranty.
    b. an implied warranty of merchantability.
    c. an implied warranty of fitness for a particular purpose.
    d. none of the above.

____ 10. **Based on a Sample CPA Exam Question.** A sales representative for Fine Office Furniture shows swatches of upholstery fabric to a customer, who says he needs chairs for an office reception area. An example of an express warranty is a warranty of

    a. conformity of goods to a sample.
    b. fitness for a particular purpose.
    c. merchantability.
    d. usage of trade.

SHORT ESSAY QUESTIONS

1.   What is the difference between the implied warranty of merchantability and the implied warranty of fitness for a particular purpose?

2.   What is the general effect of a warranty disclaimer?

ISSUE SPOTTERS

(Answers at the Back of the Book)

1.   Barb sells a car to Stan. Two months later, Ace Credit Company comes to Stan to repossess the car. Ace shows Stan papers proving that it has a security interest in the car and that Barb has missed five payments. Stan says, "I know nothing about any of this. You have to get your money from Barb. You can't take the car." Is Stan right?

2.   Dan loves Sunny Foods, which are cholesterol-rich. When Dan is diagnosed as suffering from heart disease, he sues the Sunny Company, on the ground that its foods are not fit to eat. He claims they breach the implied warranty of merchantability. Is it likely that the court will agree with Dan?

3.   Bailey Vehicles sells to Greg, a farmer, a used pick-up truck. The contract, in large type, states, "THE SALE OF THIS TRUCK IS 'AS IS.'" When the truck is delivered, it has no wheels. Can Bailey use the statement in the contract to avoid liability for delivering a truck with no wheels? Could the statement be used to hold Bailey liable?

4.   General Construction Company (GCC) tells Industrial Supplies, Inc., that it needs an adhesive to do a particular job. Industrial provides a five-gallon bucket of a certain brand. When it does not perform to GCC's specifications, GCC sues Industrial, which claims, "We didn't expressly promise anything." What should GCC argue?

5. In negotiating a sale of handicrafts to Pat, Kate insists that the buyer examine the goods. Pat refuses. Later, Pat is injured by a defect in one of the items that could have been spotted by a reasonable inspection. If Pat sues Kate for breach of the implied warranty of merchantability, will Kate be held liable?

SPECIAL INFORMATION FOR CPA CANDIDATES

The CPA examination does not cover the Magnuson–Moss Warranty Act (or similar state consumer protection legislation). The CPA exam does cover, however, the UCC's rules on warranty. These rules may be better applied if they are actually understood. That is, a rote memorization of the rules may not prove as useful as actual comprehension. To this end, it may be helpful to imagine their application in a real sales contract situation. In particular, remember that UCC warranty actions require privity of contract and that the warranty of merchantability applies only to merchants.

CUMULATIVE HYPOTHETICAL PROBLEM FOR UNIT THREE—INCLUDING CHAPTERS 19–23

(Answers at the Back of the Book)

Alpha Engineering Corporation designs products for companies in the aerospace industry. Beta Computers, Inc. , makes and sells hard drives.

____ **1.** Alpha writes to Beta to order one hundred hard drives. Beta writes to accept but adds a clause providing for interest on any overdue invoices (a common practice in the industry). If there is no further communication between the parties

   a. Beta has made a counteroffer.
   b. there is a contract but without Beta's added term.
   c. there is a contract that includes Beta's added term.
   d. there is no contract because Alpha did not expressly accept the added term.

____ **2.** Beta tenders delivery of the hard drives to Alpha. Alpha says that it cannot take possession immediately but will do so later in the day. Before Alpha takes possession, the goods are destroyed in a fire. The risk of loss

   a. passed to Alpha at the time the contract was formed.
   b. passed to Alpha on Beta's tender of delivery.
   c. remained with Beta, because Alpha had not yet taken possession.
   d. remained with Beta, because title had not yet passed to Alpha.

____ **3.** Beta tenders delivery of the hard drives to Alpha. Alpha says that it had decided not to buy them. In Beta's suit against Alpha, Beta can recover the contract price if

   a. Beta does not seek any damages in addition to the contract price.
   b. Beta identified the goods to the contract and a reasonable effort to resell the goods would not succeed.
   c. specific performance is not possible.
   d. the goods have been destroyed and Beta's insurance is inadequate.

____   **4.** Alpha tries to put the hard drives into use, but they do not do what Beta promised. In the deal between Alpha and Beta, the most important factor in determining whether an express warranty was created is whether

a. Beta intended to create a warranty.
b. Beta made the promises in the ordinary course of business.
c. Beta's promises became part of the basis of the bargain.
d. Beta's statements were in writing.

____   **5.** Under the UCC, to be subject to an implied warranty of merchantability, Beta's hard drives do NOT need to be

a. adequately packaged and labeled.
b. fit for all of the purposes for which Alpha intends to use the goods.
c. in conformity with any affirmations of fact made on the package.
d. sold by a merchant.

Chapter 24
The Function and Creation of Negotiable Instruments

WHAT THIS CHAPTER IS ABOUT

A **negotiable instrument** is a signed writing that contains an unconditional promise or order to pay an exact sum of money, when demanded or at an exact future time. This chapter outlines types of negotiable instruments and the requirements for negotiability.

CHAPTER OUTLINE

I. ARTICLE 3 OF THE UCC AND ITS REVISION

UCC Article 3 applies to transactions involving negotiable instruments. Since 1990, most states have adopted revised versions of these articles. This outline refers to the revised articles.

II. THE FUNCTION OF INSTRUMENTS

A negotiable instrument can function as a substitute for money or as an extension of credit. To do so, it must be easily transferable without danger of being uncollectible.

III. TYPES OF INSTRUMENTS

A. DRAFTS AND CHECKS (ORDERS TO PAY)

The person who signs or makes an order to pay is the **drawer**. The person to whom the order is made is the **drawee**. The person to whom payment is ordered is the **payee**.

1. Draft

An unconditional written order by one person to another to pay money. The drawee must be obligated to the drawer either by an agreement or through a debtor-creditor relationship to honor the order.

a. Time Draft

Payable at a definite future time.

b. Sight Draft (Demand Draft)

Payable on sight (when presented for payment). A draft payable at a stated time after sight is both a time and a sight draft.

    c. **Trade Acceptance**

A draft in which the seller is both the drawer and the payee. The draft orders the buyer to pay a specified sum of money to the seller, at a stated time in the future.

    d. **Banker's Acceptance**

A draft drawn by a creditor against his or her debtor, who must pay it at maturity. Typically, the term is short.

2. Check

A draft drawn on a bank and payable on demand. A **cashier's check** is a draft in which the bank is both the drawer and drawee. A **teller's check** is a draft drawn by one bank on another bank [UCC 3–104(h)].

B. PROMISSORY NOTES AND CDS (PROMISES TO PAY)

A person who promises to pay is a **maker**. A person to whom the promise is made is a **payee**. A **promissory note** is a written promise by one party to pay money to another party. A **certificate of deposit (CD)** is a note made by a bank promising to repay a deposit of funds with interest on a certain date [UCC 3–104(j)].

IV. REQUIREMENTS FOR NEGOTIABILITY

To be negotiable, an instrument must meet all of the following requirements [UCC 3–104(a)]. The instrument must be—

A. IN WRITING

A writing can be on anything that (1) is permanent and (2) has portability [UCC 3–103(a)(6)].

B. SIGNED BY THE MAKER OR DRAWER

A signature can be any place on an instrument and in any form (a mark or rubber stamp) that purports to be a signature and authenticates the writing [UCC 1–201(39), 3–401(b)].

C. AN UNCONDITIONAL PROMISE OR ORDER

1. Promise or Order

A promise must be an affirmative written undertaking—more than a mere acknowledgment of a debt (an I.O.U. does not qualify; use of the words "I promise" or "Pay" qualifies) [UCC 3–103(a)(9)].

    a. **Certificates of Deposit**

The bank's acknowledgment of a deposit and the other terms indicates a promise to repay a sum of money [UCC 3–104(j)].

    b. **More Than One Payee**

An order may be addressed to more than one person, either jointly ("Pay Joe and Jan") or alternatively ("Pay Joe or Jan") [UCC 3–103(a)(6)].

2. Unconditionality

Payment cannot be conditional, and the promise or order cannot be subject to or governed by another writing, or be subject to rights or obligations stated in another writing [UCC 3–104(a), 3–106(a)]. Negotiability is not affected by—

    a. **References to Other Writings [UCC 3–106(a)]**

    b. **Payments Only out of a Particular Fund or Source [UCC 3–106(b)(ii)]**

    c. **A Statement that an Instrument Is Secured by a Mortgage**
Destroys negotiability only if it stipulates that a promise to pay is subject to the terms of the mortgage [UCC 3–106(a)(ii)].

D. AN ORDER OR PROMISE TO PAY A FIXED AMOUNT OF MONEY
A negotiable instrument must state a fixed amount of money to be paid when the instrument is payable.

    1. **Fixed Amount**

        a. **References to Outside Sources**
Interest may be determined with reference to information not contained in the instrument but readily ascertainable by reference to a source described in the instrument [UCC 3–112(b)].

        b. **Variable Interest Rate Notes Can Be Negotiable**
The fixed-amount requirement applies only to principal [UCC 3–104].

    2. **Payable in Money**
Only instruments payable in money (not bonds, stock, gold, or goods) are negotiable [UCC 3–104(a)(3)]. *Money* is a medium of exchange recognized as the currency of a government [UCC 1–201(24)].

E. PAYABLE ON DEMAND OR AT A DEFINITE TIME

    1. **Payable on Demand**
An instrument that is payable on sight or presentment or that does not state any time for payment [UCC 3–108(a)]. A check is payable on demand [UCC 3–104(f)]. **Presentment** occurs when a person presents an instrument to a person liable on it for payment or when a person presents a draft to a drawee for acceptance.

    2. **Payable at a Definite Time**
Payable on or before a stated date or within a fixed period after sight, or on a date or time ascertainable at the time the instrument is issued [UCC 3–108(b)].

    3. **Acceleration Clause**
Allows a holder to demand payment of entire amount due if a certain event occurs. Does not affect negotiability [UCC 3–108(b)(ii)]. A **holder** is "the person in possession if the instrument is payable to bearer, or in the case of an instrument payable to an identified person, if the identified person is in possession" [UCC 1–201(20)].

    4. **Extension Clause**
The period of the extension must be specified if the right to extend is given to the maker. If the holder has the right, no period need be specified [UCC 3–108(b)(iii), (iv)].

F. PAYABLE TO ORDER OR TO BEARER
When it is issued or first comes into a holder's possession [UCC 3–104(a)(1)].

    1. **Order Instrument**
May be payable "to the order of an identified person" or to "an identified person or order" (the person must be identified with certainty) [UCC 3–109(b)].

2. Bearer Instrument
Does not designate a specific payee (but an instrument payable to a nonexistent entity is not bearer paper) [UCC 3–109(a) and Comment 3]: "Payable to the order of bearer," "Pay to the order of cash," "Pay cash"

V. FACTORS NOT AFFECTING NEGOTIABILITY

A. NO DATE
Negotiability is affected only if a date is necessary to determine a definite time for payment [UCC 3–113(b)].

B. POSTDATING
Postdating an instrument does not affect negotiability [UCC 3–113(a)].

C. HANDWRITTEN WORDS
Handwritten words prevail typewritten words, which prevail over those that are printed (such as preprinted forms) [UCC 3–114].

D. DISCREPANCY BETWEEN WORDS AND NUMBERS
An amount stated in words outweighs a contradictory number [UCC 3–114].

E. UNSPECIFIED INTEREST RATE
If a rate is unspecified, interest will be at the *judgment rate* [UCC 3–112(b)].

F. NOTATION ON A CHECK THAT IT IS NONNEGOTIABLE
This has no effect on a check, but any other instrument is made nonnegotiable by the maker or drawer adding such a notation [UCC 3–104(d)].

TRUE-FALSE QUESTIONS

(Answers at the Back of the Book)

_____ 1. The person who signs or makes an order to pay is the drawer.

_____ 2. Negotiable instruments serve as a substitute for money.

_____ 3. A bearer instrument is payable to whoever possesses it.

_____ 4. To be negotiable, an instrument must be in writing.

_____ 5. To be negotiable, an instrument must expressly state when payment is due.

_____ 6. An instrument is nonnegotiable if the time for payment can be extended indefinitely beyond the date of maturity by the *holder*.

_____ 7. An instrument that does not designate a specific payee is an order instrument.

_____ 8. Postdating an instrument does not affect negotiability.

_____ 9. An amount stated in words on an instrument prevails over different numerals.

_____ 10. A notation on a check that it is nonnegotiable renders the check nonnegotiable.

FILL-IN QUESTIONS

(Answers at the Back of the Book)

The person who signs or makes an order to pay is a _____
(drawer/drawee). The person to whom an order to pay is made is a _____
(drawee/payee). The person to whom payment is ordered is a _____
(payee/maker). A person who promises to pay a note is a _____
(payee/maker).   A person to whom the promise to pay a note is made is a
_____ (payee/drawee).

MULTIPLE-CHOICE QUESTIONS

(Answers at the Back of the Book)

_____   1.   **Based on a Sample CPA Exam Question.** Alex makes out an instrument that
states Alex promises to pay $600 and gives it to Beth. To be negotiable, this
instrument must

a.   be payable to order or to bearer.
b.   be signed by the payee.
c.   contain references to all agreements between the parties.
d.   contain necessary conditions of payment.

_____   2.   Bob makes out a check "Pay to the order of cash." This is

a.   a bearer instrument.
b.   an order instrument.
c.   both a and b.
d.   none of the above.

_____   3.   Jules owes money to Kim. Kim owes money to Larry. Larry signs an
instrument that orders Jules to pay to Larry the money that Jules owes to
Kim. This is a

a.   certificate of deposit.
b.   check.
c.   draft.
d.   note.

_____   4.   Sally signs and delivers to Tim a $5,000 negotiable note payable to "Tim or
bearer." The note is

a.   a bearer instrument.
b.   an order instrument.
c.   both a and b.
d.   none of the above.

_____   5.   Jill writes out a note and signs it. To be negotiable, it must also include a
statement of

a.   the principal, in a fixed amount.
b.   the interest, in a fixed amount.
c.   both a and b.
d.   none of the above.

_____ **6.** Owen writes out a note and signs it. The note can be negotiable if it is

    a. due on demand only.
    b. paid in full on a specific date only.
    c. paid in installments only.
    d. due on demand, paid in full on a certain date, or paid in installments.

_____ **7.** Paula writes out and signs a note that states its payment is "subject to the terms of Paula's mortgage." This note is

    a. negotiable.
    b. nonnegotiable.
    c. negotiable or nonnegotiable, depending on other, unstated information.
    d. negotiable and nonnegotiable, depending on how its recipient treats it.

_____ **8.** Ray is the owner of Espresso Express. Dan's Office Supplies sells Ray supplies for the Express. To pay, Ray signs a check "Espresso Express" in the lower left corner. The check is

    a. not negotiable, because "Espresso Express" is a trade name.
    b. not negotiable, because Ray signed the check in the wrong location.
    c. negotiable, and Ray is bound.
    d. negotiable, but Ray is not bound.

_____ **9.** Don's checks are printed "Pay to the order of" followed by a blank. On one of the checks, Don writes in the blank "Mac or bearer." The check is a

    a. bearer instrument.
    b. order instrument.
    c. both a and b.
    d. none of the above.

_____ **10.** Pam writes out a check and a note and signs them. Which of the following would render the check or the note nonnegotiable?

    a. Omitting the name of the bank on which a check is drawn
    b. Postdating a check
    c. Stating the note's amount is due "with interest" but failing to specify a rate
    d. None of the above

SHORT ESSAY QUESTIONS

1. What are the primary functions of negotiable instruments?

2. What are the requirements for an instrument to be negotiable?

ISSUE SPOTTERS

(Answers at the Back of the Book)

1. If Louis makes out a check "Pay to the order of Maria," is the check an order instrument or a bearer instrument?

2. After filling out her tax return, Pam wants to dramatize her feelings about the amount she has to pay. She writes on the back of her shirt, "Pay to the order of the

IRS" and fills in the amount. For her signature, Pam uses a rubber stamp bearing her signature. Is the shirt negotiable?

3.   Jim owes Sherry $700. Sherry asks Jim to sign a negotiable instrument regarding the debt. Which of the following, if included on that instrument, would prevent it from being negotiable: "I.O.U. $700," "I promise to pay $700," or an instruction to Jim's bank stating, "I wish you would pay $700 to Sherry"?

4.   Lisa writes out a check payable to the order of cash and gives it to Jeff. Is the check an order instrument or a bearer instrument?

5.   Jack gets his paycheck from his employer and attempts to deposit it in his account at First National Bank. Kay, the cashier, notices that on the check the amount stated in words and the amount stated in numerals are different. Which amount can the bank lawfully credit to Jack's account?

SPECIAL INFORMATION FOR CPA CANDIDATES

For the CPA examination, the two most important concepts in the area of negotiable instruments are negotiability and holder in due course (HDC) (which is discussed in the next chapter). You should fully understand both concepts to be able to answer questions involving UCC Article 3. The significance of negotiability is that it facilitates the transfer and payment of money using a contractual obligation instead of cash. As you'll learn in the next chapter, if an instrument is negotiable, a holder can be an HDC. This is an important status because of the protection it provides.

★ Key Points

The **key points** in this chapter include:

1. The process of negotiation.

2. The types of indorsements and the effects of each type.

3. The difference between holders and holders in due course (HDCs).

4. The requirements for HDC status.

5. How a person who does not qualify as an HDC can acquire the rights and privileges of an HDC.

Chapter 25
Transferability and Holder in Due Course

WHAT THIS CHAPTER IS ABOUT

A negotiable instrument is transferred more easily than a contract, and a person who acquires it is subject to less risk than the assignee of a contract. This chapter outlines the types and the effect of indorsements, defines *holder in due course* (HDC), and describes how a holder becomes an HDC.

CHAPTER OUTLINE

I. NEGOTIATION
On a transfer by negotiation, the transferee becomes a holder and receives the rights of the previous possessor (and possibly more) [UCC 3–201(a), 3–202(b), 3–203(b), 3–305, 3–306].

A. NEGOTIATING ORDER INSTRUMENTS
Order instruments are negotiated by delivery with indorsement [UCC 3–201(b)].

B. NEGOTIATING BEARER INSTRUMENTS
Bearer instruments are negotiated by delivery only [UCC 3–201(b)].

C. CONVERTING INSTRUMENTS
An instrument can be converted from a bearer to an order instrument, or vice versa, by indorsement. A check payable to "cash" subsequently indorsed "Pay to Bob" must be negotiated as an order instrument (by indorsement and delivery) [UCC 3–205(a)]. An instrument payable to a named payee ("Bob") and indorsed in blank is a bearer instrument [UCC 3–205(b)].

II. INDORSEMENTS
Indorsements are required to negotiate an order instrument. The person who indorses an instrument is an **indorser**; the person to whom the instrument is transferred is an **indorsee**.

A. WHAT AN INDORSEMENT IS
A signature with or without additional words or statements. Usually written on the back of an instrument but can be written on a separate piece of paper (an **allonge**) affixed (stapled) to it [UCC 3–204(a)].

B. BLANK INDORSEMENT

Specifies no particular indorsee and can consist of a mere signature [UCC 3–205(b)]. Converts an order instrument to a bearer instrument.

C. SPECIAL INDORSEMENT

Names the indorsee [UCC 3–205(a)]. No special words are needed. Converts a bearer instrument into an order instrument.

D. QUALIFIED INDORSEMENT

Disclaims or limits contract liability (see Chapter 19) (the notation "without recourse" is commonly used) [UCC 3–415(b)]. Often used by persons acting in a representative capacity.

1. No Payment Guarantee

Does not guarantee payment, but does transfer title. (Most blank and special indorsements are unqualified, guaranteeing payment and transferring title).

2. Further Negotiation

A *special* qualified indorsement makes an instrument order paper (and requires indorsement and delivery for negotiation). A *blank* qualified indorsement creates bearer paper (and requires only delivery).

E. RESTRICTIVE INDORSEMENTS

1. Indorsement Prohibiting Further Indorsement

Does not destroy negotiability [UCC 3–206(a)]. Has the same effect as a special indorsement.

2. Conditional Indorsement

Specifying an event on which payment depends does not affect negotiability. A person paying or taking the instrument for value can disregard the condition [UCC 3–206(b)]. (Conditional language on the face of an instrument, however, does destroy negotiability.)

3. Indorsement for Deposit or Collection

Making the indorsee (usually a bank) a collecting agent of the indorser (such as "For deposit only") locks the instrument into the bank collection process [UCC 3–206(c)].

4. Trust Indorsement (Agency Indorsement)

An indorsement by one who is to hold or use the funds for the benefit of the indorser or a third party [UCC 3–206(d), (e)]. To the extent the original indorsee pays or applies the proceeds consistently with the indorsement, he or she is a holder and can become a holder in due course (HDC). Any subsequent purchaser can qualify as an HDC (unless he or she knows the instrument was negotiated in breach of fiduciary duty).

III. MISCELLANEOUS INDORSEMENT PROBLEMS

A. FORGED OR UNAUTHORIZED SIGNATURES OR INDORSEMENTS

See Chapters 26 and 27.

B. MISSPELLED NAME

An indorsement should be the same as the name on the instrument. An indorsee whose name is misspelled can indorse with the misspelled name, the correct name, or both [UCC 3–204(d)].

C. MULTIPLE PAYEES

An instrument payable in the alternative ("Pay to the order of Bill or Joan") requires the indorsement of only one. An instrument payable jointly ("Pay to the order of Bill and Joan") requires the indorsements of both. If it is not clear how it is payable, it requires the indorsement of only one [UCC 3–110(d)].

D. AGENTS OR OFFICERS

An instrument payable to an entity ("Pay to the order of the YWCA") can be negotiated by the entity's representative. An instrument payable to a public officer ("Pay to the order of the County Tax Collector") can be negotiated by whoever holds the office [UCC 3–110(c)].

IV. HOLDER VERSUS HOLDER IN DUE COURSE (HDC)

A. HOLDER

A **holder** is "the person in possession if the instrument is payable to bearer, or in the case of an instrument payable to an identified person, if the identified person is in possession" [UCC 1–201(20)]. A holder is subject to the same defenses that could be asserted against the transferor (the party from whom the holder obtained the instrument).

B. HOLDER IN DUE COURSE

A holder who meets certain requirements becomes a **holder in due course (HDC)**, and takes an instrument free of all claims to it and most defenses against payment that could be successfully asserted against the transferor.

V. REQUIREMENTS FOR HDC STATUS

To become an HDC, a person must be a holder and take an instrument (1) for value; (2) in good faith; and (3) without notice that it is overdue, that it has been dishonored, that any person has a defense against it or a claim to it, or that the instrument contains unauthorized signatures, alterations, or is so irregular or incomplete as to call into question its authenticity [UCC 3–302].

A. TAKING FOR VALUE

A holder does not give value by receiving an instrument as a gift or inheriting it. A holder gives value by [UCC 3–303(a)]—

1. Performing a promise for which an instrument was issued or transferred.

2. Acquiring a security interest or other lien in the instrument (other than a lien obtained by a judicial proceeding).

3. Taking instrument in payment of, or as security for, an antecedent debt.

4. Giving a negotiable instrument as payment.

5. Giving an irrevocable commitment as payment.

6. **Special Situations**
   A holder can be limited to ordinary holder's rights by buying an instrument at a judicial sale or taking it under legal process; acquiring it when taking over an estate; or buying it as part of a bulk transfer [UCC 3–302(c)].

B. TAKING IN GOOD FAITH

1. **What Good Faith Is**
   Good faith is "honesty in fact and the observance of reasonable commercial standards of fair dealing."

2. **How to Apply this Requirement**
   A purchaser must honestly believe that an instrument is not defective and observe reasonable commercial standards. This applies only to the holder—a person who in good faith takes an instrument from a thief may become an HDC.

C. **TAKING WITHOUT NOTICE**

A holder must acquire an instrument without knowing, or having reason to know, that it is defective.

1. **What Constitutes Notice?**

Notice is (1) actual knowledge of a defect, (2) receipt of notice about a defect, or (3) reason to know that a defect exists [UCC 1–201(25)]. Knowledge of certain facts does not constitute notice [see UCC 3–302(b)].

2. **Overdue Instruments**

a. **Demand Instruments—What Puts a Holder on Notice**

If a holder takes an instrument knowing demand was made or takes it an unreasonable time after its issue (ninety days for a check; other instruments depend on the circumstances [UCC 3–304(a)]).

b. **Time Instruments—What Puts a Holder on Notice**

If a holder takes an instrument after its expressed due date. If, on an installment note or on a series of notes, the maker has defaulted on an installment or one of the notes [UCC 3–304(b)].

3. **Dishonored Instruments—What Puts a Holder on Notice**

A holder has notice if he or she knows an instrument has been dishonored, or if he or she knows of facts that would lead him or her to suspect that an instrument has been dishonored [UCC 3–302(a)(2)].

4. **Notice of Claims or Defenses**

A holder cannot be an HDC if he or she knows of a claim to the instrument or defense against it [UCC 3–302(a)]. Knowledge can be imputed if a claim or defense is apparent on the face of the instrument or if the purchaser otherwise had reason to know from facts surrounding the transaction.

a. **Incomplete Instruments—What Puts a Holder on Notice**

If an instrument is so incomplete that an element of negotiability is lacking (e.g., amount not filled in). Accepting an instrument without knowing it was incomplete when issued is not notice.

b. **Irregular Instruments—What Puts a Holder on Notice**

If an irregularity on the face of an instrument calls into question its validity or terms of ownership, or creates ambiguity as to who to pay.

c. **Voidable Obligations—What Puts a Holder on Notice**

Knowing a party to an instrument has a defense that entitles the party to avoid the obligation. Knowing of one defense bars HDC status to all defenses. Knowing that a fiduciary has wrongfully negotiated an instrument [UCC 3–307(b)].

VI. **HOLDER THROUGH AN HDC**

A. **SHELTER PRINCIPLE**

A person who does not qualify as an HDC but who acquires an instrument from an HDC or from someone with HDC rights receives the rights and privileges of an HDC [UCC 3–203(b)].

B. **LIMITATIONS TO THE SHELTER PRINCIPLE**

A holder who was a party to fraud or illegality affecting an instrument or who, as a prior holder, had notice of a claim or defense cannot improve his or her status by repurchasing it from a later HDC [UCC 3–203(b)].

TRUE-FALSE QUESTIONS

(Answers at the Back of the Book)

___   1.   A negotiable instrument can be transferred only by negotiation.

___   2.   Indorsements are required to negotiate order instruments.

___   3.   An instrument payable to a named payee and indorsed in blank is a bearer instrument.

___   4.   Indorsements are required to negotiate bearer instruments.

___   5.   Every person who possesses an instrument is a holder.

___   6.   Anyone who takes an instrument for value, in good faith, and without notice is a holder in due course (HDC).

___   7.   A holder has only those rights that his or her transferor had in the instrument.

___   8.   All claims to an instrument can be successfully asserted against an HDC.

___   9.   For HDC status, good faith means an honest belief that an instrument is not defective.

___   10. Knowing that an instrument has been dishonored puts a holder on notice, and he or she cannot become an HDC.

FILL-IN QUESTIONS

(Answers at the Back of the Book)

A person who does not qualify as an HDC _____ (can/cannot) acquire the rights of an HDC if a person who does not qualify as an HDC acquires an instrument from an HDC. A holder who was a party to fraud or illegality affecting an instrument _____ (can/cannot) improve his or her status by repurchasing the instrument from a later HDC. A holder who, as a prior holder, had notice of a claim or defense against the instrument _____ (can/cannot) improve his or her status by repurchasing it from a later HDC.

MULTIPLE-CHOICE QUESTIONS

(Answers at the Back of the Book)

___   1.   Alec makes out a check "Pay to the order of Bill." Bill indorses the check on the back by signing his name. Before Bill signed his name, the check was

   a.   a bearer instrument.
   b.   an order instrument.
   c.   a bearer instrument and an order instrument.
   d.   none of the above.

___   2.   **Based on a Sample CPA Exam Question.** Lee accepts a promissory note from Mike. For Lee to be a holder in due course (HDC) of the note

   a.   all prior holders must have HDCs.
   b.   Lee must be the payee of the note.
   c.   the note must be negotiable.
   d.   the note must be "Payable to Bearer."

___   3.   Donna signs and delivers to Erin a $5,000 negotiable note payable to "Erin or bearer." Erin negotiates it to Frank, indorsing it on the back by signing "Erin." The note is

   a.   a bearer instrument, and Frank can convert it to order paper by writing "Pay to the order of Frank" above Erin's signature.
   b.   a bearer instrument, and it cannot be converted to an order instrument.
   c.   an order instrument, and it cannot be converted to a bearer instrument.
   d.   none of the above.

___   4.   Jack writes out a check payable to the order of Kay. Kay receives the check but wants to negotiate it further to her friend Lee. Kay can negotiate the check further by

   a.   indorsing it only.
   b.   delivering it to the transferee only.
   c.   indorsing it and delivering it to the transferee.
   d.   none of the above.

___   5.   Bob receives from Carol a check that is made out "Pay to the order of Bob." Bob turns it over and writes on the back, "Pay to Doug. [Signed] Bob." Bob's indorsement is a

   a.   blank indorsement.
   b.   qualified indorsement.
   c.   restrictive indorsement.
   d.   special indorsement.

___   6.   Sam issues a $5,000 note to Mike due six months from the date issued. One month later, Mike negotiates the note to Julie for $2,500 in cash and a negotiable check for $2,500. Julie is an HDC of the note to the extent of

   a. $2,500.
   b. $5,000.
   c. $7,500.
   d.   none of the above.

___   7.   Don signs a note that states, "Payable in thirty days." The note is dated March 2, which means it is due April 1. Jo buys the note on April 12. She is

   a.   an HDC to the extent that she paid for the note.
   b.   an HDC to the extent that the note is not yet paid.
   c.   not an HDC.
   d.   none of the above.

___   8.   Steve opens an account at First National Bank with a $4,000 check drawn on another bank and payable to himself. He indorses the check in blank. The bank credits his account and allows him to draw on the $4,000 immediately. The bank knows of no defense to the check. The bank is

   a.   an HDC to the extent that Steve draws against the $4,000 balance.
   b.   an HDC for the full amount of the check.
   c.   an HDC to the extent of any amount that is collected on the check.
   d.   not an HDC.

___   9.   Pat writes out a check for $500, but does not specify a payee. Greg steals the check and makes it payable to himself. He negotiates the check to Nick, who takes it in good faith and without notice. Regarding payment, Pat is

   a.   not liable to Greg, because Greg is not a holder.
   b.   liable to Nick, because Nick is an HDC.
   c.   both a and b.
   d.   none of the above.

___ **10.** Ben contracts with Amy to fix her roof, and Amy writes Ben a check, but Ben never makes the repairs. Carl knows Ben breached the contract, but cashes the check anyway. Carl cannot attain HDC status as regards

a. any defense Amy might have against payment.
b. only any personal defense Amy might have against payment.
c. only Ben's breach, which is Amy's personal defense against payment.
d. none of the above.

SHORT ESSAY QUESTIONS

1. How are instruments negotiated?

2. How is a person who acquires a time instrument or a demand instrument put on notice that the instrument is overdue?

ISSUE SPOTTERS

(Answers at the Back of the Book)

1. Jill writes out a check payable to the order of Kyle. Negotiation occurs when Kyle receives the check. How does Kyle subsequently negotiate the check?

2. Tom gets his paycheck from his employer, indorses the back ("Tom"), and goes to cash it at his credit union. On the way, he loses the check. Debby finds it. Has the check been negotiated to Debby? How might Tom have avoided this loss?

3. Alan issues a $500 note to Bonnie due six months from the date issued. One month later, Bonnie negotiates the note to Carl for $250 in cash and a check for $250. To what extent is Carl an HDC of the note?

4. Joan signs a note that states, "Payable in thirty days." The note is dated March 2. Rick buys the note on April 3. Is Rick an HDC of the note?

5. Barb fraudulently induces Diane to sign a note. Barb sells the note to Ellen, who does not know of the fraud and takes the note for value and in good faith, and thus becomes an HDC. Ellen sells the note to Fred, who sells the note back to Barb. Does Barb acquire Ellen's HDC rights in the note?

SPECIAL INFORMATION FOR CPA CANDIDATES

On the CPA exam, questions concerning negotiability and holders in due course are asked nearly every time. When testing on negotiability, the exam often includes instruments with a number of different indorsements. The CPA exam will not explain the indorsements for you. You will need to work through them and determine what they mean to respond to the question. (Remember that an indorsement in blank does not mean that there is no indorsement.) Negotiability is determined from the face of an instrument; whether an instrument is order paper or bearer paper can be affected by the front and the back of the instrument (and remember that this status can change). As regards holders in due course, memorize the requirements (holder, value, good faith, no notice). Review, too, the shelter rule, which is frequently covered on the exam and defenses, including breach of contract and fraud in the inducement, which are often on the exam.

Chapter 26
Liability, Defenses, and Discharge

WHAT THIS CHAPTER IS ABOUT

Two kinds of liability are associated with negotiable instruments: signature liability and warranty liability. This chapter outlines this liability, as well as the effects of certain defenses against holders and holders in due course (HDCs) and the ways in which parties can be discharged from liability on negotiable instruments.

CHAPTER OUTLINE

I. **SIGNATURE LIABILITY**
Every party (except a qualified indorser) who signs an instrument is either primarily or secondarily liable for payment when it comes due [UCC 3–401(a)]. Each party is liable for the full amount to any later indorser or to any holder.

A. **WHAT A SIGNATURE IS**
Any name, including a trade or assumed name, or a word, mark, or symbol "executed or adopted by a person with the present intention to authenticate a writing" [UCC 1–209(39), 3–401(b)].

B. **PRIMARY LIABILITY**
A person who is primarily liable is absolutely required to pay, subject to certain defenses [UCC 3–305]. Primarily liable parties include—

1. **Maker of a Note**
If an instrument is incomplete when the maker signs it, the maker must pay it as completed if authorized or, if unauthorized, as completed to an HDC [UCC 3–407, 3–412, 3–413].

2. **Acceptor of a Draft**
When a drawee accepts a draft (by signing it), he or she becomes an acceptor and is primarily liable to all subsequent holders [UCC 3–409(a)]. (A drawee that refuses to accept a draft requiring the drawee's acceptance has dishonored the instrument.)

3. Issuer of a Draft Drawn on the Drawer
Such drafts include cashier's checks [UCC 3–412, 3–414].

C. SECONDARY LIABILITY
Drawers and unqualified indorsers are secondarily liable—they pay only if a party who is primarily liable does not pay. A drawer pays if a drawee does not; an indorser pays if a maker defaults. Secondary liability is triggered by proper presentment, dishonor, and notice of dishonor.

1. Proper Presentment

a. To the Proper Person
A note or CD is presented to the maker; a draft to the drawee for acceptance, payment, or both (whatever is required); a check to the drawee [UCC 3–501(a), 3–502(b)].

b. In the Proper Manner
Depending on the type of instrument [UCC 3–501(b)]: (1) any commercially reasonable means (oral, written, or electronic; but it is not effective until the demand is received); (2) a clearinghouse procedure used by banks; or (3) at the place specified in the instrument.

c. Timely
Failure to present on time is the most common reason for improper presentment [UCC 3–414(f), 3–415(e), 3–501(b)(4)].

2. Dishonor
Occurs when payment or acceptance is refused or cannot be obtained within the prescribed time, or when required presentment is excused and the instrument is not accepted or paid [UCC 3–502(e), 3–504].

3. Proper Notice
On dishonor, to hold secondary parties liable, notice must be given within thirty days following the day on which a person receives notice of the dishonor (except a bank, which must give notice before midnight of the next banking day after receipt) [UCC 3–503].

D. ACCOMMODATION PARTIES
An **accommodation party** signs an instrument to lend his or her name as credit to another party on the instrument [UCC 3–419(a)].

1. Primary or Secondary Liability?
Primary liability: signing on behalf of a maker. Secondary liability: signing on behalf of a payee or other holder.

2. Right of Recourse
An accommodation party is never liable to the party accommodated.

E. AGENTS' SIGNATURES
Agents can sign negotiable instruments and thereby bind their principals [UCC 3–401(a)(ii), 3–402(a)].

1. Authorized Agent—Liability of the Parties

a. When the Agent Clearly Names the Principal
The principal is liable. The agent is not—if the signature shows that it is on behalf of the principal [UCC 3–402(b)(1)].

b. Other Situations

(1) If an agent signs his or her name only; (2) if an instrument is signed in both agent's and principal's names, but does not indicate agency relation; or (3) if an agent indicates agency status but fails to name the principal [UCC 3–402(b)(2)]—

1) Agent's Liability

Agent is personally liable to an HDC who has no notice that the agent was not intended to be liable. Agent is not liable to others if the original parties did not intend it.

2) Principal's Liability

Principal is liable if a party entitled to enforce the instrument can prove the agency.

2. Unauthorized Agent—Liability of the Parties

Agent's signature is ineffective except as the signature of the unauthorized signer [UCC 3–403(a)].

F. UNAUTHORIZED SIGNATURES

An unauthorized signature does not bind the person whose name is forged. (For liability of banks paying under forged signatures, see Chapter 20.)

1. Two Exceptions

(1) An unauthorized signature is binding if the person whose name is signed ratifies it [UCC 3–403(a)]; (2) a person can be barred, on the basis of negligence, from denying liability [UCC 3–115, 3–406, 4–401(d)(2)].

2. Liability of the Signer

An unauthorized signature operates as the signature of the *signer* in favor of an HDC [UCC 3–403(a)].

G. SPECIAL RULES FOR UNAUTHORIZED INDORSEMENTS

Generally, the loss falls on the first party to take the instrument. The loss falls on the maker or drawer in cases involving—

1. Imposters

An **imposter** is one who induces a maker or drawer to issue an instrument in the name of an impersonated payee.

2. Effect of an Imposter's Indorsement

Effective against the drawer, if the instrument is transferred to an innocent party [UCC 3–404(a)].

3. Fictitious Payees

A **fictitious payee** is one to whom an instrument is payable but who has no right to receive payment. (Often, dishonest employees issue such instruments or deceive employers into doing so.)

4. Effect of a Fictitious Payee's Indorsement

Not treated as a forgery; the employer can be held liable by an innocent holder [UCC 3–404(b)(2)]. The employer has recourse against the dishonest employee.

5. Comparative Negligence Standard

Comparative negligence applies in cases involving imposters and fictitious payees (thus, a bank may be partially liable) [UCC 3–404(d), 3–405(b)].

II.   WARRANTY LIABILITY

A. TRANSFER WARRANTIES

1. **The Warranties**
    Any person who transfers an instrument for consideration warrants to the transferee and, if the transfer is by indorsement, to all later transferees and holders who take the instrument in good faith [UCC 3–416]—

    a. The transferor is entitled to enforce the instrument.

    b. All signatures are authentic and authorized.

    c. The instrument has not been altered.

    d. The instrument is not subject to a defense or claim that can be asserted against the transferor.

    e. The transferor has no knowledge of any insolvency proceedings against the maker, the acceptor, or the drawer of the instrument.

2. **To Whom the Warranties Extend**
    With order instruments, the warranties run to any subsequent holder who takes the instrument in good faith. With bearer instruments, the warranties run only to the immediate transferee [UCC 3–416(a)].

3. **When to Sue for Breach of Warranty**
    As soon as a transferee or holder who takes an instrument in good faith has reason to know of it [UCC 3–416(b), (c), (d)]. Notice of the claim must be given to the warrantor within thirty days.

4. **Disclaimer**
    With respect to any instrument, except a check, include in the indorsement such words as "without warranties" [UCC 3–416(c)].

B. PRESENTMENT WARRANTIES

1. **The Warranties**
    Any person who obtains payment or acceptance of an instrument warrants to any other person who in good faith pays or accepts the instrument [UCC 3–417(a), (d)]—

    a. The person obtaining payment or acceptance is entitled or authorized to enforce the instrument (that is, there are no missing or unauthorized indorsements).

    b. The instrument has not been altered.

    c. The person obtaining payment or acceptance has no knowledge that the signature of the issuer of the instrument is unauthorized.

2. **The Last Two Warranties Do Not Apply in Certain Cases**
    It is assumed, for example, that a drawer or a maker will recognize his or her own signature and that a maker or an acceptor will recognize whether an instrument has been materially altered.

3. **When to Sue for Breach of Warranty**
    As soon as a transferee or holder who takes an instrument in good faith has reason to know of it [UCC 3–417(e)]. Notice of the claim must be given to the warrantor within thirty days.

4. Disclaimer
Valid with respect to any instrument except a check.

III. DEFENSES

A. UNIVERSAL DEFENSES
Valid against all holders, including HDCs and holders who take by HDCs.

1. Forgery
Forgery of a maker's or drawer's signature cannot bind the person whose name is used (unless that person ratifies the signature or is precluded from denying it) [UCC 3–403(a)].

2. Fraud in the Execution
Defense is valid if a person is deceived into signing an instrument, believing that it is something else. Defense is not valid if a reasonable inquiry would have revealed the nature of the instrument.

3. Material Alteration
An alteration is material if it changes the contract terms between any two parties in any way (making any change in an unauthorized manner that relates to a party's obligation) [UCC 3–407(a)].

    a. Complete Defense against an Ordinary Holder
    A holder recovers nothing [UCC 3–407(a)]. (If an alteration is visible, a holder has notice and cannot be an HDC [UCC 3–302(a)(1)].)

    b. Partial Defense against an HDC
    If an instrument was originally incomplete and later completed in an unauthorized manner, an HDC can enforce it as completed [UCC 3–407(b)].

4. Discharge in Bankruptcy
Absolute defense [UCC 3–305(a)(1)].

5. Minority
A defense to the extent that state law recognizes it as a defense to a contract [UCC 3–305(a)(1)(i)] (see Chapter 15).

6. Illegality
A defense if the law declares that an instrument executed in connection with illegal conduct is *void* [UCC 3–305(a)(1)(ii)].

7. Mental Incapacity
An instrument issued by a person who has been adjudicated mentally incompetent by state proceedings is void [UCC 3–305(a)(1)(ii)].

8. Extreme Duress
Extreme duress is an immediate threat of force or violence [UCC 3–305(a)(1)(ii)].

B. PERSONAL DEFENSES
Personal defenses avoid payment to an ordinary holder (but not an HDC).

1. Breach of Contract or Breach of Warranty
If there is a breach of a contract for which an instrument was issued or a breach of warranty (see Chapter 25), the maker or drawer may not pay.

2. **Lack or Failure of Consideration [UCC 3–303(b), 3–305(a)(2)]**
   For example, when there is no consideration for the issuing of a note.

3. **Fraud in the Inducement (Ordinary Fraud)**
   If one issues an instrument based on false statements by the other party.

4. **Illegality**
   When a statute makes an illegal transaction *voidable*.

5. **Mental Incapacity**
   If a person drafts an instrument while mentally incompetent but before a court declares him or her so, the instrument is voidable.

6. **Others**
   Discharge by payment or cancellation; unauthorized completion of an incomplete instrument; nondelivery of an instrument; ordinary duress or undue influence.

C. **FEDERAL LIMITATIONS ON HDC RIGHTS**
   A Federal Trade Commission rule (FTC Rule 433) effectively abolished HDC protection in consumer transactions.

1. **When the Rule Applies**
   As part of a consumer credit contract, a seller or lessor of consumer goods or services receives a promissory note from a consumer or arranges with a third party for a loan for a consumer to pay for the goods or services.

2. **What the Rule Requires**
   The seller or lessor must include in the contract a notice that all holders take subject to any defenses the debtor has against the seller or lessor.

3. **Effect of the Rule**
   There can be no HDC of an instrument that contains the notice (or a similar statement required by law) [UCC 3–106(d)]. A consumer can assert any defense he or she has against the seller of a product against a subsequent holder as well.

IV. DISCHARGE

A. **DISCHARGE BY PAYMENT OR TENDER OF PAYMENT**
   All parties are discharged if the party primarily liable pays to a holder the amount due in full [UCC 3–602, 3–603]. Payment by any other party discharges only that party and subsequent parties.

1. **Paying in Bad Faith**
   A party is not discharged when paying in bad faith to a holder who got the instrument by theft or from someone who got it by theft (unless the holder has the rights of an HDC) [UCC 3–602(b)(2)].

2. **When Tender Is Refused**
   Indorsers and accommodation parties with recourse against the party making tender are discharged to the extent of the tender [UCC 3–603(b)].

B. **DISCHARGE BY CANCELLATION OR SURRENDER**
   A holder can discharge any party by intentionally destroying, mutilating, or canceling an instrument, canceling or striking out a party's signature, or adding words (such as "Paid") to the instrument indicating discharge [UCC 3–604]. A holder can also discharge by surrendering it to the person to be discharged.

C. DISCHARGE BY REACQUISITION

A person who reacquires an instrument that he or she held previously discharges all intervening indorsers against subsequent holders who do not qualify as HDCs [UCC 3–207].

D. DISCHARGE BY IMPAIRMENT OF RECOURSE OR OF COLLATERAL

If a holder adversely affects an indorser's right to recover payment from prior parties, the indorser is discharged [UCC 3–605].

TRUE-FALSE QUESTIONS

(Answers at the Back of the Book)

____   1. Generally, no one is liable on an instrument unless his or her signature appears on it.

____   2. Every party who signs an instrument is primarily liable for payment of it when it comes due.

____   3. If a drawer issues an instrument to an imposter, the later forgery of the payee's name is effective to pass good title to the instrument.

____   4. Warranty liability is subject to the same conditions of proper presentment, dishonor, and notice of dishonor as signature liability.

____   5. Writing "Paid" across the face of a negotiable instrument cancels the obligation on the instrument if it is done intentionally.

____   6. Universal defenses can be raised to avoid payment to an HDC.

____   7. All warranties can be disclaimed with respect to all instruments.

____   8. Personal defenses can be raised to avoid payment to an HDC.

____   9. An unauthorized signature usually binds the person whose name is forged.

____   10. Drawers are secondarily liable.

FILL-IN QUESTIONS

(Answers at the Back of the Book)

There are three _____ (presentment/transfer) warranties. Any person who seeks payment or acceptance of a negotiable instrument impliedly warrants to any other person who in good faith pays or accepts the instrument that: (1) the _____ (presenter/transferor) has good title to the instrument or is authorized to obtain payment or acceptance on behalf of a one who has good title; (2) the _____ (presenter/transferor) has no knowledge that the signature of _____ (any indorsee/the maker or the drawer) is unauthorized; and (3) the instrument has not been _____ _____ (materially altered/materially altered by the presenter/ materially altered by the transferor).

MULTIPLE-CHOICE QUESTIONS

(Answers at the Back of the Book)

_____ 1. Mary signs her name to one of her checks, but designates no amount or payee. She loses the check in a public place. Dick finds it, makes it payable to himself for $4,000, and presents it to the First State Bank (the drawee) for payment. The bank cashes it. If Mary sues the bank,

    a. the bank will probably _not_ be held liable for the amount of the check.
    b. the bank will probably be held liable for the amount of the check.
    c. Mary's account will be recredited. The government will reimburse the bank.
    d. none of the above.

_____ 2. **Based on a Sample CPA Exam Question.** First National Bank is an HDC of a note for $1,000 on which there is the signature "Bob Adams." Bob has a defense against payment on the note to the bank if

    a. Bob's signature was forged.
    b. the note was issued based on the false statements of another party.
    c. there was no consideration for issuing the note.
    d. there was a breach of the contract for which the note was issued.

_____ 3. Tony writes a check payable to the order of Gina. The check is stolen, and John forges Gina's name on the back. He cashes the check at the First State Bank, which presents it for payment to City Bank, the drawee. In presenting the check to City Bank, State Bank breaches the warranty that

    a. it has no knowledge of any insolvency proceedings against the drawer.
    b. the instrument had not been materially altered.
    c. the signatures are authentic and authorized.
    d. none of the above.

_____ 4. Bill issues a check for $4,000, dated June 1, to Ed. The check is drawn on the First National Bank. Ed indorses the check and transfers it to Jane. Which of the following will trigger the liability of Bill and Ed on the check, based on their signatures?

    a. Presentment only
    b. Dishonor only
    c. Both presentment and dishonor
    d. Neither presentment nor dishonor

_____ 5. Standard Company issues a draft for $500 on May 1, payable to the order of Ace Credit Corporation. The draft is drawn on the First State Bank. If the bank does not accept the draft, who is liable for payment?

    a. Standard Company
    b. Ace Credit Corporation
    c. First State Bank
    d. No one

_____ 6. Pam writes out a check payable to Bob, who attempts to cash the check at the First City Bank. The bank can refuse to pay the check without dishonor

    a. only if Bob refuses to provide identification.
    b. only if the check lacks an indorsement.
    c. if Bob refuses to provide identification or if the check lacks an indorsement.
    d. none of the above.

____ 7. Alpha Company contracts to buy supplies from Beta, Inc., and signs a note payable to Beta for $500. Beta does not deliver the supplies. Alpha obtains a discharge in bankruptcy on the note. First National Bank later acquires the note, in good faith and without notice. Alpha's defenses against payment to the bank include

    a. only Alpha's discharge of the note in bankruptcy.
    b. only Beta's breach of contract.
    c. Alpha's discharge in bankruptcy and Beta's breach of contract.
    d. none of the above.

____ 8. Ann works for Eagle Equipment, Inc., as a purchasing agent with authority to sign corporate checks. Ann pays American Suppliers, on Eagle's behalf, with a check. Ann tells American she is signing for Eagle, and signs both names. Who is liable for payment on the check?

    a. Ann only
    b. Eagle only
    c. Both Eagle and Ann
    d. American

____ 9. On the back of a check are the unqualified indorsements of "Ann", "Bill", and "Carl". Donna receives the check, strikes out Bill's signature, and adds her own indorsement. Completely discharged from liability to later indorsers is

    a. Ann.
    b. Bill.
    c. Carl.
    d. Donna.

____ 10. Pam writes out a check for $50 to Dave. Dave alters the amount to $500. Although the alteration is clearly visible, Gail cashes the check for $500. Pam is liable to pay Gail

    a. $50.
    b. $500.
    c. $550.
    d. none of the above.

SHORT ESSAY QUESTIONS

1. What are the similarities and differences between transfer and presentment warranties?

2. What are the two situations in which, when there is a forged or unauthorized indorsement, the burden of loss falls on the maker or drawer?

ISSUE SPOTTERS

(Answers at the Back of the Book)

1. Tom is an accountant with KLP Corporation. He has no authority to sign corporate checks. When Tom orders furniture from the Smith Company, he pays with a check, signing "KLP Corp. by Tom, accountant." Smith does not know that Tom has no authority to sign the check. Can KLP refuse to pay it?

2.   Jay signs corporate checks for the Clef Corporation. Jay's assistant Lena usually enters the amounts and payees' names before Jay signs the checks. Lena makes a check payable to the Cole Company, to whom Clef actually owes no money. Jay signs the check. Lena forges Cole's indorsement and cashes the check at the First National Bank, the drawee. Does Clef have any recourse against the bank for the payment?

3.   Alan transfers a note, for consideration, to George by blank indorsement and delivery. George transfers the note to Brenda, who takes it in good faith. What does Alan warrant to Brenda?

4.   Phil issues a check for $100. Andy steals it and alters the amount to $1,000. He negotiates the check to Lily, who takes it in good faith, for value, and without notice of the alteration. When Lily attempts to recover on the check, Phil refuses to pay more than $100. If Lily sues Phil, will she recover more?

5.   Neal issues a check for $4,000, dated June 1, to Ed. The check is drawn on the First National Bank. Ed indorses the check and transfers it to Will. What will trigger the liability of Neal and Ed on the check?

SPECIAL INFORMATION FOR CPA CANDIDATES

Questions can be constructed so that an apparently good faith party is liable on an instrument. This is particularly true in situations involving imposters, fictitious payees, and untrustworthy agents. You may find it helpful to review the rules concerning these culprits, and remember that a good faith party can be liable for a loss. There's one point that you may be able to forget, however: FTC Rule 433 has never been on the CPA exam.

★ Key Points

The **key points** in this chapter include:

1. Types of checks.

2. When a bank may dishonor a customer's check without liability.

3. A bank's responsibilities for stale checks, stop-payment orders, and forged or altered checks.

4. How banks collect payment o checks.

5. The laws governing electronic fund transfers.

Chapter 27
Checks and Electronic Fund Transfers

WHAT THIS CHAPTER IS ABOUT

This chapter outlines the duties and liabilities that arise when a check is issued and paid. Checks are governed by UCC Articles 3 and 4. If there is a conflict between the articles, Article 4 controls. This outline also covers electronic fund transfers.

CHAPTER OUTLINE

I. **CHECKS**

A **check** is a draft drawn on a bank, ordering the bank to pay a fixed amount of money on demand [UCC 3–104(f)]. If a bank wrongfully dishonors any of the following special types of checks, the holder can recover expenses, interest, and consequential damages [UCC 3–411].

A. **CASHIER'S CHECK**
A check drawn by a bank on itself; negotiable on issue [UCC 3–104(g)].

B. **TELLER'S CHECK**
A draft drawn by a bank on another bank, or if drawn on a nonbank, payable at or through a bank [UCC 3–104(h)].

C. **TRAVELER'S CHECK**
A check on which a financial institution is both drawer and drawee. The buyer must sign it twice (buying it and using it) [UCC 3–104(i)].

D. **CERTIFIED CHECK**
A check accepted by the bank on which it is drawn [UCC 3–409(d)]. When a bank certifies a check, it immediately charges the drawer's account and transfers those funds to its own account. The effect of certification is to discharge the drawer and prior indorsers [UCC 3–414(c), 3–415(d)].

E. MISSING CASHIER'S, TELLER'S, AND CERTIFIED CHECKS

1. Who Can Claim a Refund?

The remitter or payee of a cashier's check or a teller's check, or the drawer of a certified check, can claim a refund if one of these types of checks is lost, destroyed, or stolen [UCC 3–312]. The claim becomes enforceable ninety days after the date of the check.

2. When Is the Bank Discharged?

If a person entitled to enforce the check presents it for payment, and the bank pays, the bank is discharged. If no one presents the check for payment, the bank's refund to the claimant discharges the bank.

II. THE BANK-CUSTOMER RELATIONSHIP

A. WHAT A BANK IS

A "person engaged in the business of banking, including a savings bank, savings and loan association, credit union or trust company" [UCC 4–105(1)]. Rights and duties of bank and customer are contractual.

B. WHAT A CUSTOMER IS

A customer is a creditor of the bank (and the bank, a debtor of the customer) when the customer deposits funds in his or her account. A bank acts as an agent for the customer when he or she writes a check drawn on the bank or deposits a check in his or her account for the bank to collect [UCC 4–201(a)].

III. HONORING CHECKS

If a bank dishonors a check for insufficient funds, it has no liability. The customer is liable to the payee or holder of the check in a civil suit. If intent to defraud is proved, the customer is also subject to criminal prosecution. If a bank wrongfully dishonors a check, however, it is liable to the customer [UCC 4–402].

A. OVERDRAFTS

1. Pay or Dishonor?

If there are insufficient funds in a customer's account, the bank can pay an item drawn on it or dishonor it. If the bank pays, it can charge the customer's account (if the customer has authorized payment) [UCC 4–401(a)]. If a check "bounces," a holder can resubmit it but must notify any indorsers of the first dishonor (or they are discharged).

2. Bank's Liability for Agreeing to Pay Overdrafts

Once a bank agrees to accept overdrafts, refusal to honor checks on an overdrawn account is wrongful dishonor [UCC 4–402(b)].

B. POSTDATED CHECKS

A bank can charge a postdated check against a customer's account if the customer does not give the bank enough notice. If the bank has notice but charges the check anyway, the bank is liable [UCC 4–401(c)].

C. STALE CHECKS

A bank is not obliged to pay an uncertified check presented for payment more than six months after its date [UCC 4–404]. If a bank pays in good faith, it can charge the customer's account for the amount.

D. DEATH OR INCOMPETENCE OF A CUSTOMER

Until a bank knows of the situation and has time to act, it is not liable for paying items [UCC 4–405]. If a bank knows of a death, for ten days after the date of death it can pay items drawn on or before the date of death (unless a person claiming an interest in the account orders a stop payment).

E. STOP-PAYMENT ORDERS

1. **Who Can Order a Stop Payment and When Must It Be Received?**
    Only a customer or person authorized to draw on the account. Must be received in a reasonable time and manner [UCC 4–403(a), 4–405].

2. **How Can a Stop Payment Be Given and How Long Is It Effective?**
    In most states, it can be given orally, but it is binding for only fourteen calendar days unless confirmed in writing. In writing, it is effective for six months, when it may be renewed [UCC 4–403(b)].

3. **If the Bank Pays over an Order**
    It must recredit the customer's account for any loss, including damages for the dishonor of subsequent items [UCC 4–403(c)].

4. **The Customer's Risks**
    Possible liability to payee for the amount of the item (and damages). Defense against payment to a payee may not prevent payment to a subsequent HDC [UCC 3–305, 3–306].

5. **Cashier's Checks and Teller's Checks**
    Except in very limited circumstances, payment will not be stopped on a cashier's check or a teller's check. If the bank issuing such a check wrongfully refuses to pay it, the bank may be liable for expenses, loss of interest, and consequential damages [UCC 3–411(b)].

F. CHECKS BEARING FORGED SIGNATURES

1. **The General Rule**
    A forged signature on a check has no legal effect as the signature of a drawer [UCC 3–403(a)]. If the bank pays, it must recredit the account.

2. **Customer Negligence**
    If the customer's negligence substantially contributed to the forgery, the bank is not obligated to recredit the account [UCC 3–406(a)].

    a. **Reducing a Customer's Liability**
        A customer's liability may be reduced by a bank's negligence (if it substantially contributed to the loss) [UCC 3–406(b)].

    b. **Timely Examination of Bank Statements Required**
        The customer must examine the bank statement and canceled checks promptly and report any forged signatures [UCC 4–406(c)].

        1) **When There Is a Series of Forgeries by the Same Wrongdoer**
            To recover for all items, a customer must report the first forgery to the bank within *thirty* calendar days of receiving the statement and canceled checks [UCC 4–406(d)(2)].

        2) **When the Bank Is Also Negligent**
            If the bank fails to exercise ordinary care ("reasonable commercial standards"), it may have to recredit the customer's account for a portion of the loss (on the basis of comparative negligence) [UCC 4–406(e)].

    c. **Absolute Time Limit**
        Customer must report a forged signature within one year of the date the statement and canceled checks were available [UCC 4–406].

3. **Other Parties from Whom the Bank May Recover**

   a. **The Forger**
   A forged signature is effective as the signature of the unauthorized signer [UCC 3–403(a)].

   b. **The Customer or Collecting Bank Who Cashed the Check**
   The bank may recover from "the person to whom or for whose benefit payment was made" [UCC 4–207(a)(2), 3–418(a)(ii)]. The bank cannot recover from "a person who took the instrument in good faith and for value or who in good faith changed position in reliance on the payment or acceptance" [UCC 3–418(c)].

G. **CHECKS BEARING FORGED INDORSEMENTS**

1. **The General Rule**
   If the bank pays a check with a forged indorsement, it must recredit the account (or be held liable for breach of contract) [UCC 4–401(a)].

2. **Timely Examination of Bank Statements Required**
   The customer must examine the bank statement and canceled checks and report forged indorsements promptly. Failure to do so within three years relieves the bank of liability [UCC 4–111].

3. **Parties from Whom the Bank May Recover**
   The bank can recover for breach of warranty from the bank that cashed the check [UCC 4–207(a)(2)]. Ultimately, the loss usually falls on the first party to take the instrument.

H. **ALTERED CHECKS**
If the bank fails to detect an alteration, it is liable to its customer for the loss [UCC 4–401(d)(1)].

1. **The Customer's Negligence**
   If a bank traces its loss to the customer's negligence or, on successive altered checks, to the customer's failure to discover the first alteration, its liability is reduced (unless it was negligent) [UCC 4–401, 4–406].

2. **Parties from Whom the Bank May Recover**
   The bank can recover from the transferor, for breach of warranty. Exceptions involve cashier's, teller's, and certified checks [UCC 3–417(a)(2), 4–208(a)(2), 4–207(a)(2)].

IV. **ACCEPTING DEPOSITS**

A. **AVAILABILITY SCHEDULE FOR DEPOSITED CHECKS**
Under the Expedited Funds Availability Act of 1987 and Regulation CC—

1. **Funds That Must Be Available the Next Business Day after Deposit**

   a. **The First $100 of Any Deposit and the Next $400 of a Local Check**
   The first $100 must be available for withdrawal on the opening of the next business day. The next $400 of a local check must be available by no later than 5:00 P.M. the next business day.

   b. **Cash Deposits, Wire Transfers, and Certain Checks**
   Funds must be available on the next business day for cash deposits, wire transfers, government checks, the first $100 of a day's check deposits, cashier's checks, certified checks, and checks for which the depositary and payor banks are the same institution.

2. **Funds That Must Be Available within Five Business Days**
   All nonlocal checks and nonproprietary ATM deposits, including cash.

3. **Funds That Can Be Held for Eight Days or an Extra Four Days**
   Eight days: funds in new accounts (open less than thirty days). Four days: deposits over $5,000 (except government and cashier's checks), accounts with many overdrafts, checks of questionable collectibility (the bank must tell the depositor it suspects fraud or insolvency).

B. INTEREST-BEARING ACCOUNTS
Under the Truth-in-Savings Act of 1991 and Regulation DD—

1. **When Must a Bank Pay Interest?**
   On the full balance of a customer's account each day.

2. **What Must a Bank Tell New Customers?**
   New customers must be told, in writing, the minimum to open an interest-bearing account, the interest in terms of the annual percentage yield, whether interest is calculated daily, and fees and other charges.

3. **What Must Be Included in a Monthly Statement?**
   Interest earned, any fees that were charged, how the fees were calculated, and the number of days that the statement covers.

C. THE COLLECTION PROCESS

1. **Banks Involved in the Collection Process**
   Depositary bank: first bank to receive a check for payment. **Payor bank**: bank on which a check is drawn. **Collecting bank**: bank (except payor bank) that handles a check for collection. **Intermediary bank**: any bank (except payor and depositary banks) involved in the collection process.

2. **Check Collection between Customers of the Same Bank**
   An item payable by a depositary bank that is also the payor bank is an "on-us item." If the bank does not dishonor it by the second banking day, it is considered paid [UCC 4–215(e)(2)].

3. **Check Collection between Customers of Different Banks**
   A depositary bank must arrange to present a check either directly or through intermediary banks to the appropriate payor bank.

   a. **Midnight Deadline**
      Each bank in the collection chain must pass a check on before midnight of the next banking day following receipt [UCC 4–202(b)].

   b. **Deferred Posting and the Midnight Deadline**
      Posting of checks received after a certain time can be deferred until the next day [UCC 4–108].

   c. **Electronic Check Presentment**
      Can be done the same day a check is deposited. The check may be kept at the place of deposit with only information about the check presented for payment under a Federal Reserve agreement, clearinghouse rule, or truncation agreement [UCC 4–110].

V. ELECTRONIC FUND TRANSFERS

A. TYPES OF ELECTRONIC FUND TRANSFER (EFT) SYSTEMS

1. **Automated Teller Machines (ATMs)**
   Connected online to bank computers, ATMs accept deposits, dispense funds from accounts, make credit-card advances, and receive payments.

2. **Point-of-Sale Systems**
   Connected online to bank computers, these systems allow consumers to transfer funds to merchants to pay for purchases. The merchant inserts the customer's card into a terminal to read the coded data on the card.

3. **Direct Deposits and Withdrawals**
   Through an electronic terminal, a deposit may be made directly to a customer's account. An institution at which a customer's funds are on deposit can also make payments electronically to a third party.

4. **Pay-by-Telephone Systems**
   These systems provide access to a financial institution's computer system by telephone to direct a transfer of funds.

B. **CONSUMER FUND TRANSFERS**
   Under the Electronic Fund Transfer Act (EFTA) of 1978 and Regulation E (issued by the Federal Reserve Board of Governors)—

   1. **Who Is Subject to the EFTA?**
      Financial institutions that offer electronic fund transfers (EFTs) involving customer asset accounts established for personal, family, or household purposes. Telephone transfers are covered only if they are made pursuant to a prearranged plan involving periodic transfers.

   2. **Disclosure Requirements**
      The terms and conditions of EFTs involving a customer's account must be disclosed in readily understandable language at the time the customer contracts for services. Disclosures include—

      a. **Customer Liability**
         If a debit card is lost or stolen, and misused, a customer is liable for (1) $50—if he or she notifies the bank within two business days of learning of the loss; (2) $500—if he or she does not tell the bank until after the second day; or (3) unlimited amounts—if notice does not occur within sixty days after the transfer appears on the customer's statement.

      b. **Errors on Monthly Statements**
         Customer's and bank's responsibilities with respect to monthly statements: customer has sixty days to report an error, bank has ten days to respond or return any disputed amounts.

      c. **Receipts**
         Bank must furnish receipts for transactions made through electronic terminals,

      d. **Periodic Statements**

         1) **How Often They Must Be Provided**
            Monthly statements are required for every month in which there is an electronic transfer of funds.

2) What They Must Include

The amounts and dates of transfers, the fees, identification of the terminals, names of third parties involved, and an address and phone number for inquiries and error notices.

e. Stopping Preauthorized Transfers

A customer may stop a transfer by notifying the institution orally or in writing up to three business days before the scheduled date of the transfer. The institution may require the customer to provide written confirmation with fourteen days of oral notification.

3. Stopping Payment and Reversibility

Except for preauthorized transfers, the EFTA does not provide for the reversal of an electronic transfer of funds, once it has occurred.

4. Unauthorized Transfers

a. What an Unauthorized Transfer Is

(1) A transfer is initiated by a person who has no actual authority to initiate the transfer; (2) the consumer receives no benefit from it; and (3) the consumer did not furnish the person "with the card, code, or other means of access" to his or her account.

b. Criminal Sanctions

Unauthorized use of an EFT system access device is a federal felony, subject to fines up to $10,000 and imprisonment up to ten years.

5. Violations and Damages

Banks are held to strict compliance. Penalties include—

a. Civil

A customer may recover actual damages, as well as punitive damages of not more than $1,000 or less than $100. In a class action suit, the punitive damages limit is the lesser of $500,000 or 1 percent of the institution's net worth.

b. Criminal

Sanctions included subjecting an institution or its officials to fines of up to $5,000 and imprisonment up to one year.

C. COMMERCIAL FUND TRANSFERS

In most states, UCC Article 4A clarifies the rights and liabilities of parties involved in fund transfers not subject to the EFTA or other federal or state statutes. In those states that have not adopted Article 4A, commercial fund transfers are governed by contract law and tort law.

TRUE-FALSE QUESTIONS

(Answers at the Back of the Book)

____   **1.**   A check is a draft drawn on a bank and payable on demand.

____   **2.**   If a bank pays a stale check in good faith without consulting the customer, the bank cannot charge the customer's account.

____   **3.**   If a bank receives an item payable from a customer's account in which there are insufficient funds, the bank cannot pay the item.

____ 4. A bank in the collection chain must normally pass a check on before midnight of the next banking day following receipt.

____ 5. The Electronic Fund Transfer Act (EFTA) requires financial institutions to provide a receipt of an electronic transfer at the time of the transfer.

____ 6. A customer must examine the statements provided by the institution handling his or her account and notify it of any errors within sixty days.

____ 7. The rights and duties of a bank and its customers are partially contractual.

____ 8. All funds deposited in all bank accounts must be available for withdrawal no later than the next business day.

____ 9. If a bank pays a customer's check that has a forged indorsement, and the customer's negligence did not contribute to the forgery, the bank must recredit the customer's account.

____ 10. A forged drawer's signature on a check is effective as the signature of the person whose name is signed.

FILL-IN QUESTIONS

(Answers at the Back of the Book)

A depositor is the _____ (drawee/drawer) of a check. The depositor is the bank's _____ (creditor/debtor) as to the amount on deposit in the depositor's account. The depositor is the bank's _____ (agent/principal) in the deposit contract. The bank is the _____ (drawee/drawer) of a check. The bank is the depositor's _____ (creditor debtor) as to the amount on deposit in the depositor's account. The bank is the depositor's _____ (agent/principal) in the handling of the account and in the collection process.

MULTIPLE-CHOICE QUESTIONS

(Answers at the Back of the Book)

____ 1. Jennifer receives a check from Mary for $300. The check is drawn on a local bank. If Jennifer deposits it in her bank, the $300 will be available to her

a. immediately.
b. the next business day.
c. within four days.
d. within eight days.

____ 2. Tom is paid with a check drawn on Pete's account at the First State Bank. The check has a forged drawer's signature. Tom indorses the check to Eve, who takes it in good faith and for value, and cashes it at the bank. When Pete discovers the forgery, he notifies the bank, which recredits his account. The bank can recover the amount of its loss from Eve

a. only if she has a bank account at any bank.
b. only if she has an account at the First State Bank.
c. under any circumstances.
d. under no circumstances.

____   3.   Ann buys three $300 television sets from Gail, paying with a check. That night, one of the sets explodes. Ann phones the City Bank, the drawee, and orders a stop payment. The next day, Gail presents the check to the bank for payment. If the bank honors the check, it must recredit Ann's account for

a. $300.
b. $900.
c.   nothing, because the stop-payment order was oral.
d.   nothing, because Gail did not present the check until the next day.

____   4.   On May 1, Pat steals from Frank two checks drawn payable to the order of Beth. On May 3, Pat forges Beth's signature and cashes the checks. The checks are returned with Frank's monthly statement from his bank on June 1. Frank discovers the forgery and demands that the bank recredit his account. The bank must recredit Frank's account for

a.   both checks.
b.   the first check only.
c.   the second check only.
d.   neither of the checks.

____   5.   Colin draws a check for $500 payable to the order of Mary. Mary indorses the check in blank and transfers it to Sam. Sam presents the check to the First National Bank, the drawee, for payment. If the bank does not pay the check, the bank is liable to

a.   Sam.
b.   Colin.
c.   Mary.
d.   none of the above.

____   6.   On July 1, Liz steals two blank checks from her employer, Dave's Market. On July 3, Liz forges Dave's signature and cashes the first check. The check is returned with Dave's monthly statement from the First National Bank on August 1. Dave does not examine the statement or the checks. On August 24, Liz forges Dave's signature and cashes the second check. This check is returned with Dave's monthly statement on September 1. Dave examines both statements, discovers the forgeries, and insists that the bank recredit the account for both checks. Assuming that the bank was not negligent in paying the checks, the bank must recredit Dave's account for

a.   both checks.
b.   the first check only.
c.   the second check only.
d.   neither of the checks.

____   7.   Delta Company uses its computer system to issue payroll checks. Ed, a Delta employee, uses the system without authorization to issue himself a check for $5,000. City Bank, Delta's bank, cashes the check. The bank need not recredit Delta's account for the entire $5,000 if

a.   Delta owed Ed $5,000 in unpaid wages.
b.   the bank did not take reasonable care to determine whether the check was good.
c.   Delta did not take reasonable care to limit access to its payroll system.
d.   none of the above.

____   8.   Roy writes a check for $300 payable to the order of Gene. Pam steals the check, alters the amount to $3,000, and forges Gene's indorsement. She presents the check to State Bank, the drawee, which cashes it. Roy demands that the bank recredit his account. The bank must recredit the account for

a. $3,000.
b. $2,300.
c. $300.
d. nothing.

____   9.   **Based on a Sample CPA Exam Question.** Jay is the holder and payee of check drawn by Karen on First National Bank. Jay takes the check to the bank to have it certified. After certification

a. Karen is discharged on the check.
b. Karen is primarily liable on the check.
c. the bank is discharged on the check.
d. the bank is secondarily liable on the check.

____   10.   On January 1, Dick discovers that his debit card to City Bank's ATMs is missing. On January 7, Tim uses the card to make a $200 withdrawal from Dick's account. On January 14, Dick tells the bank that the card is missing. For Tim's unauthorized use of the access card, Dick is liable for

a. $0.
b. $50.
c. $200.
d. $10,000.

SHORT ESSAY QUESTIONS

1.   Under what circumstances might a customer be unable to recover from a bank that pays on a forged check drawn on the customer's account?

2.   What are the principal features of the Electronic Fund Transfer Act (EFTA)?

ISSUE SPOTTERS

(Answers at the Back of the Book)

1.   Lynn draws a check for $900 payable to the order of Jan. Jan indorses the check in blank and transfers it to Owen. Owen presents the check to the First National Bank, the drawee bank, for payment. If the bank does not honor the check, is Lynn liable to Owen? Could Lynn also be subject to criminal prosecution?

2.   Herb steals a check from Kay's checkbook, forges Kay's signature, and transfers the check to Will for value. Unaware that the signature is not Kay's, Will presents the check to the First State Bank, the drawee. The bank cashes the check. Kay discovers the forgery and insists that the bank recredit her account. Can the bank refuse to recredit Kay's account? If not, can the bank recover the amount paid to Will?

3.   Rose draws a check for $70 payable to the order of Serena. Serena indorses the check in blank and transfers it to Val. Val alters the check to read $700 and presents it to City Bank, the drawee, for payment. The bank cashes it. Rose discovers the alteration and sues the bank. How much can Rose recover? From whom can the bank recover?

4.   First National Bank mistakenly transfers $1,000 from a customer's account in its bank to another account in the First State Bank. The transfer is done electronically. When First National learns of the mistake, it credits its customer's account and asks First State to "return" the $1,000. First State refuses. First National sues, claiming that First State violated First National's rights under the EFTA. First State argues that the EFTA does not apply, because First National and First State are financial institutions, not consumers. Will the court agree?

5.   Carla authorizes City Bank to make transfers from her account to make her automobile payments. After three payments, the dealership repossesses the car and refuses to return it. Carla phones the bank to stop the payments and follows up with a confirming letter. The bank fails to stop the fourth and fifth payments, and the dealership refuses to refund anything. Can Carla get her money from the bank?

SPECIAL INFORMATION FOR CPA CANDIDATES

Typically, banking questions on the CPA exam concern the relationship between a bank and its customer. Remember in particular that there is no primarily liable party among the original three parties on a check; only the drawer can sue a drawee for wrongful dishonor (a payee cannot enforce a check against the drawee); and a drawee does not have to pay a stale check. Another specific matter tested on the exam has been the liability surrounding stop-payment orders. In that context, remember that a personal defense is no good against a holder in due course.

Electronic fund transfers are not tested on the CPA exam.

CUMULATIVE HYPOTHETICAL PROBLEM FOR UNIT FOUR—INCLUDING CHAPTERS 24–27

(Answers at the Back of the Book)

On May 15, 2001, Erin bought the following instrument from Beta Corporation for $1,700. Erin paid for the instrument with check. Erin knew that Alpha, Inc., disputed its liability on the instrument because of Beta's alleged breach of the computer purchase contract referred to on the face of the instrument. On May 20, First National Bank bought the instrument from Erin for $1,900. First National did not know that Alpha disputed its liability. On the back of the instrument is the indorsement "Pay to the order of First National Bank, without recourse [signed] *Erin*".

May 1, 2001

Alpha, Inc., promises to pay to Beta Corp. or bearer $2,000 on June 1, 2001, with interest at the rate of 8 % per year. Alpha may elect to extend the due date to July 1, 2001.

Alpha, Inc.

By _C.D. Jones_

C.D. Jones, president

Re: computer purchase order no. 123, dated May 1, 2001

____ **1.** This instrument is

a. a check.
b. a promissory note.
c. a sight draft.
d. a trade acceptance.

____ **2.** This instrument is

a. negotiable because it refers to the computer purchase agreement.
b. negotiable even though Alpha has the right to extend the due date.
c. nonnegotiable because Alpha has the right to extend the due date.
d. nonnegotiable because it refers to the computer purchase agreement.

____ **3.** First National Bank

a. can negotiate the instrument further only by indorsing it.
b. cannot be an HDC because Erin indorsed without recourse.
c. is an HDC only because Erin indorsed the instrument.
d. is not an HDC because the instrument is nonnegotiable.

____ **4.** First National demands payment on the instrument from Alpha. Alpha refuses, claiming that Beta breached the computer purchase agreement. First National

a. can collect from Alpha because First National is an HDC.
b. can collect from Erin, but not Alpha, because Erin knew of Alpha's claim.
c. cannot collect from Alpha because Erin was not an HDC.
d. cannot collect from Alpha because of Beta's breach.

____ **5.** Beta presents Erin's check for payment, but City Bank, the drawee, refuses to pay. The party with primary liability for payment of the check is

a. Beta.
b. City Bank.
c. Erin.
d. none of the above.

Chapter 28
Secured Transactions

WHAT THIS CHAPTER IS ABOUT

This chapter covers transactions in which the payment of a debt is secured (guaranteed) by personal property owned by the debtor or in which the debtor has a legal interest. The importance of being a secured creditor cannot be overemphasized—secured transactions are as basic to modern business as credit.

CHAPTER OUTLINE

I. THE TERMINOLOGY OF SECURED TRANSACTIONS
UCC Article 9 applies to secured transactions.

A. SECURED TRANSACTION
Transaction in which payment of a debt is guaranteed by personal property owned by the debtor or in which the debtor has a legal interest.

B. SECURITY INTEREST, SECURED PARTY, COLLATERAL, AND DEBTOR
A **security interest** is any interest "in personal property or fixtures which secures payment or performance of an obligation" [UCC 1–201(37)]. A **secured party** is any person in whose favor there is a security interest [UCC 9–105(1)(m)]. **Collateral** is the property subject to a security interest [UCC 9–105(1)(c)]. **Debtor** is the party who owes the payment [UCC 9–105(1)(d)].

II. CREATING A SECURITY INTEREST
A creditor's rights attach to collateral, creating an enforceable security interest against a debtor if the following requirements are met [UCC 9–203].

A. WRITTEN AGREEMENT
(1) It must be signed by the debtor and (2) contain a description of the collateral, (3) which the description must reasonably identify [UCC 9–110, 9–203(1)]. Or the secured party must possess the collateral.

B. SECURED PARTY MUST GIVE VALUE
Value is any consideration that supports a contract [UCC 1–201(44)]).

C. DEBTOR MUST HAVE RIGHTS IN THE COLLATERAL
The debtor must have an ownership interest or right (current or future legal interest) to obtain possession of the collateral.

III. PURCHASE-MONEY SECURITY INTEREST
A PMSI is (1) retained in, or taken by the seller of, goods to secure part or all of the price, or (2) taken by a lender, such as a bank, as part of a loan to enable a debtor to buy the collateral [UCC 9–107].

IV. PERFECTING A SECURITY INTEREST
Perfection is the process by which secured parties protect themselves against the claims of others who wish to satisfy their debts out of the same collateral.

A. PERFECTION BY FILING
Filing is the most common means of perfecting a security interest.

1. What a Financing Statement Must Contain
It must contain (1) the signature of the debtor, (2) the names and addresses of both the debtor and the creditor, and (3) a description of the collateral by type or item [UCC 9–402(1)].

2. Where to File a Financing Statement
Depending on how the collateral is classified: county clerk (consumer goods), secretary of state (other collateral), or both [UCC 9–401].

B. PERFECTION WITHOUT FILING

1. Perfection by Possession
A creditor can possess collateral and return it when the debt is paid [UCC 9–203(1)(a)]. For some securities, negotiable instruments, and nonnegotiable transferable instruments, this is the only way to perfect.

2. Purchase-Money Security Interest—Automatic Perfection
A PMSI in consumer goods (and, in some states, farm equipment under a certain value) is perfected automatically when it is created. The seller need do nothing more [UCC 9–302(1)(d)].

C. PERFECTION OF SECURITY INTERESTS IN MOTOR VEHICLES
A security interest in a motor vehicle is perfected by noting the interest on the certificate of title.

D. COLLATERAL MOVED TO ANOTHER JURISDICTION

1. Continues to Be Perfected for Up to Four Months
From the date it is moved or for the period remaining in the perfection in the original jurisdiction, whichever expires first [UCC 9–103(1)(d), (3)(e)]. Collateral moved from county to county within a state (if local filing is required) may not have a four-month limit [UCC 9–403(3)].

2. Automobiles
If the original state does not require a certificate of title, perfection automatically ends four months after the move. If the original state requires title registration, and the security interest is noted on the certifi-

cate, perfection continues after the car is moved to another state requiring a certificate until the car is registered there [UCC 9–103(2)].

E. EFFECTIVE TIME OF PERFECTION

A financing statement is effective for five years [UCC 9–403(2)]. A continuation statement filed within six months before the expiration date continues the effectiveness for five more years (and so on) [UCC 9–403(3)].

V. THE SCOPE OF A SECURITY INTEREST

A. PROCEEDS

Proceeds include whatever is received when collateral is sold or otherwise disposed of. A secured party has an interest in proceeds that perfects automatically on perfection of the security interest and remains perfected for a t least ten days after the debtor receives the proceeds. The interest remains perfected for more than ten days if—

1. A filed financing statement covers the original collateral and the proceeds are property (or cash used to acquire property) in which a security interest may be perfected by filing in the same office [UCC 9–306(3)(a)].
2. There is a filed statement that covers the original collateral and the proceeds are identifiable cash proceeds [UCC 9–306(3)(b)].
3. The security interest in the proceeds is perfected before the expiration of the ten-day period [UCC 9–306(3)(c)].

B. AFTER-ACQUIRED PROPERTY

A security agreement may cover **after-acquired property**—collateral acquired by a debtor after execution of a security agreement, including consumer goods acquired within ten days "after the secured party gives value" [UCC 9–204].

C. FUTURE ADVANCES

A security agreement may provide that future advances against a line of credit are subject to a security interest in the collateral [UCC 9–204(3)].

D. THE FLOATING-LIEN CONCEPT

A **floating lien** is a security agreement that provides for the creation of a security interest in any (or all) of the above. The concept can apply to a shifting stock of goods—the lien can start with raw materials and follow them as they become finished goods and inventories and as they are sold, turning into accounts receivable, chattel paper, or cash [UCC 9–205].

VI. RESOLVING PRIORITY DISPUTES

When several creditors claim a security interest in the same collateral of a debtor, which interest has priority?

A. SECURED PARTY V. UNSECURED PARTY

Secured parties (perfected or not) prevail over unsecured creditors and creditors who have obtained judgments against the debtor but who have not begun the legal process to collect on those judgments [UCC 9–301].

B. SECURED PARTY V. LIEN CREDITOR

1. Secured Party's Priority

Any perfected security interest has priority over lien creditors who acquired their liens after perfection.

2. **Lien Creditor's Priority**
A lien creditor has priority over an unperfected security interest. **Exception**: a PMSI filed within ten days (in many states, twenty days) after debtor receives possession of collateral has priority over lien creditor rights that arise between the time the PMSI attaches and the time of filing [UCC 9–301(2)].

C. WHEN MORE THAN ONE PARTY IS SECURED

1. **The General Rule**
The first interest to be filed or perfected has priority over other filed or perfected security interests. If none of the interests has been perfected, the first to attach has priority [UCC 9-312(5)].

2. **Exception—PMSI**
When the first in time to file or perfect is a PMSI, the PMSI is first in priority rights to the collateral. Also—

   a. **Inventory**
   A perfected PMSI prevails over a previously perfected security interest if the holder of the PMSI perfects and gives the holder of the other interest written notice of the PMSI before the debtor takes possession of the new inventory [UCC 9–312(3)].

   b. **Other Collateral**
   A PMSI has priority over a previously perfected security interest if the PMSI is perfected either before or within ten days after the debtor takes possession. No notice is required [UCC 9–312(4)].

D. SECURED PARTY V. BUYER

1. **The General Rule**
A security interest in collateral continues even after the collateral has been sold unless the secured party authorized the sale [UCC 9-306(2)].

2. **Exception—Buyer in the Ordinary Course of Business**
Takes goods free of any security interest (unless the buyer knows that the purchase violates a third party's rights) [UCC 1–201(9), 9-307(1)].

3. **Exception—Buyer of Farm Products from a Farmer**
Under the Food Security Act of 1985, the buyer takes free of a security interest unless he or she (1) receives notice of the interest within one year before the purchase; (2) fails to register with the secretary of state before the purchase, and the secured party perfects his or her interest centrally; or (3) receives notice from the secretary of state that the products are subject to an effective financing statement (EFS).

4. **Exception—Buyer of Consumer Goods from Consumer**
The consumer must not know of the original interest; the purchase must occur before the secured party files a statement [UCC 9–307(2)].

5. **Exception—Buyer of Chattel Paper and Instruments**
If chattel paper perfected by filing is sold to another purchaser who gives new value and takes possession of the paper in the ordinary course of the purchaser's business, without knowledge that it is subject to a security interest, the new purchaser will have priority over the secured creditor [UCC 9–308]. (The creditor has rights in the proceeds.)

VII. OTHER RIGHTS AND DUTIES UNDER ARTICLE 9

A. INFORMATION REQUESTS
When filing, creditors can ask the filing officer to note the file number, the date, and the hour on a copy of the statement and send it to the creditor [UCC 9–407(1)]. Others (such as prospective creditors) can ask the filing officer to provide a certificate that gives information on possible perfected financing statements [UCC 9–407(2)].

B. ASSIGNMENT, AMENDMENT, AND RELEASE
A secured party can release part or all of the collateral [UCC 9–406], or assign part or all of the security interest [UCC 9–405(2)]. A filed financing statement can be amended, if both parties sign [UCC 9–402].

C. REASONABLE CARE OF COLLATERAL
A secured party in possession of collateral must use reasonable care in preserving it [UCC 9–207(1), (3)]. If it increases in value, the party can hold the increased value or profit as additional security [UCC 9–207(2)(c)].

D. THE STATUS OF THE DEBT
When the debtor asks, the secured party must tell the debtor the amount of the unpaid debt (within two weeks of the debtor's request) [UCC 9–208].

E. TERMINATION STATEMENT
When a debt is paid, the secured party can send a termination statement to the debtor or file it with the original financing statement.

1. If the Collateral Is Consumer Goods
The statement must be filed within one month after the debt is paid, or—if the debtor requests the statement in writing—within ten days of receipt of the request, whichever is earlier [UCC 9–404(1)].

2. If the Collateral Is Other Goods
The statement must be filed or furnished to the debtor within ten days after a written request is made by the debtor.

VIII. DEFAULT
Default is whatever the parties stipulate in their agreement [UCC 9–501(1)]. It occurs most often when the debtor fails to make payments or goes bankrupt.

A. BASIC REMEDIES

1. Execution and Levy
A secured party give up the security interest and proceed to judgment on the debt (this is done if the value of the collateral is less than the debt and the debtor has other assets) [UCC 9–501(1)].

2. Take Possession of the Collateral
A secured party can take possession of the collateral [UCC 9–503] and retain it for satisfaction of the debt [UCC 9–505(2)] or resell it and apply the proceeds toward the debt [UCC 9–504] (see below).

3. When the Collateral Consists of Both Real and Personal Property
A secured party can use the Article 9 remedies against the personal property or proceed against all of the collateral under real property law (in which case, Article 9 does not apply) [UCC 9–501(4)].

4. **The Soldiers' and Sailors' Relief Act of 1940**
If a security interest is created *before* a person in the military goes on active duty, a secured party cannot repossess and dispose of the collateral while the person is on active duty and for up to six months after the active duty ends.

B. **SECURED PARTY'S RIGHT TO TAKE POSSESSION OF THE COLLATERAL**
A secured party can take possession of the collateral without a court order, if it can be done without a breach of the peace [UCC 9–503]. Generally, this means not going onto the debtor's property, which could be trespass.

C. **DISPOSITION OF COLLATERAL**

1. **Retention of Collateral by the Secured Party**

   a. **Notice**
   A secured party must give written notice to the debtor. In all cases except consumer goods, notice must also be sent to any other secured party from whom the secured party has received notice of a claim.

   b. **If Debtor or Other Secured Party Objects within Twenty-One Days**
   The secured party must sell or otherwise dispose of the collateral [UCC 9–505(2)].

2. **Consumer Goods**
If the collateral is consumer goods with a PMSI and the debtor has paid 60 percent or more on the price or loan, the secured party must sell within ninety days [UCC 9–505(1), 9–507(1)].

3. **Disposition Procedures**
(1) A sale must be in a commercially reasonable manner and (2) the debtor must be notified of the sale [UCC 9–504].

   a. **What Qualifies as a Commercially Reasonable Sale?**
   When collateral is sold in the usual manner in the usual market for selling such goods or in conformity with reasonable commercial practices among dealers in the type of property sold [UCC 9–507].

   b. **The Secured Party Must Give Written Notice to the Debtor**
   In all cases except consumer goods, notice must also be sent to any other secured party from whom the secured party has received notice of a claim [UCC 9–504(3)], unless the collateral is perishable or is customarily sold in a recognized market.

4. **Proceeds from Disposition**
Must be applied to (1) expenses stemming from the retaking, holding, or preparing for sale, (2) satisfaction of the debt, (3) creditors with subordinate security interests [UCC 9–504(1)], and (4) surplus to the debtor.

5. **Deficiency Judgment**
In most cases, if a sale of collateral does not repay the debt, the debtor is liable for any deficiency. A creditor can obtain a judgment to collect.

6. **Redemption Rights**
Before the secured party retains or disposes of the collateral, the debtor or any other secured party can take the collateral by tendering performance of all secured obligations and paying the secured party's expenses [UCC 9–506].

IX.   REVISED ARTICLE 9

Revised Article 9 becomes effective July 1, 2001. Secured transactions entered before that date are subject to the new provisions after that date. Changes that Revised Article 9 makes to the law include the following.

A.   SCOPE

Certain types of collateral and kinds of transactions in which a security interest can be perfected are added (for example, electronic chattel paper, deposit accounts, and letter-of-credit rights) [UCC 9–102, 9 109].

B.   PERFECTION

The time period to perfect a PMSI is now twenty days; possession is no longer the only perfection method for negotiable instruments and transferable nonnegotiable instruments, but it is the only method for a security interest in money; perfection by attachment runs to more types of collateral [UCC 9–104, 9–105, 9–309, 9–310, 9–312, 9–313, 9–317].

C.   CHOICE OF LAW

With some exceptions, perfection is now possible in the state in which the debtor is located [UCC 9–301 through 9–307].

D.   PERFECTION BY FILING

Filing is now done only at a central state office (except for real estate related interests); electronic filing is possible [UCC 9–501, 9–502, 9–506 through 9–509, 9–513, 9–516, 9–517, 9–521, 9–523, 9–625].

E.   DEFAULT AND ENFORCEMENT

Parties have expanded rights; secured parties who sell collateral impliedly warrant title; other provisions relate to price [UCC 9–102, 9–602, 9–610, 9–611 through 9–615, 9–620, 9–624].

TRUE-FALSE QUESTIONS

(Answers at the Back of the Book)

_____   1.   Perfection is the process by which a secured party protects his or her interest against some claims of third parties who may wish to have their debts satisfied out of the same collateral.

_____   2.   A secured party needs to file copies of a financing statement only in his or her own office to protect all of his or her rights.

_____   3.   A security interest in proceeds does not perfect automatically.

_____   4.   The descriptions of collateral in a security agreement and a financing statement must be different.

_____   5.   Generally, a security interest in collateral terminates when the debt is paid.

_____   6.   A security agreement determines most of the parties' rights and duties concerning the security interest.

_____   7.   When a debt is paid, the secured party can send a termination statement to the debtor or file one with the officer to whom the financing statement was given.

_____   8.   Default occurs most commonly when a debtor fails to repay the loan for which his or her property served as collateral.

____ 9. After a debtor has defaulted and the secured party has taken possession of the property that was the collateral, the debtor can never get it back.

____ 10. When several secured parties claim a security interest in the same collateral of a debtor, the last to have been perfected takes priority.

FILL-IN QUESTIONS

(Answers at the Back of the Book)

1. Generally, in a secured transaction, the _____ (creditor/debtor) files a financing statement with the appropriate state office. When the debt is paid, the _____ (creditor/debtor) may also send a termination statement to the officer with whom the financing statement was filed.

2. When two or more secured parties have perfected security interests in the same collateral, generally the _____ (first/last) to perfect has priority. When two conflicting security interests are unperfected, the _____ (first/last) to attach has priority.

MULTIPLE-CHOICE QUESTIONS

(Answers at the Back of the Book)

____ 1. A document reads, "Debtor (Michael's Sports, 711 Fifth Avenue, St. Paul, MN) grants to secured party (Ace Finance Company, 115 First Street, St. Paul, MN) a security interest in debtor's inventory." For this document to qualify as a *financing statement*, which of the following is NOT necessary?

a. The debtor's signature
b. The creditor 's signature
c. Both parties' addresses
d. The description of the collateral ("debtor's inventory")

____ 2. Friendly Loan Company loans $15,000 to Steve to buy a new car. Their agreement provides that Steve will repay the loan over a five-year period and that he is in default if he misses a single payment. One year later, Steve fails to make two payments, and the lender declares him to be in default. The lender may take possession of the car and

a. keep it.
b. sell it to anyone after giving Steve an opportunity to fully comply with the security agreement.
c. sell it to Steve on Steve's full compliance with the security agreement.
d. any of the above.

____ 3. Paul owns a Veggies Too restaurant. Paul wants to borrow $60,000 from First National Bank to open another Veggies Too, using his first restaurant as collateral. The bank asks Paul to sign a *security agreement*. Besides Paul's signature, to be effective the agreement must

a. contain a description that reasonably identifies the collateral.
b. include the addresses of the debtor and the creditor.
c. both a and b.
d. none of the above.

____ 4. **Based on a Sample CPA Exam Question.** A purchaser of consumer goods will own the goods free of a perfected security interest in them if he or she is

a. a consumer who purchases the goods from a consumer purchaser who gave the security interest.
b. a consumer who purchases the goods in the ordinary course of business.
c. a merchant who purchases the goods for resale.
d. a merchant who purchases the goods for use in his or her business.

____ 5. Chris defaults on a loan from EZ Loan Company. EZ takes possession of the collateral and would like to keep it. Ace Capital, which also has an interest in the collateral, sends EZ notice of its claim. EZ may

a. not retain the collateral because it would violate Ace's interest.
b. retain the collateral if it sends notice to Ace.
c. be forced to sell the collateral if Ace objects to the retention.
d. be forced to sell the collateral and be forced to pay Ace.

____ 6. Eve and Rick sign an agreement that states, "Debtor (Eve) grants to secured party (Rick) a security interest in debtor's 1997 Miata." Rick gives Eve a check for $5,000. For Rick to have an enforceable security interest, which of the following is NOT necessary?

a. Eve's giving of rights in her car
b. The written agreement
c. Rick's signature on the agreement
d. The check that Rick gave to Eve

____ 7. Amigo Credit Agency loans $10,000 to Al's Hardware. The loan is secured by Al's inventory, which includes tools and supplies that Al sells to some customers on installment payment plans. Eventually, Al defaults on the loan. Amigo is entitled to

a. all of the inventory sold to customers.
b. any remaining installment payments.
c. both a and b.
d. none of the above.

____ 8. Amy buys a car with money borrowed from Bob, who takes a security interest in the car. The transaction occurs in a state that requires title registration and Bob's interest is noted on the certificate of title. If Amy moves to another state requiring a certificate, Bob's interest is

a. no longer effective.
b. effective for five years from the date the car is moved.
c. effective for four months from the date the car is moved.
d. effective until the car is registered in the new state.

____ 9. On May 1, First State Bank lends $10,000 to Diane. On May 10, the bank files a financing statement. Before that statement is filed, however, Diane uses the same collateral to borrow $5,000 from City Bank, which files a statement on May 4. In a dispute between the banks over the collateral

a. First State Bank wins because it lent money first.
b. First State Bank wins because its interest attached first.
c. City Bank wins because it perfected first.
d. City Bank wins because its interest attached first.

_____ **10.** A security agreement for a loan from First State Bank to C.C. Computers provides for the coverage of inventory, proceeds, future advances, and after-acquired property. C.C. sells its inventory for trade-ins plus cash and buys new inventory with funds from the bank. The bank has a perfected interest in

a. the trade-ins under the *proceeds* clause.
b. the funds to buy the new inventory under the *proceeds* clause.
c. the new inventory under the *inventory* clause.
d. none of the above.

SHORT ESSAY QUESTIONS

1. What is the floating lien concept?

2. What are a secured party's rights on a debtor's default?

ISSUE SPOTTERS

(Answers at the Back of the Book)

1. Stan needs $300 to buy textbooks, notebooks, and other supplies. Duane says, "I'll lend you $300 if you'll agree that if you don't pay it back, I get your laptop." Stan agrees, they put their agreement in writing, and Duane gives Stan $300. How does Duane let other creditors know of his interest in the laptop?

2. The Money Shop loans $25,000 to Wolf's Photo, secured by the store's inventory. Wolf sells cameras and other equipment from inventory to consumers on installment payment plans. Wolf defaults on the loan, but all of the inventory has been sold. Many installment payments remain, however. How can the Money Shop recover its funds?

3. Assume that in the previous question Wolf's business was more complicated: Wolf sold inventory for trade-ins plus cash and bought new inventory with additional funds advanced from the Money Shop. How can the lender be sure that its interest isn't lost in all the transactions?

4. Imagine that in the previous question Wolf sold to Mann a camcorder covered by the Money Shop's agreement with Wolf. Before Mann's check cleared, Wolf defaulted on the loan to the Money Shop. Is the lender entitled to the camcorder or the check?

5. Avco Finance loans $5,000 to Brad to buy a computer. The loan is secured by the computer. Brad defaults on the loan. Avco can repossess and keep the computer, but Avco does not want it. What are the alternatives?

SPECIAL INFORMATION FOR CPA CANDIDATES

The importance of the material in this chapter is evident in the number of questions that are devoted to it on the CPA examination. Traditionally, the UCC has made up about 25 percent of the exam, and of that 25 percent, about a third of the questions cover secured transactions. The concentration has been in four basic topics: attachment; perfection; priorities; and the rights of debtors, creditors, and others. Also frequently covered: purchase money security interests and the classification of goods as consumer goods, inventory, equipment, or farm products. All of these topics may be touched on in a single problem (or series of questions). To have a good grasp of how these topics interrelate, it may help to keep a diagram of the typical secured transaction in mind.

Chapter 29
Other Creditors' Remedies and Suretyship

WHAT THIS CHAPTER IS ABOUT

This chapter sets out the rights and remedies available to a creditor, when a debtor defaults, under laws other than UCC Article 9. Among those remedies are rights afforded by liens, and surety and guaranty agreements.

CHAPTER OUTLINE

I. LAWS ASSISTING CREDITORS

A. LIENS IN GENERAL
A **lien** is a claim on a debtor's property that must be satisfied before the property is available to satisfy other creditor's claims. A lien has priority over an unperfected security interest. Mechanic's and artisan's liens have priority over perfected security interests.

B. MECHANIC'S LIEN
Can be placed by a creditor on real property when a person contracts for labor, services, or material to improve the property but does not pay.

1. When a Creditor Must File a Mechanic's Lien
Within a specific time period, measured from the last date on which materials or labor were provided (usually within 60 to 120 days).

2. If the Owner Does Not Pay
The property can be sold to satisfy the debt. Notice of the foreclosure and sale must be given to the debtor in advance.

C. ARTISAN'S LIEN
A security device by which a creditor can recover from a debtor for labor and materials furnished in the repair of personal property.

1. The Creditor Must Possess the Property
The lien terminates if possession is voluntarily surrendered.

2. If the Owner Does Not Pay
The property can be sold to satisfy the debt. Notice of the foreclosure and sale must be given to the debtor in advance.

D. JUDICIAL LIENS
A debt must be past due before a creditor can commence legal action. Once an action is brought, the debtor's property may be seized to satisfy the debt.

1. Attachment
Attachment is a court-ordered seizure and taking into custody of property before the entry of a final judgment for a past-due debt.

a. After a Court Issues a Writ of Attachment
A sheriff or other officer seizes nonexempt property. If the creditor prevails at trial, the property can be sold to satisfy the judgment.

b. Limitations
The due process clause of the Fourteenth Amendment limits a court's power to authorize seizure of a debtor's property without notice to the debtor or a hearing on the facts.

2. Writ of Execution
A **writ of execution** is an order, usually issued by the clerk of the court, directing the sheriff to seize and sell any of the debtor's nonexempt property within the court's geographical jurisdiction.

a. First, the Creditor Must Obtain a Judgment against the Debtor
If the debtor does not pay, proceeds from the sale pay the judgment. The debtor can redeem the property any time before it is sold.

b. Limitations
Because of laws that exempt a debtor's homestead and designated items of personal property, many judgments are uncollectible.

E. GARNISHMENT
Garnishment is when a creditor collects a debt by seizing property of the debtor (such as wages or money in a bank account) that is being held by a third party (such as an employer or a bank).

1. First, the Creditor Must Obtain a Judgment against the Debtor
The garnishment judgment is then served on a debtor's employer so that part of the debtor's paycheck will be paid to the creditor.

2. Limitations
In some states, a creditor must go back to court for a separate order of garnishment for each pay period. Both federal and state laws limit the amount of money that can be garnished from a debtor's weekly take-home pay. State limits are often higher.

F. CREDITORS' COMPOSITION AGREEMENTS
A **creditors' composition agreement** is a contract between a debtor and his or her creditors for discharge of the debtor's liquidated debts on payment of a sum less than that owed.

G. MORTGAGE FORECLOSURE
A mortgagee can foreclose on the mortgaged property if the debtor defaults. The usual method is a judicial sale. The proceeds are applied to the debt.

1. Equity of Redemption
A mortgagor can redeem the property any time before the sale (and, in some states, within a certain period of time after the sale).

2. **Deficiency Judgment**
   If the proceeds do not cover the foreclosure costs and the debt, the mortgagee can recover the difference from the mortgagor by obtaining a deficiency judgment (in a separate legal action after the foreclosure).

H. **ASSIGNMENT FOR THE BENEFIT OF CREDITORS**
   A debtor may transfer title to his or her assets to a trustee or assignee, who sells them and pays each creditor in proportion to the debt. Each creditor may accept (and discharge the debt) or reject (and attempt to collect another way). Bankruptcy may supersede the assignment (see Chapter 32).

II. SURETYSHIP AND GUARANTY

A. **SURETYSHIP**
   Suretyship is a promise by a third person to be responsible for a debtor's obligation. Does not have to be in writing. A surety is primarily liable—a creditor can demand payment from the surety the moment the debt is due.

B. **GUARANTY**
   A **guaranty** is a promise to be secondarily liable for the debt or default of another. A guarantor pays only after the debtor defaults and the creditor has made an attempt to collect from the debtor. A guaranty must be in writing unless the main-purpose exception applies (see Chapter 17).

C. **DEFENSES OF THE SURETY AND THE GUARANTOR**
   To avoid payment, a surety (guarantor) may use the following defenses.

   1. **Material Change to the Contract between Debtor and Creditor**
      Without obtaining the consent of the surety (guarantor), a gratuitous surety is discharged completely and a compensated surety is discharged to the extent he or she suffers a loss.

   2. **The Principal Obligation Is Paid or Valid Tender Is Made**
      The surety (guarantor) is discharged from the obligation.

   3. **Most of the Defenses of the Principal Debtor**
      Defenses that cannot be used: the debtor's incapacity, bankruptcy, and the statute of limitations.

   4. **A Surety or Guarantor's Own Defenses**
      For example, fraud by the creditor to induce the surety (guarantor) to guarantee the debt (such as the creditor's failure to inform the surety of facts that would substantially increase the surety's risk).

   5. **A Creditor's Surrender or Impairment of the Collateral**
      Without the surety's (guarantor's) consent, releases the surety to the extent of any loss suffered from the creditor's actions.

D. **RIGHTS OF THE SURETY AND THE GUARANTOR**
   If the surety (guarantor) pays the debt—

   1. **Right of Subrogation**
      The surety (guarantor) may pursue any remedies that were available to the creditor against the debtor.

   2. **Right of Reimbursement**
      The surety is entitled to receive from the debtor all outlays made on behalf of the suretyship arrangement.

3. Co-Sureties' Right of Contribution

A surety who pays more than his or her proportionate share on a debtor's default is entitled to recover from co-sureties.

III. PROTECTION FOR DEBTORS

A. EXEMPTIONS

1. Homestead

Each state allows a debtor to retain the family home (in some states only if debtor has a family) in its entirety or up to a specified amount.

2. Personal Property

Often exempt: household furniture up to a specified amount; clothing and other personal possessions; a vehicle (or vehicles) (up to a specified amount); certain animals, usually livestock but including pets; and equipment that the debtor uses in a business or trade.

B. SPECIAL PROTECTION FOR CONSUMER DEBTORS

A Federal Trade Commission rule limits the rights of a holder in due course (HDC) who holds a negotiable promissory note executed by a consumer as part of a consumer transaction (see Chapter 26). Other laws include the Truth-in-Lending Act, which protects consumers by requiring creditors to disclose certain information when making loans (see Chapter 44).

TRUE-FALSE QUESTIONS

(Answers at the Back of the Book)

_____ 1. A mechanic's lien always involves real property, and an artisan's lien always involves personal property.

_____ 2. Federal and state laws limit the amount that can be garnished from wages, but they cannot be applied together to determine how much is exempt.

_____ 3. A creditors' composition agreement discharges only the debtor's debts owed to those creditors who agree.

_____ 4. An innkeeper's lien is placed on the baggage of guests for agreed-on hotel charges that remain unpaid.

_____ 5. Generally, to avoid liability, a surety or a guarantor cannot use any defenses available to the principal debtor.

_____ 6. If a creditor obtains a judgment against a debtor and the debtor does not willingly pay, there is nothing that the creditor can do.

_____ 7. Under an assignment for the benefit of creditors, the creditors must accept whatever payment is offered.

_____ 8. A surety or guarantor is discharged from his or her obligation when the principal debtor pays the debt.

_____ 9. A writ of execution is issued before the entry of a final judgment.

_____ 10. A surety cannot use the principal debtor's bankruptcy as a defense against the surety's payment of the debt.

FILL-IN QUESTIONS

(Answers at the Back of the Book)

A _____ (contract of suretyship/guaranty contract) is a promise to a creditor made by a third person to be responsible for a debtor's obligation. A _____ (guarantor/surety) is primarily liable: the creditor can hold the _____ (guarantor/surety) responsible for payment of the debt when the debt is due, without first exhausting all remedies against the debtor. A _____ (contract of suretyship/guaranty contract) also includes a promise to answer for a principal's obligation, but a _____ (guarantor/surety) is secondarily liable—that is, the principal must first default, and ordinarily, a creditor must have attempted to collect from the principal, because ordinarily a debtor would not otherwise be declared in default.

MULTIPLE-CHOICE QUESTIONS

(Answers at the Back of the Book)

____ 1. Melita leaves her necklace with Berman Jewelers to be repaired. When Melita returns to pick up the necklace, she says, "I don't have the money right now, but I'll pay you for the repairs later." Berman

a. can keep the necklace until Melita pays for the repairs.
b. can keep the necklace for a reasonable time but must then return it to Melita even if she does not pay for the repairs.
c. cannot keep the necklace.
d. none of the above.

____ 2. Sam's $6,000 debt to Ace Credit Company is past due, and Ace files suit. Before the judge hears the case, Ace learns that Sam has hidden some of her property from her creditors. Ace believes that Sam is about to hide the rest of her property. To ensure there will be some assets to satisfy the debt if Ace wins the suit, Ace can use

a. garnishment.
b. a mechanic's lien.
c. an artisan's lien.
d. attachment.

____ 3. **Based on a Sample CPA Exam Question.** Ed's $2,500 debt to Owen is past due. To collect money from Ed's wages to pay the debt, Owen can use

a. an order of receivershi;p.
b. a writ of attachment.
c. a writ of execution.
d. garnishment.

____ 4. Bob obtains a judgment for $30,000 and a writ of execution against Mary. To enforce the writ, Mary's home is sold for $60,000. The homestead exemption is $35,000. All of Mary's personal property is exempt, except two motorcycles that are sold for $5,000. After applying the appropriate amounts to payment of the debt, how much of the debt will be unpaid?

a. $25,000
b. $10,000
c. $5,000
d. $0

____ 5. L&R Hardware, Inc., wants to borrow money from First National Bank. The bank refuses to lend L&R the money unless Lee, the sole stockholder, agrees to assume liability if L&R does not pay off the loan. Lee agrees. L&R makes the first four payments. When the fifth payment is due, the bank can seek payment from L&R

    a. but not Lee, because Lee is a guarantor.
    b. but not Lee, because L&R is a surety.
    c. or Lee, because Lee is a surety.
    d. or Lee, because Lee is a guarantor.

____ 6. EZ Loan Company lends $90,000 to Patty. Carl, Lynn, and Floyd are co-sureties. The maximum liability of each is: Carl $18,000, Lynn $27,000, and Floyd $45,000. Patty defaults. The balance due is $60,000. Floyd pays $45,000 and Patty pays $15,000. Floyd can recover

    a. $18,000 from Carl and $27,000 from Lynn.
    b. $13,500 from Carl and $20,250 from Lynn.
    c. $9,000 from Carl and $13,500 from Lynn.
    d. $0 from Carl and $0 from Lynn.

____ 7. Adam owes Barb $500 but refuses to pay. To collect, Barb files a suit against Adam and wins. Adam still refuses to pay. To collect the amount of the judgment, Barb can use

    a. an assignment for the benefit of creditors.
    b. a creditor's composition agreement.
    c. a foreclosure.
    d. a writ of execution.

____ 8. John owes First State Bank $40,000, secured by a mortgage on John's office building. John fails to make payments on the loan. To obtain the amount that is owed, the bank can use

    a. an assignment for the benefit of creditors.
    b. a creditor's composition agreement.
    c. a foreclosure.
    d. a writ of execution.

____ 9. Gail agrees to act, without compensation, as a surety for Mary's loan from Ace Credit. Later, without Gail's knowledge, Mary and Ace agree to extend the time for repayment and to increase the interest rate. Gail's obligation

    a. remains the same.
    b. changes to match Mary's obligation.
    c. is discharged to the extent of any loss caused by the extension of time.
    d. is discharged completely.

____ 10. Lee agrees to act, without compensation, as a guarantor for Paula's loan from Ron. Collateral for the loan is Paula's car, which Paula gives to Ron. Later, without Lee's knowledge, Paula and Ron agree to increase the interest rate and Ron returns the car to Paula. Lee's obligation

    a. remains the same.
    b. is discharged to the extent of the additional interest.
    c. is discharged to the extent of any loss caused by surrender of the car.
    d. is discharged completely.

SHORT ESSAY QUESTIONS

1.   What is a lien? What are the four ways in which a lien can arise? What is a lienholder's priority compared to other creditors?

2.   What are the differences between contracts of suretyship and guaranty contracts?

ISSUE SPOTTERS

(Answers at the Back of the Book)

1.   Joe contracts with Larry of Midwest Roofing to fix Joe's roof. Joe pays half of the contract price in advance. Larry and Midwest complete the job, but Joe refuses to pay the rest of the price. What can Larry and Midwest do?

2.   Laura wants to borrow $10,000 from the Ace Finance Company to buy a new car, but Ace refuses to lend the money unless Bob cosigns the note. Bob cosigns the note and makes three of the payments to Ace when Laura fails to do so. Can Bob get the money for these three payments from Laura?

3.   Ann borrows $1,200 from Bill. Carol, Dian, and Ernie agree to act as co-sureties for the debt in equal proportions. Ann defaults and Bill collects all of the unpaid amount ($900) from Carol. Are Dian and Ernie discharged of any obligation? If not, how much do they owe and to whom do they owe it?

4.   Al owes Don $5,000 and refuses to pay. Don obtains a garnishment order and serves it on Al's employer. If the employer complies with the order and Al stays on the job, is one order enough to garnish all of Al's wages for each pay period until the debt is paid?

5.   Rick defaults on his mortgage payments, and First National Bank, the mortgagee, brings a foreclosure action. Before the house is sold, what can Rick do to get it back?

SPECIAL INFORMATION FOR CPA CANDIDATES

Suretyship is usually tested on the CPA examination in the section covering the relationship between debtors and creditors. Questions regarding suretyship have also been included in the contracts section as part of a Statute of Frauds question or a question concerning consideration. One common fact situation presented on the exam has involved a surety who is not paid for his or her suretyship. Consideration is usually present elsewhere in the question, however, and thus, its lack is not a defense for that surety. Another frequent scenario involves co-sureties—be certain that you grasp the rights of the parties in such circumstances.

★ Key Points

The **key points** in this chapter include:

1. The Chapter 7 requirements for bankruptcy.

2. The basic steps in the bankruptcy process.

3. Preferential transfers, competing claims, and discharge.

4. The purpose of a Chapter 11 reorganization.

5. Chapter 13 plans.

Chapter 30
Bankruptcy Law

WHAT THIS CHAPTER IS ABOUT

This chapter covers bankruptcy law. Congressional authority to regulate bankruptcies comes from Article I, Section 8, of the U.S. Constitution. Current law is based on the Bankruptcy Reform Act of 1978 (the Code).

CHAPTER OUTLINE

I. BANKRUPTCY RELIEF

Bankruptcy law (1) protects a debtor by giving him or her a fresh start and (2) ensures equitable treatment to creditors competing for a debtor's assets. Bankruptcy proceedings are held in federal bankruptcy courts. Current law is based on the Bankruptcy Reform Act of 1978 (the Bankruptcy Code). Relief can be granted under the Code's Chapter 7, Chapter 11, Chapter 12, or Chapter 13.

II. LIQUIDATION PROCEEDINGS (CHAPTER 7)

This is the most familiar type of bankruptcy proceeding. A debtor declares his or her debts and gives all assets to a trustee, who sells the nonexempt assets and distributes the proceeds to creditors.

A. WHO CAN FILE FOR A LIQUIDATION

Any "person"—individuals, partnerships, and corporations (spouses can file jointly)—except railroads, insurance companies, banks, savings and loan associations, and credit unions.

B. FILING THE PETITION

1. Voluntary Bankruptcy

a. The Debtor Files a Petition with the Court
The petition includes schedules (lists) of (1) creditors and the debt to each, (2) the debtor's financial affairs, (3) the debtor's property, and (4) current income and expenses.

b. Filing of the Petition Constitutes an Order for Relief
The clerk of the court must give the trustee and creditors notice of the order within not more than twenty days.

    c. **Substantial Abuse**

A court can dismiss a petition if granting it would constitute substantial abuse (if the debtor seeks only an advantage over creditors and his or her financial situation does not warrant a discharge of debts) [11 U.S.C. Section 707(b)].

  2. **Involuntary Bankruptcy**

A debtor's creditors can force the debtor into bankruptcy proceedings.

    a. **Who Can Be Forced into Involuntary Proceedings**

A debtor with twelve or more creditors, three or more of whom (with unsecured claims of at least $10,775) file a petition. A debtor with fewer than twelve creditors, one or more of whom (with a claim of $10,775) files. Not a farmer or a charitable institution.

    b. **When an Order for Relief Will Be Entered**

If the debtor does not challenge the petition, the debtor is generally not paying debts as they come due, or a receiver, assignee, or custodian took possession of the debtor's property within 120 days before the petition was filed.

C. AUTOMATIC STAY

When a petition is filed, an **automatic stay** suspends all action by creditors against the debtor. The **adequate protection doctrine** protects secured creditors by requiring payments, or other collateral or relief, to the extent that the stay may cause the value of their collateral to decrease.

D. PROPERTY OF THE ESTATE

  1. **What Property Is Included in the Debtor's Estate**

Interests in property presently held; community property; property transferred in a transaction voidable by the trustee; proceeds and profits; after-acquired property; interests in gifts, inheritances, property settlements, and life insurance death proceeds to which the debtor becomes entitled within 180 days after filing.

  2. **What Property Is Not Included**

Property acquired after the filing of the petition except as noted above.

E. CREDITORS' MEETING AND CLAIMS

Within "not less than ten days or more than thirty days," the court calls a meeting of creditors, at which the debtor answers questions. Within ninety days of the meeting, a creditor must file a proof of claim. The proof lists the creditor's name and address, as well as the amount of the debt.

F. EXEMPTIONS

  1. **Federal Law**

Exempts such property as interests in a residence to $16,150, a motor vehicle to $2,575, household goods to $8,625, and tools of a trade to $1,625, and the rights to receive Social Security and other benefits.

  2. **State Law**

Most states preclude the use of federal exemptions; others allow a debtor to choose between state and federal. State exemptions may include different value limitations and exempt different property.

G. THE TRUSTEE

After the order for relief, an interim trustee is appointed to preside over the debtor's property until the first meeting of creditors, when a permanent trustee is elected. A trustee's duty is to collect and reduce to money the property of the estate and distribute the proceeds.

1. Trustee's Powers

A trustee has the same rights as (1) a lien creditor with priority over an unperfected secured party and (2) a bona fide purchaser of real property from the debtor.

2. Voidable Rights

Any reason that a debtor can use to obtain the return of his or her property can be used by the trustee (fraud, duress, etc.)

3. Preferences

A trustee can recover payments made by a debtor (1) within ninety days before the petition and (2) for a preexisting debt.

a. Insiders or Fraud

If a creditor is an insider (partner, corporate officer, relative) or a transfer is fraudulent, a trustee may recover transfers made within one year before filing.

b. Transfers That Are Not Preferences

Payment for services rendered within ten to fifteen days before the payment; payment received in the ordinary course of business (such as payment of a phone bill); transfer of property up to $600; property sold to an innocent third party.

4. Liens on Debtor's Property

A trustee can avoid statutory liens that first became effective when the bankruptcy petition was filed or the debtor became insolvent, and any lien against a bona fide purchaser that was not enforceable on the date of the filing.

5. Fraudulent Transfers

A trustee can avoid fraudulent transfers made within one year of the filing of the petition or if they were made with the intent to delay, defraud, or hinder a creditor. Transfers for less than reasonably equivalent consideration may also be avoided if, by making them, the debtor became insolvent or was left in business with little capital.

H. DISTRIBUTION OF PROPERTY

1. Secured Creditors

Within thirty days of the petition or before the first creditors' meeting (whichever is first), a debtor must state whether he or she will retain secured collateral (or claim it as exempt, etc.). The trustee must enforce the statement within forty-five days. If the collateral does not cover the debt, the secured creditor is an unsecured creditor for the difference.

2. Unsecured Creditors

Paid in the order of priority. Each class is paid before the next class is entitled to anything. The order of priority is—

a. Administrative expenses (court costs, trustee and attorney fees).

   b. In an involuntary bankruptcy, expenses incurred by the debtor in the ordinary course of business from the filing of the petition to the appointment of the trustee or the issuance of an order for relief.

   c. Unpaid wages, salaries, and commissions earned within ninety days of the petition, to $4,300 per claimant. A claim in excess is a claim of a general creditor (no. i below).

   d. Unsecured claims for contributions to employee benefit plans, limited to services performed within 180 days before the petition and $4,300 per employee.

   e. Claims by farmers and fishers, to $4,300, against storage or processing facilities.

   f. Consumer deposits to $1,950 given to the debtor before the petition to buy, lease, or rent property or services that were not received.

   g. Claims for paternity, alimony, maintenance, and support.

   h. Taxes and penalties due to the government.

   i. Claims of general creditors.

   3. Debtors
   Any amount remaining is turned over to the debtor.

I. DISCHARGE
A discharge voids any judgment on a discharged debt and prohibits any action to collect a discharged debt. A co-debtor's liability is not affected.

   1. Exceptions—Debts That May Not Be Discharged
   Claims for back taxes, amounts borrowed to pay back taxes, goods obtained by fraud, debts that were not listed in the petition, alimony, child support, student loans, certain cash advances, and others.

   2. Objections—Debtors Who May Not Receive a Discharge
   Those who conceal property with the intent to hinder, delay, or defraud a creditor; who fail to explain a loss of assets; or who have been granted a discharge within six years of the filing of the petition.

   3. Revocation of Discharge
   A discharge may be revoked within one year if the debtor was fraudulent or dishonest during the bankruptcy proceedings.

J. REAFFIRMATION OF DEBT
A debtor's agreement to pay an otherwise dischargeable debt must be made before a discharge is granted and must usually be approved by the court. Can be rescinded within sixty days or before the discharge is granted.

III. REORGANIZATIONS (CHAPTER 11)
The creditors and debtor formulate a plan under which the debtor pays a portion of the debts, is discharged of the rest, and continues in business.

A. WHO IS ELIGIBLE FOR RELIEF UNDER CHAPTER 11
Any debtor (except a stockbroker or a commodities broker) who is eligible for Chapter 7 relief. Used most commonly by corporate debtors. The same principles apply that govern liquidation (automatic stay, etc.).

B. WHY A CASE MAY BE DISMISSED
Creditors may prefer a **workout** (a privately negotiated settlement) to bankruptcy proceedings, or there may be other reasons (inability to effect a plan, unreasonable delay by the debtor that is prejudicial to creditors, etc.).

C. DEBTOR IN POSSESSION

On entry of an order for relief, the debtor continues to operate his or her business as a debtor in possession (DIP).

1. If Gross Mismanagement Is Shown

The court may appoint a trustee (or receiver) to operate the business. This may also be done if it is in the best interests of the estate.

2. DIP's Role Is Similar to That of a Trustee in a Liquidation

The DIP can avoid pre-petition preferential payments and fraudulent transfers and decide whether to cancel pre-petition executory contracts.

3. Strong-Arm Clause

A DIP can avoid any obligation or transfer that could be avoided by (1) a creditor who extended credit at the time of bankruptcy and who consequently obtained (a) a lien or (b) a writ of execution that was returned unsatisfied; and (2) a bona fide purchaser of real property, if the transfer was perfected at the time of the bankruptcy.

D. COLLECTIVE BARGAINING AGREEMENTS

Can be rejected if the debtor first proposes modifications to the union and the union fails to adopt them without good cause. The debtor must (1) provide the union with information needed to evaluate the proposal and (2) confer in good faith to attempt a mutually satisfactory agreement.

E. CREDITORS' COMMITTEES

A committee of unsecured creditors is appointed to consult with the trustee or DIP. Other committees may represent special-interest creditors. Some small businesses can avoid creditors' committees.

F. THE REORGANIZATION PLAN

1. What the Plan Must Do

Conserve and administer the debtor's assets in the hope of a return to solvency; be fair and equitable ("in the best interests of the creditors"); designate classes of claims and interests; specify the treatment to be afforded the classes; and provide an adequate means for execution.

2. Who Can File a Plan

Only debtor within the first 120 days (100 days in some cases) after date of the order for relief. Any other party, if debtor does not meet the deadline or fails to obtain creditor consent within 180 days (or 160 days).

3. The Plan Is Submitted to Creditors for Acceptance

Each class adversely affected by a plan must accept it (two-thirds of the total claims must approve). If only one class accepts, the court may confirm it if it "does not discriminate unfairly" against any creditors. The plan is binding on confirmation—the debtor is given a discharge from all claims not within the plan (except those that would be denied in a liquidation).

IV. INDIVIDUALS' REPAYMENT PLANS (CHAPTER 13)

A. WHO IS ELIGIBLE

Individuals (not partnerships or corporations) with regular income and unsecured debts of less than $269,000 or secured debts of less than $807,750.

B. VOLUNTARY FILING ONLY

A Chapter 13 case can be initiated by the filing of a voluntary petition only. A trustee is appointed.

C. AUTOMATIC STAY

On the filing of a petition, an automatic stay enjoins creditors from taking action against co-obligors of the debtor. If a creditor asks to vacate the stay against a co-debtor, unless written objection is filed, twenty days later the stay against the co-debtor is automatically terminated without a hearing.

D. THE REPAYMENT PLAN

The plan must provide for (1) turnover to the trustee of the debtor's future income, (2) full payment of all claims entitled to priority, and (3) the same treatment of each claim within a particular class.

1. Filing and Confirming the Plan

Only the debtor can file a plan, which the court will confirm if (1) the secured creditors accept it, (2) it provides that creditors retain their liens and the value of the property to be distributed to them is not less than the secured portion of their claims, or (3) the debtor surrenders the property securing the claim to the creditors.

2. Payments under the Plan

The time for payment must be less than three years (five years, with court approval). The payments must be timely, or the court can convert the case to a liquidation or dismiss the petition. Before completion of payments, the plan may be modified at the request of the debtor, the trustee, or an unsecured creditor.

3. Objection to the Plan

Over the objection of the trustee or an unsecured creditor, the court may approve a plan only if (1) the value of the property to be distributed is equal to the amount of the claims, or (2) all the debtor's disposable income during the plan will be used to make payments.

E. DISCHARGE

After completion of all payments, all debts provided for by the plan are discharged. A discharge obtained by fraud can be revoked within one year.

V. FAMILY-FARMER PLANS (CHAPTER 12)

Chapter 12 is nearly identical to Chapter 13. Eligible debtors include a family farmer whose gross income is at least 50 percent farm dependent and whose debts are at least 80 percent farm related (total debt must not exceed $1.5 million), and a partnership or closely held corporation (at least 50 percent owned by a farm family).

TRUE-FALSE QUESTIONS

(Answers at the Back of the Book)

____ 1. A debtor must be insolvent to file a voluntary petition under Chapter 7.

____ 2. Debtors are protected from losing the value of their property as a result of the automatic stay.

    3. In a bankruptcy proceeding, any creditor's claim is allowed automatically unless contested by the trustee, the debtor, or another creditor.

    4. The same principles cover the filing of a Chapter 7 petition and a Chapter 11 proceeding.

    5. A bankruptcy may be commenced by involuntary petition under Chapter 13.

    6. Secured creditors lose the value of their security as a result of the automatic stay in a bankruptcy proceeding.

    7. Under Chapter 13, a discharge obtained by fraud can be revoked within one year.

    8. In a bankruptcy proceeding under Chapter 11, a debtor can continue to operate his or her business as a debtor in possession.

    9. No small business can avoid creditors' committees under Chapter 11.

    10. Bankruptcy proceedings are held in federal bankruptcy courts.

FILL-IN QUESTIONS

(Answers at the Back of the Book)

Liquidation is the purpose of Chapter [C01]_____ (7/11/13). Reorganization is the purpose of Chapter [C01]_____ (7/11/13). Adjustment is the purpose of Chapter [C01]_____ (7/11/13). Under Chapter [C02]_____ (7/11/13), nonexempt property is sold, with proceeds distributed in a certain priority to classes of creditors, and dischargeable debts are terminated. Under Chapter [C03]_____ (7/11/13), a plan for reorganization is submitted, and if it is approved and followed, debts are discharged. Under Chapter [C04D01E02F03]_____ (7/11/13), a plan must be approved if the debtor turns over all disposable income for a three-year period, after which debts are discharged. The advantages of Chapter [C02D08]_____ (7/11/13) include the debtor's opportunity for a fresh start. The advantages of Chapter [C03]_____ (7/11/13) include the debtor's continuation in business under a plan that allows for reorganization of debts. The advantages of Chapter [C04D01E03]_____ (7/11/13) include "super-discharge," which allows the discharge of fraudulently incurred debt and claims resulting from malicious or willful injury.

MULTIPLE-CHOICE QUESTIONS

(Answers at the Back of the Book)

    1. Ted is the sole proprietor of Duncan's Restaurant, which owes secured debts of $225,000 and unsecured debts of $75,000. The amount is more than Ted believes he and the restaurant can reasonably repay. Most of Duncan's creditors agree that liquidating Ted and the restaurant would not be in their best interests. To stay in business, Ted could file for bankruptcy under

a. Chapter 7 only.
b. Chapter 11 only.
c. Chapter 13 only.
d. Chapter 11 or Chapter 13.

____ **2.** Jerry's monthly income is $2,500, his monthly expenses are $2,100, and his debts are nearly $15,000. If he applied the difference between his income and expenses to pay off the debts, they could be eliminated within three years. The provision in the Bankruptcy Code that covers this sort of plan is

a. Chapter 7.
b. Chapter 11.
c. Chapter 12.
d. Chapter 13.

____ **3.** General Supplies Corporation (GSC) has not paid any of its fifteen creditors, six of whom have unsecured claims of more than $8,000. Under which chapter of the Bankruptcy Code can they force GSC into bankruptcy?

a. Chapter 7 only
b. Chapter 11 only
c. Chapter 13 only
d. Chapter 7 or Chapter 11

____ **4.** Dick pays for college by taking out student loans. After graduation, he marries and works briefly before divorcing and filing for Chapter 7 bankruptcy. Dick's only debts are student loans and alimony. The debts that can be discharged in the bankruptcy are

a. the alimony only.
b. the student loans only.
c. both the alimony and the student loans.
d. none of the above.

____ **5.** Jill's monthly income is $2,000, her monthly expenses are $2,800, and her debts are nearly $40,000. To obtain a fresh start, Jill could file for bankruptcy under

a. Chapter 7.
b. Chapter 11.
c. Chapter 12.
d. Chapter 13.

____ **6. Based on a Sample CPA Exam Question.** Pat files a Chapter 7 petition for a discharge in bankruptcy. Pat may be denied a discharge if Pat

a. fails to explain a loss of assets.
b. fails to list a debt.
c. owes back taxes.
d. owes child support payments.

____ **7.** Donna and Tom make down payments on goods to be received from Eagle Furniture Store. Before the goods are delivered, Eagle files for bankruptcy. Besides consumers like Donna and Tom, Eagle owes wages to its employees and taxes to the government. In what order will these debts be paid?

a. Unpaid wages, consumer deposits, taxes
b. Taxes, consumer deposits, unpaid wages
c. Consumer deposits, unpaid wages, taxes
d. Unpaid wages, taxes, consumer deposits

____ 8. Jan is appointed trustee of Bill's estate in bankruptcy. To collect the property of Bill's estate, Jan can set aside which of the following transfers?

    a. A transfer made within ninety days of the filing of the petition in preference to one creditor over others
    b. A payment within the ordinary course of business
    c. Both a and b
    d. None of the above

____ 9. National Stores, Inc., decides to file for bankruptcy. Under which chapter of the Bankruptcy Code can a corporation file a petition for bankruptcy?

    a. Chapter 7 only
    b. Chapter 11 only
    c. Chapter 13 only
    d. Chapter 7 or Chapter 11

____ 10. A bankruptcy trustee has the power to avoid

    a. preferences.
    b. fraudulent transfers.
    c. transactions that the debtor could rightfully avoid, or cancel.
    d. all of the above.

SHORT ESSAY QUESTIONS

1. Compare Chapters 7, 11, 12, and 13, discussing, for each chapter, the purpose or function, who is eligible for relief, whether proceedings can be initiated voluntarily or involuntarily, procedures leading to discharge, and the advantages.

2. How are secured creditors protected from losing the value of their security as a result of an automatic stay?

ISSUE SPOTTERS

(Answers at the Back of the Book)

1. Northwest Company's creditors include First National Bank with a perfected security interest in Northwest's building and equipment, Trager Construction with a mechanic's lien on the building that predates First National's security interest, and Universal Supplies, Inc., with an unperfected security interest. Northwest files a petition for Chapter 7 liquidation. In what order are the creditors entitled to be paid?

2. Adam is a vice president for Beta Company. On May 1, Adam loans Beta $10,000. On June 1, the company repays the loan. On July 1, Beta files for bankruptcy. Carl is appointed trustee. Can Carl recover the $10,000 paid to Adam on June 1?

3. Jan is a farmer. Her debts are 90 percent farm-related. They total $1 million, and Jan believes that bankruptcy is the only alternative for discharging them. Jan does not want to lose the farm, however, and most of her creditors agree that liquidation would not serve their best interests. Is there a proceeding under the bankruptcy laws through which she can retain the farm and the creditors can have some of the debt repaid?

4. Al's Retail Store is a sole proprietorship. Smith & Jones is an advertising partnership. Roth & Associates, Inc., is a professional corporation. First State Savings

& Loan is a savings and loan corporation. Which of these is not eligible for reorganization under Chapter 11?

5.   After graduating from college, Tina works briefly as a salesperson before filing for bankruptcy. As part of her petition, Tina reveals her only debts as student loans, taxes accruing within the last year, and a claim against her based on misuse of customers' funds during her employment. Are these debts dischargeable in bankruptcy?

SPECIAL INFORMATION FOR CPA CANDIDATES

On the CPA examination, bankruptcy is tested as part of the section on creditors and debtors, which also tests on the material in the previous chapter. Topics that have been tested in the past include the requirements for filing for bankruptcy under Chapter 7, the basic steps of a bankruptcy, a general knowledge of Chapter 11 and Chapter 13, and specific coverage of preferential transfers, discharge, and debts that are not discharged in a bankruptcy proceeding. The priority of those with competing claims to the collateral is also usually included in questions on the exam.

CUMULATIVE HYPOTHETICAL PROBLEM FOR UNIT FIVE—INCLUDING CHAPTERS 28–30

(Answers at the Back of the Book)

Omega Computers, Inc., sells computers to consumers.

____   1.   Alan fixes the roof of Omega's office building, but Omega does not pay. Bob fixes one of Omega's trucks, but Omega does not pay. Bob does not return the truck to Omega. Alan and Bob place a mechanic's lien and an artisan's lien on Omega's property. Before foreclosure, notice must be given to Omega by

a.   Alan only.
b.   Bob only.
c.   Alan and Bob.
d.   none of the above.

____   2.   In the course of business, Omega borrows money from First National Bank. The loan is cosigned by Carl as a surety. Omega defaults on the loan, and Carl pays the entire amount. To collect from Omega, Carl has the right of

a.   contribution.
b.   exemption.
c.   exoneration.
d.   subrogation.

____   3.   Omega buys inventory from Beta Digital Products. Beta finances the purchase, accepts the inventory as security, and perfects its interest. Under UCC Article 9, perfection of a security interest will *not* affect the rights of

a.   a buyer in the ordinary course of business.
b.   a subsequent secured creditor.
c.   the trustee in Omega's bankruptcy.
d.   all of the above.

____ **4.** Omega files a voluntary petition in bankruptcy under Chapter 11. A reorganization plan is filed with the court. Normally, the court will confirm a Chapter 11 plan if it is accepted by

a. Omega.
b. Omega's secured creditors.
c. Omega's shareholders.
d. Omega's unsecured creditors.

____ **5.** Omega's Chapter 11 plan is confirmed, and a final decree is entered. Omega will

a. be discharged from all debts except as otherwise provided by the law.
b. be liquidated.
c. be operated in business by the bankruptcy trustee.
d. not be allowed to continue in the same business.

Chapter 31
Agency Formation and Duties

WHAT THIS CHAPTER IS ABOUT

This chapter covers some of the aspects of agency relationships, including how they are formed and the duties involved. An agency relationship involves two parties: the principal and the agent. Agency relationships are essential to a corporation, which can function and enter into contracts only through its agents.

CHAPTER OUTLINE

I. AGENCY RELATIONSHIPS
In an agency relationship, the parties agree that the agent will act on behalf and instead of the principal in negotiating and transacting business with third persons.

A. EMPLOYER-EMPLOYEE RELATIONSHIPS
Normally, all employees who deal with third parties are deemed to be agents. Statutes covering workers' compensation and so on apply only to employer-employee relationships.

B. EMPLOYER–INDEPENDENT CONTRACTOR RELATIONSHIPS
Those who hire independent contractors have no control over the details of their physical performance. Independent contractors can be agents.

C. CRITERIA FOR DETERMINING EMPLOYEE STATUS
The greater an employer's control over the work, the more likely it is that the worker is an employee. Another key factor is whether the employer withholds taxes from payments to the worker and pays unemployment and Social Security taxes covering the worker.

II. FORMATION OF THE AGENCY RELATIONSHIP
Consideration is not required. A principal must have capacity to contract, but anyone can be an agent. An agency can be created for any legal purpose.

A. AGENCY BY AGREEMENT

Normally, an agency must be based on an agreement that the agent will act for the principal. Such an agreement can be an express written contract or can be implied by conduct.

B. AGENCY BY RATIFICATION

A person who is not an agent (or who is an agent acting outside the scope of his or her authority) may make a contract on behalf of another (a principal). If the principal approves or affirms that contract by word or by action, an agency relationship is created by ratification (see Chapter 32).

C. AGENCY BY ESTOPPEL

1. The Principal's Actions

When a principal causes a third person to believe that another person is his or her agent, and the third person deals with the supposed agent, the principal is estopped to deny the agency relationship.

2. The Third Party's Reasonable Belief

The third person must prove that he or she reasonably believed that an agency relationship existed and that the agent had authority—that an ordinary, prudent person familiar with business practice and custom would have been justified in concluding that the agent had authority.

D. AGENCY BY OPERATION OF LAW

A court may find an agency relationship in the absence of a formal agreement. This may occur in family relationships or in an emergency, when the agent's failure to act outside the scope of his or her authority would cause the principal substantial loss.

III. DUTIES OF AGENTS AND PRINCIPALS

The principal-agent relationship is fiduciary.

A. AGENT'S DUTIES TO PRINCIPAL

1. Performance

An agent must use reasonable diligence and skill (the degree of skill of a reasonable person under similar circumstances), unless an agent claims special skills (such as those of an accountant), in which case the agent is expected to use those skills.

2. Notification

An agent must notify the principal of all matters concerning the agency. Notice to the agent is considered to be notice to the principal.

3. Loyalty

An agent must act solely for the benefit of the principal (not in the interest of the agent or a third party).

a. Confidentiality

Any information or knowledge acquired through the agency relationship is confidential. It cannot be disclosed during the agency or after its termination.

  b. Agent's Loyalty Must Be Undivided
  An agent employed by a principal to buy cannot buy from himself or herself, and an agent employed to sell cannot become the purchaser, without the principal's consent.

 4. Obedience
 When an agent acts on behalf of the principal, the agent must follow all lawful instructions of the principal. Exceptions include emergencies and instances in which instructions are not clearly stated.

 5. Accounting
 An agent must keep and make available to the principal an account of everything received and paid out on behalf of the principal. An agent must keep separate accounts for the principal's funds.

B. PRINCIPAL'S DUTIES TO AGENT

 1. Compensation
 A principal must pay an agent for services rendered (unless the agent does not act for money). Payment must be timely. If no amount has been agreed to, the principal owes the customary amount for such services.

 2. Reimbursement and Indemnification
 A principal must (1) reimburse the agent for money paid at the principal's request or for necessary expenses and (2) indemnify an agent for liability incurred because of authorized acts.

 3. Cooperation
 A principal must cooperate with and assist an agent in performing his or her duties. The principal must do nothing to prevent performance.

 4. Safe Working Conditions
 A principal must provide safe working conditions.

IV. REMEDIES AND RIGHTS OF AGENTS AND PRINCIPALS

If one party violates his or her duty to the other, remedies available to the party not in breach arise out of contract and tort law, and include damages, termination of the agency, injunction, and accounting.

A. AGENT'S RIGHTS AND REMEDIES AGAINST PRINCIPAL

For every duty of the principal, an agent has a corresponding right. Breach of a duty by the principal follows normal contract and tort remedies. If the relation is not contractual, an agent has no right to specific performance (but can recover for past services and future damages).

B. PRINCIPAL'S RIGHTS AND REMEDIES AGAINST AGENT

 1. Constructive Trust
 A court imposes a constructive trust if an agent retains benefits or profits that belong to the principal or takes advantage of the agency to obtain property the principal wants to buy. The court declares that the agent holds money or property on behalf of the principal.

 2. Avoidance
 If an agent breaches an agency agreement under a contract, the principal has a right to avoid any contract entered into with the agent.

 3. Indemnification
 A principal can be sued by a third party for an agent's negligence, and in certain situations the principal can sue the agent. The same is true if the agent violates the principal's instructions.

TRUE-FALSE QUESTIONS

(Answers at the Back of the Book)

____ 1. An agent can perform legal acts that bind the principal.

____ 2. An agency relationship is established when an agent agrees to act for a principal and the principal agrees to have the agent act for him or her.

____ 3. An agency relationship is fiduciary.

____ 4. The key feature of an employer–employee relationship is that employees have independent business discretion.

____ 5. In most states, a minor can be a principal but not an agent.

____ 6. Unless the parties agree otherwise, a principal must pay for an agent's services.

____ 7. A principal can never avoid a contract entered into with an agent.

____ 8. A principal cannot be sued by a third party for an agent's negligence.

____ 9. An agent must keep separate accounts for the principal's funds.

____ 10. Information obtained through an agency relationship is confidential.

FILL-IN QUESTIONS

(Answers at the Back of the Book)

An agent's use of reasonable diligence and skill is part of the agent's duty of _____ (obedience/performance). Informing a principal of all material matters that come to the agent's attention concerning the subject matter of the agency is an aspect of the agent's duty of _____ (accounting/notification). Acting solely for the benefit of the principal and not in the interest of the agent or a third party is part of the agent's duty of _____ (loyalty/performance). Following all lawful and clearly stated instructions of the principal is an aspect of the agent's duty of _____ (loyalty/obedience). If an agent is required to keep and make available to the principal a record of all property and money received and paid out on behalf of the principal, this is part of the agent's duty of _____ (accounting/notification).

MULTIPLE-CHOICE QUESTIONS

(Answers at the Back of the Book)

____ 1. National Supplies Company hires Linda and Brad as employees to deal with third-party purchasers and suppliers. Linda and Brad are

a. principals.
b. agents.
c. principals and agents.
d. none of the above.

____ 2. Baron Interiors, Inc., tells Jan, whose business is purchasing for others, to select and buy $200 worth of certain goods and ship them to Baron. Jan buys the goods from Adam's Store and ships them as directed, keeping an account for the expense in Baron's name. Baron and Jan

   a. have an agency relationship.
   b. do not have an agency relationship, because their agreement is not in writing.
   c. do not have an agency relationship, because Jan's business is buying for others.
   d. do not have an agency relationship, because Jan did not indicate that she was acting for Baron.

____ 3. **Based on a Sample CPA Question.** Doug agrees to act as an agent for Great Sales Corporation on a commission basis. The agreement does not call for Doug to pay expenses out of his commission. Great Sales is required to

   a. keep records, account to Doug, and pay Doug according to the agreement.
   b. reimburse Doug for all authorized expenses.
   c. both a and b.
   d. none of the above.

____ 4. EZ Sales Company hired Jill as a sales representative for six months at a salary of $5,000 per month, plus a commission of 10 percent of sales. In matters concerning EZ's business, Jill must act

   a. solely in EZ's interest.
   b. solely in Jill's interest.
   c. solely in the interest of the customers.
   d. none of the above

____ 5. Ryan agrees to buy a certain amount of goods from Desktop Suppliers, Inc. Ryan will pay for and sell the goods at prices set by Desktop, deposit 90 percent of the proceeds in an account for Desktop, and return unsold goods. Desktop will pay half of Ryan's expenses. Ryan is

   a. an agent.
   b. a principal.
   c. an agent and a principal.
   d. none of the above.

____ 6. Standard Services, Inc., and Donna wish to enter into an agency relationship for the purpose of buying computers for Standard's offices. This relationship requires

   a. a written agreement.
   b. consideration.
   c. both a and b.
   d. none of the above.

____ 7. Ann gives Bill the impression that Carol is Ann's agent, when in fact she is not. Bill deals with Carol as Ann's agent. Regarding any agency relationship, Ann

   a. can deny it.
   b. can deny it to the extent of any injury suffered by Bill.
   c. can deny it to the extent of any liability that might be imposed on Ann.
   d. cannot deny it.

____ **8.** Dave is an accountant hired by Eagle Equipment Corporation to act as its agent. In acting as an agent for Eagle, Dave is expected to use

a. reasonable diligence and skill.
b. the degree of skill of a reasonable person under similar circumstances.
c. the special skills he has as an accountant.
d. none of the above.

____ **9.** Mandy asks Bob, a real estate broker, to sell her land. Bob learns that the K.T. Mall Corporation is willing to pay a high price for the land. Without telling Mandy about K.T. Mall, Bob says that he will buy the land himself. Instead, Mandy sells the land to Ken. If Bob sues Mandy,

a. Bob will win, because Mandy breached her duty to Bob.
b. Bob will win, because he was never Mandy's agent.
c. Mandy will win, because Bob breached his duty to Mandy.
d. Mandy will win, because she was not Bob's principal.

____ **10.** While acting as an agent for American Transport Company, Kay negligently injures Lee in a traffic accident. In this situation, a lawsuit can be brought by

a. American against Kay only.
b. Lee against Kay only.
c. Lee against American and Kay only.
d. Lee against American and Kay, and American against Kay.

SHORT ESSAY QUESTIONS

1. What are the essential differences among the relationships of principal and agent, employer and employee, and employer and independent contractor? What are the factors that indicate whether an individual is an employee or an independent contractor?

2. What are the ways in which a principal–agent relationship can be formed?

ISSUE SPOTTERS

(Answers at the Back of the Book)

1. Kurt contracts with Dee to buy a certain horse for Dee, who asks Kurt not to reveal her identity. Kurt makes a deal with Country Stables, the owner of the horse, and gives Country a down payment. Dee fails to pay the rest of the price. Country sues Kurt for breach of contract. Can Dee be liable for whatever damages Kurt may have to pay?

2. Able Corporation wants to build a new mall on a specific tract of land. Able contracts with Sheila to buy the property. When Sheila learns of the difference between the price that Able is willing to pay and the price at which the owner is willing to sell, she wants to buy the land and sell it to Able herself. Can she do this?

3. Tom is a booking agent, who agrees with performers only to sign contracts with promoters, and others, on the performers' behalf. Adam is a truck driver for General Theatre Supplies Company (GTSC). Adam does exactly what GTSC tells him. Dian is a lighting technician who hires out on an *ad hoc* basis. Which of these is an employee? An independent contractor? An agent?

4. Mark agrees to act as Nora's agent for the purpose of investing Nora's money. Mark violates his duty to Nora by depositing the money in his own account and spending it. What remedies are available to Nora?

5.　Paula agrees to act as Rick's agent in settlement negotiations with an insurance company. Paula works out a profitable compromise for Rick, but deposits the company's payment in her own account and refuses to give it to Rick. Besides normal contract and tort relief, what remedy might a court impose for Rick?

SPECIAL INFORMATION FOR CPA CANDIDATES

The material covered in this and the next chapter is always included in the CPA examination. Thus, while the concepts are basic and relatively simple, they are nevertheless essential. Agency concepts are applied in questions in the context of principal-agent relationships, partnership law, and corporation law.

Among the points to keep in mind are the rights and duties of the principal and agent, the fiduciary nature of the relationship, and how an agency relationship is formed. Its formation does not need to be contractual, but if it is, it must meet the requirements of a contract.

Chapter 32

Liability to Third Parties and Termination

WHAT THIS CHAPTER IS ABOUT

This chapter deals with the liability of principals and agents to third parties in contract and tort and principals' liability to third parties for agents' torts. The chapter concludes with a section on the termination of agency relationships.

CHAPTER OUTLINE

I. SCOPE OF AN AGENT'S AUTHORITY

A principal's liability in a contract with a third party arises from the authority given the agent to enter contracts on the principal's behalf.

A. EXPRESS AUTHORITY

1. Equal Dignity Rule

In most states, if the contract being executed is or must be in writing, the agent's authority must also be in writing.

a. Exception—Executive Officer Doing Ordinary Business

A corporate executive doing ordinary business does not need written authority from the corporation.

b. Exception—Agent Acting in the Presence of the Principal

In this case, the agent does not need written authority.

2. Power of Attorney

A power of attorney can be special or general. An ordinary power terminates on the incapacity or death of the person giving it. A durable power is not affected by the principal's incapacity.

B. IMPLIED AUTHORITY

Conferred by custom, can be inferred from the position an agent occupies, or is implied as reasonably necessary to carry out express authority.

C. APPARENT AUTHORITY AND ESTOPPEL

An agent has apparent authority when a principal, by word or action, causes a third party reasonably to believe that an agent has authority, though the agent has no authority. The principal may be estopped from denying it if the third party changes position in reliance.

D. EMERGENCY POWERS

If an emergency demands action by the agent, but the agent is unable to communicate with the principal, the agent has emergency power.

E. RATIFICATION

A principal can ratify an unauthorized contract or act, if he or she is aware of all material facts. Ratification can be done expressly or impliedly (by accepting the benefits of a transaction). An entire transaction must be ratified; a principal cannot affirm only part.

1. Effect of Ratification Without Knowing All the Facts

If the third party acts in reliance to his or her detriment on the apparent ratification, the principal can repudiate but must reimburse the third party's costs.

2. Effect of Ratification

Ratification binds the principal to the agent's act and treats it as if it had been authorized from the outset.

3. Effect of No Ratification

There is no contract binding the principal; the third party's agreement with the agent is an unaccepted offer; the agent may be liable to the third party for misrepresenting his or her authority.

II. LIABILITY FOR CONTRACTS

Who is liable to third parties for contracts formed by an agent?

A. DEFINITIONS

1. Disclosed Principal

A principal whose identity is known by the third party when the contract is made.

2. Partially Disclosed Principal

A principal whose identity is not known by the third party, but the third party knows the agent is or may be acting for a principal when the contract is made.

3. Undisclosed Principal

A principal whose identity is totally unknown by the third party, who also does not know that the agent is acting in an agency capacity at the time of the contract.

B. IF AN AGENT ACTS WITHIN THE SCOPE OF HIS OR HER AUTHORITY

1. Disclosed Principal

If a principal's identity is known to a third party when an agent makes a contract, the principal is liable. The agent is not liable.

2. Partially Disclosed Principal

The principal is liable. In most states, the agent is also liable (but is entitled to indemnification by the principal).

3. Undisclosed Principal

The principal and the agent are liable. Exceptions—

    a. The principal was expressly excluded as a party in the contract.

    b. The contract is a negotiable instrument (check or note).

    c. The performance of the agent is personal to the contract.

    d. The third party would not have contracted with the principal had the third party known his or her identity, the agent or the principal knew this, and the third party rescinds the contract.

C. IF THE AGENT HAS NO AUTHORITY

The principal is not liable in contract to a third party. The agent is liable, for breach of the implied warranty of authority (not on breach of the contract), unless the third party knew the agent did not have authority.

III. LIABILITY FOR AGENT'S TORTS

An agent is liable to third parties for his or her torts. Is the principal also liable?

A. PRINCIPAL'S TORTIOUS CONDUCT

A principal may be liable for harm resulting from the principal's negligence or recklessness (giving improper instructions; authorizing the use of improper materials or tools; establishing improper rules; or failing to prevent others' tortious conduct while they are on the principal's property or using the principal's equipment, materials, or tools).

B. PRINCIPAL'S AUTHORIZATION OF AGENT'S TORTIOUS CONDUCT

A principal who authorizes an agent to commit a tortious act may be liable.

C. MISREPRESENTATION

1. Fraudulent Misrepresentation

If a principal has given an agent authority to make statements and the agent makes false claims, the principal is liable. If an agent appears to be acting within the scope of authority in taking advantage of a third party, the principal who placed the agent in that position is liable.

2. Innocent Misrepresentation

When a principal knows that an agent does not have all the facts but does not correct the agent's or the third party's impressions, the principal is liable.

D. THE DOCTRINE OF *RESPONDEAT SUPERIOR*

An employer is liable for harm caused (negligently or intentionally) to a third party by an employee acting within the scope of employment, without regard to the personal fault of the employer. This is known as **vicarious liability**.

1. Scope of Employment

    a. Factors

    In determining whether an act is within the scope of employment, a court considers—

    1) the time, place, and purpose of the act.

    2) whether the act was authorized by the employer.

    3) whether the act is one commonly performed by employees on behalf of their employers.

    4) whether the employer's interest was advanced by the act.

    5) whether the private interests of the employee were involved.

6) whether the employer furnished the means by which an injury was inflicted.

7) whether the employer had reason to know that the employee would do the act in question.

8) whether the act involved the commission of a serious crime.

b. Travel and Commuting

The travel of those whose jobs require it is considered within the scope of employment for the duration of the trip, including the return. An employee going to and from work or meals is usually considered outside the scope of employment.

2. Employer's Liability for Torts outside the Scope of Employment

An employer who knows or should know that an employee has a propensity for committing tortious acts is liable for the acts even if they are outside the scope of employment. Also, an employer is liable for permitting an employee to engage in reckless acts that can injure others.

3. Employee's Liability for His or Her Own Torts

An employee is liable for his or her own torts. An employee who commits a tort at the employer's direction can be liable with the employer, even if he or she was unaware of the wrongfulness of the act.

IV. LIABILITY FOR INDEPENDENT CONTRACTOR'S TORTS

An employer is not liable for physical harm caused to a third person by the tortious act of an independent contractor (except in cases of hazardous activities such as blasting operations, the transportation of highly volatile chemicals, and the use of poisonous gases, in which strict liability is imposed).

V. LIABILITY FOR AGENT'S CRIMES

A principal is not liable for an agent's crime, unless the principal participated. In some jurisdictions, a principal may be liable for an agent's violating, in the course and scope of employment, such regulations as those governing sanitation, prices, weights, and the sale of liquor.

VI. LIABILITY FOR SUBAGENT'S ACTS

If an agent is authorized to hire subagents for the principal (to perform simple, definite duties; when it is the business custom; or for unforeseen emergencies), the principal is liable for the acts of the subagents.

VII. TERMINATION OF AN AGENCY

A. TERMINATION BY ACT OF THE PARTIES

1. Lapse of Time

An agency agreement may specify the time period during which the agency relationship will exist. If so, the agency ends when that time expires. If no definite time is stated, an agency continues for a reasonable time and can be terminated at will by either party.

2. Purpose Achieved

An agent can be employed to accomplish a particular objective. If so, the agency automatically ends when the objective is accomplished.

3. Occurrence of a Specific Event

An agency can be created to terminate on the occurrence of a certain event. If so, the agency automatically ends when the event occurs.

4. **Mutual Agreement**
   Parties can cancel their agency by mutually agreeing to do so.

5. **Termination by One Party**
   Both parties have the *power* to terminate an agency, but they may not have the *right* and may therefore be liable for breach of contract.

   a. **Agency at Will—Principal Must Give Reasonable Notice**
      To allow the agent to recoup expenses and, in some cases, to make a normal profit.

   b. **Agency Coupled with an Interest—Irrevocable**
      This agency is created for the benefit of the agent, who acquires a beneficial interest in the subject matter, and thus it is not equitable to permit a principal to terminate at will. Also, it is not terminated by the death of either the principal or the agent.

   c. **Not an Agency Coupled with an Interest—May Be Revocable**
      An agency coupled with an interest should not be confused with an agency in which the agent derives only proceeds or profits (such as a commission) from the sale of the subject matter. This is revocable by the principal, subject to any contract between the parties.

B. **TERMINATION BY OPERATION OF LAW**

1. **Death or Insanity**
   Death or insanity of either party automatically and immediately ends an agency. Knowledge of the death is not required.

2. **Impossibility**
   When the specific subject matter of an agency is destroyed or lost, the agency terminates. When it is impossible for the agent to perform the agency lawfully because of a change in the law, the agency terminates.

3. **Changed Circumstances**
   When an event occurs that has such an unusual effect on the subject matter of the agency that the agent can reasonably infer that the principal will not want the agency to continue, the agency terminates.

4. **Bankruptcy**
   Bankruptcy of the principal or the agent usually terminates an agency. In some circumstances, as when the agent's financial status is irrelevant to the purpose of the agency, the agency relationship may continue.

5. **War**
   When the principal's country and the agent's country are at war with each other, the agency is terminated.

C. **NOTICE REQUIRED FOR TERMINATION**

1. **Notice Required**
   If the parties themselves terminate the agency, the principal must inform any third parties who know of the agency that it has ended.

   a. **Agent's Authority Continues**
      An agent's actual authority continues until the agent receives notice of termination. An agent's apparent authority continues until the third person is notified (from any source).

    b.   **What the Principal Must Do**
The principal is expected to notify directly any third person who the principal knows has dealt with the agent. For third persons who have heard about the agency but have not dealt with the agent, constructive notice is sufficient.

    c.   **Form of the Notice**
No particular form of notice is required unless the agent's authority is written, in which case it must be revoked in writing, and the writing must be shown to all who saw the written authority.

  2. **No Notice Required**
If an agency terminates by operation of law, there is no duty to notify third persons, unless the agent's authority is coupled with an interest.

TRUE-FALSE QUESTIONS

(Answers at the Back of the Book)

____   1.   A disclosed principal is liable to a third party for a contract made by an agent acting within the scope of authority.

____   2.   A principal whose agent commits a tort in the scope of his or her employment is not liable to persons injured.

____   3.   An employer is generally not expected to bear responsibility for an independent contractor's torts unless exceptionally hazardous activities are involved.

____   4.   An agent may be liable for a contract he or she enters into on behalf of an undisclosed principal.

____   5.   In an ordinary agency relationship, the agency terminates automatically on the death of the principal.

____   6.   An employer is liable for *any* harm caused to a third party by an employee acting within the scope of employment.

____   7.   Both parties to an agency have the right to terminate the agency at any time.

____   8.   The only way a principal can ratify a transaction is by a written statement.

____   9.   An agent is not liable for his or her own torts.

____ 10.   An employee may be liable for his or her own tort, even if it is committed within the scope of employment.

FILL-IN QUESTIONS

(Answers at the Back of the Book)

If an agent is authorized to hire subagents, the principal _____ (is/is not) liable for the subagents' acts. An agent who hires for _____ (a disclosed/an undisclosed) principal is responsible to the subagent in contract for such things as wages, but the _____ (disclosed/undisclosed) principal is generally liable for _____ (the subagent's crimes/tort injuries) under the doctrine of *respondeat superior*. An agent's unauthorized hiring of a subagent _____ (also results/generally does not result) in a legal relationship between principal and subagent.

MULTIPLE-CHOICE QUESTIONS

(Answers at the Back of the Book)

____ 1. Bass Corporation hires Ellen to manage one of its stores. Bass does not specify the extent, if any, of Ellen's authority to contract with third parties. The express authority that Bass gives Ellen to manage the store implies authority to do whatever

a. is customary to operate the business.
b. can be inferred from the manager's position.
c. both a and b.
d. none of the above.

____ 2. **Based on a Sample CPA Exam Question.** Kay acts within the scope of her authority to enter into a contract with First National Bank on behalf of Kay's undisclosed principal, Digital Engineering, Inc. Digital is

a. liable on the contract only if Digital ratifies the contract.
b. liable on the contract only if Digital's identity is later disclosed.
c. liable on the contract under the stated circumstances.
d. not liable on the contract.

____ 3. Security Guns & Ammo, Inc., directs its salespersons never to load a gun during a sale. Bert, a salesperson, loads a gun during a sale. The gun fires, negligently injuring Kathy, who is in the store. Security is

a. not liable, because Bert was not acting within the scope of employment.
b. not liable, because employers are not responsible for their employees' torts.
c. liable under the doctrine of *respondeat superior*.
d. liable under the doctrine of *res ipsa loquitur*.

____ 4. Ron orally engages Dian to act as his agent. During the agency, Ron knows that Dian deals with Mary. Ron also knows that Pete and Brad are aware of the agency but have not dealt with Dian. Ron decides to terminate the agency. Regarding notice of termination,

a. Dian need not be notified in writing.
b. Dian's actual authority terminates without notice to her of Ron's decision.
c. Dian's apparent authority terminates without notice to Mary.
d. Pete and Brad must be directly notified.

____ 5. Smith Petroleum, Inc., contracts to sell oil to Jones Petrochemicals, telling Jones that it is acting on behalf of "a rich Saudi Arabian who doesn't want his identity known." Smith signs the contract, "Smith, as agent only." In fact, Smith is acting on its own. If the contract is breached, Smith may

a. not be liable, because Smith signed the contract as an agent.
b. not be liable, unless Jones knew Smith did not have authority to act.
c. be liable, unless Jones knew Smith did not have authority to act.
d. be liable, because Smith signed the contract as an agent.

____ 6. Al is Eve's agent for the purpose of buying a certain parcel of land. Al learns that an adjacent parcel is for sale at a favorable price. Unable to contact Eve, Al buys the adjacent property on Eve's behalf. Eve can be liable if she contacts the property owner to

    a. ratify the contract.
    b. disapprove of the contract.
    c. disaffirm the contract.
    d. all of the above.

____ 7. In which of the following situations is the agency relationship terminated?

    a. Sam engages Taylor to sell Sam's car. Two years pass, during which Sam and Taylor do not communicate and the car is not sold.
    b. Tom, the owner of Home & Yard, Inc., decides to close the business and engages Ace Liquidators to sell the remaining inventory. Ace sells the inventory, after which Tom decides to go into a different business.
    c. Lee, the owner of Exotic Imports, engages Don to buy carvings to be imported from the Far East. Lee dies, effectively putting Exotic Imports out of business, but Don is not aware of the death.
    d. All of the above

____ 8. National Manufacturing, Inc., employs Mark as an assembly worker. While attempting, without National's knowledge, to steal a forklift from National's property, Mark has an accident, negligently injuring Pam. Who is liable to Pam?

    a. National only
    b. Mark only
    c. Both National and Mark
    d. None of the above

____ 9. Northwest Timber Company employs Tom to cut down specific trees. Tom mistakenly cuts down an unspecified tree, negligently injuring Carol. Who is liable to Carol?

    a. Northwest only
    b. Tom only
    c. Both Northwest and Tom
    d. None of the above

____ 10. Jill is employed by American Grocers to buy and install a computer system for American's distribution network. When the system is set up and running, the agency

    a. terminates automatically.
    b. terminates after fourteen days.
    c. continues for one year.
    d. continues indefinitely.

SHORT ESSAY QUESTIONS

1. Identify and describe the categories of authority by which an agent can bind a principal and a third party in contract.

2. What are some of the situations in which a principal is liable for an agent's torts?

ISSUE SPOTTERS

(Answers at the Back of the Book)

1. Marie, owner of the Consumer Goods Company, employs Rachel as an administrative assistant. In Marie's absence, and without authority, Rachel represents herself as Marie and signs a promissory note in Marie's name. Under what circumstance could Marie be liable on the note?

2. First Union Bank encourages its depositors to ask its advice concerning their investments. Ian, one of the bank's investment counselors, advises Bill to invest in Spectre Corporation, although Ian knows that Spectre's financial situation is precarious. If Bill loses money on the deal, can the bank be held liable?

3. The United Delivery Service employs Otis as a driver. One afternoon, United tells Otis to deliver a certain package within the hour. While making the delivery, to bypass a traffic jam, Otis recklessly drives onto the sidewalk, injuring Bea. Is United liable to Bea? Is Otis liable to Bea?

4. First State Bank employs Tim as an information clerk. Tim has authority only to answer customers' questions. During the bank's renovation, the bank temporarily puts Tim in a teller's window. Nora, a customer, believes that Tim is a teller and leaves a deposit with him. If Tim keeps the money, is the bank liable?

5. Jack hires Cathy to sell Jack's land. Before the land is sold, Cathy discovers that there is a rich vein of gold in a hill on the property. Can Cathy reasonably infer that under this circumstance Jack would not want to continue the agency to sell the property?

SPECIAL INFORMATION FOR CPA CANDIDATES

The CPA examination covers agency principles in three contexts: agency law, partnership law, and corporation law. The scope of an agent's authority is virtually certain to be part of the exam. In particular, an agent's implied authority and an agent's apparent authority are among the most common topics on the test. It is thus important to be clear about the differences between these two concepts of authority. Implied authority is derived from express authority. Apparent authority arises from what a principal tells or shows a third party. Apparent authority can result from as little as the title or position that a principal gives an agent.

Another important point to keep in mind when applying these principles to questions on the exam is the size and type of the business at issue—the manager of a large store normally has more authority than the employee of a small store. Also, while a principal is ordinarily liable for the unintentional torts of his or her employees, the principal is not ordinarily liable for an employee's crimes.

On the termination of an agency relationship—as on the termination of a partnership—remember that actual notice must be given to creditors, but constructive notice is sufficient for others.

CUMULATIVE HYPOTHETICAL PROBLEM FOR UNIT SIX—INCLUDING CHAPTERS 31–32

(Answers at the Back of the Book)

Delta Products, Inc., hired Erin as a sales representative for six months at a salary of $3,000 per month, plus a 10 percent commission.

____ **1.** To satisfy the legal elements of a principal and agent relationship, Delta's hiring of Erin requires

    a. a meeting of the minds and consent to act.
    b. a power of attorney.
    c. a written agreement.
    d. specified consideration.

____ **2.** As Delta's agent, Erin

    a. cannot be dismissed during the six-month period without cause.
    b. cannot enforce the agency unless it is in writing and signed by Delta.
    c. is an agent coupled with an interest.
    d. must act solely in Delta's interest in matters concerning Delta's business.

____ **3.** Erin enters into a contract with Gamma Sales Company in excess of Erin's authority. Erin disclosed Delta's identity. To ratify the contract,

    a. Delta must expressly communicate its intent to be bound.
    b. Delta must know the relevant facts concerning the deal.
    c. Erin must have had capacity to enter into the contract.
    d. the contract must be in Delta's best interest.

____ **4.** Erin enters into a contract with Omega Computers, Inc., within the scope of her authority but without disclosing Delta's identity. Delta repudiates the contract. Omega

    a. can hold either Delta or Erin liable on the contract.
    b. can obtain specific performance to force Delta to go through with the deal.
    c. cannot enforce the contract against Delta.
    d. cannot enforce the contract against Erin if she discloses Delta's identity.

____ **5.** Delta terminated its relationship with Erin and notified all of Erin's known customers. Alpha Company knew of Erin's representation but had never dealt with her and was not notified of the end of her relationship with Delta. Later, Alpha placed an order with Erin, purportedly to be received from Delta, and paid her for the goods, which were not delivered. In a suit against Delta to enforce the contract, Alpha will

    a. lose, because Delta is not liable for Erin's fraud.
    b. lose, because Erin did not have authority to enter into the contract.
    c. win, because as a principal, Delta is bound to its agents' actions.
    d. win, because Delta's notice did not terminate Erin's apparent authority.

Chapter 33
Sole Proprietorships and Partnerships

WHAT THIS CHAPTER IS ABOUT

This chapter outlines part of the law of partnerships. In the absence of express agreement, partnerships are governed by the Uniform Partnership Act (UPA). The Revised Uniform Partnership Act (RUPA) significantly changes some of the rules. Besides these statutes, agency concepts (see Chapters 31 and 32) apply.

CHAPTER OUTLINE

I. **SOLE PROPRIETORSHIPS**
The simplest form of business—the owner is the business.

    A. **ADVANTAGES**
The proprietor takes all the profits. Easier to start than other kinds of businesses (few legal forms involved); has more flexibility (proprietor is free to make all decisions); owner pays only personal income tax on profits.

    B. **DISADVANTAGES**
The proprietor has all the risk (unlimited liability for all debts); limited opportunity to raise capital; the business dissolves when the owner dies.

II. **THE LAW GOVERNING PARTNERSHIPS**
A partnerships arises from an agreement between two or more persons to carry on a business for profit. A partnership is governed by this agreement, the principles of agency law, and the Uniform Partnership Act (UPA) or the Revised Uniform Partnership Act (RUPA).

III. **DEFINITION OF PARTNERSHIP**

    A. **ELEMENTS OF A PARTNERSHIP**
"[A]n association of two or more persons to carry on as co-owners a business for profit" [UPA 6(1)]. There are three essential elements:

        1. A sharing of profits or losses.
        2. A joint ownership of the business.
        3. An equal right in the management of the business.

B. SHARING PROFITS IS NOT ENOUGH

Sharing profits from a business does not imply a partnership, if the profits were received as payment of a debt by installments or interest on a loan, wages of an employee, rent to a landlord, an annuity to a widow or representative of a deceased partner, or a sale of goodwill of a business or property [UPA 7(4)]. Sharing profits from the joint ownership of property is not enough to create a partnership [UPA 7(2), (3)].

IV. THE NATURE OF PARTNERSHIPS

A. PARTNERSHIP AS AN ENTITY

In many states, and under the UPA, the RUPA, and federal law, a partnership can be treated as an entity for certain purposes.

1. Legal Capacity

Some states (and federal courts, when a federal question is at issue) permit a partnership to sue and be sued in the firm name; others allow a partnership to be sued as an entity but not to sue others in its firm name (it must use the names of the individual partners).

2. Judgments

When a judgment is against a firm name, the liability is paid first out of partnership assets and then out of general partners' personal assets.

3. Marshaling Assets

Partnership creditors have first priority to the partnership's assets, and personal creditors of the individual partners have first priority to the individual assets of each partner.

4. Bankruptcy

In federal court, a bankruptcy in the firm name applies only to the partnership entity—it is not personal bankruptcy for the partners.

5. Conveyance of Property

A partnership can own property as an entity [UPA 8(3)] and can convey it without each individual partner's joining in the transaction.

B. AGGREGATE THEORY OF PARTNERSHIP

If a partnership is not regarded as a separate entity, it is treated as an aggregate of the individual partners.

V. PARTNERSHIP FORMATION

A partnership agreement generally states the intention to create a partnership, contribute capital, share profits and losses, and participate in management.

A. FORMALITIES

A partnership agreement can be oral, written, or implied by conduct. Some must be in writing under the Statute of Frauds (see Chapter 15). Partners can agree to any terms that are not illegal or contrary to public policy.

B. DURATION

1. Partnership for a Term

The agreement can specify the duration of the partnership in terms of a date or the completion of a particular project. Dissolution without all partners' consent before expiration is a breach of the agreement.

2. **Partnership at Will**
No duration is set; any partner can dissolve a partnership at any time.

C. CAPACITY

Any person having capacity to enter a contract can become a partner. Minors and mentally incompetent persons can avoid their partnership contracts (see Chapter 13). If a partner is adjudicated mentally incompetent during the partnership, dissolution can be decreed by a court.

D. A CORPORATION AS PARTNER

Many states (not the UPA) restrict the ability of corporations to become partners. In those states, courts sometimes validate such arrangements by characterizing them as joint ventures.

E. PARTNERSHIP BY ESTOPPEL

When parties who are not partners hold themselves out as partners and make representations that third persons rely on in dealing with them, liability is imposed on the alleged partner. A partner who consents to the misrepresentation is also liable to third persons who extend credit in good faith reliance [UPA 16] (but the partnership is not).

VI. PARTNERSHIP OPERATION

A. RIGHTS AMONG PARTNERS

1. **Management**

   a. **Ordinarily, the Majority Rules**
   "All partners have equal rights in the management and conduct of partnership business" [UPA 18(e)]. Each partner has one vote.

   b. **When Unanimous Consent Is Required**
   Unanimous consent is required to (1) alter the essential nature of the firm's business or capital structure; (2) admit new partners or enter a new business [UPA 18(g), (h)]; (3) assign property into a trust for the benefit of creditors; (4) dispose of the firm's goodwill; (5) confess judgment against the firm or submit firm claims to arbitration; (6) undertake any act that would make conduct of partnership business impossible [UPA 9(3)]; or (7) amend partnership articles.

2. **Interest in the Partnership**
   Unless the partners agree otherwise, profits and losses are shared equally [UPA 18(a)].

3. **Compensation**
   Doing partnership business is a partner's duty and not compensable. On the death of a partner, a surviving partner is entitled to compensation to wind up partnership affairs [UPA 18(f)].

4. **Inspection of Books**
   A partner has a right to complete information concerning the conduct of partnership business [UPA 20]. Partnership books must be kept at the principal business office [UPA 19].

5. **Accounting**
   A partner has a right to a formal accounting (1) on dissolution [UPA 22]; (2) when the partnership agreement provides for it; (3) when a partner

is wrongfully excluded from the business, the books, or both; (4) when a partner withholds profits or benefits belonging to the partnership; or (5) when circumstances "render it just and reasonable."

6. **Property Rights**
A partner has an interest in the partnership, a right in partnership property, and a right to participate in management [UPA 24].

    a. **Partner's Interest in the Firm**
    A personal asset consisting of a proportionate share of the profits [UPA 26] and a return of capital.   The interest can be assigned, and creditors can attach it by obtaining a charging order [UPA 28].

    b. **Partnership Property**
    A partner is co-owner with his or her partners of partnership property, holding it as a tenant in partnership [UPA 25(1)].

        1) **If a Partner Dies**
        Surviving partners, not the heirs of the deceased, have a right of survivorship to the property (they must account to the decedent's estate for the value [UPA 25(2)(d), (e)]).

        2) **Each Partner Has Equal Rights**
        Each partner can possess partnership property for business purposes or in satisfaction of firm debts, but cannot sell, assign, or deal with the property other than for partnership purposes [UPA 25(2)(a), (b)], without the consent of all of the partners.

B. **DUTIES AND POWERS OF PARTNERS**

1. **Fiduciary Duties**
Partners (1) must act in good faith for the benefit of the partnership, (2) cannot engage in independent competitive activities without the other partners' consent, and (3) must account to the partnership for profits or benefits derived in a partnership transaction [UPA 21].

2. **General Agency Powers**
Each partner is an agent of every other partner and of the partnership in carrying out partnership business [UPA 9(1)].

    a. **Authority of Partners**
    Agency concepts apply to partners' authority (see Chapter 32).

    b. **Scope of Implied Powers**
    Implied authority is determined by the character and scope of the partnership business and the customary nature of the business. Normally, partners exercise all implied powers reasonably necessary to carry on the business [UPA 11].

3. **Joint Liability**
In most states, partners are jointly liable for partnership debts and contracts [UPA 15(b)] (each partner is liable for the entire debt; if one pays, the partnership or the other partners must reimburse that partner [UPA 18(b)]). To bring a successful claim against the partnership, a plaintiff must name all the partners as defendants.

4. **Joint and Several Liability**

In some states, partners are jointly and severally liable for partnership debts and contracts [see RUPA 306]. In all states, partners are jointly and severally liable for torts and breaches of trust [UPA 15(a)] (a partner who commits a tort must reimburse the partnership for any damages it pays). To bring a successful claim, a plaintiff need not name all the partners as defendants—a judgment against one partner does not extinguish the others' liability.

5. **Liability of Incoming Partner**

A newly admitted partner is liable for partnership debts incurred before his or her admission only to the extent of his or her interest in the partnership [UPA 17].

VII. PARTNERSHIP TERMINATION

Termination is caused by any change in the relations of the partners that demonstrates unwillingness or inability to carry on partnership business [UPA 29]. To continue the business, a partner can organize a new partnership.

A. DISSOLUTION

Occurs when a partner ceases to be associated with the carrying on of the business. Dissolution terminates the right of a partnership to exist as a going concern, but the partnership exists long enough to wind up its affairs.

1. **Dissolution by Acts of the Partners**

    a. **Dissolution by Agreement**

    The partnership agreement can stipulate events that will dissolve the firm. Partners can agree to dissolve the partnership early.

    b. **Partner's Power to Withdraw**

    No person can be compelled to be a partner. Under the UPA, a partner's withdrawal dissolves the partnership. Under the RUPA, dissolution results only if the partnership must be liquidated, not if a partner only quits the business [RUPA 601, 701, 801].

    c. **Admission of a New Partner**

    Admitting a new partner (without the consent of the others) causes dissolution. If the remaining or new partners continue the business, a new partnership arises (taking on the debts of the old [UPA 41]).

    d. **Transfer of a Partner's Interest**

    A transfer of a partner's interest or a sale of the interest for the benefit of creditors [UPA 28] leads to judicial dissolution (see below).

2. **Dissolution by Operation of Law**

    a. **Death**

    The death of a partner dissolves the firm, even if the partnership agreement provides for carrying on the business. (The surviving partners can form a new partnership.) Under the RUPA, death is not an automatic ground for dissolution [RUPA 601].

    b. **Bankruptcy**

    Bankruptcy of a partner (or the firm) will dissolve a partnership.

c. **Illegality**
Dissolution is caused by (1) an event that makes it unlawful for the partnership to continue, unless the partners decide to change the nature of the business and continue, or (2) an event that makes it illegal for any partner to carry on.

3. **Dissolution by Judicial Decree**
A court can dissolve a partnership for a partner's mental incompetency, incapacity, or improper conduct; impracticality of the firm's business (if it can be run only at a loss); or other circumstances [UPA 32].

4. **Notice of Dissolution**
The intent to dissolve (or to withdraw) must be communicated to each partner. Unless the other partners have notice, a withdrawing partner will continue to be bound as a partner to all contracts created for the firm. Notice must also be given to all affected third persons. A third person who has extended credit to the partnership must receive actual notice. For others, constructive notice is sufficient.

B. **WINDING UP**
Involves collecting and preserving partnership assets, paying debts, and accounting to each partner for the value of his or her interest.

1. **No New Obligations**
Once dissolution has occurred and partners have been notified, they cannot create new obligations on behalf of the partnership. Their only authority is to complete transactions begun but not finished at the time of dissolution and to wind up the business of the partnership.

2. **Interest of a Partner Who Violates the Partnership Agreement**
The other partners can buy out the interest and continue the business.

3. **If Dissolution Is Caused by the Death of a Partner**
All partnership assets vest in the surviving partners, who must settle partnership affairs and account to the estate of the deceased for the value of his or her interest. The surviving partners are entitled to payment for their services in winding up and for any costs [UPA 18(f)].

C. **DISTRIBUTION OF ASSETS**

1. **UPA Distribution**
Priority for the distribution of a partnership's assets is [UPA 40(b)]: (1) payment to third party creditors; (2) refund of loans made to or for the firm by a partner; (3) return of capital contribution to a partner; and (4) distribution of the balance, if any, to partners proportionate to their shares in the profits.

2. **RUPA Distribution**
Partner creditors are included among creditors who take first priority [RUPA 808]. Capital contributions and profits or losses are then calculated together to determine the amounts that the partners receive or the amounts that they must pay.

3. **If the Partnership's Liabilities Are Greater Than Its Assets**
Partners bear losses (in the absence of a contrary agreement) in the same proportion in which they shared profits. If the firm is insolvent, part-

ners must still contribute their respective shares. If a partner does not contribute, the others must make the extra payments but have a **right of contribution** against whoever does not pay.

D. PARTNERSHIP BUY-SELL AGREEMENTS

1. UPA Buy-out
Partners may agree that one or more partners may buy out the others. The agreement may state who buys what, under what circumstances, and at what price, or that one or more partners will determine the value of the interest, and the others can decide whether to buy or sell.

2. RUPA Buy-out
If a partner's dissociation does not result in a dissolution of the partnership, a buy-out of the partner's interest is mandatory [RUPA 701] at basically the same price as he or she would get on dissolution.

TRUE-FALSE QUESTIONS

(Answers at the Back of the Book)

____ 1. In a sole proprietorship, the owner and the business are entirely separate.

____ 2. A partnership is an association of two or more persons to carry on, as co-owners, a business for profit.

____ 3. A partnership cannot exist unless a certificate of partnership is filed with a state.

____ 4. The sharing of profits from joint ownership of property is usually enough to create a partnership.

____ 5. A writing is always necessary to form a partnership.

____ 6. Unless a partnership agreement specifies otherwise, each partner has one vote in management matters.

____ 7. A partner is co-owner with his or her partners of partnership property.

____ 8. A partner can dissolve a partnership at any time without liability to the other partners for losses due to the termination.

____ 9. A partnership pays income tax on its profits.

____ 10. Partners pay income tax on the partnership's profits that are passed to them.

FILL-IN QUESTIONS

(Answers at the Back of the Book)

In most states, partners _____ (are/are not) subject to joint liability on partnership debts, contracts, and torts. Joint liability means that if a third party sues a partner on a partnership _____ (obligation/tort), the partner has the right to insist that the other partners be sued with him or her. If the third party does not sue all of the partners, those partners who are _____ (not sued/sued) cannot be required to pay a judgment. In that circumstance, the assets of the partnership _____ (can/cannot) be used to satisfy the judgment. The third party's release of one partner _____ (does not release/releases) the other partners. In most states, to bring a successful claim against a partnership on a debt or contract, a plaintiff _____ (may/must) name all the partners as defendants.

MULTIPLE-CHOICE QUESTIONS

(Answers at the Back of the Book)

____ 1. Dave and Paul agree to go into business together. They do not formally declare that their business has a specific form of organization. Dave and Paul's business is

   a. a proprietorship.
   b. a partnership.
   c. a sole proprietorship.
   d. none of the above.

____ 2. To obtain a contract with Dick, Cindy misrepresents that she is a partner with Karl. Karl overhears Cindy's misrepresentation, but says nothing to Dick. Cindy breaches the contract. Who is liable to Dick?

   a. Cindy only
   b. Karl only
   c. Cindy and Karl
   d. None of the above

____ 3. Greg, Kim, and Pete are partners in Northern Mines. Greg sells the ore extracted from the mines to Yukon Resources, Inc. Regarding the funds that Greg receives from Yukon for the ore, he

   a. must account for the funds to Yukon only.
   b. must account for the funds to Kim and Pete only.
   c. must account for the funds to Yukon, Kim, and Pete.
   d. is free to dispose of the funds in any manner.

____ 4. Mark owns M Carpets, a home furnishings store. He hires Lois as a salesperson, agreeing to pay her $8.50 per hour plus 10 percent of her sales. Mark and Lois are

   a. partners, because Lois receives a share of the store's profits.
   b. partners, because Lois is responsible for some of the store's sales.
   c. not partners, because Lois does not have an ownership interest or management right in the store.
   d. not partners, because Lois does not receive an equal share of the store's profits.

____ 5. **Based a Sample CPA Exam Question.** Alan, Bill, and Carol are partners in ABC Accountants. Dissolution would be caused by

   a. Alan joining another partnership.
   b. Bill's interest in the partnership being attached by a court.
   c. Carol being adjudicated bankrupt.
   d. any partner being sued by the other partners for an accounting.

____   **6.**   Nick and Laura are partners in Cafe Ole, a coffee shop. On the petition of one of the partners, a court could dissolve the partnership

    a. only if Nick or Laura becomes mentally incompetent.
    b. only if Nick or Laura engage in improper conduct.
    c. only if Cafe Ole can be run at a loss.
    d. under any circumstances that makes dissolution equitable.

____   **7.**   Don and Sue are partners in AAA Investments, a partnership. Don convinces Tim, a customer, to invest heavily in a nonexistent gold mine. Don absconds with Tim's money. If Tim sues Sue, Tim will

    a. win, because partners are jointly and severally liable.
    b. win, because partnership assets are available to pay the judgment.
    c. lose, because partners are not jointly and severally liable.
    d. lose, because only partnership assets are available to pay the judgment.

____   **8.**   Jack and Mary do business as J&M Marketing. In resolving a dispute over whether the business is a partnership, a court will normally look for all of the following EXCEPT

    a. sharing of profits or losses.
    b. joint ownership of the business.
    c. payment of wages to employees.
    d. equal rights in the management of the business.

____   **9.**   Lee and Mike do business as a partnership under the name Southern Investments. Southern

    a. cannot sue others in its own name.
    b. cannot collect judgments in its own name.
    c. is not a tax-paying entity for federal income tax purposes.
    d. cannot hold title to real property.

____   **10.**   April, Brady, and Carol are partners in an accounting firm. April tells Brady and Carol that effective immediately, she is quitting the firm. Later the same day, at Brady's insistence, Brady and Carol sign a contract with a supplier. The contract is binding on

    a. Brady only.
    b. Brady and Carol only.
    c. April, Brady, and Carol.
    d. none of the partners.

SHORT ESSAY QUESTIONS

1.   What are the rights held by partners in terms of management, interest in the partnership, compensation, inspection of books, accounting, and property rights?

2.   How do the concepts of joint liability, and joint and several liability relate to partnerships?

ISSUE SPOTTERS

(Answers at the Back of the Book)

1. Lon's Music leases space in the Mall of the Americas. As part of the rent, Lon pays the mall a percentage of its gross receipts. One of the elements of a partnership is the sharing of profits or losses from a business. Is the mall a partner in Lon's business? Is Lon a partner in the mall's business?

2. Logan and Murphy are partners in a computer peripherals operation. Logan dies. Logan's widow calls Murphy and says, "As Logan's heir, I'm entitled to take Logan's place as your partner." Murphy says, "No, you're not." Logan says, "Ok, then, as Logan's heir, I'm entitled to all the CD-ROM drives in the warehouse." Murphy says, "No, you're not. As Logan's heir, all you're entitled to is the *value* of Logan's interest in partnership property." Who's right?

3. Hal and Gretchen are partners in a delivery business. When business is slow, without Gretchen's knowledge, Hal leases out the delivery vehicles as moving vans. Because the vehicles would otherwise be sitting idle in a parking lot, can Hal keep the lease money or does Hal have to account to Gretchen?

4. Dave and Ira agree to become partners in an investment firm. Their written agreement states that the partnership dissolves on each being paid $1 million from partnership earnings. Ten years later, when the goal is reached, Dave and Ira decide that they want to continue the firm. Can they do so, despite what their agreement says?

5. Sam plans to open a sporting goods store, and to hire Gil and Art. Sam will invest only his own capital. He does not expect to make a profit for at least eighteen months and to make little profit for the first three years. He hopes to expand eventually. Which form of business organization would be most appropriate?

SPECIAL INFORMATION FOR CPA CANDIDATES

For the CPA exam, it is important to know the differences among the types of business organizations, including sole proprietorships and partnerships.

As of the time of this writing, the CPA examination tested candidates' knowledge of the UPA, not the RUPA. The UPA definition of *partnership* has frequently been on the exam. Remember that it represents an example of the aggregate theory (you may as well also review aspects of the entity theory). Keep in mind, too, that unless partners agree otherwise, they share profits, losses, and management rights equally, and that only surviving partners are entitled to a salary. Other important points include that partners are jointly and severally liable for torts committed by copartners carrying on the business but jointly liable for all partnership contracts.

For the CPA examination, an important point in the material in this chapter is the liability of partners to each other and to third parties—remember that every partner is an agent of the partnership and of the other partners. Review the liability of withdrawing partners and new partners.

Chapter 34 Corporations— Formation and Financing

WHAT THIS CHAPTER IS ABOUT

This chapter covers corporate rights, powers, classifications, formation, and financing. Most corporations are formed under state law, and a majority of states follow some version of the Revised Model Business Corporation Act (RMBCA).

CHAPTER OUTLINE

I. THE NATURE OF THE CORPORATION

A. CORPORATE PERSONNEL
Shareholders elect a board of directors, which is responsible for overall management and hires corporate officers to run daily operations.

B. CORPORATE TAXATION
Corporate profits are taxed twice: as income to the corporation and, when distributed as dividends, as income to the shareholders.

C. CONSTITUTIONAL RIGHTS OF CORPORATIONS
A corporation is recognized by the law as a "person" and, under the Bill of Rights, has the same rights as a natural person (see Chapter 4). Only officers and employees have the right against self-incrimination, however, and the privileges and immunities clause does not protect corporations.

D. TORTS AND CRIMINAL ACTS
A corporation is liable for the torts committed by its agents within the course and scope of employment. A corporation may be held liable for the crimes of its employees and agents if the punishment for the crimes can be applied to a corporation.

E. CORPORATE SENTENCING GUIDELINES
The guidelines cover thirty-two levels of offenses. Punishment depends on the seriousness of a charge, the amount of money involved, and the extent to

which corporate officers are involved. Sanctions are reduced when corporations cooperate to prevent, investigate, and punish wrongdoing.

II. CORPORATE POWERS

A. EXPRESS AND IMPLIED POWERS
Express powers are in (in order of priority) the U.S. Constitution, state constitution, state statutes, articles of incorporation, bylaws, and board resolutions. A corporation has the *implied* power to perform all acts reasonably appropriate and necessary to accomplish its purposes.

B. *ULTRA VIRES* DOCTRINE
Ultra vires acts are beyond the purposes stated in the articles. Most such acts have involved contracts (which generally are enforced [RMBCA 3.04]). Courts usually allow any legal action a firm takes to profit shareholders.

III. CLASSIFICATION OF CORPORATIONS

A. DOMESTIC, FOREIGN, AND ALIEN CORPORATIONS
A corporation is a **domestic corporation** in the state in which it incorporated, a **foreign corporation** in other states, and an **alien corporation** in other countries. A foreign corporation normally must obtain a certificate of authority to do business in any state except its home state.

B. PUBLIC AND PRIVATE CORPORATIONS
A **public corporation** is formed by the government to meet a political or governmental purpose (the U.S. Postal Service, AMTRAK). A **private corporation** is created for private benefit and is owned by private persons.

C. NONPROFIT CORPORATIONS
Corporations formed without a profit-making purpose (private hospitals, educational institutions, charities, and religious organizations).

D. CLOSE CORPORATIONS
To qualify as a **close corporation**, a firm must have a limited number of shareholders, and restrict its issue and transfer of stock.

1. Advantage
Exempt from most of the nonessential formalities of corporate operation (bylaws, annual meetings, etc. [RMBCA 7.32]).

2. Management
Resembles that of a sole proprietorship or a partnership—one or a few shareholders usually hold the positions of directors and officers.

3. Transfer of Shares
Often restricted by stipulating that shareholders offer their shares to the corporation or other shareholders before offering them to outsiders.

E. S CORPORATIONS

1. Requirements
Must be a domestic corporation; must not be a member of an affiliated group of corporations; shareholders must be individuals, estates, or certain trusts; must have thirty-five or fewer shareholders; can have only one class of stock; no shareholder can be a nonresident alien.

2. Advantages
Shareholders can use corporate losses to offset other income; only a single tax on corporate income is imposed at individual income tax rates a t the shareholder level (whether or not it is distributed).

F. PROFESSIONAL CORPORATIONS
Generally subject to the law governing ordinary corporations.

1. Limited Liability
A shareholder in a professional corporation is protected from liability for torts (except malpractice) committed by other members.

2. Unlimited Liability
A court might regard a professional corporation as a partnership, in which each partner may be liable for the malpractice of the others.

IV. CORPORATE FORMATION

A. PROMOTIONAL ACTIVITIES
Promoters take the first steps in organizing a corporation: issue a prospectus (see Chapter 37) and secure the corporate charter (see below).

1. Promoter's Liability
Personally liable on preincorporation contracts, unless the contracting party agrees otherwise. This liability continues after incorporation unless the third party releases the promoter or the corporation assumes the contract by novation (see Chapter 17).

2. Subscribers and Subscriptions
Subscribers (who agree to buy stock in a future corporation) become shareholders as soon as the corporation is formed or as soon as the corporation accepts their subscription agreement with the promoter.

a. Subscribers' Liability
A subscription is irrevocable for six months unless the parties agree otherwise [RMBCA 6.20]. In some states, a subscriber can, without liability, revoke an offer to buy before the corporation accepts.

b. Corporation's Liability
Preincorporation subscriptions are continuing offers to buy stock. On or after its formation, a corporation can choose to accept the offer.

B. INCORPORATION PROCEDURES

1. State Chartering
Some states offer more advantageous tax or incorporation provisions.

2. Articles of Incorporation
The articles include basic information about the corporation and serve as a primary source of authority for its organization and functions.

a. Corporate Name
Cannot be the same as, or deceptively similar to, the name of a corporation doing business in the state.

b. Nature and Purpose
The intended business activities of the corporation must be specified. Stating a general corporate purpose is usually sufficient.

    c. **Duration**
A corporation can have perpetual existence in most states.

    d. **Capital Structure**
The amount of stock authorized for issuance; its valuation; and other information as to equity, capital, and credit must be outlined.

    e. **Internal Organization**
Management structure can be described in bylaws later.

    f. **Registered Office and Agent**
Usually, the registered office is the principal office of the corporation; the agent is a person designated to receive legal documents on behalf of the corporation.

    g. **Incorporators**
Incorporators (some states require only one) must sign the articles when they are submitted to the state; often this is their only duty, and they need have no other interest in the corporation.

3. **Certificate of Incorporation (Corporate Charter)**
The articles of incorporation are sent to the appropriate state official (usually the secretary of state). Many states issue a certificate of incorporation authorizing the corporation to conduct business.

4. **First Organizational Meeting (After the Charter Is Granted)**

    a. **Who Holds the Meeting**
The incorporators or the board; the business conducted depends on state law, the nature of the corporation's business, the provisions of the articles, and the wishes of the promoters.

    b. **Adoption of the Bylaws**
The most important function of the first organizational meeting.

V.   IMPROPER INCORPORATION

A. POSSIBLE RESULTS OF IMPROPER INCORPORATION
On the basis of improper incorporation—

1. **Shareholders May Be Personally Liable for Corporate Obligations**
A person attempting to enforce a contract or bring a tort suit against the corporation could seek to make the shareholders personally liable.

2. **Third Parties May Avoid Liability to the Corporation**
If a corporation seeks to enforce a contract, the defaulting party who learns of a defect in incorporation may be able to avoid liability.

B. *DE JURE* AND *DE FACTO* CORPORATIONS

1. *De Jure* **Existence**
Occurs if there is substantial compliance with all requirements for incorporation. In most states, the certificate of incorporation is evidence that all requirements have been met, and neither the state nor a third party can attack the corporation's existence.

2. *De Facto* **Existence**

The existence of a corporation cannot be challenged by third persons (except the state) if (1) there is a statute under which the firm can be incorporated, (2) the parties made a good faith attempt to comply with it, and (3) the firm has attempted to do business as a corporation.

C. CORPORATION BY ESTOPPEL

If an association that is neither an actual corporation nor a *de facto* or *de jure* corporation holds itself out as being a corporation, it will be estopped from denying corporate status in a lawsuit by a third party.

VI. DISREGARDING THE CORPORATE ENTITY

A. PIERCING THE CORPORATE VEIL

A court may ignore the corporate structure (pierce the corporate veil) if—

1. A party is tricked or misled into dealing with the corporation rather than the individual.
2. The corporation is set up never to make a profit or always to be insolvent, or it is too thinly capitalized.
3. Statutory corporate formalities are not followed.
4. Personal and corporate interests are commingled to the extent that the corporation has no separate identity.

B. RESULT

Personal liability for corporate debts is imposed on shareholders.

VII. CORPORATE FINANCING

A. BONDS

Bonds are issued as evidence of funds that business firms borrow from investors. A lending agreement called a **bond indenture** specifies the terms (maturity date, interest). A trustee ensures that the terms are met.

B. STOCKS

The most important characteristics of stocks are (1) they need not be paid back, (2) stockholders receive dividends only when voted by the directors, (3) stockholders are the last investors to be paid on dissolution, and (4) stockholders vote for management and on major issues.

TRUE-FALSE QUESTIONS

(Answers at the Back of the Book)

_____ 1. A corporation is an artificial person.

_____ 2. A corporation that is formed in a country other than the United States, but which does business in the United States, is a foreign corporation.

_____ 3. Generally, a promoter is personally liable on a preincorporation contract until the corporation assumes it by novation or adopts it by performance.

_____ 4. When conflicts arise among documents involving corporations, resolutions of the board of directors have the highest priority.

_____   **5.**   Stocks are certificates that evidence corporate ownership.

_____   **6.**   Bonds are certificates that evidence corporate debt.

_____   **7.**   Unlike a sole proprietorship and many partnerships, a corporation is not a legal entity separate and distinct from its owners.

_____   **8.**   A corporation enjoys many of the same rights and privileges that U.S. citizens enjoy.

_____   **9.**   A corporation is liable for the torts of its employees committed within the scope of their employment.

_____   **10.**   One disadvantage of an S corporation is that tax is imposed on income at the corporate and shareholder levels.

FILL-IN QUESTIONS

(Answers at the Back of the Book)

Those who, for themselves or others, take the preliminary steps in organizing a corporation are _____ (promoters/incorporators). These persons enter into contracts with professionals, whose services are needed in planning the corporation, and are personally liable on these contracts, _____ (unless/even if) the third party issues a release or the corporation assumes the contract. A person who applies to the state on behalf of the corporation to obtain its certificate of incorporation is _____ (a promoter/an incorporator). This person _____ (must/need not) have any interest in the corporation.

MULTIPLE-CHOICE QUESTIONS

(Answers at the Back of the Book)

_____   **1.**   Adam, Barb, Cathy, and Dave want to form Eagle Corporation. Which of the following is NOT a step in forming the corporation?

   a.   The promoters make preincorporation contracts.
   b.   The incorporators execute the articles of incorporation.
   c.   The shareholders approve or disapprove of corporate business matters at a shareholders' meeting.
   d.   The incorporators (or the board of directors) hold an organizational meeting to complete details of incorporation.

_____   **2.**   When Best Products Corporation was organized, the directors were chosen by the organizers. During the first three years of business, however, Best's shareholders become dissatisfied with the directors' management. The directors can be replaced by

   a.   organizing Best into a new corporation.
   b.   a vote of the shareholders.
   c.   a vote of the organizers.
   d.   the board of directors.

____ 3. Omega, Inc., incorporated in Ohio, its only place of business. Its stock is owned by ten shareholders. Two are resident aliens. Three of the others are the directors and officers. The stock has never been sold to the public. If a shareholder wants to sell his or her shares, the other shareholders must be given the opportunity to buy them first. Omega is

a. a close corporation.
b. a foreign corporation.
c. an alien corporation.
d. none of the above.

____ 4. ABC Equipment, Inc., is a corporation. Which of the following statements concerning the implied powers of ABC is FALSE?

a. ABC officers have the authority to bind the corporation in matters of great significance to the corporate purpose.
b. ABC officers have the authority to bind the corporation in matters directly connected to the ordinary business affairs of the corporation.
c. ABC has implied power to borrow money within certain limits.
d. ABC has implied power to extend credit to those with whom it has a legal or contractual relationship.

____ 5. Mike, Nora, and Paula are shareholders in National Business, Inc. All of the shareholders are National's

a. incorporators.
b. managers.
c. owners.
d. promoters.

____ 6. National Distribution Company issues common stock, preferred stock, and bonds. Regarding these investments, which of the following is TRUE?

a. Bondholders will be the last investors paid if National dissolves.
b. Bonds and preferred stock are identical from an investment standpoint.
c. Bonds need not be repaid, and their owners receive interest payments only when so voted by the directors of National.
d. Common stock represents a proportionate interest in National with regard to control, earning capacity, and net assets.

____ 7. TV Corporation is a small audio and video equipment repair business owned and operated by Hal and Bert. Their prices are very competitive, and business is expanding. TV wants to open more repair facilities but lacks the money to do so. To raise funds, TV may wish to issue

a. assets.
b. dividends.
c. liabilities.
d. securities.

____ 8. As a corporation, International Sales, Inc. (ISI), has all of the following characteristics EXCEPT

a. ISI officers answer to the board rather than to the shareholders.
b. ISI profits may be passed to shareholders as tax-free dividends.
c. ISI substitutes itself for its shareholders in conducting corporate business.
d. responsibility for the management of ISI rests with a board of directors.

____ 9. **Based on a Sample CPA Exam Question.** Sam and Tina form Digital Express, Inc., a computer equipment company. If Digital's articles of incorporation are like those of most corporations, the articles will include

    a. the name of the registered agent only.
    b. the number of authorized shares only.
    c. the name of the registered agent and the number of authorized shares.
    d. none of the above.

____ 10. Frank is the sole shareholder of General Supplies Corporation (GSC). A court will look behind the corporate structure, or pierce the corporate veil, and hold Frank personally liable for a corporate debt if

    a. a party is misled into dealing with GSC rather than Frank.
    b. GSC is set up never to make a profit or always to be insolvent or is too thinly capitalized.
    c. personal and corporate interests are commingled to the extent that GSC has no separate identity.
    d. all of the above.

SHORT ESSAY QUESTIONS

1. What is the significance of the following items as they relate to a company's articles of incorporation: (1) corporate name, (2) nature and purpose, (3) duration, (4) capital structure, (5) internal organization, (6) registered office and agent, and (7) incorporators?

2. Describe the primary features of nonprofit, close, S, and professional corporations.

ISSUE SPOTTERS

(Answers at the Back of the Book)

1. Midwest Products Corporation is formed in Iowa. Midwest wants to do business through sales representatives in Illinois. Does Midwest have an automatic right to do business in Illinois? If not, what must the firm do to obtain the right?

2. Northwest Brands, Inc., is a small business. Incorporated in Minnesota, its one class of stock is owned by twelve members of a single family. Ordinarily, corporate income is taxed at the corporate and shareholder levels. Is there a way for Northwest to avoid this double income taxation?

3. Ann, Greg, and Brian form Consumer Investments, Inc., and elect its directors, Diane, Erin, and Frank. During the first year of business, Consumer shareholders become dissatisfied with Diane. How can Diane be replaced?

4. ACS Corporation is an Internet service provider. How can ACS obtain capital to finance its operations?

5. Apple Corporation is convicted of conspiring with Orange Corporation to violate a federal law that is punishable by a term of imprisonment and a fine. The prosecutor argues that the firms should be subject to both types of punishment. The attorneys for the defendants argue that a corporation cannot be imprisoned and thus should be subject only to a fine. How might the prosecutor's request be carried out?

SPECIAL INFORMATION FOR CPA CANDIDATES

Over time, the CPA examination has come to emphasize statutory principles (such as the MBCA and the RMBCA) and deemphasize common law principles (such as *de jure* and *de facto* corporations and the *ultra vires* doctrine—the most likely application of the latter is in a question that involves an executory contract).

Other important points to keep in mind include the liability of a promoter who organizes a new corporation (and how a promoter can avoid liability), the liability of the corporation in regard to preincorporation contracts, the relationship of the promoters to shareholders and the corporation, and the circumstances under which a shareholder may be liable for the debts of a corporation.

Chapter 35
Corporations— Directors, Officers, and Shareholders

WHAT THIS CHAPTER IS ABOUT

This chapter outlines the rights and responsibilities of all participants—directors, officers, and shareholders—in a corporate enterprise. Also noted are the ways in which conflicts among these participants are resolved.

CHAPTER OUTLINE

I. **ROLE OF DIRECTORS**
The board of directors governs a corporation. Officers handle daily business.

A. **ELECTION OF DIRECTORS**

1. **Number of Directors**
Set in a corporation's articles or bylaws. Corporations with fewer than fifty shareholders can eliminate the board of directors [RMBCA 8.01].

2. **How Directors Are Chosen**
The first board (appointed by the incorporators or named in the articles) serves until the first shareholders' meeting. Subsequent directors are elected by a majority vote of the shareholders (see below).

3. **Removal of Directors**
A director can be removed for cause by shareholder action (or the board may have the power). In most states, a director cannot be removed without cause, unless the shareholders have reserved the right.

B. **BOARD OF DIRECTORS' MEETINGS**

1. **Formal Minutes and Notice**
A board conducts business by holding formal meetings with recorded minutes. The dates for regular meetings are usually set in the articles

and bylaws or by board resolution, and no other notice is required. Special meetings require notice to all directors.

2. Quorum Requirements and Voting

Quorum requirements vary. If the firm specifies none, in most states a quorum is a majority of the number of directors authorized in the articles or bylaws. Voting is done in person, one vote per director.

C. RIGHTS OF DIRECTORS

1. Participation and Inspection

A director has a right to participate in corporate business. A director must have access to all corporate books and records to make decisions.

2. Compensation and Indemnification

Nominal sums may be paid to directors, and there is a trend to provide more. Most states permit a corporation to indemnify a director for costs and fees in defending against corporate-related lawsuits. Many firms buy insurance to cover indemnification.

D. MANAGEMENT RESPONSIBILITIES

1. Areas of Responsibility

Major policy and financial decisions; appointment, supervision, pay, and removal of officers and other managerial employees.

2. Executive Committee

Most states permit a board to elect an executive committee from among the directors to handle management between board meetings. The committee is limited to ordinary business matters.

II. ROLE OF CORPORATE OFFICERS AND EXECUTIVES

Officers and other executive employees are hired by the board. Officers act as agents of the corporation (see Chapters 31 and 32).

A. QUALIFICATIONS

At the discretion of the firm; included in the articles or bylaws. A person can hold more than one office and also be a director.

B. RIGHTS AND DUTIES

The rights of corporate officers and other high-level managers are defined by employment contracts. Officers normally can be removed by the board at any time (but the corporation could be liable for breach of contract). Officers' duties are the same as those of directors.

III. FIDUCIARY DUTIES OF DIRECTORS AND OFFICERS

Directors and officers are fiduciaries of the corporation.

A. DUTY OF CARE

Directors and officers must act in good faith, in what they consider to be the best interests of the corporation, and with the care that an ordinarily prudent person would exercise in similar circumstances.

1. Duty to Make Informed and Reasonable Decisions

Directors must be informed on corporate matters and act in accord with their knowledge and training. A director can rely on information furnished by competent officers, or others, without being accused of acting in bad faith or failing to exercise due care [RMBCA 8.30].

   2. **Duty to Exercise Reasonable Supervision**
      Directors must exercise reasonable supervision when work is delegated.

   3. **Dissenting Directors**
      Directors must attend board meetings; if not, he or she should register a dissent to actions taken (to avoid liability for mismanagement).

B. DUTY OF LOYALTY

Directors and officers cannot use corporate funds or confidential information for personal advantage. Specifically, they cannot—

   1. Compete with the corporation.

   2. Usurp a corporate opportunity.

   3. Have an interest that conflicts with the interest of the corporation.

   4. Engage in insider trading (see Chapter 37).

   5. Authorize a corporate transaction that is detrimental to minority shareholders.

   6. Sell control over the corporation.

C. CONFLICTS OF INTEREST

Directors and officers must disclose fully any conflict of interest that might occur in a deal involving the corporation. A contract may be upheld if it was fair and reasonable to the firm when it was made, there was full disclosure of the interest of the officers or directors involved, and it was approved by a majority of disinterested directors or shareholders.

IV.   LIABILITY OF DIRECTORS AND OFFICERS

A. THE BUSINESS JUDGMENT RULE

Honest mistakes of judgment and poor business decisions do not make directors and officers liable to the firm for poor results, if the decision complies with management's fiduciary duties, has a reasonable basis, and is within managerial authority and the power of the corporation.

B. LIABILITY FOR TORTS AND CRIMES

Directors and officers are personally liable for their torts and crimes, and may be liable for those of subordinates (under the "responsible corporate officer" doctrine or the "pervasiveness of control" theory). The corporation is liable for such acts when committed within the scope of employment.

V.   ROLE OF SHAREHOLDERS

A. SHAREHOLDERS' POWERS

Shareholders own the corporation, approve fundamental corporate changes, and elect and remove directors.

B. SHAREHOLDERS' MEETINGS

Regular meetings must occur annually; special meetings can be called to handle urgent matters.

   1. **Notice of Meeting Must be in Writing in Advance**
      Notice of a special meeting must state the purpose.

2. Proxies

Rather than attend a meeting, shareholders normally authorize third parties to vote their shares. A proxy may be revocable and may have a time limit. When a firm sends proxy materials to its shareholders, it must allow them to vote on pending policy proposals.

C. SHAREHOLDER VOTING

1. Quorum Requirements

At the meeting, a quorum must be present. A majority vote of the shares present is required to pass resolutions. Fundamental changes require a higher percentage.

2. Voting Techniques

Each common shareholder has one vote per share. The articles can exclude or limit voting rights.

a. Cumulative Voting

The number of members of the board to be elected is multiplied by the total number of voting shares. This is the number of votes a shareholder has and can be cast for one or more nominees.

b. Shareholder Voting Agreements

A group of shareholders can agree to vote their shares together. A shareholder can vote by proxy. Any person can solicit proxies.

c. Voting Trust

Exists when legal title (recorded ownership on the corporate books) is transferred to a trustee who is responsible for voting the shares. The shareholder retains all other ownership rights.

VI. RIGHTS OF SHAREHOLDERS

A. STOCK CERTIFICATES

Notice of shareholder meetings, dividends, and corporate reports are distributed to owners listed in the corporate books, not on the basis of possession of stock certificates (which most states do not require).

B. PREEMPTIVE RIGHTS

Usually apply only to additional, newly issued stock sold for cash and must be exercised within a specified time (usually thirty days). When new shares are issued, each shareholder is given **stock warrants** (transferable options to acquire a certain number of shares at a stated price).

C. DIVIDENDS

Dividends can be paid in cash, property, or stock. Once declared, a cash dividend is a corporate debt. Dividends are payable only from (1) retained earnings, (2) current net profits, or (3) any surplus.

1. Illegal Dividends

A dividend paid when a corporation is insolvent is illegal and must be repaid. A dividend paid from an unauthorized account or causing a corporation to become insolvent may have to be repaid. In any case, the directors can be held personally liable.

2. **If the Directors Fail to Declare a Dividend**
Shareholders can ask a court to compel a declaration of a dividend, but to succeed, the directors' conduct must be an abuse of discretion.

D. **INSPECTION RIGHTS**
Shareholders (or their attorney, accountant, or agent) can inspect and copy corporate books and records for a proper purpose, if the request is made in advance [RMBCA 16.02]. This right can be denied to prevent harassment or to protect confidential corporate information.

E. **TRANSFER OF SHARES**
Any restrictions on transferability must be noted on the face of a stock certificate. Restrictions must be reasonable—for example, a right of first refusal remains with the corporation or the shareholders for only a specified time or a reasonable time.

F. **RIGHTS ON DISSOLUTION**
Shareholders can petition a court to dissolve a firm if [RMBCA 14.30]—

1. The directors are deadlocked, shareholders are unable to break the deadlock, and there is or could be irreparable injury to the firm.

2. The acts of the directors or those in control of the corporation are illegal, oppressive, or fraudulent.

3. Corporate assets are being misapplied or wasted.

4. The shareholders are deadlocked in voting power and have failed, for a specified period (usually two annual meetings), to elect successors to directors.

G. **SHAREHOLDER'S DERIVATIVE SUIT**
If directors fail to sue in the corporate name to redress a wrong suffered by the firm, shareholders can do so (after complaining to the board). Any recovery normally goes into the corporate treasury.

VII. LIABILITY OF SHAREHOLDERS
In most cases, if a corporation fails, shareholders lose only their investment. Exceptions include (see also Chapter 37)—

A. **STOCK-SUBSCRIPTION AGREEMENTS**
Once a subscription agreement is accepted, any refusal to pay is a breach, resulting in personal liability.

B. **WATERED STOCK**
In most cases, a shareholder who receives watered stock (stock sold by a corporation for less than par value) must pay the difference to the corporation. In some states, such shareholders may be liable to creditors of the corporation for unpaid corporate debts.

VIII. DUTIES OF MAJORITY SHAREHOLDERS
A single shareholder (or a few acting together) who owns enough shares to control the corporation owes a fiduciary duty to the minority shareholders and creditors when they sell their shares.

TRUE-FALSE QUESTIONS

(Answers at the Back of the Book)

____ **1.** Both directors and officers may be immunized from liability for poor business decisions under the business judgment rule.

____ **2.** Because their positions involve similar decision making and control, officers have the same duties as directors.

____ **3.** The rights of shareholders are established solely in the articles of incorporation.

____ **4.** Dividends can be paid in cash or property.

____ **5.** Any damages recovered in a shareholder's derivative suit are normally paid to the shareholder or shareholders who brought the suit.

____ **6.** As a general rule, shareholders are not personally responsible for the debts of the corporation.

____ **7.** Officers, but not directors, owe a duty of loyalty to the corporation.

____ **8.** The business judgment rule makes a director liable for losses to the firm that result from the director's authorized, good faith business decisions.

____ **9.** Shareholders may vote to elect directors and they may vote to remove directors.

____ **10.** Par-value shares have a specific face value.

FILL-IN QUESTIONS

(Answers at the Back of the Book)

A stock certificate may be lost or destroyed, _____ (and ownership is/but ownership is not) destroyed with it.   A new certificate _____ (can/cannot) be issued to replace one that has been lost or destroyed. Notice of meetings, dividends, and operational and financial reports are all distributed according to the individual _____·_____ _____ (in possession of the certificate/recorded as the owner in the corporation's books).

MULTIPLE-CHOICE QUESTIONS

(Answers at the Back of the Book)

____ **1.** Jill is a shareholder of United Manufacturing Company. As a shareholder, Jill's rights include all of the following EXCEPT a right to

   a. one vote per share, subject to any limitation in the articles.
   b. access to corporate books and records, subject to the firm's right to protect itself from potential abuse.
   c. transfer shares, subject to any valid restriction.
   d. take title to and sell corporate property when directors are mishandling corporate assets, subject to any limitation in the articles.

____ 2. Jim is a director of Facts & Figures, Inc. As a director, Jim has a right to

a. participate in board meetings.
b. inspect all corporate books and records.
c. both a and b.
d. none of the above.

____ 3. The board of directors of U.S. Goods Corporation announces that the corporation will pay a cash dividend to its shareholders. Once declared, a cash dividend is

a. a corporate debt.
b. a personal debt of the directors.
c. a personal debt of the shareholders.
d. an illusory promise.

____ 4. The board of Consumer Sales Corporation delegates work to corporate officers and employees. If the directors do not use a reasonable amount of supervision, they could be held liable for

a. negligence only.
b. mismanagement of corporate personnel only.
c. negligence or mismanagement of corporate personnel.
d. none of the above.

____ 5. **Based on a Sample CPA Exam Question.** The management of National Brands, Inc., is at odds with the shareholders over some recent decisions. The shareholders may file a shareholders' derivative suit to

a. compel dissolution of National.
b. compel payment of a properly declared dividend.
c. enforce a right to inspect corporate records.
d. recover damages from the management for an *ultra vires* act.

____ 6. Federated Products Corporation uses cumulative voting in its elections of directors. Mary owns 3,000 Federated shares. At an annual meeting at which three directors are to be elected, how many votes may Mary cast for any one candidate?

a. 1,000
b. 3,000
c. 9,000
d. 27,00

____ 7. Bob is a director and shareholder of Eagle Corporation and of American Goods, Inc. If a resolution comes before the Eagle board to enter into a contract with American, Bob

a. must resign the directorship with Eagle.
b. must resign the directorship with American.
c. must disclose the potential conflict of interest.
d. need not disclose the potential conflict of interest.

____   8.   Nationwide Company's chief financial officer resigns. After a personnel search, an investigation, and an interview, the board of directors hires Ed. Ed turns out to be dishonest. Nationwide's shareholders sue the board. The board's best defense is

    a.   the business judgment rule.
    b.   the directors' duty of care.
    c.   the directors' duty of loyalty.
    d.   a shareholder's derivative suit.

____   9.   Julio and Gloria are officers of World Export Corporation. As corporate officers, their rights, with respect to the corporation, are set out in

    a.   state corporation statutes.
    b.   World Export's certificate of authority.
    c.   their employment contracts with World Export.
    d.   international agreements with non-resident shareholders.

____   10.   Mike is a director of Allcom, Inc. Mike buys stock in Techron, an Allcom competitor. As to Mike's relationship to Allcom, this is a breach of

    a.   Mike's duty of care.
    b.   the business judgment rule.
    c.   Mike's duty of loyalty.
    d.   none of the above.

SHORT ESSAY QUESTIONS

1.   How do the duty of care and the duty of loyalty govern the conduct of directors and officers in a corporation?

2.   What are the rights of the shareholders of a corporation?

ISSUE SPOTTERS

(Answers at the Back of the Book)

1.   Glen is a director and shareholder of the Diamond Corporation and of Ruby Rock, Inc. If a resolution comes before the Ruby board to compete with Diamond, what is Glen's responsibility?

2.   Joe is a director and officer of United Products, Inc. Joe makes a decision about the marketing of United products that results in a dramatic decrease in profits for United and its shareholders. The shareholders accuse Joe of breaching his fiduciary duty to the corporation. What is Joe's best defense?

3.   Medtech Corporation's board of directors—among whom are Tom and Kate, officers of the firm—is deadlocked over whether to market a new product. Consequently, corporate investment is frozen. Ed, a minority shareholder, suspects that Tom and Kate are taking advantage of the deadlock to use corporate assets—offices, equipment, supplies, staff time—to initiate a competing enterprise. Is Ed powerless to intervene?

4.   JKL Development Corporation has an opportunity to buy stock in Delong Properties, Inc. The directors decide that, instead of JKL buying the stock, the directors will buy it. After they buy the stock, Franco, a JKL shareholder, learns of the circumstances and wants to sue the directors on JKL's behalf. Can he do so?

5.   Pam is Mayer Corporation's majority shareholder.   Pam owns enough stock in Mayer that if she were to sell it, the sale would be a transfer of control of the firm. Does Pam owe any duty to Mayer or the minority shareholders in selling her shares?

SPECIAL INFORMATION FOR CPA CANDIDATES

For the CPA examination, be sure that you understand the relationship of directors and officers to the corporation. These individuals have fiduciary duties and agency authority that shareholders do not have. Officers and directors must exercise reasonable care, subject to the business judgment rule (which absolves those who act in good faith).

Note that this is not the same as the due diligence standard of the Securities Exchange Commission (SEC) (see Chapter 37). For that reason, pay close attention to which standard a question involves. Regarding shareholders, you should know their rights, and in what circumstances a shareholder may be personally liable for the obligations of a corporation.

Chapter 36
Corporations— Merger, Consolidation, and Termination

WHAT THIS CHAPTER IS ABOUT

This chapter covers corporate mergers, consolidations, purchase of another corporation's assets, and purchase of a controlling interest in another corporation. The chapter also touches on the reasons for, and methods used in, terminating a corporation.

CHAPTER OUTLINE

I. MERGER AND CONSOLIDATION

Whether a combination is a merger or a consolidation, the rights and liabilities of shareholders, the corporation, and its creditors are the same.

A. MERGER

1. What a Merger Is
The combination of two or more corporations, often by one absorbing the other. After a merger, only one of the corporations exists.

2. The Results of a Merger
The surviving corporation has all of the rights, assets, liabilities, and debts of itself and the other corporation. Its articles of incorporation are deemed amended to include changes stated in the articles of merger.

B. CONSOLIDATION
In a **consolidation**, two or more corporations combine so that each corporation ceases to exist and a new one emerges. The results of a consolidation are essentially the same as the results of a merger.

C. PROCEDURE FOR MERGER OR CONSOLIDATION

1. The Basic Steps
(1) Each board approves the merger or consolidation plan; (2) each firm's shareholders vote on the plan at a shareholders' meeting; (3)

the plan is filed, usually with the secretary of state; and (4) the state issues a certificate of merger or consolidation.

2. **Short-Form Mergers**
A substantially owned subsidiary corporation can merge into its parent corporation without shareholder approval, if the parent owns at least 90 percent of the subsidiary's outstanding stock.

3. **Appraisal Rights**
If provided by statute, a shareholder can dissent from a merger, consolidation, sale of substantially all the corporate assets not in the ordinary course of business, and (in some states) amendments to articles.

   a. **Procedure**
   A shareholder must file written notice of dissent before the shareholders vote on the proposed transaction. If the transaction is approved, the shareholder must make a written demand for payment.

   b. **Fair Value**
   Value on the day before the date the vote is taken [RMBCA 13.01]. The corporation must make a written offer to buy the shareholder's stock. If fair value cannot be agreed to, a court will set it.

II. PURCHASE OF ASSETS

A. IS SHAREHOLDER APPROVAL REQUIRED?
A corporation that buys all or substantially all of the assets of another corporation does not need shareholder approval. The corporation whose assets are acquired must obtain approval of its board and shareholders.

B. ASSUMPTION OF LIABILITY
An acquiring corporation is not responsible for the seller's liabilities, unless there is (1) an implied or express assumption, (2) a sale amounting to a merger or consolidation, (3) a buyer retaining the seller's personnel and continuing the business, or (4) a sale executed in fraud to avoid liability.

III. PURCHASE OF STOCK
A purchase of a substantial number of the voting shares of a corporation's stock enables an acquiring corporation to control a target corporation. The acquiring corporation deals directly with shareholders to buy shares.

A. TENDER OFFERS
A tender offer is a public offer. The offer can turn on the receipt of a specified number of shares by a specified date.

1. **The Price Offered for the Target's Stock**
Generally higher than the stock's market price before the tender offer. May involve an exchange of stock or cash for stock in the target.

2. **Federal and State Securities Laws**
Federal laws control the terms, duration, and circumstances in which most tender offers are made. Most states also impose regulations.

B. TARGET RESPONSES

1. **Good Faith Decision**
The directors of the target firm must make a good faith decision as to whether the shareholders' acceptance or rejection of the offer would be most beneficial. The directors must fully disclose all material facts.

2. To Resist a Takeover

Among other tactics, a target may make a self-tender (offer to buy its own stock). A target may also sell its most desirable assets or take other defensive measures (such as a poison pill: give its shareholders the right to buy additional shares at low prices).

IV.   TERMINATION

A. DISSOLUTION

1. Voluntary Dissolution

a. To Initiate Dissolution

Shareholders can initiate dissolution by a unanimous vote. Directors may propose dissolution to the shareholders for a vote.

b. To Dissolve

The corporation files articles of dissolution with the secretary of state [RMBCA 14.03]. The effective date of dissolution will be the date of the articles. The corporation notifies its creditors and sets a date (at least 120 days following the date of dissolution) by which all claims against the corporation must be received [RMBCA 14.06].

2. Involuntary Dissolution

a. By the State

In an action brought by the secretary of state or the state attorney general, a corporation may be dissolved for [RMBCA 14.20]—

1) Failing to comply with corporate formalities or other statutory requirements.

2) Procuring a charter through fraud or misrepresentation.

3) Abusing corporate powers (*ultra vires* acts).

4) Violating the criminal code after a demand to discontinue the violation has been made by the secretary of state.

5) Failing to commence business operations.

6) Abandoning operations after starting up.

b. By a Shareholder

The articles of a close corporation may empower any shareholder to dissolve the corporation at will or on the occurrence of a certain event (such as the death of another shareholder).

c. By a Court

Courts can also dissolve a corporation when a board is deadlocked or for mismanagement [RMBCA 14.30].

B. LIQUIDATION

Corporate assets are converted into cash and distributed among creditors and shareholders according to specific rules.

1. Board Supervision

If dissolution is by voluntary action, the members of the board act as trustees of the assets, and wind up the affairs of the corporation for the benefit of corporate creditors and shareholders.

   2. **Court Supervision**
   If dissolution is involuntary, the board does not wish to act as trustee, or shareholders or creditors can show why the board should not act as trustee, a court will appoint a receiver to wind up the corporate affairs.

TRUE-FALSE QUESTIONS

(Answers at the Back of the Book)

____   1. If a parent corporation owns are least 90 percent of the outstanding shares of its subsidiary corporation, the subsidiary can be merged into its parent without the approval of the shareholders of either corporation.

____   2. Appraisal rights are available only when a statute specifically provides for them.

____   3. Shareholders must normally approve actions that will substantially change a corporation's business position.

____   4. Shareholders must normally approve the purchase of all or substantially all of another corporation's assets.

____   5. Federal laws strictly control the terms, duration, and circumstances under which most tender offers are made.

____   6. During the liquidation of a corporation, corporate assets are converted to cash and distributed to creditors and shareholders.

____   7. Shareholders who disapprove of a merger or a consolidation may be entitled to the fair value of their shares.

____   8. A corporation that purchases the assets of another corporation always assumes the selling corporation's liabilities as part of the deal.

____   9. A board of directors can file articles of merger or consolidation without shareholder approval.

____   10. Appraisal rights are not ordinarily available in sales of substantially all of a corporation's assets.

FILL-IN QUESTIONS

(Answers at the Back of the Book)

   If provided by statute, a shareholder _____ (can/cannot) dissent from becoming an unwilling shareholder in a corporation that has been substantially altered by a merger or consolidation. To do so, the _____ (corporation/shareholder) must file a written notice of dissent _____ (after/before) the shareholders vote on the proposed change. If the change is approved, the shareholder must make a written demand for payment. The fair value of shares is usually their value on the day _____ (after/before) the date on which _____ _____ (the change is made/the vote is taken).

MULTIPLE-CHOICE QUESTIONS

(Answers at the Back of the Book)

____ 1. National Sales, Inc., merges with American Distribution Corporation. As the result of a merger, one firm

a. acquires all assets previously held by two firms, without a formal transfer.
b. becomes subject to the provisions of two sets of articles.
c. both a and b.
d. none of the above.

____ 2. Bob, Jane, and Grant are the shareholders of Federated Products, Inc. Federated sells off all its assets, except for one store. When Grant, the company president, contracts to sell the last store for what he believes is a fair price, Bob and Jane object. If they sue, they will

a. win, because their approval is required to sell the store.
b. win, because the store is Federated's last asset and thus cannot be sold.
c. lose, because their approval is not required to sell the store.
d. lose, because Grant contracted for what he believed was a fair price.

____ 3. **Based on a Sample CPA Exam Question.** Digital Equipment, Inc., sells computer products. Which of the following may Digital's board of directors do without shareholder approval?

a. Amend the articles of incorporation
b. Buy substantially all of the assets of another corporation
c. Dissolve the corporation
d. Sell substantially all of the assets of Digital

____ 4. Best Design, Inc., wants to merge or consolidate with Software Engineering, Inc. Which of the following is NOT part of a merger or a consolidation?

a. The board of directors of each corporation approves the combination.
b. The shareholders of each corporation approve the combination.
c. The officers of each corporation approve the combination.
d. The articles of merger or consolidation are filed with the appropriate state official.

____ 5. EZ, Inc., does not pay its annual franchise fees nor does it file an annual report. The attorney general of the state of EZ's incorporation might seek a court decree to dissolve EZ for its failure to

a. pay annual franchise fees.
b. file an annual report.
c. both a and b.
d. none of the above.

____ 6. Sugar Corporation and Spice Products, Inc., decide to combine. Afterwards, Sugar will cease to exist—only Spice will function, as the surviving corporation. The combination of Sugar and Spice is

a. a consolidation.
b. a merger.
c. both a and b.
d. none of the above.

___ 7. Mary and Adam are the directors and majority shareholders of U.S. Imports, Inc., and Overseas Corporation. U.S. Imports owes $5,000 to International Transport, Inc. (IT). To avoid the debt, Mary and Adam vote to sell all U.S. Imports' assets to Overseas. If IT sues Overseas on the debt, IT will

    a. win, because an acquiring corporation automatically assumes a selling corporation's liabilities.
    b. win, because the sale was fraudulently executed to avoid liability.
    c. lose, because Overseas refused to assume U.S. Imports' debt.
    d. lose, because U.S. Imports has ceased to exist.

___ 8. Consumer Sales Corporation and Nationwide Products Company decide to combine. Afterwards, Consumer and Nationwide will cease to exist—a new organization, CSNP, Inc., will function in their place. The combination of these firms is

    a. a consolidation.
    b. a merger.
    c. both a and b.
    d. none of the above.

___ 9. American Goods, Inc., and National Trucking Company consolidate. As the result of a consolidation, one of the firms

    a. has all the rights and powers previously held by two firms.
    b. is liable for all the debts previously owed by two firms.
    c. both a and b.
    d. none of the above.

___ 10. Nationwide Investments, Inc., incorporates in Delaware. Delaware's state attorney general may seek a court decree to dissolve Nationwide if the firm

    a. does not file an annual report.
    b. does not commence business operations.
    c. attempts to take over another corporation through stock acquisition.
    d. both a and b.

SHORT ESSAY QUESTIONS

1. Define these takeover defense terms: greenmail; Pac-man; poison pill; scorched-earth tactic; shark repellant; and white knight.

2. What are the steps in the process by which a corporation is dissolved and liquidated?

ISSUE SPOTTERS

(Answers at the Back of the Book)

1. NB Corporation combines with MC, Inc. MC ceases to exist—NB is the surviving firm. Warner Corporation and Special Animation Company combine. Afterwards, Warner and Special Animation cease to exist. Fine Points, Inc., a new firm, functions in their place. Which of these is a merger and which is a consolidation?

2.   Delacroix Corporation asks its shareholders to vote on a proposed merger with Hugo, Inc.   Deb, a Delacroix shareholder, votes against it, but is outvoted by Delacroix's other shareholders.   Deb is unwilling to become a Hugo shareholder.   Is there anything she can do to avoid being forced to go along with the transaction?

3.   Champ Sports Corporation buys the assets of Athletic Authority Company (AAC). Champ continues AAC's business and retains the same personnel.   AAC is a firm on paper only, with many unpaid debts.   Is Champ liable for AAC's debts?

4.   Beloit Corporation makes a public offer to buy Fort, Inc., stock.   The price of the offer is higher than the market price of the stock, but Fort's board believes that it should be resisted.   What can Fort do to retain control over itself?

5.   Dee and Jim form Home Remodeling, Inc.   After three years, they decide to cease business and go their separate ways.   Can they simply dissolve Home at will?   Could Dee or Jim seek dissolution of Home alone (as a partner can dissolve a partnership)?

SPECIAL INFORMATION FOR CPA CANDIDATES

One of the most important aspects of the material in this chapter, to remember for the CPA examination, is the role of shareholders.   Note particularly the events that require shareholder approval (and those that don't).   Also, review the section on appraisal rights: they are available *only* when specifically provided by statute.

★ **Key Points**

The **key points** in this chapter include:

1. What is meant by the term *securities*.

2. The purpose and provisions of the Securities Act of 1933.

3. The purpose and provisions of the Securities Exchange Act of 1934.

4. Federal laws that specifically regulate investment companies.

5. State securities laws.

Chapter 37
Corporations— Securities Regulation and Investor Protection

WHAT THIS CHAPTER IS ABOUT

The general purpose of securities laws is to provide sufficient, accurate information to investors to enable them to make informed buying and selling decisions about securities. This chapter provides an outline of federal securities laws.

CHAPTER OUTLINE

I. THE SECURITIES AND EXCHANGE COMMISSION (SEC)
Administers the federal securities laws and regulates the sale and purchase of securities.

A. THE SEC'S BASIC FUNCTIONS

1. Require disclosure of facts concerning offerings of certain securities.

2. Regulate national securities trading.

3. Investigate securities fraud.

4. Regulate securities brokers, dealers, and investment advisers.

5. Supervise mutual funds.

6. Recommend sanctions in cases involving violations of securities laws. (The U.S. Department of Justice prosecutes violations.)

B. THE SEC'S REGULATORY POWERS
Congress has expanded the SEC's powers to include the power to seek sanctions against those who violate foreign securities laws; to suspend trading if prices rise and fall in short periods of time; and to exempt persons, securities, and transactions from securities law requirements.

II. SECURITIES ACT OF 1933
Requires that all essential information concerning the issuance (sales) of new securities be disclosed to investors.

A. WHAT IS A SECURITY?

1. Courts' Interpretation of the Securities Act
A security exists in any transaction in which a person (1) invests (2) in a common enterprise (3) reasonably expecting profits (4) derived *primarily* or *substantially* from others' managerial or entrepreneurial efforts.

2. A Security Is an Investment
Examples: stocks, bonds, investment contracts in condominiums, franchises, limited partnerships, and oil or gas or other mineral rights.

B. REGISTRATION STATEMENT
Before offering securities for sale, issuing corporations must (1) file a registration statement with the Securities and Exchange Commission (SEC) and (2) provide investors with a prospectus that describes the security being sold, the issuing corporation, and the investment or risk.

1. Contents of a Registration Statement

a. Description of the significant provisions of the security and how the registrant intends to use the proceeds of the sale.

b. Description of the registrant's properties and business.

c. Description of the management of the registrant; its security holdings; its remuneration and other benefits, including pensions and stock options; and any interests of directors or officers in any material transactions with the corporation.

d. Financial statement certified by an independent public accountant.

e. Description of pending lawsuits.

2. Twenty-Day Waiting Period after Registration
Securities cannot be sold for twenty days (oral offers can be made).

3. Advertising
During the waiting period, very limited written advertising is allowed. After the period, no written advertising is allowed, except a tombstone ad, which simply tells how to obtain a prospectus.

C. EXEMPT SECURITIES
Securities that can be sold (and resold) without being registered include—

1. Small Offerings under Regulation A
An issuer's offer of up to $5 million in securities in any twelve-month period (including up to $1.5 million in nonissuer resales). The issuer must file with the SEC a notice of the issue and an offering circular (also provided to investors before the sale). A company can **test the waters** (determine potential interest) before preparing the circular.

2. Other Exempt Securities

a. All bank securities sold prior to July 27, 1933.

b. Commercial paper if maturity does not exceed nine months.

c. Securities of charitable organizations.

    d. Securities resulting from a reorganization issued in exchange for the issuer's existing securities and certificates issued by trustees, receivers, or debtors in possession in bankruptcy (see Chapter 30).

    e. Securities issued exclusively in exchange for the issuer's existing securities, provided no commission is paid (such as stock splits).

    f. Securities issued to finance the acquisition of railroad equipment.

    g. Any insurance, endowment, or annuity contract issued by a state-regulated insurance company.

    h. Government-issued securities.

    i. Securities issued by banks, savings and loan associations, farmers' cooperatives, and similar institutions.

D. EXEMPT TRANSACTIONS

Securities that can be sold without being registered include those sold in transactions that consist of—

1. Small Offerings under Regulation D

Offers that involve a small amount of money or are not made publicly.

    a. Offerings Up to $1 Million

    Noninvestment company offerings up to $1 million in a twelve-month period [Rule 504].

    b. Blank-Check Company Offerings Up to $500,000

    Offerings up to $500,000 in any one year by companies with no specific business plans are exempt if (1) no general solicitation or advertising is used, (2) the SEC is notified of the sales, and (3) precaution is taken against nonexempt, unregistered resales [Rule 504a].

    c. Offerings Up to $5 Million

    Private, noninvestment company offerings up to $5 million in a twelve-month period if (1) no general solicitation or advertising is used; (2) the SEC is notified of the sales; (3) precaution is taken against nonexempt, unregistered resales; and (4) there are no more than thirty-five unaccredited investors. If the sale involves any unaccredited investors, all investors must be given material information about the company, its business, the securities [Rule 505].

    d. Private Offerings in Unlimited Amounts

    Essentially the same requirements as Rule 505, except (1) there is no limit on the amount of the offering and (2) the issuer must believe that each unaccredited investor has sufficient knowledge or experience to evaluate the investment [Rule 506].

    e. Offerings to Qualified Purchasers

    Offerings up to $5 million per transaction to qualified purchasers (wealthy, sophisticated investors) only [Rule 1001].

2. Small Offerings to Accredited Investors Only

An offer up to $5 million is exempt if (1) no general solicitation or advertising is used; (2) the SEC is notified of the sales; (3) precaution is taken against nonexempt, unregistered resales; and (4) there are no unaccredited investors [Section 4(6)].

3. **Intrastate Issues**
Offerings in the state in which the issuer is organized and doing business are exempt [Rule 147] if, for nine months after the sale, no resale is made to a nonresident.

4. **Resales ("Safe Harbors")**
Most securities can be resold without registration. Resales of blank-check company offerings [Rule 504a], small offerings [Rule 505], private offerings [Rule 506], and offers to accredited investors only [Section 4(6)] are exempt from registration if—

   a. **The Securities Have Been Owned for Two Years or More**
   If seller is not an **affiliate** (in control with the issuer) [Rule 144].

   b. **The Securities Have Been Owned for at Least One Year**
   There must be adequate public information about the issuer, the securities must be sold in limited amounts in unsolicited brokers' transactions, and the SEC must be notified of the resale [Rule 144].

   c. **The Securities Are Sold Only to an Institutional Investor**
   The securities, on issue, must not have been of the same class as securities listed on a national securities exchange or a U.S. automated interdealer quotation system, and the seller on resale must take steps to tell the buyer they are exempt [Rule 144A].

E. **VIOLATIONS OF THE 1933 ACT**
If registration statement or prospectus contains material false statements or omissions, liable parties include anyone who signed the statement.

1. **Defenses**
Statement or omission was not material; plaintiff knew of misrepresentation and bought stock anyway; *due diligence* (Chapter 51).

2. **Penalties**
Fines up to $10,000; imprisonment up to five years; injunction against selling securities; order to refund profits; damages in civil suits.

III. **SECURITIES EXCHANGE ACT OF 1934**
Regulates the markets in which securities are traded by requiring disclosure by Section 12 companies (corporations with securities on the exchanges and firms with assets in excess of $10 million and five hundred or more shareholders).

A. **INSIDER TRADING—SECTION 10(b) AND SEC RULE 10b-5**
Section 10(b) proscribes the use of "any manipulative or deceptive device or contrivance in contravention of such rules and regulations as the [SEC] may prescribe." Rule 10b-5 prohibits the commission of fraud in connection with the purchase or sale of any security (registered or unregistered).

1. **What Triggers Liability**
Any material omission or misrepresentation of material facts in connection with the purchase or sale of any security.

2. **Who Can Be Liable**
Those who take advantage of inside information when they know that it is unavailable to the person with whom they are dealing.

a. **Insiders**

Officers, directors, majority shareholders, and persons having access to or receiving information of a nonpublic nature on which trading is based (accountants, attorneys).

b. **Outsiders**

1) **Tipper/Tippee Theory**

One who acquires inside information as a result of an insider's breach of fiduciary duty to the firm whose shares are traded can be liable, if he or she knows or should know of the breach.

2) **Misappropriation Theory**

One who wrongfully obtains inside information and trades on it to his or her gain can be liable, if a duty to the lawful possessor of information was violated and harm to another results.

B. **INSIDER REPORTING AND TRADING—SECTION 16(b)**

Officers, directors, and shareholders owning 10 percent of the securities registered under Section 12 are required to file reports with the SEC concerning their ownership and trading of the securities.

1. **Corporation Is Entitled to All Profits**

A firm can recapture *all* profits realized by an insider on *any* purchase and sale or sale and purchase of its stock in any six-month period.

2. **Applicability of Section 16(b)**

Applies to stock, warrants, options, securities convertible into stock.

C. **PROXY STATEMENTS—SECTION 14(A)**

Regulates the solicitation of proxies from shareholders of Section 12 companies. Whoever solicits a proxy must disclose, in the proxy statement, all of the pertinent facts.

D. **VIOLATIONS OF THE 1934 ACT**

1. **Criminal Penalties**

Maximum jail term is ten years; fines up to $1 million for individuals and to $2.5 million for partnerships and corporations.

2. **Civil Sanctions**

a. **Insider Trading Sanctions Act of 1984**

SEC can bring suit in federal court against anyone violating or aiding in a violation of the 1934 act or SEC rules. Penalties include triple the profits gained or the loss avoided by the guilty party.

b. **Insider Trading and Securities Fraud Enforcement Act of 1988**

Enlarged the class of persons subject to civil liability for insider-trading violations, increased criminal penalties, and gave the SEC authority to (1) reward persons providing information and (2) make rules to prevent insider trading.

IV. REGULATION OF INVESTMENT COMPANIES

Investment companies and mutual funds are regulated by the SEC under the Investment Company Act of 1940, the Investment Company Act Amendments of 1970, the Securities Act Amendments of 1975, and later amendments.

A. WHAT AN INVESTMENT COMPANY IS

Any entity that (1) is engaged primarily "in the business of investing, reinvesting, or trading in securities" or (2) is engaged in such business and has more than 40 percent of the company's assets in investment securities. (Does not include banks, finance companies, and others).

B. WHAT AN INVESTMENT COMPANY MUST DO

Register with the SEC by filing a notification of registration and, each year, file reports with the SEC. All securities must be in the custody of a bank or stock-exchange member.

C. WHAT AN INVESTMENT COMPANY CANNOT DO

No dividends may be paid from any source other than accumulated, undistributed net income. There are restrictions on investment activities.

V. STATE SECURITIES LAWS

All states regulate the offer and sale of securities within individual state borders. Exemptions from federal law are not exemptions from state laws, which have their own exemptions. Under the National Market Securities Improvement Act of 1996, the SEC regulates most national securities activities.

TRUE-FALSE QUESTIONS

(Answers at the Back of the Book)

_____ 1. Generally, if a security does not qualify for an exemption, it must be registered before it is offered to the public.

_____ 2. A nonexempt security must be accompanied by a prospectus to investors.

_____ 3. Securities issued by banks are normally exempt from the SEC registration requirements.

_____ 4. Securities resulting from a corporate reorganization issued for exchange with the issuer's existing security holders are exempt from the SEC registration requirements.

_____ 5. The Securities Act of 1933 is concerned primarily with the _resale_ of securities, and the Securities Exchange Act of 1934 is concerned primarily with disclosure on the _issuance_ of securities.

_____ 6. Rules requiring full and accurate disclosure of all pertinent facts apply to proxy statements under the Securities Exchange Act of 1934.

_____ 7. All states regulate the offer and sale of securities within their borders.

_____ 8. Penalties for insider trading may include triple the profits gained or the loss avoided by the guilty party.

_____ 9. SEC Rule 10b-5 prohibits the commission of fraud in connection with the purchase or sale of registered securities only.

_____ 10. No security can be resold without registration.

FILL-IN QUESTIONS

(Answers at the Back of the Book)

The SEC can award "bounty" payments to persons providing information leading to the _____ (conviction/prosecution) of insider-trading violations. Civil penalties include _____ (double/triple) the profits gained or the loss avoided. Criminal penalties include maximum jail terms of _____ (five/ ten) years. Individuals and corporations _____ (may/may not) also be subject to million dollar fines.

MULTIPLE-CHOICE QUESTIONS

(Answers at the Back of the Book)

____   1. **Based a Sample CPA Question.** Under the Securities Exchange Act of 1934, the Securities and Exchange Commission is responsible for all of the following activities EXCEPT

a. investigating securities fraud.
b. prosecuting criminal violations of federal securities laws.
c. regulating the activities of securities brokers.
d. requiring disclosure of facts concerning offerings of securities listed on national securities exchanges.

____   2. Gene is an officer for Max Software, Inc. In April, Gene learns that market tests indicate Max's new product will sell well. He buys 1,000 shares of Max stock. In May, the product is released, and sales exceed expectations. In July, as part of a corporate reorganization, Gene is laid off. In August, he sells his stock at a profit. If Max sues Gene under Section 16(b), Max will

a. win, because Gene was a Max officer who bought and sold Max stock within a six-month period.
b. win, because Gene used inside information in connection with the purchase and sale of Max stock.
c. lose, because Gene was not a Max officer when he realized the stock profit.
d. lose, because Gene did not use inside information in connection with the purchase and sale of Max stock.

____   3. Superior, Inc., is a private, noninvestment company. In one year, Superior advertises a $300,000 offering. This offering is

a. exempt from registration because of the low amount of the issue.
b. exempt from registration because the offering was advertised.
c. exempt from registration because the issuer is a private company.
d. not exempt from registration.

____   4. Ontario, Inc., in one year, advertises two $2.25 million offerings. Buying the stock are twelve accredited investors. This offering is

a. exempt from registration because of the low amount of the issue.
b. exempt from registration because the offering was advertised.
c. exempt from registration because only accredited investors bought stock.
d. not exempt from registration.

____ 5. A registration statement for National Distributors, Inc., must include

a. a description of the security and its relationship to the registrant's other securities.
b. how the registrant intends to use the proceeds from the sale of the issue.
c. both a and b.
d. none of the above.

____ 6. Huron, Inc., makes a $5.5 million private offering to twenty accredited investors and less than thirty unaccredited investors. Huron advertises the offering and believes that the unaccredited investors are sophisticated enough to evaluate the investment. Huron gives material information about itself, its business, and the securities to all investors. This offering is

a. exempt from registration because of the low amount of the issue.
b. exempt from registration because the offering was advertised.
c. exempt from registration because the issuer believed that the unaccredited investors were sophisticated enough to evaluate the investment.
d. not exempt from registration.

____ 7. Ed is an officer of Cafe Corporation (CC). Ed learns that CC has developed a new process for its products. Ed believes that when the process is announced, CC stock's price will increase. Ed tells Lyn, Ed's attorney, who tells Dick, Lyn's accountant. Lyn and Dick are aware that Ed has breached a fiduciary duty to CC in disclosing this information. Ed, Lyn, and Dick each buy CC stock through a national exchange without telling the sellers of the new process. When the process is announced, the price increases, and Ed, Lyn, and Dick sell their stock. Who may be liable under Rule 10b-5?

a. All of them
b. Ed and Lyn only
c. Ed only
d. None of them

____ 8. Erie, Inc., is a noninvestment company. In one year, Erie advertises two $1.75 million offerings. Buying the issues are sixty accredited investors and twenty unaccredited investors. Erie gives information about itself, its business, and the securities to unaccredited investors only. This offering is

a. exempt from registration because of the low amount of the issue.
b. exempt from registration because the offering was advertised.
c. exempt from registration because the unaccredited investors were informed.
d. not exempt from registration.

____ 9. Great Lakes Company is a private, noninvestment company. Last year, as part of a $250,000 advertised offering, Great Lakes sold stock to John, a private investor. John would now like to sell the shares. This resale is

a. exempt from registration because of the low amount of the original issue.
b. exempt from registration because the offering was advertised.
c. exempt from registration because all resales are exempt.
d. not exempt from registration.

____ 10. Digital Products Corporation's registration statement must include

a. a description of the registrant's properties and management.
b. a description of pending lawsuits.
c. both a and b.
d. none of the above.

SHORT ESSAY QUESTIONS

1. What do federal securities laws require of a company that sells nonexempt securities to the public? Be sure to state what a registration statement must include and what a company can do before, during, and after the required waiting period.

2. How do Section 10(b), SEC Rule 10b-5, and Section 16(b) regulate insider trading?

ISSUE SPOTTERS

(Answers at the Back of the Book)

1. Is it possible for a "security" to be something other than a share of stock or a corporate bond? What is the definition of a security?

2. When a corporation wishes to issue certain securities, it must provide sufficient information for an unsophisticated investor to evaluate the financial risk involved. Specifically, the law imposes liability for making a false statement or omission that is "material." What sort of information would an investor consider material?

3. Mel is a vice president of Flax, Inc. Mel knows that a Flax engineer has just discovered a new lode of platinum, an element essential to Flax operations. Mel believes that when the news is made public, the price of Flax's stock will increase. Can Mel take advantage of this information to buy and sell Flax stock?

4. The Securities Act of 1933, the Securities Exchange Act of 1934, and other securities regulation is federal law. Mott Assembly Corporation incorporated in Ohio, does business exclusively in Ohio, and offers its securities for sale only in Ohio. Are there state securities laws to regulate the sale of securities within individual state borders?

5. What is a investment company?

SPECIAL INFORMATION FOR CPA CANDIDATES

Securities law is an important part of the CPA examination. Among the significant details you should pick up from your study of this chapter are the basic differences between the two federal securities acts, the definition of a security, and the requirements for selling securities that are not exempt—registration statement, prospectus, and the twenty-day waiting period. Among the regulations that exempt certain securities and transactions from the registration requirements, the most important for purposes of the CPA exam are Regulation A and Regulation D. These rules are consistently tested. In your study of the Securities Exchange Act of 1934, emphasize insider trading but be aware that other aspects of the act may be tested.

★ Key Points

The **key points** in this chapter include:

1. The advantages of limited liability companies and partnerships.

2. What a limited liability company is and how it operates.

3. How limited liability partnerships can limit the tort liability of partners.

4. What a family limited liability partnership is.

5. How a limited partnership differs from a general partnership.

Chapter 38
Limited Liability Companies and Limited Partnerships

WHAT THIS CHAPTER IS ABOUT

This chapter sets out the law relating to relatively new business organizations: limited liability companies (LLCs), limited liability partnerships (LLPs), limited partnerships, and limited liability limited partnerships (LLLPs). The chief features of these business forms are limited liability and tax advantages.

CHAPTER OUTLINE

I. **LIMITED LIABILITY COMPANIES**
A limited liability company (LLC) is a hybrid form of business enterprise that offers limited liability of a corporation with tax advantages of a partnership.

   A. **FORMATION OF AN LLC**
   Articles of organization must be filed with the state. Certain information is required.

   B. **JURISDICTION OVER AN LLC**
   An LLC is a citizen of every state of which its members are citizens.

   C. **ADVANTAGES**
   Taxed as a partnership; liability of members is limited to the amount of their investment; members can participate in management; corporations, partnerships, and foreign investors can be members; no limit on the number of members (in many states, one is enough).

   D. **DISADVANTAGES**
   Statutory restrictions on the transfer of ownership; because the LLC is a new form, little case law exists; until uniform statutes are adopted by most states, an LLC with multistate operations may face difficulties.

   E. **THE LLC OPERATING AGREEMENT**
   Provisions relate to management, division of profits, transfer of membership, what events trigger dissolution, and so on. In the absence of an

agreement, state statutes govern. If there is no statute, the principles of partnership law apply.

F. MANAGEMENT OF AN LLC

1. Member-Managed LLC
Unless members agree otherwise, all members participate in management and voting rights are usually proportional to capital contributions. An agreement may set governing procedures (in contrast to corporations, which are subject to specific state requirements).

2. Manager-Managed LLC
Members may designate a group to run the firm. If so, the members' interests in the firm may qualify as securities.

II. LIMITED LIABILITY PARTNERSHIPS
Professionals may organize as a limited liability partnership (LLP) to enjoy the tax advantages of a partnership, while avoiding personal liability for the wrongdoing of other partners.

A. LIABILITY IN AN LLP
In an LLP, professionals avoid personal liability for malpractice of other partners.

1. Liability outside the State of Formation
If a state has not adopted the LLP form, its courts may not recognize the LLP's limits on liability. If a state provides different LLP liability protection, there may be a dispute as to which state's law to apply.

2. Supervising Partner's Liability
A partner who commits a wrongful act is liable for the results. Also liable is the partner who supervises the party who commits the act. Some states provide that each partner is liable only up to the proportion of his or her responsibility for the result.

B. FAMILY LIMITED LIABILITY PARTNERSHIPS
This is a limited liability partnership (LLP) in which most of the partners are related. All partners must be natural persons or persons acting in a fiduciary capacity for natural persons. Family-owned farms may benefit from the use of the family limited liability partnership (FLLP) form.

III. LIMITED PARTNERSHIPS
Limited partnerships must include at least one general partner and one or more limited partners. General partners assume management responsibility and liability for all partnership debts.

A. FORMATION OF A LIMITED PARTNERSHIP
The partners sign a certificate of limited partnership, which requires information similar to that found in a corporate charter (see Chapter 34). The certificate is filed with the secretary of state [RULPA 101(7), 201].

B. RIGHTS AND LIABILITIES OF LIMITED PARTNERS

1. Rights of Limited Partners
Essentially the same rights as general partners. Can generally assign their interests in the partnership [RULPA 702, 704]. Can also sue on behalf of the firm if general partners refuse [RULPA 1001].

2. Liabilities of Limited Partners

a. Limited Liability to Creditors of the Partnership
Liable to the extent of any contribution that is promised to the firm or any part of a contribution that was withdrawn [RULPA 502].

b. Personal Liability for Defects in Formation

1) If a Firm Is Organized in an Improper Manner
If the limited partner fails to withdraw on discovery of the defect, he or she can be personally liable to the firm's creditors.

2) If There Is a False Statement in the Partnership Certificate
If a limited partner knows of the statement, he or she may be liable to any person who relies on it [RULPA 207].

3) How to Avoid Future Liability
File an amendment or corrected certificate or renounce an interest in the profits of the partnership [RULPA 304].

3. Limited Partners and Management
Generally, participating in management results in personal liability for partnership debt, if creditors knew of participation [RULPA 303].

C. DISSOLUTION

1. General Partners—Dissolution
Retirement, death, or mental incompetence of a general partner dissolves the firm, unless continued by other general partners [RULPA 801]. Illegality, expulsion, or bankruptcy of general partner dissolves a firm.

2. Limited Partners—No Dissolution
Death or assignment of interest of a limited partner does not dissolve the firm [RULPA 702, 704, 705], nor does personal bankruptcy.

3. Court Decree
A limited partnership can be dissolved by court decree [RULPA 802].

4. Priority to Assets on Dissolution
(1) Creditors, including partners who are creditors; (2) partners and former partners receive unpaid distributions of partnership assets and, except as otherwise agreed, a return on their contributions and amounts proportionate to their share of distributions [RULPA 201(a)(10), 804].

IV. LIMITED LIABILITY LIMITED PARTNERSHIPS
This form is similar to a limited partnership, except that the liability of all partners in a limited liability limited partnership (LLLP) is limited to the amount of their investment in the firm.

V. MAJOR BUSINESS FORMS COMPARED
To decide which form of business organization is appropriate involves the consideration of such factors as the ease of creation, the liability of the owners, tax considerations, and the need for capital. Each form has advantages and disadvantages that indicate when it is most useful.

TRUE-FALSE QUESTIONS

(Answers at the Back of the Book)

____   1.   If, in forming a limited partnership, the limited partnership statute is not followed exactly, a general partnership will result.

____   2.   An assignment of a limited partner's interest in a limited partnership will dissolve the firm.

____   3.   To form a limited liability company, articles of organization need not be filed with the state.

____   4.   A limited liability company is a citizen of every state of which its members are citizens.

____   5.   One disadvantage of a limited liability company is that it cannot include the limited liability of a corporation.

____   6.   The partners in a limited liability partnership cannot avoid personal liability for the malpractice of other partners.

____   7.   The liability of all of the partners in a limited partnership is limited to the amount of their investment in the firm.

____   8.   The liability of all of the partners in a limited liability limited partnership is limited to the amount of their investment in the firm.

____   9.   The members of a limited liability company have more flexibility in terms of governing procedure than the owners of a corporation.

____   10.   The principles of partnership law may, in some cases, apply to a limited liability company.

FILL-IN QUESTIONS

(Answers at the Back of the Book)

Unless the participants agree otherwise, all of the _____ (members/limited partners) of a _____ (limited liability company/limited partnership) may participate in management without assuming liability for the obligations of the firm. In contrast, the _____ (members/limited partners) of a _____ (limited liability company/limited partnership) who participate in management may be personally liable for the debts of the firm.

MULTIPLE-CHOICE QUESTIONS

(Answers at the Back of the Book)

____   1.   **Based on a Sample CPA Question.** Kim is a limited partner in LP Sales, a limited partnership. Ace Credit Company, an LP creditor, claims that Kim is subject to personal liability for LP's debts because Kim has the right, as a limited partner to take control of the firm. Ace is correct about

a.   Kim's liability only.
b.   Kim's right to control the firm only.
c.   Kim's liability and Kim's right to control the firm.
d.   none of the above.

_____ **2.** Dan is a general partner, and Erin and Fred are limited partners in Net.com, a limited partnership. Dan pays personal income taxes on

a. all of the firm's income.
b. his share of the firm's income.
c. only the amount of the firm's income that is actually paid to him.
d. none of the above.

_____ **3.** Betty and Ron form B&R Computers, LLC, a limited liability company. One of the advantages of a limited liability company is that it is taxed as

a. a corporation.
b. a partnership.
c. a sole proprietorship.
d. none of the above.

_____ **4.** Larry, Mary, and Ned form Speedy Delivery Service as a limited liability company. Mary and Ned are liable for the company's debts

a. only to the extent of their investment in the company.
b. only to the extent that Larry cannot pay the debts.
c. to the full extent.
d. none of the above.

_____ **5.** Adam, Bill, and Cathy form Eagle Equipment Company as a limited liability company. Bill and Cathy can participate in management

a. only to the extent that they assume personal liability for the firm's debts.
b. only to the extent of the amount of their investment in the firm.
c. to any extent.
d. to no extent.

_____ **6.** Sam, Jill, and Karl form Sam & Partners, a limited partnership. Sam is a general partner. Jill and Karl are limited partners. Dissolution of the firm would result from Karl's

a. death.
b. bankruptcy.
c. assignment of his interest in the firm to a third party.
d. none of the above.

_____ **7.** Dr. Jones and Dr. Smith are partners in a medical clinic. Jones manages the clinic, which is organized as a limited liability partnership. A court holds Smith liable in a malpractice suit. Jones is

a. not liable.
b. liable only to the extent of her share of that year's profits.
c. liable only to the extent of her investment in the firm.
d. liable beyond her investment in the firm, because she managed the clinic.

_____ **8.** Mike, Nora, and Pat want to form a limited partnership to invest in mutual funds. Mike will be the general partner. All of the following are required to form the partnership EXCEPT

a. at least one general partner and at least one limited partner.
b. either Nora or Pat designated as manager of the firm.
c. a certificate of limited partnership signed by all of the partners.
d. a certificate of limited partnership filed with a designated state official.

____ 9. Greg is a general partner, and Lee and Carol are limited partners in GLC Associates, a limited partnership. Lee and Carol

    a. have less managerial powers than Greg.
    b. cannot sue on behalf of the firm if Greg refuses to do so.
    c. are personally liable only for the debts of the firm, unlike Greg.
    d. risk nothing if they participate in the management of the partnership.

____ 10. Rod, Sara, and Tim form A+ Goods, LLC, a limited liability company. A disadvantage of this form of business organization is that

    a. the income of a limited liability company is taxed twice.
    b. the members are subject to personal liability for the firm's debts.
    c. state laws concerning limited liability companies are not yet uniform.
    d. none of the above.

SHORT ESSAY QUESTIONS

1. What are the advantages of doing business as a limited liability company?

2. Describe the following characteristics of limited partnerships: creation, sharing of profits and loses, liability, capital contribution, management, duration, assignment, and priorities on liquidation.

ISSUE SPOTTERS

(Answers at the Back of the Book)

1. Carol, Donna, and Earl are partners in an accounting firm that is a limited liability partnership. Carol is Donna's supervising partner. Donna obtains $50,000 by committing fraud against Fred, one of the firm's clients. Who may be liable for the $50,000?

2. Olga is a limited partner, and Anton is a general partner of Platinum Fitness Club, a limited partnership. Anton manages the firm. Olga has some expertise in the area and believes that she could do a better job than Anton at managing, but she abstains from becoming actively involved. Why might she choose to keep away from management activities?

3. Greg, Harry, and Ida are members of Best Products, LLC (limited liability company). What are their options with respect to the management of Best Products?

4. Bob and Dian are partners in PC Parts, a computer peripherals mail-order firm. When they decide to end their partnership, the firm's creditors and their personal creditors make claims to partnership assets. At the same time, Bob files for bankruptcy. What is the priority of the creditors to Bob's and the partnership's assets?

5. Jill. Kyle, and Laura want to form Digital Software, LLC (limited liability company). What should they provide in their operating agreement? If they fail to include some important operating details, what determines these details?

SPECIAL INFORMATION FOR CPA CANDIDATES

For the CPA exam, it is most important to know the differences among the types of business organizations, including limited partnerships and limited liability companies.

★ Key Points

The **key points** in this chapter include:

1. Characteristics of joint ventures, syndicates, joint stock companies, business trusts, and cooperatives.

2. How a franchising relationship arises.

3. Federal and state laws that govern franchising arrangements.

4. Some concerns of franchisors and franchisees with respect to franchise contracts.

5. Circumstances in which franchisors may be liable under agency law.

Chapter 39
Special Business Forms and Private Franchises

WHAT THIS CHAPTER IS ABOUT

This chapter sets out features of other forms for doing business—joint ventures, business trusts, cooperatives, and so on. The chapter also discusses private franchises.

CHAPTER OUTLINE

I. SPECIAL BUSINESS FORMS

A. JOINT VENTURE
An enterprise in which two or more persons combine their efforts or property for a single transaction or project, or a related series of transactions or projects. Unless otherwise agreed, joint venturers share profits and losses equally.

1. Characteristics
Same as a partnership except members have less implied and apparent authority than partners, and death of a member does not terminate a joint venture.

2. Duration
Depending on the circumstances: members specify a duration, venture terminates when project for which it is formed is completed, or venture is terminable at the will of any of its members.

3. Duties, Rights, and Liabilities among Joint Venturers

a. Duties
Same as partners (see Chapter 33).

b. Conflicts When Members Are Competitors
(1) Each may face a choice between disclosing trade secrets to a competitor and breaching the duty to disclose, and (2) there is potential for violation of antitrust laws (see Chapter 47).

c. Rights
Each joint venturer has an equal right to manage the activities of the enterprise (though control may be given to one member).

d. Liability
Each joint venturer is liable to third parties for the actions of the other members in pursuit of the goal of the venture.

B. SYNDICATE
A group of individuals financing a project; may exist as a corporation, a partnership, or no legally recognized form.

C. JOINT STOCK COMPANY
Usually treated like a partnership (formed by agreement, members have personal liability, etc.), but members are not agents of one another, and has many characteristics of a corporation: (1) ownership by shares of stock, (2) managed by directors and officers, and (3) perpetual existence.

D. BUSINESS TRUST
Legal ownership and management of the property of the business is in one or more trustees; profits are distributed to beneficiaries, who are not personally responsible for the debts of the trust. Resembles a corporation.

E. COOPERATIVE
An association that is organized to provide an economic service without profit to its members (or shareholders).

1. Incorporated Cooperative
Subject to state laws governing nonprofit corporations. Distributes profits to owners on the basis of their transactions with the cooperative rather than on the basis of the amount of capital they contributed.

2. Unincorporated Cooperatives
Often treated like partnerships. The members have joint liability for the cooperative's acts.

II. PRIVATE FRANCHISES
A **franchise** is any arrangement in which the owner of a trademark, a trade name, or a copyright has licensed others to use it in selling goods or services.

A. TYPES OF FRANCHISES

1. Distributorship
When a manufacturer licenses a dealer to sell its product (such as an automobile dealer). Often covers an exclusive territory.

2. Chain-Style Business Operation
When a franchise operates under a franchisor's trade name and is identified as a member of a group of dealers engaged in the franchisor's business (such as most fast-food chains). The franchisee must follow standardized or prescribed methods of operations, and may be obligated to obtain supplies exclusively from the franchisor.

3. Manufacturing or Processing-Plant Arrangement
When a franchisor transmits to the franchisee the essential ingredients or formula to make a product (such as Coca-Cola), which the franchisee makes and markets according to the franchisor's standards.

B. LAWS GOVERNING FRANCHISING

1. Federal Protection for Franchisees

a. Automobile Dealers' Franchise Act of 1965
Dealership franchisees are protected from manufacturers' bad faith termination of their franchises.

b. Petroleum Marketing Practices Act (PMPA) of 1979
Prescribes the grounds and conditions under which a gasoline station franchisor may terminate or decline to renew a franchise.

c. Antitrust Laws
May apply if there is an anticompetitive agreement (see Chapter 45).

d. Federal Trade Commission (FTC) Regulations
Franchisors must disclose material facts necessary to a prospective franchisee's making an informed decision concerning a franchise.

2. State Protection for Franchisees
Similar to federal law. State deceptive practices acts may apply, as may Article 2 of the Uniform Commercial Code.

C. THE FRANCHISE CONTRACT
A franchise relationship is created by a contract between the franchisor and the franchisee.

1. Payment for the Franchise
A franchisee pays (1) a fee for the franchise license, (2) fees for products bought from or through the franchisor, (3) a percentage of sales, and (4) a percentage of advertising and administrative costs.

2. Business Premises
The agreement may specify whether the premises for the business are leased or purchased and who is to supply equipment and furnishings.

3. Location of the Franchise
The franchisor determines the territory to be served and its exclusivity.

4. Business Organization of the Franchisee
A franchisor may specify requirements for the form and capital structure of the business.

5. Quality Control
A franchisor may specify standards of operation (such as quality standards) and personnel training methods. Too much control may result in a franchisor's liability for torts of a franchisee's employees.

6. Pricing Arrangements
A franchisor may require a franchisee to buy certain supplies from the franchisor at an established price. A franchisor may also set retail prices for the goods that the franchisee sells.

7. Termination of the Franchise
Determined by the parties. Usually, termination must be "for cause" (such as breach of the agreement, etc.) and notice must be given. A franchisee must be given reasonable time to wind up the business.

TRUE-FALSE QUESTIONS

(Answers at the Back of the Book)

____ 1. A joint stock company is usually treated like a partnership.

____ 2. A syndicate may exist in the form of a corporation.

____ 3. The termination of a franchise is always determined by a court.

____ 4. A joint venture can be sued as an entity.

____ 5. A cooperative may take the form of a partnership or a corporation, but its distinguishing feature is that it is organized to provide an economic service without profit.

____ 6. A franchise is an arrangement in which the owner of a trademark, a trade name, or a copyright has licensed others to use it in selling goods or services.

____ 7. A franchisee is not subject to the franchisor's control in the area of product quality.

____ 8. The members of a joint venture have the same power as partners in a partnership to bind other members in the firm.

____ 9. As a form of business organization, a business trust resembles a corporation.

____ 10. There is no state law covering franchises.

FILL-IN QUESTIONS

(Answers at the Back of the Book)

An automobile dealership is an example of a _____ (chain-style/distributorship/manufacturing) franchise. McDonald's is an example of a _____ (chain-style/distributorship/manufacturing) franchise. Coca-Cola is an example of a _____ (chain-style/distributorship/manufacturing) franchise.

MULTIPLE-CHOICE QUESTIONS

(Answers at the Back of the Book)

____ 1. **Based on a Sample CPA Exam Question.** Acme Corporation and U.S. Goods, Inc., form a joint venture to develop and market business software. A joint venture is

a. a corporate enterprise for a single undertaking of limited duration.
b. an association limited to no more than two persons in business for profit.
c. an association of persons engaged as co-owners in a single undertaking for profit.
d. an enterprise of numerous co-owners in a nonprofit undertaking.

____ **2.** Don, Eve, and Frank form a syndicate to finance Village Office Park, a real estate development project. A syndicate

a. is similar to a corporation.
b. is similar to a partnership.
c. is a hybrid of a corporation and a partnership.
d. may exist as a partnership or a corporation.

____ **3.** Lee and Mike form a joint stock company to manage investments for businesses' pension funds. A joint stock company

a. is similar to a corporation.
b. is similar to a partnership.
c. is a hybrid of a corporation and a partnership.
d. may exist as a partnership or a corporation.

____ **4.** American Products, Inc., and National Manufacturing Corporation pool their assets to form a business trust. A business trust

a. is similar to a corporation.
b. is similar to a partnership.
c. is a hybrid of a corporation and a partnership.
d. may exist as a partnership or a corporation.

____ **5.** Kay invests in a franchise with Go Gas Stations, Inc. Regarding the prices at which Kay can sell Go products, the franchisor can set

a. maximum prices only.
b. minimum prices only.
c. maximum or minimum prices.
d. none of the above.

____ **6.** Paul invests in a franchise with Office Copy Centers, Inc. The franchise agreement may require Paul to pay a percentage of Office Copy's

a. administrative expenses only.
b. advertising expenses only.
c. administrative and advertising expenses.
d. none of the above.

____ **7.** Doug wants the exclusive right to sell Computech software in a specific area. If Computech agrees, the franchisor may require Doug to pay Computech

a. only a fee for the license to sell the software.
b. only a percentage of the receipts from sales of the software.
c. a fee for the license and a percentage of the receipts.
d. none of the above.

____ **8.** Nora buys a franchise from Global Services, Inc. In their franchise agreement, Global may specify

a. requirements for the business form of the organization only.
b. standards of operation only.
c. requirements for the form of business and standards of operation.
d. none of the above.

_____   **9.**   Barb buys a franchise from Sports Club Corporation.   If their franchise agreement is like most franchise agreements, it will allow Sports Club to

    a.   terminate the franchise for cause.
    b.   terminate the franchise for any reason without notice.
    c.   not terminate the franchise.
    d.   none of the above.

_____   **10.**   Mark invests in a franchise with Best Foods Corporation. With respect to the franchise, Mark may have legal protection under

    a.   federal law only.
    b.   state law only.
    c.   federal and state law.
    d.   none of the above.

SHORT ESSAY QUESTIONS

1.   What are the principal characteristics of a cooperative?

2.   Explain how franchise agreements generally deal with the following: (1) payment for the franchise, (2) location, (3) price controls, (4) quality control, and (5) termination.

ISSUE SPOTTERS
(Answers at the Back of the Book)

1.   S&R Automobiles, a dealership in Rice County, and National Automobile Company (NAC) enter into a franchise agreement. The agreement gives S&R the right to buy NAC cars for resale. NAC's area manager orally tells S&R that it will be the county's exclusive NAC dealer. Six months later, NAC grants another dealership in Rice County to Bob's Cars. S&R sues, claiming a violation of the Automobile Dealers' Franchise Act, which defines franchise as a "written agreement." Will S&R win?

2.   American Bottling Company and U.S. Beverages, Inc., enter into a franchise agreement that provides it may be terminated at any time "for cause." American fails to meet the specified sales quota of U.S. Does this constitute "cause" for termination?

3.   Jones Construction and Smith Developers form a joint venture.   Machine Manufacturing and Statewide Distributors form a joint stock company. Red's Market and White's Produce form an unincorporated cooperative. What do these forms of business organization have in common?

4.   Great States Mining Corporation and National Ore, Inc., form a business trust. Eagle Equipment Company and Flag Supply Corporation form a joint stock company. Health Resources, Inc., and State Medical Clinics, Inc., form an incorporated cooperative. What do these forms of business organization have in common?

5.   Fine Restaurants, Inc., sells franchises. Fine imposes on its franchisees standards of operation and personnel training methods. What is the potential pitfall to Fine if it exercises too much control over its franchisees?

SPECIAL INFORMATION FOR CPA CANDIDATES

For the CPA exam, it is most important to know the differences among the types of business organizations. Not traditionally tested on the exam are franchises. Of course, they may some day appear in a question on the test.

Chapter 40
Ethics and Business Decision Making

WHAT THIS CHAPTER IS ABOUT

The concepts set out in this chapter include the nature of business ethics and the relationship between ethics and business. Ultimately, the goal of this chapter is to provide you with basic tools for analyzing ethical issues in a business context.

CHAPTER OUTLINE

I. THE NATURE OF BUSINESS ETHICS

A. WHAT IS ETHICS?
Ethics is the branch of philosophy that focuses on morality (right and wrong behavior) and the application of moral principles in everyday life.

B. DEFINING BUSINESS ETHICS
Business ethics focuses on what constitutes ethical behavior in the world of business. Business ethics is *not* a separate kind of ethics.

C. CONFLICTING DUTIES

1. **Duties Owed to Many Groups**
    Ethical decision making is complex in business because duties are owed to a number of groups, including a firm's owners (in a corporation, the shareholders), its employees, its suppliers, its customers, the community in which it operates, and society. These duties may conflict.

2. **Corporate Restructuring and Employee Welfare**
    For example, does an employer have an ethical duty to loyal, long-term employees not to replace them with workers who will accept lower pay? Should this duty prevail over a duty to improve profitability by restructuring?

D. PUBLIC OPINION AND BUSINESS ETHICS
Behaving ethically can protect a firm's reputation and profits.

II. APPROACHES TO ETHICAL REASONING

A. DUTY-BASED ETHICS

1. Religious Standards

Religious standards provide that when an act is prohibited by religious teachings, it is unethical and should not be undertaken, regardless of the consequences. Religious standards also involve compassion.

2. Philosophical Principles

Immanual Kant believed that people should be respected because they are qualitatively different from other physical objects. Individuals should evaluate their actions in light of what would happen if everyone acted the same way.

3. Principle of Rights

According to the principle that persons have rights (to life and liberty, for example), a key factor in determining whether a business decision is ethical is how that decision affects the rights of others, including employees, customers and society.

B. OUTCOME-BASED ETHICS

Utilitarianism is a belief that an action is ethical if it produces the greatest good for the greatest number. This approach is often criticized, because it tends to reduce the welfare of people to plus and minus signs on a cost-benefit worksheet.

III. ETHICAL DECISION MAKING

A. IS THE CONTEMPLATED ACTION LEGAL?

1. Laws Regulating Business

Because there are many laws regulating business, it is possible to violate one without realizing it. The best course is to act responsibly and in good faith.

2. "Gray Areas"

There are also many "gray areas" in which it is difficult to predict how a court will rule. For example, if a consumer is harmed by a product because he or she misused the product, should the manufacturer bear the responsibility?

B. IS THE CONTEMPLATED ACTION ETHICAL?

The minimal acceptable standard for ethical business behavior is compliance with the law. Ethical standards, such as those in a company's policies or codes of ethics, must also guide decision making.

1. Ethical Codes

Most large corporations have codes of conduct that indicate the firm's commitment to legal compliance and to the welfare of those who are affected by corporate decisions and practices. Large firms may also emphasize ethics in other ways (for example, with training programs).

2. Ethical Priorities

To sort out conflicting ethical duties, priorities must be established. Balancing profits and ethics requires sacrificing some profit. Many firms aim for optimum, rather than maximum, profits.   Being ethical can protect a firm's reputation and profits, in light of public opinion.

IV.   MAXIMUM VERSUS OPTIMUM PROFITS

As noted above, behaving ethically can protect a firm's reputation and profits. Behaving ethically may also result in less harsh treatment by the government. Many firms thus attempt to strike a balance between ethics and profits, and aim for optimum, rather than maximum, profits.

V.   THE EVER-CHANGING ETHICAL LANDSCAPE

Our sense of what is ethical—what is fair or just or right in a given situation—changes over time. Conduct that was considered ethical ten years ago might be considered unethical today.

A.   MONITORING THE EMPLOYMENT PRACTICES OF FOREIGN SUPPLIERS

Concerns include the treatment of foreign workers who make goods imported and sold in the United States by U.S. firms. Should a U.S firm refuse to deal with certain suppliers or monitor their workplaces to make sure that the workers are not being mistreated?

B.   THE FOREIGN CORRUPT PRACTICES ACT

The Foreign Corrupt Practices Act (FCPA) of 1977 applies to—

1.   U.S. Companies

Including their directors, officers, shareholders, employees, and agents.

a.   What Is Prohibited

Bribery of most foreign government officials to get an official to act in an official capacity to provide business opportunities.

b.   What Is Permitted

Payments to (1) minor officials whose duties are ministerial, (2) foreign officials if the payments are lawful in the foreign country, or (3) private foreign companies or other third parties unless the U.S. firm knows payments will be made to a foreign government.

2.   Accountants

a.   What Is Required

All companies must (1) keep detailed records that "accurately and fairly" reflect the company's financial activities and (2) have an accounting system that provides "reasonable assurance" that a l l transactions are accounted for and legal.

b.   What Is Prohibited

False statements to accountants and false entries in accounts.

3.   Penalties

Firms: fines up to $2 million. Officers or directors: fines up to $100,000 (cannot be paid by the company); imprisonment up to five years.

C.   OTHER NATIONS

A treaty signed by members of the Organization for Economic Cooperation and Development makes the bribery of foreign officials a crime.

TRUE-FALSE QUESTIONS

(Answers at the Back of the Book)

____ 1. Ethics is the study of what constitutes right and wrong behavior.

____ 2. The study of business ethics is fundamentally different from the general study of ethics.

____ 3. According to religious standards, certain moral standards are universal.

____ 4. In determining how ethical an act is according to utilitarian standards, it does not matter how many people benefit from the act.

____ 5. A socially responsible firm will often aim for optimum profits instead of maximum profits.

____ 6. Ethical problems that arise in a business context normally involve clear choices between good and bad alternatives.

____ 7. If a corporation fails to conduct itself ethically, its profits may suffer.

____ 8. Under the Foreign Corrupt Practices Act, an accountant could be fined up to $100,000.

____ 9. When the legality of an action is not clear, a businessperson should take an action that is at least ethically defensible.

____ 10. Business conduct that was considered acceptable in the past is always acceptable today.

FILL-IN QUESTIONS

(Answers at the Back of the Book)

A law is what society considers _____
(proper behavior/a principle that never changes). An ethical value is an expression of
what is considered _____ (proper behavior/a
principle that never changes). Our sense of what is ethical _____
(changes/does not change) over time.

MULTIPLE-CHOICE QUESTIONS

(Answers at the Back of the Book)

____ 1. Business ethics focuses on the application of

a. moral principles.
b. business philosophies.
c. law.
d. none of the above.

____ 2. Which ethical standards derive from religious sources?

a. Duty-based ethics
b. Utilitarianism
c. Outcome-based ethics
d. None of the above

____   **3.**   Religious ethical standards are generally viewed as absolute but may also involve an element of

a.   cost-benefit analysis.
b.   discretion.
c.   compassion.
d.   none of the above.

____   **4.**   Which ethics is premised on acting so as to do the greatest good for the greatest number of people?

a.   Duty-based ethics
b.   Utilitarianism
c.   Religious-based ethics
d.   None of the above

____   **5.**   Steve does not agree with the principles of utilitarianism. Which of the following would be Steve's best criticism of utilitarianism?

a.   It requires choosing among conflicting ethical principles.
b.   It tends to focus on society as a whole rather than on individuals.
c.   It is overly concerned with ideals of perfection.
d.   It is an outdated philosophy.

____   **6.**   ABC Corporation responds to what it sees as a moral obligation to correct for past discrimination by adjusting pay differences among employees. This likely raises an ethical conflict between which parties?

a.   Employees only
b.   ABC and employees only
c.   ABC and shareholders only
d.   ABC and employees, and ABC and shareholders

____   **7.**   **Based on a Sample CPA Exam Question.** Ethical standards would most likely be considered to have been violated if Acme Services, Inc., represents to Best Production Company that certain services will be performed for a stated fee, but it is apparent at the time of the representation that

a.   Acme cannot perform the services alone.
b.   the actual charge will be substantially higher.
c.   the actual charge will be substantially lower.
d.   the fee is a competitive bid.

____   **8.**   In deciding on a course of action, Erin, an officer with Federated Industries, Inc., is confronted with conflicting ethical duties. A decision may have to be made as to which duty should prevail. Such a decision

a.   does not normally have clear answers.
b.   may involve choices between equally good and bad alternatives.
c.   both a and b.
d.   none of the above.

___ **9.** Don, an executive with Eagle Transport Company, must consider the consequences of an Eagle act that would be illegal. If the act benefits a large number of people, the act may be considered

    a. legal.
    b. ethical under a duty-based standard.
    c. ethical under a utilitarian-based standard.
    d. all of the above.

___ **10.** Alpha, Inc., a U.S. corporation, is looking for business opportunities abroad. The minister of commerce of one country offers to use his official power to provide those opportunities for a "personal contribution." The Foreign Corrupt Practices Act prohibits bribery

    a. to all foreigners.
    b. to foreign officials to influence official acts.
    c. by corporations only.
    d. by foreign officials to U.S. corporations.

SHORT ESSAY QUESTIONS

What is the difference between legal and ethical standards? How are legal standards affected by ethical standards?

ISSUE SPOTTERS

(Answers at the Back of the Book)

1. If, like Robin Hood, a person robs the rich to pay the poor, does his or her benevolent intent make his or her actions ethical?

2. Gamma Manufacturing, Inc., has to decide whether to close a plant. Gamma may weigh the costs of doing against the benefits. If the benefits are greater than the costs, can closing the plant be ethically justified, considering the effect on the employees?

3. Paula, an executive with Worldwide Products Corporation, has to decide whether to market a product that might have undesirable side effects for a small percentage of users. What is the balance that must be struck?

4. Delta Tools, Inc., markets a product that under some circumstances is capable of seriously injuring consumers. Does Delta owe an ethical duty to remove this product from the market, even if the injuries result only from misuse?

5. Acme Corporation decides to respond to what it sees as a moral obligation to correct for past discrimination by adjusting pay differences among its employees. Does this raise an ethical conflict between Acme's employees? Between Acme and its employees? Between Acme and its shareholders?

SPECIAL INFORMATION FOR CPA CANDIDATES

Ethics is tested in the business law and professional responsibilities portion of the CPA examination. The general outline provided in this chapter can serve as a jumping-off point for a more specific study of professional ethics. In the past, the CPA has covered the legal implications to CPAs, of certain business transactions, as well as the CPA's professional responsibility to clients and the accounting profession. The Foreign Corrupt Practices Act has been tested in the securities portion of the exam.

Specific topics in the area of professional responsibility can be divided into two categories: (1) the code of conduct and other professional responsibilities and (2) the law relating to CPA responsibilities. The first category can be further split into such topics as the code of professional conduct; proficiency and due care; consulting responsibilities; and tax practice responsibilities. The second category includes such topics as potential common law liability to clients and third parties, liability under federal statutes, and liability relating to working papers, privileged communications with clients, and confidentiality. These topics are covered in Chapter 51.

CUMULATIVE HYPOTHETICAL PROBLEM FOR UNIT SEVEN—INCLUDING CHAPTERS 33–40

(Answers at the Back of the Book)

Adam, Beth, and Carl are sole proprietors who decide to pool their resources to produce and maintain an Internet portal Web site, "i-World."

____ **1.** Adam, Beth, and Carl decide to form a partnership. They transfer their business assets and liabilities to the firm and start business on May 1, 2001. The parties execute a formal partnership agreement on July 1. The partnership began its existence

   a. on May 1.
   b. on July 1.
   c. when each partner's individual creditors consented to the asset transfer.
   d. when the parties initially decided to form a partnership.

____ **2.** After six months in operation, Adam, Beth, and Carl decide to change the form of their partnership to a limited partnership. To form a limited partnership, they must

   a. accept limited liability for all of the partners.
   b. create the firm according to specific statutory requirements.
   c. designate one general partner to be a limited partner.
   d. each make a capital contribution.

____ **3.** Adam, Beth, and Carl's i-World is very successful. In March 2002, they decide to incorporate. The articles of incorporation must include all of the following except

   a. the name of a registered agent.
   b. the name of the corporation.
   c. the names of the incorporators.
   d. the names of the initial officers.

____ **4.** In January 2003, Adam, Beth, and Carl decide to issue additional stock in i-World, Inc. The registration statement must include

   a. a copy of the corporation's most recent proxy statement.
   b. the names of prospective accredited investors.
   c. the names of the current shareholders.
   d. the principal purposes for which the proceeds from the offering will be used.

_____ **5.** The issue of shares that i-World, Inc., plans to make qualifies under Rule 504 of Regulation D of the Securities Act of 1933. Under this rule, i-World

   a. may not make the offering through general advertising.
   b. may sell the shares to an unlimited number of investors.
   c. must offer the shares for sale for more than twelve months.
   d. must provide all prospective investors with a prospectus.

Chapter 41
Labor and Employment Law

WHAT THIS CHAPTER IS ABOUT

This chapter outlines the most significant laws regulating employment relationships. Other significant laws regulating the workplace—those prohibiting employment discrimination—are dealt with in Chapter 42.

CHAPTER OUTLINE

I. WAGE-HOUR LAWS

Davis-Bacon Act of 1931 requires "prevailing wages" for employees of some government contractors. Walsh-Healey Act of 1936 requires minimum wage and overtime for employees of some government contractors. Fair Labor Standards Act of 1938 (FLSA) covers all employees and regulates—

A. CHILD LABOR
Children under fourteen can deliver newspapers, work for their parents, and work in entertainment and agriculture. Children fourteen and older cannot work in hazardous occupations.

B. MAXIMUM HOURS
Employees who work more than forty hours per week must be paid no less than one and a half times their regular pay for all hours over forty. Executives, administrative employees, professional employees, and outside salespersons are exempt.

C. MINIMUM WAGE
A specified amount (periodically revised) must be paid to employees in covered industries. Wages include the reasonable cost to furnish employees with board, lodging, and other facilities.

II. LABOR UNIONS

A. FEDERAL LABOR LAWS

1. **Norris-LaGuardia Act**
   Enacted in 1932. Restricts federal courts' power to issue injunctions against unions engaged in peaceful strikes, picketing, and boycotts.

2. **National Labor Relations Act (NLRA) of 1935**
   Established rights to bargain collectively and to strike, and—

   a. **Unfair Employer Practices**
   Prohibits interfering with union activities, discriminating against union employees, refusing to bargain with union, other practices.

   b. **National Labor Relations Board (NLRB)**
   Created to oversee union elections, prevent employers from engaging in unfair practices, investigate employers in response to employee charges of unfair labor practices, issue cease-and-desist orders.

3. **Labor-Management Relations Act (LMRA) of 1947**
   Prohibits unions from refusing to bargain with employers, engaging in certain types of picketing, featherbedding, and other unfair practices. Preserves union shops, but allows states to pass right-to-work laws, which make it illegal to require union membership for employment.

4. **Labor-Management Reporting and Disclosure Act (LMRDA) of 1959**

   a. **Union Business**
   Requires elections of union officers under secret ballot; prohibits ex-convicts and Communists from holding union office; makes officials accountable for union property; allows members to participate in union meetings, nominate officers, vote in proceedings.

   b. **Hot-Cargo Agreements**
   Outlaws hot-cargo agreements (in which employers agree not to handle, use, or deal in non-union goods of other employers).

B. **UNION ORGANIZATION**
   If a majority of workers sign authorization cards and the employer refuses to recognize the union, unionizers can petition the NLRB for an election.

   1. **Union Elections**
   For an election to be held, there must be support for the union by at least 30 percent of the workers. NLRB ensures secret voting.

   2. **Union Election Campaigns**
   Employers may limit campaign activities (fairly) and may campaign against union.

C. **COLLECTIVE BARGAINING**
   The process by which labor and management negotiate terms and conditions of employment. Each side must bargain in good faith (be willing to meet and to consider the other's offers and proposals). Refusing to bargain in good faith without justification is an unfair labor practice.

D. **STRIKES**
   A strike occurs when workers leave their jobs and refuse to work.

   1. **Right to Strike**
   Guaranteed by the NLRA, within limits. Strike activities, such as picketing, are protected by the First Amendment. Nonworkers have a

right to participate in picketing. Workers can also refuse to cross a picket line of fellow workers who are engaged in a lawful strike.

2. Replacing or Rehiring Strikers
An employer may hire substitute workers to replace strikers.

a. Economic Strikes over Working Conditions
Strikers have no right to return to their jobs, but must be given preference to any vacancies and also retain their seniority rights.

b. Employer Unfair Labor Practice Strikes
Strikers must be given their jobs back.

III. WORKER HEALTH AND SAFETY

A. OCCUPATIONAL SAFETY AND HEALTH ACT OF 1970
Attempts to ensure safe and healthful work conditions for most employees.

1. Enforcement Agencies

a. Occupational Safety and Health Administration (OSHA)
Inspects workplaces and issues safety standards, including standards covering employee exposure to harmful substances.

b. National Institute for Occupational Safety and Health
Researches safety and health problems and recommends standards for OSHA to adopt.

c. Occupational Safety and Health Review Commission
Hears appeals from actions taken by OSHA administrators.

2. Procedures and Violations
Employees file complaints of OSHA violations (employers cannot retaliate); employers must keep injury and illness records; employers must file accident reports directly to OSHA. Penalties are limited.

B. STATE WORKERS' COMPENSATION LAWS
State laws establish procedure for compensating workers injured on the job.

1. No State Covers All Employees
Often excluded are domestic workers, agricultural workers, temporary employees, and employees of common carriers.

2. Requirements for Recovery
There must be an employment relationship, and the injury must be accidental and occur on the job or in the course of employment.

3. Filing a Claim
An employee must notify the employer of an injury (usually within thirty days), and file a claim with a state agency within a certain period (sixty days to two years) from the time the injury is first noticed.

4. Acceptance of Workers' Compensation Benefits Bars Suits
An employee's acceptance of benefits bars the employee from suing for injuries caused by the employer's negligence.

IV. INCOME SECURITY

A. SOCIAL SECURITY AND MEDICARE

1. Social Security
The Social Security Act of 1935 provides for payments to persons who are retired, widowed, disabled, etc. Employers and employees must contribute under the Federal Insurance Contributions Act (FICA).

2. Medicare
A health insurance program administered by the Social Security Administration for people sixty-five years of age and older and for some under sixty-five who are disabled.

B. PRIVATE PENSION PLANS
The Employee Retirement Income Security Act (ERISA) of 1974 empowers the Labor Management Services Administration of the Department of Labor to oversee those who operate private pension funds.

1. Vesting
Generally, employee contributions to pension plans vest immediately; employee rights to employer contributions vest after five years.

2. Investing
Pension-fund managers must be cautious in investing and refrain from investing more than 10 percent of the fund in securities of the employer.

C. UNEMPLOYMENT COMPENSATION
The Federal Unemployment Tax Act of 1935 created a state system that provides unemployment compensation to eligible individuals.

V. COBRA
The Consolidated Omnibus Budget Reconciliation Act (COBRA) of 1985 prohibits the elimination of a worker's medical, optical, or dental insurance on the termination of most workers' employment. Coverage must continue for up to 18 months (29 months in some cases). A worker pays the premium plus 2 percent.

VI. FAMILY AND MEDICAL LEAVE ACT (FMLA) OF 1993
Employers with fifty or more employees must provide them with up to twelve weeks of family or medical leave during any twelve-month period, continue health-care coverage during the leave, and guarantee employment in the same, or a comparable, position when the employee returns to work.

VII. EMPLOYEE PRIVACY RIGHTS
A right to privacy has been inferred from constitutional guarantees provided by the First, Third, Fourth, Fifth, and Ninth Amendments to the Constitution.

A. LIE-DETECTOR TESTS
Under the Employee Polygraph Protection Act of 1988, employers cannot, among other things, require, request, or suggest that employees or applicants take lie-detector tests. Employers may use polygraph tests when investigating theft, including theft of trade secrets.

B. DRUG TESTING

1. Protection for the Privacy Rights of Private Employees
Some state constitutions may prohibit, or some state statutes may restrict, private employers from testing for drugs. Other protection

includes collective bargaining agreements and tort actions for invasion of privacy. There may be little recourse for "false positives," however.

2. Protection for Government Employees
Constitutional limitations (the Fourth Amendment) apply. Drug tests have been upheld when there was a reasonable basis for suspecting employees of using drugs, or when drug use could threaten public safety.

C. AIDS TESTING
Some state laws restrict AIDS testing. The federal Americans with Disabilities Act of 1990 and other statutes protect employees or applicants who have tested positive from discrimination.

D. SCREENING PROCEDURES
A key factor in determining whether preemployment screening tests violate privacy rights is whether there is a connection between the questions and the job for which an applicant is applying.

VIII. EMPLOYMENT-RELATED IMMIGRATION LAWS

A. IMMIGRATION REFORM AND CONTROL ACT (IRCA) OF 1986
The IRCA prohibits employers from hiring illegal immigrants.

B. IMMIGRATION ACT OF 1990
Employers recruiting workers from other countries must complete a certification process, satisfy the Department of Labor that there is a shortage of qualified U.S. workers to perform the work, and show that bringing aliens into this country will not adversely affect the labor market.

IX. WRONGFUL DISCHARGE
Under the employment at-will doctrine, either the employer or the employee may terminate an employment relationship at any time and for any reason (unless a contract or the law provides to the contrary).

A. EXCEPTIONS BASED ON CONTRACT THEORY

1. Implied Contract
Some courts have held that an implied contract exists between an employer and an employee (if, for example, a personnel manual states that no employee will be fired without good cause).

2. Implied Covenant of Good Faith
A few states have held that all employment contracts contain an implied covenant of good faith.

B. EXCEPTIONS BASED ON TORT THEORY
Discharge may give rise to a tort action for wrongful discharge.

C. EXCEPTIONS BASED ON PUBLIC-POLICY
An employer may not fire a worker for reasons that violate a public policy of the jurisdiction (for example, for refusing to violate the law).

X. STATUTORY PROTECTION FOR WHISTLEBLOWERS
An employer cannot fire an employee in violation of a federal or state statute. If so, the employee may bring an action for wrongful discharge. Some state and federal statutes protect whistleblowers from retaliation. The False Claims Act of 1986 gives a whistleblower 15 to 25 percent of proceeds recovered from fraud.

TRUE-FALSE QUESTIONS

(Answers at the Back of the Book)

____ 1. Employers can agree with unions not to handle, use, or deal in non-union-produced goods.

____ 2. In some circumstances, the Constitution allows employers to test their employees for drugs.

____ 3. Employment considered to be "at will" means that employers cannot fire employees without good cause.

____ 4. Employers are required by federal statute to establish health insurance and pension plans.

____ 5. Management serves as the representative of workers in bargaining with a union over the rights of employees.

____ 6. Children fourteen and older can work in hazardous occupations.

____ 7. Under the FLSA, all nonexempt employees who work more than forty hours per week must be paid at least one and a half times their regular pay for all hours over forty.

____ 8. Peaceful strikes, picketing, and boycotts are protected under federal law.

____ 9. Employees have no right to engage in collective bargaining through elected representatives.

____ 10. Requiring union membership as a condition of employment is prohibited by federal law.

FILL-IN QUESTIONS

(Answers at the Back of the Book)

Under the employment-at-will doctrine, _____ (either/neither) party may terminate an employment relationship at any time and for any reason _____ (unless/even if) a contract provides to the contrary. An employee who is fired in violation of a federal or state statute _____ (may/may not) bring an action for wrongful discharge. _____ (Some/No) courts have held that an implied contract exists between an employer and an employee. _____ (All/A few states) have held that all employment contracts contain an implied covenant of good faith. An employer _____ (may/may not) fire a worker for reasons that violate a public policy of the jurisdiction.

MULTIPLE-CHOICE QUESTIONS

(Answers at the Back of the Book)

____ 1. **Based on a Sample CPA Exam Question.** Fast Jack is a fast-food restaurant. To verify Fast Jack's compliance with statutes governing employees' wages and hours, personnel records should be checked against the provisions of

a. the Fair Labor Standards Act.
b. the Family and Medical Leave Act.
c. the National Labor Relations Act.
d. the Taft-Hartley Act.

_____ 2. Erin, an employee of CamCorp, is injured. For Erin to receive *workers' compensation*, the injury must be

a. accidental and arise out of a preexisting disease or condition.
b. accidental and occur on the job or in the course of employment.
c. intentional and arise out of a preexisting disease or condition.
d. intentional and occur on the job or in the course of employment.

_____ 3. U.S. Goods, Inc. (USG), recruits workers from other countries to work in its U.S. plant. To comply with the Immigration Act of 1990, USG must show that

a. there is a shortage of qualified U.S. workers to perform the work.
b. bringing aliens into the country will not adversely affect the existing labor market in that area.
c. both a and b.
d. none of the above.

_____ 4. Ron is an employee of National Sales Company. Both Ron and National make contributions to the federal social security system under

a. the Federal Unemployment Tax Act.
b. the Federal Insurance Contributions Act.
c. the Employment Retirement Income Security Act.
d. none of the above.

_____ 5. Eagle Products, Inc., sets up a pension fund for its employees. Eagle's operation of the fund is regulated by

a. the Federal Unemployment Tax Act.
b. the Federal Insurance Contributions Act.
c. the Employment Retirement Income Security Act.
d. none of the above.

_____ 6. ABC Box Corporation provides health insurance for its 150 employees, including Diana. When Diana takes twelve weeks' leave to care for her new baby, she

a. can continue her heath insurance at her expense.
b. can continue her heath insurance at ABC Box Corporation's expense.
c. loses her heath insurance immediately on taking leave.
d. is entitled to "leave pay" equal to twelve weeks' of health insurance coverage.

_____ 7. Mega Corporation provides health insurance for its employees. When Mega closes one of its offices and terminates the employees, the employees

a. can continue their heath insurance at their expense.
b. can continue their heath insurance at Mega's expense.
c. lose their heath insurance immediately on termination of employment.
d. are entitled to "severance pay" equal to twelve weeks' of health insurance coverage.

____ **8.** Don works for American Tools Company. Don and other employees designate the National Machinists Union (NMU) as their bargaining representative. Without violating federal labor law, American Tools can

    a. refuse to bargain with NMU.
    b. fire Don for "choosing the wrong side."
    c. both a and b.
    d. none of the above.

____ **9.** Assembly Workers Union (AWU) represents the employees of National Manufacturing, Inc. When AWU calls an economic strike, National Manufacturing hires replacement workers. After the strike

    a. the former strikers must be rehired.
    b. the replacement workers must be fired.
    c. both a and b.
    d. none of the above.

____ **10.** Standard Machine Company production employees are to vote on whether to be represented by the Production Workers Union (PWU). During the election campaign, the company may

    a. campaign against the union.
    b. announce that it will refuse to bargain with the union if the union wins.
    c. restrict union campaigning but permit other solicitation.
    d. threaten employees with the loss of their jobs if the union wins the vote.

SHORT ESSAY QUESTIONS

1. What is the employment-at-will doctrine? What are its exceptions?

2. What are important federal laws concerning labor unions? What specifically does each law provide?

ISSUE SPOTTERS

(Answers at the Back of the Book)

1. American Manufacturing Company (AMC) issues an employee handbook that states employees will be discharged only for good cause. One day, Greg, an AMC supervisor, says to Larry, "I don't like your looks. You're fired." May AMC be held liable for breach of contract?

2. Workers' compensation laws establish a procedure for compensating workers who are injured on the job. Instead of suing, the worker files a claim with the appropriate state agency. Does the injury have to have been caused by the employer's negligence?

3. Rose applies for work with National Packaging Company (NPC). NPC tells her that it requires union membership as a condition of employment. Rose applies for work with U.S. Goods Corporation (USG). USG does not require union membership as a condition of employment but requires employees to join a union after six months on the job. Are these conditions legal?

4. Arlene, a waitress at the Good Eats Cafeteria, notices that the kitchen staff is not wearing protective gloves while preparing food, a violation of state law. Arlene reports this to her manager, but no steps are taken. Arlene then tells a friend of hers who works for the local newspaper. After the paper runs a story on the violations, business at the Good Eats Cafeteria drops by 65 percent. Can the Good Eats Cafeteria fire Arlene for her actions?

5. The Employee Retirement Income Security Act (ERISA), passed by Congress in 1974, granted the Labor Management Services Administration of the U.S. Department of Labor the power to oversee the operators of private pension funds. What are the two most important provisions of this law?

SPECIAL INFORMATION FOR CPA CANDIDATES

The CPA examination has never covered the employment-at-will doctrine, the laws protecting whistleblowers, the laws related to employee privacy rights, or labor law. FICA, FUTA, and the law governing workers' compensation have been often tested, however. FICA questions concern coverage and benefits; FUTA questions relate to the source of funds for unemployment compensation; workers' compensation questions often concern the basis for recovery under applicable laws. Some of the other material touched on in this chapter has been covered on recent CPA exams. This material includes FLSA, OSHA, and ERISA—their objectives, coverage, and application.

Chapter 42
Employment Discrimination

WHAT THIS CHAPTER IS ABOUT

The law restricts employers and unions from discriminating against workers on the basis of race, color, religion, national origin, gender, age, or handicap. A class of persons defined by one or more of these criteria is known as a **protected class**. This chapter outlines these laws.

CHAPTER OUTLINE

I.   TITLE VII OF THE CIVIL RIGHTS ACT OF 1964
Prohibits employment discrimination against employees, applicants, and union members on the basis of race, color, national origin, religion, and gender.

A.   WHO IS SUBJECT TO TITLE VII?
Employers with fifteen or more employees, labor unions with fifteen or more members, labor unions that operate hiring halls, employment agencies, and federal, state, and local agencies.

B.   PROCEDURES UNDER TITLE VII
(1) A victim files a claim with the Equal Employment Opportunity Commission (EEOC); (2) the EEOC investigates and seeks a voluntary settlement; (3) if no settlement is reached, the EEOC may sue the employer; (4) if the EEOC chooses not to sue, the victim may file a lawsuit.

C.   INTENTIONAL AND UNINTENTIONAL DISCRIMINATION
Title VII prohibits both intentional and unintentional discrimination.

1.   Disparate-Treatment Discrimination
Intentional discrimination by an employer against an employee.

a.   *Prima Facie* Case—Plaintiff's Side of the Case
Plaintiff must show (1) he or she is a member of a protected class, (2) he or she applied and was qualified for the job, (3) he or she

344

was rejected by the employer, (4) the employer continued to seek applicants or filled the job with a person not in a protected class.

b. **Defense—Employer's Side of the Case**
Employer must articulate a legal reason for not hiring the plaintiff. To prevail, the plaintiff must show that the employer's reason is a pretext and that discriminatory intent motivated the decision.

2. **Disparate-Impact Discrimination**

a. **Types of Disparate-Impact Discrimination**
Disparate-impact discrimination results if, because of a requirement or hiring practice—

1) an employer's work force does not reflect the percentage of members of protected classes that characterizes qualified individuals in the local labor market, or

2) members of protected class are excluded from employer's work force at substantially higher rate than nonmembers (under EEOC's "four-fifths rule," selection rate for protected class must be at least 80 percent of rate for group with the highest rate).

b. *Prima Facie* **Case—Plaintiff's Side of the Case**
Plaintiff must show a connection between a requirement or practice and a disparity; no evidence of discriminatory intent is needed.

D. **DISCRIMINATION BASED ON RACE, COLOR, AND NATIONAL ORIGIN**
Employers cannot effectively discriminate against employees on the basis of race, color, national origin, or religion (unless there is a substantial, demonstrable relationship between the trait and the job, etc.).

E. **DISCRIMINATION BASED ON RELIGION**
Title VII prohibits employers and unions from discriminating against persons because of their religions.

F. **DISCRIMINATION BASED ON GENDER**
Employers cannot discriminate against employees on the basis of gender (unless the gender of the applicant can be proved essential to the job, etc.). The Pregnancy Discrimination Act of 1978 amended Title VII: employees affected by pregnancy or related conditions must be treated the same as persons not so affected but similar in ability to work.

G. **SEXUAL HARASSMENT**

1. **Forms of Harassment**
(1) *Quid pro quo* harassment: when promotions, etc., are doled out on the basis of sexual favors; (2) hostile-environment harassment: when an employee is subjected to offensive sexual comments, etc.

2. **Harassment by Supervisors, Co-Workers, or Nonemployees**

a. **When an Employer May Be Liable**
If anyone (employee or nonemployee) harasses an employee, and the employer knew, or should have known, and failed to take immediate corrective action, the employer may be liable.

b. **Employer's Defense**
(1) Employer took "reasonable care to prevent and correct promptly any sexually harassing behavior," and (2) employee suing for harassment failed to follow employer's policies and procedures.

H. REMEDIES UNDER TITLE VII
Reinstatement, back pay, retroactive promotions, and damages.

1. **Damages**
Compensatory damages are available only in cases of intentional discrimination. Punitive damages are available only if an employer acted with malice or reckless indifference

2. **Limitations**
Total damages are limited to specific amounts against specific employers (from $50,000 against those with one hundred or fewer employees to $300,000 against those with more than five hundred employees).

II.   EQUAL PAY ACT OF 1963
Prohibits gender-based discrimination in wages for equal work (work requiring equal skill, effort, and responsibility under similar conditions). Different wages are acceptable because of any factor but gender (seniority, merit, etc.).

III.   DISCRIMINATION BASED ON AGE

A. AGE DISCRIMINATION IN EMPLOYMENT ACT (ADEA) OF 1967
Prohibits employment discrimination on the basis of age (including mandatory retirement), by employers with twenty or more employees, against individuals forty years of age or older. Administered by the EEOC, but private causes of action are also possible.

B. PRINCIPLES ARE SIMILAR TO TITLE VII
Requires the establishment of a *prima facie* case: plaintiff must show that he or she was (1) forty or older, (2) qualified for a position, and (3) rejected in circumstances that infer discrimination. The employer must articulate a legal reason; the plaintiff may show it is a pretext.

C. STATE EMPLOYERS
Under the Eleventh Amendment to the Constitution, a state is immune from suits brought by private individuals in federal court unless the state consents to the suit. A state agency sued by a state employee for age discrimination may have the suit dismissed on this ground.

IV.   DISCRIMINATION BASED ON DISABILITY
Under the Americans with Disabilities Act (ADA) of 1990, an employer cannot refuse to hire a person who is qualified but disabled.

A. PROCEDURES AND REMEDIES UNDER THE ADA

1. **Procedures**
A plaintiff must show he or she (1) has a disability, (2) is otherwise qualified for a job and (3) was excluded solely because of the disability. A suit may be filed only after a claim is pursued through the EEOC.

2. Remedies

Reinstatement, back pay, some compensatory and punitive damages (for intentional discrimination), and certain other relief. Repeat violators may be fined up to $100,000.

B. WHAT IS A DISABILITY?

"(1) [A] physical or mental impairment that substantially limits one or more of the major life activities . . . ; (2) a record of such impairment; or (3) being regarded as having such an impairment." Includes AIDS, morbid obesity, etc.; not homosexuality or kleptomania.

C. REASONABLE ACCOMMODATION

For a person with a disability, an employer may have to make a reasonable accommodation (more flexible working hours, new job assignment, different training materials or procedures)—but not an accommodation that will cause **undue hardship** (impose "significant difficulty or expense").

1. Job Applications

The application process must be accessible to those with disabilities.

2. Preemployment Physical Exams

Employers cannot require a disabled person to take a preemployment physical (unless all applicants do). Disqualification must be from problems that render a person unable to perform the job.

3. Dangerous Workers

An employer need not hire disabled workers who would pose a "direct threat to the health or safety" of co-workers or to themselves.

4. Substance Abusers

The ADA protects addicts who have completed or are in supervised rehabilitation, and alcoholics to the extent of equal treatment.

5. Health Insurance Plans

Workers with disabilities must be given equal access to insurance plans provided to other workers. If a plan includes a disability-based distinction, an employer must show (1) limiting coverage keeps the plan financially sound, (2) coverage would otherwise be too expensive for many workers, or (3) the distinction is justified by the risk and costs.

V. DEFENSES TO EMPLOYMENT DISCRIMINATION

The first defense is to assert that the plaintiff did not prove discrimination. If discrimination is proved, an employer may attempt to justify it as—

A. BUSINESS NECESSITY

An employer may show that there is a legitimate connection between a job requirement that discriminates and job performance.

B. BONA FIDE OCCUPATIONAL QUALIFICATION (BFOQ)

Another defense applies when discrimination against a protected class is essential to a job—that is, when a particular trait is a BFOQ. Generally restricted to cases in which gender is essential. Race can never be a BFOQ.

C. SENIORITY SYSTEMS

An employer with a history of discrimination may have no members of protected classes in upper-level positions. If no present intent to discriminate is shown, and promotions, etc., are distributed according to a fair seniority system, the employer has a good defense.

D. AFTER-ACQUIRED EVIDENCE

An employer who discovers, after discharging an employee, that the worker engaged in misconduct in applying for the job or while on the job may use that misconduct to limit the amount of damages to the plaintiff.

VI. AFFIRMATIVE ACTION

An affirmative action program attempts to make up for past discrimination by giving members of protected classes preferential treatment in hiring or promotion. Such an employment program cannot use quotas or preferences for unqualified persons, and once it has succeeded, it must be changed or dropped.

VII. STATE LAWS PROHIBITING DISCRIMINATION

Most states have statutes that prohibit the kinds of discrimination prohibited under federal law. Also, state laws often protect individuals, such as those under forty years of age or those who work at very small firms, who are not protected under federal law, and may provide for damages in addition to those allowed under federal law.

TRUE-FALSE QUESTIONS

(Answers at the Back of the Book)

_____ 1. Once an affirmative action program has succeeded, it must be changed or dropped.

_____ 2. In a sexual harassment case, an employer cannot be held liable if an employee did the harassing.

_____ 3. In a sexual harassment case, an employer cannot be held liable if a nonemployee did the harassing.

_____ 4. Women affected by pregnancy must be treated for all job-related purposes the same as persons not so affected but similar in ability to work.

_____ 5. Employment discrimination against persons with a physical or mental impairment that substantially limits their everyday activities is prohibited.

_____ 6. Discrimination complaints brought under federal law must be filed with the Equal Opportunity Employment Commission.

_____ 7. If the Equal Employment Opportunity Commission decides not to investigate a claim, the victim has no other option.

_____ 8. All employers are subject to Title VII of the Civil Rights Act of 1964 regardless of the number of their employees.

_____ 9. Disparate-treatment discrimination occurs when an employer intentionally discriminates against an employee.

_____ 10. Title VII prohibits employers and unions from discriminating against persons because of their religions.

FILL-IN QUESTIONS

(Answers at the Back of the Book)

Compliance with the federal antidiscrimination laws is monitored by the Equal Employment Opportunity Commission (EEOC), which _____ (can/cannot) sue organizations that violate these laws. A victim files a claim with the EEOC, which investigates and _____ (must sue/may sue if a settlement between the parties is not reached). If the EEOC does not sue, the victim may sue. On proof of discrimination, a victim may be awarded _____ (reinstatement and back pay/reinstatement, back pay, and retroactive promotions).

MULTIPLE-CHOICE QUESTIONS

(Answers at the Back of the Book)

____ 1. Tina believes that she has been discriminated against because she is a woman. She attempts to resolve the dispute with her employer, who decides that her claim has no basis. Tina's next best step is to

    a. file a lawsuit.
    b. for get about the matter.
    c. contact a state or federal agency to see whether a claim is justified.
    d. ask the Equal Opportunity Employment Commission to issue a guideline.

____ 2. Greg and Nora work for SeeCo as software engineers. Greg is paid more than Nora because, according to SeeCo, he is a man with a family to support. This distinction is prohibited by

    a. the Age Discrimination in Employment Act of 1967.
    b. the Equal Pay Act of 1963.
    c. the Americans with Disabilities Act of 1990.
    d. none of the above.

____ 3. **Based on a Sample CPA Exam Question.** Under the Age Discrimination in Employment Act of 1967, Alpha Corporation is prohibited from

    a. committing unintentional age discrimination.
    b. forcing an employee to retire.
    c. terminating an employee between the ages of sixty-five and seventy for cause.
    d. terminating an employee as part of a rational business decision.

____ 4. Janet, who is hearing impaired, applies for a position with Beta Company. Janet is qualified but is refused the job because, she is told, "We can't afford to accommodate you with an interpreter." If Janet sues Beta, she will

    a. win, if Beta has installed ramps for disabled persons.
    b. win, if an interpreter would be a "reasonable accommodation."
    c. lose, because an interpreter would not be a "reasonable accommodation."
    d. lose, if Beta has never done anything to accommodate any disabled person.

____ 5. LaBrea Correctional Institution, a women's prison, is in the process of hiring a correctional officer. Dave applies for the job and is told that the position is only open to female applicants. This is due in large part to the fact that the position calls for body-searches of inmates, and state law prohibits men from searching women in that manner. Dave files a claim, charging that he was discriminated against on the basis of his gender. LaBrea's best defense is

a. disparate-impact discrimination .
b. business necessity.
c. BFOQ.
d. none of the above.

____ 6. Digital Software, Inc., prefers to hire Asian Americans, because, according to its personnel director, "they're smarter and work harder" than other minorities. Showing a preference for one minority over another is prohibited by

a. Title VII of the Civil Rights Act of 1964 .
b. the Equal Pay Act of 1963.
c. the Americans with Disabilities Act of 1990.
d. none of the above.

____ 7. Dan and Mary work for Gamma Software, Inc. Dan is Mary's supervisor. During a review of her work, Dan makes comments and touches her in a way that she perceives as sexually offensive. She says nothing to the company, but suffers anxiety, quits less than a year later, and sues Gamma. Mary will

a. win, because Dan's conduct constituted sexual harassment.
b. win, because Gamma failed to take corrective action.
c. lose, because Mary overreacted—a few comments and a little touching never hurt anyone.
d. lose, because Mary said nothing to Gamma.

____ 8. Eagle Sales, Inc., requires that all its secretaries be able to type. Alice, a member of a minority, applies to Eagle for a secretarial job. She cannot type but tells Eagle that she is willing to learn. When Eagle does not hire her, she sues. She will

a. win, if Eagle's work force does not reflect the same percentage of members of a protected class that characterizes qualified individuals in the local labor market.
b. win, because she was willing to learn and an employer is obligated to hire and train unqualified minority employees.
c. lose, because in this case being a member of the majority is a BFOQ.
d. lose, because Eagle has a valid business necessity defense.

____ 9. U.S. Tech, Inc., discharges Mike. He believes that he was discriminated against because of his age. To bring a lawsuit based on age discrimination, Mike must show that he

a. is forty or older and qualified for the job.
b. was discharged in circumstances that imply discrimination.
c. both a and b.
d. none of the above.

_____ **10.** National Mining Company requires job applicants to pass certain physical tests. Only a few women who apply to work for National can pass the tests, but it they pass, they are hired. National's best defense in a suit charging that the tests discriminate against women would be that

a. gender is a BFOQ.
b. some men cannot pass the tests.
c. any discrimination is not intentional.
d. passing the tests is a business necessity.

SHORT ESSAY QUESTIONS

1. Define disparate-treatment discrimination and disparate-impact discrimination, and compare and contrast Title VII's response to each in the context of employment.

2. What does the Americans with Disabilities Act require employers to do?

ISSUE SPOTTERS
(Answers at the Back of the Book)

1. Lani, a member of a minority, learns of a job opening at Belco Engineering for which she is well-qualified. She applies for the job but is rejected. Belco continues to seek applicants for the position and eventually fills the position with a person who is not a member of a minority. Could Lani succeed in a suit against Belco for discrimination?

2. Grant is a supervisor for Subs & Suds, a restaurant. Judy is a Subs employee. When the owner announces that sales are down and some employees will be discharged, Grant tells Judy that if she has sex with him, she can keep her job. Is this sexual harassment?

3. Dick, a disabled person, learns of a job opening at the Bond Company for which he is well-qualified. He applies for the job but is rejected. Bond continues to seek applicants for the position and eventually fills the position with a person who is not disabled. Could Dick succeed in a suit against Belco for discrimination?

4. Hector, managing editor of the Springfield News, has a fairly lenient policy when it comes to employee tardiness. He would prefer that they be at their desks at 9 a.m., but he usually does not enforce this policy. One week Ned, who had spent time in an alcohol rehabilitation program the previous month, was late three days in a row. Given his appearance, it was obvious that he had been drinking the night before. Hector suspended him without pay for two weeks. Is Ned protected by the ADA?

5. On the night of the first Tuesday of every month, the law firm of Smith & Smith holds an "update session" for junior partners. This session is designed to keep the employees up-to-date on various changes in statutes that impact the firm. Jenna, a junior partner, is a member of a local religious group that practices druidism, a religion based on the practices of the ancient Celts. Because her group meets on Tuesday nights, Jenna does not attend the update sessions. Can Smith & Smith fire Jenna for missing the mandatory meetings?

SPECIAL INFORMATION FOR CPA CANDIDATES

The CPA examination has included an occasional question on discrimination—what is prohibited and what individuals are protected. These questions have concerned the broad coverage of the law, rather than specific details.

CUMULATIVE HYPOTHETICAL PROBLEM FOR UNIT EIGHT—INCLUDING CHAPTERS 41–42

(Answers at the Back of the Book)

Donna, Earl, Frank, Gail, Hal, Ira, Jane, Karen, Larry, and Mike are employees of International Sales Corporation (ISC).

____ 1. Donna, who works in ISC's warehouse, is injured on the job. Donna may NOT collect workers' compensation benefits if she

   a. files a civil suit against a third party based on the injury.
   b. intentionally caused her own injury.
   c. was injured as a result of a co-worker's act.
   d. worked for ISC for less than sixty days.

____ 2. Earl retires from ISC at the age of sixty-five. Frank retires at sixty-seven. Because of a disability, Gail, after fifteen years, is unable to continue working for ISC. Hal is discharged from ISC as part of a reduction in force. All of the following benefits are part of Social Security EXCEPT

   a. Earl's government retirement payments.
   b. Frank's Medicare payments.
   c. Gail's government disability payments.
   d. Hal's unemployment benefits.

____ 3. Ira voluntarily resigns from ISC. Under COBRA, Ira's group health insurance that was in effect when he worked for ISC

   a. ceases if Ira was not at the normal retirement age when he resigned.
   b. ceases if Ira was not part of an ISC reduction in force.
   c. may be continued for at least eighteen months at Ira's expense.
   d. may be continued for at least eighteen months at ISC's expense.

____ 4. Four employees file suits against ISC, alleging discrimination. Title VII of the Civil Rights Act of 1964 covers all of the following EXCEPT Jane's suit alleging discrimination on the basis of

   a. age.
   b. gender.
   c. race.
   d. religion.

____ 5. Karen, an ISC manager, wants to institute a policy of mandatory retirement for all employees at age sixty-four. Larry, an ISC manager, wants to discharge Mike, who is age sixty-seven, for cause. Under federal antidiscrimination law

   a. only Karen's wish can be granted.
   b. only Larry's wish can be granted.
   c. both Karen's and Larry's wishes can be granted.
   d. none of the above.

Administrative Law

WHAT THIS CHAPTER IS ABOUT

Federal, state, and local administrative agencies regulate virtually every aspect of a business's operation. Agencies' rules, orders, and decisions make up the body of administrative law. How agencies function is the subject of this chapter.

CHAPTER OUTLINE

I. **AGENCY CREATION AND POWERS**
Congress delegates some of its authority to make and implement laws, particularly in highly technical areas, to administrative agencies.

A. **ENABLING LEGISLATION**
To create an agency, Congress passes enabling legislation, which specifies the powers of the agency.

B. **TYPES OF AGENCIES**

1. **Executive Agencies**
Includes cabinet departments and their subagencies. Subject to the authority of the president, who can appoint and remove their officers.

2. **Independent Regulatory Agencies**
Includes agencies outside the major executive departments. Their officers serve for fixed terms and cannot be removed without just cause.

C. **AGENCY POWERS AND THE CONSTITUTION**
Agency powers include functions associated with the legislature (rulemaking), executive branch (enforcement), and courts (adjudication). Under Article I of the Constitution and the delegation doctrine, Congress has the power to establish agencies to create rules for implementing laws.

II.   ADMINISTRATIVE PROCESS

Rulemaking, investigation, and adjudication make up the administrative process. The Administrative Procedure Act (APA) of 1946 imposes procedural requirements that agencies must follow.

A.   RULEMAKING

Rulemaking is the formulation of new regulations. **Legislative rules** are as legally binding as the laws that Congress makes. Interpretive rules are not binding but indicate how an agency will apply a certain statute.

1.   Notice of the Proposed Rulemaking

An agency begins by publishing, in the *Federal Register*, a notice that states where and when proceedings will be held, terms or subject matter of the proposed rule, the agency's legal authority for making the rule.

2.   Comment Period

Interested parties can express their views. The agency must respond to significant comments by modifying the final rule or explaining, in the statement accompanying the final rule, why it did not.

3.   The Final Rule

The agency publishes the final rule in the *Federal Register*. The final rule has binding legal effect unless overturned by a court.

B.   INVESTIGATION

Agencies must have knowledge of facts and circumstances pertinent to proposed rules. Agencies must also obtain information and investigate conduct to ascertain whether its rules are being violated.

1.   Inspections and Tests

Through on-site inspections and testing, agencies gather information to prove a regulatory violation or to correct or prevent a bad condition.

2.   Subpoenas

With subpoenas, agencies compel witnesses to testify and compel individuals or organizations to hand over specified books, papers, records, or documents. Limits on agency demands include—

a.   An investigation must have a legitimate purpose.

b.   The information that is sought must be relevant.

c.   Demands must be specific.

d.   The party from whom the information is sought must not be unduly burdened by the request.

3.   Search Warrants

A search warrant directs an officer to search a specific place for a specific item and present it to the agency.

a.   Fourth Amendment

The Fourth Amendment protects against unreasonable searches and seizures by requiring that in most instances a physical search must be conducted under the authority of a search warrant.

b. Warrantless Searches
Warrants are not required to conduct searches in businesses in highly regulated industries, in certain hazardous operations, and in emergencies.

C. ADJUDICATION
Adjudication involves the resolution of disputes by an agency.

1. Negotiated Settlements
The purpose of negotiation is (1) for agencies: to eliminate the need for further proceedings; and (2) for parties subject to regulation: to avoid publicity and the expense of litigation.

2. Formal Complaints
If there is no settlement, the agency may issue a formal complaint. The party charged in the complaint may respond with an answer. The case may go before an administrative law judge (ALJ).

3. The Role of an Administrative Law Judge (ALJ)
Presides over the hearing. Has the power to administer oaths, take testimony, rule on questions of evidence, and make determinations of fact. An ALJ works for the agency, but must be unbiased. Certain safeguards in the APA prevent bias and promote fairness.

4. Hearing Procedures
Procedures vary widely from agency to agency. Agencies exercise substantial discretion over the type of procedures used. A formal hearing resembles a trial, but more items and testimony are admissible in an administrative hearing.

5. Agency Orders
After a hearing, the ALJ issues an initial order. Either side may appeal to the commission that governs the agency and ultimately to a federal appeals court. If there is no appeal or review, the initial order becomes final.

III. LIMITATIONS ON AGENCY POWERS
Because of the concentration of so much authority in administrative agencies, the three branches of the government exercise control over agency powers.

A. JUDICIAL CONTROLS
The APA provides for judicial review of most agency decisions.

1. Requirements for Judicial Review

a. The action must be reviewable (under the APA, agency actions are presumed reviewable).

b. The party must have standing (a direct stake in the outcome).

c. The party must have exhausted all administrative remedies.

d. An actual controversy must be at issue.

2. Scope of Review
In most cases, a court defers to the facts as found in an agency proceeding. A court will review whether an agency has —

a. Exceeded its authority under its enabling legislation.

      b. Properly interpreted laws applicable to the action under review.

      c. Violated any constitutional provisions.

      d. Acted in accord with procedural requirements.

      e. Taken actions that were arbitrary, capricious, or an abuse of discretion.

      f. Reached conclusions that are not supported by substantial evidence.

B. EXECUTIVE CONTROLS

The president may veto enabling legislation or subsequent modifications to agency authority that Congress seeks to enact. The president appoints and removes many federal officers, including those in charge of agencies.

C. LEGISLATIVE CONTROLS

Congress can give power to an agency, take power away, reduce or increase agency finances, abolish an agency, investigate the implementation of the laws, investigate agencies, and affect policy through individual legislators' attempts to help their constituents deal with agencies.

IV. PUBLIC ACCOUNTABILITY

A. FREEDOM OF INFORMATION ACT (FOIA) OF 1966

The federal government must disclose certain records to any person on request. A failure to comply may be challenged in federal district court.

B. GOVERNMENT-IN-THE-SUNSHINE ACT OF 1976

Requires (1) that "every portion of every meeting of an agency" that is headed by a "collegial body" is open to "public observation" and (2) procedures to ensure that the public is provided with adequate advance notice of meetings and agendas (with exceptions).

C. REGULATORY FLEXIBILITY ACT OF 1980

Whenever a new regulation will have a "significant impact upon a substantial number of small entities," the agency must conduct a regulatory flexibility analysis. The analysis must measure the cost imposed by the rule on small businesses and must consider less burdensome alternatives.

D. SMALL BUSINESS REGULATORY ENFORCEMENT FAIRNESS ACT

Under this act, passed in 1996—

1. Congress Reviews New Federal Regulations

Congress reviews new regulations for at least sixty days before they take effect. Opponents have time to present arguments to Congress.

2. Agencies Must Issue "Plain English" Guides

Agencies must prepare guides that explain how small businesses can comply with their regulations.

3. Regional Boards Rate Federal Agencies

The National Enforcement Ombudsman receives comments from small businesses about agencies. Based on the comments, Regional Small Business Fairness Boards rate the agencies.

4. Small Businesses May Recover Expenses and Fees

Small businesses may recover expenses and legal fees from the government if an agency makes excessive demands for fines or penalties.

V.   STATE ADMINISTRATIVE AGENCIES

A state agency often parallels a federal agency, providing similar services on a localized basis. The supremacy clause requires that the federal agency's operation prevail over an inconsistent state agency's action.

TRUE-FALSE QUESTIONS

(Answers at the Back of the Book)

____   1.   Enabling legislation specifies the powers of an agency.

____   2.   Most federal agencies are part of the executive branch of government.

____   3.   To create an agency, Congress enacts enabling legislation.

____   4.   Agency rules are not as legally binding as the laws that Congress enacts.

____   5.   After an agency adjudication, the administrative law judge's order must be appealed to become final.

____   6.   Congress has no power to influence agency policy.

____   7.   The Administrative Procedure Act provides for judicial review of most agency actions.

____   8.   When a new regulation will have a significant impact on a substantial number of small entities, an analysis must be conducted to measure the cost imposed on small businesses.

____   9.   State administrative agency operations prevail over federal agency actions.

____   10.   An agency cannot conduct a search without a warrant.

FILL-IN QUESTIONS

(Answers at the Back of the Book)

The rulemaking process begins with the publication in the _____ _____ (*Congressional Record/Federal Register*) of a notice of the proposed rulemaking. The agency may conduct a public hearing at which it presents evidence to justify the proposed rule, and _____ (anyone/no one) may present opposing evidence. The agency _____ (must/need not) respond to significant comments. After the hearing, the agency publishes the final draft of the rule in the _____ (*Congressional Record/Federal Register*).

MULTIPLE-CHOICE QUESTIONS

(Answers at the Back of the Book)

____   1.   Alan, a congressperson, believes a new federal agency is needed to perform a certain function. Congress has the power to establish an agency to

a.   make administrative rules only.
b.   adjudicate disputes arising from administrative rules only.
c.   make rules and adjudicate disputes arising from those rules.
d.   none of the above.

____   **2.** Like other federal agencies, the Securities and Exchange Commission may obtain information concerning activities and organizations that it oversees by compelling disclosure through

a. a subpoena only.
b. a search only.
c. a subpoena and a search.
d. neither a subpoena nor a search.

____   **3.** In making rules, the procedures of the Equal Employment Opportunity Commission and other federal agencies normally includes

a. notice.
b. opportunity for comments by interested parties.
c. publication of the final draft of the rule.
d. all of the above.

____   **4.** The Occupational Safety and Health Administration (OSHA) issues a subpoena for Triplex Corporation to hand over all of its files. Triplex's possible defenses against the subpoena include

a. OSHA is a federal agency, but Triplex only does business locally.
b. an administrative agency cannot issue a subpoena.
c. the demand is not specific enough.
d. none of the above.

____   **5.** The National Oceanic and Atmospheric Administration (NOAA) is a federal agency. To limit the authority of NOAA, the president can

a. abolish the agency.
b. take away the agency's power.
c. veto legislative modifications to the agency's authority.
d. refuse to appropriate funds to the agency.

____   **6.** The Bureau of Indian Affairs (BIA) wants to close a series of its meetings to the public. To open the meetings, a citizen would sue the BIA under

a. the Freedom of Information Act.
b. the Government-in-the-Sunshine Act.
c. the Regulatory Flexibility Act.
d. the Administrative Procedure Act.

____   **7.** The U.S. Fish and Wildlife Service orders Ed to stop using a certain type of fishing net from his fishing boat. Before a court will hear Ed's appeal of the order, he must

a. exhaust all administrative remedies.
b. bypass all administrative remedies and appeal directly to the court.
c. appeal simultaneously to the agency and the court.
d. ignore the agency and continue using the net.

____   **8.** The Federal Trade Commission (FTC) issues an order relating to the advertising of Midtron Corporation. Midtron appeals the order to a court. The court may review whether the FTC has

a. exceeded its authority.
b. taken an action that is arbitrary, capricious, or an abuse of discretion.
c. violated any constitutional provisions.
d. any of the above.

____ 9. The Environmental Protection Agency (EPA) publishes notice of a proposed rule. When comments are received about the rule, the EPA must respond to

    a. all of the comments.
    b. any significant comments that bear directly on the proposed rule.
    c. only comments by businesses engaged in interstate commerce.
    d. none of the comments.

____ 10. Tom is an administrative law judge (ALJ) for the National Labor Relations Board. In hearing a case brought before him, Tom has the authority to

    a. administer oaths only.
    b. rule on questions of evidence only.
    c. make determinations of fact only.
    d. administer oaths, rule on questions of evidence, and make determinations of fact.

SHORT ESSAY QUESTIONS

1. What are the conditions to judicial review of an agency enforcement action?

2. How does Congress hold agency authority in check?

ISSUE SPOTTERS

(Answers at the Back of the Book)

1. The Securities and Exchange Commission (SEC) makes rules regarding what disclosures must be made in a stock prospectus, prosecutes and adjudicates alleged violations, and prescribes punishment. This gives the SEC considerable power. What checks are there against this power?

2. Administrative agencies—like the Securities and Exchange Commission, the Federal Trade Commission, and the Food and Drug Administration—make rules. What are these rules called, and how binding are they? What must such a rule NOT do?

3. The U.S. Department of Transportation (DOT) sometimes hears appeals from those whose contracts with the DOT are canceled. Such an appeal is heard in a proceeding overseen by an administrative law judge (ALJ). The ALJ is a member of the DOT. What safeguards promote the ALJ's fairness?

4. The U.S. Department of Justice holds formal hearings concerning the deportation and exclusion of immigrants. How do such formal hearings resemble a trial? How are they different?

5. Digitech Corporation would like to know what information federal agencies have about Digitech's business operations, so that Digitech will know what its competitors may be able to learn about it. Under what federal law can Digitech require the agencies to disclose whatever information they may have concerning it?

SPECIAL INFORMATION FOR CPA CANDIDATES

The material in this chapter has not been part of the CPA examination in the past. Regarding specific administrative agencies, however, you will be expected to know that the commerce clause supports the Securities Exchange Commission's regulation of interstate buying and selling of securities.

Although you should plan on taking the CPA examination as soon as possible after completing your undergraduate education (because the exam is an academic test, covering material that is part of the curriculum in the accounting programs in business schools), you should find some relief in the fact that the exam does not cover new law for at least one year after the law is enacted. If a question is posed on the test on a topic on which a new law has been enacted within the twelve months preceding the test, you will be given credit for answering the question in accord with the old law or the new law.

Chapter 44:
Consumer and Environmental Law

WHAT THIS CHAPTER IS ABOUT

Federal and state laws protect consumers from unfair trade practices, unsafe products, discriminatory or unreasonable credit requirements, and other problems related to consumer transactions. This chapter focuses on *federal* consumer law. This chapter also covers the law that relates to environmental protection.

CHAPTER OUTLINE

I. CONSUMER PROTECTION LAWS

A. DECEPTIVE ADVERTISING
The Federal Trade Commission Act of 1914 created the Federal Trade Commission (FTC) to prevent unfair and deceptive trade practices. **Deceptive advertising**: advertising that would mislead a consumer.

1. Advertising That Is Deceptive
Scientifically untrue claims; misleading half-truths; **bait-and-switch** ads (if a seller refuses to show an advertised item, fails to have adequate quantities on hand, fails to promise to deliver within a reasonable time, or discourages employees from selling the item.).

2. Advertising That Is Not Deceptive
Puffing (vague generalities, obvious exaggeration).

3. FTC Actions against Deceptive Advertising
If the FTC believes that an ad is unfair or deceptive, it sends a complaint to the advertiser, who may settle. If not, the FTC can, after a hearing, issue a cease-and-desist order or require counteradvertising.

B. TELEMARKETING AND ELECTRONIC ADVERTISING

1. Telephone Consumer Protection Act (TCPA) of 1991
Prohibits (1) phone solicitation using an automatic dialing system or a prerecorded voice and (2) transmission of ads via fax without the recipient's permission. Consumers can recover actual losses or $500 for each

violation, whichever is greater. If a defendant willfully or knowingly violated the act, a court can award treble damages.

2. **Telemarketing and Consumer Fraud and Abuse Prevention Act of 1994**
    Authorized FTC to set rules for telemarketing and bring actions against fraudulent telemarketers. The FTC's Telemarketing Sales Rule of 1995 makes it illegal to misrepresent information and requires disclosure.

3. **State Laws**
    Most states also have laws regulating phone solicitation.

C. **LABELING AND PACKAGING**

1. **Fair Packaging and Labeling Act of 1966**
    Requires that labels identify the product; net quantity of contents; quantity of servings, if the number of servings is stated; manufacturer; and packager or distributor. More can be required (such as fat content).

2. **Other Federal Laws**
    Fur Products Labeling Act of 1951, Wool Products Labeling Act of 1939, Flammable Fabrics Act of 1953, Smokeless Tobacco Health Education Act of 1986, Nutrition Labeling and Education Act of 1990.

D. **SALES**
Federal agencies that regulate sales include the FTC and the Federal Reserve Board of Governors (Regulation Z governs credit provisions in sales contracts). All states have some form of consumer protection laws.

1. **Door-to-Door Sales**
    States' cooling-off laws permit a buyer to rescind a purchase within a certain time; the FTC has a three-day period (consumers can choose the most favorable). The FTC requires a seller to notify a buyer of the right to cancel (in Spanish, if the sale is in Spanish).

2. **Telephone and Mail-Order Sales**
    Consumers are partly protected by federal laws prohibiting mail fraud (see Chapter 5) and by state law that parallels federal law.

    a. **FTC "Mail or Telephone Order Merchandise Rule" of 1993**
       For goods bought via phone lines or through the mail, merchants must ship orders within the time promised in their ads, notify consumers when orders cannot be shipped on time, and issue a refund within a specified time if a consumer cancels an order.

    b. **Postal Reorganization Act of 1970**
       Unsolicited merchandise sent by mail may be retained, used, discarded, or disposed of, without obligation to the sender.

E. **CREDIT PROTECTION**

1. **Truth-in-Lending Act (TILA)**
    Enacted in 1968, Title I of the Consumer Credit Protection Act (CCPA), administered by the Federal Reserve Board, requires the disclosure of credit terms.

    a. **Who Is Subject to TILA?**
       Creditors who, in the ordinary course of business, lend money or sell goods on credit to consumers, or arrange for credit for consumers.

b. **What Does TILA Require?**
Under Regulation Z, in any transaction involving a sales contract in which payment is to be made in more than four installments, a lender must disclose all the credit terms clearly and conspicuously.

c. **Equal Credit Opportunity Act of 1974**
Prohibits (1) denial of credit on the basis of race, religion, national origin, color, sex, marital status, age and (2) credit discrimination based on whether an individual receives certain forms of income.

d. **Credit-Card Rules**
Liability of a cardholder is $50 per card for unauthorized charges made before the issuer is notified the card is lost. An issuer cannot bill for unauthorized charges if a card was improperly issued. If a cardholder wishes to withhold payment for a faulty product, there are specific procedures to follow.

e. **Consumer Leasing Act of 1988**
Those who lease consumer goods in the ordinary course of their business, if the goods are priced at $25,000 or less and the lease term exceeds four months, must disclose all material terms in writing.

2. **Fair Credit Reporting Act (FCRA) of 1970**

a. **What the FCRA Provides**
Consumer credit reporting agencies may issue credit reports only for certain purposes (extension of credit, etc.); a consumer denied credit, or charged more than others would be, on the basis of a report must be notified and told of the agency that issued the report.

b. **Consumers Can Have Inaccurate Information Deleted**
If a consumer learns that the report contains inaccurate information, the agency must delete it within a reasonable period of time.

3. **Fair Debt Collection Practices Act (FDCPA) of 1977**
Applies only to debt-collection agencies that, usually for a percentage of the amount owed, attempt to collect debts on behalf of someone else.

a. **What the FDCPA Prohibits**

1) Contacting the debtor at the debtor's place of employment if the employer objects.
2) Contacting the debtor during inconvenient times or at any time if the debtor is represented by an attorney.
3) Contacting third parties other than the debtor's parents, spouse, or financial advisor about payment unless a court agrees.
4) Using harassment, or false and misleading information.
5) Contacting the debtor any time after the debtor refuses to pay the debt, except to advise of further action to be taken.

b. **What Does the FDCPA Require?**
Collection agencies must notify a debtor that he or she has thirty days to dispute the debt and request written verification of it.

c. **Remedies**
A debt collector may be liable for actual damages, plus additional damages not to exceed $1,000 and attorneys' fees.

4. **Garnishment**
   To collect a debt, a creditor may use garnishment, which involves attaching a debtor's assets that are in the possession of a third party (employer, bank). The debtor must be notified and have an opportunity to respond. The amount that may be garnished is limited.

F. **CONSUMER HEALTH AND SAFETY**

1. **Federal Food, Drug, and Cosmetic Act of 1938**
   Sets food standards, levels of additives, classifications of food and food ads; regulates medical devices. Drugs must be shown to be effective and safe. Enforced by the Food and Drug Administration (FDA).

2. **Consumer Product Safety Act of 1972**
   Includes a scheme for the regulation of consumer products and safety by the Consumer Product Safety Commission (CPSC). The CPSC—

   a. Conducts research on product safety.
   b. Sets standards for consumer products and bans the manufacture and sale of a product that is potentially hazardous to consumers.
   c. Removes from the market any products imminently hazardous and requires manufacturers to report on any products already sold or intended for sale if the products have proved to be hazardous.
   d. Administers other product safety legislation.

G. **STATE CONSUMER PROTECTION LAWS**
   State laws (typically directed at deceptive trade practices) may provide more protection for consumers than do federal laws. UCC warranty and unconscionability provisions offer protection. The Uniform Consumer Credit Code (UCCC) includes sections on truth in lending, fine-print clauses, etc.

II. **ENVIRONMENTAL LAW**

A. **COMMON LAW ACTIONS**

1. **Nuisance**
   Persons cannot use their property in a way that unreasonably interferes with others' rights to use or enjoy their own property. An injured party may be awarded damages or an injunction.

2. **Negligence and Strict Liability**
   A business that fails to use reasonable care may be liable to a party whose injury was foreseeable. Businesses that engage in ultrahazardous activities are strictly liable for whatever injuries the activities cause.

B. **STATE AND LOCAL REGULATION**
   States regulate the environment through zoning or more direct regulation. Local governments control some aspects through zoning laws, waste removal and disposal regulations, aesthetic ordinances, and so on.

C. **FEDERAL REGULATION**

1. **Environmental Protection Agency (EPA)**
   Coordinates federal environmental responsibilities and administers most federal environmental policies and statutes.

2. **National Environmental Policy Act (NEPA) of 1969**
Requires that all federal agencies consider environmental factors when making significant decisions.

   a. **When an Environmental Impact Statement (EIS) Must Be Prepared**
   When a major federal action significantly affects the quality of the environment. An action is *major* if it involves substantial commitment of resources. An action is *federal* if a federal agency has the power to control it.

   b. **What an EIS Must Analyze**
   (1) Impact on the environment that the action will have, (2) any adverse effects to the environment and alternative actions that might be taken, (3) irreversible effects the action might generate.

   c. **When an Agency Decides That an EIS Is Unnecessary**
   It must issue a statement supporting this conclusion.

3. **Other Federal Laws**
Other federal laws that require the consideration of environmental values in agency decision making include the Fish and Wildlife Coordination Act of 1958 and the Endangered Species Act of 1973.

D. **AIR POLLUTION**
The Clean Air Act of 1963 (and amendments) is the basis for regulation.

1. **Mobile Sources**
Regulations governing air pollution from automobiles and other mobile sources specify standards and time schedules. For example, under the 1990 amendments to the Clean Air Act—

   a. **New Automobiles' Exhaust**
   Manufacturers had to cut emission of nitrogen oxide by 60 percent and emission of other pollutants by 35 percent. By 2007, new cars must cut nitrogen oxide emissions by 10 percent.

   b. **Sport Utility Vehicles and Light Trucks**
   These vehicles are now subject to the same standards as cars.

   c. **Gasoline**
   Service stations must sell gasoline with a higher oxygen content.

   d. **New Standards**
   The EPA attempts to update these and other standards when new scientific evidence is available.

2. **Stationary Sources**
The EPA sets air quality standards for stationary sources (such as industrial plants), and the states formulate plans to achieve them. For example, under the 1990 amendments to the Clean Air Act—

   a. **Major New Sources**
   Must use the maximum achievable control technology (MACT) to reduce emissions from the combustion of fossil fuels (coal and oil).

   b. **110 of the Oldest Coal-burning Power Plants in the United States**
   Must cut emissions by 40 percent by the year 2001 to reduce acid rain.

    c. Utilities

       Granted "credits" to emit certain amounts of sulfur dioxide. Those that emit less can sell their credits to other polluters.

    d. Other Factories and Businesses

       Must reduce emissions to cut ground-level ozone in 96 cities by 2005. Production of chlorofluorocarbons, carbon tetrachloride, and methyl chloroform (linked to depleting the ozone layer) must stop by 2002.

    e. Hazardous Air Pollutants

       Industrial emissions of 189 specific hazardous air pollutants must be reduced by 90 percent by 2000. Under 1996 rule, certain landfills must install air-pollution collection and control systems.

3. Penalties

Civil penalties up to $25,000 per day, or an amount equal to a violator's economic benefits from noncompliance, plus up to $5,000 per day for other violations. Criminal fines up to $1 million and imprisonment up to two years are possible. Private citizens can sue.

E. WATER POLLUTION

1. Navigable Waters

The Clean Water Act of 1972 amended the Federal Water Pollution Control Act (FWPCA) of 1948 to provide—

    a. Goals

       (1) Make waters safe for swimming, (2) protect fish and wildlife, (3) eliminate the discharge of pollutants into the water.

    b. Limits on Discharges

       Timetables (extended by amendment in 1977 and by the Water Quality Act of 1987) limit discharges of pollutants. New sources must install best available control technology (BACT). Existing sources must first install best practical control technology (BPCT).

    c. Permits

       Municipal and industrial polluters must obtain permits before discharging wastes into navigable waters.

    d. Penalties and Remedies

       Civil penalties from $10,000 per day (up to $25,000 per violation) to $25,000 per day. Criminal penalties from fines of $2,500 per day to $1 million total and one to fifteen years' imprisonment. Injunctions, damages, and clean-up costs can be imposed.

2. Drinking Water

The Safe Drinking Water Act of 1974 requires the EPA to set maximum levels for pollutants in public water systems. Operators must come as close as possible to the standards using the best available technology.

3. Ocean Dumping

The Marine Protection, Research, and Sanctuaries Act of 1972—

    a. Radiological Waste and Other Materials

       Dumping of radiological, chemical, and biological warfare agents, and high-level radioactive waste is prohibited. Transporting and dumping other materials (with exceptions) requires a permit.

b. Penalties
Civil penalties of not more than $50,000 or revocation or suspension of a permit. Criminal penalties of up to $50,000 fine, imprisonment for not more than a year, or both. Injunctions can be imposed.

4. Oil Pollution
The Oil Pollution Act of 1990 provides that any oil facility, oil shipper, vessel owner, or vessel operator that discharges oil may be liable for clean-up costs, damages, and fines of up to $25,000 per day.

F. NOISE POLLUTION
Under the Noise Control Act of 1972, the EPA sets maximum levels for noise. The act requires use of the best available technology. Injunctions may be imposed. Penalties include fines of up to $50,000 per day and up to two years' imprisonment.

G. TOXIC CHEMICALS

1. Pesticides and Herbicides
Federal Insecticide, Fungicide, and Rodenticide Act (FIFRA) of 1947—

a . Registration, Certification, and Use
Pesticides and herbicides must be (1) registered before they can be sold, (2) certified and used only for approved applications, and (3) used in limited quantities when applied to food crops.

b. Labels
Must include directions for use of a pesticide or herbicide, warnings to protect human health and the environment, a statement of treatment in the case of poisoning, and a list of the ingredients.

c. Penalties
For registrants and producers: suspension or cancellation of registration, up to a $50,000 fine, imprisonment up to one year. For commercial dealers: up to a $25,000 fine, imprisonment up to one year. For private users: a $1,000 fine, imprisonment up to thirty days.

d. 1996 Amendments to Federal Food, Drug, and Cosmetic Act
To stay on the market, pesticide must have a "reasonable certainty of no harm" (one-in-a-million risk to people of cancer from exposure). Grocery stores must display brochures about pesticides.

2. Toxic Substances
Under the Toxic Substances Control Act of 1976, for substances that potentially pose an imminent hazard or an unreasonable risk of injury to health or the environment, the EPA may require special labeling, set production quotas, or limit or prohibit the use of a substance.

H. HAZARDOUS WASTES

1. Resource Conservation and Recovery Act (RCRA) of 1976
The EPA determines which forms of solid waste are hazardous, and sets requirements for disposal, storage, and treatment. Penalties include up to $25,000 (civil) per violation, $50,000 (criminal) per day, imprisonment up to two years (may be doubled for repeaters).

2. Superfund

The Comprehensive Environmental Response, Compensation, and Liability Act (CERCLA) of 1980 regulates the clean-up of leaking hazardous waste disposal sites. If a release or a threatened release occurs, the EPA can clean up the site and recover the cost from—

a. Potentially Responsible Parties

(1) The person who generated the wastes disposed of at the site, (2) the person who transported the wastes to the site, (3) the person who owned or operated the site at the time of the disposal, or (4) the current owner or operator.

b. Joint and Several Liability

One party can be charged with the entire cost (which that party may recover in a contribution action against others).

TRUE-FALSE QUESTIONS

(Answers at the Back of the Book)

____ **1.** Advertising will be deemed deceptive if a consumer would be misled by the advertising claim.

____ **2.** In general, labels must be accurate—they must use words as those words are understood by the ordinary consumer.

____ **3.** Under no circumstances can a consumer rescind a contract freely entered into.

____ **4.** The TILA applies to creditors who, in the ordinary course of business, lend money or sell goods on credit to consumers.

____ **5.** A consumer can include a note in his or her credit file to explain any misinformation in the file, but the misinformation cannot be deleted.

____ **6.** No common law doctrines apply against polluters today.

____ **7.** Local governments can control some aspects of the environment through zoning laws.

____ **8.** Under federal environmental laws, there is a single standard for all polluters and all pollutants.

____ **9.** The Toxic Substances Control Act of 1976 regulates the clean up of leaking hazardous waste disposal sites.

____ **10.** If a release of hazardous waste occurs at a hazardous waste disposal site, the Environmental Protection Agency can clean it up and recover the entire cost from a potentially responsible party.

FILL-IN QUESTIONS

(Answers at the Back of the Book)

The Truth-in-Lending Act contains provisions regarding credit cards. One provision limits the liability of the cardholder to _____ ($50/$500) per card for unauthorized charges made _____ (after/before) the credit card issuer is notified that the card has been lost. Another provision _____ (allows/prohibits) a credit card company _____ (from billing/to bill) a consumer for any unauthorized charges _____ (unless/if) the credit card was improperly issued by the company.

MULTIPLE-CHOICE QUESTIONS

(Answers at the Back of the Book)

____ 1. Rich Foods Company advertises that its cereal, "Fiber Rich," reduces cholesterol. After an investigation and a hearing, the FTC finds no evidence to support the claim. To correct the public's impression of Fiber Rich, which of the following would be most appropriate?

   a. Counteradvertising
   b. Cease-and-desist order
   c. Civil fine
   d. Criminal fine

____ 2. ABC Corporation sells a variety of consumer products. Generally, the labels on its products must

   a. only be accurate.
   b. only use words as they are ordinarily understood by consumers.
   c. both a and b.
   d. none of the above.

____ 3. Maria does not speak English. Burt comes to her home and, after a long presentation in Spanish, sells her a vacuum cleaner. He hands her a paper that contains only in English a notice of the right to cancel a sale within three days. This transaction was

   a. proper, because the salesperson gave the buyer notice of her rights.
   b. not proper, because the deal was in Spanish but the notice was in English.
   c. proper, because ignorance of your rights is no defense.
   d. not proper, because ignorance of your rights is a defense.

____ 4. Bob takes out a student loan from First National Bank. After graduation, Bob goes to work, but he does not make payments on the loan. The bank agrees with Ace Collection Agency that if Ace collects the debt, it can keep a percentage of the amount. To collect the debt, Ace can contact

   a. Bob at his place of employment, even if his employer objects.
   b. Bob at unusual or inconvenient times or any time if he retains an attorney.
   c. third parties, including Bob's parents, unless ordered otherwise by a court.
   d. Bob only to advise him of further action that Ace will take.

____ 5. The ordinary business of Ace Credit Company is to lend money to consumers. Ace must disclose all credit terms clearly and conspicuously in

   a. no credit transaction.
   b. any credit transaction in which payments are to be made in more than four installments.
   c. any credit transaction in which payments are to be made in more than one installment.
   d. all credit transactions.

____ 6. The U.S. Department of the Interior's approval of coal mining operations in several eastern states requires an environmental impact statement

a. only because it affects the quality of the environment.
b. only because it is "major."
c. only because it is "federal."
d. because it affects the quality of the environment, is "major," and is "federal."

____ 7. **Based on a Sample CPA Exam Question.** Federated Industries' factories emit toxic air pollutants. Under the Clean Air Act and EPA regulations, Federated is required to

a. eliminate all air polluting emissions.
b. install emission control equipment on its products.
c. reduce emissions by installing the best available technology.
d. remove all pollutants from its factories.

____ 8. In the 1990s, All-Waste Company owned a hazardous waste disposal site, which it sold to ABC Properties, Inc., in 2000. In 2002, the EPA discovers a leak at the site and cleans it up. The EPA can recover from All-Waste

a. the entire cost to clean up the site.
b. about half of the cost to clean up the site.
c. the portion of the cost attributable to the extent of the leak in the 1990s.
d. none of the cost to clean up the site.

____ 9. Eagle Industries, Inc., fails to obtain a permit before discharging waste into navigable waters. Under the Clean Water Act, Eagle can be required

a. only to clean up the pollution.
b. only to pay for the cost of cleaning up the pollution.
c. to clean up the pollution or pay for the cost of doing so.
d. none of the above.

____ 10. Petro, Inc., ships unlabeled containers of hazardous waste to off-site facilities for disposal. If the containers later leak, Petro could be found to have violated

a. the Resource Conservation and Recovery Act (RCRA) only.
b. the Comprehensive Environmental Response, Compensation, and Liability Act (CERCLA) only.
c. both the RCRA and CERCLA.
d. none of the above.

SHORT ESSAY QUESTIONS

1. What are some of the more common deceptive advertising techniques and the ways in which the FTC may deal with such conduct?

2. What federal laws regulate toxic chemicals and what do those laws require?

ISSUE SPOTTERS

(Answers at the Back of the Book)

1.   Top Electronics, Inc., advertises GEM computers at a low price. Top keeps only a few in stock and tells its sales staff to switch consumers attracted by the price to more expensive brands. Top tells its staff that if all else fails, refuse to show the GEMs, and if a consumer insists on buying one, do not promise delivery. Has Top violated a law?

2.   Sweet Candy Company wants to sell its candy in a normal-sized package labeled "Gigantic Size." Fine Fabrics, Inc., wants to advertise its sweaters as having "That Wool Feel," but does not want to specify on labels that the sweaters are 100 percent polyester. What stops these firms from marketing their products as they would like?

3.   General Tobacco Corporation (GTC) sells tobacco products. On the packages of its smokeless tobacco products, what must GTC include?

4.   Erin buys a laptop computer from Top Electronics. She pays for it with her credit card. When it proves defective, she asks Top to repair or replace it, but Top refuses. What can Erin do?

5.   ChemCorp generates hazardous wastes from its operations. Central Trucking Company transports those wastes to Intrastate Disposal, Inc., which owns a hazardous waste disposal site. Intrastate sells the property on which the disposal site is located to ABC Properties, Inc. If the EPA cleans up the site, from whom can it recover the cost?

SPECIAL INFORMATION FOR CPA CANDIDATES

The CPA examination tests some concepts of environmental law. Environmental impact statements—their purpose and use—is one part of the material in this chapter that should be understood. You should have an awareness of the major environmental laws, too. Most important, however, is the Comprehensive Environmental Response, Compensation, and Liability Act (CERCLA) of 1980 (Superfund). Of specific significance is the use of the term "owner or operator" to subject many parties to liability for the clean-up costs of hazardous waste sites. In particular, you should remember the possibility that a lender may be held liable.

★ Key Points

The **key points** in this chapter include:

1. The purpose of antitrust law, and the major federal antitrust statutes.

2. The types of activities prohibited by the Sherman Act.

3. The types of activities prohibited by the Clayton Act.

4. How the antitrust laws are enforced.

5. Exemptions to the antitrust laws.

Chapter 45
Antitrust Law

WHAT THIS CHAPTER IS ABOUT

This chapter outlines aspects of the major antitrust statutes—the Sherman Act, the Clayton Act, and the Federal Trade Commission Act. Keep in mind that the basis of the antitrust laws is a desire to foster competition (to result in lower prices and so on).

CHAPTER OUTLINE

I. THE SHERMAN ANTITRUST ACT
Enacted in 1890, the Sherman Act is one of the government's most powerful weapons to maintain a competitive economy.

A. MAJOR PROVISIONS OF THE SHERMAN ACT
Section 1 requires two or more persons; cases often concern agreements (written or oral) that have a wrongful purpose and lead to a restraint of trade. Section 2 cases deal with monopolies that already exist.

B. JURISDICTIONAL REQUIREMENTS
The Sherman Act applies to restraints that substantially affect interstate commerce. The act also covers activities by U.S. nationals abroad that have an effect on U.S. foreign commerce.

II. SECTION 1 OF THE SHERMAN ACT

A. *PER SE* VIOLATIONS VERSUS THE RULE OF REASON
Some trade restraints are deemed *per se* violations. Others are subject to analysis under the rule of reason.

1. *Per Se* Violations
Agreements that are blatantly anticompetitive are illegal *per se*.

2. Rule of Reason
A court considers the purpose of an agreement, the power of the parties, the effect of the action on trade, and in some cases, whether there are less restrictive alternatives to achieve the same goals. If the competi-

tive benefits outweigh the anticompetitive effects, the agreement is held lawful.

3. **Soft or Limited *Per Se* Rule (Narrow Rule of Reason)**
   In some cases, the United States Supreme Court has stated that it is applying a *per se* rule, but the Court's analysis suggests that it is weighing benefits against harms under a rule of reason.

B. HORIZONTAL RESTRAINTS
Agreements that restrain competition between rivals in the same market.

1. **Price Fixing**
   Any agreement among competitors to fix prices is a *per se* violation.

2. **Group Boycotts**
   An agreement by two or more sellers to refuse to deal with a particular person or firm is a *per se* violation, if it is intended to eliminate competition or prevent entry into a given market.

3. **Horizontal Market Division**
   An agreement between competitors to divide up territories or customers is a *per se* violation.

4. **Trade Associations**
   Businesses within the same industry or profession organized to pursue common interests. The rule of reason is applied.

5. **Joint Ventures**
   An undertaking by two or more individuals or firms for a specific purpose. If it does not involve price fixing or market divisions, the agreement will be analyzed under the rule of reason.

C. VERTICAL RESTRAINTS
A restraint of trade that results from an agreement between firms at different levels in the manufacturing and distribution process.

1. **Territorial or Customer Restrictions**
   An agreement between a manufacturer and a distributor or retailer to restrict sales to certain areas or customers. Judged under a rule of reason.

2. **Resale Price Maintenance Agreements**
   An agreement between a manufacturer and a distributor or retailer in which the manufacturer specifies the retail prices of its products. Subject to the rule of reason.

3. **Refusals to Deal**
   A firm is free to deal, or not, unilaterally, with whomever it wishes.

III. SECTION 2 OF THE SHERMAN ACT
Applies to individuals and to several people; cases concern the structure of a monopoly in the marketplace and the misuse of monopoly power. Covers two distinct types of behavior: monopolization and attempts to monopolize.

A. MONOPOLIZATION
Requires two elements: (1) the possession of monopoly power in the relevant market and (2) the willful acquisition or maintenance of that power.

1. **Monopoly Power**
   Sufficient market power to control prices and exclude competition.

   a. **Market-Share Test**
      A firm has monopoly power if its share of the relevant market is 70 percent or more.

   b. **The Relevant Market Has Two Elements—**

      1) **Relevant Product Market**
         All products with identical attributes and those that are sufficient substitutes for each other.

      2) **Relevant Geographical Market**
         If competitors sell in only a limited area, the geographical market is limited to that area.

2. **The Intent Requirement**
   If a firm has market power as a result of a purposeful act to acquire or maintain that power through anticompetitive means, it is a violation of Section 2. Intent may be inferred from evidence that the firm had monopoly power and engaged in anticompetitive behavior.

B. **ATTEMPTS TO MONOPOLIZE**
   Any action challenged as an attempt to monopolize must (1) be intended to exclude competitors and garner monopoly power and (2) have a dangerous probability of success.

IV. THE CLAYTON ACT

Enacted in 1914, the Clayton Act is aimed at practices not covered by the Sherman Act. Conduct is illegal only if it substantially tends to lessen competition or create monopoly power.

A. **SECTION 2—PRICE DISCRIMINATION**
   Price discrimination occurs when a seller charges different prices to competitive buyers for identical goods.

   1. **Elements**
      (1) The seller must be engaged in interstate commerce, (2) the effect of the price discrimination must be to substantially lessen competition or create a competitive injury, and (3) a seller's pricing policies must include a reasonable prospect of the seller's recouping its losses.

   2. **Exceptions**
      (1) When a lower price is charged temporarily and in good faith to meet another seller's equally low price to the buyer's competitor or (2) a buyer's purchases saved the seller costs in producing and selling goods.

B. **SECTION 3—EXCLUSIONARY PRACTICES**

   1. **Exclusive-Dealing Contracts**
      A contract under which a seller forbids the buyer to buy products from the seller's competitors. Prohibited if the effect is "to substantially lessen competition or tend to create a monopoly."

   2. **Tying Arrangements**
      When a seller conditions the sale of a product on the buyer's agreement to buy another product produced or distributed by the same seller.

Legality depends on the agreement's purpose and its likely effect on competition in the relevant markets. Subject to the "soft" *per se* rule.

C. SECTION 7—MERGERS

A person or firm cannot hold stock or assets in another firm if the effect may be to substantially lessen competition. A crucial consideration in most cases is market concentration (percentage of market shares of firms in the relevant market).

1. Horizontal Mergers

Mergers between firms that compete with each other in the same market. If a merger creates an entity with more than a small percentage market share, it is presumed illegal. Factors include—

a. The degree of concentration in the relevant market.

b. The ease of entry into the relevant market.

c. Economic efficiency.

d. The financial condition of the merging firms.

e. The nature and prices of the products.

2. Vertical Mergers

When a company at one stage of production acquires a company at a higher or lower stage of production. Legality depends on market concentration, barriers to entry into that market, and the parties' intent.

3. Conglomerate Mergers

a. **Market-Extension Merger**

When a firm seeks to sell its product in a new market by merging with a firm already established in that market.

b. **Product-Extension Merger**

When a firm seeks to add a closely related product to its existing line by merging with a firm already producing that product.

c. **Diversification Merger**

When a firm merges with another firm that offers a product or service wholly unrelated to the first firm's existing activities.

D. SECTION 8—INTERLOCKING DIRECTORATES

No person may be a director in two or more corporations at the same time if either firm has capital, surplus, or undivided profits of more than $16,732,000 or competitive sales of $1,673,200 or more (as of 2000).

V. THE FEDERAL TRADE COMMISSION ACT

Enacted in 1914. Section 5 condemns all forms of anticompetitive behavior that are not covered under other federal antitrust laws.

VI. ENFORCEMENT OF ANTITRUST LAWS

A. DEPARTMENT OF JUSTICE (DOJ)

Prosecutes violations of the Sherman Act as criminal or civil violations. Violations of the Clayton Act are not crimes; the DOJ can enforce it only through civil proceedings. Remedies include divestiture and dissolution.

B. **FEDERAL TRADE COMMISSION (FTC)**
Enforces the Clayton Act; has sole authority to enforce the Federal Trade Commission Act; issues administrative orders; can seek court sanctions.

C. **PRIVATE PARTIES**

1. **Treble Damages and Attorneys' Fees**
Can sue for treble damages and attorneys' fees under the Clayton Act if injured by a violation of any federal antitrust law (except the FTC Act).

2. **Injunctions**
May seek an injunction to prevent antitrust violations if the violation injured business activities protected by the antitrust laws.

VII. U.S. ANTITRUST LAWS IN A GLOBAL CONTEXT
For U.S. courts to exercise jurisdiction over a foreign entity under U.S. antitrust laws, a violation must (1) have a substantial effect on U.S. commerce or (2) constitute a *per se* violation. Foreign governments and persons can also sue U.S. firms and persons for antitrust violations.

VIII. EXEMPTIONS FROM ANTITRUST LAWS

A. **LABOR ACTIVITIES**
A labor union can lose its exemption if it combines with a nonlabor group.

B. **AGRICULTURAL ASSOCIATIONS AND FISHERIES**
Except exclusionary practices or restraints of trade against competitors.

C. **INSURANCE COMPANIES**
Exempt in most cases when state regulation exists.

D. **FOREIGN TRADE**
U.S. exporters may cooperate to compete with similar foreign associations (if it does not restrain trade in the U.S. or injure other U.S. exporters).

E. **PROFESSIONAL BASEBALL**
Other professional sports are not exempt.

F. **OIL MARKETING**
States set quotas on oil to be marketed in interstate commerce.

G. **COOPERATIVE RESEARCH AND PRODUCTION**
Cooperative research among small business firms is exempt.

H. **JOINT EFFORTS TO OBTAIN LEGISLATIVE OR EXECUTIVE ACTION**
Joint efforts by businesspersons to obtain executive or legislative action are exempt (*Noerr-Pennington* doctrine). Exception: an action is not protected if "no reasonable [person] could reasonably expect success on the merits" and it is an attempt to make anticompetitive use of government processes.

I. **OTHER EXEMPTIONS**

1. Activities approved by the president in furtherance of defense.

2. State actions, when the state policy is clearly articulated and the policy is actively supervised by the state.

3. Activities of regulated industries when federal commissions, boards, or agencies have primary regulatory authority.

TRUE-FALSE QUESTIONS

(Answers at the Back of the Book)

____ 1. A horizontal restraint results from an agreement between firms at different levels in the manufacturing and distribution process.

____ 2. An agreement that restrains competition between rivals in the same market is a vertical restraint.

____ 3. Monopoly power is market power sufficient to control prices and exclude competition.

____ 4. An exclusive dealing contract is a contract under which competitors agree to divide up territories or customers.

____ 5. Price discrimination occurs when a seller forbids a buyer from buying products from the seller's competitors.

____ 6. A horizontal merger results when a company at one stage of production acquires another company at a higher or lower stage in the chain of production and distribution.

____ 7. A merger between firms that compete with each other in the same market is a vertical merger.

____ 8. A relevant product market consists of all products with identical attributes and those that are sufficient substitutes for each other.

____ 9. An agreement that is inherently anticompetitive is illegal *per se*.

____ 10. An agreement between competitors to fix prices is a *per se* violation.

FILL-IN QUESTIONS

(Answers at the Back of the Book)

_____ (Monopoly power/A restraint of trade) is any agreement that has the effect of reducing competition in the marketplace. _____
_____ (Monopoly power/ Restraint of trade) is an extreme amount of market power. A firm that can raise its prices somewhat without too much concern for its competitors' response has some degree of market power. Whether such power is sufficient to call it _____ (monopoly power/ a restraint of trade) is one of the most difficult tasks in antitrust law.

MULTIPLE-CHOICE QUESTIONS

(Answers at the Back of the Book)

____ 1. The National Coal Association (NCA) is a group of independent coal mining companies. Demand for coal falls and so the price drops. The Coal Refiners Association, a group of coal refining companies, agrees to buy NCA's coal and sell it according to a schedule that will increase the price. This agreement is

a. exempt from the antitrust laws.
b. subject to evaluation under the rule of reason.
c. a *per se* violation of the Sherman Act.
d. none of the above.

____   **2.** International Sales, Inc. (ISI), is charged with a violation of antitrust law. ISI's conduct is a *per se* violation

    a. only if it qualifies as an exemption.
    b. if the competitive benefits outweigh the anticompetitive harms.
    c. if the anticompetitive harms outweigh the competitive benefits.
    d. if the conduct is blatantly anticompetitive.

____   **3.** Comtech, Inc., sells its brand-name computer equipment directly to its franchised retailers. Depending on how existing franchisees do, Comtech may limit the number of franchisees in a given area to reduce intrabrand competition. Comtech's restrictions on the number of dealers is

    a. exempt from the antitrust laws.
    b. subject to evaluation under the rule of reason.
    c. a *per se* violation of the Sherman Act.
    d. none of the above.

____   **4.** Delta Corporation is charged with a violation of antitrust law that requires evaluation under the rule of reason. In that case, a court considers

    a. only the purpose of the conduct.
    b. only the effect of the conduct on trade.
    c. only the power of the parties to accomplish what they intend.
    d. the purpose of the conduct, the effect of the conduct on trade, and the power of the parties to accomplish what they intend.

____   **5.** Adams, Inc., controls 80 percent of the market for telecommunications equipment in the southeastern United States. To show that Adams is monopolizing that market in violation of the Sherman Act requires proof of

    a. only the possession of monopoly power in the relevant market.
    b. only the willful acquisition or maintenance of monopoly power.
    c. the possession of monopoly power in the relevant market and the willful acquisition or maintenance of that power.
    d. none of the above.

____   **6.** Federated Tools, Inc., charges Jack's Hardware five cents per item and Eve's Home Store ten cents per item for the same product. The two stores are competitors. If this substantially lessens competition, it constitutes

    a. a market division.
    b. an exclusionary practice.
    c. price discrimination.
    d. none of the above.

____   **7.** A group of foreign manufacturers organize to control the price for video cameras in the United States. Liberty Company, a U.S. firm, joins the group. If their actions have a substantial effect on U.S. commerce, which of the parties may be sued for violation of U.S. antitrust laws?

    a. Only Liberty
    b. Only the foreign manufacturers
    c. Both Liberty and the foreign manufacturers
    d. None of the above

____ 8. Super Software Corporation and Tech Products, Inc., are competitors. They form a joint venture to research, develop, and produce new software for a particular line of computers. This joint venture is

   a. exempt from the antitrust laws.
   b. subject to evaluation under the rule of reason.
   c. a *per se* violation of the Sherman Act.
   d. none of the above.

____ 9. AMT Company is charged with a violation of antitrust law subject to evaluation under the rule of reason. In that case, AMT's conduct is unlawful

   a. only if it qualifies as an exemption.
   b. if the competitive benefits outweigh the anticompetitive harms.
   c. if the anticompetitive harms outweigh the competitive benefits.
   d. if the conduct is blatantly anticompetitive.

____ 10. American Goods, Inc., and Consumer Products Corporation are competitors. They merge, and after the merger, Consumer Products is the surviving firm. To assess whether this is in violation of the Clayton Act requires a look at

   a. market division.
   b. market concentration.
   c. market power.
   d. none of the above.

SHORT ESSAY QUESTIONS

1. How does Section 1 of the Sherman Act deal with horizontal restraints?

2. How does the Clayton Act deal with exclusionary practices?

ISSUE SPOTTERS

(Answers at the Back of the Book)

1. Wheels Company, a bicycle manufacturer, refuses to deal with Bob's Bikes, a retailer. A manufacturer is generally free to deal (or not) with whomever it wants. In what circumstances might Wheels's refusal to deal with Bob violate antitrust law?

2. Alpha, Inc., Beta Corporation, and Omega Company compete against each other in Illinois, Indiana, and Ohio. To reduce marketing costs, they agree that Alpha will sell products only in Illinois, Beta only in Indiana, and Omega only in Ohio. This allows each firm to raise the price of the goods in its state and increase profits. Is this a violation of antitrust law? If so, is it a *per se* violation or is it subject to evaluation under the rule of reason?

3. Under what circumstances would M&P Market, a small store in a small, isolated town, be considered a monopolist? If M&P is a monopolist, is it in violation of Section 2 of the Sherman Act?

4. Maple Corporation conditions the sale of its syrup on the buyer's agreement to purchase Maple's pancake mix. What factors would a court consider to decide whether this arrangement violates the Clayton Act?

5. Syntech Corporation is a manufacturer of computers. Digital, Inc., is a chain of retail computer stores. Syntech and Digital merge. Syntech is the surviving entity. What factors determine whether this merger is illegal under the Clayton Act?

SPECIAL INFORMATION FOR CPA CANDIDATES

Most of the material in this chapter is not tested on the CPA examination. For the purposes of the exam, restraints of trade are acceptable in only two situations, both involving covenants not to compete (discussed in Chapter 13).

CUMULATIVE HYPOTHETICAL PROBLEM FOR UNIT NINE—INCLUDING CHAPTERS 43–45

(Answers at the Back of the Book)

Beta Chemical Corporation manufactures and sells chemical products to industrial customers and individual consumers.

___ 1. Beta advertises its products with slogans that consist of vague generalities. Because of this advertising, the Federal Trade Commission may

    a. issue a cease-and-desist order only.
    b. require counteradvertising only.
    c. issue a cease-and-desist order or require counteradvertising.
    d. none of the above.

___ 2. To determine whether Beta is violating regulations issued by the Environmental Protection Agency (EPA), the EPA may NOT

    a. arbitrarily order Beta to shut its manufacturing site down.
    b. conduct an on-site inspection of Beta's manufacturing site.
    c. test Beta's products on its manufacturing site.
    d. none of the above.

___ 3. Beta's manufacturing process generates hazardous waste that is transported to Gamma Company's disposal site by Omega Trucking, Inc. If the EPA cleans up Gamma's site, liability for the cost may be assessed against

    a. Beta or Gamma only.
    b. Gamma or Omega only.
    c. Beta or Omega only.
    d. Beta, Gamma, or Omega.

___ 4. As a for-profit corporation that does business in interstate commerce, Beta may be subject to regulations issued by

    a. federal administrative agencies only.
    b. state administrative agencies in states in which Beta does business only.
    c. federal agencies or state agencies in states in which Beta does business.
    d. none of the above.

___ 5. Beta charges National Refining, Inc., less per item than Beta charges International Export Corporation for the same product. The two industrial buyers are competitors. This pricing difference violates antitrust law

    a. if both buyers' customers pay the same price for the buyers' products.
    b. if National and International know what each other pays.
    c. if the pricing substantially lessens competition.
    d. under no circumstances.

Chapter 46
Personal Property and Bailments

WHAT THIS CHAPTER IS ABOUT

This chapter covers the nature of personal property, forms of property ownership, the acquisition of personal property, and bailments. Note that personal property can be tangible (such as a car) or intangible (such as securities or patents).

CHAPTER OUTLINE

I. PROPERTY CLASSIFICATION
Personal property can be tangible (a television set) or intangible (stocks, computer program). Real property consists of land and everything permanently attached to it.

II. FIXTURES
Personal property so closely associated with certain real property that it is viewed as part of it (such as plumbing in a building). Fixtures are included in a sale of land if the contract does not provide otherwise.

A. FACTORS IN DETERMINING THAT AN ITEM IS A FIXTURE
The intent of the parties, whether the item can be removed without damaging the real property, and whether the item is sufficiently adapted so as to have become a part of the real property.

B. TRADE FIXTURES
Installed for a commercial purpose by a tenant, whose property it remains, unless removal would irreparably damage the real property.

III. PROPERTY OWNERSHIP
Ownership can be viewed as the rights to possess property and to dispose of it.

A. FEE SIMPLE
A person who holds all of the rights is an owner in fee simple (see Chapter 47); on death, the owner's interest descends to his or her heirs.

B. CONCURRENT OWNERSHIP

1. **Tenancy in Common**
   Each of two or more persons owns an *undivided* interest (each has rights in the whole—if each had rights in specific items, the interests would be *divided*). On death, a tenant's interest passes to his or her heirs. Most states presume that a co-tenancy is a tenancy in common unless there is a clear intention to establish a joint tenancy.

2. **Joint Tenancy**
   Each of two or more persons owns an undivided interest in the property; a deceased joint tenant's interest passes to the surviving joint tenant or tenants. Can be terminated at any time before a joint tenant's death by gift, by sale, or by partition (divided into equal parts).

3. **Tenancy by the Entirety**
   Created by a transfer of real property to a husband and wife; neither spouse can transfer separately his or her interest during his or her life. In some states, this tenancy has been effectively abolished. A divorce, either spouse's death, or mutual agreement will terminate this tenancy.

4. **Community Property**
   Each spouse owns an undivided half interest in property acquired by either spouse during their marriage (except property acquired by gift or inheritance). Recognized in only some states, on divorce the property is divided equally in a few states and at a court's discretion in others.

IV. ACQUIRING OWNERSHIP OF PERSONAL PROPERTY

A. PURCHASE
Outlined in Chapters 19 through 23.

B. POSSESSION
An example of acquiring ownership by possession is the capture of wild animals. (Exceptions: (1) wild animals captured by a trespasser are the property of the landowner, and (2) wild animals captured or killed in violation of statutes are the property of the state.)

C. PRODUCTION
Those who produce personal property have title to it. (Exception: employees do not own what they produce for their employers.)

D. GIFT
A **gift** is a voluntary transfer of property ownership not supported by consideration.

1. **The Three Requirements for an Effective Gift**

   a. **Delivery**

      1) **Constructive Delivery**
         If a physical object cannot be delivered, an act that the law holds to be equivalent to an act of real delivery is sufficient (a key to a safe-deposit box for the contents of the box, for example).

      2) **Delivery by a Third Person**
         If the person is the donor's agent, the gift is effective when the agent delivers the property to the donee. If the person is the

donee's agent, the gift is effective when the donor delivers the property to the agent.

3) Giving Up Control
Effective delivery requires giving up control over the property.

b. Donative Intent
Determined from the language of the donor and the surrounding circumstances (relationship between the parties and the size of the gift in relation to the donor's other assets).

c. Acceptance
Courts assume a gift is accepted unless shown otherwise.

2. Gifts *Inter Vivos* and Gifts *Causa Mortis*
Gifts *inter vivos* are made during one's lifetime. Gifts *causa mortis* are made in contemplation of imminent death, do not become effective until the donor dies, and are automatically revoked if the donor does not die.

E. WILL OR INHERITANCE
Outlined in Chapter 50.

F. ACCESSION
Occurs when someone adds value to a piece of personal property by use of labor or materials. Ownership can be at issue in the following situations.

1. When Accession Occurs without Permission of the Owner
Courts tend to favor the owner over the one who improved the property (and deny the improver any compensation for the value added).

2. When Accession Greatly Increases the Value or Changes the Identity
The greater the increase, the more likely that ownership will pass to the improver who must compensate the original owner for the value of the property before the accession.

G. CONFUSION
Commingling goods so that one person's cannot be distinguished from another's. Frequently involves fungible goods. If goods are confused due to a wrongful act, the innocent party acquires all. If confusion is by agreement, mistake, or a third party's act, the owners share as tenants in common.

V. MISLAID, LOST, OR ABANDONED PROPERTY

A. MISLAID PROPERTY
Property that has been voluntarily placed somewhere by the owner and then inadvertently forgotten. When the property is found, the owner of the place where it was mislaid (not the finder) becomes the caretaker.

B. LOST PROPERTY
Property that is involuntarily left. A finder can claim title against the whole world, except the true owner. Many states require the finder to make a reasonably diligent search to locate the true owner. **Estray statutes** allow finders, after passage of a specified time, to acquire title to the property if it remains unclaimed.

C. ABANDONED PROPERTY
Property that has been discarded by the true owner, who has no intention of claiming title to it. A finder acquires title good against the whole world, including the original owner. A trespasser does not acquire title, however; the owner of the real property on which it was found does.

D. TREASURE TROVE
Money, gold, silver, or bullion hidden in some private place, owner unknown. In the absence of a statute, a finder (who was not trespassing) has title to treasure trove against all but the true owner.

VI. BAILMENTS
The elements of a bailment are the following.

A. PERSONAL PROPERTY
Only personal property (tangible or intangible) is bailable.

B. DELIVERY OF POSSESSION (WITHOUT TITLE)
A bailee must (1) be given exclusive possession and control of the property and (2) knowingly accept it. Delivery may be actual or constructive.

C. AGREEMENT THAT THE PROPERTY BE RETURNED OR DISPOSED OF
The agreement must provide for the return of the property to the bailor or a third person, or for its disposal by the bailee.

VII. ORDINARY BAILMENTS
The three types of ordinary bailments are: (1) Bailment for the sole benefit of the bailor, (2) bailment for the sole benefit of the bailee, and (3) bailment for their mutual benefit.

A. RIGHTS OF THE BAILEE

1. Right of Possession
Temporary control and possession of property that ultimately is to be returned to the owner. During a bailment, a bailee can recover damages from any third persons for damage or loss to the property.

2. Right to Use Bailed Property
The extent to which bailees can use the property depends on the contract. If no provision is made, the extent depends on how necessary it is for the goods to be at the bailee's disposal.

3. Right of Compensation
A bailee has a right to be compensated as agreed and to be reimbursed for costs and services in the keeping of the property. To enforce this right, a bailee can place a lien on the property (see Chapter 31).

4. Right to Limit Liability
Bailees can limit their liability as long as—

a. Limitations Are Called to the Attention of the Bailor
Fine print on the back of a ticket stub is not sufficient.

b. Limitations Are Not Against Public Policy
Exculpatory clauses are carefully scrutinized by the courts and, in bailments, often held to be illegal. If a bailee attempts to exclude liability for his or her own negligence, the clause is unenforceable.

B. DUTIES OF THE BAILEE

1. Duty of Care
Bailees must exercise care over the property in their possession (or be liable in tort—see Chapter 5). The appropriate standard is—

a. Slight Care
In bailments for the sole benefit of the bailor, the bailee is liable only for gross negligence.

b. Great Care
In bailments for the sole benefit of the bailee, the bailee is liable for even slight negligence.

c. Ordinary Care
In bailments for the mutual benefit of both parties, the bailee is liable for a failure to use reasonable care.

2. Duty to Return Bailed Property
When a bailment ends, the bailee must relinquish the property. Failure to do so is a breach of contract and could constitute conversion.

a. Delivery of Goods to the Wrong Person
A bailee may be liable if the property is given to the wrong person.

b. Exceptions
The property is destroyed, lost, or stolen through no fault of the bailee, or given to a third party with a superior claim.

3. Presumption of Negligence
When the bailee has the property and damage occurs that normally results only from someone's negligence, the bailee's negligence is presumed. The bailee must prove that he or she was not at fault.

C. RIGHTS OF THE BAILOR
Complementary to the bailee's duties—

1. The property will be protected with reasonable care while in the bailee's possession.

2. The bailee will use the property as agreed (or not at all).

3. The property will be relinquished according to the bailor's directions.

4. The bailee will not alter the goods except as agreed.

5. The bailor will not be bound by any limitations on the bailee's liability unless these limitations are known and are enforceable by law.

6. Repairs or service will be done without defective workmanship.

D. DUTIES OF THE BAILOR
A bailor has a duty to provide the bailee with goods that are free from hidden defects that could injure the bailee.

1. Bailor's Duty Has Two Aspects

a. In a mutual-benefit bailment, bailor must notify bailee of all known defects and any hidden defects that the bailor knew of or could have discovered with reasonable diligence and proper inspection.

      b. In a bailment for the sole benefit of the bailee, the bailor must notify the bailee of any known defects.

    2. To Whom Does Liability Extend?
To anyone who might be expected to come in contact with the goods. A bailor may also be liable under UCC Article 2A's implied warranties.

E. TERMINATION OF BAILMENTS
Bailments for a specific term end when the term ends. If no term is specified, a bailment can be terminated by mutual agreement of the parties, a demand by either party, completion of the bailment's purpose, an act by the bailee inconsistent with the terms of the bailment, or operation of law.

VIII. SPECIAL TYPES OF BAILMENTS

A. DOCUMENTS OF TITLE AND ARTICLE 7
Documents of title are subject to UCC Article 7 (unless federal law applies).

    1. What a Document of Title Is
A receipt for goods in the charge of a bailee-carrier or a bailee-warehouser and a contract for the shipment or storage of identified goods. Includes bills of lading, warehouse receipts, and delivery orders.

    2. Negotiability of a Document of Title
A document of title is negotiable if it specifies that goods are to be delivered to bearer or to the order of a named person. If so—

      a. The possessor of the document is entitled to receive, hold, and dispose of the document and the goods it covers.

      b. A good faith purchaser of the document may acquire greater rights to the document and the goods it covers than the transferor had or had the authority to convey (he or she may take free of the claims and defenses of prior parties).

    3. Due Negotiation
Due negotiation means that the buyer of a document of title takes it (1) in good faith, for value, and without notice of a defense against or a claim to it, and (2) in the regular course of business or financing (not in settlement or payment of a money obligation).

    4. Goods Delivered According to a Thief's Instructions
A bailee who receives goods from a thief and acts according to that individual's instructions is not liable to the goods' true owner (if he or she acted in good faith and observed reasonable commercial standards).

B. COMMON CARRIERS
Common carriers are publicly licensed to provide transportation services to the general public.

    1. Strict Liability
Common carriers are absolutely liable, regardless of negligence, for all loss or damage to goods in their possession, except if it is caused by an act of God, an act of a public enemy, an order of a public authority, an act of the shipper, or the nature of the goods.

2. **Limits to Liability**

    Common carriers can limit their liability to an amount stated on the shipment contract. The shipper bears any loss occurring through its own fault or improper crating or packaging procedures.

3. **Connecting Carriers**

    When connecting carriers are involved under a through bill of lading, the shipper can recover from the original carrier or any connecting carrier. Normally, the last carrier is presumed to have received the goods in good condition.

C. WAREHOUSE COMPANIES

Warehouse companies are liable for loss or damage to property resulting from negligence [UCC 7–204(1)]. A warehouse company can limit the dollar amount of liability, but the bailor must be given the option of paying an increased storage rate for an increase in the liability limit [UCC 7–204(2)].

D. INNKEEPERS

Those who provide lodging to the public for compensation as a regular business are strictly liable for injuries to guests (not permanent residents).

1. **Hotel Safes**

    In many states, innkeepers can avoid strict liability for loss of guests' valuables by providing a safe. Statutes often limit the liability of innkeepers for articles that are not kept in the safe.

2. **Parking Facilities**

    If an innkeeper provides parking facilities, and the guest's car is entrusted to the innkeeper, the innkeeper will be liable under the rules that pertain to parking lot bailees (ordinary bailments).

TRUE-FALSE QUESTIONS

(Answers at the Back of the Book)

_____ 1. Generally, those who produce personal property have title to it.

_____ 2. If goods are confused due to a wrongful act and the innocent party cannot prove what percentage is his or hers, the wrongdoer gets title to the whole.

_____ 3. To constitute a gift, a voluntary transfer of property must be supported by consideration.

_____ 4. If an accession is performed in good faith, the improver keeps the property as improved, whether or not there has been any change in the value.

_____ 5. One who finds abandoned property acquires title to it good against the whole world, including the true owner.

_____ 6. Any delivery of personal property from one person to another creates a bailment.

_____ 7. A bailee is not responsible for the loss of bailed property in his or her care.

_____ 8. A bailee has only one duty: to surrender the property at the end of the bailment.

_____ 9. In some ordinary bailments, bailees can limit their liability.

_____ **10.** Warehouse companies have the same duty of care as ordinary bailees.

FILL-IN QUESTIONS

(Answers at the Back of the Book)

A gift made during the donor's lifetime is a gift _____ (*causa mortis/inter vivos*). A gift _____ (*causa mortis/inter vivos*) is made in contemplation of imminent death. Gifts _____ (*causa mortis/inter vivos*) do not become absolute until the donor dies from the contemplated illness or disease. A gift _____ (*causa mortis/inter vivos*) is revocable at any time up to the death of the donor and is automatically revoked if the donor recovers. A gift _____ (*causa mortis/inter vivos*) is revocable at any time before the donor's death.

MULTIPLE-CHOICE QUESTIONS

(Answers at the Back of the Book)

_____ **1.** Eve designs an Internet home page to advertise her services as a designer of home pages. Tim hires her to design a homepage for his business. Eve has title to

   a. her home page only.
   b. Tim's home page only.
   c. her homepage, Tim's home page, and any other home page she creates.
   d. none of the above.

_____ **2.** Nancy sells her boat to Chris and Nora. Chris and Nora are not married. The contract of sale says that the buyers each have a right of survivorship in the boat. Chris and Nora own the boat as

   a. tenants in common.
   b. joint tenants.
   c. tenants by the entirety.
   d. community property.

_____ **3.** Meg wants to give Lori a pair of diamond earrings that Meg has in her safe-deposit box at First National Bank. Meg gives Lori the key to the box and tells her to go to the bank and take the earrings from the box. Lori does so. Two days later, Meg dies. Who do the earrings belong to?

   a. Lori
   b. Meg's heirs
   c. First National Bank
   d. The state government

_____ **4.** John is employed in remodeling homes bought and sold by Best Sale Realty. In one of the homes, John finds an item of jewelry and takes it to Hall Gems, Inc., to be appraised. The appraiser removes some of the jewels. Who has the best title to the jewels that were removed?

   a. John
   b. Hall Gems, Inc.
   c. Best Sale Realty
   d. John's employer

___ 5. Jane, Mark, and Guy are farmers who store their grain in three silos. Jane contributes half of the grain, Mark a third, and Guy a sixth. A tornado hits two of the silos and scatters the grain. If each farmer can prove how much he or she deposited in the silos, how much of what is left belongs to each?

   a. Jane owns half, Mark a third, and Guy a sixth
   b. Because only a third is left, Mark owns it all
   c. Because Jane and Mark lost the most, they split what is left equally
   d. Jane, Mark, and Guy share what is left equally

___ 6. Doug wants to give Kim a laptop computer in a locker at the airport. Doug gives Kim the key to the locker and tells her to take the laptop from the locker. Kim says that she doesn't want the computer and leaves the key on Doug's desk. The next day, Doug dies. Who gets the computer?

   a. Kim
   b. Doug's heirs
   c. The airport
   d. The state government

___ 7. Eve parks her car in an unattended lot behind Bob's store, which is closed. Eve locks the car and takes the keys. This is NOT a bailment because

   a. no money is involved.
   b. no personal property is involved.
   c. there is no transfer of possession.
   d. neither party signed a contract.

___ 8. Marcy goes to Don's Salon for a haircut. Behind a plant on a table in the waiting area, Marcy finds a wallet containing $5,000. Who is entitled to possession of the wallet?

   a. Marcy because the money was lost
   b. Don because the money was mislaid
   c. The state under an estray statute
   d. The police under the local finders' law

___ 9. Kay checks her coat at a restaurant. Hidden in the sleeve is her purse. By accepting the coat, the restaurant is a bailee of

   a. the coat only.
   b. the purse only.
   c. both the coat and the purse.
   d. none of the above.

___ 10. **Based on a Sample CPA Exam Question.** Adams Corporation ships goods via Baker Transport Company. Baker will NOT be liable for the loss of the goods if they are

   a. crushed in a warehouse accident that is the fault of Baker's crane operator.
   b. damaged because Adams failed to package the goods properly.
   c. destroyed in a traffic accident that is the fault of Baker's truckdriver.
   d. stolen by an unknown person

SHORT ESSAY QUESTIONS

1. State the principal features of the four forms of concurrent property ownership: tenancies in common, joint tenancies, tenancies by the entirety, and community property.

2. What are the three elements involved in creating a valid gift?

ISSUE SPOTTERS

(Answers at the Back of the Book)

1. Mac wants to give Rita a pearl necklace that Mac has in his safe deposit box at First State Bank. The bank is closed for a holiday. Mac gives Rita a key to the box and tells her to go to the bank after the holiday and take the necklace. Rita does so. The next day, Mac dies. Mac's heirs want the necklace. Can Rita keep it?

2. Dave and Paul share ownership rights in a multimedia computer set-up. When they acquired the computer, they agreed in writing that if one dies, the other inherits his interest. Are Dave and Paul tenants in common or joint tenants?

3. Kane Corporation sends important documents to Trager, Inc., via Speedy Messenger Service. While the documents are in Speedy's care, Al causes an accident to Speedy's delivery vehicle that results in the loss of the documents. Does Speedy have a right to recover from Al for the loss of the documents?

4. Bob leaves his clothes with Corner Dry Cleaners to be cleaned. When the clothes are returned, some are missing and others are greasy and smell bad. Is Corner liable?

5. Cambridge Corporation ships a load of goods via Southern Cartage Company. The load is lost in a hurricane in Florida. Who suffers the loss?

SPECIAL INFORMATION FOR CPA CANDIDATES

The CPA examination has questions that involve personal property ownership, including such aspects as the acquisition of ownership (especially gifts) and the types of ownership. Fixtures are covered (remember that the more difficult it is to remove an item, the more likely it will be regarded as a fixture). Trade fixtures are judged differently—be sure that you understand the difference.

Personal property, its ownership, and its transfer may also be at issue on such parts of the exam as those that test on sales of goods under the Uniform Commercial Code, sales involving the common law of contracts, commercial paper (negotiable instruments), securities law, secured transactions, and bailments (the subject of the next chapter). You may find it helpful to briefly review those topics from the frame of reference of the principles in this chapter.

Bailments are also tested on the CPA examination. You should be thoroughly familiar with what degree of care (slight, great, or reasonable) is required in which type of bailment (gratuitous for the bailor, gratuitous for the bailee, or mutual). The concepts related to documents of title may also be included in the questions on this part of the CPA exam.

★ Key Points

The **key points** in this chapter include:

1. Basic interests in real property ownership.

2. The priorities of competing claims under recording statutes.

3. The acquisition of title to property by adverse possession.

4. Limitations on the rights of property owners.

Chapter 47
Real Property

WHAT THIS CHAPTER IS ABOUT

This chapter covers ownership rights in real property, including the nature of those rights and their transfer. The chapter also outlines the right of the government to take private land for public use, zoning laws, and other restrictions on ownership.

CHAPTER OUTLINE

I. THE NATURE OF REAL PROPERTY
Real property consists of land and the buildings, plants, and trees on it.

A. LAND
Includes the soil on the surface of the earth, natural products or artificial structures attached to it, the water on or under it, and the air space above.

B. AIR AND SUBSURFACE RIGHTS
Limitations on air rights or subsurface rights normally have to be indicated on the deed transferring title at the time of purchase.

1. Air Rights
Flights over private land do not normally violate the owners' rights.

2. Subsurface Rights
Ownership of the surface can be separated from ownership of the sub-surface. In excavating, if a subsurface owner causes the land to subside, he or she may be liable to the owner of the surface.

C. PLANT LIFE AND VEGETATION
A sale of land with growing crops on it includes the crops, unless otherwise agreed. When crops are sold by themselves, they are personal property.

II. OWNERSHIP INTERESTS IN REAL PROPERTY

A. FEE SIMPLE
A **fee simple absolute** owner has the most rights possible—to give the property away, sell it, transfer it by will, use it for virtually any purpose, and possess it to the exclusion of all the world—potentially forever.

B. LIFE ESTATES

Lasts for the life of a specified individual ("to A for his life"). A life tenant can use the land (but cannot commit waste), mortgage the life estate, and create liens, easements, and leases (but not longer than the life defining the estate).

C. LEASEHOLD ESTATES

Created when an owner or landlord conveys the right to possess and use property to a tenant for a certain period of time. The rights and duties of landlord and tenant are outlined in Chapter 51.

1. Tenancy for Years

Created by contract (which can sometimes be oral) by which property is leased for a specific period (a month, a year, a period of years). At the end of the period, the lease ends (without notice). If the tenant dies during the lease, the lease interest passes to the tenant's heirs.

2. Periodic Tenancy

Created by a lease that specifies only that rent is to be paid at certain intervals. Automatically renews unless terminated. Can arise if a landlord allows a tenant for years to hold over. Terminates, at common law, on one period's notice.

3. Tenancy at Will

A tenancy for as long as the landlord and tenant agree. Exists when a tenant for years retains possession after termination with the landlord's consent before payment of the next rent (when it becomes a periodic tenancy). Terminates on the death of either party.

4. Tenancy at Sufferance

Possession of land without right (without the owner's permission).

D. NONPOSSESSORY INTERESTS

1. Easements and Profits

Easement: the right of a person to make limited use of another person's land without taking anything from the property. **Profit**: the right to go onto another's land and take away a part or product of the land.

a. Creation of an Easement or Profit

By deed, will, contract, implication, necessity, or prescription.

b. Effect of a Sale of Property

The benefit of an easement or profit goes with the land. The burden goes with the land only if the new owner recognizes it, or knew or should have known of it.

c. Termination of an Easement or Profit

Terminates when deeded back to the owner of the land that is burdened; its owner becomes the owner of the property burdened; or it is abandoned with the intent to relinquish the right to it.

2. Licenses

The revocable right of a person to come onto another person's land.

III. TRANSFER OF OWNERSHIP

A. DEEDS

Possession and title to land can be passed by deed without consideration.

1. **Requirements**

   (1) Names of the grantor and grantee, (2) words evidencing an intent to convey, (3) legally sufficient description of the land, (4) grantor's (and usually the spouse's) signature, and (5) delivery of the deed.

2. **Warranty Deed**

   Provides the most protection against defects of title—covenants that the grantor has title to, and the power to convey, the property; that the buyer will not be disturbed in his or her possession of the land; and that transfer is made without unknown adverse claims of third parties.

3. **Special Warranty Deed**

   Warrants only that the grantor has done nothing to lessen the value of the property. If all liens and encumbrances are disclosed, the seller is not liable if a third person interferes with the buyer's ownership.

4. **Quitclaim Deed**

   Warrants less than any other deed. Conveys to the grantee only whatever interest the grantor had.

5. **Grant Deed**

   By statute, may impliedly warrant that the grantor owns the property and has not encumbered it or conveyed it to another.

6. **Sheriff's Deed**

   Gives ownership rights to a buyer at a sheriff's sale.

7. **Recording Statutes**

   Require transfers to be recorded in public records (generally in the county in which the property is located) to prevent fraud. Many states require the grantor's signature and two witnesses' signatures.

   a. **Race Statute**

   The first person to record a deed has superior rights to the property, whether he or she knew of another previous, unrecorded transfer.

   b. **Pure Notice Statute**

   A person who does not know of a previous, unrecorded transfer can claim priority, whether or not he or she records first.

   c. **Notice-Race Statute**

   A person who does not know of a previous, unrecorded transfer and who files first can claim priority.

B. **CONTRACTS FOR THE SALE OF REAL ESTATE**

1. **Formation of the Contract**

   An offer to buy includes a deposit of earnest money (forfeited if the offer is withdrawn). Normally, the contract must be in writing to be enforceable; the writing should identify the parties, describe the property, and state the price.

   a. **Marketable Title**

   A contract for a sale of land includes an implied warranty that the seller will deliver marketable title. Defects that render title unmarketable include breaks in the chain of title and liens. Buyers buy title insurance against the risk of undiscovered defects.

      b.   Risk of Loss
      Unless the parties agree otherwise, in most states the risk is on the buyer until title passes. The buyer must pay the contract price even if the property is destroyed (unless the destruction is due to the seller's negligence).

   2.   Escrow
   The seller may give the deed to an escrow agent to deliver to the buyer when the conditions of sale are met, and the closing occurs. Once those conditions are met, passage of title relates back to the time of delivery of the deed to escrow (thus, if the grantor dies, title still passes).

   3.   Financing
   A **mortgage** is a loan for which real property is given as security. If payments are not made, the mortgagee loses the right to title.

   4.   Fitness of the Property

      a.   *Caveat Emptor*
      In a few states, the seller makes no warranties with respect to fitness (unless the deed or contract specifies otherwise). The buyer takes the property "as is."

      b.   Implied Warranty of Habitability
      In most states, the seller of a new house impliedly warrants that it will be fit for human habitation (in reasonable working order and of reasonably sound construction). In a few states, a later buyer can recover from the original builder under this warranty.

      c.   Duty to Disclose
      In most states, sellers must disclose any known defect that materially affects the value of the property and that the buyer could not reasonably discover.

C.   TRANSFER BY INHERITANCE
Outlined in Chapter 50.

D.   ADVERSE POSSESSION
A person who possesses another's property acquires title good against the original owner if the possession is (1) actual and exclusive; (2) open, visible, and notorious; (3) continuous and peaceable for a statutorily required period of time; and (4) hostile, as against the whole world.

IV.   LIMITATIONS ON THE RIGHTS OF PROPERTY OWNERS

A.   EMINENT DOMAIN
The government can take private property for public use. To obtain title, a condemnation proceeding is brought. The Fifth Amendment requires that just compensation be paid for a taking; thus, in a separate proceeding a court determines the land's fair value (usually market value) to pay the owner.

B.   ZONING
Under its police power, a state can pass zoning laws to regulate uses of land without having to compensate the landowner.

   1.   Limits on the State's Power
   Regulation cannot be (1) confiscatory (or the owner must be paid just compensation); (2) arbitrary or unreasonable (taking without due pro-

cess under the Fourteenth Amendment); or (3) discriminatory, under the Fourteenth Amendment.

2. Variances
An owner can obtain a variance if (1) it is impossible to realize a reasonable return on the land as zoned, (2) the ordinance adversely affects only the owner (and not all owners), and (3) granting a variance will not substantially alter the essential character of the zoned area.

C. RESTRICTIVE COVENANTS

1. Covenants Running with the Land
A covenant runs with the land (the original parties and their successors are entitled to its benefit or burdened with its obligation) if—

a. It is created in a written agreement (usually the document that conveys the land).

b. Parties intend that it run with the land (agreement states that all promisor's "successors, heirs, or assigns" will be bound).

c. Covenant touches and concerns the land (limits on burdened land must have some connection to the land).

d. Original parties are in privity of estate when covenant is created.

2. Illegal Restrictive Covenants
A covenant cannot be discriminatory.

TRUE-FALSE QUESTIONS

(Answers at the Back of the Book)

_____ 1. A fee simple absolute is potentially infinite in duration and can be disposed of by deed or by will.

_____ 2. The owner of a life estate has the same rights as a fee simple owner.

_____ 3. An easement allows a person to use land and take something from it, but a profit allows a person only to use land.

_____ 4. Deeds offer different degrees of protection against defects of title.

_____ 5. Private property may be taken for public use without just compensation under the government's power of eminent domain.

_____ 6. The government has the power to take _private_ property for _private_ uses only.

_____ 7. A periodic tenancy is a tenancy for a specified period of time, such as a month, a year, or a period of years.

_____ 8. To obtain a variance, a landowner must show that his or her alternative use of the land would substantially alter its essential character.

_____ 9. In most states, the seller of a new house impliedly warrants that it will be fit for human habitation.

_____ 10. A license is a revocable right of a person to come onto another person's land.

FILL-IN QUESTIONS

(Answers at the Back of the Book)

The deed that provides the most protection against defects of title is the _____ _____ (warranty/special warranty/quitclaim) deed. Among other things, it covenants that the transfer is made without any unknown adverse claims of third parties. The deed that warrants only that the grantor has done nothing to lessen the value of the property is the _____ (warranty/special warranty/quitclaim) deed. Under this deed, the seller may not be liable if a third person interferes with the buyer's ownership. The deed that warrants less than any other deed is the _____ (warranty/special warranty/quitclaim) deed. This deed conveys to the grantee only whatever interest the grantor had.

MULTIPLE-CHOICE QUESTIONS

(Answers at the Back of the Book)

_____ 1. Lou owns two hundred acres next to Brook's lumber mill. Lou sells to Brook the privilege of removing timber from his land to refine into lumber. The privilege of removing the timber is

a. an easement.
b. a profit.
c. a license.
d. none of the above.

_____ 2. Evan owns an apartment building in fee simple. Evan can

a. give the building away.
b. sell the building for a price or transfer it by a will.
c. both a and b.
d. none of the above.

_____ 3. Gina conveys her warehouse to Sam under a warranty deed. Later, Rosa appears, holding a better title to the warehouse than Sam's. Rosa proceeds to evict Sam. Sam can recover from Gina

a. the purchase price of the property.
b. damages from being evicted.
c. both a and b.
d. none of the above.

_____ 4. Jan sells the eastern half of her land to Ken. According to the deed, Ken agrees to maintain a fence along the common boundary. Later, Jan sells the rest of her land to Ed, and Ken sells his land to Tina. Under the deed, Tina agrees to maintain the fence. If Ed sues Tina to repair the fence, Ed will

a. win, because the covenant runs with the land to Ed and Tina through Jan and Ken.
b. win, because Ed bought his half of Jan's land before Tina bought her half.
c. lose, because the original covenant was in the deed given by Jan to Ken.
d. lose, because there is no privity between Ed and Tina.

____ 5. Dan owns a half acre of land that fronts on Blue Lake. Rod owns the property behind Dan's land. No road runs to Dan's land, but Rod's driveway runs between a road and Dan's property, so Dan uses Rod's driveway. The right-of-way that Dan has across Rod's property is

    a. an easement.
    b. a profit.
    c. a license.
    d. none of the above.

____ 6. **Based on a Sample CPA Exam Question.** Dave owns an office building. Dave sells the building to P&I Corporation. To be valid, the deed that conveys the property from Dave to P&I must include

    a. only a description of the property.
    b. only the purchase price.
    c. a description of the property and the purchase price.
    d. none of the above.

____ 7. Susan signs a lease for an apartment, agreeing to make rental payments before the fifth of each month. The lease does not specify a termination date. This tenancy is

    a. a periodic tenancy.
    b. a tenancy for years.
    c. a tenancy at will.
    d. a tenancy at sufferance.

____ 8. Rick sells his property to Ben, a good faith purchaser, on Monday. Rick sells the same property to Jill, also a good faith purchaser, on Tuesday. Ben records his interest on Wednesday. Jill records her interest on Thursday. The property is in a state with a notice-race statute. Who owns it?

    a. Rick
    b. Ben
    c. Jill
    d. The state

____ 9. Home Corporation builds a new house, constructing the roof improperly. Before buying the house, Lee asks Pat (Home's sales agent) about the roof. Pat says that it was carefully constructed. Lee buys the house. The roof blows off in the first storm. Lee may successfully sue Home for

    a. breach of an implied warranty of habitability only.
    b. misrepresentation or fraud only.
    c. breach of an implied warranty of habitability, misrepresentation, or fraud.
    d. none of the above.

____ 10. Lana owns a cabin on Long Lake. Bob takes possession of the cabin without Lana's permission and puts up a sign that reads "No Trespassing by Order of Bob, the Owner." The statutory period for adverse possession is ten years. Bob is in the cabin for eleven years. Lana sues to remove Bob. She will

    a. win, because she sued Bob after the statutory period for adverse possession.
    b. win, because Bob did not have permission to take possession of the cabin.
    c. lose, because the no-trespassing sign misrepresented ownership of the cabin.
    d. lose, because Bob acquired the cabin by adverse possession.

SHORT ESSAY QUESTIONS

1.   Describe the power of eminent domain and the process by which private property is condemned for a public purpose.

2.   What does the implied warranty of habitability require, and when does it apply?

ISSUE SPOTTERS

(Answers at the Back of the Book)

1.   Rob owns a commercial building in fee simple. Rob transfers temporary possession of the building to the Alliance Corporation. Can Alliance transfer possession for even less time to the Web Company?

2.   Charles sells his house to Diane under a warranty deed. Later, Carol appears, holding a better title to the house than Diane. Carol wants Diane off the property. What can Diane do?

3.   Tyler owns an orchard behind Ruth's house and property. The only access to the orchard is Ruth's driveway, which Tyler uses to get to his land. Tyler sells the orchard to Sheila. Can Sheila now use the right-of-way across Ruth's property?

4.   Ann leases an office in Al's building for a one-year term. If Ann dies during the period of the lease, what happens to the leased property?

5.   River City designates certain areas within its limits for industrial, commercial, residential, and mixed uses. Dick owns a small plot of land in a mixed-use area in the city. Can the city limit only Dick's land to residential use?

SPECIAL INFORMATION FOR CPA CANDIDATES

Real property and property interests are covered on the CPA examination.

Of the material in this chapter, you should know the basic rights and interests of real property ownership, including the different types of tenancies. Regarding deeds, you should know the priorities of competing claims under the recording statutes and the differences among a warranty deed, a special warranty deed, and a quitclaim deed. You should also know the elements of adverse possession.

Life estates are included in questions about trusts (see Chapter 51). Other material to review in relation with this chapter for the real property questions on the exam include the types of property ownership, especially joint tenancy with the right of survivorship (Chapter 46); the law of landlord and tenant (Chapter 48); mortgage law (see Chapter 29); and insurance (Chapter 50).

Chapter 48
Landlord-Tenant Relationships

WHAT THIS CHAPTER IS ABOUT

This chapter outlines laws behind the landlord-tenant relationship, including contract doctrines, and state and local statutes and ordinances. More than one-fourth of the states have adopted the Uniform Residential Landlord and Tenant Act (URLTA).

CHAPTER OUTLINE

I. CREATING THE LANDLORD-TENANT RELATIONSHIP

    A. FORM OF THE LEASE
    To ensure the validity of a lease, it should be in writing and—

        1. Express an intent to establish the relationship.

        2. Provide for transfer of the property's possession to the tenant at the beginning of the term.

        3. Provide for the landlord to retake possession at the end of the term.

        4. Describe the property.

        5. Indicate the length of the term and the amount and due dates of rent.

    B. ILLEGALITY
    A landlord cannot discriminate against tenants on the basis of race, color, religion, national origin, or sex. A tenant cannot promise to do something counter to these laws. There may be other state or local restrictions.

    C. UNCONSCIONABILITY
    Some jurisdictions (and URLTA 1.303) apply UCC 2–302, under which a court may declare an entire contract or any of its clauses unconscionable and thus illegal (see Chapters 13 and 14).

II.   PARTIES' RIGHTS AND DUTIES

A. POSSESSION

1.   Landlord's Duty to Deliver Possession

A landlord must give a tenant possession of the property that the tenant has agreed to lease. Many states require a landlord to provide physical possession. Some require only the legal right to possession.

2.   Tenant's Right to Retain Possession

The tenant retains possession exclusively until the lease expires, unless the lease provides otherwise or the tenant defaults. (A landlord can come onto the property for some purposes—for example, repairs.)

3.   Covenant of Quiet Enjoyment

The landlord promises that during the lease term no one having superior title to the property will disturb the tenant's use and enjoyment of it. If so, the tenant can sue for damages for breach.

4.   Eviction

If the landlord deprives the tenant of possession of the property or interferes with his or her use or enjoyment of it, the tenant can (1) sue for damages or possession or (2) stop paying rent or terminate the lease.

5.   Constructive Eviction

Constructive eviction occurs when this results from a landlord's failure to perform adequately his or her duties under the lease..

6.   Retaliatory Eviction

Retaliatory eviction occurs when a landlord evicts a tenant for complaining to a government agency about the premises' condition.

B. USE OF THE PREMISES

Unless the parties agree otherwise, a tenant may make any use of the property (but no waste), so long as it is legal, relates to the purpose for which the property is adapted or ordinarily used, does not injure the landlord's interest (no alterations without consent), and does not create a nuisance.

C. MAINTAINING THE PREMISES

1.   Statutory Requirements

A landlord must comply with safety and health standards. In most states, a landlord must repair damage not caused by the tenant. A landlord is responsible for maintaining common areas, including defects the landlord knows of and those the landlord should know of.

2.   Implied Warranty of Habitability

In most states, a landlord must furnish residential premises that are habitable. This applies to substantial defects that the landlord knows or should know about and has had a reasonable time to repair. In deciding whether a defect is sufficiently substantial, courts ask—

a. Whether the tenant caused the defect.

b. How long the defect has existed.

c. The age of the building.

    d. The defect's impact on the tenant's health and safety.

    e. Whether a defect violates housing, building, or sanitation statutes.

3. Remedies for Landlord's Failure to Maintain Leased Property
In some circumstances, a tenant may withhold rent, pay for a repair and deduct the amount from the rent, cancel the lease, or sue for damages.

D. RENT
A tenant must pay rent even if he or she refuses to occupy the property or moves out (if the refusal or move is unjustified).

1. Security Deposits and Late Charges
These are legal. A landlord may withhold an amount from the deposit to cover damages.

2. Rent Escalation and Property Taxes
Unless the lease states otherwise, a landlord cannot raise rent during the term or charge the tenant for property taxes.

3. Landlord's Remedies for Tenant's Failure to Pay Rent
If a tenant fails to pay rent or refuses to give up wrongful possession of leased property, the landlord can resort to—

    a. **Landlord's Lien**
In some states, a landlord can exercise a lien on the tenant's personal property (and sell it to recoup unpaid rent).

    b. **Lawsuit**
In some states, a landlord must wait for up to ten days after the rent is due (and give notice) before suing for damages or termination.

    c. **Recovery of Possession**
A landlord may bring an action in ejectment or, in most states, an unlawful detainer action (shorter and faster than ejectment).

4. Landlord's Duty to Mitigate Damages
In many states, even if a tenant vacates leased property unjustifiably, the landlord must make a reasonable attempt to lease the property to another party.

III. LIABILITY FOR INJURIES ON THE PREMISES
Liability usually depends on who controls the area where the injury occurred; the standard is reasonable care under all circumstances (see Chapter 5).

A. LANDLORD'S LIABILITY

1. Injuries Caused by Defects on the Premises
A landlord is liable for injuries resulting from a dangerous condition that the landlord knew about or should have known about, when the landlord fails to tell the tenant about it or actually conceals it. (Exception—obvious conditions or conditions the tenant knows about.)

2. Common Areas
A landlord is liable for injuries occurring on property within the landlord's control (common areas, such as hallways and elevators). This includes a duty to inspect and repair. (Exception—areas where people could not be reasonably expected to go.)

3. **Injuries Caused by Crimes of Third Persons**
   If crimes are reasonably foreseeable and the landlord takes no steps to prevent them, he or she may be liable for negligence if an injury results. Foreseeability may depend on recent, prior, similar, criminal activity.

B. **TENANT'S LIABILITY**
   A tenant must maintain in a reasonably safe condition those areas under his or her control. Under a commercial lease, the tenant's duty may coincide with the landlord's (and both may be liable).

IV. TRANSFERRING RIGHTS TO LEASED PROPERTY

A. **TRANSFERRING THE LANDLORD'S INTEREST**
   A landlord can sell, give away, or otherwise transfer his or her real property (see Chapter 47), or transfer only the lease, only the reversionary interest, only the rent, or any of these rights in combination. If complete title is transferred, the tenant becomes the tenant of the new owner.

B. **TRANSFERRING THE TENANT'S INTEREST**
   Before a tenant can assign or sublet his or her interest, the lease may require the landlord's consent (it cannot be unreasonably withheld). If the assignee or sublessee later defaults, the tenant must pay the rent.

V. TERMINATION OR RENEWAL OF THE LEASE

A. **TERMINATION**
   On termination, a tenant is no longer liable for rent and is no longer entitled to possession of the property. A lease terminates when its term ends or by—

   1. **Notice**
      A periodic tenancy (see Chapter 47) will renew automatically unless one of the parties gives timely notice of termination.

   2. **Release and Merger**
      If a landlord conveys his or her interest in the property to the tenant, the transfer is a release, and the tenant's interest in the property merges into the title to the property (which he or she holds).

   3. **Surrender by Agreement**
      The parties may agree to end a tenancy before it would otherwise terminate.

   4. **Abandonment**
      A landlord may treat a tenant's moving out with no intent of returning before the end of the term as an offer of surrender. The landlord's re-taking of possession relieves the tenant of the duty to pay rent.

   5. **Forfeiture**
      If a tenant fails to fulfill a condition under the lease, the tenant may forfeit his or her interest in it. Generally, if neither the lease nor a statute provides for forfeiture, a landlord may claim only damages.

   6. **Destruction of the Property by a Cause beyond the Landlord's Control**
      Usually, a landlord is not obligated to restore the premises. Depending on the terms of a lease, a commercial tenant may be responsible for restoring the premises, however.

B. RENEWAL

If a lease does not contain an option for renewal and the parties have not agreed that the tenant may stay on, the tenant has no right to remain.

TRUE-FALSE QUESTIONS

(Answers at the Back of the Book)

____   1.   The covenant of quiet enjoyment guarantees that a tenant will not be disturbed in the possession of the premises by the landlord or any third person.

____   2.   If the covenant of quiet enjoyment is breached, the tenant can sue the landlord for damages.

____   3.   Generally, a tenant must pay rent when he or she moves out, if the move is unjustifiable.

____   4.   If a lease states the time it will end, a landlord must give a tenant notice that the lease is going to expire as the time approaches.

____   5.   A tenant does not have to pay rent if there is anything wrong with leased property, no matter how slight the defect.

____   6.   In most states, a tenant can alter leased premises without the landlord's consent.

____   7.   A landlord is liable for injuries occurring on property within the landlord's control.

____   8.   A tenant is liable for injuries occurring on property within the tenant's control.

____   9.   When a landlord sells leased premises to a third party, any existing leases terminate automatically.

____   10. When a tenant assigns or sublets a lease to a third party, the tenant's obligations under the lease terminate automatically.

FILL-IN QUESTIONS

(Answers at the Back of the Book)

In many states, judicial decisions or statutes impose a duty on a landlord who leases _____ (commercial/residential) property to furnish premises that are habitable and to make repairs not caused by the _____ (landlord's/tenant's) actions. Under most circumstances, a _____ (commercial/residential) tenant is not required to make such major repairs as replacing a roof or a foundation. Thus, without a lease clause under which the _____ _____ (commercial/residential) tenant assumes a duty to maintain the leased property, the tenant is under no obligation to do so. Normally, the tenant is liable for repairs required only as a result of the _____ (landlord's/tenant's) intentional or negligent actions.

MULTIPLE-CHOICE QUESTIONS

(Answers at the Back of the Book)

____ 1. **Based on a Sample CPA Exam Question.** Paul leases a house from John for a two-year term. To be enforceable, their lease must include

a. a description of the premises.
b. a due date for the payment of the property taxes.
c. a requirement that John will perform any structural repairs to the property.
d. a requirement that Paul carry liability insurance.

____ 2. Jim leases an apartment from Maria. With Maria's consent, Jim assigns the lease to Nell for the last two months of the term, after which Nell exercises an option under the original lease to renew for three months. One month later, Nell moves out. Regarding the rent for the rest of the term

a. no one is liable.
b. Jim can be held liable.
c. only Nell is liable.
d. Maria is liable.

____ 3. Dian leases an apartment from Tom. The lease provides that Tom is not liable for any injury if the heating system fails to function. In January, the system breaks down. Dian becomes seriously ill. If Dian sues Tom, she will

a. win, because Dian is the tenant.
b. win, because the clause absolving Tom of liability is unconscionable.
c. lose, because the lease absolves Tom of responsibility.
d. lose, because Tom is the landlord.

____ 4. Jill reports housing code violations in her apartment to local authorities. In retaliation, her landlord Ken changes the lock on her door, refuses to give her a new key, and starts eviction proceedings. If Jill sues Ken, she will

a. win, because Jill is the tenant.
b. win, because Ken is attempting a retaliatory eviction.
c. lose, because Ken is attempting a retaliatory eviction.
d. lose, because Tom is the landlord.

____ 5. National Coffee Brokers leases an office from RP Properties, Inc. Before the end of the lease term, National does not pay the rent for three months and then, without justification, vacates the office. RP can

a. retake possession of the office only.
b. sue the tenant for the unpaid rent only.
c. retake possession of the office and sue the tenant for unpaid rent.
d. do nothing until the lease term expires.

____ 6. Discount Sales leases a store from Commercial Mall, Inc. While installing trade fixtures, Discount's workers damage some floor tiles and fail to fix them. Later, Adam, a customer, trips on a tile and injures himself. If Adam sues Discount, he will

a. win, because he was injured.
b. win, because Discount failed maintain an area under its control.
c. lose, because he failed to exercise reasonable care.
d. lose, because Commercial Mall is liable, not Discount.

_____ 7. Ron signs a one-year lease for an apartment. Kim is the landlord. Six months later, Ron moves out of the apartment with no intent of returning. Ron has no more obligation to pay rent if Kim

    a. moves into the apartment.
    b. enters the apartment to make a repair.
    c. does not ask for the rent.
    d. does nothing.

_____ 8. Cassie leases an apartment from Tom. Their lease contains a clause relieving Tom from any liability for any injury Cassie might suffer while living in the apartment. One winter night, the pipes burst because Tom has failed to tend to them, and the heat goes out because he forgot to pay the gas bill. Cassie slips on the ice in her living room and breaks her leg. Tom

    a. will be liable for Cassie's injury because of his negligence.
    b. will not be liable for Cassie's injury in spite of his negligence.
    c. will only be liable is prior tenants had been similarly injured.
    d. will not be liable because Cassie's living room is not a common area.

_____ 9. Dick rents an apartment from Sue. Two months later, Dick moves out, and arranges with Lee to move in and pay the rent to Sue for the rest of the term. This is

    a. an assignment.
    b. a sublease.
    c. an eviction.
    d. a release and merger.

_____ 10. Ray operates Family Restaurant in space that he leases in Village Mall. Village Mall is owned by VM Associates. VM Associates sells the mall to BB Properties. For the rest of the lease term, Ray owes rent to

    a. VM Associates.
    b. BB Properties.
    c. Family Restaurant.
    d. no one.

SHORT ESSAY QUESTIONS

1. In what circumstances is the landlord liable for injuries on the leased premises?

2. What are the ways in which a lease may be terminated?

ISSUE SPOTTERS

(Answers at the Back of the Book)

1. Barb leases a store in Dan's Town Mall. Dan sells Town Mall to Eagle Properties, Inc. Does Barb owe rent for the remainder of the lease term to Dan, or is Barb now Eagle's tenant? If Eagle collects rent from Barb, is Eagle bound by the terms of the original lease?

2. Eve orally agrees to rent an apartment to Nancy for a six-month term. Is this lease enforceable if it is not in writing?

3. Ann leases an apartment from Ed. When Ann arrives to take possession, Lou, the previous tenant, is still on the premises. Ann asks Ed to get rid of Lou. Ed says that Lou is Ann's problem. Is Ed right?

4. Bob wants to lease a store in Rita's mall. Rita insists that the lease include a rent escalation clause, indexing future increases to Bob's sales. Bob claims that such a clause is illegal, that rent cannot be increased during a lease term, and that even if such a clause were legal, the amounts must be stated in exact dollar amounts. Is Bob right?

5. Lisa owns a building in an area in which there has been a few automobile thefts. When a break-in occurs in Lisa's building, she installs an alarm and hires a security guard. If more crimes occur in the building and an injury results, is Lisa liable?

SPECIAL INFORMATION FOR CPA CANDIDATES

The section of the CPA examination on property law includes questions on land-lord-tenant law. Of the material covered in this chapter, it is important for you to know that a tenant is entitled to exclusive possession of the premises for the term of the lease. Eviction may result for using the property for illegal or prohibited purposes or for failing to pay the rent. You should the difference between an assignment and a sub-lease (the former involves the tenant's entire interest under the lease; the later involves all or part of the premises for a shorter term). Unless the lease prohibits it, a tenant can assign or sublet without the landlord's consent.

Material in other chapters that you may wish to review for the exam includes the types of tenancies covered in Chapter 47.

On the contracts section of the exam, there may be a question about a lease that cannot be completed within a year. Of course, any such lease must be in writing to be enforceable under the Statute of Frauds.

CUMULATIVE HYPOTHETICAL PROBLEM FOR UNIT TEN—INCLUDING CHAPTERS 46–48

(Answers at the Back of the Book)

As joint tenants, Eve and Frank own twenty acres of land, on which there is a warehouse surrounded by a fence.

____ **1.** In determining whether the fence is a fixture, the most important factor is

a. the adaptability of the fence to the land.
b. the intent of Eve and Frank.
c. the manner in which the fence is attached to the land.
d. the value of the fence.

____ **2.** Frank wants to sell the land and the warehouse. He executes and delivers a deed to Greg. Eve will

a. own all of the land and the warehouse because she did not sign the deed.
b. own exactly twenty acres and half a warehouse.
c. retain a 1/2 undivided interest in the property.
d. share ownership of the property with Greg as a joint tenant.

____ **3.** For the deed between Frank and Greg to be effective, one of the conditions is that the deed must

a. be delivered by Frank with the intent to transfer title.
b. be recorded within certain statutory time limits.
c. include the sale price.
d. include the signatures of both Frank and Greg.

____ **4.** Before Greg records the deed, Frank deeds the same interest in the property to Helen. Helen is aware of the prior transfer to Greg and records her deed first. Under a race-notice recording statute, the prevailing party is

a. Eve.
b. Frank.
c. Greg.
d. Helen.

____ **5.** International Sales, Inc. (ISI), rents the warehouse from the owners, under a two-year lease that requires ISI to pay the property taxes. At the start of the second year, ISI agrees with J&J Transport to allow it to occupy the warehouse and pay rent to ISI. No one pays the property taxes for the second year. In a suit to collect, the owners would most likely

a. lose and have to pay the taxes themselves.
b. prevail against ISI because the agreement with J&J was a sublease.
c. prevail against ISI and J&J because they are jointly and severally liable.
d. prevail against J&J because the lease was assigned to J&J.

Chapter 49
Insurance

WHAT THIS CHAPTER IS ABOUT

Insurance is a contract in which one party agrees to compensate the other for any future loss on a specified subject by a specified peril. Essentially, insurance is an arrangement for managing—transferring and allocating—risk. This chapter covers the law relating to insurance.

CHAPTER OUTLINE

I. TERMINOLOGY AND CONCEPTS

    A. RISK MANAGEMENT
    Risk management consists of plans to protect personal and financial interests should an event undermine their security. The most common method is to transfer risk from a business or individual to an insurance company.

    B. INSURANCE TERMINOLOGY
    An insurance company is an **underwriter** or an **insurer**; the party covered by insurance is the **insured**; an insurance contract is a **policy**; consideration paid to an insurer is a **premium**; policies are obtained through an **agent** or **broker**.

    C. RISK POOLING
    Insurance companies spread the risk among a large number of people—the pool—to make the premiums small compared with the coverage offered.

    D. CLASSIFICATIONS OF INSURANCE
    Insurance is classified according to the nature of the risk involved.

    E. INSURABLE INTEREST
    To obtain insurance, one must have a sufficient interest in what is insured.

        1. Life Insurance
        One must have a reasonable expectation of benefit from the continued life of another. The benefit may be related to money or may be founded on a relationship (by blood or affinity).

a. Key-person Insurance
An organization (partnership, corporation) can insure the life of a person who is important to that organization (partner, officer).

b. When the Insurable Interest Must Exist
An interest in someone's life must exist *when the policy is obtained*.

2. Property Insurance
One has an insurable interest in property when one would sustain a pecuniary loss from its destruction. An insurable interest in property must exist *when the loss occurs*.

II. THE INSURANCE CONTRACT
Policies generally are standard; in some states, this is required.

A. APPLICATION FOR INSURANCE
The application is part of the contract. Misstatements can void a policy, especially if the insurer shows that it would not have issued the policy if it had known the facts.

B. EFFECTIVE DATE OF COVERAGE
A policy is effective when (1) a binder is written, (2) the policy is issued, or (3) a certain time elapses.

1. When a Policy Is Obtained from a Broker
A broker is the agent of the applicant. Until the broker obtains a policy, the applicant is normally not insured.

2. When a Policy Is Obtained from an Agent
An agent is the agent of the insurer. One who obtains a policy from an agent can be protected from the moment the application is made (under a binder), or the parties may agree to delay coverage until a policy is issued or some condition is met (such as a physical exam).

C. PROVISIONS AND CLAUSES
Some important clauses include—

1. Provisions Mandated by Statute
A court will deem that a policy contains such a clause even if it is not actually included in the language of the contract.

2. Incontestability Clause
After a life or health policy has been in force for a certain time (two or three years), the insurer cannot cancel the policy or avoid a claim on the basis of statements made in the application.

3. Coinsurance Clause
A standard provision in fire insurance policies; applies only in cases of *partial* loss. If an owner insures property up to a specified percentage (usually 80 percent) of its value, he or she will recover any loss up to the face amount of the policy. If the insurance is for less than this percentage, the owner is responsible for a proportionate share.

4. Appraisal and Arbitration Clauses
If insurer and insured disagree about the value of a loss, they can demand separate appraisals, to be resolved by a third party (*umpire*).

5. **Multiple Insurance Coverage**
If policies with several companies cover the same risk and the amount of coverage exceeds the loss, the insured collects from each insurer its proportionate share of the liability to the total amount of insurance.

6. **Antilapse Clause**
Provides grace period for insured to pay an overdue premium.

D. INTERPRETING PROVISIONS
Words in an insurance contract have their ordinary meanings. If there is an ambiguity or uncertainty, it is interpreted against the insurer.

E. CANCELLATION
A policy may be canceled for nonpayment of premiums, fraud or misrepresentation, conviction for a crime that increases the hazard insured against, or gross negligence that increases the hazard insured against. An insurer may be required to give advance written notice.

F. BASIC DUTIES AND RIGHTS
Parties must act in good faith and disclose all material facts. If there is a claim, the insurer must investigate. Insurer and insured must fulfill the terms of the policy.

G. DEFENSES AGAINST PAYMENT
Fraud, misrepresentation, violation of warranties, and actions that are against public policy or that are otherwise illegal.

III.   TYPES OF INSURANCE

A. LIFE INSURANCE
A fixed amount is paid to a beneficiary on an insured's death.

1. **Types of Life Insurance**
Basic types—**whole life**: has cash surrender value that grows at a predetermined rate and can be used as collateral for a loan; **term**: provides protection for a specified period; has no cash surrender value.

2. **Liability**
Unless excluded, any cause of death is the insurer's risk. Typical exclusions: death by suicide, when the insured is a passenger in a commercial vehicle, in military action in war, or execution by the government.

3. **Misstatement of Age**
This does not void a policy, but premiums or benefits are adjusted.

4. **Assignment**
An insured can change beneficiaries, with notice to the insurer.

5. **Creditors' Rights**
Generally, a judgment creditor can reach an insured's interest in life insurance. The creditor cannot compel the insured to obtain cash surrender value or change the beneficiary to the creditor.

6. **Termination**
Usually occurs only on default in premium payments (policy lapses), payment of benefits, expiration of term, or cancellation by insured.

B. FIRE INSURANCE

Protects the homeowner against fire, lightning, and damage from smoke and water caused by the fire or the fire department.

1. Liability

Usually, recovery is limited to losses resulting from hostile fires. In some cases, the insured must file proof of a loss as a condition for recovery. In most cases, premises must be occupied at the time of loss, unless the parties agree otherwise.

2. Assignment

Not assignable without the consent of the insurer (because it would materially change the insurer's risk).

C. HOMEOWNERS' INSURANCE

1. Property Coverage

The garage; the house; other private buildings; personal possessions at home, in travel, or at work. Includes expenses for living away from home because of a fire or some other covered peril.

2. Liability Coverage

Injuries occurring on the insured's property; damage or injury by the insured to others or their property. Excludes professional malpractice.

D. AUTOMOBILE INSURANCE

1. Liability Insurance

Covers bodily injury and property damage.

2. Collision Insurance

Covers damage to the insured's car in any type of collision. Most people agree to pay a deductible before the insurer becomes liable.

3. Comprehensive Insurance

Covers loss, damage, and destruction by fire, hurricane, hail, vandalism, and theft.

4. Uninsured Motorist Insurance

Covers the driver and passengers against injury caused by any driver without insurance or by a hit-and-run driver. Some states require it all automobile policies sold to drivers.

5. Other-Driver Coverage

Protects vehicle owner and anyone who drives the vehicle with owner's permission.

6. No-fault Insurance

Provides that claims arising from an accident are made against the claimant's own insurer, regardless of whose fault the accident was.

E. BUSINESS LIABILITY INSURANCE

1. Key-person Insurance

See above (I, E, 1, a).

2. **General Liability Insurance**
   Covers as many risks as the insurer agrees to cover. Policies can be drafted to meet special needs, such as specific risks of product liability (see Chapter 6).

3. **Professional Malpractice Insurance**
   Protects professionals against malpractice claims.

4. **Workers' Compensation Insurance**
   Covers payments to employees who are injured in accidents occurring on the job or in the course of employment (see Chapter 35).

TRUE-FALSE QUESTIONS

(Answers at the Back of the Book)

____ 1. Risk management involves the transfer of certain risks from an individual or a business to an insurance company.

____ 2. Insurance is classified by the nature of the person or interest protected.

____ 3. An insurance broker is always an agent of an insurance company.

____ 4. An insurance applicant is usually protected from the time an application is made, if a premium has been paid.

____ 5. A person can insure anything in which he or she has an insurable interest.

____ 6. An application for insurance is not part of the insurance contract.

____ 7. An insured can change beneficiaries under a life insurance policy without the insurer's consent.

____ 8. A coinsurance clause in a fire insurance policy reduces the amount of the insured's recovery only in a case of total loss.

____ 9. More than one party can have an insurable interest in, for example, the same property.

____ 10. Under an antilapse clause, an insurance policy lapses unless the insured pays a premium exactly on time.

FILL-IN QUESTIONS

(Answers at the Back of the Book)

The words used in an insurance contract have their _____ (ordinary/special) meaning and are interpreted by the courts in light of the _____ _____ (insured's conduct/nature of the coverage) involved. When there is an ambiguity in a policy, a provision is interpreted against the _____ _____ (insurance company/insured). When it is unclear whether an insurance contract actually exists because the written policy has not been delivered, the uncertainty will be determined against the _____ (insurance company/insured). A court presumes the policy _____ (is/is not) in effect unless the _____ (insurance company/insured) can show otherwise.

MULTIPLE-CHOICE QUESTIONS

(Answers at the Back of the Book)

____ 1. Satellite Communications, Inc., takes out an insurance policy on its plant. For which of the following reasons could the insurer cancel the policy?

a. Satellite's president appears as a witness in a case against the company.
b. Satellite begins using grossly careless manufacturing practices.
c. Two of Satellite's drivers have their driver's licenses suspended.
d. All of the above

____ 2. Sue applies to A&I Insurance Company for a fire insurance policy for her warehouse. To obtain a lower premium, she misrepresents the age of the property. The policy is granted. After the warehouse is destroyed by fire, A&I learns the true facts. A&I can

a. refuse to pay on the ground of fraud in the application.
b. refuse to pay on the ground that the warehouse has been destroyed by fire.
c. not refuse to pay, because an application is not part of an insurance contract.
d. not refuse to pay, because the warehouse has been destroyed by fire.

____ 3. Jim is an executive with E-Tech Corporation. Because his death would cause a financial loss to E-Tech, the firm insures his life. Later, Jim resigns to work for DigiCom, Inc., one of E-Tech's competitors. Six months later, Jim dies. Regarding payment for the loss, E-Tech can

a. collect, because its insurable interest existed when the policy was obtained.
b. not collect, because its insurable interest did not exist when a loss occurred.
c. not collect, because it suffered no financial loss from the death of Jim, who resigned to work for one of its competitors.
d. none of the above.

____ 4. **Based on a Sample CPA Exam Question.** Tom buys a house and obtains a fire insurance policy on the property. If the house is destroyed by fire, to collect payment under the policy, Tom's insurable interest

a. exists only if the property is owned by Tom or a related individual.
b. exists only if the property is owned in fee simple.
c. must exist when the loss occurs.
d. must exist when the policy is issued and when the loss occurs.

____ 5. Pam states, on her application for life insurance, that she has not been hospitalized within the last five years, forgetting that two years earlier she was hospitalized briefly. One year later, Pam dies for a cause unrelated to the earlier hospitalization. The insurer denies payment. If Pam's beneficiary sues the insurer, the beneficiary will

a. win, because an insurer cannot use a misstatement on an application to avoid payment.
b. win, because Pam's misstatement did not concern a material fact.
c. lose, because Pam's misstatement concerned a material fact.
d. lose, because an insurer can use any misstatement on an application to avoid payment.

____ **6.** Deb takes out a fire insurance policy on her $200,000 warehouse. The policy contains a coinsurance clause with a specified percentage of 80 percent. Deb insures the property for $160,000. In a fire, she suffers a $100,000 loss. She can recover

    a. $200,000.
    b. $160,000.
    c. $100,000.
    d. $80,000.

____ **7.** Techron Corporation manufactures computers. To insure its products to cover injuries to consumers if the products prove defective, Techron should buy

    a. group insurance.
    b. liability insurance.
    c. major medical insurance.
    d. term life insurance.

____ **8.** Eagle Company has insurance policies with General Insurance, Inc., and InsurCorp covering the risk of loss of its building in a fire. Each policy has a multiple insurance clause. If the building is partially destroyed in a fire, Eagle can collect from each insurer

    a. the full amount of the loss.
    b. half of the amount of the loss.
    c. each insurer's proportionate share of the loss to the total amount of insurance.
    d. nothing.

____ **9.** Ace Manufacturing, Inc., has property insurance with National Insurer, Inc. When Ace suffers a loss in a burglary, Ace and National cannot agree on the amount of recovery. Under an appraisal and arbitration clause

    a. each party can demand separate appraisals to be resolved by a third party.
    b. Ace can demand an appraisal which National must pay.
    c. National can demand an appraisal which Ace must accept.
    d. the government sets the value of the loss which both parties must accept.

____ **10.** Lee buys BizNet, a company that provides Internet access, and takes out property insurance with InsCo to cover a loss of the equipment. Two years later, Lee sells BizNet. Six months after the sale, BizNet's equipment is stolen. Under InsCo's policy, Lee can recover

    a. the total amount of the insurance.
    b. the total amount of the loss.
    c. InsCo's proportionate share of the loss to the total amount of insurance.
    d. nothing.

SHORT ESSAY QUESTIONS

1. Define the concept of insurable interest. What is its effect on insurance payments?

2. What are some of the types of insurance policies that businesses carry to protect themselves from risk?

ISSUE SPOTTERS

(Answers at the Back of the Book)

1. Why is an insurance premium small relative to the amount of coverage that an insurance company offers?

2. Neal applies to Farm Insurance Company for a life insurance policy. On the application, Neal understates his age. Neal obtains the policy, but for a lower premium than he would have had to pay had he disclosed his actual age. The policy includes an incontestability clause. Six years later, Neal dies. Can the insurer refuse payment?

3. Al is divorced and owns a house. Al has no reasonable expectation of benefit from the life of Beth, his ex-spouse, but applies for insurance on her life anyway. Al obtains a fire insurance policy on the house, then sells the house. Ten years later, Beth dies and the house is destroyed by fire. Can Al obtain payment for these events?

4. Umbrella insurance policies are bought separately from regular insurance coverage and can provide coverage for as much as $5 million. Under what circumstances might an individual want to buy umbrella insurance coverage?

5. KT Electronics Corporation discovers a defect in its recently marketed hard drives. KT decides to recall the product and replace it with another. KT's insurance will cover any harm to customers that occurs before the drives are returned. Will the insurance also pay for the recall and replacement?

SPECIAL INFORMATION FOR CPA CANDIDATES

Insurance is part of the property section of the CPA examination. The most important points for your review are the warranties that an insured makes when applying for a policy, the workings of coinsurance clauses, and the concept of insurable interest. When must a party have an insurable interest to obtain insurance? Can more than one party have an insurable interest in, for example, the same property? (Yes.) Does a coinsurance clause apply in a case of total loss? Except for questions concerning insurable interest, the CPA exam does not cover automobile or life insurance.

Chapter 50
Wills, Trusts, and Elder Law

WHAT THIS CHAPTER IS ABOUT

This chapter covers some of the laws governing the succession of property. (See also Chapter 46 on joint tenancy and Chapter 49 on insurance.) A person can direct the passage of property after death by will. If no valid will has been executed, state intestacy laws apply. A person can also transfer property with a trust. Elder law, which relates to the needs of older persons, is also covered in this chapter.

CHAPTER OUTLINE

I. WILLS

A **will** is a declaration of how a person wants property disposed of after death; a formal instrument that must follow the statutory requirements to be effective.

A. TERMINOLOGY OF WILLS

A **testator** is a person who makes a will; a **probate court** oversees the administration of a will by an **executor** (appointed by the testator in the will) or by an **administrator** (appointed by the court).

B. LAWS GOVERNING WILLS

Vary from state to state. Some of the law includes—

1. Uniform Probate Code (UPC)

Codifies principles and procedures for the resolution of conflicts in settling estates and relaxes some of the requirements for a will.

2. Revised UPC

In 1990, the UPC was revised to further relax formal will requirements and to provide for the interpretation of will substitutes and other *inter vivos* transfers (see below).

C. TYPES OF GIFTS

A gift of real estate by will is a **devise**; the recipient is a **devisee**. A gift of personal property is a **bequest** or **legacy**; a recipient is a **legatee**. Gifts can be specific, general, or residuary. If there are not enough assets to pay all general bequests, an **abatement** reduces the gifts.

D. REQUIREMENTS FOR A VALID WILL

1. **A Testator Must Have Capacity**
   When a will is made, the testator must be of legal age (in most states, at least eighteen years old) and sound mind (a person can be adjudged mentally incompetent or have delusions about certain subjects and, during lucid moments, still be of sound mind).

2. **A Testator Must Have Intent**
   A testator must (1) intend a document to be his or her will, (2) understand the property being distributed, and (3) remember the "natural objects of his or her bounty" (family members and others for whom the testator has affection).

3. **A Will Must Be in Writing**
   An outside document can be incorporated by reference if it exists when the will is executed and is identified in the will. In a few states, an oral (nuncupative) will is valid to pass personal property below a certain value if made in the expectation of imminent death.

4. **A Will Must Be Signed by the Testator**
   The testator must sign with the intent to validate the will; the signature need not be at the end.

5. **A Will Must Be Witnessed**
   The number of witnesses, their qualifications, and the manner in which it must be done vary from state to state.

6. **In a Few States, a Will Must Be "Published"**
   Publication is an oral declaration by the maker to the witnesses that the document they are about to sign is his or her will.

E. REVOCATION OF WILLS

A will is revocable, in whole or in part, by its maker any time during the maker's lifetime by physical act (intentionally obliterating or destroying a will, or directing someone else to do so); by a document (a codicil, a new will); or by operation of law (marriage, divorce, annulment, birth of child).

F. RIGHTS UNDER A WILL

A surviving spouse can renounce the amount given by will and elect a forced share, if the share is larger than the gift. In most states, a forced share is one-third of an estate or an amount equal to a spouse's share under intestacy laws (see below). A beneficiary can renounce his or her share.

G. PROBATE PROCEDURES

Probate: establish the validity of a will and administer the estate. The UPC includes rules and procedures for resolving conflicts in settling estates and relaxes some of the will requirements.

1. **Informal Probate**
   In some states, cars, bank accounts, etc., can pass by filling out forms, or property can be transferred by affidavit. Most states allow heirs to distribute assets themselves after a will is admitted to probate.

2. **Formal Probate**
   For large estates, a probate court supervises distribution.

3. **Property Transfers outside the Probate Process**
   Will substitutes include living trusts (see below), life insurance, and joint tenancies.

II. INTESTACY LAWS

Statutes of descent and distribution regulate how property is distributed when a person dies without a valid will. The rules vary widely from state to state, but typically, the debts of the decedent are satisfied out of his or her estate, and the remaining assets pass to the surviving spouse and children.

A. SURVIVING SPOUSE AND CHILDREN

1. Legitimate Heirs

The spouse usually receives a share of the estate (such as one-half if there is a surviving child); the children receive the rest. If no children or grandchildren survive, the spouse succeeds to the entire estate.

2. Illegitimate Children

In some states, intestate succession between a parent and an illegitimate child can occur only if the child is legitimized by ceremony or was acknowledged by the parent.

B. ORDER OF DISTRIBUTION

1. Lineal Descendants

If there is no surviving spouse or child, grandchildren are next in line, then parents. Generally, title descends (to children, etc.) before it ascends (to parents, etc.).

2. Collateral Heirs

If there are no lineal descendants, brothers, sisters, nieces, nephews, aunts, and uncles inherit. If none survive, property goes to collateral heirs' next of kin (relatives by marriage are not considered kin).

3. Methods of Distribution

Per stirpes: a class or group of distributees take the share that their deceased parent would have been entitled to inherit had that parent lived. *Per capita*: each person takes an equal share of the estate.

III. TRUSTS

Arrangements by which a grantor (settlor) transfers legal title to the trust property to a trustee, who administers the property as directed by the grantor for the benefit of the beneficiaries.

A. ESSENTIAL ELEMENTS

1. A designated beneficiary.

2. A designated trustee.

3. A fund sufficiently identified to enable title to pass to the trustee.

4. Actual delivery to the trustee with the intention of passing title.

B. EXPRESS TRUSTS

1. Living Trust (or *Inter Vivos* Trust)

Created by trust deed to exist during the settlor's lifetime.

2. Testamentary Trust

Created by will to come into existence on the settlor's death (if the will is invalid, the trust is invalid). If not named in the will, a trustee is appointed by a court. Trustee's actions are subject to judicial approval.

3. **Charitable Trust**
   Designed to benefit a segment of the public or the public in general, usually for charitable, educational, religious, or scientific purposes. Identities of the beneficiaries are uncertain.

4. **Spendthrift Trust**
   Prevents a beneficiary's transfer of his or her right to future payments of income or capital by expressly placing restraints on the alienation of trust funds.

5. **Totten Trust**
   Created when one person deposits money in his or her own name as trustee. Revocable at will until the depositor dies or completes the gift (for example, by delivery of the funds to the beneficiary).

C. IMPLIED TRUSTS

1. **Constructive Trust**
   An equitable remedy that enables plaintiffs to recover property (and sometimes damages) from defendants who would otherwise be unjustly enriched. A court declares the legal owner of the property to be a trustee for parties entitled to the benefit of the property.

2. **Resulting Trust**
   Arises when the conduct of the parties raise an inference that the party holding legal title to the property does so for the benefit of another.

D. THE TRUSTEE
Anyone capable of holding title to, and dealing in, property can be a trustee

1. **Trustee's Duties**
   Preserve the trust property; make the trust property productive; and if required by the terms of the trust agreement, pay income to the beneficiaries.

   a. **General Duties**
      Honesty, good faith, and prudence in administering the trust for the exclusive interest of the beneficiary; invest and manage the trust assets as a prudent investor would manage his or her own assets.

   b. **Specific Duties**

      1) **Keep Accurate Accounts of the Trust's Administration**
         Furnish complete information to the beneficiary. Keep trust assets separate from his or her own assets. Pay to an income beneficiary the net income of the trust at reasonable intervals.

      2) **Invest the Trust Property**
         Distribute the risk of loss from investments by diversification and dispose of assets that do not represent prudent investments.

2. **Trustee's Powers**
   Whatever the settlor prescribes. State law applies only to the extent that it does not conflict with the terms of the trust.

   a. **If State Law Applies**
      May restrict the investment of trust funds, confining trustees to investments in conservative debt securities.

       b. Discretion to Distribute the Principal or Invest the Income
          Subject to trust purposes, a trustee may make adjustments in annual distributions to provide the beneficiary with predictable income.

    3. Allocations between Principal and Income
       Ordinary receipts and expenses (rent, royalties) are chargeable to income; extraordinary receipts and expenses (proceeds from the sale of property, stock dividends) are allocated to principal.

E. TRUST TERMINATION
Typically, a trust instrument specifies a termination date. If the trust's purpose is fulfilled before that date, a court may order the trust's termination. If no date is specified, a trust terminates when its purpose is fulfilled (or becomes impossible or illegal).

IV. ESTATE ADMINISTRATION

The procedure used to collect and distribute assets when a person dies, subject to the oversight of a probate court. Rules vary from state to state.

A. BASIC STEPS
(1) Did the decedent leave a will? (2) Does it name a executor? If so, the court must approve; if not, the court appoints an administrator.

B. DUTIES OF A PERSONAL REPRESENTATIVE

    1. What to Do with the Decedent's Assets
       Inventory and collect them; if necessary, have them appraised; manage them during administration to avoid waste or depletion.

    2. What to Do with Claims
       Pay federal and state income taxes, estate or inheritance taxes, and the valid claims of creditors.

       a. Federal Estate Tax
          Tax on the total value of the estate (not the beneficiaries) after debts, expenses, and exemptions (including gifts to charity). The lowest tax rates are applied to a surviving spouse and the children of the decedent.

       b. State Inheritance Tax
          Generally, imposed on the recipient of a bequest (not the estate). Tax rates are graduated according to the relationship between the beneficiary and decedent (lowest rates and largest exemptions are applied to a surviving spouse and children).

    3. Other Duties
       Post a bond, if required (the will can waive it). Distribute the estate pursuant to court order. Render an accounting to the court.

V. ELDER LAW

A. PLANNING FOR DISABILITY
In anticipation of becoming incapacitated, persons sometimes plan for others to manage their affairs.

    1. Durarble Power of Attorney
       Authorizes a person to act on behalf of an incompetent person when he or she becomes incapacitated.

2. **Health-Care Power of Attorney**
    Designates a person to choose medical treatment for a person who is unable to make such a choice.

3. **Living Will**
    Designates whether or not a person wants certain life-saving procedures to be taken if they will not result in a reasonable quality of life.

B. **MEDICAID**
    In anticipation of the cost of long-term care, persons sometimes plan to meet the requirements of Medicaid so their assets can go to others.

1. **What Medicaid Is**
    Health-care services for the poor of all ages. Administered by state agencies; regulations vary from state to state. At the federal level, administered by the Health Care Financing Administration.

2. **Planning for Medicaid**
    A person who accepts Medicaid pays his or her income to the state. Exceptions include a home, a car, and assets up to $75,000. Assets may also be transferred to others, but not within less than three years (five years if a trust is involved). A penalty "waiting period" may apply.

3. **Advising Others to Plan for Medicaid**
    It is a crime for an attorney to advise elderly clients to give away assets to get Medicaid coverage of nursing-home costs, but at least one court has ruled that the law is unconstitutional.

TRUE-FALSE QUESTIONS

(Answers at the Back of the Book)

_____   1.   A will is revocable only after the testator's death.

_____   2.   The testator generally must sign a will.

_____   3.   If a person dies without a will, all of his or her property automatically passes to the state in which that person lived most of his or her life.

_____   4.   An *inter vivos* trust is a trust created by a grantor during his or her lifetime.

_____   5.   A testamentary trust is created by will to begin on the settlor's death.

_____   6.   A will can only distribute property.

_____   7.   If a person marries after executing a will that does not include the spouse, the will must be revoked or the spouse gets nothing on the person's death.

_____   8.   A beneficiary can renounce his or her share of property under a will.

_____   9.   A trustee has a duty to dispose of trust assets that do not represent prudent investments.

_____   10.   A trust terminates on the trustee's death.

FILL-IN QUESTIONS

(Answers at the Back of the Book)

When a person dies, a personal representative settles the decedent's affairs. A personal representative named in a will is an _____ (administrator/executor). A personal representative appointed by a court for a decedent who dies without a will, who fails to name a personal representative in a will, who names a personal representative lacking the capacity to serve, or who writes a will that the court refuses to admit to probate is an _____ (administrator/executor).

MULTIPLE-CHOICE QUESTIONS

(Answers at the Back of the Book)

___ 1. Joe's will provides for specific items of property to be given to certain individuals, including employees of Joe's business. The will also provides for certain sums of money to be given to Joe's daughters, Gail and Laura. Because Joe's assets are insufficient to pay in full all of the bequests

a. all of the property must be sold and the proceeds distributed to the heirs.
b. the employees, who are not in a blood relationship with Joe, get nothing.
c. Gail and Laura get nothing.
d. the gifts to Gail and Laura will be reduced proportionately.

___ 2. **Based on a Sample CPA Exam Question.** Carol dies without a will, but is survived by her brother Dan, her child Erin, and her parents. The party with the first priority to receive Carol's estate is

a. her brother.
b. her child.
c. her parents.
d. the state.

___ 3. Paul executes a will that leaves all his property to Dave. Two years later, Paul executes a will that leaves all his property to Nora. The second will does not expressly revoke the first will. Paul dies. Who gets his property?

a. Dave, because he was given the property in the first will
b. Dave, because the second will did not expressly revoke the first will
c. Nora, because the first will was revoked by the second will
d. Nora, because two years separated the execution of the wills

___ 4. Tony dies intestate, survived by Lisa, his mother; Grace, his wife; Abby and Selena, their two daughters; and Brock, the son of Cliff, their son, who predeceased his father. Under intestacy laws,

a. Grace receives one-third of Tony's estate, and Abby, Selena, and Brock receive equal portions of the rest.
b. Abby and Selena receive half of Tony's estate, and Grace receives the rest.
c. Lisa and Grace receive equal portions of Tony's estate.
d. Grace receives all of Tony's estate.

    5. Kate wants Bev and Nina, her daughters, to get the benefit of Kate's farm when she dies. She believes that her daughters cannot manage the farm effectively, because they live in other states. She can provide for them to get the farm's income, under another party's management, by setting up

    a. a constructive trust.
    b. a resulting trust.
    c. a testamentary trust.
    d. an interstate trust.

    6. Al's will provides, "I, Al, leave all my computer equipment to my good friend, Ray." When Al dies, the personal representative gives Ray the computer equipment. Ray is

    a. a devisee.
    b. a legatee.
    c. a residuary.
    d. none of the above.

    7. Ellen believes that probate is too time-consuming and costly, and wishes that her assets pass to her heirs as quickly and inexpensively as possible. To avoid probate, Ellen can

    a. have her heirs decide among themselves who will get what on her death.
    b. create a testamentary trust.
    c. hold the assets in joint tenancy.
    d. none of the above.

    8. Don is the trustee of a testamentary trust. The trust grants Don discretion to invest the assets. In most states, this means that

    a. Don must confine trust investments to conservative securities.
    b. Don's investment decisions are subject to the prudent person rule.
    c. Don is entitled to invest the assets however he sees fit.
    d. Don must invest as aggressively as possible.

    9. Kim is the trustee of a testamentary trust. Ordinary trust expenses, such as the rent for Kim's office, are chargeable to

    a. trust income.
    b. trust principal.
    c. Kim.
    d. the court that oversees Kim's administration.

    10. Annette is Kevin's adult daughter. Kevin decides that he wants Annette to act on his behalf should he become incapacitated by old age. Kevin should arrange for Annette to have

    a. his Medicare benefits.
    b. a living trust.
    c. power of trustee.
    d. durable power of attorney.

SHORT ESSAY QUESTIONS

1. What requirements must be satisfied to create a valid will?

2.   In what ways may a will be revoked?

ISSUE SPOTTERS

(Answers at the Back of the Book)

1.   Sheila makes out a will, leaving her property in equal thirds to Mark and Paula, her children, and Carol, her niece. Two years later, Sheila is adjudged mentally incompetent, and that same year, she dies. Can Mark and Paula have Sheila's will revoked, on grounds that she did not have the capacity to make a will?

2.   Lee's will provides for a distribution of Lee's property. First, the assets need to be collected and inventoried, however. They may also need to be appraised. Creditors' claims must be sorted out. Federal and state income taxes must be paid. Finally, the assets must be distributed. Who does these things?

3.   Dick dies. Dick's will provides for specific property to be given to certain individuals, including Dick's family and employees. The will also provides for certain amounts of money to be given to Emily, Ed, and Pat. The estate's assets are not quite enough to pay Emily, Ed, and Pat in full. Who gets what?

4.   When Barb dies, it is discovered that she has no will. She does have, however, many relatives—a spouse, children, adopted children, sisters, brothers, uncles, aunts, cousins, nephews, nieces. How is it determined who gets what?

5.   Chloe, an elderly woman, has been diagnosed with lung cancer. She realizes her condition may worsen, and that there is a chance that at some point she will become so weak the only way she will be able to breathe is with the help of medical machinery. She does not want to be kept alive in such a "vegetative state." What are Chloe's options?

SPECIAL INFORMATION FOR CPA CANDIDATES

The CPA examination has not traditionally asked questions about the requirements or validity of a will. The exam has covered, however, estate and trust administration. You should know what makes up an estate (property that is part of the estate for tax purposes may not be part of the estate under the will—for example, property held in joint tenancy is subject to estate taxes but is not subject to a will).

In the property section of the exam, trusts have been much emphasized. You should know the essential elements of a trust, and the difference between *inter vivos* and testamentary trusts. You should be familiar with the definition of a spendthrift trust. Also important are the fiduciary duties of the trustee, who must, among other responsibilities, make allocations between principal and income. Finally, you should know what terminates a trust.

★ **Key Points**

The **key points** in this chapter include:

1. Areas in which professionals may be liable at common law.

2. Liability that may be imposed on accountants under the securities laws.

3. Accountants' potential criminal liability.

4. Professionals' privileges concerning working papers.

5. The protection of professionals and their clients for their communications.

Chapter 51
Liability of Accountants and Other Professionals

WHAT THIS CHAPTER IS ABOUT

This chapter outlines the potential common law liability of professionals, the potential liability of accountants under securities laws and the Internal Revenue Code, and the duty of professionals to keep their clients' communications confidential.

CHAPTER OUTLINE

I. COMMON LAW LIABILITY TO CLIENTS

A. LIABILITY FOR BREACH OF CONTRACT
For a professional's breach of contract, a client can recover damages, including expenses incurred to secure another professional to provide the services and other reasonable and foreseeable losses.

B. LIABILITY FOR NEGLIGENCE
Professionals must exercise the standard of care, knowledge, and judgment generally accepted by members of their professional group.

1. Accountant's Duty of Care

a. Comply with Accounting Principles and Standards
Accountants must comply with generally accepted accounting principles (GAAP) and generally accepted auditing standards (GAAS) (though compliance does not guarantee relief from liability). Violation of either is *prima facie* evidence of negligence. Note: there may be a higher state law standard.

b. Act in Good Faith
If an accountant conforms to GAAP and acts in good faith, he or she will not be liable to a client for incorrect judgment.

c. **Investigate Suspicious Financial Transactions**
An accountant who uncovers suspicious financial transactions and fails to investigate the matter fully or to inform his or her client of the discovery can be held liable to the client for the resulting loss.

d. **Defenses to Negligence**

1) The accountant was not negligent.

2) If the accountant was negligent, the negligence was not the proximate cause of the client's loss.

3) The client was also negligent.

e. **Qualified Opinions and Disclaimers**
An accountant is not liable for damages resulting from whatever is qualified or disclaimed.

2. **Attorney's Duty of Care**

a. **General Duty**
All attorneys owe a duty to provide competent and diligent representation. The standard is that of a reasonably competent general practitioner of ordinary skill, experience, and capacity.

b. **Specific Responsibilities**
Attorneys must be familiar with well-settled principles of law applicable to a case, discover law that can be found through a reasonable amount of research, and investigate and discover facts that could materially affect the client's legal rights.

C. **PROFESSIONALS' LIABILITY FOR FRAUD**

1. **Actual Fraud**
A professional may be liable if he or she intentionally misstates a material fact to mislead his or her client and the client justifiably relies on the misstated fact to his or her injury.

2. **Constructive Fraud**
A professional may be liable for constructive fraud whether or not he or she acted with fraudulent intent (for example, an accountant who is grossly negligent; gross negligence includes the intentional failure to perform a duty in reckless disregard of the consequences).

II.   AUDITORS' LIABILITY TO THIRD PARTIES
Most courts hold that auditors can be held liable to third parties for negligence.

A. **THE *ULTRAMARES* RULE**

1. **The Privity Requirement**
An accountant owes a duty only to a third person with whom he or she has a direct contractual relationship (privity) or a relationship "so close as to approach that of privity."

2. **The "Near Privity" Rule**
In a few states, if a third party has a sufficiently close relationship or nexus with an accountant, the *Ultramares* privity requirement may be satisfied without establishing an accountant-client relationship.

B. THE *RESTATEMENT* RULE

Most courts hold accountants liable for negligence to persons whom the accountant "intends to supply the information or knows that the recipient intends to supply it" and persons whom the accountant "intends the information to influence or knows that the recipient so intends" [*Restatement (Second) of Torts*, Section 552].

C. LIABILITY TO REASONABLY FORESEEABLE USERS

A few courts hold accountants liable to any users whose reliance on an accountant's statements or reports was reasonably foreseeable.

III. LIABILITY OF ACCOUNTANTS UNDER SECURITIES LAWS

A. LIABILITY UNDER THE SECURITIES ACT OF 1933

1. Misstatements or Omissions in Registration Statements

An accountant may be liable for misstatements and omissions of material facts in registration statements (which they often prepare for filing with the Securities and Exchange Commission (SEC) before an offering of securities—see Chapter 37) [Section 11].

a. To Whom an Accountant May Be Liable

Anyone who acquires a security covered by the statement. A plaintiff must show that he or she suffered a loss on the security. There is no requirement of privity or proof of reliance.

b. Due Diligence Defense

An accountant may avoid liability by showing that, in preparing the financial statements, he or she had—

1) Reasonable Grounds to Believe that the Statements Were True

After a reasonable investigation, the accountant believed that the statements were true and omitted no material facts.

2) Followed GAAP and GAAS

Failure to follow GAAP and GAAS is proof of a lack of due diligence.

3) Verified Information Furnished by Officers and Directors

This defense requires that accountants verify information furnished by the offering firm's officers and directors.

c. Other Defenses to Liability

1) There were no misstatements or omissions.

2) The misstatements or omissions were not of material facts.

3) The misstatements or omissions had no causal connection to the purchaser's loss.

4) The purchaser invested in the securities knowing of the misstatements or omissions.

2. Misstatements or Omissions in Other Communications in an Offer

Anyone offering or selling a security may be liable for fraud for communicating to an investor a misstatement or omission [Section 12(2)].

3. **Penalties and Sanctions for Violations**
   The U.S. Department of Justice brings criminal actions against willful violators. Penalties: fines up to $10,000; imprisonment up to five years. The SEC can seek an injunction and other relief (such as an order to refund profits).

B. **LIABILITY UNDER THE SECURITIES EXCHANGE ACT OF 1934**

   1. **False or Misleading Statements in Certain SEC Documents**
      An accountant may be liable for making or causing to be made in an application, report, document, or registration statement filed with the SEC a statement that at the time and in light of the circumstances was false or misleading with respect to any material fact [Section 18].

      a. **To Whom an Accountant May Be Liable**
         Only sellers and purchasers who can prove (1) the statement affected the price of the security and (2) they relied on the statement and were unaware of its inaccuracy.

      b. **Defenses**

         1) **Proof of Good Faith**
            Proof that the accountant did not know the statement was false or misleading. This can be refuted by showing the accountant's (1) intent to deceive or (2) reckless conduct and gross negligence.

         2) **Buyer or Seller Knew the Statement Was False or Misleading**

         3) **Statute of Limitations Tolled**
            An action must be brought within one year after the discovery of facts constituting the cause and within three years after the cause accrues.

   2. **Misstatements or Omissions under Section 10(b) and Rule 10b-5**
      Covers written and oral statements.

      a. **Section 10(b)**
         Makes it unlawful for any person to use, in connection with the purchase or sale of any security, any manipulative or deceptive device or contrivance in contravention of SEC rules and regulations.

      b. **Rule 10b-5**
         Makes it unlawful for any person, by use of any means or instrumentality of interstate commerce, to—

         1) Employ any device, scheme, or artifice to defraud.

         2) Make any untrue statement of a material fact or to omit to state a material fact necessary to make the statements made, in light of the circumstances, not misleading.

         3) Engage in any act, practice, or course of business that operates or would operate as a fraud or deceit on any person, in connection with the purchase or sale of any security.

        c. To Whom An Accountant May Be Liable
            Only to sellers or purchasers. Privity is not required. To recover, a plaintiff must prove (1) *scienter*, (2) a fraudulent action or deception, (3) reliance, (4) materiality, and (5) causation.

C. THE PRIVATE SECURITIES LITIGATION REFORM ACT OF 1995

    1. Adequate Procedures and Disclosure
        An auditor must use adequate procedures in an audit to detect any illegal acts. If something is detected, the auditor must disclose it to the board, audit committee, or SEC, depending on the circumstances.

    2. Proportionate Liability
        A party is liable only for the proportion of damages for which he or she is responsible.

    3. Aiding and Abetting
        An accountant who knows that he or she is participating in an improper activity and knowingly aids the activity (even by silence) is guilty of aiding and abetting. The SEC may obtain an injunction or damages.

IV. POTENTIAL CRIMINAL LIABILITY OF ACCOUNTANTS

A. THE SECURITIES ACTS
An accountant may be subject to imprisonment of up to five years and a fine of up to $10,000 under the 1933 act and up to $100,000 under the 1934 act.

B. THE INTERNAL REVENUE CODE

    1. Aiding or Assisting in the Preparation of a False Tax Return
        A felony punishable by a fine of $100,000 ($500,000 in the case of a corporation) and imprisonment for up to three years [Section 7206(2)].

    2. Understatement of a Client's Tax Liability
        Liability is limited to one penalty per taxpayer per tax year.

        a. Negligent or Willful Understatement
            A tax preparer is subject to a penalty of $250 per return for negligent understatement and $1,000 for willful understatement or reckless or intentional disregard of rules or regulations [Section 6694].

        b. Aiding and Abetting an Individual's Understatement
            $1,000 per document ($10,000 in corporate cases) [Section 6701].

    3. Other Liability Related to Tax Returns
        A tax preparer may be subject to penalties for failing to furnish the taxpayer with a copy of the return, failing to sign the return, or failing to furnish the appropriate tax identification numbers [Section 6695].

C. STATE LAW
Most states impose criminal penalties for knowingly certifying false or fraudulent reports; falsifying, altering, or destroying books of account; and obtaining property or credit through the use of false financial statements.

V. WORKING PAPERS
In a number of states, working papers are the accountant's property. The client has a right of access to them, and they cannot be transferred to another accoun-

tant or otherwise disclosed without the client's permission (or a court order). Unauthorized disclosure is a ground for a malpractice suit.

VI. CONFIDENTIALITY AND PRIVILEGE

A. ATTORNEY-CLIENT
The confidentiality of attorney-client communications is protected by law. The client holds the privilege, and only the client may waive it.

B. ACCOUNTANT-CLIENT
In response to a federal court order, an accountant must provide the information sought; there is no privilege. In most states, on a court order, an accountant must disclose information about his or her client. In a few states, no disclosure is allowed (even in a court) without the client's permission.

VII. LIMITING PROFESSIONALS' LIABILITY
Professionals may limit their liability for misconduct of other professionals with whom they work by organizing as a professional corporation (see Chapter 34) or a limited liability partnership (see Chapter 38).

TRUE-FALSE QUESTIONS

(Answers at the Back of the Book)

____ 1. Professionals must exercise the standard of care, knowledge, and judgment generally observed by their peers.

____ 2. A violation of GAAP and GAAS is *prima facie* evidence of negligence.

____ 3. Compliance with GAAP and GAAS will relieve an accountant of liability.

____ 4. In all states, an accountant is liable to anyone who relies on the accountant's negligently prepared reports.

____ 5. Accountants are not subject to criminal penalties under the Securities Act of 1933 or the Securities Exchange Act of 1934.

____ 6. A tax preparer may be subject to penalties under the Internal Revenue Code for assisting in filing a false tax return.

____ 7. There is no penalty under the Internal Revenue Code for failing to give the taxpayer a copy of the return.

____ 8. State-provided rights to confidentiality of accountant-client communications are not recognized in federal cases.

____ 9. Under the Private Securities Litigation Reform Act of 1995, a party is liable only for the proportion of damages for which he or she is responsible.

____ 10. For an accountant to be liable to a seller or purchaser for misstatements or omissions under SEC Rule 10b-5, there must be privity.

FILL-IN QUESTIONS

(Answers at the Back of the Book)

Accountants must comply with generally accepted accounting principles (GAAP) and generally accepted auditing standards (GAAS). An accountant who conforms to GAAP and acts in good faith _____ (may/will not) be liable to a client for incorrect judgment. An accountant who uncovers suspicious financial transactions but fails to investigate fully or to inform the client _____ (may/will not) be liable. If a client suffers a loss due to fraud that an accountant negligently fails to discover, the accountant _____ (may/will not) be liable.

MULTIPLE-CHOICE QUESTIONS

(Answers at the Back of the Book)

____   1. Betty, an accountant, accumulates working papers in performing an audit for her client, Multimedia Corporation. Under which of the following circumstances is Betty entitled to release those papers?

   a. Only with Multimedia's permission
   b. Only on the request of another accountant
   c. Under any circumstances
   d. Under no circumstances

____   2. **Based on a Sample CPA Exam Question.** Digital, Inc., asks Ed, an accountant, to prepare its financial statements. Ed conducts the audit negligently. The firm uses the statements to obtain a loan from First National Bank. The loan is not repaid. In most states, Ed is

   a. liable only to Digital for the negligent audit.
   b. liable to any possible foreseeable user of the statements.
   c. liable to the bank if Ed knew the bank would rely on the statements.
   d. liable to the bank only if it was in privity of contract with Ed.

____   3. National Distribution, Inc., includes financial statements prepared by Sam, an accountant, in a registration statement filed with the SEC as part of a public stock offer. Bob buys 100 shares and later suffers losses due to misstatements of fact in the statements prepared by Sam. Bob sues Sam under the Securities Act of 1933. Bob will

   a. win, if the misstatements were material.
   b. win, if Sam prepared the statements with knowledge of the misstatements.
   c. lose, if Sam and Bob were not in privity.
   d. lose, because Bob relied on the statements.

____   4. Dick, an accountant, audits financial statements for Eagle Corporation and issues an unqualified opinion on them. Fiona buys 100 shares of Eagle stock and later suffers losses due to misrepresentations in the statements. Fiona sues Dick under the Securities Exchange Act of 1934. Fiona will

   a. win, if the misstatements were material.
   b. win, if Dick prepared the statements knowing of the misstatements.
   c. lose, if Dick and Fiona were not in privity.
   d. lose, because Fiona relied on the statements.

_____ 5. In auditing Federated Retail, Inc.'s books, Mary is assisted by Ann, a Federated employee. Mary does not discover Ann's theft of Federated funds because Ann hides records that would reveal it. When Ann absconds with the funds, Federated sues Mary. Federated will

  a. win, because Mary did not discover the theft.
  b. win, because Mary did not inform Federated of the theft.
  c. lose, because Mary could not reasonably have been expected to discover the theft.
  d. lose, because Mary is not liable for the results once she has performed.

_____ 6. Ron is an accountant. In most states, under which of the following circumstances can Ron be compelled to disclose a client's communication?

  a. Only with the client's permission
  b. Only on a court order
  c. Under any circumstances
  d. Under no circumstances

_____ 7. Dan, an accountant, breaches his contract with Harrigan's, a local restaurant chain. Damages that Harrigan's may recover include

  a. only the cost to secure the contracted-for services elsewhere.
  b. only penalties imposed for failing to meet deadlines.
  c. the cost to secure services elsewhere and penalties for missing deadlines.
  d. none of the above.

_____ 8. Polly is injured in an automobile accident, but the insurance company refuses to pay her claim. She hires Doug, an attorney, to handle her case. Doug fails to file Polly's suit against the insurance company before the time for filing the suit runs out. Polly sues Doug. She will

  a. win, because the insurance company refused to pay her claim.
  b. win, because Doug committed malpractice.
  c. lose, because Doug could not reasonably have been expected to file on time.
  d. lose, because clients are ultimately responsible for such deadlines.

_____ 9. Rick's Auto Repairs hires Hillary, an accountant, to perform an audit. In the course of the audit, Hillary accumulates several hundred pages of notes, computations, and other memoranda. Following completion of the audit

  a. Hillary has the right to retain all working papers.
  b. Rick's Auto Repairs has the right to access these working papers.
  c. both a and b.
  d. none of the above.

_____ 10. Jane is an accountant whom Gail, a former client, charges with negligence. Jane's defenses include

  a. only that she was not negligent.
  b. only that if she was negligent, it was not the proximate cause of Gail's loss.
  c. that she was not negligent, and if she was negligent, it was not the proximate cause of the client's loss.
  d. none of the above.

SHORT ESSAY QUESTIONS

1. Contrast an accountant's past and present potential common law liability to third persons.

2. Contrast the attorney-client privilege and the accountant-client privilege.

ISSUE SPOTTERS

(Answers at the Back of the Book)

1. What is a professional liable for, at common law, if he or she *un*intentionally misstates a material fact that misleads a client?

2. Rita, an accountant, prepares a financial statement for Toby & Company, a client, knowing that Toby will use the statement to obtain a loan from the First National Bank. If Rita makes negligent omissions in the statement that results in a loss to the bank, could the bank successfully sue Rita?

3. Phil, an accountant, prepares a financial statement as part of a registration statement that MMF, Inc., files with the Securities and Exchange Commission before making a public offering of securities. In the statement is a misstatement of material fact not attributable to Phil's fraud or negligence. Gina relies on the misstatement, buys some of the securities, and suffers a loss. Can Phil be held liable to Gina?

4. Can an accountant who prepares a tax return for a client be held liable for any false statements in the return? Can a person who is not an accountant and who prepares a tax return for someone else be held liable for any false statements in the return?

5. Professionals are restrained by the ethical tenets of their professions from disclosing communications with their clients. In some instances, professional-client communications are privileged under state and federal law. What professional is most restricted from disclosing a client's communication?

SPECIAL INFORMATION FOR CPA CANDIDATES

Of course, the material in this chapter is part of the CPA examination. Among the most important points for you to know for the test are the accountant's potential tort liability to third parties—of the three basic approaches to liability, the CPA exam has in the past followed the *Ultramares* rule. With respect to liability under the Securities Acts, "mere" negligence is a defense under the 1934 act (which, as you may recall, requires "gross" negligence for liability). With respect to the possible criminal penalties, the CPA exam expects you to know them. Also keep in mind that unless a state provides for an accountant-client privilege, there is none. Related material on professional responsibility tested in the business law portion of the exam is covered in your auditing course.

Chapter 52
International and Comparative Law

WHAT THIS CHAPTER IS ABOUT

This chapter notes sources of international law, some of the ways in which U.S. businesspersons do business in foreign countries, and how that business is regulated. This chapter also compares the legal systems of various nations and specific legal concepts and principles related to contracts, torts, and employment relationships.

CHAPTER OUTLINE

I. **INTERNATIONAL LAW**
To facilitate commerce, sovereign nations agree to be governed in certain respects by international law.

A. SOURCES OF INTERNATIONAL LAW

1. **International Customs**
Customs that have evolved among nations in their relations with one another. "[E]vidence of a general practice accepted as law" [Article 38(1) of the Statute of the International Court of Justice].

2. **Treaties and International Agreements**
A treaty is an agreement or contract between two or more nations that must be authorized and ratified by the supreme power of each nation. A bilateral agreement occurs when only two nations form an agreement; multilateral agreements are those formed by several nations.

3. **International Organizations and Conferences**
Composed mainly of nations (such as the United Nations); usually established by treaty; such entities adopt resolutions that require particular behavior of nations (such as the 1980 United Nations Convention on Contracts for the International Sale of Goods).

B. LEGAL PRINCIPLES AND DOCTRINES
The following are based on courtesy and respect and are applied in the interest of maintaining harmony among nations.

1. **The Principle of Comity**
   One nation defers and gives effect to the laws and judicial decrees of another country, so long as those laws and judicial decrees are consistent with the law and public policy of the accommodating nation.

2. **The Act of State Doctrine**
   A doctrine under which the judicial branch of one country will not examine the validity of public acts committed by a recognized foreign government within its own territory. Often used in cases involving—

   a. **Expropriation**
      This occurs when a government seizes a privately owned business or goods for a proper public purpose and pays just compensation.

   b. **Confiscation**
      This occurs when a government seizes private property for an illegal purpose or without just compensation.

3. **The Doctrine of Sovereign Immunity**
   Exempts foreign nations from the jurisdiction of domestic courts. In the United States, the Foreign Sovereign Immunities Act (FSIA) of 1976 exclusively governs the circumstances in which an action may be brought against a foreign nation.

   a. **When Is a Foreign State Subject to U.S. Jurisdiction?**
      When it has waived its immunity, or when the action is based on commercial activity in the U.S. by the foreign state [Section 1605].

   b. **What Entities Fall within the Category of Foreign State?**
      A political subdivision and an instrumentality (an agency or entity acting for the state) [Section 1603].

   c. **What Is a Commercial Activity?**
      Courts decide whether an activity is governmental or commercial.

II. DOING BUSINESS INTERNATIONALLY

A. INTERNATIONAL BUSINESS OPERATIONS

1. **Exporting**
   The simplest way to do business internationally is to export to foreign markets. **Direct exporting**: signing a sales contract with a foreign buyer. **Indirect exporting**: selling directly to consumers through a foreign agent or foreign distributor.

2. **Manufacturing Abroad**
   A domestic firm can establish a manufacturing plant abroad by—

   a. **Licensing**
      A firm may license its technology to a foreign manufacturer to avoid the process, product, or formula being pirated. The foreign firm agrees to keep the technology secret and to pay royalties for its use.

   b. **Franchising**
      Franchising (see Chapter 39) is a form of licensing in which the owner of a trademark, trade name, or copyright conditions its use in the selling of goods or services.

c. **Investing in a Wholly Owned Subsidiary or a Joint Venture**
When a wholly owned subsidiary is established, the domestic firm retains ownership of the foreign facilities and control over the entire operation. In a joint venture, a domestic firm and one or more foreign firms share responsibilities, profits, and liabilities.

B. REGULATION OF INTERNATIONAL BUSINESS ACTIVITIES

1. **Investing**
For property confiscated by a government without just compensation, few remedies are available. Many countries guarantee compensation to foreign investors in their constitutions, statutes, or treaties. Some countries provide insurance for their citizens' investments abroad.

2. **Export Control**

a. **Restricting Exports**
Under the Constitution, Congress cannot tax exports, but may set quotas. Under the Export Administration Act of 1979, restrictions can be imposed on the flow of technologically advanced products and technical data.

b. **Stimulating Exports**
Devices to stimulate exports include incentives and subsidies.

3. **Import Control**
Laws prohibit, for example, importing illegal drugs and agricultural products that pose dangers to domestic crops or animals.

a. **Quotas and Tariffs**
Quotas limit how much can be imported. Tariffs are taxes on imports (a percentage of the value or a flat rate per unit).

b. **Dumping**
A tariff may be assessed on imports to prevent **dumping** (sales of imported goods at "less than fair value," usually determined by prices in the exporting country).

4. **International Organizations and Agreements**

a. **World Trade Organization (WTO)**
The principal instrument for regulating international trade. Each member country agrees to grant **most-favored-nation status** to other members (the most favorable treatment with regard to trade).

b. **European Union (EU)**
A regional trade association that minimizes trade barriers among the fifteen European member nations.

c. **North American Free Trade Agreement (NAFTA)**
Created a regional trading unit consisting of Mexico, the United States, and Canada. The goal is to eliminate tariffs in the region on substantially all goods over a period of fifteen to twenty years, while retaining tariffs on goods imported from other countries.

C. DISPUTE SETTLEMENT IN THE INTERNATIONAL CONTEXT

1. **Arbitration**

   Arbitration clauses (see Chapter 2) are often in international contracts.

   a. **The Arbitrator**

      May be a neutral entity, a panel of individuals representing both parties' interests, or another group.

   b. **Enforcement of Arbitration Clauses**

      The United Nations Convention on the Recognition and Enforcement of Foreign Arbitral Awards assists in the enforcement of arbitration clauses, as do provisions in specific treaties between nations.

2. **Litigation**

   May be subject to forum-selection and choice-of-law clauses (Chapter 19). If no forum and law are specified, litigation may be complex and uncertain (held simultaneously in two countries, for example, without regard of one for the other; a judgment may not be enforced).

III. COMPARATIVE LAW

Comparative law is the study of legal systems and laws across nations.

A. COMPARATIVE LEGAL SYSTEMS

1. **Common Law and Civil Law Systems**

   Legal systems are generally divided into common law and civil law systems.

   a. **Common Law Systems**

      Based on case law. Common law systems exist in countries that were once a part of the British Empire (such as Australia, India, the United States). The judges of different common law nations have produced differing common law principles.

   b. **Civil Law Systems**

      Civil law systems are based on codified law (statutes). Courts interpret the code and apply the rules without developing their own laws. Civil law systems exist in most European nations, in Latin American, African, and Asian countries that were colonies of those nations; Japan; South Africa; Muslim countries; Louisiana.

   c. **Similarities between Common and Civil Law Systems**

      Much of the law in a common law system is statutory. In a civil law system, judges must develop some law because codes cannot address every issue.

   d. **Differences among Common Law Systems**

      The judges of different common law nations have produced differing common law principles. For example, the principles governing contracts differ in the United States and India.

   e. **Differences among Civil Law Systems**

      The French code sets out general principles of law; the German code is more specific. In some Middle Eastern countries, the code is grounded in religious, Islamic directives, known as *shari'a*. This makes it difficult to change.

B. JUDGES AND PROCEDURES
In all countries, the primary function of judges is the resolution of litigation.

1. Differences among Judges
In the United States, a judge normally does not actively participate in a trial, but in many countries, judges are involved, such as by questioning witnesses. In the United States, a federal judge is less likely to be influenced by politics (he or she serves for life and cannot be removed by impeachment except in extreme cases). In India, judges ruling contrary to the prime minister have been transferred or demoted.

2. Differences among Procedures
The procedures employed in resolving cases varies from country to country. For example, in Saudi Arabia, a defendant can "demand the oath"—swear before God that he did not do what he is charged with doing—and be released.

C. NATIONAL LAWS COMPARED
Even when statutory language is similar, application of the law varies among nations.

1. Tort Law
Tort law allows persons to recover damages for harms or injuries caused by the wrongful actions of others (see Chapters 5 and 6).

a. Failure to Act
In Germany, one is normally not liable for failing to rescue someone in distress. Some nations provide liability for negligent omissions.

b. Damages
Swiss and Turkish courts reduce damages if an award of full damages would cause undue hardship to a party who was found negligent. In some nations of northern Africa, different amounts of damages are awarded depending on the type of tort.

c. Statutes of Limitations
Generally, the period is longer than in the United States.

d. Burden of Proof
In the United States, the burden of proof is on the plaintiff. In Russia, the defendant must prove that he or she was not at fault.

2. Contract Law
For requirements of contracts in the United States, see Chapters 11–13.

a. United Nations Convention for the International Sale of Goods
Some contract law has been internationalized through the CISG (see Chapter 19), but parties can agree to apply other law.

b. Agreement (Offer and Acceptance)
In Germany, a written offer must be held open for a reasonable time, unless the offer states otherwise. Oral offers must be accepted immediately or they expire. In Mexico, if a time for acceptance is not stated in an offer, the offer is deemed to be held open for three days (plus whatever time is necessary for the mails).

    c. **Consideration**
In Germany, consideration is not required for a contract to be binding—agreements to make gifts may thus be enforceable by the recipient. In India, some contracts are lawful in the absence of consideration, such as promises in exchange for a past act.

    d. **Remedies**
Germany's typical remedy for breach of contract is specific performance (breaching party does what was promised). In the United States, this is granted only if the remedy of damages (money) is inadequate.

    e. **Defenses**
Defenses include lack of a writing (United States, Saudi Arabia) or witnesses (Saudi Arabia), and lack of consideration (India).

3. **Employment Law**
Under the employment-at-will doctrine (see Chapter 41), employers can hire and fire employees "at will" (for any reason or no reason).

    a. **Reasons for Discharging Employees**
Employers may fire employees without notice only for causes such as violence, imprisonment, excessive absenteeism, or lying on a job application (Taiwan), or if the worker commits a criminal offense, loses a license or other employment qualification, or seriously breaches his or her duties (Poland).

    b. **Discharge Procedures**
In some countries, to discharge an employee for cause, an employer must first submit the proposed discharge to mediators (France) or a committee (Egypt).

    c. **Wages and Benefits**
Wages are typically lower in other countries, but workers are often entitled to more paid time off.

    d. **Equal Employment Opportunity**
In Indonesia, Japan, and Mexico, employers cannot discriminate against employees or job applicants on some bases. Discrimination is not prohibited in Argentina, Brazil, Egypt, or Turkey.

D. **CULTURAL AND BUSINESS TRADITIONS**

1. **Communication**
Language differences and different understandings of body movements, gestures, facial expressions, colors, and numbers can confound efforts to do business abroad. For example, advertising slogans translated word-for-word may be nonsense in other languages.

2. **Ethics**

    a. **Gift Giving and Bribery**
In many countries, gift giving is common among companies or between companies and government. U.S. firms are prohibited from offering payments to foreign officials to secure favorable contracts (see Chapter 40). Payments to minor officials to, for example, facilitate paperwork are not prohibited.

b. Women in Business

Some countries reject any role for women professionals. Others impose cultural restrictions. Because of these restrictions, many U.S. companies are reluctant to assign women to work overseas. Equal employment opportunity is a fundamental policy in the United States, however (see Chapter 42).

TRUE-FALSE QUESTIONS

(Answers at the Back of the Book)

_____ 1. All nations must give effect to the laws of all other nations.

_____ 2. Under the act of state doctrine, foreign nations are subject to the jurisdiction of U.S. courts.

_____ 3. Under the doctrine of sovereign immunity, foreign nations are subject to the jurisdiction of U.S. courts.

_____ 4. The Foreign Sovereign Immunities Act states the circumstances in which the United States can be sued in foreign courts.

_____ 5. A member of the World Trade Organization must usually grant other members most-favored nation status, with regard to trade.

_____ 6. U.S. firms are prohibited from offering payments to foreign officials to secure favorable contracts.

_____ 7. Legal systems are generally divided into criminal law and civil law systems.

_____ 8. In all countries, the primary function of judges is the resolution of litigation.

_____ 9. All international contracts are subject exclusively to the CISG.

_____ 10. Congress cannot tax exports but may set export quotas.

FILL-IN QUESTIONS

(Answers at the Back of the Book)

_____ (A confiscation/An expropriation) occurs when a national government seizes a privately owned business or privately owned goods for a proper public purpose. _____ (A confiscation/An expropriation) occurs when the taking is made for an illegal purpose. When _____ _____ (a confiscation/an expropriation) occurs, the government pays just compensation. When _____ (a confiscation/an expropriation) occurs, the government does not pay just compensation.

MULTIPLE-CHOICE QUESTIONS

(Answers at the Back of the Book)

____   **1.**   Chile issues bonds to finance the construction of an international airport. Chile sells some of the bonds in the United States to Bob. A terrorist group destroys the airport, and Chile refuses to pay interest or principal on the bonds. Bob files suit in a U.S court. The court will hear the suit if Chile

a.   is a "foreign state" and selling bonds is a "commercial activity."
b.   in effect confiscated Bob's funds when it refused to pay on the bonds.
c.   in effect expropriated Bob's funds when it refused to pay on the bonds.
d.   none of the above.

____   **2.**   To install new computers in government offices, Mexico accepts bids from U.S. firms, including Paco, Inc., and NuCorp. Paco wins the contract. NuCorp sues Paco in a U.S. court, on the ground that Paco's sole shareholder is the brother of the wife of Mexico's minister of commerce. The U.S. court

a.   must hold the contract illegal under the principle of commercial relations.
b.   must hold the contract illegal under the act of state doctrine.
c.   cannot rule on the legality of the contract, under the act of state doctrine.
d.   cannot rule on the legality of the contract, under the principle of commercial relations.

____   **3.**   A Polish seller and a U.S. buyer form a contract. The buyer breaches. The seller sues in a Polish court and wins damages, but the buyer's assets are in the United States. If a U.S. court enforces the judgment, it will be because of

a.   the doctrine of sovereign immunity.
b.   the act of state doctrine.
c.   the principle of comity.
d.   none of the above.

____   **4.**   Digital, Inc., makes supercomputers that feature advanced technology. To inhibit Digital's export of its products to other countries, Congress can

a.   tax exported supercomputers heavily.
b.   set quotas on exported supercomputers.
c.   expropriate all profits on exported supercomputers.
d.   tax exports and set quotas.

____   **5.**   MotoCorp manufactures cars in the United States. To boost the sales of MotoCorp and other domestic car manufacturers, Congress can

a.   tax imported vehicles heavily.
b.   set quotas on imported vehicles.
c.   expropriate all profits on imported vehicles.
d.   tax imports and set quotas.

____   **6.**   Common law systems

a.   are based on codified law.
b.   are based on case law.
c.   have produced differing common law principles in different countries.
d.   both b and c.

___ 7. Civil law systems

    a. are based on codified law.
    b. are based on case law.
    c. require that courts apply the rules without developing their own laws.
    d. both a and c.

___ 8. Nora is a judge in the United States. As a U.S. judge, Nora

    a. normally actively participates in a trial.
    b. normally does not actively participate in a trial.
    c. is likely to be influenced by politics.
    d. can be impeached, except in extreme cases.

___ 9. In the area of contract law

    a. there are so few differences among nations that the law is, for all practical purposes, uniform.
    b. some of the basic principles are similar among nations, but some are very different.
    c. there is an international law enforced by the United Nations that applies to all international contracts.
    d. there are no basic principles that any two nations share.

___ 10. Discrimination in employment is

    a. prohibited in all countries.
    b. prohibited in some countries.
    c. not prohibited in any country.
    d. required in all countries.

SHORT ESSAY QUESTIONS

1. Describe ways in which a company may conduct international business.

2. What effect does the Foreign Sovereign Immunities Act have on commercial activities by foreign governments?

ISSUE SPOTTERS

(Answers at the Back of the Book)

1. Japan and other countries agree to abide by tariff reductions and other provisions of the World Trade Organization (WTO). What is the chief advantage to these countries of cooperating with the WTO?

2. MacMill, Inc., owns substantial assets in Tagistan, a new Asian country. The government of Tagistan wants to nationalize all assets owned by foreign investors. What can MacMill do? Can it at least get paid for the assets?

3. Cafe Rojo, Ltd., a Colombian firm, agrees to sell coffee beans to Java Corporation, a U.S. company. Java accepts the beans, but refuses to pay. Cafe Rojo sues Java in a Colombian court and is awarded damages, but Java's assets are in the United States. Under what circumstances would a U.S. court enforce the Colombian court's judgment?

4. Hi-Cola Corporation, a U.S. company, markets a popular soft drink. The formula is secret, but with careful chemical analysis, its ingredients could be discovered. What can Hi-Cola do to prevent its product from being pirated abroad?

5. Pygo International, Ltd., is a foreign firm that has a 12-percent share of the U.S. market for diamonds. To capture a larger share, Pygo offers its products at a below-cost discount to U.S. buyers (and inflates the prices in its own country to make up the difference). How can this attempt to undersell U.S. businesses be defeated?

SPECIAL INFORMATION FOR CPA CANDIDATES

Most of the material in this chapter is not covered in the CPA examination (although in the business world, an accountant will likely encounter many aspects of international business and law). The Foreign Corrupt Practices Act has been tested in the securities portion of the exam.

The CPA examination is designed to test technical competence in at least three areas: (1) technical knowledge and the application of this knowledge, (2) an understanding of professional responsibilities, and (3) the exercise of good judgment. The material in this chapter can contribute to an understanding of the law as it applies in all three of these areas. This chapter provides background to a study of business law by underscoring the point that the law is not static. This material illustrates that the law changes—from time to time and from place to place within a given time. Basic principles may change only slowly and over relatively long periods of time, but there is otherwise the same fluidity in the law as there is in any other field of knowledge.

Overall, in the past, the CPA exam has tested heavily in the following areas of business law: contracts, sales, commercial paper, bankruptcy, agency, partnerships, corporations, securities, accountant's professional liability, and real and personal property. The CPA exam has tested less heavily in these areas: documents of title, secured transactions, suretyship, employment laws, insurance, and estates and trusts.

Chapter 53
Law for Entrepreneurs

WHAT THIS CHAPTER IS ABOUT

For entrepreneurs, business law takes on special significance, in part because of the small size of most entrepreneurial businesses. This chapter covers some aspects of the law as it applies in that context.

CHAPTER OUTLINE

I. THE IMPORTANCE OF LEGAL COUNSEL

A. FINDING AN ATTORNEY
Sources include friends, business associates, other entrepreneurs, business networks (chambers of commerce or bar organizations), Yellow Pages, *Martindale-Hubbell Law Directory* (available in libraries or at http://www.martindale.com).

B. INTERVIEWING AND EVALUATING ATTORNEYS
Ask: did the attorney seem knowledgeable about what you need? Did he or she seem willing to investigate the relevant law? Did you communicate well with each other? Did the attorney perceive what issues were of foremost concern and address those issues?

C. RETAINING AN ATTORNEY
Benefits of retaining an attorney include the lawyer's contacts (such as potential investors), business expertise, confidentiality of attorney-client communications, and flexibility of payment plans (for example, regular monthly billing, as opposed to one-time lump sum).

D. RETAINING AN ACCOUNTANT
A professional accountant is more expensive than bookkeeping software, but may be more accurate and adds to credibility with investors.

II.   **SELECTING AN APPROPRIATE BUSINESS FORM**
Factors to consider when choosing a business form (see Chapters 33–39) include:

A.   **LIMITATIONS ON LIABILITY**
Some business forms limit liability if, for example, a court awards damages to a customer injured on the premises (the owner is not personally liable). Corporations, limited partnerships, limited liability corporations (LLCs), and limited liability partnerships (LLPs) limit personal liability.

B.   **TAX CONSIDERATIONS**

1.   **Sole Proprietorships**
A sole proprietor pays taxes on business income as an individual.

2.   **Partnerships**
Partnerships do not pay tax, but the partners pay income tax on the firm's profits.

3.   **Corporations**
Most corporations pay double taxes (the corporation pays tax on profits, and the shareholders pay tax on distributions).   S corporations and LLCs are taxed like partnerships.

C.   **CONTINUITY OF LIFE**
In most cases, corporations survive their owners.   In a partnership, the death or withdrawal of a partner may terminate the partnership unless the partners have expressly provided otherwise.   A sole proprietorship ends with the death of the sole proprietor.

D.   **LEGAL FORMALITY AND EXPENSE**

1.   **Benefits of Formal Business Arrangements**
These include an agreement setting out ownership rights if a dispute arises, and the advantages (or disadvantages) provided by existing statutes and case law relating to particular business forms.

2.   **Forms That Avoid Formality and Expense**
Sole proprietorships and general partnerships avoid formalities and expense of incorporating or creating a limited partnership.

3.   **All Businesses**
Any business must meet such legal requirements as business name registration, occupational licensing, state tax registration, health and environmental permits, zoning and building codes, import/export regulations, and laws governing the workplace.

III.   **CREATING THE BUSINESS ENTITY**
There are no special requirements for creating a sole proprietorship.   A general partnership requires only an agreement between the partners.   Forming a limited partnership or corporation (see Chapter 34) is more complicated.

A.   **CHOOSING A CORPORATE NAME**
Must be different from those of existing businesses (even unincorporated businesses) and should include the word *corporation*, *company*, or *incorporated*.   Should be filed with the appropriate state office (usually secretary of state) to protect it as a trade name within the state.

B. ARTICLES OF INCORPORATION, BYLAWS, AND INITIAL MEETINGS

1. Articles of Incorporation
States vary with respect to what provisions must be included in the articles. S corporations must file additional forms with the IRS and (in most states) with the appropriate state agency.

2. Bylaws
Include provisions for the dates on which annual meetings will be held, terms for voting quorums, and other rules.

3. Initial Meeting
Directors adopt bylaws, appoint corporate officers and define their authority, issue stock, open bank accounts, take other necessary steps.

C. CREATING A CORPORATE RECORDS BOOK
Organizes important documents, such as articles of incorporation and minutes of director and shareholder meetings. Stock certificates may need to be created and a corporate seal may need to be obtained.

IV. INTELLECTUAL PROPERTY
Protecting rights in intellectual property (see Chapter 7) is a central concern to some new businesses, such as software companies.

A. CHOOSING AND PROTECTING A TRADEMARK
A trademark cannot be too similar to another mark or mislead customers to think that a product was made by someone else. Generally, the first to use a trademark owns it.

1. Choosing a Trademark
A mark should be distinctive (for example, a made-up word such as Exxon or Kodak). Name-consulting companies help in selecting marks, but may be too expensive for small business entrepreneurs.

2. Undertaking a Trademark Search
To ensure that a mark is not too similar to existing marks, check the Yellow Pages in the relevant area, consult *Gale's List of Tradenames*, look at the federal and state trademark registers, etc.

3. Registering a Trademark
A trademark can be registered with the U.S. Patent and Trademark Office (PTO). This provides nationwide protection for a mark that is in use or will be within six months. If a logo consists of a distinctive name as well as a graphic, each can be registered independently.

4. Protecting a Trademark

a. Symbols to Put Others on Notice
If a mark is federally registered, the symbol ® may be used. If a mark is not registered, the symbol ™ can be used.

b. Renewal of Registration
Five years after the initial registration, registration may be renewed, and every ten years thereafter.

c. Abandonment
Allowing others to use a mark without restrictions or without protest can constitute abandonment. Abandonment is presumed if a mark registered with the PTO is not used for two years.

B. PROTECTING TRADE SECRETS

1. What a Trade Secret Is
Trade secrets (see Chapter 7) are anything that makes an individual company unique and that would have value to a competitor.

2. What a Firm Can Do to Protect Its Trade Secrets
Require employees to agree not to (1) divulge trade secrets, and (2) work for a competitor, or set up a competing business, in which the company's trade secrets will likely be disclosed.

V.   RAISING FINANCIAL CAPITAL

A. LOANS
Capital can be raised through a bank loan, but this may not be possible for many entrepreneurs. Loans may be available from the Small Business Administration (SBA).

B. VENTURE CAPITAL
Most new businesses raise capital by exchanging ownership rights (equity) in the firm for capital (the investor may be called a **venture capitalist**).

1. Procedure
Plan describing company, products, and anticipated performance is presented; investor examines the firm's books and assets (the investor should sign a confidentiality agreement not to disclose trade secrets).

2. Points for Negotiation
Terms of financing, how much ownership and control the venture capitalist will receive, type and quantity of stock, and related issues.

C. SECURITIES REGULATION
When an investor exchanges capital for an interest in an enterprise and the interest consists of shares of stock (or otherwise qualifies as a security—see Chapter 37), it is subject to securities laws.

1. Private Offering
A limited amount of money can be raised from a limited number of investors without registering shares as securities with the Securities and Exchange Commission.

2. Public Offering
Making shares available for purchase by members of the public is highly regulated (but may raise a lot of capital). The securities must be registered. A simplified registration form for small businesses is the Small Corporate Offering Registration (SCOR).

VI. BUY-SELL AGREEMENTS AND KEY-PERSON INSURANCE
For any enterprise, a written agreement establishes what happens if partners or shareholders die, go bankrupt, get divorced, have their ownership interest attached, become disabled, or are so at odds that they cannot work together.

A. BUY-SELL AGREEMENT (KEY TERM OF SHAREHOLDER AGREEMENT)
Enables buy-out of a shareholder and provides for the price to be paid. Might include (1) a right of first refusal (prevents sale to a third party without first giving the other owners a right to buy), or (2) a "take-along" right (allows an investor to participate in sale of shares to a third party).

B. KEY-PERSON INSURANCE

To protect against the risk that a key person (manager, for example) may become disabled or die. Key-person insurance (see Chapter 52) helps cover losses caused by the death or disability.

VII. CONTRACT LAW AND THE ENTREPRENEUR

A. BASIC CONTRACT PRINCIPLES APPLY

Basic contract law (see Chapters 10 through 18) applies to leases and sales of real property and equipment. A contract should be in writing in case of a dispute, or in some cases (see Chapter 15) so it can be enforced.

B. AGENCY PRINCIPLES APPLY

If a firm is organized in a form other than a sole proprietorship, persons who sign contracts or negotiable instruments (Chapter 26) on its behalf will want to do so as agents to avoid personal liability.

VIII. CREDIT AND PAYMENT

A. FREE SHIPPING AND PRICE DISCOUNTS

To encourage prompt payment or payment in advance, a firm may offer free shipping or price discounts.

B. LATE CHARGES AND INTEREST

To get customers to pay on time, a firm may assess late charges. If a firm charges interest on overdue balances, the Truth-in-Lending Act may require certain disclosures (see Chapter 44).

C. COLLECTION OF OVERDUE DEBTS

A contract may provide that a buyer is responsible for all costs to collect overdue payments. State debt-collection laws typically prevent the use of abusive efforts, such as threatening individuals.

IX. EMPLOYMENT ISSUES

A. HIRING EMPLOYEES

Some important considerations are:

1. **Disclosure of Trade Secrets**

    Employees should not disclose trade secrets of former (or current) employers.

2. **Promises of Job Security**

    Employees should not unintentionally be promised job security. (Such promises can be implied from statements in employment manuals.) All terms could be put in writing (for example, that employment is at-will—see Chapter 41), including grounds for termination.

3. **Screening Applicants**

    If appropriate, an applicant may be required to take a drug test. Credentials and job experience should be verified (to avoid a negligent-hiring lawsuit—for example, hiring someone as a driver who has no driver's license).

4. **Compliance with INS Requirements**

    The Immigration and Naturalization Service (INS) has certain requirements with respect to employing noncitizens.

B. EMPLOYEE COMPENSATION

1. Fair Labor Standards Act (FLSA)
Applies to businesses with $500,000 or more in sales or engaged in interstate commerce. Requires minimum wage, plus time-and-a-half for overtime (with exceptions), and wage and hour records.

2. State Law
May require a meal break or rest breaks.

C. WORKERS' COMPENSATION INSURANCE
In most states, an employee injured in the course of employment receives workers' compensation (and cannot sue the employer for more). Employers pay premiums for this insurance based in part on their safety records.

D. UNEMPLOYMENT COMPENSATION
Unemployment compensation (see Chapter 41) tax rates are based in part on the size of a payroll and the number of claimants. Compensation is not payable if an employee quits a job or is fired for misconduct.

E. FIRING EMPLOYEES

1. Wrongful Termination

a. Employment Contracts
Unless otherwise specified, an employee can be fired for any reason. If termination is in bad faith, an employee may bring an action for wrongful discharge. Defense: having good cause for termination.

b. Antidiscrimination Laws
Employers with fewer than fifteen employees are not covered by federal antidiscrimination laws, but may be covered by state laws.

2. Severance Pay
Severance pay is not required, but most states specify when an employee must be given his or her final paycheck.

3. Employer's False Statements to Others
An employer may be liable for (1) defamation if a negative false statement is made to others (such as other employers) about the reason for an employee's termination, or (2) misrepresentation if a positive false statement is made about the employee.

F. COVENANTS NOT TO COMPETE
Covenants not to compete (see Chapter 13), are generally enforceable so long as they are not unreasonably restrictive in terms of time or geographic area.

G. USING INDEPENDENT CONTRACTORS
Independent contractors are not employees (see Chapter 31) and an employer cannot control how they do their work.

1. Taxes
Income taxes and Social Security/Medicare taxes do not have to be withheld or paid. Employers need not pay premiums for workers' compensation insurance or unemployment insurance.

2. Antidiscrimination Laws
An independent contractor cannot sue an employer for discrimination.

3. **Misclassification of Employees as Independent Contractors**
   If a government agency determines that workers are employees, not independent contractors, there may be tax liability and penalties.

TRUE-FALSE QUESTIONS

(Answers at the Back of the Book)

_____ 1. The most important factor is choosing an attorney is the price.

_____ 2. In most cases, corporations survive their owners.

_____ 3. A corporation's name can be the same as that of another existing business.

_____ 4. Allowing others to use a trademark without protesting that use can constitute abandonment of the mark.

_____ 5. No money can be raised through an offering of stock without registering the shares as securities with the Securities and Exchange Commission.

_____ 6. Key-person insurance helps to cover business losses caused by the death or disability of an essential employee.

_____ 7. No contract needs to be in writing to be enforceable.

_____ 8. To charge interest on an overdue account, a business must make certain disclosures relating to those charges before entering into the contract.

_____ 9. An employer's promises of job security are never binding.

_____ 10. If appropriate, a job applicant can be required to take a drug test.

FILL-IN QUESTIONS

(Answers at the Back of the Book)

An employer must withhold and pay federal and state income taxes and Social Security/Medicare taxes for _____ (employees/independent contractors/employees and independent contractors). An employer must pay premiums for workers' compensation insurance and unemployment insurance to cover _____ _____ (employees/independent contractors/employees and independent contractors). An employer can be sued for discrimination by _____ (employees/independent contractors/employees and independent contractors).

MULTIPLE-CHOICE QUESTIONS

(Answers at the Back of the Book)

_____ 1. Ben is starting his own financial planning business. He hires Eve, an attorney, to handle the initial paperwork. The advantages of retaining an attorney at this point in Ben's business include the lawyer's

a. business contacts.
b. legal and business expertise.
c. confidentiality.
d. all of the above.

_____ 2. Carol is starting her own business to design and maintain home pages on the Internet. Carol can avoid all business-related legal requirements if she organizes the business as

a. a sole proprietorship only.
b. a partnership only.
c. either a sole proprietorship or a partnership.
d. none of the above.

_____ 3. Dave and Franco decide to open a restaurant and to operate the business as a corporation. At the corporate directors' initial meeting, the directors may

a. adopt articles of incorporation.
b. adopt bylaws.
c. choose a corporate name.
d. all of the above.

_____ 4. Donna starts a business to market nationally an exercise package called "Santa Fe Fitness." Donna registers her trademark with the U.S. Patent and Trademark Office. This provides nationwide protection for the mark

a. only if the mark is currently in use.
b. only if the mark is not yet in use but will be within six months.
c. if the mark is currently in use or will be in use within six months.
d. under any circumstances.

_____ 5. Tom designs a new baseball bat and decides to incorporate to make and sell it. To sell a limited number of shares of stock in his new corporation to the public, Tom must register the shares with

a. the Securities and Exchange Commission.
b. an attorney with securities law expertise.
c. a venture capitalist.
d. none of the above.

_____ 6. **Based on a Sample CPA Exam Question.** Andrews goes into business as Best Goods, Inc., to sell goods throughout the United States. The Fair Labor Standards Act regulates

a. only Best's employees' minimum wages and overtime pay.
b. only the records of the hours in Best's employees' workweek.
c. Best's employees' minimum wages, overtime pay, and recorded hours.
d. none of the above.

_____ 7. Deb's job is to buy supplies for BT Corporation. To avoid personal liability for contracts and negotiable instruments signed on BT's behalf, Deb must sign

a. as a agent only.
b. as a party to the contract only.
c. as both an agent and a party to the contract.
d. none of the above.

_____ 8. To encourage its customers to pay on time, Ace Products Company may provide in the customers' contracts that

a. Ace may resort to abusive efforts to collect overdue accounts.
b. the customer is responsible for all collection costs on overdue accounts.
c. both a and b.
d. none of the above.

____   **9.**   Jones Manufacturing, Inc., fires Paul. If Jones is asked by other employers to make a statement about the reason for Paul's termination, Jones might be held liable for making

    a.   a negative statement only.
    b.   a positive statement only.
    c.   a negative statement or a positive statement.
    d.   none of the above.

____   **10.**   The four shareholders of Eagle, Inc., want to prevent each other from selling the shares to third parties without first being given the opportunity to buy them. The shareholders can provide for this in

    a.   a buy-sell agreement that includes a "take-along" clause.
    b.   a buy-sell agreement that includes a right of first refusal.
    c.   a key-person clause that specifies who can sell what to whom.
    d.   none of the above.

SHORT ESSAY QUESTIONS

1.   What are the primary factors to consider when choosing a business form?

2.   What are some of the important considerations in discharging an employee?

ISSUE SPOTTERS

(Answers at the Back of the Book)

1.   Kay and Carl are going into business as KC's Pizza Palace. To find an attorney to help them select a business form and organize it properly, where should they look?

2.   Maria has been running MC^3 Computers as a sole proprietorship, but would now like to limit her liability for obligations of the firm. Which organizational form might Maria want to adopt for MC^3 Computers?

3.   Jim owns Copyshop and wants to sell Copyshop franchises throughout the United States. In doing so, Jim wants to prevent competitors from imitating the distinctive Copyshop logo and thereby misleading consumers. How can Jim protect the logo?

4.   Oxen, Inc., sells parts and service to local Internet access providers. How can Oxen prevent its employees from revealing its customer lists and pricing policies if the employees go to work for a competitor or go into the same business for themselves?

5.   Rick opened his first Bagels & Coffee shop several years ago and has been successful. To open shops in more locations, Rick needs capital and wants to attract investors. How can he do this?

SPECIAL INFORMATION FOR CPA CANDIDATES

The CPA requires knowledge of some of the concepts discussed in this chapter. Many of these topics are discussed in more detail in other chapters. For example, for the exam, it is important to understand the differences among the basic forms of business organizations. These forms and their differences are discussed in more detail in Chapters 33 through 39. Securities law is an important part of the exam and is covered in detail in Chapter 47. Employment topics that may be part of the exam include unemployment compensation, workers' compensation, and the Fair Labor Standards Act (see Chapter 41). For specific information about the relevance, as regards the CPA exam, of other topics discussed in other chapters, see those chapters.

CUMULATIVE HYPOTHETICAL PROBLEM FOR UNIT ELEVEN—INCLUDING CHAPTERS 49–53

(Answers at the Back of the Book)

Earl, in his will, establishes a trust and designates First National Bank to be the trustee. The property of the trust includes warehouses and other commercial property.

____ 1. On a warehouse, the trustee obtains a $300,000 fire insurance policy from American Insurance Company that includes an 80 percent coinsurance clause. At the time, the warehouse is valued at $400,000. When the warehouse is valued at $500,000, it sustains fire damage of $60,000. Recovery under the policy is

   a. $45,000.
   b. $60,000.
   c. $75,000.
   d. $300,000.

____ 2. While operating as the trustee, the bank incurs charges that include ordinary expenses and extraordinary expenses. These are allocated

   a. entirely to income.
   b. entirely to principal.
   c. extraordinary expenses to income and ordinary expenses to principal.
   d. ordinary expenses to income and extraordinary expenses to principal.

____ 3. On behalf of the trust, the trustee loans money to General Sales, Inc. (GSI). GSI's financial statements were audited by Holly, an accountant. The bank files a suit against Holly based on fraud. Holly's best defense is

   a. a disclaimer included with the financial statements.
   b. contributory negligence on the part of GSI.
   c. lack of privity between Holly and the trust.
   d. lack of reliance on the statements on the part of the bank.

____ 4. The bank retains Ira, an outside accountant, to prepare the trust's federal tax forms. The bank asks Ira to help it evade some of the taxes by providing false information. If Ira helps the bank, he may be subject to

   a. an injunction prohibiting him from acting as a tax preparer only.
   b. federal criminal prosecution only.
   c. an injunction prohibiting him from acting as a tax preparer and federal criminal prosecution.
   d. none of the above.

____ 5. Jill, an accountant, prepares financial statements for a registration statement for Mega Industries, Inc. To be successful against Jill in a civil action under the Securities Act of 1933 for misleading statements in the registration statement, the trustee must prove

a. Jill's intent to deceive only.
b. the bank's reliance on the registration statement only.
c. Jill's intent to deceive and the bank's reliance on the registration statement.
d. none of the above.

Business Law for the Uniform CPA Examination

THE UNIFORM CPA EXAMINATION

To obtain a Certified Public Accountant (CPA) certificate or license, accountants must meet certain requirements. State boards of accountancy set these requirements. In every state, one of the requirements is passing the Uniform CPA Examination. The Board of Examiners of the American Institute of Certified Public Accountants (AICPA) is responsible for the preparation and advisory grading of the Uniform CPA Examination. The examination, which is given over a two-day period twice a year (in May and November), contains four sections: business law and professional responsibilities, auditing, accounting and reporting (taxation, managerial, and governmental not-for-profit organizations), and financial accounting and reporting.

The business law and professional responsibilities portion of the examination is given on the first day of the examination—Wednesday—from 9 A.M. until noon. The format consists of questions in a multiple-choice or other objective format and essay or problem-type questions. The multiple-choice questions are similar to some of the multiple-choice questions in this *Study Guide*. Normally, essay questions have two or more parts that test candidates' knowledge of different business law topics. Generally, an essay question consists of a fact situation involving a number of legal issues. Candidates are expected to discuss these issues and should provide reasons for their conclusions.

Distinctions about subject matter are not always clear-cut. That is, there may be some overlap of subjects within the four sections of the examination and within the seven areas of the business law section of the examination. For instance, the factual situation in a business law question may require knowledge of accounting or auditing, and the answers may involve a response based in part on this knowledge.

THE SUBJECT MATTER OF THE UNIFORM CPA EXAMINATION

Knowledge of business law is necessary to pass the test. Detailed information about the subject matter of the examination and the approximate percentage of the examination devoted to each of seven broad topics is provided in specifications adopted by the Board of Examiners of the AICPA. The business law and professional responsibilities section tests the candidates' knowledge of the legal implications of business transactions, particularly as they relate to accounting and auditing, and candidates' knowledge of the CPA's professional responsibilities to the public and the profession.

As outlined by the Board of Examiners of the AICPA, the section includes a CPA's professional responsibilities, business organizations, contracts, debtor-creditor relationships, government regulation of business, the Uniform Commercial Code, and property. The subjects on the examination normally are covered in standard textbooks on business law, auditing, taxation, and accounting. Candidates are expected to recognize the existence of legal implications and the applicable basic legal principles, and they are usually asked to indicate the probable result of the application of such basic principles.

The business law and professional responsibilities section is chiefly conceptual in nature and is broad in scope, as determined by the Board of Examiners of the AICPA. The examination is not intended to test competence to practice law or expertise in legal matters, but is intended to determine that the candidates' knowledge is sufficient (1) to recognize relevant legal issues, (2) to recognize the legal implications of business situations, (3) to apply the underlying principles of law to accounting and auditing situations, and (4) to seek legal counsel or recommend that it be sought.

The section deals with federal and widely adopted uniform laws. If there is no federal or applicable uniform law on a subject, the questions ask for knowledge of the majority rules. Federal tax elements may be covered in the overall context of a question.

Writing skills are assessed on selected essay responses. Five percent of the total points for the business law and professional responsibilities portion will be allocated to writing skills. Writing skills include such characteristics as the ability to organize a response coherently, brevity, clarity, use of standard English, responsiveness to the requirements of the question, and appropriateness for the reader. Standard English is the language of business and the professions.

STUDY TIP ☞ Effective Writing Skills

In answering essay questions on the Uniform CPA Examination, responses should be organized in short paragraphs, each limited to the explanation of a single main point, with short sentences. Short sentences and simple wording also demonstrate the ability to write concisely—that is, the ability to express an important point in as few words as possible. Clarity involves using words of precise meaning in well-constructed sentences. These words include terms that are appropriate for the subject being tested. Correct grammar—including punctuation, capitalization, spelling, and word usage—enhance clarity. In responding to a question, do not broadly discuss general subject matter. Address a question directly.

THE BUSINESS LAW CONTENT OF THE EXAMINATION

The specific content of the Business Law and Professional Responsibilities portion of the Uniform CPA Examination is as follows:[1]

I. Professional and Legal Responsibilities (15 percent)

   A. Code of Professional Conduct
   B. Proficiency, Independence, and Due Care
   C. Responsibilities in Other Professional Services
   D. Disciplinary Systems within the Profession
   E. Common Law Liability to Clients and Third Parties
   F. Federal Statutory Liability
   G. Privileged Communications and Confidentiality
   H. Responsibilities of CPAs in Business and Industry, and in the Public Sector

II. Business Organizations (20 percent)

   A. Agency

      1. Formation and Termination
      2. Duties of Agents and Principals
      3. Liabilities and Authority of Agents and Principals

   B. Partnerships, Joint Ventures, and Other Unincorporated Associations

      1. Formation, Operation, and Termination
      2. Liabilities and Authority of Partners and Joint Owners

   C. Corporations

      1. Formation and Operation
      2. Stockholders, Directors, and Officers
      3. Financial Structure, Capital, and Distributions
      4. Reorganization and Dissolution

   D. Estates and Trusts

      1. Formation, Operation, and Termination
      2. Allocation between Principal and Income
      3. Fiduciary Responsibilities
      4. Distributions

III. Contracts (10 percent)

   A. Formation
   B. Performance
   C. Third Party Assignments
   D. Discharge, Breach, and Remedies

---

[1] This and other information pertaining to the CPA examination is available at the Web site of the American Institute of Certified Public Accountants (AICPA) at www.aicpa.org.

IV. Debtor-Creditor Relationships (10 percent)

    A. Rights, Duties, and Liabilities of Debtors and Creditors

        1. Liabilities and Defenses
        2. Release of Parties
        3. Remedies of Parties

    B. Rights, Duties, and Liabilities of Guarantors

        1. Liabilities and Defenses
        2. Release of Parties
        3. Remedies of Parties

    C. Bankruptcy

        1. Voluntary and Involuntary Bankruptcy
        2. Effects of Bankruptcy on Debtor and Creditors
        3. Reorganizations

V. Government Regulation of Business (15 percent)

    A. Federal Securities Acts

        1. Securities Registration
        2. Reporting Requirements
        3. Exempt Securities and Transactions

    B. Employment Regulation

        1. Payroll Taxes
        2. Employee Safety
        3. Employment Discrimination
        4. Wage and Hour
        5. Pension and Other Fringe Benefits

    C. Environmental Regulation

VI. Uniform Commercial Code (20 percent)

    A. Negotiable Instruments

        1. Types of Negotiable Instruments
        2. Requisites of Negotiability
        3. Transfer and Negotiation
        4. Holders and Holders in Due Course
        5. Liabilities, Defenses, and Rights
        6. Discharge

B. Sales

1. Contracts Covering Goods
2. Warranties
3. Product Liability
4. Risk of Loss
5. Performance and Obligations
6. Remedies and Defenses

C. Secured Transactions

1. Attachment of Security Interests
2. Perfection of Security Interests
3. Priorities
4. Rights of Debtors, Creditors, and Third Parties

D. Documents of Title

VII. Property (10 percent)

A. Real Property

1. Types of Ownership
2. Lessor-Lessee
3. Deeds, Recording, Title Defects, and Title Insurance
4. Mortgages and Other Liens
5. Fixtures
6. Environmental Liability

B. Personal Property, Bailments, and Computer Technology Rights

1. Types of Ownership
2. Bailments
3. Computer Technology Rights

Cross References:
Business Law Subjects in the Uniform CPA Examination—
Chapters in *West's Business Law, Eighth Edition*

SUBJECTS	CHAPTERS
PROFESSIONAL AND LEGAL RESPONSIBILITIES	
A. Code of Professional Conduct	40, 51
B. Proficiency, Independence, and Due Care	40, 51
C. Responsibilities in Other Professional Services	40, 51
D. Disciplinary Systems Imposed by the Profession and State Regulatory Bodies	40, 51
E. Common Law Liability to Clients and Third Parties	40, 51
F. Federal Statutory Liability	40, 51
G. Privileged Communications and Confidentiality	40, 51
H. Responsibilities of CPAs in Business and Industry, and in the Public Sector	40, 51
BUSINESS ORGANIZATIONS	
A. Agency	31, 32
B. Partnerships, Joint Ventures, and Other Unincorporated Associations	33, 38, 39
C. Corporations	34, 35, 36, 37
D. Estates and Trusts	50
CONTRACTS	
A. Formation	10, 11, 12, 13, 14, 15
B. Performance	17
C. Third-Party Assignments	16
D. Discharge, Breach, and Remedies	17, 18
DEBTOR-CREDITOR RELATIONSHIPS	
A. Rights, Duties, and Liabilities of Debtors and Creditors	29
B. Rights, Duties, and Liabilities of Guarantors	29
C. Bankruptcy	30
GOVERNMENT REGULATION OF BUSINESS	
A. Federal Securities Acts	37
B. Employment Regulation	41, 42
C. Environmental Regulation	44
UNIFORM COMMERCIAL CODE	
A. Negotiable Instruments	24, 25, 26, 27
B. Sales	19, 20, 21, 22, 23
C. Secured Transactions	28
D. Documents of Title	46

PROPERTY

A. Real Property, including Insurance   47, 49
B. Personal Property, including Bailments and Computer
    Technology Rights   9, 46

UNIFORM CPA EXAMINATION DATES

Uniform CPA Examinations are scheduled for the following dates:

2000—	May 3, 4	2002—	May 8, 9
	November 1, 2		November 6, 7
2001—	May 2, 3	2003—	May 7, 8
	November 7, 8		November 5, 6

Students who plan to sit for any of the Uniform CPA Examinations should obtain copies of *Information for Uniform CPA Examination Candidates* issued by the AICPA.[2]

---

[2] Copies may be obtained by writing to:

American Institute of Certified Public Accountants, Inc.
1211 Avenue of the Americas
New York, New York 10036-8775

Answers

Chapter 1

True-False Questions

1. T
2. F. Legal positivists believe that there can be no higher law that a nation's positive law (the law created by a particular society at a particular point in time). The belief that law should reflect universal moral and ethical principles that are part of human nature is part of the natural law tradition.
3. T
4. T
5. T
6. F. Each state's constitution is supreme within each state's borders, so long as it does not conflict with the U.S. Constitution.
7. F. The National Conference of Commissioners on Uniform State Laws drafted the Uniform Commercial Code and proposed it for adoption by the states.
8. T
9. T
10. T

Fill-in Questions

with similar facts; precedent; permits a predictable

Multiple-Choice Questions

1. C. Legal realists believe that judges are influenced by the beliefs and attitudes unique to their individual personalities, that the application of precedent should be tempered by each case's specific circumstances, and that extra-legal sources should be considered in making decisions.
2. C. The use of precedent—the doctrine of *stare decisis*—permits a predictable, relatively quick, and fair resolution of cases. If the application of the law was unpredictable, there would be no consistent rules to follow and no stability.
3. C. In addition to case law, when making decisions, courts may consider other sources of law, including the U.S. Constitution, state constitutions, and administrative agency rules and regulations. A court may also take into consideration the principles of other areas

of study, including science, economics, psychology, and others.

4.   A.   The doctrine of *stare decisis* attempts to harmonize the results in cases with similar facts.   When the facts are sufficiently similar, the same rule is normally applied.

5.   A.   Equity and law do provide different remedies—injunctions and specific performance, for example, are equitable remedies, and damages is a remedy at law.   Most states no longer maintain separate courts of law and equity.

6.   C.   How a court interprets a particular statute determines how that statute will be applied.   To learn what a statute says, a person needs to study it.   To learn how that statute will be applied, a person needs to see what precedents have been established in regard to it.

7.   B.   Using the principles behind the decisions in previous legal disputes, courts develop rules to apply in current disputes.   These rules are known as the common law.

8.   A.   Statutory law is a primary source of law that includes the statutes passed by Congress and the various state legislative bodies, as well as the ordinances passed by cities and counties.   It does not include the rules, orders, and decisions of administrative agencies, which makes up what is known as administrative law.

9.   A.   In reasoning by analogy, a judge compares the facts in one case to the facts in another case and to the extent that the facts are similar, applied the same legal principle.   If the facts can be distinguished, different legal rules may apply.   In either case, a judge will ordinarily state his or her reasons for applying a certain principle and arriving at a certain conclusion.

10.   A.   In a common law system, the basis for law is case law—the rulings in cases decided by judges.   Case precedents are binding on lower courts in the jurisdictions in which they are issued, unlike the effect of court decisions in a civil law system.

Issue Spotters

1.   Case law includes courts' interpretations of statutes, as well as constitutional provisions and administrative

rules.   Statutes often codify common law rules.   For these reasons, a judge might rely on the common law as a guide to the intent and purpose of a statute.

2.   No.   The U.S. Constitution is the supreme law of the land.   A law in violation of the Constitution (in this question, the First Amendment to the Constitution) will be declared unconstitutional.

3.   This case could be found in volume 26 of the *Wisconsin Reports, Second Series*, on page 683, or in volume 133 of the *North Western Reporter, Second Series*, on page 267.

4.   No.   If this were the title of a case in a trial court, Jones would be the plaintiff (the person who filed the suit) and Smith the defendant.   Some appellate courts place the name of the party appealing a decision first, so that this same case on appeal may be called *Smith v. Jones*.

5.   An opinion contains the reasons for a court's decision.   When all the judges or justices unanimously agree on an opinion, it is written for the entire court as a unanimous opinion.   When they do not agree, a majority opinion is written to outline the views of the majority.   A judge who agrees with the majority's decision, but for different reasons, may write a concurring opinion.   Whichever judges disagree with the majority may write a dissenting opinion.

Chapter 2

True-False Questions

1.   T

2.   F.   A particular court may have jurisdiction but not venue.   They are separate questions.   Jurisdiction relates to the authority of a court to hear a case.   Venue relates to the appropriate location for a case to be heard.

3.   T

4.   T

5.   T

6.   T

7.   F.   The Supreme Court has original jurisdiction in controversies between states, controversies involving ambassadors and other public ministers, controversies between the U.S. and a state, and controversies between a state and the citizens of another state or country. In other cases, the Supreme Court has appellate jurisdiction, subject to regulation by Congress.

8. F. The jury verdict after a summary jury trial (SJT) is not binding. SJT is a form of alternative dispute resolution in which the parties' attorneys present their cases to a jury, but no witnesses are called, and the verdict is advisory only.

9. F. Negotiation typically does not involve a third party. The major difference between negotiation and mediation is that mediation does involve the presence of a third party—a mediator—who assists the parties in reaching an agreement and who often suggests solutions towards that end.

10. T

Fill-in Questions

trial; reviewing; factual issues; the law to the facts; of law but not of fact

Multiple-Choice Questions

1. A. A corporation is subject to the jurisdiction of the courts in any state in which it is incorporated, in which it has its main office, or in which it does business. The court may be able to exercise personal jurisdiction, *in rem* jurisdiction, or *quasi in rem* jurisdiction, or the court may reach a defendant corporation with a long arm statute.

2. A. A court that has jurisdiction may not have venue. Essentially, the court that tries a case should be in the geographic area in which the incident occurred or the parties reside.

3. B. Cases are generally not retried on appeal. An appeals court examines the record of a case, looking at questions of law and procedure for errors by the court below. If it determines that a retrial is necessary, the case is sent back to the lower court.

4. C. A suit can be brought in a federal court if it involves a question arising under the Constitution, a treaty, or a federal law. A suit can also be brought in a federal court under the court's diversity jurisdiction—that is, if the suit involves citizens of different states, a foreign country and an American citizen, or a foreign citizen and an American citizen, and the amount in controversy is more than $75,000.

5. C. A case involving diversity of citizenship is an example. When cases can be tried only in federal courts or only in state courts, exclusive jurisdiction exists. For instance, federal courts have exclusive jurisdiction in cases involving bankruptcy, patents, and copyrights and other areas of the law.

6. A. A party bringing a lawsuit must have suffered a harm or been threatened with a harm by the action about which he or she has complained. (Sometimes, a party may bring a suit on behalf of another, such as his or her child.) This is the requirement of standing. Also, a controversy must be justiciable, which means it must be real and not merely hypothetical.

7. A. Every state has at least one court of appeals, which may be an intermediate appellate court or the state's highest court. If a federal or constitutional issue is involved, the case may ultimately be appealed to the United States Supreme Court.

8. B. Neither the amount involved nor the parties' satisfaction is relevant. An arbitrator's award will be set aside if it violates pubic policy. Other grounds on which an award may be set aside arise from the arbitrator's conduct—for example, if his or her bad faith substantially prejudices the rights of one of the parties, or if he or she decides issues that the parties did not agree to submit to arbitration.

9. A. Arbitration is the settling of a dispute by an impartial third party (whose decision can be legally binding). The amount of money involved is immaterial, and the dispute need not arise from a written agreement.

10. D. In mediation, the parties settle their dispute themselves—a mediator gives only his or her opinion, which the parties can disregard. The goal of mediation is to resolve a dispute to the satisfaction of both parties. The amount of money involved is immaterial, and the dispute need not arise from a written agreement.

Issue Spotters

1. Before a court will hear a case, it must be established that the court has subject matter and personal jurisdiction and that the matter at issue is justiciable.

The party bringing the suit must also have standing to sue.

2. Yes. Whenever a suit involves citizens of different states, diversity of citizenship exists, and the suit can be brought in a federal court. In diversity of citizenship suits, Congress has set an additional requirement—the amount in controversy must be more than $75,000.

3. Yes. There is no absolute right of appeal to the United States Supreme Court. A party may ask the Supreme Court to issue a writ of *certiorari* (an order to a lower court to send the Court the record of the case for review), but the Court may deny the request.

4. Litigating is costly and it can be years before a case is tried. Resolving a dispute outside the courts is usually less expensive and quicker. It is usually more private, unlike court proceedings, which are public. It also allows a more flexible result. Normally, the parties can control how a dispute is settled, what procedures are used, and whether the result is binding.

5. Unlike litigation, negotiation involves no third parties. Partly for this reason, negotiation is less expensive and can be less time-consuming, Also, negotiation is not subject to the same rules of procedure as litigation.

Chapter 3

True-False Questions

1. F. Pleadings inform each party of the other's claims and specify the issues. Pleadings consist of a complaint and an answer, not a motion to dismiss.

2. F. In ruling on a motion for summary judgment, a court can consider evidence outside the pleadings, such as answers to interrogatories.

3. T

4. F. A defendant can file an answer that includes an affirmative defense. The defendant can also file a motion to dismiss or an answer that includes a counterclaim. A defendant will be held in default if he or she fails to file *any* response to a complaint.

5. F. The process that involves obtaining access to documents and other materials in the hands of an opposing party prior to trial is the *discovery* process.

6. T

7. F. The plaintiff in a civil case must prove a case by a preponderance of the evidence (the claim is more likely to be true than the defendant's). Some claims (such as fraud) must be proved by clear and convincing evidence (the truth of the claim is highly probable). The standard in a criminal trial is *beyond a reasonable doubt*.

8. T

9. T

10. T

Fill-in Questions

to dismiss; for judgment on the pleadings; summary judgment

Multiple-Choice Questions

1. D. The considerations for whether to take a case to court involve primarily time and money. Even settling out of court for less than you are owed may be wise in terms of future expenses, time waiting, time lost, and frustration.

2. D. A complaint contains a statement alleging jurisdictional facts, a statement of facts entitling the complainant to relief, and a statement asking for a specific remedy. It is filed with the court that has proper jurisdiction and venue. A copy of the complaint is served, with a summons, on the defendant named in the complaint.

3. C. Discovery saves time by preserving evidence, narrowing the issues, preventing surprises at trial, and avoiding a trial altogether in some cases. The current trend is toward allowing more discovery and thus fewer surprises.

4. C. A defendant may file a motion to dismiss if he or she is not properly served with the complaint, if the court lacks personal or subject matter jurisdiction, if the venue is improper, if the complaint does not state a claim for which relief can be granted, or other specific reasons.

5. B. If a motion to dismiss is filed before a defendant answers a complaint and the motion is granted, the case is at an end. If the motion is denied, the defendant must file an answer, or a default judgment will be entered against him or her.

6. A. An important part of the discovery process is a deposition, which is sworn testimony. Interrogatories are a series of written questions for which written answers are prepared and signed under oath by the plaintiff or defendant. A pretrial conference involves the plaintiff, the defendant, their attorneys, and judge.

7. A. Once a jury is chosen, a trial begins with the parties' opening statements, after which the plaintiff presents his or her case. The defendant then presents his or her case. The plaintiff can refute the defendant's case in a rebuttal, and the defendant then has the opportunity to present a rejoinder.

8. A. After a plaintiff calls and questions the first witness on direct examination, the defendant questions the witness on cross-examination. The plaintiff may then question the witness again (redirect examination), and the defendant may follow (recross-examination). Then the plaintiff's other witnesses are called, and the defendant presents his or her case.

9. C. After a verdict, the losing party can move for a new trial or for a judgment notwithstanding the verdict. If these motions are denied, he or she can appeal.

10. C. For obvious reasons, a losing party may wish to appeal a judgment. A winning party has the same right to appeal if he or she is dissatisfied with the relief granted.

Issue Spotters

1. First, Jan should consult an attorney. The attorney will help Jan to consider the merits and the costs of a possible lawsuit and other alternatives. If Jan wishes to proceed with the suit, the next steps will include serving Dean with a complaint and summons.

2. Jan needs to make use of the discovery process to see her opponent's relevant papers and obtain answers to her questions. The papers may be released in response to a request for documents. The questions may be answered in response to interrogatories.

3. Dean could file a motion for a directed verdict. This motion asks the judge to direct a verdict for Dean on the ground that Jan presented no evidence that would justify granting Jan relief. The judge grants the motion if there is insufficient evidence to raise an issue of fact.

4. This is not necessarily the end of their case. Either a plaintiff or a defendant, or both, can appeal a judgment to a higher court. An appellate court can affirm, reverse, or remand a case, or take any of these actions in combination. To appeal successfully, it is best to appeal on the basis of an error of law, because appellate courts do not usually reverse on findings of fact.

5. Jan can ask the court to order a sheriff to seize property owned by Dean and hold it until Dean pays the judgment. If Dean fails to pay, the property can be sold at a public auction and the proceeds given to Jan, or the property can be transferred to Jan in lieu of payment.

Chapter 4

True-False Questions

1. F. A federal form of government is one in which separate states form a union and divide sovereign power between themselves and a central authority. The United States has a federal form of government.

2. F. The executive branch of the government enforces the law. The judicial branch interprets the law.

3. T

4. T

5. T

6. F. Under the supremacy clause, when there is a direct conflict between a federal law and a state law, the federal law takes precedence over the state law, which is invalid.

7. T

8. F. Advertising can be restricted as long as the restriction (1) seeks to implement a substantial government interest, (2) directly advances that interest, and (3) goes no further than necessary to accomplish its objective.

9. T

10. F. Due process relates to the limits that the law places on the liberty of *everyone*. Equal protection relates to the limits that the law places on only *some people*.

Fill-in Questions

states; states; state; state; validity

Multiple-Choice Questions

1. B. Under Articles I, II, and III of the Constitution, the legislative branch makes the law, the judicial branch interprets the law, and the executive branch enforces the law.

2. B. The first ten amendments to the Constitution, known as the Bill of Rights, embody protections against various types of interference by the federal government. Through the Fourteenth Amendment, most of these guarantees apply to states as well.

3. C. When a state law impinges on interstate commerce, a court will balance the state's interest in the merit and purpose of the law against the burden on interstate commerce. If the law is not a substantial interference, it does not violate the commerce clause.

4. D. The Fifth Amendment privilege against self-incrimination is available only to natural persons, and a corporation is not a natural person. Business corporations can be compelled to produce their records even if they are incriminating.

5. A. Commercial speech that is neither related to illegal activities nor misleading may not be restricted unless a state has a substantial interest that cannot be achieved by less restrictive means.

6. D. Under the establishment and free exercise clauses, the government must accommodate all religions and cannot be hostile toward any religion—that is, government action must be neutral toward religion.

7. A. For example, if a law prohibits all persons from buying contraceptive devices, it raises a substantive due process question. Substantive due process is protected by two clauses in the Constitution. The due process clause of the Fourteenth Amendment applies to state and local governments, and the due process clause of the Fifth Amendment applies to the federal government.

8. C. If a law prohibits only some persons from buying contraceptive devices, for example, it raises an equal protection issue. Equal protection means that the government must treat similarly situated individuals in a similar manner. The equal protection clause of the Fourteenth Amendment applies to state and local governments, and the due process clause of the Fifth Amendment guarantees equal protection by the federal government.

9. A. Under the supremacy clause, if Congress chooses to act exclusively in an area in which states have concurrent power, Congress is said to preempt the area. The federal law takes precedence over a state law on the same subject.

10. B. To obtain a warrant, an officer must convince a judge there is evidence that would convince a reasonable person a search or seizure is justified. Probable cause is also required to search business premises, but the standard is different—a general, neutral enforcement plan is sufficient.

Issue Spotters

1. Under the commerce clause, according to the Supreme Court, Congress has the power to regulate any activity—interstate or intrastate—that affects interstate commerce. Thus, under that clause, Congress could regulate this farmer's activity.

2. No. Even if commercial speech is not related to illegal activities nor misleading, it may be restricted if a state has a substantial interest that cannot be achieved by less restrictive means. In this case, the interest in energy conservation is substantial, but it could be achieved by less restrictive means.

3. No. The First Amendment requires that the government not prohibit the free exercise of religious practices. But an individual's religious beliefs are not considered to excuse him or her from compliance with an otherwise valid law. That would inhibit the government's ability to enforce prohibitions of socially harmful conduct.

4. Yes, the law would violate both types of due process. The law would be unconstitutional on substantive due process grounds, because it abridges freedom of speech. The law would be unconstitutional on procedural due process grounds, because it imposes a penalty without giving an accused a chance to defend his or her actions.

5. Yes. The tax would limit the liberty of some persons (out of state businesses), so it is subject to a review under the equal protection clause. Protecting local businesses from out-of-state competition is not a legitimate government objective. Thus, such a tax would violate the equal protection clause.

Chapter 5

True-False Questions

1. T
2. F. This is an element of a battery. A *reasonable apprehension or fear* of immediate harmful or offensive contact is an essential element of assault.
3. F. Defamation may be committed orally, in writing, or in a form of communication that has the potentially harmful qualities characteristic of writing—pictures, signs, statues, and films.
4. T
5. F. Justified or permissible interference is not wrongful. Defenses to wrongful interference torts include bona fide competitive behavior and other legal conduct.
6. T
7. F. Disparagement of property is a general term for torts that can be more specifically referred to as slander of quality or slander of title.
8. F. The statement is seller's talk, or puffery—the seller's *opinion*. For fraud to occur, there must be a misrepresentation of a *fact*.
9. T
10. F. An individual with knowledge, skill, or intelligence superior to that of an ordinary person has a higher standard of care—his or her duty is that which is reasonable in light of those capabilities.

Fill-in Questions

1. negligence;
2. defense of assumption of risk
3. contributory;
4. comparative

Multiple-Choice Questions

1. A. To satisfy the elements of a negligence cause of action, a breach of a duty of care must cause the harm. If an injury would not have occurred without the breach, there is causation in fact. Causation in fact can usually be determined by the but-for test: But for the wrongful act, the injury would not have occurred.
2. C. To delay a customer suspected of shoplifting, a merchant must have probable cause (which requires more than a mere suspicion). A customer's concealing merchandise in his or her bag and leaving the store without paying for it would constitute probable cause.
3. C. A person may not be liable for defamatory statements if he or she enjoys a privilege. Absolute privilege exists in limited situations, including judicial proceedings.
4. D. Other acts that constitute intrusion into another's affairs or seclusion include invading someone's home, illegally searching someone's belongings, eavesdropping by wiretap, unauthorized scanning of a bank account, compulsory blood testing, and window peeping.
5. D. Trespass to land occurs when a person, without permission, enters onto another's land, or remains on the land. Harm to the land is not required. A trespasser can be removed by reasonable force.
6. A. The basis of the tort of defamation is publication of a statement that holds an individual up to contempt, ridicule, or hatred. Publication means that statements are made to or within the hearing of persons other than the defamed party. Dictating a letter to a secretary constitutes publication; a secretary reading a letter constitutes publication.
7. B. Failing to exercise reasonable care is potentially tortious conduct. Whether conduct is unreasonable depends on a number of factors, including how easily the injury could have been guarded against. Unless a retail firm has taken all reasonable precautions against injuries to its customers, it may be held to have breached its duty of care to those invitees.
8. C. Joe is guilty of assault—an intentional, unexcused act that creates in another person a reasonable apprehension of immediate harmful or offensive contact.

9. A. False or misleading statements about a competitor's products are actionable as trade libel, or slander of quality. Actual damages must be proved to have proximately resulted from the slander.

10. D. Advertising is bona fide competitive behavior, which is not a tort even if it results in the breaking of a contract. Obtaining more customers is one of the goals of effective advertising.

Issue Spotters

1. Yes. Adam is guilty of battery—an unexcused, harmful, or offensive physical contact intentionally performed. A battery may involve contact with any part of the body and anything (a blouse, in this problem) attached to it.

2. Yes. Trespass to personal property occurs when an individual unlawfully harms another's personal property or otherwise interferes with the owner's right to exclusive possession and enjoyment.

3. The question is one of proximate cause. Proximate cause is a question not of fact but of law and policy for a court to decide: should a negligent actor's responsibility extend to consequences that could not have been anticipated? In this problem, the death seems too far removed from the careless act to result in liability.

4. Yes. If the employer with the broken contract can show that its competitor induced its employee to break the contract, the employer can recover damages. This is wrongful interference with a contractual relationship.

5. Yes. Passing on false information about a person's credit standing or business reputation that impairs the person's ability to obtain further credit is defamation and entitles the defamed person to damages.

Chapter 6

True-False Questions

1. T

2. F. In an action based on strict product liability, a plaintiff does not have to prove that there was a failure to exercise due care. That distinguishes a product liability action based on strict liability from one based on negligence, which requires proof of a lack of due care.

3. T

4. F. A defendant may be liable for the result of his or her act regardless of intent—that is part of the basis of the doctrine of strict liability. Similarly, it usually does not matter whether the defendant exercised reasonable care. Strict liability is liability without regard to fault or intent.

5. T

6. F. Product liability may be imposed for defects in the design or construction of products that cause injuries, but it may also be imposed for a failure to include a reasonable warning.

7. F. Strict product liability for personal injuries caused by defective goods does extend to those who lease the goods.

8. T

9. T

10. T

Fill-in Questions

limitations; does not begin until; repose; repose; limitations

Multiple-Choice Questions

1. D. Assumption of risk is a defense in an action based on strict liability if the plaintiff knew and appreciated the risk created by the defect and voluntarily undertook the risk, even though it was unreasonable to do so.

2. A. All courts extend the doctrine of strict liability to injured bystanders. A defendant does not have to prove that the manufacturer or seller failed to use due care, nor is there a requirement of privity. The defense of assumption of risk does not apply, because one cannot assume a risk that one does not know about.

3. B. The manufacturer was clearly negligent to sell a product with a defective safety switch. As a defendant in a product liability suit on the ground of negligence, the manufacturer would be liable. The plaintiff knew about the defect, however, and used the treadmill anyway. Under the defense of comparative negligence, the amount of the defendant's liability may be reduced in proportion to the amount by which the plaintiff's injury was the result of the plaintiff's own negligence.

4. B. Liability would be based on the circumstance that the pharmacy, through its pharmacist, misrepresented the character of the contents of the bottle.

5. D. All of the choices are public policy reasons for imposing the doctrine of strict liability. In terms of spreading the costs, manufacturers and others who might be liable typically have insurance to cover any losses. To pay for the insurance, the insured may simply raise its prices to its customers.

6. D. A manufacturer may be held liable if its product is unsafe as a result of negligence in the manufacture or when the design makes it unreasonably dangerous for the use for which it is made. A manufacturer also has a duty to warn and to anticipate reasonably foreseeable misuses. There is no liability, however, with respect to unforeseeable, improper misuses.

7. B. A less dangerous alternative was economically feasible—a grid could have been placed over the auger's opening—but the manufacturer failed to include it.

8. C. In an action based on strict liability, the plaintiff does not need to prove that anyone was at fault. Privity of contract is also not an element of an action for strict liability. A plaintiff does have to show, however, in a suit against a seller, that the seller was a merchant engaged in the business of selling the product on which the suit is based.

9. C. The doctrine of strict liability extends to suppliers of component parts as well as the manufacturers, sellers, and distributors of the products made with those components.

10. C. Misrepresentation must be of a material fact, there must be an intent to induce a buyer's reliance, and the buyer must rely on the misrepresentation. Nonfraudulent misrepresentation occurs when a merchant innocently misrepresents the character or quality of goods—the misrepresentation does not have to be knowing.

Issue Spotters

1 Yes. Mac is liable for the injuries to Keith and his passengers. A manufacturer is liable for its failure to exercise due care to any person who sustains an injury proximately caused by a negligently made (defective) product. In this problem, the failure to inspect is a failure to use due care. Rollco may also be liable.

2. Yes. Under the doctrine of strict liability, persons may be held liable for the results of their acts regardless of their intentions or their exercise of reasonable care—that is, regardless of fault.

3. Yes. Suppliers are generally required to expect reasonably foreseeable misuses and to design products that are either safe when misused or marketed with some protective device.

4. Yes. The manufacturer of the component part may be held liable. The strict liability doctrine has been expanded to include suppliers of component parts.

5. Yes. Most courts will consider a plaintiff's negligence in apportioning liability, resulting in an application of the doctrine of comparative negligence in strict liability cases.

Chapter 7

True-False Questions

1. T

2. F. A copyright is granted automatically.

3. T

4. T

5. F. The policies and restrictions that apply to trademarks apply to service, certification, and collective marks.

6. F. Unlike copyright and trademark protection, protection of trade secrets extends to ideas *and* their expression.

7. T

8. F. These principles apply to trade names. Trade names cannot be registered with the federal government, but they are protected under the common law (when used as trademarks or service marks).

9. T

10. F. A copy does not have to be the same as an original to constitute copyright infringement. In other words, a copyright is infringed if a substantial part of a work is copied without the copyright holder's permission.

Fill-in Questions

70; 95; 120; 70

Multiple-Choice Questions

1.   A. A firm that makes, uses, or sells another's patented design, product, or process without the patent owner's permission commits patent infringement. It is not required that an invention be copied in its entirety. The object that is copied does not need to be trademarked or copyrighted, in addition to being patented.

2.   A. Registration is not necessary to obtain protection from trademark infringement. A trademark receives protection to the degree that it is distinctive. Using a fanciful symbol for a product, as here, is the most distinctive sort of mark.

3.   A. One of the requirements for copyright protection is that a work be original. There is nothing original about a telephone directory that lists persons in alphabetical order. Such raw facts may be copied without liability.

4.   C. In applying and interpreting the Computer Software Copyright Act of 1980, courts have extended protection to all of the listed items. Courts have not extended protection to computer programs' "look and feel," however.

5.   C. Software products often do not meet the "novel" and "not obvious" requirements for a patent because much software simply automates procedures that can be performed manually. Also, the basis for a computer program is often a mathematical equation or formula, which is not patentable.

6.   B. To obtain a patent, an applicant must satisfy the U.S. Patent and Trademark Office that the invention or design is genuine, novel, useful, and not obvious in light of contemporary technology. A patent is granted to the first person to create whatever is to be patented, rather than the first person to file for a patent.

7.   B. Patent infringement occurs by making, using, or selling another's patented design, product, or process without the patent owner's permission. The entire product does not need to be copied. Copying a part of it is enough.

8.   C. Business processes and information that cannot be patented, copyrighted, or trademarked are protected against appropriation by others as trade secrets. These include production techniques.

9.   C. Trademark law protects a distinctive symbol that a manufacturer stamps, prints, or otherwise affixes to the goods it produces to distinguish them from the goods of others. A trademark does not need to be registered to be protected.

10.   B. A certification mark certifies the region, materials, mode of manufacture, quality, or accuracy of goods or services. A collective mark is a certification mark used by members of a cooperative, association, or other organization (a union, in this problem).

Issue Spotters

1.   The developer cannot prevent a competitor from producing another game that is based on gladiators, but the developer can prevent competitors from copying the graphics. An idea itself may not be granted a copyright, but the way in which an idea is expressed may be.

2.   Under the Berne Convention, if an American writes a book, his or her copyright is recognized by every country that has signed the convention. If a citizen of a country that has not signed the convention first publishes a book in a country that has, all other countries that have signed the convention must recognize the author's copyright.

3.   Unlikely. "Apple Balls" is a generic term, and a court will only protect Crabb if consumers are misled into believing that Green's products are in fact manufactured by Crabb. In no event could Apple Balls be a trademark, even if the term had acquired secondary meaning. Generic terms cannot be trademarks.

4.   North King can sue Burley for the theft of trade secrets. Trade secrets include customer lists. Liability extends to those who misappropriate trade secrets by any means, including modems.

5.   This is patent infringement. A software maker in this situation might best protect its product, save litigation costs, and profit from its patent by the use of a license. In the context of this problem, a license would grant permission to sell a patented item. (A license can be limited to certain purposes and to the licensee only.)

Chapter 8

True-False Questions

1. T
2. F. Crime requires the performance of a prohibited act. Most crimes require an act of commission, but some acts of omission (such as not filing a tax return when it is required) are crimes.
3. T
4. T
5. F. Once a state grants immunity from prosecution, a person cannot be prosecuted. He or she can be compelled to answer questions, however.
6. F. These are elements of the crime of robbery.
7. T
8. F. Although the "property" at the heart of the theft of a computer program consists only of magnetic impulses, stealing the program can be larceny.
9. T
10. T

Fill-in Questions

unreasonable; probable; due process of law; jeopardy; trial; trial by; witnesses; bail and fines

Multiple-Choice Questions

1. A. The state prosecutes criminal cases against defendants, whom the prosecution must prove are guilty. Tort law actions are generally intended to compensate the victims. Criminal law actions are generally intended to punish the wrongdoer. This is one of the essential differences between civil and criminal law. A crime is usually declared in a statute, the violation of which is the crime.
2. C. The elements of a crime are the performance of a prohibited act (*actus reus*) and a specified state of mind (*mens rea*).
3. A. In considering the defense of entrapment, the important issue is whether a person who committed a crime was pressured by the police to do so. Entrapment occurs when the police suggest that a crime be committed, pres-sure an individual to commit it, and arrest the individual for it.
4. C. A person in police custody who is to be interrogated must be informed that he or she has the right to remain silent; anything said can and will be used against him or her in court; and he or she has the right to consult with an attorney. The person also must be told that if he or she is indigent, a lawyer will be appointed. These rights may be waived if the waiver is knowing and voluntary.
5. C. Plea bargaining occurs when a defendant in a criminal case is granted immunity in exchange for information, or agrees to plead guilty in exchange for the prosecutor's promise to grant concessions (such as a reduced sentence), or at least seek them.
6. D. April committed larceny. Larceny is the wrongful or fraudulent taking and carrying away by any person of the personal property of another. There was no entrapment, and there is no distance requirement to the crime of larceny—three steps is enough.
7. A. Embezzlement is the fraudulent conversion of property or money owned by one person but entrusted to another. The company entrusted its equipment to its employee; the employee stole it.
8. C. Under the Fourth Amendment to the U.S. Constitution, no warrants for a search (or an arrest) can be issued without probable cause. Proximate cause and causation in fact are parts of the element of causation in a negligence suit. Whether or not an officer intends to search certain premises is not relevant to obtaining a warrant.
9. D. The Fifth Amendment to the U.S. Constitution prohibits double jeopardy. A person may be tried more than once, however, if there is no verdict in the first trial. A person may also be tried separately in state and federal courts for separate crimes arising from the same occurrence. A person may also be subject to a civil suit in addition to criminal prosecution.
10. D. If a confession is obtained after an illegal arrest, the confession is normally excluded. This is known as the exclusionary rule, under which all evidence obtained in violation of the constitutional rights spelled out in the Fourth, Fifth, and Sixth Amendments

normally is excluded, as well as all evidence derived from the illegally obtained evidence. The purpose of the rule is to deter police misconduct.

Issue Spotters

1. No. A mistake of fact, as opposed to a mistake of law, will constitute a defense if it negates the mental state required for the crime. The mental state required for theft involves the knowledge that the property is another's and the intent to deprive the owner of it.

2. Yes. Duress constitutes a defense to a criminal charge if: the threat is of serious bodily harm or death, the harm that is threatened is greater than the harm that will be caused by the crime, the threat is immediate and inescapable, and the situation arose through no fault of the accused.

3. Yes. Forgery is the fraudulent making or altering of any writing that changes the legal liability of another. In some instances, however, authorization to sign another's name negates a charge of forgery.

4. Yes. With respect to the gas station, she has obtained goods by false pretenses. She might also be charged with forgery, and most states have special statutes covering illegal use of credit cards.

5. Yes. Federal law makes it a crime to use the mails, a telegram, a telephone, radio, or television to defraud. Carl has committed a violation of federal wire fraud statutes.

Chapter 9

True-False Questions

1. F. Whether a party outside the geographical limits of a court's jurisdiction can be compelled to appear depends on the contacts that the party has within those limits.

2. F. Courts do not always consider encryption code to be "speech." U.S. Department of Commerce regulations of encryption code have been challenged as violations of the First Amendment's protection for freedom of speech, but the challenges have not generally been successful.

3. T

4. F. Harassing a person in cyberspace—cyberstalking—is prohibited by federal law and by about half the states.

5. T

6. F. What the government can do to restrict spam, or junk e-mail, is limited by the First Amendment's protection for freedom of speech. The sending of spam may constitute trespass to personal property, however, and thus could be curtailed by private lawsuits.

7. T

8. F. This is the making of a "copy" for purposes of U.S. copyright law, but it is not clear what constitutes the making of a "copy" in electronic form for purposes of international law.

9. F. The security of e-money payment information is not specifically guaranteed by federal, state, or international laws. In fact, although some statutes and common law principles apply to situations involving e-money, it is not otherwise entirely clear what law applies to this means of payment.

10. T

Fill-in Questions

trademark; trademark; patent; copyright

Multiple-Choice Questions

1. A. On a "sliding scale" test, a court's exercise of personal jurisdiction depends on the amount of business that an individual or firm transacts over the Internet. Jurisdiction is most likely proper when there is substantial business, most likely improper when a Web site is no more than an ad, and may or may not be appropriate when there is some interactivity. "Any" interactivity with "any resident" of a state would likely not be enough, however.

2. C. Under the First Amendment, a library can impose content-based restrictions on access to the Internet only on showing "a compelling state interest" (preventing children from viewing obscene materials, for example) and "a means narrowly drawn to achieve that end." The means must be a reasonable response that will alleviate the targeted harm in a direct and material way. The other choices here are too broad, or given the nature of the Internet, unrealistic, and therefore unreasonable.

3. D. Under the Communications Decency Act, an Internet service provider (ISP) may not be held liable for defamatory statements made by its customers online. Congress provided this immunity as an incentive to ISPs to "self-police" the Internet for offensive material.

4. D. Trespass to personal property is intentional physical contact with another's personal property that causes damage. Sending spam through an Internet service provider (ISP) is intentional contact with the ISP's computer systems. A negative impact on the value of the ISP's equipment, by using its processing power to transmit e-mail, constitutes damage (the resources are not available for the ISP's customers). Also, service cancellations harm an ISP's business reputation and goodwill.

5. B. A party can use another's trademark that describes, and is used fairly and in good faith only to describe, the party using the mark. This is "fair use." The party using the mark as a tag must not attempt to confuse visitors to its Web site into believing that it is related to the owner of the mark.

6. C. In this problem, the license is an agreement that permits the use of a trademark for certain purposes. The licensee is allowed to use the mark of the licensor as part of the licensee's domain name. The licensee broke the terms of the license, however, by redesigning its Web site to resemble the licensor's. This is trademark infringement.

7. D. Publishers can put the contents of their periodicals into online databases and other electronic resources, including CD-ROMs, without securing the permission of the writers whose contributions are included, if the "new" versions qualify as "revisions" under the Copyright Act. To qualify, the "new" publication has to be an original selection or arrangement, which can be accomplished by, for example, retaining an original selection of articles.

8. B. Although data may be legally compiled with the awareness and consent of consumers, it may not be distributed to others if the collector of the data represents that it will not. The Federal Trade Commission Act, for example, prohibits unfair or deceptive practices in, or affecting, commerce. This can include misrepresentation.

9. A. A product that is offered for sale on the Web and for which payment is collected, but which is never delivered, is a common type of cyber fraud. Other types include phony bidding in Web auctions, false promises of profits for investing in scams, and schemes in which profits are made from recruiting others instead of from sales of goods or services.

10. A. By disseminating fictitious testimonials, a business commits fraud. It is the falsity of the content of the testimonial that serves as the basis for the violation. If the violation is online, it is cyber fraud. This may violate the Federal Trade Commission Act, as well as a state false advertising statute.

Issue Spotters

1. Some courts have upheld exercises of jurisdiction on the basis of the accessibility of a Web page. Other courts have concluded that without more, a presence on the Web is not enough to support jurisdiction over a nonresident. The standard that is generally accepted for evaluating the exercise of jurisdiction based on contacts over the Internet, however, is a "sliding scale." On the scale, a court's exercise of personal jurisdiction depends on the amount of business that an individual or firm transacts over the Internet. A passive ad would not be enough to exercise jurisdiction.

2. No. Law enforcement authorities are afraid that the wrong persons (criminals or terrorists) would use encryption software to engage in illegal activities. U.S. Department of Commerce regulations ban the export of encryption software. It is also a violation of a federal criminal statute. The law has been challenged on the ground that encryption code is speech protected by the First Amendment. Courts have held, however, that encryption code is not speech, because its purpose is functional (not communication).

3. Yes. The National Information Infrastructure Protection Act of 1996 amended the Counterfeit Access Device and Computer Fraud and Abuse Act of 1984. The statute provides that a person who accesses a computer online, without permission, to obtain classified data (such as consumer credit files in a credit agency's database) is subject to criminal prosecution. The crime has two elements: accessing the computer without permission and taking data. It is a felony if done for private financial gain. Penalties include fines and imprisonment for up to twenty years. The victim of the theft can also bring a civil suit against the criminal to obtain damages and other relief.

4.   Yes. This may be an instance of trademark dilution. Dilution occurs when a trademark is used, without permission, in a way that diminishes the distinctive quality of the mark. Dilution does not require proof that consumers are likely to be confused by a connection between the unauthorized use and the mark. The products involved do not have to be similar. Dilution does require, however, that a mark be famous when the dilution occurs.

5.   Yes. The agreement between these parties is a licensing agreement. This is a way by which a party can make use of another's patented product, trademark, copyrighted work, or trade secret. A license is an agreement to permit the use of the object of the agreement for certain purposes. A licensee might be allowed to incorporate the product of the licensor into its own products, for example, without otherwise altering the licensed product. Breaking the terms of the license, however, could result in liability.

Cumulative Hypothetical Problem for Unit One—Including Chapter s 1–9

1.   C. Intellectual property law protects such intangible rights as copyrights, trademarks, and patents, which include the rights that an individual or business firm has in the products it produces. Protection for software comes from patent law and from copyright law. Protection for the distinguishing trademarks on the software come from, of course, trademark law.

2.   D. Of these choices, the firm most likely violated tort law, which includes negligence and strict liability, both as distinct torts and as a part of product liability. Negligence requires proof of intent. Strict liability does not. These firms may also have breached their

contracts and their warranties, topics which are discussed in the next Unit.

3.   D. These state and federal courts would all have jurisdiction over the defendant. The customer's state could exercise jurisdiction over the firm through its long arm statute. The firm's state would have jurisdiction over it as a resident. A federal court could hear the case under its diversity jurisdiction: the parties are residents of different states and the amount in controversy is at least $75,000.

4.   B. This is cyber theft. Accessing a computer online, without authority, to obtain classified, restricted, or protected data, or attempting to do so is prohibited by the National Information Infrastructure Protection Act of 1996. Penalties include fines and imprisonment for up to twenty years.

5.   A. A corporation cane be held liable for the crimes of its employees, officers, or directors. Imprisonment is not possible, in a practical sense, as a punishment for a corporation. A business firm can be fined or denied certain privileges, however.

Chapter 10

True-False Questions

1.   F. All contracts involve promises, but all promises do not establish legal contracts. Contract law reflects society's determination of the kinds of promises that should be legally enforced.

2.   T

3.   F. Consideration is the inducement—reason, cause, motive, or price—to a contract.

4.   T

5.   F. Formal contracts require a special form or method of formation to be enforceable. All other contracts are informal contracts.

6.   F. An unenforceable contract is a valid contract that cannot be enforced due to certain defenses. A voidable contract is a valid contract in which one or both of the parties has the option of avoiding his or her legal obligations.

7.   T

8.   T

9.   T

10.   T

Fill-in Questions

objective; objective; did; circumstances surrounding; in a particular transaction

Multiple-Choice Questions

1. A. An express contract is a contract in which the terms are fully expressed in words, but those words do not necessarily have to be in writing. A contract that is implied from conduct is an implied-in-fact contract. Implied-in-law (or quasi) contracts are not actual contracts but are imposed on parties by courts.

2. D. An obligation to pay Don will be imposed by law to prevent Mick from being unjustly enriched at Don's expense. Mick *knew* of the benefit being conferred by Don and accepted it, even though there was no contract between them.

3. A. According to the objective theory of contracts, a party's intention to enter into a contract is judged by outward, objective facts as they would be interpreted by a reasonable person, rather than by the party's own subjective intentions. Forgetfulness on the part of a party making an offer is part of the party's subjective intent—a reasonable person in the position of a party receiving an offer can know what is in the offer only from what is offered.

4. B. Rona has performed; Greg has not. If one party has fully performed but the other has not, the contract is said to be executed on the one side and executory on the other, and it is classified as executory.

5. B. An implied-in-fact contracts looks at actions leading up to what happened. Lee furnished services, expecting to be paid, which Mary should have known, and Mary had a chance to reject Lee's services and did not.

6. A. The four requirements that constitute what are known as the elements of a contract include agreement, consideration, contractual capacity, and legality. Defenses to the enforcement of a contract include a lack of genuineness of assent and the use of the wrong form for the contract (for example, a contract that should be in writing is not).

7. B. The primary purpose of the rules for the interpretation of contracts is to give effect to the parties' intent as expressed in their contract. When a contract is clear and unequivocal, a court will enforce it according to its plain meaning.

8. C. One of the rules for the interpretation of contracts is that all writings that are part of the same transaction will be interpreted together. Terms that were negotiated separately will be given greater consideration, however, than standardized terms and terms that were not negotiated separately.

9. D. A minor can choose to avoid his or her obligations under a contract. This makes a minor's contracts voidable. A voidable contract is, however, a valid contract—that is, it can be enforced if, in this case, the minor does not choose to avoid the obligations.

10. D. A contract is an agreement that can be enforced in a court. It is formed by two or more parties who promise to do or not do something now or in the future.

Issue Spotters

1. Under the objective theory of contracts, if a reasonable person would have thought that Ellen accepted Buck's offer when Ellen signed and returned the letter, a contract was made, and Ellen is bound. This depends in part on what was said in the letter—was it a valid offer?—and what was said in response—was it a valid acceptance? The issue is not whether either party subjectively believed that they did, or did not, have a contract.

2. Yes. A person who is unjustly enriched at the expense of another can be required to account for the benefit under the theory of quasi contract. The parties here did not have a contract, but the law will impose one to avoid the unjust enrichment.

3. No. This "contract" is for an illegal purpose and therefore void. A void contract gives rise to no legal obligation on the part of any party. A contract that is void is no contract. There is nothing to enforce.

4. The handwritten term controls. The rules of contract interpretation favor handwritten terms over printed ones. Terms that are the subject of separate negotiation (as a handwritten term added to a contract would almost certainly be) are given greater consideration than terms that are standardized (as imprinted terms in a standard form contract would almost certainly be).

5. Under the plain meaning rule (when a writing is clear and unequivocal, it will be enforced according to its plain meaning), the court could agree with Lou. The court might reason that the language in the contract was chosen by the bank (an ambiguous term is interpreted against the party who drafted the contract).

Chapter 11

True-False Questions

1. T

2. F. One of the elements for a valid offer is that the terms be definite enough to be enforced by a court. The term "a fair share" is too indefinite to constitute an enforceable term.

3. T

4. F. Irrevocable offers—offers that must be kept open for a period of time—include option contracts. Other irrevocable offers include a merchant's firm offer and, under the doctrine of promissory estoppel, an offer on which an offeree has changed position in reliance.

5. F. The mirror image rule (according to which the terms of an acceptance must exactly match the terms of an offer) is still effective over contracts not governed by the UCC, as well some UCC contracts.

6. F. Normally, silence cannot be acceptance, but it can operate as acceptance when: an offeree takes the benefit of offered goods or services (even though he or she had an opportunity to reject and knew that they were offered with the expectation of compensation); the parties have had prior dealings in which the offeree has led the offeror reasonably to understand that the offeree will accept all offers unless he or she sends notice to the contrary; or if one has agreed that his or her failure to respond will constitute acceptance.

7. F. An offer terminates automatically when the time specified in the offer has passed. The offeree does not need to be given "one last chance" to accept.

8. F. Except in certain special circumstances, only the person to whom an offer is made can accept it.

9. T

10. T

Fill-in Questions

serious; offeror; reasonably definite; offeree

Multiple-Choice Questions

1. B. In these circumstances, the rule of acceptance on dispatch (the mailbox rule) dictates that the acceptance is effective when sent. When an offeree uses a method of communication expressly authorized by an offeror, acceptance is effective on dispatch.

2. C. In general, ads are treated as invitations to negotiate, not offers. This question and answer are based on a question that appeared in the CPA exam in May 1981.

3. B. This statement makes a second offer without rejecting the first offer. An offeree may make an offer without rejecting the original offer, in which case two offers exist, each capable of acceptance.

4. A. The other replies are conditional. When an acceptance is made conditional, it constitutes a rejection.

5. C. An offer terminates on the offeror's death.

6. C. Generally, an offer may be revoked any time before acceptance. Most offers are revocable even if they say that they are not.

7. C. In an auction with reserve, the bidder is the offeror. The auctioneer may reject a bid before the auctioneer strikes the hammer, which constitutes acceptance of the bid.

8. B. Silence can constitute acceptance in only a few circumstances, as is the case when the parties expect it—if, for example, a prior course of dealing indicates that notice is not required.

9. B. Under the mailbox rule, if an offeree uses a mode of communication expressly or impliedly authorized by the offeror, acceptance is effective when sent. Here, the mode was impliedly authorized because the offeror did not specify a particular mode. In such circumstances, whatever mode the offeror used to make the offer is reasonable to use to accept.

10. B. Traditional rules of contract apply to new forms of communication. Under the mailbox rule, using a mode of communication impliedly authorized by the offeror makes an acceptance effective when sent. Here, the offeror did not specify a certain mode, so the mode the offeror used to make the offer was a reasonable means of acceptance.

Issue Spotters

1. No. Taking into account Jane's frustration and the obvious difference between the value of her car and the purchase price, a reasonable person would declare that her offer was not made with serious intent and that you did not have an agreement.

2. Yes. An offer must be communicated to the offeree, so that the offeree knows it. For example, a reward must be communicated so that the offeree knows of it. If so, the offeree can claim the reward for doing whatever the reward was offered for doing.

3. No. Revocation of an offer may be implied by conduct inconsistent with the offer. When the corporation hired someone else, and the offeree learned of the hiring, the offer was revoked. The acceptance was too late.

4. No. An offer terminates if the offeror dies.

5. No. The offeree's power to accept the offer was strictly limited to a specific time and method. If that method is not used and that time is not met, the power to accept lapses.

Chapter 12

True-False Questions

1. F. Ordinarily, courts will not evaluate the adequacy of consideration, unless it is grossly inadequate or so unfair as to indicate the existences of fraud, duress, incapacity, undue influence, or a lack of bargained-for exchange.

2. T

3. F. Promises based on past consideration—that is, promises made with respect to events that have already happened—are unenforceable. They lack the element of bargained-for consideration.

4. T

5. F. A promise does have value as consideration. Consideration may consist of goods, money, performance, or a promise.

6. T

7. F. Unlike a release, a covenant not to sue does not always bar further recovery. If one party does not do what he or she promised, the other party can file a suit for breach of contract.

8. F. When a debt is liquidated, it is not in dispute—it is a preexisting obligation. A preexisting obligation cannot be consideration. For an accord and satisfaction, a debt must be disputed. The consideration is the parties' giving up their legal right to contest the amount of debt.

9. T

10. T

Fill-in Questions

promise; detriment; promisor; promise; enforced; promisee; substantial

Multiple-Choice Questions

1. A. To constitute consideration, the value of whatever is exchanged for the promise must be legally sufficient. Its economic value (its "adequacy") is rarely the basis for a court's refusal to enforce a contract.

2. B. Consideration must be bargained for. Performance or a promise is bargained for if, as in this problem, the promisor seeks it in exchange for his or her promise and the promisee gives it in exchange for that promise.

3. D. Generally, a promise to do what one already has a legal duty to do is not legally sufficient consideration, because no legal detriment or benefit has been incurred or received. This is the preexisting duty rule.

4. A. Past consideration is no consideration. Promises made with respect to past consideration are not enforceable. This question and answer are based on a question that appeared in the May 1995 CPA exam.

5. A. In a covenant not to sue, the parties substitute a contractual obligation for some other type of legal action, such as a tort. A covenant not to sue does not always bar further recovery, unlike a release.

6.   C. John signed a valid, enforceable release. No fraud was involved. Consideration was given in the form of the insurance company's promise to pay John $5,000 in return for John's promise not to sue for a larger amount.

7.   A. This is an example of an accord and satisfaction. An unliquidated debt is one whose amount is not settled, and acceptance of payment of a lesser sum can operate as a satisfaction, or discharge, of it.

8.   A. A debtor who promises to pay a debt barred by a statute of limitations makes an enforceable promise. In effect, the promise extends the limitations period, and the creditor can sue to recover the amount promised. Such a promise covers only the debt to which it relates, however.

9.   A. A person who reasonably relies on the promise of another to that person's detriment can recover under the doctrine of promissory estoppel. There must be (1) a promise, (2) reliance on the promise, (3) reliance of a substantial, definite nature, and (4) justice in the enforcement of the promise.

10.   C. A release is generally binding if it is (1) given in good faith, (2) stated in a signed writing (which is required in many states), and (3) accompanied by consideration.

Issue Spotters

1.   Yes. The original contract was executory. The parties rescinded it and agreed to a new contract. If the employee had broken the contract to accept a contract with another employer, she might have been held liable for damages for the breach.

2.   No. The promise is illusory, because performance is uncertain—it depends solely on the discretion of management. There is no bargained-for consideration, and thus, there is no enforceable promise.

3.   Yes. Under the doctrine of promissory estoppel(or detrimental reliance), the promisee is entitled to payment of $5,000 when she graduates. There was a promise, on which she relied, her reliance was substantial and definite (she

went to college for nearly four years, incurring considerable expenses), and it would only be fair to enforce the promise.

4.   Yes. The forbearance to drink liquor is a performance and, assuming that it was bargained for, is consideration for the promise to pay money.

5.   No. An unliquidated debt is one whose amount is in dispute, and acceptance of a lesser sum can discharge it. In this case, consideration is given: the parties give up the right to contest the amount in dispute.

Chapter 13

True-False Questions

1.   T

2.   T

3.   F. A contract entered into by a person intoxicated enough to lack mental capacity is voidable at the option of the intoxicated person.

4.   F. When parents relinquish control over their children, the children assume full contractual capacity and lose the right to disaffirm.

5.   T

6.   T

7.   F. An adhesion contract may be deemed unconscionable if its terms are so unfair as to be harsh and oppressive. The typical case involves an agreement between parties with unequal bargaining power.

8.   F. An illegal contract is void.

9.   T

10.   F. A covenant not to compete may be upheld if the length of time and the size of the area in which the party agrees not to compete are reasonable.

Fill-in Questions

ratification; disaffirm; indicates; ratification

Multiple-Choice Questions

1.   C. Ratification is accepting and thus giving legal force to an obligation that was previously unenforceable. Most contracts with minors are not fully enforceable until the minor reaches the age of majority. Similarly, a minor cannot effectively ratify a contract until he

or she attains majority. This question and answer are based on a question that appeared in the May 1993 CPA exam.

2.   A.   If a person was intoxicated enough to lack mental capacity, the contract is voidable at his or her option. Being intoxicated enough to lack mental capacity means being so impaired as not to comprehend the consequences of entering into a contract. Otherwise, the contract is enforceable.

3.   C.   A guardian can enter into legally binding contracts on a person's behalf if the person has been adjudged mentally incompetent by a court of law.

4.   A.   To disaffirm a fully executed contract, a minor must return whatever he or she received under the contract. A minor can never partially disaffirm a contract. That is, he or she must return all of whatever he or she received and still has in his or her possession or control.

5.   C.   The general rule is that an illegal contract is void. If an illegal agreement is executory, with the illegal part not yet performed, the party whose performance has not been rendered can withdraw. The person cannot be held in breach, and the contract cannot be enforced.

6.   C.   Al's promise—a covenant not to compete—is not unenforceable, because it is no broader than necessary for Dan's protection. Such promises may be considered contracts in restraint of trade, illegal on grounds of public policy, when they are broader than necessary, or are not accompanied by a sale of a business.

7.   A.   A contract with an unlicensed individual is illegal when the purpose of a licensing statute is to protect the public from unauthorized practitioners. If the purpose of the statute is to raise revenue, however, the contract is enforceable.

8.   D.   The reasonableness of a covenant not to compete, accompanied by the sale of a business, is determined by the length of time and the size of the area in which the party agrees not to compete. In most cases, one year and one county would be very reasonable.

9.   D.   An exculpatory clause—a contract clause attempting to absolve a party of negligence or other wrongs—is often held unconscionable, especially in cases in which an employer is attempting to avoid liability for injury to an employee. A contract clause that is held to be unconscionable is not enforced.

10.   B.   A contract with an unlicensed individual may be enforceable depending on the nature of the applicable licensing statute. If the statute bars the enforcement of such contracts, of course they are not enforceable. They are also not enforceable if the statute's purpose is to protect the public from unlicensed practitioners. Otherwise, if the statute is intended only to raise revenue, such contracts may be enforceable.

Issue Spotters

1.   No. Joan may disaffirm this contract. Because the apartment was a necessary, however, she remains liable for the reasonable value of her occupancy of the apartment.

2.   Yes. A contract made by a person who is so intoxicated that he or she does not know what he or she is doing is voidable, particularly if the other party has reason to know of the intoxication. The circumstances indicate that Nick did not know what he was doing and that Dave took advantage of the situation—the consideration was inadequate, and the transaction was not one that a reasonably competent person would have made.

3.   Yes. The effect of mental incompetency on executory contracts is similar to that of minority. Regardless of the other party's knowledge and of the fairness of contractual terms, an incompetent person, on regaining competency, can affirm or disaffirm a contract, if he or she does so within a reasonable time.

4.   No. A contract that calls for something that is prohibited by statute is illegal and thus void and unenforceable.

5.   No. Generally, An exculpatory clause (a clause attempting to absolve parties of negligence or other wrongs) is not enforced if the party seeking its enforcement is involved in a business that is important to the public as a matter of practical necessity, such as an airline. Because of the essential nature of these services, they have an advantage in bargaining strength and could insist that anyone contracting for their services agree not to hold them liable.

Chapter 14

True-False Questions

1.   T
2.   F. If the parties to both sides of a contract are mistaken as to the same material fact, the contract can be rescinded by any party at any time.
3.   T
4.   T
5.   T
6.   T
7.   F. If the parties to the contract had substantially unequal bargaining positions and enforcement would be unfair or oppressive, the contract will not be enforced. A court may base its decision on the doctrine of unconscionability, or on traditional concepts of fraud, undue influence, or duress.
8.   F. A person can misrepresent a material fact without intending to defraud. This is known as innocent misrepresentation. A party who contracts with the person in reliance on the statement may be able to rescind the contract.
9.   F. If a defect is serious (such as the risks of a medical procedure), it must be disclosed. The general rule is, however, that neither party to a contract has a duty to speak. Also, if a defect is obvious, a buyer cannot justifiably rely on a seller's representations.
10.   F. When both parties to a contract make a mistake as to the market value or quality of the object of their deal, the contract can be *enforced* by either party. Mutual mistakes of *material fact* permit rescission by either party.

Fill-in Questions

value; value; cannot; value

Multiple-Choice Questions

1.   A.   Generally, a unilateral mistake—a mistake on the part of only one of the parties—does not give the mistaken party any right to relief. There are two exceptions. One of the exceptions is that the rule does not apply if the other party knew or should have known that a mistake was made. This question and answer are based a question that appeared in the CPA exam in May 1995.
2.   B. One of the elements of fraudulent misrepresentation is an innocent party's reliance on the deceiving party's false statements. Such reliance can occur when the innocent party does not know the true facts and has no way of finding them out.
3.   B. When parties contract, their agreement establishes the value of the object of their transaction for the moment. Each party is considered to assume the risk that the value will change or prove to be different from what he or she thought. In this case, the buyer assumed the risk of a drop in the price.
4.   C. The contract may be avoided on the ground of undue influence. The inexperienced seller is justified, in these circumstances, in assuming that her nephew will not act in a manner inconsistent with her best interests.
5.   B. The elements of fraudulent misrepresentation are misrepresentation of a material fact, intent to deceive, and the innocent party's justifiable reliance on the misrepresentation. The misrepresentation must be an important factor in inducing the party to contract—reliance is not justified if the party knows or should know the truth.
6.   C. Fraudulent misrepresentation refers to misrepresentation that is intended to mislead another. The perpetrator must know or believe that the assertion is not true. Representations of future facts, statements of opinion, and most laypersons' statements about the law are generally not subject to claims of fraud.
7.   A. An adhesion contract (which is what a standard form contract often is) may not be enforced if the adhering party (the buyer, in this problem) shows that the parties had substantially unequal bargaining positions and enforcement would be unfair or oppressive. Such a contract may be avoided on grounds of unconscionability (the most likely possibility here), fraud, undue influence, or duress.
8.   B. Proof of an injury is required to recover damages on the ground of misrepresentation. Proof of an injury is not generally required to rescind a contract on that basis.

9. B. Normally, a party to a contract does not have a duty to disclose defects. If a serious defect is known to the seller that is not known or could not be reasonably suspected by the buyer, however, the contract may be avoided by the buyer on the basis of misrepresentation.

10. D. Threatening to exercise a legal right, such as the right to sue to enforce a contract, is not duress. It is also not misrepresentation or undue influence.

Issue Spotters

1. No. When parties base their contract on a common assumption about a material fact that proves false, the transaction may be avoided if because of the mistake a different exchange of values occurs from the exchange of values that the parties contemplated. In other words, what the buyer actually found on the property was not part of the bargain between the buyer and the seller.

2. No. The accountant exerted economic duress on the other party. The threat to break a contract on the eve of the deadline in this problem was sufficiently coercive to constitute duress. Duress involves coercive conduct—forcing a party to enter into a contract by threatening the party with a wrongful act.

3. Yes. Rescission may be granted on the basis of fraudulent misrepresentation. The elements of fraudulent misrepresentation include intent to deceive, or *scienter*. *Scienter* exists if a party makes a statement recklessly, without regard to whether it is true or false, or if a party says or implies that a statement is made on some basis such as personal knowledge or personal investigation when it is not.

4. Yes. The accountant may be liable on the ground of negligent misrepresentation. A misrepresentation is negligent if a person fails to exercise reasonable care in disclosing material facts or does not use the skill and competence required by his or her business or profession.

5. Yes. The attorney's conduct may not amount to misrepresentation (a statement of value is generally considered an opinion, not a representation, if the individual making it has no experience in the particular matter) or duress (the advice was unfairly persuasive, not coercive). The conduct does amount to undue influence, however, because the seller is justified in assuming that the attorney will not act in a manner inconsistent with the seller's welfare.

Chapter 15

True-False Questions

1. T

2. F. A promise ancillary to a principal transaction and made by a third party to assume the debts or obligations of the primary party must generally be in writing to be enforceable. But there is an exception: an oral promise to answer for the debt of another is enforceable if the guarantor's main purpose is to secure a personal benefit.

3. F. Under the doctrine of promissory estoppel, an oral contract may be enforced if a promisor makes a promise on which the promisee justifiably relies to his or her detriment, the reliance was foreseeable to the promisor, and injustice can be avoided only by enforcing the promise..

4. T

5. F. A contract for customized goods may be enforceable under the UCC even if it is only oral. Also, oral agreements between merchants that have been confirmed in writing may be enforceable.

6. F. The Statute of Frauds requires that contracts for all transfers of interests in land be in writing to be enforceable. Included are sales, mortgages, leases, and other transfers.

7. F. The UCC's Statute of Frauds requires that contracts for sales of goods priced at $500 or more be in writing to be enforceable.

8. T

9. F. A writing sufficient to satisfy the Statute of Frauds may be an invoice, a confirmation memo, a letter, or a combination of documents, typewritten, imprinted, or handwritten. Generally, such a writing must state the essential terms and be signed by the party against whom the contract is being enforced (although the requirements vary with the type of contract).

10. F. Under the parol evidence rule, if the parties' contract is completely integrated into a writing (which they intend to be the embodiment of their agreement), evidence of their prior negotiations, prior agreements, or contemporaneous oral agreements that contradicts or varies the terms of the contract is not admissible.

Fill-in Questions

ancillary; primary; must; need not

Multiple-Choice Questions

1. B. This contract could not be performed within one year. (The contracts in answer choices *a* and *c* are of uncertain duration and thus could terminate within a year.)

2. C. A contract that cannot be performed within one year must be in writing to be enforceable. Because the employee was hired to work for one year several days before the employment began, the contract cannot be performed within a year.

3. B. Under the parol evidence rule, if a writing that is determined to constitute a contract includes everything that the parties intended, no evidence of prior negotiations, prior agreements, or contemporaneous oral negotiations may be used to change the terms. A later oral agreement is admissible, however. This question and answer are based on a question that appeared as part of the CPA exam in May 1995.

4. D. Under the Statute of Frauds, a contract for the sale of an interest in land must be in writing to be enforceable. A party to an oral contract involving an interest in land cannot force the other party to buy or sell the property.

5. C. This is an exception to the rule that a contract for a transfer of an interest in land is not enforceable unless it is in writing. If a buyer pays part of the price, takes possession, and makes permanent improvements and the parties cannot be returned to their pre-contract status quo, a court may grant specific performance of an oral contract for the transfer of an interest in land.

6. A. The Statute of Frauds requires only a writing signed by the party against whom enforcement is sought. Thus, a signed sales receipt may be enough. A purchase order that is not signed by either party would not qualify, regardless of the details that are included on the form.

7. D. Letterhead stationery, and even a business card, might qualify as a signed writing. But neither would be sufficient proof on which to enforce a contract without proof of the necessary terms—parties, subject matter, price, and consideration. In the case of a sale of property, in some states those terms include price and a description of the property.

8. C. Under the Uniform Commercial Code, a contract for a sale of goods for the price of $500 *or more* must be in writing to be enforceable.

9. A. A collateral promise must be in writing to be enforceable unless the main purpose of the guarantor is to secure a benefit for himself or herself. Because the main purpose of the guarantor here does not appear to be to secure a benefit for himself, this promise must be in writing.

10. A. If the main purpose of a guarantor in accepting secondary liability is to serve a benefit for himself or herself, the contract need not be in writing to be enforceable. Here, the guaranty is to serve the guarantor's purpose, so it does not need to be in writing to be enforced.

Issue Spotters

1. No. Under the parol evidence rule, if a writing that is determined to constitute a contract includes a clause that no oral statements are incorporated, then no evidence of prior negotiations, prior agreements, or contemporaneous oral statements may be used to change the terms.

2. Yes. Letterhead stationery can constitute a signature. If the memo names the parties, the subject matter, the consideration, and the quantity involved in the transaction, it may be sufficient to be enforced against the party whose letterhead appears on it.

3. No. Under the UCC, a contract for a sale of goods priced at $500 or more must be in writing to be enforceable. In this case, the contract is not enforceable beyond the quantity already delivered and paid for.

4. The court might conclude that under the doctrine of promissory estoppel, the employer is estopped from claiming the lack of a written contract as a defense. The oral contract may be enforced because the employer made a promise on which the employee justifiably relied in moving to New York, the reliance was foreseeable, and injustice can be avoided only by enforcing the promise. If the court strictly enforces the Statute of Frauds, however, the employee may be without a remedy.

5. Possibly. If a party admits in pleadings, testimony, or in court that a contract was made, in some states the contract will be enforceable even if it was originally oral.

Chapter 16

True-False Questions

1. F. Intended beneficiaries have legal rights in the contract under which they benefit. Third parties who benefit from a contract only incidentally—that is, incidental beneficiaries—normally do not.

2. T

3. F. In an assignment, the party assigning the rights is the *assignor*. The *obligor* is the party who was originally obligated to perform for the assignor. The party who receives the rights on an assignment is the assignee (who may also be the obligee).

4. F. A right cannot be assigned if (1) a statute expressly prohibits its assignment; (2) a contract stipulates that it cannot be assigned; (3) it is under a contract that is uniquely personal; or (4) assignment would materially increase or alter the risk of the obligor.

5. T

6. T

7. F. An assignment is effective with or without notice. Until the obligor has notice of the assignment, however, the obligor can discharge his or her obligation by performance to the assignor. Also, if the same right is assigned without notice to more than one party, there may be a question as to who has priority.

8. T

9. T

10. T

Fill-in Questions

an assignment; a delegation; assigned; assign

Multiple-Choice Questions

1. A. GMC is an incidental beneficiary because GMC cannot enforce the contract between Greg and Dan. The benefit that GMC will receive from the contract is unintentional.

2. D. Ben is the assignor, Carol is the obligor, and Doug is the assignee. An assignee has a right to demand performance from the obligor, but the assignee takes only those rights that the assignor originally had, and these rights are subject to defenses that the obligor has against the assignor. The obligor's assent is not necessary for an effective assignment.

3. B. The rights of an intended third party beneficiary to a contract vest when the original parties cannot rescind or change the contract without the third party's consent. This occurs when the beneficiary learns of the contract and manifests assent to it.

4. A. Burt can sell the business just as Jenny did, and assign the right not to have her compete. A contract right that consists of protection against the impairment of a business (the covenant not to compete, in this problem) is assignable.

5. C. Delegating a duty does not normally free the delegator of the obligation to perform if the delegatee does not do so. Ordinarily, if a delegatee (Sally, in this problem) fails to perform, the delegator (Dick) remains liable to the obligee (Jane).

6. D. The presence of one or more of any of these factors strongly indicates that a third party is an intended, rather than an incidental, beneficiary.

7. D. An assignment is not valid if it materially increases or alters the risk or duties of the obligor. An assignment is also invalid if a statute prohibits it, if it involves a contract for personal services, or if, with some exceptions, the contract stipulates that it cannot be assigned. This question and answer are based on a question that appeared in the CPA exam in May 1995.

8. A. An anti-assignment contract clause is generally effective, but there are exceptions. One of those exceptions concerns the right to receive damages for the breach of a sales contract. The assignment of such a right is valid, even if the contract prohibits it.

9. D. The effect of an unconditional assignment is to extinguish the rights of the assignor. Such an assignment also gives the assignee a right to demand performance from the obligor. Of course, the assignee's rights are subject to the defenses the obligor has against the assignor.

10. C. An assignment does not require notice. When an assignor assigns the same right to different persons, in most states the first to receive the assignment is the first in right.

Issue Spotters

1. Yes. When one person makes a promise with the intention of benefiting a third person, the third person can sue to enforce it. This is a third party beneficiary contract. The third party is the intended beneficiary.

2. Yes. When Penny assigns her right to Charlie, Penny's right to the money is extinguished, and Charlie acquires the right against Abby to receive the money.

3. Yes. An assignee takes only those rights that the assignor originally had, and those rights are subject to any defenses that the obligor has against the assignor.

4. Yes. Generally, if a contract makes it clear that a right is not assignable, no assignment will be effective, but there are exceptions, and assignment of the right to receive money cannot be prohibited.

5. No. Performance of the duty under this contract is personal.

Chapter 17

True-False Questions

1. T
2. T
3. F. A material breach of contract—which occurs when performance is not at least substantial—excuses the nonbreaching party from performance. A *minor* breach of contract does not discharge the nonbreaching party's duty to

perform, however, although it will affect his or her performance.

4. F. An executory contract can be rescinded. The parties must make a new agreement. This agreement must qualify to be a contract. (The parties' promises not to perform are consideration for the new contract.)

5. T
6. T
7. T
8. T
9. F. This is anticipatory repudiation and can discharge the nonbreaching party, who can sue to recover damages immediately. The nonbreaching party can also seek a similar contract elsewhere.

10. F. Statutes of limitations limit the period during which a party can sue based on a breach of contract. UCC 2–725, for example, limits the time to four years.

Fill-in Questions

Rescission; Novation; Substitution of a new contract; An accord; accord

Multiple-Choice Questions

1. C. A breach of contract entitles the nonbreaching party to damages, but only a material breach discharges the nonbreaching party from his or her duty to perform under the contract. In this problem, the builder has a claim for the amount due on the contract, but the buyer is entitled to have set off the difference in the value of the building as constructed (that is, to subtract the expense to finish the construction).

2. D. The failure of the bank does not discharge or suspend Gil's duty. The failure was an ordinary business risk—none of the grounds for applying the doctrine of impossibility, commercial impracticability, or temporary impossibility exist.

3. B. Contracts that involve construction need only be performed to the satisfaction of a reasonable person. When a contract requires performance to the satisfaction of a third party, a minority of courts require the personal satisfaction of the third party (who must act honestly and in good faith). A majority of courts require the work to be satisfactory to a reasonable person. In this problem, if the work would satisfy a reasonable person, it must be paid for, regardless of the subjective motivation of the party to whom performance was rendered.

4. A. An accord is an executory contract to perform an act to satisfy a contractual duty that has not been discharged. An accord suspends the original obligation. A satisfaction is the performance of the accord.

5. A. Reneging on an employment contract before the employment starts is anticipatory repudiation of the contract and discharges the nonbreaching party from performance. The nonbreaching party can treat the anticipatory breach as a material breach and sue for damages immediately.

6. A. A condition that must be fulfilled before a party is required to perform is a condition precedent. In other words, the condition precedes the absolute duty to perform.

7. C. Novation substitutes a new party for an original party, by agreement of all the parties. The requirements are a previous valid obligation, an agreement of all the parties to a new contract, extinguishment of the old obligation, and a new, valid contract .

8. C. Agreement and operation of law are valid bases on which contracts are discharged, but most contracts are discharged by the parties' doing what they promised to do.

9. B. On this basis, a contract may be discharged if, for example, after it is made, performance becomes objectively impossible because of a change in the law that renders that performance illegal. This is also the result if one of the parties dies or becomes incapacitated, or the subject matter of the contract is destroyed. This question and answer is based on a question in the May 1995 CPA exam.

10. D. Contracts that have not been fully performed on either side can be rescinded. The parties must make another agreement (which must satisfy the legal requirements for a contract). The parties' promises not to perform are consideration for the new agreement. A contract that has been fully performed on one side can be rescinded only if the party who has performed receives ad-ditional consideration to call off the deal.

Issue Spotters

1. No. General Construction has substantially performed its duties under the contract. For the sake of justice and fairness, Federated will be held to its duty to pay, less damages for the deviation from the contract deadline.

2. Contracts that are executory on both sides—contracts on which neither party has performed—can be rescinded solely by agreement. Contracts that are executed on one side—contracts on which one party has performed—can be rescinded only if the party who has performed receives consideration for the promise to call off the deal.

3. Their deaths before fulfilling the contract discharge both the contract and their estates' liability for their nonperformance.

4. The raising of capital is a condition precedent to performance of the contract. If it is not satisfied, the obligations of the parties are discharged. In other words, under this contract, if the money is not raised, neither party needs to do anything.

5. Yes. Statutes of limitations limit the period during which a party can sue on a cause of action. The running of a limitations statute does not extinguish the contractual obligation, however—the obligor can revive it by making a new promise to perform. Thus, if the time has run out, the breaching party can make a new promise to perform, for which it can be held liable.

Chapter 18

True-False Questions

1. T

2. T

3. F. Nominal damages may be awarded when no actual loss results from a breach of contract—but the breach must be proved. This award establishes that the breaching party acted wrongfully.

4. F. Liquidated damages are certain amounts of money estimated in advance of, and payable on, a breach of contract.

Liquidated means determined, settled, or fixed.

5. T

6. F. Limitation-of-liability clauses may be enforced. Such clauses typically provide that the only remedy for a breach of contract is the replacement or repair of damaged goods, or the refund of the price.

7. T

8. F. There can be no enforceable contract if the doctrine of quasi contract is to be applied. Under this doctrine, to prevent unjust enrichment, the law implies a promise to pay the reasonable value for benefits received.

9. T

10. F. To obtain specific performance, damages must *not* be an adequate remedy. If goods are unique, or a contract involves a sale of land, damages would not adequately compensate an innocent party for a breach of contract, so specific performance is available.

Fill-in Questions

the contract price and the market price; specific performance; the contract price and the market price

Multiple-Choice Questions

1. B. The school is entitled to compensatory damages, which compensate an injured party for the loss of their bargain—that is, for injuries proved to arise directly from the loss. In this case, the loss of the bargain is the loss of the tuition.

2. C. A failure to perform entitles the nonbreaching party to rescind the contract, and the parties must make restitution by returning whatever goods, property, or money were transferred. The bank's failure has no effect on the nonbreaching party's rights.

3. B. The measure of damages on breach of a construction contract depends on which party breaches and when the breach occurs. If, as in this problem, the owner breaches during construction, normally the contractor may recover its profit plus the costs incurred to that point.

4. C. Under a contract for a sale of goods, the usual measure of compensatory damages is the difference between the contract price and the market price—on a seller's breach, the difference between what the seller would have been owed if he or she had performed and what the buyer would have to pay in the current market for the goods.

5. D. On the breach of a contract, the buyer is entitled to be compensated for the loss of the bargain. When, as in this problem, a seller also knew that the buyer would lose business if the goods were not delivered on time, the buyer is entitled to consequential damages. Incidental damages include the rental costs for the substitute goods.

6. D. Specific performance is an award of the act promised in a contract. This remedy is granted when the legal remedy (damages) is inadequate. Damages are generally inadequate for a buyer on the breach of a contract for a sale of land, because every piece of land is considered unique.

7. A. A quasi contract may be imposed when a party has partially performed under a contract that is unenforceable. (An oral contract, the terms of which cannot be performed within one year, is unenforceable under the one-year rule of the Statute of Frauds.) To obtain quasi-contractual relief, a party must show that: (1) he or she conferred a benefit on another, (2) he or she conferred the benefit with the reasonable expectation of being paid, (3) he or she did not act as a volunteer in conferring the benefit, and (4) the party receiving the benefit would be unjustly enriched by retaining the benefit without paying for it.

8. B. If the area or time constraints in a covenant not to compete are unreasonable, some courts will reform the restraints to make them reasonable. Other courts will throw the covenant out altogether. In this problem, the constraints are very likely unreasonable and would be reformed, if not eliminated.

9. A. Under the election of remedies doctrine, a nonbreaching party must choose which remedy to pursue. The purpose of the doctrine is to prevent double recovery: a party may not recover twice for the same harm. This contract provided that keeping the deposit was a remedy. The seller cannot also collect damages.

10. D. If the clause is determined to be a penalty clause, it will be unenforceable. To determine whether a clause is a liquidated damages clause or a penalty clause, consider first whether, when the contract was made, damages would clearly be difficult to estimate in the event of a breach. Second, consider whether the amount set as damages is a reasonable estimate. Two "yeses" mean the clause is enforceable. One "no" means the provision is an unenforceable penalty. This question and answer are based on a question that was in the May 1993 CPA exam.

Issue Spotters

1. Ron is entitled to the benefit of the bargain that was made with George—that is, Ron is entitled to be put in as good a position as he would have been in if the contract had been fully performed. The measure of the benefit is the cost to complete the work ($500). These are compensatory damages.

2. No. To recover damages that flow from the consequences of a breach but that are caused by circumstances beyond the contract (consequential damages), the breaching party must know, or have reason to know, that special circumstances will cause the nonbreaching party to suffer the additional loss.

3. Yes. Contracts for the sale of goods rarely qualify for specific performance, because substantially identical goods can be bought in the market. If goods are unique, however, such as the works of art in this problem, specific performance can be obtained.

4. The doctrine of quasi contract provides a basis for relief when there is no enforceable contract. To recover, a party must show that he or she conferred a benefit on the other party, with the reasonable expectation of being paid. It must also be shown that he or she did not act as a volunteer in conferring the benefit, and the party receiving the benefit would be unjustly enriched by retaining it without paying.

5. This clause is known as an exculpatory clause. In many cases, such clauses are not enforced, but to be effective in any case, all contracting parties must have consented to it. A clause excluding liability for negligence may be enforced if the contract was made by parties in roughly equal bargaining positions, as two large corporations would be.

Cumulative Hypothetical Problem for Unit Two—Including Chapters 10–18

1. D. An offeror can revoke an offer for a bilateral contract, which is what this offer is, any time before it is accepted. This may be after the offeree is aware of the offer.

2. C. Courts impose an objective, or reasonable, analysis in determining whether or not a contract was made and in interpreting its terms. This is known as the objective theory of contracts.

3. B. A mutual mistake of fact may be a ground for relief, but it is not the only mistake for which relief may be granted. Although a party to a contract is not normally granted relief for a unilateral mistake, if the other party knew, or should have known, of the mistake, the law allows for relief.

4. C. A novation completely discharges a party to a contract. Another party assumes the discharged party's obligations. If a party has assigned his or her rights under a contract, he or she may still be liable in the event the assignee defaults. A *executed* accord would allow a party to avoid liability under a contract, but an *unexecuted* accord does not.

5. A. Damages, the remedy at law, is the usual remedy for a breach of contract. Specific performance is granted only if the remedy at law is inadequate, as it is when, for example, the goods that are the subject of a contract are unique. Courts are also reluctant to award specific performance in cases involving contracts for services.

Chapter 19

True-False Questions

1. T
2. T
3. F. If a transaction involves only a service, the common law usually applies (one exception is the serving of food or drink, which is governed by the UCC). When goods and services are combined, courts have disagreed over whether a particular transaction involves a sale of

goods or a rendering of service. Usually, a court will apply the law that applies to whichever feature is dominant.

4. F. Unlike the common law rule that contract modification must be supported by new consideration, the UCC requires no consideration for an agreement modifying a contract.

5. F. A writing will be sufficient if indicates that a contract was intended, if it includes a quantity term, and—except for transactions between merchants—if it is signed by the party against whom enforcement is sought. Most terms can be proved by oral testimony or be supplied by the UCC's open term provisions—a contract is not enforceable beyond the quantity of goods shown in the writing, however, except for output and requirements contracts.

6. T

7. F. Under the CISG, the price term must be specified, or provisions for its specification must be included, in the agreement; a court will not supply a price term. In other words, under the CISG, without a price term, there is no contract.

8. T

9. T

10. T

Fill-in Questions

Course of dealing; Usage of trade; trade; consistent; terms in the agreement

Multiple-Choice Questions

1. D. A sale is defined as "the passing of title from the seller to the buyer for a price." The price may be payable in money or in goods, services, or real estate.

2. B. A merchant is a person who acts in a mercantile capacity, possessing or using expertise specifically related to the goods being sold. A merchant for one type of goods—such as the products the merchant is in business to sell (beverages, in this problem)—is not necessarily a merchant for another type (carbon dioxide, here).

3. A. Under the UCC, a sales contract will not fail for indefiniteness even if one or more terms are left open, as long as the parties intended to make a contract and there is a reasonably certain basis for the court to grant an appropriate remedy. If the price term is left open, for example, and the parties cannot later agree on a price, a court will set the price according to what is reasonable. One exception is the quantity term. If no quantity is specified, in most cases the contract will fail.

4. B. A finance lease involves a lessor who leases (or buys) goods from a supplier and subleases (or leases) them to a lessee. The lessor is typically the financier of the deal. Remember that under a finance lease, the lessee must perform his or her part of the bargain, whether the financier does or not.

5. C. The contract is subject to the Statute of Frauds, and thus should be in waiting to be fully enforceable. A contract that is subject to the Statute of Frauds but is not in writing will be enforceable, however, if payment is made and accepted—but only to the extent of the payment actually made.

6. C. In a transaction between merchants, additional terms in the acceptance of an offer become part of a contract *unless* they materially alter the contract, the offer expressly states that no terms other than those in the offer will be accepted, or the offeror objects to the added terms in a timely fashion.

7. C. A contract in writing that was intended to be a final expression cannot be contradicted by evidence of prior agreements or contemporaneous oral agreements. Some evidence outside the contract is admissible, however. Besides the evidence noted in the correct answer, evidence of what the parties did under the contract—their course of performance—is also admissible.

8. C. A firm offer can only be made by a merchant in a signed writing. The other party does not need to be a merchant. Consideration is not necessary, and no definite period need be specified. This question and answer are based on a question that appeared in the CPA exam in November 1995.

9. A. This is a requirements contract. The UCC imposes a good faith limitation on requirements (and output) contracts: the quantity is the amount that is required (or put out) during a normal production year. Note: output and requirements contracts are exceptions to the rule that contracts without specified quantities are not enforceable.

10. A. Under the CISG—which governs this transaction—international contracts for sales of goods need not be in writing to be enforceable. That is one of the differences between the CISG and the UCC (which requires a writing for contracts involving goods priced at $500 or more).

Starbucks Coffee Co. International Sales Contract Applications

1. B. As stated in the "Breach or Default of Contract" clause on the second page, this contract is subject to Article 2 of the UCC. If the parties to a sales contract do not express some of the terms in writing, including the price term, the contract is still enforceable. A sales contract that must be in writing is only enforceable, however, to the extent of the quantity stated in writing. If these parties did not state the amount of product ordered, the contract may not be enforced because if a quantity term is left out, the court would have no basis for determining a remedy.

2. B. When a seller, as a party to a sales contract, states or otherwise expresses what the goods will be, then the goods must be that. The goods must at least conform to the seller's description of them, wherever that descriptions is, whether in the contract, in promotional materials, on labels, by salespersons, by comparison to a sample, etc. A seller's subjective belief is not the standard. The buyer's subjective belief may be the standard if the contract specifies that the goods must personally satisfy the buyer.

3. C. This clause states the terms for payment under this sales contract and indicates that the buyer has two days after the day of tender in which to pay for the goods or will be considered in breach. The "BREACH OR DEFAULT OF CONTRACT" clause sets out what happens "if either party hereto fails to perform." These are all incentives for the buyer to pay on time.

4. A. This clause allows the buyer to reject nonconforming product, although this is limited to a specific number of days. (Note that the buyer' right to reject does not need to be stated in a contract for the buyer to have that right.) This clause details the procedures that the parties may follow if the product does not meet its description. These are

incentives for the seller to deliver conforming goods.

5. D. This is a destination contract, as indicated by the "ARRIVAL," "DELIVERY," "INSURANCE," and "FREIGHT" clauses. This means that the seller bears the risk of loss until the coffee is delivered to its destination (a "Bonded Public Warehouse" in Laredo, Texas). Risk of loss is discussed in more detail in the following chapter.

Issue Spotters

1. It is a sale of goods. A contract for the sale of a building is a contract for a sale of goods if removal is to be made by the seller. If the buyer is to sever the subject of the contract from the land, the contract is considered a sale of real estate subject to the principles of real property law, not the UCC. Because the contract involved goods priced at less than $500, it did not need to be in writing to be enforceable.

2. Yes. Under the UCC, if a merchant gives assurances in a signed writing that an offer will remain open, the offer is irrevocable. As a car dealer, Lena is a merchant. She promised to keep the offer open for seven days and did not do so.

3. A shipment of nonconforming goods constitutes an acceptance and a breach, unless the seller seasonably notifies the buyer that the nonconforming shipment does not constitute an acceptance and is offered only as an accommodation. Without the notification, the shipment is an acceptance and a breach. Thus, here, the shipment was both an acceptance and a breach.

4. Yes. In a transaction between merchants, the requirement of a writing is satisfied if one of them sends to the other a signed written confirmation that indicates the terms of the agreement, and the merchant receiving it has reason to know of its contents. If the merchant who receives it does not object in writing within ten days after receipt, the writing will be enforceable against him or her even though he or she has not signed anything.

5. Yes. The fourth contract called for the delivery of steel of a different description. Without more, this description is language with an express meaning. Express terms control over a course of dealing, unless they are construed as consistent with each other, which, in this problem, is unlikely, given the different contract terms.

Chapter 20

True-False Questions

1. T
2. F. If contracting parties do not expressly agree to when and under what conditions title will pass, title passes at the time and place at which *the seller delivers the goods.*
3. T
4. T
5. F. A buyer has an insurable interest in goods the moment they are identified to the contract by the seller. A seller has an insurable interest in goods as long as he or she has title. After title has passed, a seller who has a security interest in goods retains an insurable interest. Thus, a buyer and a seller can both have an insurable interest in goods at the same time.
6. T
7. F. In a sale on approval, the risk of loss remains with the seller until the buyer accepts the goods.
8. F. Generally, a buyer acquires whatever title the seller has to the goods. If a seller (or lessor) stole the goods, he or she has no title, and the buyer (or lessee) gets nothing. The real owner can reclaim the goods.
9. F. Under a *shipment* contract, title passes at time and place of shipment. Under a destination contract, title passes when the goods are tendered at a certain destination.
10. T

Fill-in Questions

F.O.B.; F.O.B.; F.O.B.; F.A.S.

Multiple-Choice Questions

1. D. Identification of goods does not in itself determine whether the risk of loss has passed from seller to buyer. There are other considerations. The contract may state when the risk passes. If it does not, and the goods are to be shipped, the UCC may determine when the risk passes based on the type of contract—shipment or destination. If the goods are not to be shipped, risk may pass subject to the merchant status of the parties. If the sale qualifies as a sale or return, or a sale on approval, there are other factors that may determine when risk passes.
2. B. Under a shipment contract, risk passes when the seller puts the goods into a carrier's possession. Under a destination contract, risk passes when the seller tenders delivery to the buyer. This question and answer are based on a question that appeared in the November 1995 CPA exam.
3. A. When goods are to be picked up by a buyer, if a seller is a nonmerchant, risk passes on the seller's tender of delivery, absent a contrary agreement. The goods were tendered on Monday, before the theft, so the buyer suffered the risk and the loss.
4. C. If a bailee holds goods for a seller and the goods are delivered without being moved, risk passes when the buyer receives a negotiable document of title for the goods. This buyer received the title document on Tuesday, before the loss.
5. D. The buyer has good title against the dealer, from whom the buyer bought the car, and the thief, who sold the car to the dealer. None of the parties has good title against the true owner, however, who is the rightful owner of the vehicle and is entitled to reclaim it.
6. C. Entrusting goods to a merchant who deals in goods of the kind gives the merchant power to transfer all rights to a buyer in the ordinary course of business. Entrustment includes leaving purchased goods with a merchant for later delivery or pickup.
7. B. Under a destination contract, risk passes when the seller tenders delivery. These goods were tendered at their destination on Tuesday.
8. C. A buyer has an insurable interest in goods as soon as they are identified to the contract, even before risk of loss passes. A seller has an insurable interest as long as he or she still has title to the goods. More than one party can have an insurable interest at the same time.
9. D. Generally, the party who breaches a contract bears the risk of loss.

Here, the seller breached. The risk passed to the buyer when the buyer accepted the goods in spite of their defect (the defect is that they were the wrong model).

10. B. If the contracting parties do not specify a time for title to pass, then it passes on delivery, according to the contract's delivery terms. Under a shipment contract, according to which a seller is required to ship goods by carrier, title passes at the time and place of shipment.

Issue Spotters

1. If Silk bore the risk, Silk must pay and seek indemnification from its insurance company. If Adams bore the risk, Adams must seek indemnification from its insurance company and may still have an obligation to deliver conforming goods to Silk.

2. The result would be the same as if the contract stated, "F.O.B. New York." For the risk to remain with the seller, a seller must specifically agree to deliver goods to a particular destination. Remember, all contracts are assumed to be shipment contracts unless they state otherwise.

3. Butler Farms—the seller. If goods are so nonconforming that a buyer has the right to reject them, the risk of loss will not pass from the seller to the buyer until the defects are cured or the buyer accepts the defective goods. Here, the defects had not been cured and the buyer had not yet accepted the goods.

4. George suffers the loss of the horse. If a bailee—in this case, Gold Spur—holds goods for a seller and the goods are to be delivered without being moved, the risk of loss passes when the bailee acknowledges the buyer's right to possess the goods. Gold Spur acknowledged George's right to possess Blaze when it said, "Ok," to Paula's call about the sale.

5. No. A seller has voidable title if goods that he or she is selling were paid for with a bad check (a check that is later dishonored). Although normally a buyer of goods acquires only the title that the seller had or had the power to transfer, a seller with voidable title can transfer good title to a good faith purchaser for value because an owner can-

not recover goods from a good faith purchaser for value. Chip's is a good faith purchaser for value.

Chapter 21

True-False Questions

1. T
2. T
3. T
4. F. When a sale is on credit, a buyer must pay according to credit terms, not when the goods are received. Credit terms may provide for payment within thirty days, for example. A credit period usually begins on the date of shipment.
5. F. After having had a reasonable opportunity to inspect, a buyer has only a reasonable time within which to reject goods. Also, once goods are accepted, they cannot be rejected. (Acceptance can be revoked, however.)
6 F. Merchants are held to a higher standard than nonmerchants are. For a merchant, good faith means honesty in fact and the observance of reasonable commercial standards of fair dealing in the trade.
7. T
8. T
9. F. A buyer's principal obligation is to pay for goods that he or she accepts. It is the seller's chief duty to tender delivery (to hold goods for the buyer and notify the buyer that the goods are ready).
10. F. A buyer can reject an installment only if its value is *substantially impaired* by a nonconformity that cannot be cured (in which case, the seller has breached the contract).

Fill-in Questions

conforming; and; buyer; receipt; unless

Multiple-Choice Questions

1. B. If a contract leaves open some particular of performance and permits one of the parties to specify it, the specification must be made in good faith and within limits set by commercial reasonableness. If the party does not make the specification, the other party may be excused from whatever performance depends on it (in this problem, the performance required is on-time delivery).

2. C. If a contract that involves a sale of identified goods does not specify a place of delivery, and the buyer is to pick up the goods, and the parties know when they contract that the goods are located somewhere other than the seller's place of business, the location of the goods is the place for their delivery. Here, the goods are in a warehouse in Barstow.

3. D. When tender is rejected because goods are nonconforming, a seller cannot exercise the right to cure by offering other nonconforming goods after the contracted time for performance. In this problem, the seller has breached the contract, and the buyer may seek a remedy.

4. C. The buyer must designate defects that are ascertainable by reasonable inspection, or those defects cannot be used to justify rejection or to establish breach if the seller could have cured them on being seasonably notified. In this problem, the seller could have cured quickly if it had known the reason for the buyer's rejection, and thus, the buyer cannot win a suit for damages.

5. C. If, before the time of performance, a party to a contract informs the other party that he or she will not perform, the nonbreaching party can treat the repudiation as a final breach and seek a remedy or wait, hoping that the breaching party will decide to honor the contract. If the party decides to wait, the breaching party can take back the repudiation.

6. A. In this problem, the seller is the beneficiary. Under a letter of credit, if the documents presented by the beneficiary comply with the terms, the issuing bank must pay the beneficiary. The buyer (or account party) has promised to repay the issuer for amounts it pays to the beneficiary in these circumstances.

7. C. The parties to a contract can stipulate the time, place, and manner of delivery. In the absence of specified details, however, tender of delivery must be at a reasonable hour and in a reasonable manner. The buyer must be notified, and the goods must be kept available for a reasonable time. This question and answer are based on a question that appeared in the CPA exam in November 1995.

8. D. Unless the parties agree otherwise, a buyer must make payment at the time and place that he or she receives the goods. Of course, before making payment, the buyer can inspect the goods and verify that they are what was ordered.

9. C. Acceptance of goods under a sales contract can be express or implied. A buyer can accept goods by words ("I accept," "the goods are what I ordered," etc.) or conduct (any act, such as using the goods, inconsistent with the seller's ownership).

10. C. It is the seller's obligation to tender delivery of goods. Under a shipment contract, a seller must contract for the transport of goods, tender to the buyer documents necessary to obtain possession of goods from the carrier, and notify the buyer that shipment has been made. Under a destination contract, a seller must also arrange for transport (or deliver the goods himself), and give the buyer the documents and notice.

Issue Spotters

1. Yes. Normally, goods must be tendered in a single delivery, but the parties can agree otherwise or the circumstances may be such that either party can rightfully request delivery in lots. The seller's proposal to work around the circumstances in this problem seems reasonable.

2. Yes. A seller is obligated to deliver goods in conformity with a contract in every detail. This is the perfect tender rule. The exception of the seller's right to cure does not apply here, because the seller delivered too little too late to take advantage of this exception.

3. No. An installment contract is breached only if one or more nonconforming installments *substantially* impair the value of the whole contract. Also, a buyer cannot reject an installment unless a nonconformity *substantially* impairs the value of the installment and cannot be cured. The nonconforming tender here, under the circumstances as stated, does not substantially impair the value of the installment or the whole contract and seems easily curable.

4. Yes. In a case of anticipatory repudiation, a buyer can resort to any remedy for breach even though the buyer told the seller—the repudiating party in this problem—that the buyer would wait for the seller's performance.

5. When a party has reason to believe another party will not perform, the first party may demand assurance of performance from the other party and suspend performance until that assurance is received. Reasonable assurance might consist of, for example, a third party's guaranty of payment or a report from a bank showing good financial condition.

Chapter 22

True-False Questions

1. F. Ordinarily, specific performance is considered inappropriate if damages will place the buyer or lessee in the position that he or she would have been in if the seller or lessor had fully performed. In other words, in most cases only if damages is an inadequate remedy is specific performance awarded.

2. T.

3. T

4. T

5. T

6. F. When a seller delivers nonconforming goods, the buyer can reject the goods with timely notice. The buyer can then recover any payments for the goods, as well as the expense of keeping or returning them. Or, in some circumstances, the buyer can resell the goods.

7. F. If a seller breaches a contract, under the UCC the buyer can cancel it and retains all rights to any other remedy against the seller.

8. F. A buyer can revoke acceptance, when a seller delivers nonconforming goods, only if the nonconformity substantially impairs the value of the goods, and it cannot be seasonably cured or it was difficult to discover before acceptance. Also, the buyer must notify the buyer of the breach within a reasonable time.

9. F. Before goods are delivered, a seller can cancel a contract only if the buyer breaches it. And even in that circumstance, the seller must notify the buyer.

10. F. Under the United Nations Convention on Contracts for the International Sale of Goods (CISG), remedies include damages, the right to avoid the contract, and the right to specific performance. These are similar to remedies available under the UCC.

Fill-in Questions

an automobile under warranty; value or use; within a certain number of opportunities; a new car, replacement of defective parts, or return of all consideration paid

Multiple-Choice Questions

1. C. If a buyer repudiates a contract or wrongfully refuses to accept goods, a seller can cancel the contract, which discharges the seller's obligations, or sue for damages: the difference between the contract price and the market price at the time and place of tender. The seller can also recover incidental damages. If the market price is less than the contract price, damages include the seller's lost profits. This question and answer are based on a question from the November 1995 CPA exam.

2. C. If a buyer is forced to obtain substitute goods for those that were due under a contract, the buyer can recover from the seller the difference between the cost of the cover and the contract price, plus incidental and consequential damages, less whatever expenses (such as delivery costs) were saved as a result of the seller's breach.

3. D. Depending on the circumstances, when a seller or lessor delivers nonconforming goods, the buyer or lessee can reject the part of the goods that does not conform (and rescind the contract or obtain cover). The buyer or lessee may revoke acceptance, or he or she may recover damages for accepted goods.

4. D. Under the UCC, contracting parties can provide for additional remedies or different remedies, including a change in the measure of damages. There are some limits. If a buyer is a consumer, for example, limiting consequential damages may be unconscionable.

5. A. When a seller (or lessor) refuses to deliver (or repudiates the contract), the buyer or lessee may obtain, depending on the circumstances, damages or cover.

6. C. If the quantity shipped is a truckload or more, a seller can stop delivery of goods if the buyer is insolvent or in breach of the contract. Of course, if the buyer is in possession of the goods, the buyer's rights to the goods have been acknowledged by the carrier or another bailee, or the buyer has received a document of title to the goods, the seller must use some other remedy.

7. C. When a seller has delivered goods that are in the possession of the buyer and the buyer refuses to pay, the seller has two choices: he or she can bring an action for the price or reclaim the goods. There are limits on the availability of the right to reclaim, however, and use of this remedy bars the seller from pursuing other remedies.

8. A. When a seller refuses to deliver goods that the parties have contracted for, the buyer can rescind the contract. The buyer must notify the seller, but is then discharged from any contractual obligations.

9. C. To use this remedy, the buyer must give the seller seasonable notice and tell the seller what the defect is. The buyer must then follow the seller's instructions as to what to do with the nonconforming goods. Of course, the buyer should be reimbursed for the expense of storage or return and so on.

10. A. If a lessee (or buyer) wrongfully refuses to accept, the lessor (or seller) can recover the difference between the contract price and the market price (at the time and place of tender), plus incidental damages. If the market price is less than the contract price, the lessor (or seller) can recover lost profits.

Issue Spotters

1. Yes. Withholding delivery is a remedy available to a seller when a buyer wrongfully rejects goods. Wrongful rejection is a breach of contract. If a breach is material and deliveries are to be made in installments, the seller can withhold the entire undelivered balance of the goods.

2. In all three instances, because the seller would be unable to resell the goods, the seller could bring an action to recover the purchase price and incidental damages. Of course, the seller must hold the goods for buyer so that if the seller is awarded damages, it can turn the goods over to the buyer.

3. The buyer should get the difference between the substitute goods' price and the contract price ($.20 per item). The buyer should also get any incidental damages, and, because the seller knew the purpose of the purchase, the buyer should get consequential damages, which could include the profits lost on the unmade sales.

4. The buyer can recover the difference between the market price—at the time that the buyer learned of the breach, at the place for tender—and the contract price, plus incidental damages (reasonable expenses incident to the breach) and consequential damages (of which the seller knew at the time of the breach), less any expenses saved by the breach. Thus, in this problem, the buyer can recover $2,000 ($10,000 x $.20), plus incidental damages and consequential damages (for the halt to the buyer's operation), less any expenses saved by the breach.

5. If a buyer wrongfully refuses to accept conforming goods, the seller can recover damages. The measure is the difference between the contract price and the market price (at the time and place of tender), plus incidental damages. If the market price is less than the contract price, the seller gets lost profits.

Chapter 23

True-False Questions

1. T

2. F. Warranties are not exclusive. A contract can include both an implied warranty of merchantability, an implied warranty of fitness for a particular purpose, and any number of express warranties.

3. F. Unless there is evidence to the contrary, when the parties know of a well-recognized trade custom, a court will infer that they intended the custom to apply to their contract.

4. T

5. T

6. T

7. T

8. F. A seller's statement of opinion or recommendation about the goods is an express warranty only if the seller who makes it is an expert and gives the opinion as an expert.

9. T

10. F. There is no implied warranty with respect to defects that a reasonable examination would reveal if a buyer examines goods before entering a contract. This is also true if the seller demands that the buyer examine the goods and the buyer refuses.

Fill-in Questions

can; can; can; need not; must

Multiple-Choice Questions

1. B. An implied warranty of merchantability arises in every sale of goods by a merchant who deals in goods of the kind. It makes no difference whether the merchant knew of or could have discovered a defect that makes a product unsafe. The warranty is that the goods are "reasonably fit for the ordinary purposes for which such goods are used."

2. A. An implied warranty of fitness for a particular purpose arises when any seller—merchant or nonmerchant—knows a particular purpose for which a buyer will use goods and that the buyer is relying on the seller's skill and judgment. Here, the buyer was relying on the seller to choose a dependable vehicle for off-road driving, and the seller knew it.

3. B. To disclaim an implied warranty of fitness for a particular purpose, a warranty must be conspicuous, but the word *fitness* does not have to be used. A disclaimer of the implied warranty of merchantability must mention *merchantability*. Warranties of title can be disclaimed only by specific language (or by circumstances that indicate no warranties of title are made).

4. C. When an express warranty is made in a sales contract, the Magnuson-Moss Warranty Act prevents sellers from disclaiming or modifying the implied warranties of merchantability and fitness for a particular purpose. Sellers can impose a time limit on an implied warranty, but it must correspond to the duration of an express warranty.

5. A. The other warranties of title are that the goods are free of the security interest of a third party of which the buyer has no knowledge and that the goods are also free of any third party's copyright, patent, or trademark claim. The choice concerning the quality of the goods at the price is a statement of opinion, and a seller's statement of opinion is not a warranty.

6. A. A label is an affirmation of fact, which is an express warranty and a standard that the labeled goods must meet. Regarding the other choices, an implied warranty is not express. An implied warranty of merchantability arises in every sale (or lease) in which the merchant selling the goods deals in goods of the kind. An implied warranty of fitness for a particular purpose arises when the merchant knows (or has reason to know) the particular purpose for which the customer is buying the goods.

7. A. As part of the warranty of title, sellers warrant that they have good and valid title and that, in a sale, the transfer of title is rightful. This warranty may be disclaimed, but only by specific contractual language.

8. A. The statement in the brochure is an affirmation of fact and thus a warranty that the goods will meet that standard. Statements that attest to the quality of the goods ("the best on the market") would not qualify.

9. D. This is a statement of opinion (puffing) and creates no warranty. If the salesperson had said something factual about the vehicle—its miles per gallon, its total mileage, whether it had been in an accident, etc.—it would be more than puffing and could qualify as an express warranty.

10. A. Showing a sample to a customer creates a warranty that the goods delivered to the customer will in fact match the sample. A sample represents a standard that the goods must meet. Warranties of fitness for a particular purpose, merchantability, and usage of trade are implied warranties. This question and answer are based on a question that appeared on the CPA exam in 1997.

Issue Spotters

1. No. A creditor with a valid security interest can repossess goods from a subsequent purchaser. If a creditor repossesses goods, however, a buyer who had no actual knowledge of the security interest can recover from the seller for breach of warranty. Thus, Ace can repossess the car from Stan, and Stan can recover from Barb.

2. No. Merchantable food means food that is fit to eat. Food containing cholesterol is merchantable—that is, it is fit to eat—if it is similar to all other food of the kind on the market.

3. The seller's description of the item as a "truck" creates an express warranty that it is a truck, and selling the item "as is" cannot disclaim this warranty—a seller cannot normally deliver a truck without wheels and avoid liability.

4. The buyer should argue that the seller breached an implied warranty of fitness for a particular purpose. An implied warranty of fitness for a particular purpose arises when a seller knows a particular purpose for which a buyer will use goods and that the buyer is relying on the seller's skill and judgment to select suitable goods.

5. No. If a seller demands that a buyer examine goods, and the buyer refuses to do so, the seller will not be held liable for breach of the implied warranty of merchantability if a defect that could have been discovered by a reasonable inspection leads to an injury.

Cumulative Hypothetical Problem for Unit Three—Including Chapters 19–23

1. C. The modification would not be considered a rejection. Under UCC 2–207, a merchant can add an additional term to a contract, with his or her acceptance, as part of the contract, unless the offeror expressly states otherwise.

2. C. If nothing is stated in a contract about the risk of loss, then the UCC determines when the risk of loss passes. Under the UCC, if there are no contract terms to the contrary, the risk of loss passes on delivery, if the seller is a merchant.

3. B. Under UCC 2–709, a seller can demand enforcement of a contract if the buyer breaches, the goods have been identified, and the seller cannot resell the goods for a reasonable price. From the perspective of the seller, recovery of the contract price is specific performance.

4. C. A seller makes an express warranty by providing an assertion, an affirmation, a promise, or a similar statement about the quality of the goods that becomes a part of the basis of the bargain. The promises may be oral, and the seller's intent is not relevant.

5. B. To be subject to the UCC's implied warranty of merchantability, goods must be fit for their ordinary or intended use, but they do not need to be fit for ALL of the possible purposes that a buyer might have in mind. The other choices are part of this implied warranty.

Chapter 24

True-False Questions

1. T
2. T
3. T
4. T
5. F. To be negotiable, an instrument must be payable on demand or at a definite time. Instruments that say nothing about when payment is due are payable on demand.
6. F. The length of the extension does not have to be specified if the option to extend is solely that of the *holder*. After the specified date passes, the note becomes, in effect, a demand instrument. The period of an extension must be specified, however, if the option is given to the maker.
7. F. An instrument that contains any indication that does not purport to designate a specific payee is a bearer instrument. An order instrument is payable to a named payee.
8. T
9. T
10. F. This notation would have no effect on a check. Any other instrument can be made nonnegotiable if the maker or drawer adds this notation to it, however.

Fill-in Questions

drawer; drawee; payee; maker; payee

Multiple-Choice Questions

1. A. One of the requirements of negotiability is that an instrument be payable to order or to bearer. An instrument that is payable to the order of an identified person is an order instrument. An instrument that is payable to bearer is a bearer instrument. A bearer instrument can be negotiated further without a payee's signature. References to other agreements do not affect an instrument's negotiability. Conditioning payment would render an instrument nonnegotiable, however. This question and answer are based on a question from the May 1995 CPA exam.

2. A. An instrument that is not payable to the order of an identified person is a bearer instrument. Although this instrument uses order language, it does not desginate a specific payee.

3. C. A draft is created when the party creating it orders another party to pay money, usually to a third party. The drawee (the party on whom the draft is drawn) must be obligated to the drawer, either by an agreement or through a debtor-creditor relationship, for the drawee to be obligated to the drawer to honor the draft.

4. A. Although this instrument includes among the possible payees a specific person, the "or bearer" language makes it payable to others as well. Also, the instrument does not contain order language, which it would need to be an order instrument.

5. A. To be negotiable, an instrument must state the principal in a fixed amount to be paid when the instrument is payable. Interest can be made calculable by reference to information not contained in the instrument if it is readily found in a source described in the instrument. (In other words, variable interest rate notes can be negotiable.)

6. D. The requirements of negotiability allow parties to set most of the terms of an instrument to suit themselves. There is no requirement that payment be made in any certain way—the parties can agree to payment in a variety of ways. Also, installment payments can be interest only, or they can be allocated between principal and interest.

7. B. To be negotiable, payment on an instrument cannot be conditional, and the promise or order cannot be subject to or governed by another writing, or be subject to rights or obligations stated in another writing. An instrument might state, however, that it is "secured" by a mortgage, but it cannot be "subject" to a mortgage.

8. C. A maker or drawer is bound even if he or she signs a trade name. The location of the signature is unimportant.

9. A. A check printed "Pay to the order of" and on which the drawer inserts in the blank "Mac or bearer" is a bearer instrument.

10. D. The omission of the name of the bank on which an instrument is drawn or payable will not render the instrument nonnegotiable. That an instrument is undated does not affect its negotiability, nor does postdating or antedating an instrument affect negotiability. When interest is provided for, the rate is the judgment rate, unless otherwise specified.

Issue Spotters

1. The check is order paper, because it is made payable to the order of a specific, named payee. (As will be explained in the next chapter, the check can be converted to bearer simply be the payee's signature on the back.)

2. Yes. To be negotiable, an instrument must be in written form and have a relative degree of permanence and portability. To be negotiable, an instrument must also be signed by the drawer. Rubber stamps bearing signatures are common in business.

3. "I.O.U. $700" or an instruction to Jim's bank stating, "I wish you would pay $700 to Sherry," would render the instrument nonnegotiable. To be negotiable, an instrument must contain an express promise to pay. An I.O.U. is only an acknowledgment of indebtedness. An order stating, "I wish you would pay," is not sufficiently precise.

4. The check is a bearer instrument. Although the drawer gave the check to a specific person, the check itself does not designate a specific payee, which it would need to do to be an order instrument. Either way, the check is negotiable, however.

5. An amount stated in words on a check prevails over an amount stated in numerals on the same instrument. Thus, the bank can lawfully credit the depositor's account for the amount stated in words.

Chapter 25

True-False Questions

1. F. A negotiable instrument can be transferred by assignment or negotiation. When a transfer fails to qualify as a negotiation, it becomes an assignment and is governed by the rules of assignment under contract law.

2. T

3. T

4. F. Bearer instruments can be negotiated by delivery alone. That is why a bearer instrument is considered payable to whoever possesses it.

5. F. To be a holder, a person must have possession and good title. The definition of a holder, from UCC 1–201(20), is "the person in possession if the instrument is payable to bearer, or in the case of an instrument payable to an identified person, if the identified person is in possession."

6. F. Despite taking an instrument for value, in good faith, and without notice, a transferee cannot be a holder in due course (HDC) unless he or she is a holder.

7. T

8. F. If a holder is an HDC, all claims to an instrument and most defenses against payment of other parties cannot be successfully asserted against him or her.

9. T

10. T

Fill-in Questions

can; cannot; cannot

Multiple-Choice Questions

1. B. Before the payee indorsed the back of the check, it was an order instrument. It could be negotiated further only with the payee's signature on it (and with delivery).

2. C. The first step in becoming a holder in due course (HDC) is that a party must be a holder. To be a holder, the instrument must be negotiable. The requirements for HDC status are that a party take the instrument for value, in good faith, and without notice of any claims to it or defenses against payment on it. This question and answer are based on a question that appeared in the CPA exam in May 1995.

3. A. A party can convert a blank indorsement to a special indorsement "by writing over the signature of the indorser in blank any contract consistent with the character of the indorsement." In other words, the payee can do what is stated in this example.

4. C. An instrument that is payable to the order of a specific payee is negotiated by delivery of the instrument to that payee. The payee negotiates the instrument further by indorsing it and delivering it to the transferee.

5. D. A special indorsement names the indorsee. No special words are needed. A special indorsement makes an instrument order paper.

6. B. A holder takes an instrument for value when he or she pays cash for it, gives a negotiable instrument for it, or makes an irrevocable commitment to a third person. He or she is an HDC to the extent that he or she gives value for the instrument (and meets the other requirements for HDC status).

7. C. A holder of a time instrument who takes it after its due date is "on notice" that it is overdue. Such a holder cannot become an HDC. Nonpayment by the due date should indicate to any purchaser who is obligated to pay that there is a defense to payment.

8. A. A bank can become an HDC when honoring other banks' checks to the extent it has given value. Thus, a bank becomes an HDC when it permits a customer to draw against a credited instrument, but only to the extent that the customer draws on the credit.

9. C. A thief cannot be a holder. A party who takes in good faith and without notice from a thief is an HDC, however. A party in the situation of the drawer of this check might also avoid liability to an ordinary holder by as-

serting the personal defense of unauthorized completion of an incomplete instrument (discussed in the next chapter).

10. A, A party who takes an instrument with knowledge of one defense that the maker or drawer has against payment on the instrument prevents the party from attaining HDC status as to all defenses. The party does not satisfy the requirement for HDC status that he or she must take the instrument without notice.

Issue Spotters

1. A payee negotiates an order instrument further by indorsing and delivering it. A specific payee's indorsing a check—which is an order instrument initially—converts it to a bearer instrument, A bearer instrument is negotiated by delivery alone—indorsement is not necessary.

2. When the payee signed the back of his check, he converted it to a bearer instrument. Because a bearer instrument can be negotiated by delivery alone, the check was negotiated to the finder. To avoid such a loss, the payee could have indorsed it "For deposit only." In this way, the check would have remained an order instrument.

3. This party is an HDC to the full extent of the note. One of the requirements for becoming an HDC is taking an instrument for value. A party may attain HDC status to the extent that he or she gives value for the instrument. Paying with cash or with a check is giving value.

4. No. Generally, the time that a due date on an instrument begins to run is the day after the date of an instrument, which would mean that this note is due April 1. That means the note is overdue. One of the requirements for becoming an HDC is that a party take an instrument without notice that it is overdue. (Nonpayment by a due date indicates to any purchaser that the maker or drawer has a defense against payment.)

5. No. A person who does not qualify as an HDC but who acquires an instrument from an HDC or from someone with HDC rights receives the rights and privileges of an HDC, but a holder who was a party to fraud affecting the instrument knows of a defense against payment on it and cannot improve his or her status by buying it from a later HDC.

Chapter 26

True-False Questions

1. T
2. F. Some parties are secondarily liable.
3. T
4. F. Warranty liability is not subject to the conditions of proper presentment, dishonor, and notice of dishonor.
5. T
6. T
7. F. Warranties cannot be disclaimed with respect to checks. To disclaim transfer warranties with respect to any instrument except a check, such words as "without warranties" must be included in the indorsement.
8. F. Personal defenses can be used to avoid payment to an ordinary holder, but only universal defenses are good against an HDC.
9. F. An unauthorized signature usually does *not* bind the person whose name is forged. An unauthorized signature can be binding, however, if the person whose name is signed ratifies it. The person's negligence may also prevent him or her from denying liability.
10. T

Fill-in Questions

presentment; presenter; presenter; the maker or the drawer; materially altered

Multiple-Choice Questions

1. A. A person who writes and signs a check, leaving blank the amount and the name of the payee, and who then leaves the check in a place available to the public, can be precluded, on the basis of negligence, from denying liability for its payment. Only if Mary can prove that the bank failed to exercise ordinary care in cashing the check might she succeed in a suit against the bank.
2. A. Forgery of the signature of the maker of a note is a real defense and thus good against an HDC. This is only

if the person whose signature was forged has not ratified it or is precluded from denying it. The other choices are personal defenses, which are good against ordinary holders but not HDCs. This question and answer are based on a question that appeared in the November 1992 CPA exam.

3. C. Good title stopped with Gina: Tony ordered the check payable to Gina. Gina did not receive payment or order payment to another.

4. C. Bill and Ed have secondary liability. Parties who are secondarily liable on an instrument promise to pay only if the following events occur: (1) the instrument is properly and timely presented; (2) the instrument is dishonored; and (3) notice of dishonor is given in a timely manner to the secondarily liable party.

5. A. When a drawee fails to accept or pay an instrument, the drawer's (secondary) liability arises. The party holding the draft can then attempt to obtain payment from the drawer.

6. C. Returning a check because it lacks a proper indorsement or because the holder refuses to provide reasonable identification is not dishonor. Payment can also be refused without dishonor if the holder refuses to sign the check as a receipt for payment.

7. A. A discharge in bankruptcy is a real defense to payment on an instrument, which means that the person who received the discharge can avoid payment even to an HDC. A breach of contract is a personal defense, however, good only against an ordinary holder of the instrument.

8. B. The principal is liable. The agent is not. On a check an agent is not liable if the agent clearly identifies the principal, discloses the agency relation, and the signature shows that it is on behalf of the principal.

9. B. These parties are unqualified indorsers of a check, which means that under ordinary circumstances they are secondarily liable on the instrument to later indorsers. When a party's indorsement on an instrument is struck, or otherwise cancelled, however, that party is completely discharged from liability on the instrument.

10. D. If a check has been materially altered and the alteration is clearly visible, a party who takes the check has notice of a defense against payment on it and cannot become an HDC. He or she can recover nothing on the check. (If the alteration was not visible and the party could otherwise become an HDC, he or she could enforce the check according to the original terms.)

Issue Spotters

1. Yes. As in cases of forgery, in which the person whose name is used is not liable, KLP can assert the defense of the unauthorized signature against any HDC, because Tom exceeded his authority in signing the check on behalf of KLP.

2. No. When a drawer's employee provides the drawer with the name of a fictitious payee (a payee whom the drawer does not actually intend to have any interest in an instrument), a forgery of the payee's name is effective to pass good title to subsequent transferees.

3. Alan warrants to Brenda that he is entitled to enforce the note, all signatures are authentic and authorized, the note has not been altered, the note is not subject to a defense or claim that can be asserted against him, and he has no knowledge of any insolvency proceedings against the maker.

4. No. Material alteration is a partial defense against an HDC. An HDC can enforce an instrument that has been materially altered against the maker or drawer according to the original terms only. Of course, if the alteration had been visible, the result would be different—the party would be on notice and could not recover anything on the check.

5. They are secondarily liable parties. A party who is secondarily liable on an instrument promises to pay it only if the following events occur: (1) the instrument is properly and timely presented; (2) the instrument is dishonored; and (3) notice of dishonor is given in a timely manner to the party.

Chapter 27

True-False Questions

1. T

2. F. If a bank pays a stale check in good faith without consulting the customer, it has the right to charge the customer's account for the amount of the check.

3. F. When a bank receives an item payable from a customer's account, but there are insufficient funds in the account to cover the amount, the bank can either dishonor the item or pay it and charge the customer's account.

4. T

5. T

6. T

7. T

8. F. Under the Expedited Funds Availability Act of 1987, there are different availability schedules for different funds, depending on such factors as the location of the bank on which an item is drawn, what type of item it is, the age and activity of an account, and the amount of the item.

9. T

10. F. A forged drawer's signature on a check has no legal effect as the signature of the party whose name is signed. If the bank pays the check, the bank must recredit the customer's account.

Fill-in Questions

drawer; creditor; principal; drawee; debtor; agent

Multiple-Choice Questions

1. B. For the deposit of a local check, the first $100 must be available for withdrawal by the opening of the next business day. The next $400—or the rest of the check, in this case—must be available by no later than 5:00 P.M. the next business day.

2. D. A bank may have a right to recover the amount of a check containing the forged signature of a drawer from a customer who cashes the check, but this right is limited. A drawee bank cannot recover from a person who took the instrument in good faith and for value or who in good faith changed position in reliance on the payment or acceptance.

3. A. If a drawee bank pays a check over a customer's stop-payment order, the bank is obligated to recredit the account of the customer, but the bank is liable for no more than the actual loss suffered by the drawer (the price of one television set).

4. A. A bank that pays a customer's check bearing a forged indorsement must recredit the customer's account or be liable to the drawer customer for breach of contract.

5. B. A drawee bank's contract is with its customer, not with those who present its customers' checks for payment. Thus, a drawee bank is not liable to a holder who presents a check for payment, even if the drawer has sufficient funds on deposit to pay the check. The holder's recourse is against the drawer, who may subsequently hold the bank liable for a wrongful refusal to pay.

6. D. To recover for all forged items, a bank customer must discover and report a forgery to the bank within thirty days of the receipt of the bank statement and canceled checks that contain the first forged item. Failure to notify the bank within this period of time discharges the bank's liability for all similar forged checks that are paid by the bank before notification.

7. C. If the bank can show that its customer failed to take reasonable care in controlling access to its checks (or check-writing program on the computer), the bank cannot be required to recredit the customer's account for the amount of a forged check. The bank's own negligence can shift the loss, however.

8. A. If a drawee bank fails to detect an alteration on a check of its customer-drawer and cashes the check, or cashes a customer's check over a forged indorsement, the bank is liable for the loss. (The customer's negligence can shift the loss, however.)

9. A. The certification of a check by the bank on which it is drawn discharges the drawer, who was secondarily liable on the check. The bank remains primarily liable and has now guaranteed payment. This question and answer are based on a question that appeared in the November 1981 CPA exam.

10. C. Dick is liable for the full amount because he did not notify the bank that the card was missing until after the withdrawal. If a customer does not inform the institution in less than two business days after learning of a card's loss or theft, the customer's liability for unauthorized transactions is up to $500.

Issue Spotters

1. Yes, to both questions. In a civil suit, a drawer is liable to a payee or to a holder of a check that is not honored. If intent to defraud can be proved, the drawer can also be subject to criminal prosecution for writing a bad check.

2. The general rule is that the bank must recredit a customer's account when it pays on a forged signature. The bank has no right to recover from a holder who, without knowledge, cashes a check bearing a forged drawer's signature. Thus, the bank in this problem can collect from neither its customer nor the party who cashed the check. The bank's recourse is to look for the thief.

3. Rose is entitled to $630—the amount to which the check was altered ($700) less the amount that Rose ordered the bank to pay ($70). The bank may recover the $630 from Val, the party who presented the altered check for payment.

4. Yes. The EFTA covers only electronic fund transfers made by consumers; transfers between financial institutions are not covered by the act. First National may recover under other legal theories, however.

5. Yes. An institution is liable for failing to stop payment of a preauthorized transfer from a customer's account when instructed to do so under the account's terms and conditions.

Cumulative Hypothetical Problem for Unit Four—Including Chapters 24–27

1. B. A promissory note is a written promise by one party to pay money to another party. This instrument is not a draft: there is no drawee. Because it is not a draft, it cannot be a sight draft, a check, or a trade acceptance, all of which are drafts.

2. B. This instrument meets all of the requirements for negotiability: it is in writing, it is signed by the maker, it is an unconditional promise to pay a fixed amount of money, it is payable to bearer, and it is payable at a definite time. The extension clause does not affect its negotiability because, although

the right to extend is given to the maker, the period of the extension is specified.

3. A. The instrument is negotiable, but it can be negotiated further only by the bank's indorsement, because it was converted from a bearer instrument to an order instrument with the indorsement to pay to the order of the bank. Because it was a bearer instrument, it could have been negotiated by delivery only, without indorsement. The indorsement "without recourse" does not affect the negotiability of the instrument.

4. A. The bank is an HDC because it took the instrument (1) for value, (2) in good faith, and (3) without notice that any person had a defense against payment on it. The party from whom the bank bought the instrument was not an HDC, however, because that party did take the instrument with knowledge of the contract dispute.

5. D. No party to a check has primary liability with respect to payment on it. The drawer is secondarily liable to the payee. If the drawer has sufficient grounds, he or she may sue the drawee for wrongful dishonor, but the payee cannot successfully sue the drawee.

Chapter 28

True-False Questions

1. T

2. F. In most cases, a creditor must file a copy of a financing statement locally (with the county clerk), centrally (with the secretary of state), or both, depending on the classification of the collateral.

3. F. A security interest in proceeds perfects automatically and remains perfected, in most cases, for at least ten days after the debtor's receipt of the proceeds.

4. F. To avoid problems arising from different descriptions, a secured party can repeat the security agreement's description in the financing statement or file the security agreement as the financing statement (or file a combination of the two).

5. T

6. T

7. T

8. T

9. F. A debtor who has defaulted has redemption rights. Before the secured party decides to retain the collateral or before it is disposed of, the debtor can take back the collateral by tendering performance of all secured obligations and paying the secured party's expenses. (Other secured parties have this same right.)

10. F. When several creditors claim a security interest in the same collateral of a debtor, the first interest to be filed takes priority. The first to attach has priority if none of the interests has been perfected.

Fill-in Questions

1. creditor; creditor
2. first; first

Multiple-Choice Questions

1. B. A *financing statement* must be signed by the debtor, but the creditor's signature is not necessary.

2. D. Of course, the exercise of these rights depends on the terms of the security agreement, the existence of other parties with a security interest in the same collateral, and other factors.

3. A. To be effective, a written security agreement must (1) be signed by the debtor, (2) contain a description of the collateral, and (3) the description must reasonably identify the collateral.

4. B. The general rule is that a perfected security interest in any type of collateral continues even after the collateral has been sold unless the secured party authorized the sale. The exceptions include consumers who buy in the ordinary course of business (unless they know that a purchase violates a third party's rights). This question and answer is based on a question from the November 1994 CPA exam.

5. C. To retain collateral that a secured party repossessed on a debtor's default, the party must notify the debtor and (in all cases except consumer goods) any other secured party of whom the party has notice of a claim. If the debtor or other secured party objects, the collateral must be sold, or otherwise disposed of, within twenty-one days.

6. C. A *security agreement* must be signed by the debtor, but the creditor's signature is not necessary.

7. B. A secured party automatically has an interest in proceeds—whatever is received—from the sale, exchange, or other disposal of collateral. Thus Amigo is entitled to whatever installment payments remain.

8 D. When a security interest exists in a car in a state in which title registration is required and the interest is noted on the certificate, perfection continues after the car is moved to another state requiring a certificate until the car is registered in the new state. If a state does *not* require a certificate of title as part of its perfection process, perfection automatically ends four months after a car is moved into another state.

9. C. The first interest to be filed or to be perfected has priority over other filed or perfected security interests. Although the second lender was not the first to provide funds to the debtor, it was the first to file. Sometimes, such circumstances are characterized as a race to the filing office.

10. A. Also, the bank gets a perfected interest in the funds to buy the new inventory under the *future-advances* clause (so B is false) and in the new inventory under the *after-acquired property* clause (so C is false).

Issue Spotters

1. Duane can put other creditors on notice by perfecting his interest—by filing a statement in the appropriate public office, or by taking possession of the laptop until Stan repays the loan.

2. The Money Shop can recover its losses, at least in part, by collecting the remaining installment payments. A secured party automatically has an interest in proceeds on a sale (or other disposal) of collateral. When Wolf sold its goods, the lender's interest continued in the seller's right to receive payments.

3. The Money Shop can protect its interest by providing in the security agreement for coverage of proceeds, after-acquired property, inventory, and future advances.

4. A consumer who buys a good from a retailer takes the item free of any security interest, created by the retailer, in the retailer's inventory. The Money Shop gets the check—the proceeds.

5. Avco can dispose of the collateral in a commercially reasonable manner, which generally requires notice of the place, time, and manner of sale—although a public sale is not necessary, and there are no specific time requirements. Brad must be notified if he has not renounced or modified, in writing, the right to notice. Before the computer is sold, Brad can redeem it by fulfilling the terms of the agreement with Avco and paying whatever expenses Avco reasonably incurred.

Chapter 29

True-False Questions

1. T
2. F. State and federal statutory exemptions can be applied together.
3. T
4. T
5. F. This is the most important concept in suretyship: a surety can use any defenses available to the principal, except personal defenses.
6. F. If the debtor does not or cannot pay, a creditor can go back to court and obtain a writ of execution through which property of the debtor can be seized and sold to satisfy the judgment.
7. F. Under an assignment for the benefit of creditors, a debtor transfers title to his or her property to a trustee or assignee, who sells the property and offers payment to each of the debtor's creditors in proportion to what is owed. Each creditor can accept the tender, and discharge the debt, or reject it, and attempt to collect in another way.
8. T
9. F. A writ of execution is issued *after* the entry of a final judgment and usually only if the debtor does not pay the judgment. A writ of attachment is issued *before* the entry of a final judgment.
10. T

Fill-in Questions

Contract of suretyship; surety; surety; guaranty contract; guarantor

Multiple-Choice Questions

1. A. Berman can keep the necklace until Melita pays for the repair. If Melita fails to pay, Berman has an artisan's lien on the necklace for the amount of the bill and can sell the necklace in satisfaction of the lien.
2. D. The creditor can use prejudgment attachment. Attachment occurs at the time of or immediately after commencement of a suit but before entry of a final judgment. The court issues a writ of attachment, directing the sheriff or other officer to seize property belonging to the debtor. If the creditor prevails at trial, the property can be sold to satisfy the judgment.
3. D. The creditor can use garnishment, a collection remedy directed at a debtor's property or rights held by a third person. A garnishment order can be served on the employer so that part of debtor's paycheck will be paid to the creditor. This question and answer are based on a question that was part of the CPA exam in 1996.
4. D. The debt is $30,000. The amount of the homestead exemption ($35,000) is subtracted from the sale price of the house ($60,000), and the remainder ($25,000) is applied against the debt. The proceeds from the sale of the nonexempt personal property ($5,000) is also applied against the debt. $25,000 + $5,000 = $30,000.
5. A. A guarantor is secondarily liable—that is, the principal must first default. Usually, a creditor must have attempted to collect from the principal, because usually a debtor would not otherwise be declared in default.
6. C. If there are co-sureties, a surety who pays more than his or her proportionate share on a debtor's default is entitled to recover from the co-sureties the amount paid above the surety's obligation. To determine the proportionate amounts, divide the contractual liability of each co-surety ($18,000 and $27,000) by the total amount borrowed ($90,000) and multiply each quotient by the amount the other co-surety paid above the surety's obligation ($45,000).
7. D. At the request of a creditor who obtains a judgment against a debtor, a writ of execution is issued after the entry of the judgment if the debtor still

does not pay. A sheriff, or other officer, executes the writ by seizing the debtor's nonexempt property, selling it, and using the proceeds to pay the amount of the judgment.

8. C. When a debtor defaults on a mortgage, the mortgagee can foreclose on the property. The usual method of foreclosure is a judicial sale. The property is sold, and the proceeds are applied to the debt. The mortgagor can pay the debt and redeem the property before the sale. If the proceeds do not cover the debt, the mortgagee can recover the difference by obtaining a deficiency judgment in a separate legal action after the foreclosure.

9. D. A surety agrees to be primarily liable to pay a debtor's debt. If the debtor and the creditor materially alter the terms of their contract without the surety's consent, a surety who agreed to act without being compensated is discharged completely. (A surety who accepted payment is discharged to the extent that he or she suffers a loss under the contract as modified.)

10. C. If a creditor in possession of a debtor's collateral surrenders it without the guarantor's consent, the guarantor is released to the extent of any loss attributable to the surrender. This protects a guarantor who agrees to the obligation only because the debtor's collateral is in the creditor's possession.

Issue Spotters

1. Larry and Midwest can place a mechanic's lien on Joe's property. If Joe does not pay what he owes, the property can be sold to satisfy the debt. The only requirements are that the lien be filed within a specific time from the time of the work, depending on the state statute, and notice of the foreclosure and sale must be given to Joe in advance.

2. Yes. Bob is a surety. A surety has a right of reimbursement from the debtor for all outlays the surety makes on behalf of the suretyship arrangement.

3. Co-sureties may be required to reimburse any co-surety who pays more than his or her proportionate share on a debtor's default. In such a case, the co-sureties are liable in proportion to their promise to pay the debt. If co-sureties have agreed to be obligated for the debt

in equal proportions, then that is the amount for which they are indebted to the surety who pays the debt. In this problem, Dian and Ernie can each be held liable to pay $300 to Carol.

4. No. In some states, a creditor must go back to court for a separate order of garnishment for each pay period. Also, federal and state laws limit the amount of money that can be garnished from a debtor's pay.

5. A mortgagor has redemption rights. These vary from state to state, but typically, before a foreclosure sale, the mortgagor can regain possession of the property by paying the debt, plus any interest and costs that have accrued. In some states, a mortgagor may redeem the property within a certain time after the sale.

Chapter 30

True-False Questions

1. F. Anyone liable to a creditor can file.

2. F. The adequate protection doctrine protects secured creditors from losing the value of their security as a result of the automatic stay.

3. T

4. T

5. F. Under Chapter 13 (and 12), a bankruptcy may be commenced only by voluntary petition. Involuntary petitions may be used to start bankruptcy proceedings under either Chapter 7 or Chapter 11.

6. F. The adequate protection doctrine protects secured creditors from losing the value of their security as a result of an automatic stay. The doctrine requires payments, or other relief, to protect secured creditors from any decreasing value of their collateral.

7. T

8. T

9. F. Some small businesses—those who do not own or manage real estate and do not have debts of more than $2 million—can choose to avoid creditors' committees under Chapter 11. Those who choose to do so, however, are subject to shorter deadlines with respect to filing a reorganization plan.

10. T

Fill-in Questions

7; 11; 13; 7; 11; 13; 7; 11; 13

Multiple-Choice Questions

1.   D.   Under Chapter 11, creditors and debtor plan for the debtor to pay some debts, be discharged of the rest, and continue in business. Under Chapter 13, with an appropriate plan, a small business debtor can also pay some (or all) debts, be discharged of the rest, and continue in business.

2.   D.   Under Chapter 13 of the Bankruptcy Code, a debtor can submit a plan under which he or she continues in possession of his or her assets, but turns over disposable income for a three-year period, after which most debts are discharged.

3.   D.   Under Chapter 7 or Chapter 11, a corporate debtor (or an individual debtor or a partnership, but not a farmer or a charitable institution) who has twelve or more creditors can be forced into bankruptcy by three or more of them, who collectively have unsecured claims for at least $10,775. A debtor with fewer than twelve creditors can be involuntarily petitioned into bankruptcy by one or more of them, if the petitioner (or petitioners) has a claim for at least $10,775.

4.   D.   Debts that are not dischargeable in bankruptcy include the claims listed in this problem—claims for alimony and claims for certain student loans—as well as claims for child support and claims for back taxes accruing within three years before the bankruptcy.

5.   A.   Any individual can file a petition for bankruptcy under Chapter 7. The debtor does not have to be insolvent. A court can dismiss a petition, however, if granting it would constitute substantial abuse or if the court finds that the debtor could pay off his or her debts under Chapter 13.

6.   A.   Other grounds on which a discharge may be denied include concealing property with the intent to defraud a creditor, fraudulently destroying financial records, and refusing to obey a lawful court order. Having obtained a discharge in bankruptcy six years earlier is also a ground for denial. The other choices represent individual debts that are not dischargeable in bankruptcy. This question and answer are based on a question from the 1997 CPA exam.

7.   A.   The first unsecured debts to be paid are the administrative expenses of the bankruptcy proceeding. Among the debts listed in this problem, the order of priority is then unpaid wages, consumer deposits, and taxes. Each class of creditors is fully paid before the next class is entitled to anything.

8.   A.   Other transfers that a trustee can set aside include a transfer made with the intent to hinder, delay, or defraud a creditor; transfers made to an insider within a year of the debtor's filing a petition in bankruptcy; payments within days before the petition for a preexisting debt; any reason that the debtor could use to get the property back.

9.   D.   Most corporations can file for bankruptcy under Chapter 7 or 11. The same principles that govern liquidation cases also govern reorganizations. Chapter 11 is used most commonly by corporate debtors. One important difference between the two chapters is that in a Chapter 11 proceeding, the debtor can continue in business.

10.   D.   A bankruptcy trustee has the power to avoid preferential payments, fraudulent transfers, and transactions that the debtor could rightfully avoid.

Issue Spotters

1.   The order of their priority is Trager, First National, and Universal. Mechanic's liens (and artisan's liens) have priority over perfected security interests. Secured parties have the next highest priority. Unsecured creditors are generally paid last.

2.   Yes. A debtor's payment to a creditor made for a preexisting debt, within ninety days (one year in the case of an insider or fraud) of the bankruptcy filing , can be recovered if it gives a creditor more than he or she would have received in the bankruptcy proceedings.

3.   Yes. Congress created Chapter 12 to help relieve economic pressure on family farmers whose gross income is at least 50 percent farm-dependent and whose debts are at least 80 percent farm-related. Total debt must not exceed $1.5 million. A Chapter 12 filing is similar to a Chapter 13 filing.

4. The savings and loan corporation is not eligible to file under Chapter 11. Debtors who can file under Chapter 11 are generally the same as those who can file under Chapter 7—any person, including individuals, partnerships, and corporations, except railroads, insurance companies, banks, savings and loan associations, and credit unions. Also excepted from Chapter 11 are stockbrokers and commodities brokers.

5. No. Besides the claims listed in this problem, the debts that cannot be discharged in bankruptcy include amounts borrowed to pay back taxes, goods obtained by fraud, debts that were not listed in the petition, alimony, child support, certain cash advances, and others.

Cumulative Hypothetical Problem for Unit Five—Including Chapters 28–30

1. C. A mechanic's lien can be placed by a creditor on real property when a person contracts for labor to repair the property but does not pay. An artisan's lien entitles a creditor to recover from a debtor for the repair of personal property. In both cases, the property can be sold to satisfy the debt, but notice of the foreclosure and sale must first be given to the debtor.

2. D. With the right of subrogation, a surety, or a guarantor, may pursue any remedies that were available to the creditor against the debtor. These rights include collection of the debt. A right of contribution is available to a co-surety, who pays more than his or her proportionate share of a debt, to recover from any other co-sureties. An exemption, in the context of a debt, is property that a debtor can protect from being used to pay the debt. Exoneration is not a term that applies to this circumstance.

3. A. Unless a buyer in the ordinary course of business knows that a purchase violates a third party's rights, the buyer takes goods free of any security interest. This is an exception to the general rule that a security interest in collateral continues even after the collateral is sold.

4. B. Only a debtor can file a plan under Chapter 11, but for the court to confirm it, the secured creditors must accept it. There is another condition that the plan must meet. It must provide that creditors retain their liens and the value of the property to be distributed to them is not less than the secured portion of their claims, or the debtor must surrender to the creditors the property securing those claims.

5. A. A Chapter 11 plan must provide for the full payment of all claims entitled to priority and the same treatment of each claim within a particular class. After the payments are completed, all debts provided for by the plan are discharged.

Chapter 31

True-False Questions

1. T
2. F. Agency by ratification and agency by estoppel do not require such an agreement.
3. T
4. F. The key feature of an employer–employee relationship is that the employer has the right to control the employee in the performance of tasks involved in the employment. Employees do not have independent business discretion.
5. F. In most states, a minor can be an *agent* but not a principal.
6. T
7. F. When an agent breaches an agency contract, the principal can choose to avoid the contract.
8. F. If an agent is negligent and harms a third party, the principal can be sued by the third party. In some circumstances, the principal may also sue the agent. The same principles apply when an agent violates a principal's instructions.
9. T
10. T

Fill-in Questions

Performance; notification; loyalty; obedience; accounting

Multiple-Choice Questions

1. B. The problem states that the two are hired as employees. The employer is the principal. Normally, all employees who deal with third parties are deemed to be agents.

2. A. This is an agency relationship. An agency agreement does not have to be in writing, and an agent does not need to indicate that he or she is an agent. The business of the agent is not a determining factor in whether an agency relationship exists.

3. C. Unless an agent is a gratuitous agent (one who does not perform for money), a principal always owes an agent compensation for services rendered. In this problem, if nothing had been agreed to, the principal would owe the agent the customary amount for his or her services. Also, payment must be timely. Another of a principal's duties is to reimburse an agent for expenses related to the agency, unless the parties have agreed otherwise. This question and answer are based on a question that appeared in the CPA exam in 1996.

4. A. An agent's duties to a principal include a duty to act solely in the principal's interest in matters concerning the principal's business. This is the duty of loyalty.

5. A. Ryan is an agent, and Desktop is a principal. Ryan may also be an employee, depending primarily on the degree of control that Desktop will exercise over the physical performance of the job.

6. D. Neither consideration nor a written agreement is required to form an agency relationship. Normally, an agency relationship must be based on an agreement that the agent will act for the principal, but the agreement can be oral or implied by conduct.

7. D. If a principal causes a third person to believe that another person is his or her agent, and the third person deals with the supposed agent, the principal is estopped to deny the agency relationship. The third person must reasonably believe that the relationship existed and that the agent had authority. An ordinary, prudent person familiar with business practice and custom would have been justified in making the same conclusion.

8. C. The first two choices in response to this problem are the same answer: in performing an agency, an agent is expected to use reasonable diligence and skill, which is the degree of skill of a reasonable person under similar circumstances. If an agent claims special skills—such as those of an accountant—he or she is expected to use those skills.

9. C. A failure to disclose material information bearing on an agency relationship is a breach of an agent's duties, and the agency is voidable at the option of the principal.

10. D. A third party can sue a principal for an agent's negligence, and in some situations, the principal can also sue the agent. This is also true if the agent violates the principal's instructions.

Issue Spotters

1. Yes. A principal has a duty to indemnify an agent for liabilities incurred because of authorized and lawful acts and transactions and for losses suffered because of the principal's failure to perform his or her duties.

2. No. An agent is prohibited from taking advantage of the agency relationship to obtain property that the principal wants to purchase. This is the duty of loyalty that arises with every agency relationship.

3. As set out in the problem, the truck driver is an employee, and the lighting technician and the booking agent are independent contractors. The booking agent is an agent, but either the employee or the independent contractor may at times also act in the capacity of an agent.

4. In an agency relationship, when one party violates his or her duty to the other, remedies available to the party not in breach include damages, termination of the agency, injunction, and accounting. Any of these remedies, which are normal contract and tort remedies, might be used in this situation.

5. When an agent retains benefits that belong to the principal, a court can impose a constructive trust and declare that the agent holds the benefit on behalf of the principal. A constructive trust may also be imposed when an agent retains profits that belong to the principal or takes advantage of the agency to obtain property the principal wants to buy.

Chapter 32

True-False Questions

1. T
2. F. Due to the doctrine of *respondeat superior*, a principal may be liable for any harm caused to a third party by an agent who is acting within the scope of her or his employment.
3. T.
4. T
5. T
6. F. Criminal acts by an agent are not the responsibility of the principal.
7. F. The parties to an agency may always have the *power* to terminate the agency at any time, but they may not always have the *right*. If a party who terminates an agency does not have the right to do so, he or she may be liable for breach of contract.
8. F. A principal can expressly ratify a transaction by a writing, but a principal can also ratify a transaction in other ways. A principal may impliedly ratify a transaction by, for example, failing to object to an unauthorized act within a reasonable time.
9. F. An agent is liable for his or her own torts. The principal may also be liable, depending on the circumstances.
10. T

Fill-in Questions

is; an undisclosed; undisclosed; tort injuries; generally does not result

Multiple-Choice Questions

1. C. In determining whether an agent has the implied authority to do a specific act, the question is whether it is reasonable for the agent to believe that he or she has the authority.
2. C. When an agent acts within the scope of his or her authority to enter into a valid contract on behalf of an undisclosed principal, the principal is liable on the contract. Ratification is not necessary. The agent may also be liable on the contract. This question and answer are based on a question included in the May 1995 CPA exam.
3. C. Under the doctrine of *respondeat superior*, an employer (or principal) is vicariously liable for the wrongful acts of his or her employee (or agent) committed within the scope of employment (or agency).
4. A. Unless an agency is in writing—in which case, it must be terminated in writing—an agent can learn of a termination through any means. Until an agent is notified of the principal's decision to terminate the agency relationship, the agent's authority continues. Similarly, third parties with whom the agent deals must be informed of the termination to end the agent's apparent authority, as regards those third parties.
5. C. When an agent acts without authority and a third party relies on the agency status, the agent may be liable for breach of any contract purportedly signed on behalf of a principal. The agent may not be liable, however, if the third party knew that the agent did not have authority to contract on behalf of the principal. In either case, the principal is not liable, unless he or she ratifies the contract.
6. A. When an agent contracts purportedly on behalf of a principal but outside the scope of his or her authority, the principal can ratify the contract (approve or affirm it by word or by deed) and thereby be liable on it.
7. D. An agency can terminate in several ways. These choices illustrate three of those ways—termination by lapse of time, by the achievement of the agency's purpose, and by death.
8. B. An employer is liable for harm to a third party by an employee acting within the scope of employment. Here, the question is whether the employee was acting within that scope. Factors that indicate he was not include that the act (theft) was not authorized, did not advance the employer's interest, is not commonly performed by employees for their employers, and involved a serious crime. The employer might be liable if it knew that the employee would commit a tort or allowed it. In this problem, the employee acted without the employer's knowledge.
9. C. An employer is liable for harm caused to a third party by an employee acting within the scope of employment. The issue is whether an act is within that scope. In this problem, factors that indicate the employee acted within that scope include that the act (cutting down

the wrong tree) was within the employer's time, place, and purpose; and the employer furnished the means. An employee is also liable for his or her own tort.

10. A. When an agent is employed to accomplish a particular objective, the agency automatically terminates when the objective is accomplished.

Issue Spotters

1. A person in whose name a contract is made by one who is not an agent may be liable on the contract if he or she approves or affirms that contract. In other words, Marie could be held liable on the note if she ratifies it on her return.

2. Probably. A principal is liable for a loss due to an agent's knowing misrepresentation if the representation was made within the scope of the agency and the agent's scope of authority.

3. Third persons injured by an employee's negligence can sue the employee or the employer, if the tort was committed while the employee was acting within the scope of employment. Thus, United is liable unless Otis's sidewalk driving is found to be outside the scope of his employment. Otis himself is liable, because an individual is always liable for his own torts.

4. Yes. When a principal causes a third party reasonably to believe that an agent has authority, and the third party changes position in reliance on the principal's representations, the principal may be estopped from denying that the agent had authority. Here, the bank put the clerk in the teller's window, the customer left money with the clerk believing that he was a teller because he was in the window, and the customer suffered a loss thereby.

5. Yes. When an event has such an unusual effect on the subject matter of an agency, an agent can consider the agency terminated.

Cumulative Hypothetical Problem for Unit Six—Including Chapters 31–32

1. A. Unless an agency relationship falls within the Statute of Frauds, it does not need to be in writing. It does not even need to be express (it may be implied in certain circumstances). The consideration does not need to be specified; consideration is not even required. A power of attorney is a type of agency relationship; it is not a requirement for all agency relationships.

2. D. One of the agent's fiduciary duties to the principal is the duty of loyalty. This means that the agent must not engage in conflicts of interest, and the agent cannot compete with the principal without informing the principal and obtaining the principal's consent.

3. B. When an agent enters into a contract onto behalf of a disclosed principal, without authority or in excess of his or her authority, the principal can be bound to the contract if he or she ratifies it. To ratify a contract, a principal must know the relevant facts, the principal must have capacity, the principal must ratify the whole transaction, and the principal must act before the other party withdraws from the deal.

4. A. In the case of an undisclosed principal, or in the case of a partially disclosed principal, a third party with whom an agent has contracted on the principal's behalf may elect to hold either the agent or the principal liable. Of course, the third party must first learn the principal's identity.

5. D. The notice to the agent's customers was sufficient. When an agent personally deals with third parties, those parties need actual notice of the agent's termination. When there is no contact, however, the principal still needs to give notice, but constructive notice, such as notice by publication, is enough.

Chapter 33

True-False Questions

1. F. In a sole proprietorship, the owner and the business are the same. If the owner dies, the business ceases to exist.

2. T

3. F. As stated in the previous question, a partnership is an association of two or more persons to carry on, as co-owners, a business for profit. A writing is not required (unless the Statute of Frauds applies): an agreement to enter into a partnership can be oral or implied by conduct. In other words, a certificate of partnership does not have to be filed with a state to form a general partnership (although a filed certificate is necessary to form a *limited* partnership, discussed in a later chapter).

4. F. Joint ownership of property does not alone create a partnership, nor is the sharing of gross returns and profits from joint ownership usually enough to create a partnership.

5. F. In forming a partnership, a writing is necessary only if the partnership would otherwise be in violation of the Statute of Frauds. For example, if the business of the partnership is to invest in land, the partnership agreement must be in writing to be enforceable.

6. T

7. T

8. T

9. F. A partnership files an informational return with the Internal Revenue Service, but the firm does not pay taxes on its profits. The income is passed through to the partners, who pay taxes on it on their individual returns.

10. T

Fill-in Questions

are; obligation; sued; cannot; releases; must

Multiple-Choice Questions

1. B. A partnership arises from an agreement between two or more persons to carry on a business for profit. No formal declaration is necessary. A proprietorship can have only a single owner. A sole proprietorship is another name for a proprietorship.

2. C. Under a partnership by estoppel theory, a person who is not a partner, but who represents himself or herself as a partner, is liable to a third person who acts in reasonable reliance on that representation. A partner who consents to the misrepresentation is also liable. Karl impliedly consented to the misrepresentation when he said nothing.

3. B. A partner holds all partnership property (and proceeds from its sale) as a tenant in partnership for all of the partners. A partner's fiduciary duty requires him or her to hold in trust for the others all funds realized from transactions connected with the business of

the partnership and to account for the profits.

4. C. This arrangement for the payment of an employee (a base wage and a sales commission) does not make the employee a partner in the employer's business. There are three attributes of a partnership—sharing profits is only one of them.

5. C. There are many ways to cause the dissolution of a partnership. Partners may expressly agree to dissolve their partnership, or dissolution may be caused by (with or without all partners' knowledge or consent) the addition of a new partner or the transfer of a partner's interest. Depending on a particular state's law, dissolution may also result from the withdrawal of a partner. Of the choices in this problem, however, the only one that would cause dissolution is a partner's bankruptcy. This question and answer are based on a question from a CPA exam in 1998.

6. D. On the petition of a partner, a judge can dissolve a partnership under any circumstances that render a decree of dissolution equitable. The other choices indicate some of the possibilities (insanity, misconduct, commercial impracticability), but there is no specified limit on causes.

7. A. In all states, partners are jointly and severally liable for torts and breaches of trust.

8. C. The other three factors are implicit in the UPA's definition of a partnership as "an association of two or more persons to carry on as co-owners a business for profit."

9. C. For most purposes, a partnership is regarded as an entity. A partnership can sue and collect judgments in its own name (rather than in the names of the individual partners). A partnership can own real estate in its name. For federal income tax purposes, however, a partnership is considered an aggregate: the firm pays no income tax. The partners pay taxes individually.

10. B. After a partner informs the other partners that he or she is withdrawing from the partnership, the withdrawing partner is not liable for contracts entered into by his or her former partners. The parties who sign the contract are, of course, liable, however.

Issue Spotters

1. No. The receipt of profits as payment of rent to a landlord is specifically excepted from the definition of partnership.

2. Logan's widow has no right to take Logan's place. No one can become a partner without the unanimous consent of the partners. Also, if a partner dies, the surviving partners, not the heirs of the deceased partner, have the right of survivorship to the specific property, such as the CD-ROM drives. Surviving partners must account to the decedent's estate for the *value* of the deceased partner's interest in the property.

3. Under the partners' fiduciary duty, a partner must account to the partnership for any personal profits or benefits derived without the consent of all the partners in connection with the use of any partnership property. Hans may not keep the money.

4. Yes. Partners do not have to abide by the stipulations in the agreement—they can mutually agree to dissolve the partnership early or to extend it.

5. When a business is relatively small and is not diversified, employs relatively few people, has modest profits, and is not likely to expand significantly or require extensive financing in the immediate future, the most appropriate form for doing business may be a sole proprietorship.

Chapter 34

True-False Questions

1. T

2. F. A corporation formed in a country other than the United States, but that does business in the United States, is an alien corporation.

3. T

4. F. When conflicts arise among documents involving corporations the U.S. Constitution has the highest priority, followed by state constitutions, state statutes, the certificate of incorporation, corporate bylaws, and resolutions of the board of directors, in that order.

5. T

6. T

7. F. Sole proprietorships and many partnerships are not separate legal entities, but corporations are.

8. T

9. T

10. F. An S corporation has tax imposed only at the shareholder level. Other corporations are subject to double taxation, however, which is one of the reasons for the enactment of the S corporation statute.

Fill-in Questions

promoters; unless; an incorporator; need not

Multiple-Choice Questions

1. C. A shareholders' meeting cannot be held until there are shareholders, and there can be no shareholders until the corporation is formed and accepts the subscribers' offers to buy stock.

2. B. After the initial board of directors is chosen, the retention or removal of directors is accomplished by a vote of the shareholders. Similarly, shareholders elect later directors to their positions.

3. A. This corporation has the characteristics of a close corporation—a corporation with a small number of shareholders and restrictions on the transfer of its shares. This corporation is also a domestic corporation.

4. A. Corporate officers do not have the authority to bind the corporation in matters of great significance to the corporate purpose.

5. C. Shareholders are a corporation's owners. Shareholders may or may not be the corporation's managers, promoters, or incorporators.

6. D. The other choices are false: Bonds must be repaid, stock is equity, bonds are debt, and holders of common stock are the last to be paid on a corporation's dissolution.

7. D. To obtain capital, a corporation issues securities, principally stocks and bonds. Essentially, a security represents either an ownership interest in a firm or a debt owed by the firm.

8. B. Dividends are taxed as ordinary income to the shareholders.

9. C. Articles of incorporation serve as a primary source of authority for a corporation's organization and functions. Besides the choices in the correct answer to this problem, the information contained in the articles includes the firm's name, its duration, its nature and purpose, and its capital structure. This question and answer are based on a question that was included in the November 1995 CPA exam.

10. D. These are just some of the factors that a court may use to pierce the corporate veil.

Issue Spotters

1. A corporation does *not* have an automatic right to do business in a state other than its state of incorporation. Normally, a firm incorporated in one state must obtain a certificate of authority in any other state in which the firm plans to do business. If a corporation does business without a certificate of authority, the state can fine the corporation, deny it the privilege of using the state's courts, and hold its officers, directors, or agents personally liable for corporate obligations incurred in that state.

2. Yes. Small businesses that meet certain requirements can qualify as S corporations, created specifically to permit small businesses to avoid double taxation. The six requirements of an S corporation are (1) the firm must be a domestic corporation, (2) the firm must not be a member of an affiliated group of corporations, (3) the firm must have less than a certain number of shareholders, (4) the shareholders must be individuals, estates, or qualified trusts, (5) there can be only one class of stock, and (6) no shareholder can be a nonresident alien.

3. The election or removal of directors is subject to a vote by the shareholders. The typical term for a director is one year. Sometimes, although all of the initial directors begin to serve at the same time, their terms are staggered, so that all directors do not stand for election simultaneously.

4. To obtain capital, a corporation issues securities, principally stocks and bonds. A security usually represents either an ownership interest in a firm or a debt owed by the firm.

5. Under certain circumstances, corporate directors and officers may themselves be imprisoned for their own criminal acts or the criminal acts of employees under their direct supervision.

Chapter 35

True-False Questions

1. T
2. T
3. F. The rights of shareholders are established in articles of incorporation and under the state's general incorporation law.
4. T
5. F. Any damages recovered in a shareholder's derivative suit are normally paid to the corporation on whose behalf the shareholder or shareholders who exercised the derivative right.
6. T
7. F. Officers and directors owe the same fiduciary duties to the corporations for which they work. They both owe a duty of loyalty. This duty requires them to subordinate their personal interests to the welfare of the corporation.
8. F. The business judgment rule immunizes directors (and officers) from liability for poor business decisions and other honest mistakes that cause a corporation to suffer a loss.
9. T
10. T

Fill-in Questions

but ownership is not; can; recorded as the owner in the corporation's books

Multiple-Choice Questions

1. D. There is no such right. The ownership of a corporation by shareholders does not include the actual ownership of specific corporate property.
2. C. Directors have rights to participate in board meetings and to inspect corporate books. Rights that directors do not have include an inherent right to compensation. That is, directors may be compensated for their efforts, but they have no inherent right to compensation.
3. A. This debt is then enforceable at law like any other debt. Generally, state law allows dividends to be paid as long as a corporation can pay its other debts

as they come due and the amount of the dividend is not more than the net worth of the corporation.

4. C. Directors are expected to use a reasonable amount of supervision over corporate officers and employees when they delegate work. This is part of the fiduciary duty of care that they owe to their corporation. Their liability for breach of this duty could be grounded in negligence or mismanagement of corporate personnel.

5. D. The other choices do not represent proper purposes for which a shareholders' derivative suit may be filed. A shareholder's derivative suit is a claim filed on behalf of the corporation. Such a suit may allege, for example, that officers or directors misused corporate assets. Of course, any damages that are awarded must be paid to the corporation. This question and answer are based on a question that appeared in a CPA exam in 1998.

6. C. Cumulative voting can often be used in the election of directors to enhance the power of minority shareholders in electing a representative. In calculating a shareholder's votes under the cumulative voting method, in this problem, Mary's number of shares is multiplied by the number of directors to be elected.

7. C. A director's fiduciary duty requires him or her to make a full disclosure of any potential conflicts of interest that might arise in any corporate transaction. If a contract between the corporations is fair and reasonable at the time it is made, and it is approved by a majority of the disinterested directors or shareholders, it will likely be upheld.

8. A. The board's best defense in this case is to assert the business judgment rule—that is, that an honest mistake of judgment on its part does not make it liable to the corporation for resulting damages. If this is not a valid defense, the directors may be held to have violated their fiduciary duties, which include the duties of loyalty and care. A shareholder's derivative suit is a shareholder's remedy for a wrong done to the corporation.

9. C. Officers and other executive employees are hired by a corporation's board of directors. The rights of the officers and other high-level managers are defined by their employment contracts with the corporation.

10. C. Under their duty of loyalty, directors cannot compete with their corporation or have an interest that conflicts with the interest of the corporation. Owning the stock of a competitor would constitute an interest that conflicts with the interest of the corporation on whose board a director serves.

Issue Spotters

1. A director cannot support a business that competes directly with a corporation on the board of which the director sits. The director's fiduciary duty requires him to fully disclose the conflict of interest. Most likely, the director in these circumstances will have to resign from one of the boards.

2. The best defense in this context is the business judgment rule. As long as a director or officer acts in good faith, it what he or she considers to be the best interests of the corporation, and with the care that an ordinarily prudent person would use in similar circumstances, he or she is not liable simply because the decision had a negative result.

3. Under these circumstances, a minority shareholder can petition a court to appoint and receiver and liquidate the assets of the corporation.

4. Yes. A shareholder can bring a derivative suit on behalf of a corporation, if some wrong is done to the corporation. Normally, any damages recovered go into the corporate treasury.

5. Yes. A single shareholder—or a few shareholders acting together—who owns enough stock to exercise *de facto* control over a corporation owes the corporation and minority shareholders a fiduciary duty when transferring those shares.

Chapter 36

True-False Questions

1. T
2. T
3. T
4. F. Shareholder approval is not normally required to buy all or substantially all of another corporation's assets.

It is necessary, however, that the selling corporation's shareholders approve the sale of all or substantially all of its assets to another corporation.

5. T
6. T
7. T
8. F. Ordinarily, a corporation that purchases the assets of another corporation does not assume the other's liabilities. In some cases, however, the purchasing corporation may be held responsible for the seller's liabilities—for example, if the purchasing corporation continues the seller's business with the same personnel.
9. F. Shareholder approval is required before filing articles of merger or consolidation.
10. F. In those states that provide for shareholder appraisal rights, they are usually available in sales of substantially all of a corporation's assets.

Fill-in Questions

Can; shareholder; before; before; the vote is taken.

Multiple-Choice Questions

1. A. In a merger or consolidation, the surviving corporation acquires all the assets of both corporations without a formal transfer. In a merger, the surviving corporation's articles of incorporation are considered to be *amended* by the articles of merger, and in a consolidation, the articles of consolidation *replace* the previous corporations' articles.
2. A. Shareholder approval is required to sell all of a corporation's assets.
3. B. Without shareholder approval, one corporation may buy all, or substantially all, of the assets of another corporation. The other choices are actions that a board of directors cannot undertake without shareholder approval. This question and answer are based on a CPA exam question that appeared in a 1997 exam.
4. C. The officers do not have to approve a merger.
5. C. A corporation's failure to comply with administrative requirements could result in a court-ordered dissolution. Both a and b are administrative requirements.

6. B. This combination is a merger—only one corporation continues to exist.
7. B. Usually, a corporation that buys the assets of another corporation does not assume the other's liabilities, unless, as in this case, the sale is fraudulently executed to avoid liability.
8. A. This combination is a consolidation—both corporations continue to exist as a new entity.
9. C. In a merger or consolidation, the surviving corporation acquires all of the assets and assumes all of the debts of its predecessors (the corporations that formed it).
10. D. A corporation's failure to comply with administrative requirements could result in a court-ordered dissolution. Filing an annual report is an administrative requirement. Dissolution may be sought if a corporation fails to commence business operations after forming. Other reasons include obtaining a corporate charter through fraud and abuse of corporate powers.

Issue Spotters

1. The first combination is a merger. One of the previously existing corporations absorbed the other. The second combination is a consolidation. Neither of the combining corporations continue after the combination: a new firm continues in their place.
2. Shareholders who disapprove of a merger or a consolidation may be entitled to be paid fair value for their shares. These are known as appraisal rights.
3. Generally, a corporation that buys the assets of another corporation does not assume the other's liabilities. In this case, however, the purchasing corporation continued the seller's business with the same personnel. The purchaser may be held responsible for the seller's liabilities because of the use of the same personnel.
4. To retain control over itself, a target corporation can take any one or more of a number of defensive measures. The target may attempt to take over the acquiring corporation, it may sell off its most attractive assets, or it may seek to be taken over by a more desirable acquiring corporation, among other courses of action.

5. Generally, only shareholders acting unanimously can dissolve a corporation. Close corporations may be dissolved by a single shareholder if the articles of incorporation provide for it. Thus, an individual shareholder's ability to dissolve a corporation depends on these factors.

Chapter 37

True-False Questions

1. T
2. T
3. T
4. T
5. F. The Securities Act of 1933 concerns primarily disclosure on the issuance of securities, and the Securities Exchange Act of 1934 concerns primarily the resale of securities.
6. T
7. T
8. T
9. F. SEC Rule 10b-5 applies to registered and unregistered securities. Fraud in connection with the purchase or sale of *any* security is prohibited under this rule.
10. F. Most securities can be resold without registration. Also, under Rule 144 and 144A ("Safe harbor" provisions), there are specific exemptions for securities that might otherwise require registration with the SEC.

Fill-in Questions

prosecution; triple; ten; may

Multiple-Choice Questions

1. B. Under the Securities Exchange Act of 1934, the Securities and Exchange Commission all of the other duties and more, including regulating national securities trading, supervising mutual funds, and recommending sanctions in cases involving violations of securities laws. This question and answer are based on a question that was included in a 1996 CPA exam.
2. A. These are the elements under Section 16(b). Whether the officer used the inside information is irrelevant.
3. A. Because of the low amount of the issue, it qualifies as an exemption from registration under Rule 504—no specific disclosure document is required, and there is no prohibition on solicitation.
4. D. This issue might qualify under Rule 505 or Section 4(6), except that again, the issuer advertised the offering, which it cannot do and remain exempt from registration. In other words, the amount of this offering disqualified the issuer from advertising it without filing a registration statement.
5. C. A registration statement must supply enough information so that an unsophisticated investor can evaluate the financial risk involved. Besides the description of management, there must also be disclosure of any of their material transactions with the firm.
6. D. The amount of this offering is too high to exempt it from the registration requirements except possibly under Rule 506 or Section 4(6). This issuer advertised the offering, however, and Rule 506 prohibits general solicitation. Thus, without filing a registration statement, the issuer could not legally solicit *any* investors (whatever it may have believed about the unaccredited investors). This offering does not qualify under Section 4(6), because unaccredited investors participated.
7. A. The executive officer is the traditional inside trader. The attorney and the accountant are a tippee and a remote tippee and will be liable because they know of the executive officer's misconduct.
8. D. The chief problem with this offering is that the issuer advertised it. Under Rule 506, private offerings in unlimited amounts may qualify for an exemption from registration, but no general solicitation is permitted without registration. Even if this issuer complied with all other SEC requirements, however, it should have given the required information to *all* investors, not only the unaccredited investors. (This offering does not qualify under Section 4(6), because unaccredited investors participated.)
9. A. Most resales are exempt from registration if they are undertaken by persons other than issuers or underwriters. Resales of restricted securities acquired under Rule 504a, Rule 505, Rule 506, or Section 4(6) may trigger registration requirements, but the original

sale in this problem came under Rule 504.

10. C. There must be disclosure of any of management's material transactions with the firm. Besides a description of the security and its relationship to the registrant's other securities, how the registrant intends to use the proceeds from the sale of the issue, a description of the registrant's properties and management, and a description of pending lawsuits, a registration statement must include a certified financial statement.

Issue Spotters

1. Yes. Under the Securities Act of 1933, a security exists when a person invests in a common enterprise with the reasonable expectation of profits derived primarily or substantially from the managerial or entrepreneurial efforts of others. In other words, securities do not include only corporate stocks and bonds.

2. The average investor is not concerned with minor inaccuracies but with facts that if disclosed would tend to deter him or her from buying the securities. This would include facts that have an important bearing on the condition of the issuer and its business—liabilities, loans to officers and directors, customer delinquencies, and pending lawsuits.

3. No. The Securities Exchange Act of 1934 extends liability to officers and directors in their personal transactions for taking advantage of inside information when they know it is unavailable to the persons with whom they are dealing.

4. Yes. All states have their own corporate securities laws.

5. Under the Investment Company Act of 1940, investment companies include any entity that is "engaged primarily . . . in the business of investing, reinvesting, or trading in securities." The act excludes banks, insurance companies, savings and loan associations, finance companies, oil and gas drilling firms, charitable foundations, tax-exempt pension funds, closely held corporations, and other institutions. Generally, an investment company buys and sells securities for the benefit of its shareholders. A mutual fund is a type of investment company that sells shares of ownership in a portfolio.

Chapter 38

True-False Questions

1. T

2. F. Similarly, a limited partnership will not dissolve on the personal bankruptcy or death of a limited partner. These same events occurring to a general partner can dissolve the firm, however.

3. F. Like the formation of a corporation and other forms of limited liability organizations, the formation of a limited liability company (LLC) requires that articles of organization be filed in the state of formation. Otherwise, an LLC will not be held to exist, and its members will not enjoy the features that they wanted.

4. T

5. F. One of the chief advantages of a limited liability company (LLC) is that it offers the limited liability of a corporation. Because an LLC also offers the tax advantages of a partnership, many businesses are using this form of organization.

6. F. The feature that makes a limited liability partnership attractive to professionals is that its partners can avoid liability for the malpractice of other partners. Of course, each partner is liable for his or her own wrongful acts. All of the partners may be held liable for other obligations of the partnership, however.

7. F. The liability of the limited partners in a limited partnership is limited to the amount of their investment in the firm, but the liability of the general partners is the same as that of the partners in a general partnership—unlimited.

8. T

9. T

10. T

Fill-in Questions

members; limited liability company; limited partners; limited partnership

Multiple-Choice Questions

1. D. Ordinarily, limited partners are liable for the debts of their limited partnerships only to the extent of their capital contributions to the firms. A general partner, in contrast, may be held personally liable for the full amount of the firm's obligations. Similarly, a limited partner, unlike a general partner does not have a right to control the partnership. This question and answer are based on a question that appeared in the November 1989 CPA exam.

2. B. A partner (general or limited) pays personal income taxes on his or her share of the firm's income, regardless of whether or not it is distributed to him. The other partners pay taxes on their shares of the firm's income.

3. B. A limited liability company is taxed as a partnership. The income is passed through to its members without being taxed at the company level. Generally, there is no particular advantage to being taxed as a corporation. In fact, avoiding corporate taxes is one reason for forming a limited liability company.

4. A. Normally, the members of a limited liability company are liable for the debts of their company only to the extent of their investment in the firm, like corporate shareholders. Sole proprietors and general partners, in contrast, may be personally liable for the full amount of their firms' obligations.

5. C. One of the advantages of the limited liability company form of business organization is that it members are not personally liable for the debts of their firm regardless of the extent of their participation in management (unlike a limited partnership). Another advantage is that there is generally no limit on the number of members that a firm can have (unlike an S corporation).

6. D. Limited partnerships may be dissolved by many causes but not by any of these choices. Partners may expressly agree to dissolve their partnership, or dissolution may be caused by the withdrawal, death, or mental incompetence of a general partner (unless the others agree to continue the business). A *general* partner's death or bankruptcy causes the firm to dissolve, as would an event that makes it impossible to operate the partnership lawfully. Dissolution can also result from a court decree.

7. C. Professionals who organize as a limited liability partnership avoid per-

sonal liability for the wrongdoing of other partners. They have only the same liability as a limited partner in a limited partnership.

8. B. A limited partner does not need to be designated as the manager of the firm to form a limited partnership. (In fact, a limited partner may forfeit limited liability by taking part in managing the business.) The other choices are requirements, however.

9. A. Limited partners essentially have fewer rights than general partners. (In return, they assume less liability for the debts of the firm.) One of the important rights of general partners that limited partners usually do not have is the right to participate in the management of the firm.

10. C. It is expected that eventually, state laws governing limited liability companies will be made relatively uniform. As for the other choices, the members are not subject to personal liability for the firm's obligations. Also, unlike corporate income, limited liability company income passes through the firm and is taxed only once.

Issue Spotters

1. A partner who commits a wrongful act, such as fraud, is liable for the results. The partner who supervises the party who commits the act may also be held liable. Some states limit this liability so that each partner is liable only up to the proportion of his or her responsibility for the result.

2. There is no law that expressly bars the participation of limited partners in the management of a limited partnership. Limited partners are, however, normally exempt from personal liability for partnership debts, torts, breaches of contract, and breaches of trust. This exemption rests primarily on the limited partner's not participating in the management of the partnership. Thus, it is the threat of personal liability that deters their participation.

3. The members of a limited liability company (LLC) may designate a group to run their firm, in which situation the firm would be considered a *manager*-managed LLC. The group may include only members, only nonmembers, or members and nonmembers. If instead, all members participate in management, the firm would be a *member*-managed LLC. In fact, unless the members agree otherwise, all members are considered to participate in the management of the firm.

4. Creditors of the partnership including partners who are creditors, have priority to partnership assets. Partners and former partners then receive (1) unpaid distributions of partnership assets and (2) except as otherwise agreed, a return on their contributions and amounts proportionate to their share of distributions.

5. The provisions of a limited liability company operating agreement typically set out the firm's management, the division of profits, how membership may be transferred, what events cause dissolution, etc. If there is no agreement, the applicable state statutes determine these issues. In the absence of a statute, the principles of partnership law apply.

Chapter 39

True-False Questions

1. T
2. T
3. F. The termination of a franchise is determined by the parties. Generally, the parties provide that termination is "for cause" and notice is required. Of course, in the case of a dispute, litigation may ensue and the parties may end up in court where the franchise may be terminated. That is not the usual course, however.
4. F. The members of a joint venture may be sued individually, but the joint venture cannot be sued as an entity.
5. T
6. T
7. F. A franchisor can exercise greater control in this area, because the *franchisor* has a legitimate interest in maintaining the quality of the product or service to protect its name and reputation.
8. F. Partners in a partnership can bind other partners to contracts and other obligations to third parties. The members of a joint venture have limited power to bind other members.

9. T
10. F. There is state law covering franchises, and it is very similar to federal law on the subject, requiring certain disclosures, limiting termination without cause, and so on.

Fill-in Questions

distributorship; chain-style; manufacturing

Multiple-Choice Questions

1. C. This definition is like the definition of a partnership. A joint venture is similar to a partnership, and is generally subject to partnership law, but unlike a partnership, a joint venture is created in contemplation of a limited activity. A joint venture may have more than two members, and a joint venture is not a corporate enterprise, although its members may be corporations. This question and answer are based on a question that appeared in the November 1989 CPA exam.
2. D. A syndicate may exist as a partnership, a corporation, or no legally recognized form. As in this problem, a syndicate is a group of individuals financing a project.
3. C. A joint stock company is a hybrid of a partnership and a corporation in that it is usually treated like a partnership, but its members are not treated like agents of each other and it has many characteristics of a corporation: (1) ownership by shares of stock, (2) managed by directors and officers, and (3) perpetual existence.
4. A. A business trust is similar to a corporation. Like corporate shareholders, the owners hold shares in the trust and they are not personally liable for the organization's debts and obligations.
5. C. At one time, it was held that a franchisor's setting of prices would violate federal antitrust laws. A recent decision of the United States Supreme Court has changed this rule.
6. C. Under the contract between the franchisor and the franchisee, the latter may be required to pay a fee for the franchise license, fees for products bought from or through the franchisor, and a percentage of advertising and administrative costs.

7. C. In this type of franchise, a franchisor typically requires a franchisee to pay it a fee for the right to sell its products. The franchisor also usually requires that the franchisee pay the franchisor a percentage of the receipts from the sales of the products.

8. C. Of the choices here, again the franchisor can set the terms. There may be little for a franchisee to negotiate with some franchises, but perhaps the chief advantage of a franchise is that the franchisee is obtaining the opportunity to profit from the sales of a proven product or service.

9. A. Franchise agreements typically that the franchisor can terminate a franchise for cause. If no set time for termination is provided, a reasonable time will be implied. A franchisor cannot usually terminate without notice.

10. C. A franchisee may have some protection under Federal Trade Commission regulations with respect to what the franchisor must disclose before the franchisee invests in a franchise. A franchisee may have additional protection under federal law, depending on the nature of the products or services being sold. State protection, while similar to federal law, may include more protection under deceptive practices acts or Article 2 of the UCC.

Issue Spotters

1. Probably not. If a franchise is a "written agreement," an oral promise would not be part of a franchise agreement.

2. Yes. If the franchisor acts in good faith, "cause" may also include the death or disability of the franchisee, the insolvency of the franchisee, and a breach of the franchise agreement.

3. There are differences between these forms of business organization, but all of them are treated under the law like partnerships. The differences include that the members of joint ventures have less authority than partners, and the members of a joint stock company are not agents of each other.

4. Although there are differences, all of these forms of business organizations resemble corporations. A joint stock company, for example, features ownership by shares of stock, it is managed by

directors and officers, and it has perpetual existence. A business trust, like a corporation, distributes profits to persons who are not personally responsible for the debts of the organization, and management of the business is in the hands of trustees, just as the management of a corporation is in the hands of directors and officers. An incorporated cooperative, which is subject to state laws covering nonprofit corporations, distributes profits to its owners.

5. Too much control may result in the franchisor's liability for torts of a franchisee's employees. For example, if the employee performs in a manner that is attributed to the control of the franchisor, and this performance results in an injury to another, the franchisor may be held liable.

Chapter 40

True-False Questions

1. T

2. F. Business ethics is concerned with right or wrong behavior in business—how general ethical principles are applied to situations that arise in business.

3. T

4. F. According to utilitarianism, it is the consequences of an act that determine how ethical the act is. Applying this theory requires determining who will be affected by an action, assessing the positive and negatives effects of alternatives, and choosing the alternative that will provide the greatest benefit for the most people. Utilitarianism is premised on acting so as to do the greatest good for the greatest number of people.

5. T

6. F. In situations involving ethical decisions, a balance must sometimes be struck between equally good or equally poor courses of action. The choice is often between equally good alternatives—benefiting shareholders versus benefiting employees, for example.

7. T

8. T

9. T

10. F. Conduct that would have been considered acceptable ten or more years ago may not be considered acceptable today. A sense of what is ethical varies from individual to individual and from group to group, and these ethics vary over time. Most of the major ethical issues confronting businesses today were of little public concern one hundred years ago.

Fill-in Questions

proper behavior; proper behavior; changes

Multiple-Choice Questions

1.   A. Business ethics focuses on the application of moral principles in a business context. Business ethics is a subset of ethics that relates specifically to what constitutes right and wrong in situations that arise in business.

2.   A. Traditionally, ethical reasoning relating to business has been characterized by two fundamental approaches—duty-based ethics and utilitarianism, or outcome-based ethics. Duty-based ethics derive from religious sources.

3.   C. Under religious ethical standards, it is the nature of an act that determines how ethical the act is, not its consequences. This is considered an *absolute* standard. This standard is tempered by compassion (the Golden Rule).

4.   B. Utilitarianism is premised on acting so as to do the greatest good for the greatest number of people.

5.   B. Utilitarianism requires determining who will be affected by an action, assessing the positive and negatives effects of alternatives, and choosing the alternative that will provide the greatest benefit for the most people. This approach has been criticized as tending to reduce the welfare of human beings to plus and minus signs on a cost-benefit worksheet.

6.   D. A corporate employer who responds to what the employer sees as a moral obligation to correct for past discrimination by adjusting pay differences raises an ethical conflict between employer and employee and between corporation and shareholder. Increasing the pay of some employees may reduce profits and the ability of the employer to give pay increases to other employees.

Lower profits will also decrease dividends to shareholders.

7.   B. In any profession, there is a responsibility, both legal and ethical, not to misrepresent material facts, even at the expense of some profits. This is a clear ethical standard in the legal profession and in the accounting profession. This question and answer are based on a question that was included in the CPA exam in November 1994.

8.   C. Despite the difficulties of some dilemmas, decisions must be made. Only through a well-thought-out consideration of the all of the factors can an intelligent choice be made. Recognizing the nature of the balance between such factors as profitability, legality, and ethics is one of the first steps in making an ethical decision.

9.   C. No matter how many people benefit from an illegal act, the act will still be considered illegal. Whether the act is ethical depends on which standard of ethics is applied. Under a duty-based standard, it is not the consequences of an act that determine how ethical the act is; it is the nature of the act itself. In contrast, utilitarianism is premised on acting so as to do the greatest good for the greatest number of people. It is the consequences of an act that determine how ethical the act is.

10.   B. The Foreign Corrupt Practices Act prohibits any U.S. firm from bribing foreign officials to influence official acts to provide the firm with business opportunities. Such payments are allowed, however, if they would be lawful in the foreign country. Thus, to avoid violating the law, the firm in this problem should determine whether "personal contributions" are legal in the minister's country.

Issue Spotters

1.   The answer depends on which system of ethics is used. Under a duty-based ethical standard, it is not the consequences of an act that determine how ethical the act is; it is the nature of the act itself. Stealing would be unethical regardless of whether the fruits of the crime are given to the poor. In contrast, utilitarianism is premised on acting so as to do the greatest good for the greatest number of people. It is the consequences of an act that determine how ethical the act is.

2. The answer depends on which system of ethics is used. From a utilitarian perspective, the plant will likely be closed, because closing it would benefit the greatest number of persons—future and other current employees, as well as shareholders.

3. When a corporate executive has to decide whether to market a product that might have undesirable side effects for a small percentage of users but would be beneficial for most users, the decision turns on the benefit to the many versus the harm to the few. Of course, all possible precautions should be taken to protect the few.

4. Maybe. On the one hand, it is not the company's "fault" when a product is misused. Also, keeping the product on the market is not a violation of the law, and stopping sales would hurt profits. On the other hand, suspending sales could reduce suffering and could stop potential negative publicity if sales continued.

5. When a corporation decides to respond to what it sees as a moral obligation to correct for past discrimination by adjusting pay differences among its employees, an ethical conflict is raised between the firm and its employees and between the firm and its shareholders. This dilemma arises directly out of the effect such a decision has on the firm's profits. If satisfying this obligation increases profitability, then the dilemma is easily resolved in favor of doing "the right thing."

Cumulative Hypothetical Problem for Unit Seven—Including Chapters 33–40

1. A. A partnership is an association of two or more persons who manage a business and share profits. Here, the partnership began when the parties combined their assets and commenced business. Before that time, there was no sharing of profits, no joint ownership of a business, and no equal right in the management of a business (because there was no business). The execution of a formal partnership agreement is not necessary, nor is the consent of creditors.

2. B. Unlike general partnerships, which can come into existence even when the parties do not intend to form a partnership, a limited partnership can only be created pursuant to the provisions of a state statute. This statute sets out exactly what partners must do to form a limited partnership, which must include at least one general partner who assumes personal liability for the debts of the firm.

3. D. The information that each state requires to be in articles of incorporation differs somewhat, but the information represented by the choices in this problem is generally required. It is not necessary to name the initial officers in the articles. Other information that might be required includes the number of authorized shares. Other information that is not required includes quorum requirements.

4. D. Other information that must be included in a registration statement, under the Securities Act of 1933, includes a description of the issuer's business, a description of the security, the capital structure of the business, the underwriting arrangements, and the certified financial statements.

5. B. Rule 504 exempts certain stock offerings from the registration requirements of the Securities Act of 1933. To qualify, a noninvestment company offering may not exceed $1 million in any twelve-month period, the Securities and Exchange Commission must be notified of the sale.

Chapter 41

True-False Questions

1. F. Secondary boycotts—including hot-cargo agreements, which are described in the question—are illegal.

2. T

3. F. Employment "at will" means that either party may terminate the employment at any time, with or without good cause.

4. F. Employers are free to offer employees no benefits. Federal and state governments participate in insurance programs designed to protect employees and their families by covering some of the financial impact of retirement, disability, death, and hospitalization.

5. F. It is the central legal right of a *union* to serve as the bargaining representative of employees in negotiations with management.

6. F. Under the Fair Labor Standards Act, minors (persons under the age of eighteen) cannot work in hazardous occupations.

7. T

8. T

9. F. Employees' right to engage in collective bargaining through elected representatives, like their right to organize and their right to engage in concerted activities for those and other purposes, was established in the National Labor Relations Act.

10. T

Fill-in Questions

either; unless; may; Some; A few states; may not

Multiple-Choice Questions

1. A. Child-labor, minimum-wage, and maximum-hour provisions are included in the Fair Labor Standards Act (also known as the Wage-Hour Law), covering virtually all employees. The employer may also be subject to the other laws given as choices in this problem, but those laws concern other rights and duties of employees and employers. This question and answer are based on a question that was included in the May 1995 CPA exam.

2. B. Intentionally inflicted injuries are not covered by workers' compensation. Many states cover problems arising out of preexisting conditions, but that is not part of the test for coverage. To collect benefits, an employee must notify the employer of an injury and file a claim with the appropriate state agency.

3. C. Under the Immigration Act, employers recruiting workers from other countries must complete a certification process with the U.S. Department of Labor. Part of the process is to show that there is a shortage of qualified U.S. workers in the particular area and that hiring aliens will not have a negative impact on the labor market in the area.

4. B. The Federal Unemployment Tax Act of 1935 concerns the system that provides unemployment compensation. The Employee Retirement Income Security Act (ERISA) of 1974 concerns the regulation of private pension plans.

5. C. The Employment Retirement Income Security Act (ERISA) covers such employers. ERISA is enforced by the Labor Management Services Administration of the Department of Labor. The other laws mentioned in the choices in this problem regulate other areas of retirement and security income.

6. B. Under the Family and Medical Leave Act (FMLA) of 1993, employees can take up to twelve weeks of family or medical leave during any twelve-month period and are entitled to continued health insurance coverage during the leave. Employees are also guaranteed the same, or a comparable, job on returning to work.

7. A. Under the Consolidated Omnibus Budget Reconciliation Act (COBRA) of 1985, most workers' medical, optical, or dental insurance is not automatically eliminated on termination of employment. The workers can choose to continue the coverage at the employer's group rate, if they are willing to pay the premiums (and a 2 percent administrative fee).

8. D. The National Labor Relations Act protects employees who engage in union activity and prohibits employers from refusing to bargain with employees' designated representative. Violations of these provisions are employer unfair labor practices.

9. D. An employer can hire permanent replacement workers during an economic strike. After the strike, the replacement workers do not have to be fired to make way for the strikers. Temporary replacement workers may be hired during any strike.

10. A. An employer may campaign against a union during a union election campaign. An employer cannot limit union campaigning unless it also limits other solicitation. An employer commits an unfair labor practice when it threatens employees with the loss of their jobs if a union wins an election or refuses to bargain with a union that wins a vote.

Issue Spotters

1. Yes. Some courts have held that an implied employment contract exists between employer and employee under an employee handbook that states employees will be dismissed only for good cause. An employer who fires a worker contrary to this promise can be held liable for breach of contract.

2. No. Generally, the right to recover under workers' compensation laws is determined without regard to negligence or fault. Unlike the potential for recovery in a lawsuit based on negligence or fault, however, recovery under a workers' compensation statute is limited to the specific amount designated in the statute for the employee's injury.

3. No. A closed shop (a company that requires union membership as a condition of employment) is illegal. A union shop (a company that does not require union membership as a condition of employment but requires workers to join the union after a certain time on the job) is illegal in a state with a right-to-work law, which makes it illegal to require union membership for continued employment.

4. Generally, no. Most states and the federal government protect employees such as Arlene who "blow the whistle" on the wrongdoing of their employers through so-called whistleblowing statutes. In some instances, these statutes encourage whistleblowing by offering a monetary reward if the employee's charges lead to a successful government lawsuit.

5. One of the most important provisions of ERISA concerns vesting. Generally, employee contributions to pension plans vest immediately; employee rights to employer contributions to those plans vest after five years. Another important ERISA provision concerns investing: pension-fund managers must be cautious in investing and refrain from investing more than 10 percent of the fund in securities of the employer.

Chapter 42

True-False Questions

1. T

2. F. An employer may be liable even though an employee did the harassing, if the employer knew, or should have known, and failed to take corrective action, or if the employee was in a supervisory position.

3. F. Just as an employer may be liable for an employee's misconduct, the employer may be liable for harassment by a nonemployee, if the employer knew, or should have known, and failed to take corrective action.

4. T

5. T

6. T

7. F. If the Equal Employment Opportunity Commission (EEOC) decides not pursue a claim, the victim can file a suit against alleged violator. The EEOC can pursue a claim in federal district court, however, in its own name against alleged violators. The EEOC can also intervene in a suit filed by a private party.

8. F. Title VII covers only employers with fifteen or more employees, labor unions with fifteen or more members, labor unions that operate hiring halls, employment agencies, and federal, state, and local agencies.

9. T

10. T

Fill-in Questions

can; may sue if a settlement between the parties is not reached; reinstatement, back pay, and retroactive promotions

Multiple-Choice Questions

1. C. Before filing a lawsuit, the best step for a person who believes that they may be a victim of discrimination is to contact a state or federal agency to see whether their claim is justified. The appropriate federal agency is the Equal Employment Opportunity Commission. Most states have similar agencies that evaluate claims under state law.

2. B. The Equal Pay Act of 1963 prohibits gender-based discrimination in wages for equal work. Different wages are acceptable because of any factor but gender, including seniority and merit.

3. A. The other choices would not subject the employer to liability under the Age Discrimination in Employment Act (ADEA). Discrimination is prohibited against persons forty years of age or older, even if the discrimination is unintentional. Mandatory retirement may be instituted, but not on account of an employee's age, and an employee may be discharged for cause at any age. This question and answer are based on a question that appeared in the CPA exam in 1996.

4. B. An employer cannot exclude arbitrarily a person who, with reasonable accommodation, could do what is required of a job. If an interpreter would be a reasonable accommodation, this employer must use one. What the employer may or may not have done for other disabled persons is irrelevant.

5. C. An employer can justify discrimination when a particular trait is essential to a job, or a bona fide occupational trait (BFOQ). In this case, because Dave is a man, he is justifiably disqualified from applying for the position.

6. A. Title VII prohibits showing a preference for members of one minority for members of another. Title VII also prohibits making distinctions according to the race of a person's spouse, friends, or other contacts.

7. A. Sexual harassment occurs when, in a workplace, an employee is subject to comments and contact that is perceived as sexually offensive. An employer may be liable even though an employee did the harassing, if the employee was in a supervisory position.

8. D. Here, the employer has a valid business necessity defense. An employer can demand that an employee possess the actual skills required for a job.

9. C. The Age Discrimination in Employment Act (ADEA) of 1967 requires, for the establishment of a *prima facie* case, that the plaintiff was forty or older, was qualified for the job, and was discharged or otherwise rejected in circumstances that imply discrimination. The difference between a *prima facie* case under the ADEA and under Title VII is that the ADEA does not require a plaintiff to show the position was filled by someone who is not a member of a protected class.

10. D. The employer's best defense in this case would be that being able to pass the tests is a business necessity—it is a necessary requirement for the job.

Discrimination may be illegal even if it is not intentional, and whether or not some men cannot pass the tests is not relevant to whether there is discrimination against women. If the employer hires some women for the job, it could not argue successfully that gender is a BFOQ for the job.

Issue Spotters

1. Yes. These circumstances include all of the elements of a *prima facie* under Title VII of the Civil Rights Act of 1964: (1) the applicant is a member of a protected class, (2) she applied and was qualified for the job, (3) she was rejected, and (4) the employer continued to seek applicants or filled the job with a person not in a protected class. The employer would then have to offer a legitimate reason for its action, and the applicant would have to show that this is a pretext, that discriminatory intent was the motivation.

2. Yes. One type of sexual harassment occurs when a request for sexual favors is a condition of employment, and the person making the request is a supervisor or acts with the authority of the employer.

3. Yes, if he can show that he was not hired solely because of the disability. The other elements for a discrimination suit based on a disability are that the plaintiff (1) has a disability and (2) is otherwise qualified for the job. Both of these elements are satisfied in this case.

4. Probably. Under the ADA, employers cannot legally discriminate against employees who are alcoholics. Alcoholism is considered a disability. If Ned can prove that he was disciplined more harshly than his colleagues would have been under similar circumstances (arriving late without providing an excuse) because of his alcoholism, the ADA would protect him.

5. No. As long as Jenna's beliefs are sincerely held, and she makes a reasonable effort to obtain the information disseminated at the update sessions, Smith & Smith must make a reasonable effort to accommodate her religion.

Cumulative Hypothetical Problem for Unit Eight—Including Chapters 41–42

1. B. The requirements for recovery under state workers' compensation laws include the existence of an employment relationship and an accidental injury that occurs on the job or within the scope of employment. Accepting benefits precludes an employee from suing his or her employer, but it does not bar the employee from suing a third party for causing the injury.

2. D. The Social Security Act of 1935 provides payments for persons who are retired or disabled. The Social Security Administration is a federal agency that also administers the Medicare program. Unemployment benefits, however, are part of a state system created by the Federal Unemployment Tax Act of 1935.

3. C. At the termination of most workers' employment, their group health insurance cannot be terminated, and may be continued for as much as twenty-nine months in some cases, if the worker is willing to pay the premium plus an administrative cost. There is no additional requirement that the employee be at the "normal" retirement age or that he or she be part of a general layoff.

4. A. Title VII of the Civil Rights Act of 1964 covers many forms of discrimination, including discrimination based on gender, race, religion, color, and national origin. But Title VII does not prohibit discrimination based on age, which is the subject of the Age Discrimination in Employment Act of 1967.

5. B. The Age Discrimination in Employment Act of 1967 prohibits discrimination against persons age forty or more. This includes mandatory retirement of such individuals. In most circumstances, however, an employer can discharge an employee for cause, regardless of his or her age, without running afoul of this, or any other, federal antidiscrimination law.

Chapter 43

True-False Questions

1. T

2. T

3. T

4. F. Agencies formulate and issue their rules under the authority of Congress. These rules are as legally binding as the laws enacted by Congress. It is for this reason, in part, that rulemaking

procedures generally include opportunities for public comment, that the rules are subject to review by the courts, and that agencies are subject to other controls by the three branches of government.

5. F. Appeal is not mandatory, although either side may appeal, to the agency commission or ultimately to a federal court. If there is no appeal, the initial order becomes final.

6. F. Congress can influence agency policy in several ways. These include that Congress can create or abolish an agency, or influence policy by the appropriation of funds for certain purposes. Congress can also revise the functions of an agency.

7. T

8. T

9. F. State and federal agency actions often parallel each other. When there is a conflict, the supremacy clause of the Constitution requires that the federal agency's operation prevail over an inconsistent state agency's action.

10. F. In most circumstances, a warrant is required for a search. Warrants are not required, however, to conduct searches in businesses in highly regulated industries, in certain hazardous operations, and in emergencies.

Fill-in Questions

Federal Register; anyone; must; *Federal Register*

Multiple-Choice Questions

1. D. Agency powers include functions associated with the legislature (rulemaking), executive branch (investigation), and courts (adjudication). Under Article I of the Constitution and the delegation doctrine, Congress has the power to establish administrative agencies with these powers.

2. C. Information may be obtained through subpoenas or searches. A subpoena may compel the appearance of a witness or the provision of certain documents and records. In some cases, searches may be conducted without warrants.

3. D. Procedures vary widely, even within agencies, but under the Administrative Procedure Act, rulemaking typically includes notice, opportunity for comment, and publication in the *Federal Register* of a final draft of the rule.

4. C. An agency has authority to issue subpoenas. There are limits on agency demands, however. An investigation must have a legitimate purpose. The information that is sought must be relevant. The party from whom the information is sought must not be unduly burdened by the request. And a demand must be specific.

5. C. The president's veto is a method by which agency authority can be checked. The limits listed in the other responses are alternatives available to Congress to limit the authority of administrative agencies.

6. B. The Government-in-the-Sunshine Act requires "every portion of every meeting of an agency" that is headed by a "collegial body" to be open to "public observation."

7. A. The Administrative Procedure Act provides for court review of most agency actions, but first a party must exhaust all other means of resolving a controversy with an agency. Also, the action must be reviewable, the party must have standing, and an actual controversy must be at issue.

8. D. Depending on the circumstances, when a court reviews an act of an administrative agency, the court may also determine whether the agency has properly interpreted laws applicable to the action under review, acted in accord with procedural requirements, or reached conclusions that are not supported by substantial evidence.

9. B. After an agency publishes notice of a proposed rule, any interested parties can express their views in writing or orally, if a hearing is held. The agency must respond to significant comments by modifying the final rule or explaining, in the statement accompanying the final rule, why it did not modify the rule.

10. D. An administrative law judge (ALJ) presides over hearings when cases are brought to the agency. Like other judges, an ALJ has the power to administer oaths, take testimony, rule on questions of evidence, and make determinations of fact. It is important to note that an ALj works for the agency but must not be biased in the agency's favor.

Issue Spotters

1. Checks against the arbitrary use of agency power include the courts' power to review agency actions. Congress also has considerable power over agencies. Among other things, Congress can create, restrict, or abolish an agency. Congress can also limit the funds that it gives to an agency. The president can exercise control over an agency through the appointment of its officers.

2. These rules are called legislative rules, and they are binding as the laws that Congress makes. Such rules, like laws, must not violate the Constitution. Unlike laws, however, such rules must not exceed the power conferred on the agency by its enabling legislation.

3. Under the Administrative Procedure Act (APA), the ALJ must be separate from the agency's investigative and prosecutorial staff. *Ex parte* communications between the ALJ and a party to a proceeding are prohibited. Under the APA, an ALJ is exempt from agency discipline except on a showing of good cause.

4. A formal adjudicatory hearing resembles a trial in that, in both types of proceedings, the parties can undertake extensive discovery (involving depositions, interrogatories, etc.) and during the hearing they may give testimony, present other evidence, and cross-examine witnesses. An administrative proceeding differs from a trial in that in the former, more information, including hearsay, can be introduced as evidence.

5. The Freedom of Information Act requires the federal government to reveal certain "records" to "any person" on request.

Chapter 44

True-False Questions

1. T
2. T
3. F. Under certain circumstances, consumers have a right to rescind their contracts. This is particularly true when a creditor has not made all required disclosures. A contract entered into as part of a door-to-door sale may be rescinded

within three days, regardless of the reason.

4. T

5. F. Under the Fair Credit Reporting Act, consumers are entitled to have deleted from their files any misinformation that leads to a denial of credit, employment, or insurance. Consumers are also entitled to receive information about the source of the misinformation and about anyone who was given the misinformation.

6. F. Common law doctrines that were applied against polluters centuries ago may be applicable today. These include nuisance and negligence doctrines.

7. T

8. F. There are different standards for different pollutants and for different polluters. There are even different standards for the same pollutants and polluters in different locations. The standards cover the amount of emissions, the technology to control them, the notice that must be given to the public, and the penalties that may be imposed for noncompliance.

9. F. The Toxic Substances Control Act of 1976 regulates substances that the production and labeling of substances of that potentially pose an imminent hazard or an unreasonable risk of injury to health or the environment. The clean-up of leaking hazardous waste disposal sites is regulated by the Comprehensive Environmental Response, Compensation, and Liability Act (CERCLA) of 1980.

10. T

Fill-in Questions

$50; before; prohibits; from billing; if

Multiple-Choice Questions

1. A. The FTC has the power to issue a cease-and-desist order, but in some cases, such an order is not enough to stop the harm. With counteradvertising (also known as corrective advertising), an advertiser attempts to correct earlier misinformation by admitting that prior claims about a product were untrue.

2. C. A regular-size box of laundry soap, for example, cannot be labeled "super-size" to exaggerate the amount of product in the box. Labels on consumer goods must identify the product, the manufacturer, the distributor, the net quantity of the contents, and the quantity of each serving (if the number of servings is given). Other information may also be required.

3. B. In a door-to-door sale, a consumer generally has at least a three-day cooling-off period within which to rescind the transaction. Salespersons are required to give consumers written notice of this right. If a sales presentation is to a consumer who speaks only Spanish, the notice must be in Spanish, too

4. D. Under the Fair Debt Collection Practices Act, once a debtor has refused to pay a debt, a collection agency can contact the debtor *only* to advise him or her of further action to be taken.

5. B. This is required under Regulation Z (which was issued by the Federal Reserve Board under the Truth in Lending Act) and applies to any creditor who, in the ordinary course of business, lends money or sells goods on credit to consumers, or arranges for credit for consumers. The information that must be disclosed includes: the specific dollar amount being financed; the annual percentage rate of interest; any financing charges, premiums or points; the number, amounts, and due dates of payments; and any penalties imposed on delinquent payments or prepayment.

6. D. An environmental impact statement (EIS) must be prepared when a major federal action significantly affects the quality of the environment. An action that affects the quality of the environment is "major" if it involves a substantial commitment of resources and "federal" if a federal agency has the power to control it.

7. C. Under the 1990 amendments to the Clean Air Act, different standards apply to existing sources and major new sources. Major new sources must use the maximum achievable control technology to reduce emissions from the combustion of fossil fuels. Other factories and businesses must reduce emissions of hazardous air pollutants with the best available technology. This question and answer are based on a question that appeared in the CPA exam in 1996.

8. A. Any potentially responsible party can be charged with the entire cost to clean up a hazardous waste disposal site. Potentially responsible parties include former owners. Of course, a party held responsible for the entire cost may be able to recoup some of it in a contribution action against other potentially responsible parties.

9. C. Besides ordering a polluter to clean up the pollution or to pay for the clean-up costs, other penalties may be imposed. For example, fines may be assessed and imprisonment ordered.

10. C. Under the Resource Conservation and Recovery Act, producers of hazardous waste must properly label and package waste to be transported. Under the Comprehensive Environmental Response, Compensation, and Liability Act, the party who generated the waste disposed of at a site can be held liable for clean-up costs.

Issue Spotters

1. Yes. The FTC has issued rules to govern advertising techniques, including rules designed to prevent bait-and-switch advertising. Under the FTC guidelines, bait-and-switch advertising occurs if the seller refuses to show the advertised item, fails to have in stock a reasonable quantity of the item, fails to promise to deliver the advertised item within a reasonable time, or discourages employees from selling the item.

2. There are a number of federal and state laws that deal specifically with information given on labels and packages, including the Fair Packaging and Labeling Act of 1966 and the Wool Products Labeling Act of 1939.

3. Under the Smokeless Tobacco Health Education Act of 1986, packages of smokeless tobacco products must include warnings about the health hazards associated with the use of smokeless tobacco similar to warnings contained on cigarette packages.

4. Under the Truth-in-Lending Act, a buyer who wishes to withhold payment for a faulty product purchased with a credit card must follow specific procedures to settle the dispute. The credit card issuer then must intervene and attempt to settle the dispute.

5. The Comprehensive Environmental Response, Compensation, and Liability Act of 1980 regulates the clean-up of hazardous waste disposal sites. Any potentially responsible party can be charged with the entire cost to clean up a hazardous waste disposal site. Potentially responsible parties include the person who generated the waste (ChemCorp) the person who transported the waste to the site (Central), the person who owned or operated the site at the time of the disposal (Intrastate Disposal), and the current owner or operator of the site (ABC). A party held responsible for the entire cost may be able to recoup some of it in a lawsuit against other potentially responsible parties.

Chapter 45

True-False Questions

1. F. This is a vertical restraint.
2. F. This is a horizontal restraint.
3. T
4. F. Exclusive dealing contracts are those under which a seller forbids a buyer from purchasing products from the seller's competitors.
5. F. Price discrimination occurs when sellers charge competitive buyers different prices for identical goods.
6. F. This is a *vertical* merger. A horizontal merger is a merger between firms that compete with each other in the same market.
7. F. This is a *horizontal* merger. A vertical merger occurs when a company at one stage of production acquires another company at a higher or lower stage in the chain of production and distribution.
8. T
9. T
10. T

Fill-in Questions

A restraint of trade; Monopoly power; monopoly power

Multiple-Choice Questions

1. C. An agreement to set prices in the manner described in the problem is a price-fixing agreement, which is a re-

straint of trade and a *per se* violation of Section 1 of the Sherman Act.

2. D. Conduct that is blatantly anti-competitive is a *per se* violation of antitrust law. Such conduct typically includes price-fixing agreements, group boycotts, horizontal market divisions, and resale price maintenance agreements.

3. B. Territorial or customer restrictions, like the restriction described in the problem, are judged under a rule of reason. The rule of reason involves a weighing of competitive benefits against anticompetitive harms. Here, the manufacturer's restriction on its dealers would likely be considered lawful because, although it reduces *intra*brand competition, it promotes *inter*brand competition.

4. D. In applying the rule of reason, courts consider the purpose of the conduct, the effect of the conduct on trade, the power of the parties to accomplish what they intend, and in some cases, whether there are less restrictive alternatives to achieve the same goals.

5. C. The elements of the offense of monopolization include monopoly power and its willful acquisition. Market domination that results from legitimate competitive behavior—such as foresight, innovation, skill, and good management—is not a violation.

6. C. Price discrimination occurs when a seller charges different buyers different prices for identical goods. To violate the Clayton Act, among other requirements, the effect of the price discrimination must be to substantially lessen competition or otherwise create a competitive injury.

7. C. Of course, a U.S. firm is subject to the jurisdiction of a U.S. court. For a U.S. court to hear a case against a foreign entity under U.S. antitrust laws, the entity's alleged violation of the law must have a substantial effect on U.S. commerce (or be a *per se* violation). In other words, foreign and domestic firms may be sued for violations of U.S. antitrust laws.

8. A. Similar exemptions from the antitrust laws include cooperative research among small business firms, cooperation among U.S. exporters to compete with comparable foreign associations, and joint efforts by businessper-sons to obtain legislative, judicial, or executive action.

9. C. Conduct evaluated under the rule of reason is unlawful if its anticompetitive harms outweigh its competitive benefits. Conduct typically subject to a rule of reason analysis includes trade association activities, joint ventures, territorial or customer restrictions, refusals to deal, price discrimination, and exclusive-dealing contracts.

10. B. An important consideration in determining whether a merger substantially lessens competition and hence violates the Clayton Act is market concentration (the market chares among the firms in the market). If a merger creates an entity with more than a small percentage market share, it is presumed illegal.

Issue Spotters

1. A unilateral refusal to deal violates antitrust law if it involves offenses proscribed under Section 2 of the Sherman Act. This occurs if the firm refusing to deal has, or is likely to acquire, monopoly power and the refusal is likely to have an anticompetitive effect on a particular market.

2. This arrangement is a market division. It is a violation of Section 1 of the Sherman Act. The same violation would occur if the competitors agree that one of them would sell only to institutions (schools, government agencies, utilities) in all three states, another only to wholesalers, and the third only to retailers. Dividing up territories or customers among competitors is a *per se* violation.

3. Size alone does not determine whether a firm is a monopoly—size in relation to the market is what matters. A small store in a small, isolated town is a monopolist if it is the only store serving that market. Monopoly involves the power to affect prices and output. If a firm has sufficient market power to control prices and exclude competition, that firm has monopoly power. Monopoly power in itself is not a violation of Section 2 of the Sherman Act. The offense also requires an intent to acquire or maintain that power through anticompetitive means.

4. This agreement is a tying arrangement. The legality of a tying arrangement depends the purpose of the agreement, the agreement's likely effect on competition in the relevant markets (the market for the tying product and the market for the tied product), and other factors. Tying arrangements for commodities are subject to Section 3 of the Clayton Act. Tying arrangements for services can be agreements in restraint of trade in violation of Section 1 of the Sherman Act.

5. Whether a vertical merger is considered illegal depends on several factors, including market concentration, barriers to entry into the market, and the apparent intent of the merging parties. A merger that prevents competitors of either firm from competing in a segment of the market is considered to foreclose competition and to be illegal.

Cumulative Hypothetical Problem for Unit Nine—Including Chapters 43–45

1. D. Advertising that consists of vague generalities is not illegal. This is also true of advertising that includes obvious exaggerations. Advertising that may lead to sanctions by the Federal Trade Commission is deceptive advertising: advertising that misleads consumers.

2. A. An administrative agency has a number of options to determine whether a manufacturer is complying with the agency's rules, but the agency may not use its powers arbitrarily or capriciously or abuse its discretion. The options that an agency may choose include those in the other answer choices, as well as obtaining a search warrant to search the premises for a specific item and return it to the agency.

3. D. Under the Comprehensive Environmental Response, Compensation, and Liability Act of 1980, any "potentially responsible party" can be charged with the entire cost to clean up a hazardous waste disposal site. Potentially responsible parties include the party who generates the waste, the party who transports the waste to the site, and the party who owns or operates the site.

4. C. A business firm may be subject to regulations issued by federal and state administrative agencies. The firm is no less subject to those regulations if they are conflicting or if the firm does not know of the regulations. Federal agencies include the Federal Trade Commission, the Environmental Protection Agency, and the U.S. Department of Justice, all of which have counterparts at the state level in most states. A business firm is also subject to local regulations at the county and city levels.

5. C. It is price discrimination when a seller charges different buyers different prices for identical products. Price discrimination is a violation of the Clayton Act if the effect of the pricing is to substantially lessen competition or otherwise create a competitive injury.

Chapter 46

True-False Questions

1. T

2. F. If goods are confused due to a wrongful act, it is the *wrongdoer* who must prove what percentage of the whole belongs to him or her to acquire title to any of the goods. Otherwise, the *innocent party* gets title to the whole.

3. F. The essence of a gift is that it is a voluntary transfer without consideration. The elements of a gift are donative intent, delivery, and acceptance.

4. F. If an accession is performed in good faith, ownership depends on the change in the value of the property. The greater the increase, the more likely that the improver will own the property.

5. T

6. F. To constitute a bailment, a delivery must be of possession without any transfer of title and there must be an agreement that the property be returned or otherwise disposed of according to the owner's directions.

7. F. In most cases, a bailee is subject to a reasonable standard of care. Depending on the specific type of bailment, that standard may range from slight care (bailment for the sole benefit of the bailor) to great care (bailment for the sole benefit of the bailee).

8. F. A bailee has *two* basic responsibilities: to take proper care of the property and to surrender or dispose of the property at the end of the bailment.

9. T
10. T

Fill-in Questions

inter vivos; *causa mortis*; *causa mortis*; *causa mortis*; *inter vivos*

Multiple-Choice Questions

1. A. Personal property includes such items as computer software and home pages. Those who produce personal property have title to it. Because the creator of the property produced it, she owns it. There is an exception, however. Employees do not own what they produce for their employers. Here, she was hired to create property for another; the other owns what she created.

2. B. A right of survivorship, in which a deceased joint tenant's interest passes to the surviving joint tenant, is the distinguishing feature of a joint tenancy. Generally, to acquire or own property as joint tenants, the owners must specify that as the form they want their ownership to take. If these buyers had not specified that form, they would own the property as tenants in common.

3. A. The three elements for an effective gift are donative intent, delivery, and acceptance. Here, the giver had the intent, and the recipient clearly accepted, if delivery was effective, which it was. Delivery of the key to the box was constructive delivery of the earrings. Thus, the gift would have been effective even if the giver had died before the recipient had taken them from the box.

4. A. John found what appears to be lost property. Generally, the finder of lost property has good title against all *but the true owner*. Therefore, John has title.

5. A. When goods are commingled, and the goods are lost, the owners bear the loss in the same proportion that they contributed to the whole. This is assuming that they can prove how much they contributed to the whole. Thus, the farmers take out the same proportions that they put in.

6. B. The three elements for an effective gift are donative intent, delivery, and acceptance. Here, the giver had the intent and clearly delivered the object of the gift (by constructive delivery). Thus, the gift would have been effective if the recipient accepted it. Acceptance is generally presumed unless proven otherwise. In the problem, the recipient announced that she did not want the gift and left they key in the possession of the donor. In this case, there was no gift. The property belongs to the donor's heirs.

7. C. A bailee must be given exclusive possession and control of the property and knowingly accept it. Here, there is no delivery of possession. Regarding the other choices, money does not need to be involved for a transaction to be a bailment, a car is personal property, and a signed contract is not necessary for a bailment (the bailment agreement may be oral).

8. B. The wallet appears to have been placed behind the plant intentionally and thus is classified as mislaid property. The owner of the premises on which mislaid property is found is entitled to possession as against the finder.

9. A. A bailment involves delivery of personal property in such a way that the bailee is given, and knowingly accepts, exclusive possession and control over it. By accepting the coat, the restaurant is given exclusive possession and control over the purse, but it the restaurant does not *knowingly* accepts the purse.

10. B. A common carrier is liable for damage caused by the willful acts of third persons or by an accident when the goods are in the carrier's possession. Thus, the carrier is liable for most of the losses among these answer choices. The other loss is caused by an act of the shipper and must be borne by the shipper. This question and answer are based on a question that appeared in the November 1995 CPA exam.

Issue Spotters

1. Yes. The necklace could not be physically delivered, because the bank was closed. Delivery of the key to the box was constructive delivery of the necklace.

2. Dave and Paul are the joint tenants. The main distinguishing feature between the tenancies in common and joint tenancies is that a joint tenancy includes a right of survivorship. This is

what Dave and Paul provided for themselves when they acquired their computer.

3. Yes. A bailee's right of possession, even though temporary, permits the bailee to recover damages from any third persons for damage or loss to the property.

4. Yes. As an ordinary bailee, the dry cleaner owes a duty to take proper care of the clothes left in its charge. To recover from a party who does not fulfill his or her duty of care, the injured party must normally prove a lack of care. In this case, that would be difficult, because the bailor is unaware as to why the clothes were returned in bad condition. Under the law of bailments, proof of damage or loss raises a presumption that a bailee is guilty of negligence (or conversion), and the bailee must prove that he or she exercised due care.

5. The shipper suffers the loss. A common carrier is liable for damage caused by the willful acts of third persons or by an accident. Other losses must be borne by the shipper (or the recipient, depending on the terms of their contract). This shipment was lost due to an act of God.

Chapter 47

True-False Questions

1. T

2. F. The owner of a life estate has the same rights as a fee simple owner except that the value of the property must be kept intact for the holder of the future interest.

3. F. An easement merely allows a person to use land without taking anything from it, while a profit allows a person to take something from the land.

4. T

5. F. Under the Fifth Amendment, private property may not be taken for public use without "just compensation."

6. F. The government has the power to take private property, but the purposes for which such property may be taken must be *public*. When taking private property, the government is also required to pay the owner just compensation.

7. F. This is a tenancy for years. A periodic tenancy does not specify how long it will last.

8. F. To be entitled to a variance, a landowner must show that a granting of the variance would *not* substantially alter the essential character of the zoned area.

9. T

10. T

Fill-in Questions

warranty; special warranty; quitclaim

Multiple-Choice Questions

1. B. A *profit* is the right to go onto land in possession of another and take away some part of the land itself or some product of the land. In contrast, an easement is a right to make limited use of another person's land without taking anything from the property. A license is a revocable right to come onto another person's land.

2. C. The rights that accompany ownership in fee simple include the right to sell the land or give it away, as well as the right to use the land for whatever purpose the owner sees fit, subject, of course, to the law's limitations.

3. C. Warranty deeds include a number of promises, including a covenant of quiet enjoyment, which guarantees that the buyer will not be disturbed in his or her possession of the land by the seller or any third persons. If this covenant is breached, the buyer can recover from the seller the purchase price and any damages for the eviction.

4. A. A covenant runs with the land so that the successors to the original parties are entitled to its benefit (or burdened with its obligation) if it meets four requirements. It must be created in writing (in the problem, the deeds). The parties must intend that it run with the land (in the problem, each successive owner agreed to maintain the fence). The limits on the "burdened" land (maintaining the fence) must have a connection to the land (the fence is built on the land and marks the common boundary). The original parties must have been in privity of estate when the covenant was created. All of these requirements are met here.

5. A. An easement is a right to make limited use of another's real property without taking anything from it. In this case, it is an easement by necessity—the owner needs access to his property. The right to take something from the property is a profit. A revocable right to come onto the property is a license.

6. C. Besides a legally sufficient description of the property and the price, a valid deed must contain the names of the grantee (buyer) and grantor (seller), words evidencing an intent to convey the property, and the grantor's (and usually the spouse's) signature. This question and answer are based on a question that was included in the CPA exam in November 1995.

7. A. A lease that does not specify how long it is to last but does specify that rent is to be paid at certain intervals creates a periodic tenancy. The tenancy is automatically renewed for each rental period unless it has been properly terminated.

8. B. Under a notice-race statute, a good faith purchaser who records his or her deed first can claim priority. In this problem, the result would be the same if the state had a pure race statute. In that circumstance, the first person to record a deed would have superior rights to the property, whether he or she knew of another previous, unrecorded transfer. Under a pure notice statute, however, the result might be different. In that circumstance, a person who does not know of a previous, unrecorded transfer can claim priority, whether or not he or she records first.

9. C. Sellers of most new houses are subject to an implied warranty of habitability. That means that the house is fit for human habitation (in reasonable working order and of reasonably sound construction). A seller of any house—old or new—may be liable for fraud or misrepresentation, particularly if, as in this problem, the buyer relied on the statements of the seller or the seller's agent.

10. D. This possession meets all the requirements for acquiring property by adverse possession: the possession was (1) actual and exclusive; (2) open, visible, and notorious; (3) continuous and peaceful for the statutory period; and (4) hostile, against the whole world, including the original owner.

Issue Spotters

1. Yes. An owner of a fee simple has the most rights possible—he or she can give the property away, sell it, transfer it by will, use it for almost any purpose, possess it to the exclusion of all the world, or as in this case, transfer possession for any period of time. The party to whom possession is transferred can also transfer his or her interest (usually only with the owner's permission) for any lesser period of time.

2. This is a breach of the warranty deed's covenant of quiet enjoyment. The buyer can sue the seller and recover the purchase price of the house, plus any damages.

3. Yes. When a parcel of land that is benefited by an easement appurtenant is sold, the property carries the easement with it. The new owner can use the easement just as the old owner did.

4. The tenant's heirs inherit the lease and can fulfill its term. (A lease passes to a tenant's heirs as personal property.) This rule protects the landlord's interest, which is to realize the full benefits of the lease, and the tenant's interest, which is also to realize the benefits of the lease. Of course, both parties must continue to abide by the terms of the lease.

5. Probably not. A zoning ordinance is considered discriminatory if it affects one parcel of land in a way unlike surrounding parcels if there is no rational basis for the difference. The facts as stated in the problem do not indicate any basis for zoning this land differently.

Chapter 48

True-False Questions

1. T

2. T

3. T

4. F. If a lease states the time that it will end, the landlord is not required to give the tenant notice. The lease terminates automatically.

5. F. A tenant can withhold rent only under a breach of the lease or, in most states, the implied warranty of habitability. Typically, this requires a major defect.

6. F. In most states, a tenant can make any use of property that is legal, relates to the purpose for which the property is adapted or ordinarily used, does not create a nuisance, and *does not injure the landlord's interest*. This last requirement means that a tenant cannot make alterations without the landlord's consent.

7. T

8. T

9. F. A landlord can sell, give away, or otherwise transfer his or her property without affecting a tenant's obligations under a lease, except that the tenant becomes the tenant of the new owner.

10. F. If an assignee or a sublessee later defaults on the obligation to pay rent, the tenant must pay it. (Also, before a tenant can assign or sublet the property, he or she must have the landlord's consent if the lease requires it).

Fill-in Questions

residential; tenant's; residential; residential; tenant's

Multiple-Choice Questions

1. A. A residential lease, to be enforceable, must include a description of the leased property. The other choices are only options. Note, too, that this lease is for a two-year term. A lease that cannot be completed within a year must be in writing to be enforceable (under the Statute of Frauds). This question and answer are based on a question that was part of the November 1995 CPA exam.

2. B. An assignment does not relieve an assigning tenant from the obligation to pay rent during the original term or during an extension under an option in the original lease.

3. B. A court would likely declare this clause unconscionable. The clause attempts to exculpate a residential landlord from fulfilling the important duty of providing habitable premises. Of course, a tenant has a duty to notify the landlord of a failure of a heating system, if the landlord has no other way of knowing of it (but this is not the same as a duty to mitigate damages).

4. B. If a tenant can prove that a landlord's primary purpose in attempting to evict the tenant is retaliation for complaining about the condition of leased premises, the tenant can stop the eviction proceedings. He or she can then collect damages, terminate the lease, or regain possession of the premises.

5. C. A tenant has exclusive possession until a lease expires, but the tenant must pay rent even if he or she moves out (assuming the move is unjustified). A landlord may treat a tenant's moving out with no intent of returning (as evidenced, for example, by a failure to pay rent) as an offer of surrender. The landlord's retaking of possession relieves the tenant of any further duty to pay rent, although the landlord may sue for previously unpaid rent.

6. B. A landlord is liable for injuries occurring on property within the landlord's control (common areas). A tenant must maintain in a reasonably safe condition those areas under his or her control. Here, the area where the injury occurred was under the tenant's control. (Depending on the terms of a commercial lease, a tenant's duty may coincide with the landlord's and both may be liable. The obviousness of a condition, its cause, and the requirement to give notice may be taken into consideration).

7. A. A landlord may treat a tenant's moving out with no intent of returning before the end of the term as an offer of surrender (assuming the move out is unjustified). The landlord's retaking of possession is considered acceptance of the surrender. A landlord can be considered to retake possession of the property by moving into it, or by changing the lock and renting it to a new tenant. In any case, this relieves the tenant of the duty to pay rent.

8. B. Despite the clause in the lease agreement, Tom will be held liable for his negligence. This type of clause is known as an exculpatory clause, and is unenforceable when the landlord fails to fulfill her or his statutory duties.

9. A. The difference between an assignment and a sublease is that an assignment involves a tenant's entire interest under the lease (the right to possession for the rest of the term), while a sublease involves all or part of the premises for a shorter term (only one of two rooms for the sixth and seventh months of a one-year lease, for example). Unless the lease prohibits it, a tenant can assign or sublet without the landlord's consent.

10. B. When a landlord transfers his or her interest in leased property, the tenant becomes the tenant of the new owner. It is to this new owner that the tenant owes rent. Both parties must continue to follow the terms of the lease.

Issue Spotters

1. When a landlord transfers his or her interest in leased property, the tenant becomes the tenant of the new owner. The new owner is entitled to any subsequent rent but must follow the terms of the existing lease.

2. Yes. A lease may be oral. In most states, however, some leases must be in writing (such as those that cannot be completed within a year, in which situation the Statute of Frauds requires that a writing). As with other oral agreements, a party who wants to enforce an oral lease may have a hard time proving its existence.

3. In many states, no. Those states require a landlord to provide actual physical possession of property that a tenant has agreed to lease. Other states require a landlord to transfer only the legal right to possession, and a new tenant is responsible for removing a previous tenant.

4. No. Rent cannot be increased during a lease term if the lease does not provide for it. But a lease may provide for increases in rent, and the amount may be indexed to increases in a commercial tenant's business activity. The amounts may be stated as percentages, rather than an exact dollar amount.

5. Probably not. If the landlord had not taken no steps against crime, in an area in which there had been some crime, the landlord may have been liable if an injury resulted. In the problem, however, the landlord installed an alarm and hired a security guard. Unless there was some other reasonable precaution that the landlord should have taken, there would likely be no liability for an injury in the building due to crime.

Cumulative Hypothetical Problem for Unit Ten—Including Chapters 46–48

1. B. The most important factor in determining whether an item is a fixture is the intent of the owners. Other factors include whether the item can be removed without damaging the real property, and whether the item is sufficiently adapted so as to have become a part of the real property. If removal would irreparably damage the property, the item may also be considered a fixture.

2. C. If a joint tenant transfers his or her interest by deed to a third party, the third party becomes a tenant in common with the remaining joint tenant or tenants. (If there is more than one remaining joint tenant, they are still joint tenants among themselves.)

3. A. The elements for a transfer of real property ownership by deed include the names of the grantor and grantee, the intent of the grantor to convey ownership, the legal description of the property, the signature of the grantor, delivery, and acceptance. Elements that are not required include consideration, the signature of the grantee, a recording of the deed, and a purchase price.

4. C. The purpose of a recording statute is to determine the priority of two deeds to the same property. Under a race-notice recording statute, the party who records his or her deed firs has priority if he or she did not have notice of a prior conveyance. Because the second transferee in this problem had notice of the first transfer, she does not have priority.

5. B. If a tenant transfers only part of a lease—that is, if the tenant transfer the right to occupy leased premises for less than the whole term—the arrangement is a sublease. (If the transfer is for the whole term, it is an assignment.) In a sublease, the original tenant is still liable to the landlord for the rent and other conditions of the original lease despite the transfer of the right to occupy the property.

Chapter 49

True-False Questions

1. T

2.   F. Insurance is classified according to the nature of the risk involved.

3.   F. A broker is normally the agent of the applicant. If the broker fails to obtain coverage and the applicant is damaged as a result, the broker is liable for the loss.

4.   T

5.   T

6.   F. The application is part of the contract. Misstatements in the application can void a policy, especially if the insurer would not have issued the policy if it had known the facts (although under an incontestability clause, the insurer may have a limited time within which to void a policy on that basis).

7.   T

8.   F. Coinsurance provisions are standard clauses in fire insurance policies, but they reduce recovery only in cases of *partial* loss and then only if the insured has less insurance than a specified percentage. The dollar amount of recovery is equal to the dollar amount of loss multiplied by the quotient of the dollar amount of insurance and (the total value of the property multiplied by the specified percentage). In other words, if the specified percentage is 80 percent, the total value of the property is $100,000, the amount of insurance is $40,000, and the loss is $30,000, the amount of recovery is $15,000—$30,000 x [$40,000/ ($100,000 x 80 percent)].

9.   T

10.   F. An antilapse clause provides a grace period for an insured to pay an overdue premium. A typical period is thirty days, and even then notice may be required to cancel the insurance.

Fill-in Questions

ordinary; nature of the coverage; insurance company; insurance company; is; insurance company

Multiple-Choice Questions

1.   B. Property insurance can be canceled for gross negligence that increases the hazard insured against. Other reasons for canceling insurance include nonpayment of premiums, fraud or misrepresentation, and conviction for a crime that, like gross negligence, increases the hazard insured against.

2.   A. An insurance company evaluates risk factors based on the information in an insurance application. For this reason, misrepresentation can void a policy, especially if the company can show that it would not have extended insurance if it had known the facts.

3.   A. The insurable interest in life insurance must exist at the time the policy is obtained. Under a key-person life insurance policy, it will not matter if the key person is no longer in the business's employ at the time of the loss (the person's death).

4.   C. To recover for a loss under a property insurance policy, an insurable interest in the property must exist when the loss occurs. It does not make any difference whether or not the property is owned in fee simple, or by an individual, or when an insurance policy is issued. This question and answer are based on a question that was included in the CPA exam in November 1995.

5.   B. When applying for insurance, an applicant must disclose all material facts, which include all facts that would influence an insurer in determining whether to charge a higher premium or to refuse to issue a policy altogether. The correct response to this problem requires determining whether the misstatement was material. Under the circumstances stated in the problem, it was not.

6.   C. When a coinsurance clause provides that if an owner insures the property up to a specified percentage of its value (80 percent, in this problem), he or she will recover any loss up to the face amount of the policy. Because in this problem the insured's coverage was up to the specified percentage ($160,000), and the loss was for less, the insured can recover the entire amount of the loss.

7.   B. Liability insurance protects against liability imposed on a company resulting from injuries to the person or property of another. Coverage under a liability policy may also include expenses involved in recalling and replacing a product that has proved to be defective.

8.   C. If policies with several companies cover the same risk and the amount of coverage exceeds the loss, under a multiple insurance clause the insured collects from each insurer its propor-

tionate share of the liability to the total amount of insurance. If each insurer covers the full value of the property, each insurer's share of the loss will be equal.

9. A. Under an appraisal and arbitration clause, if the insurer and the insured disagree about the amount of recovery (the value of a loss), they can demand separate appraisals. If they still cannot come to terms, the appraisals are assessed and resolved by a third party (called an umpire).

10. D. To obtain insurance, one must have a sufficient interest in what is insured. In this problem, the insured had a sufficient interest in the property when the policy was obtained. That is, when the policy was taken out, the insured would have sustained a monetary loss from the property's loss. To collect for a property loss, the insured must likewise have an insurable interest in the property *when the loss occurs*. Here, the insured sold the property *before* the loss.

Issue Spotters

1. Insurance companies use the principle of risk pooling. The risk that an event will occur requiring payments under an insurance contract is spread among a large number of people to make the premiums small compared with the coverage offered.

2. No. An incorrect statement as to the age of an insured is a misrepresentation. Under an incontestability clause, however, after a policy has been in force for a certain time (usually two or three years), the insurer cannot cancel the policy or avoid a claim on the basis of statements made in the application.

3. No. To obtain insurance, one must have a sufficiently substantial interest in whatever is to be insured. One has an insurable interest in property if one would suffer a pecuniary loss from its destruction. This interest must exist *when the loss occurs*. To obtain insurance on another's life, one must have a reasonable expectation of benefit from the continued life of the other. The benefit may be founded on a relationship, but "ex-spouse" alone is not such a relationship. An interest in someone's life must exist *when the policy is obtained*.

4. Those who are dissatisfied with the maximum liability limits offered by regular insurance coverage may want to buy separate coverage under an umbrella policy. Umbrella policies often cover personal liability in excess of an automobile or a homeowners' policy's liability limits.

5. Coverage under a general comprehensive liability policy or a specific product liability policy may include expenses involved in recalling and replacing a product that has proved to be defective. Of course, the coverage may involve a higher premium.

Chapter 50

True-False Questions

1. F. A will is revocable by the testator (or by operation of law) at any time during his or her life.

2. T

3. F. Intestacy statutes regulate how property is distributed when a person dies without a will. These statutes typically provide that after payment of the decedent's debts, the remaining property passes to the decedent's surviving wife, children, or other relatives. If there are no living relatives, the property passes to the state.

4. T

5. T

6. F. A will can appoint a guardian for minor children or incapacitated adults and can also appoint a personal representative to settle the affairs of the deceased.

7. F. The spouse—or child, if a child is born after a will is executed—is entitled to receive whatever portion of the testator's estate that he or she is permitted to take under the state's intestacy laws.

8. T

9. T

10. F. Unless the trust expressly provides otherwise, it will not terminate on the trustee's death. Normally, a trust does specify its own termination date. If its purpose is fulfilled before that date, a court may order termination. If no date is stated, a trust terminates when its purpose is fulfilled, or becomes impossible or illegal.

Fill-in Questions

executor; administrator

Multiple-Choice Questions

1. D. When assets are insufficient to pay in full all that a will provides, the gifts of general property, such as sums of money, are reduced proportionately. Thus, the gifts to the testator's daughters will be reduced. This is known as abatement.

2. B. Under intestacy statutes, each state regulates how property is distributed when a person dies without a will. These statutes attempt to carry out the likely intent of the decedent, setting out rules by which the deceased's natural heirs (such as children, siblings, parents, or other family members) inherit his or her property. This question and answer are based on a question that appeared in the CPA exam in 1997.

3. C. If an express declaration of revocation is missing from a second will, the wills are read together, and if a disposition in the second will is inconsistent with the prior will, the language of the second will controls.

4. A. A surviving spouse usually receives a share of the estate—one-half if there is also a surviving child and one-third if there are two or more children, and the remaining property passes to the children and the children of deceased children.

5. C. Under a testamentary trust, which is set up in a will, a designated, court-approved trustee would manage the property for the daughters' benefit.

6. B. A gift of personal property by will is a legacy (or a bequest)—its recipient is a legatee. A gift of real estate by will is a devise—its recipient is a devisee. Gifts can be specific, general, or residuary (paid out of the assets remaining in the estate after all taxes and bills have been paid, and specific and general gifts have been made..

7. C. On the death of a joint tenant, property held in joint tenancy passes to the surviving joint tenant or tenants without probate. In the other instances, probate is not avoided, and in the case of the trust, ongoing court supervision is required. (Note—property held in joint tenancy is not subject to a will or to probate, but it is subject to estate taxes.)

8. B. Among a trustee's duties is the responsibility to dispose of assets that do not represent prudent investments. A trustee must also distribute the risk of loss from investments by diversification. Thus, when a trustee is granted discretionary investment power, he or she must *not* invest *only* in conservative securities. (If *no* discretion is granted to a trustee, however, most states require conservative investments.)

9. A. A trust's ordinary receipts and expenses, such as rent, are chargeable to trust income (unless the trust provides otherwise). Extraordinary expenses and receipts, such as proceeds from the sale of property, are allocated to principal.

10. D. A durable power of attorney authorizes a person to act on behalf of an incompetent person.

Issue Spotters

1. No. The general test for testamentary capacity is that the testator comprehend and remember the "natural objects of his or her bounty" (usually family members and others), that the testator comprehend the kind and character of the property being distributed, and that the testator understand and formulate a plan for disposing of the property. In this problem, the testator passes the test.

2. The will may name an executor to administer the estate. If the will does not name an executor, or if there is no will, the court must appoint an administrator. Under the UPC, the term personal representative refers to either an executor or an administrator.

3. The specific gifts will pass as directed. When estate assets are insufficient to pay in full all that a will provides, the gifts of general property, such as the sums of money, are reduced proportionately. Thus, the gifts to Emily, Ed, and Pat will be reduced.

4. The estate will pass according to the state's intestacy laws. Intestacy laws set out how property is distributed when a person dies without a will. Their purpose is to carry out the likely intent of the decedent. The laws determine which of the deceased's natural heirs (including first the surviving spouse, second lineal descendants, third parents, and finally collateral heirs) inherit his or her property.

5. Chloe has several options. She could give health-care power of attorney to an adult child or some other person who understands her wishes and will see that they are carried out. Or, if her home state allows it, she could create a living will, in which she can designate that she does not want certain lifesaving procedures to be undertaken in her case.

Chapter 51

True-False Questions

1. T
2. T
3. F. Compliance with GAAP and GAAS may be required, but it is no guarantee of freedom from liability. Also, there may be a higher standard of conduct under a state statute or judicial decision.
4. F. The majority view is that accountants are subject to liability for negligence to foreseeable users. In some states, however, the view is to extend liability only to users whose use of, and reliance on, an accountant's statements or reports was reasonably foreseeable.
5. F. Under the securities acts, an accountant may be subject to criminal penalties for willful violations.
6. T
7. F. Tax preparers may be subject to penalties if they fail to furnish a taxpayer with a copy of the return.
8. T
9. T
10. F. No privity is not required. To recover, a plaintiff must prove five elements, including *scienter*, a fraudulent act or deception, reliance, materiality, and causation.

Fill-in Questions

will not; may; may

Multiple-Choice Questions

1. A. Working papers are the property of the accountant whose work they represent, but working papers cannot be released without the permission of the client for whom they were accumulated.

2. C. Generally, an auditor can be held liable to a third party for negligence. In most states, however, an accountant is liable only to users whom the accountant knew or should have known about. In some states, privity is required; in others, "near privity" is the requirement. This question and answer are based on a question that appeared in the CPA exam in 1997.
3. A. Under the Securities Act of 1933, an accountant may be liable for any false statement of material fact or omission of a material fact in a registration statement. The other elements indicated in the other choices are not requirements for liability under this statute.
4. B. Under the Securities Exchange Act of 1934, an accountant may be liable for any false statement of material fact or omission of a material fact made with the intent to defraud.
5. C. The client assigned the employee who was committing the wrongful act to assist the accountant, who failed to discover the wrongdoing because the employee covered it up. The client's loss was thus due to the client's own error. This generally reduces or eliminates any potential liability on the part of the accountant.
6. B. In most states, under a court order an accountant must disclose information about his or her client, including communications between the accountant and the client.
7. C. Besides the cost to obtain the accountant's contracted-for services elsewhere and the amount of any penalties for failing to meet deadlines, the client may recover other reasonable and foreseeable losses.
8. B. In this problem, the attorney failed to exercise reasonable care and professional judgment, thereby breaching the duty of care owed to clients. If a statute of limitations runs out, a client can no longer file a suit and loses a potential award of damages.
9. C. In a number of states, working papers remain the property of the accountant. These papers may act as crucial evidence in case the accountant needs to defend himself or herself against charges of negligence or fraud. At the same time, because the working papers reflect the client's financial

situation, the client does have the right of access to them.

10. C. Another possible defense that an accountant or other professional may assert against a charge of negligence, in a state that allows contributory negligence as a defense, is that the client was negligent.

Issue Spotters

1. Unintentionally misstating a material fact may lead to liability based on constructive fraud. A professional may be liable for constructive fraud whether or not he or she acted with fraudulent intent. Constructive fraud may exist, for instance, if a professional intentionally fails to perform a duty in reckless disregard of the consequences.

2. Yes. In these circumstances, when the accountant knows that the bank will use the statement, the bank is a foreseeable user. A foreseeable user is a third party within the class of parties to whom an accountant may be liable for negligence.

3. No. In the circumstances described in the problem, the accountant will not be held liable to a purchaser of the securities. To avoid liability, however, the accountant must prove that he is free of fraud and negligence.

4. Yes, in both cases. Aiding or assisting in the preparation of a false tax return and understating a client's tax liability are both crimes under the Internal Revenue Code. Liability does not depend on a person's professional or nonprofessional status.

5. An attorney is the most restricted professional. Without a client's permission, an attorney cannot disclose the client's communication. Disclosure is prohibited under federal law, state law, and the ethical tenets of the legal profession.

Chapter 52

True-False Questions

1. F. According to the principle of comity, however, a nation will give effect to the laws of another nation if those laws are consistent with the law and public policy of the accommodating nation.

2. F. The act of state doctrine tends to immunize foreign nations from the jurisdiction of U.S. courts—that is, foreign nations are often exempt from U.S. jurisdiction under this doctrine.

3. F. As with the act of state doctrine, the doctrine of sovereign immunity tends to immunize foreign nations from the jurisdiction of U.S. courts

4. F. The Foreign Sovereign Immunities Act sets forth the major exceptions to the immunity of foreign nations to U.S. jurisdiction.

5. T

6. T

7. F. Legal systems in all nations can be generally divided into *common* law and civil law systems.

8. T

9. F. Some contract law has been internationalized through the CISG, but parties contracting internationally can agree to apply other law to their contract disputes.

10. T

Fill-in Questions

An expropriation; A confiscation; an expropriation; a confiscation

Multiple-Choice Questions

1. A. Under certain conditions, the doctrine of sovereign immunity prohibits U.S. courts from exercising jurisdiction over foreign nations. Under the Foreign Sovereign Immunities Act, a foreign state is not immune when the action is based on a commercial activity carried on in the United States by the foreign state.

2. C. Under the act of state doctrine, the judicial branch of one country will not examine the validity of public acts committed by a recognized foreign government within its own territory. The awarding of a government contract under the circumstances described in the problem meets this criteria.

3. C. U.S. courts give effect to the judicial decrees of another country under the principle of comity, if those decrees are consistent with the laws and public policies of the United States.

4. B. The U.S. Congress cannot tax exports, but it may establish export quotas. In particular, under the Export

Administration Act of 1979, restrictions can be imposed on the export of technologically advanced products.

5.   D.   Unlike exports, imports can be taxed.   A tax on an import is a tariff (generally set as a percent of the value). Imports can also be subject to quotas, which limit how much can be imported.

6.   D.   Although increasingly influenced by statutory law, common law systems are based on judicial decisions and precedent.   Despite this general frame of reference, common law courts in different nations have developed different principles.

7.   D.   Civil law systems are based on statutory law. In a civil law system, courts are permitted to interpret the code and apply the rules, but they are not to develop their own body of law.

8.   B.   In many countries, however, judges are actively involved in trials, such as by questioning witnesses. In the United States, besides a less participatory role at trial, a federal judge is less likely to be influenced by politics, in part because he or she cannot be removed by impeachment except in extreme cases.

9.   B.   For example, mutual assent (offer and acceptance) is a common element for an enforceable contract.   But the details of its application varies in different countries.   In Germany, for instance, a written offer must be held open for a reasonable time, unless the offer states otherwise, and oral offers must be accepted immediately or they expire.   In Mexico, if a time for acceptance is not stated in an offer, the offer is deemed to be held open for three days (plus whatever time is necessary for the mails).

10.   B.   In some countries, employers cannot discriminate against employees or job applicants, to varying degrees. The prohibited bases for discrimination differ among nations. Discrimination is not prohibited in all countries, however.

Issue Spotters

1.   The World Trade Organization (WTO)—formerly known as the General Agreement on Tariffs and Trade (GATT)—is the principal instrument for regulating international trade.   The chief advantage of participating in the WTO is that each member country is granted most-favored-nation status by the other members.   This status is the most favorable treatment with regard to trade.

2.   If a government decides to confiscate property within its borders, and not to pay for it, there are few remedies available.   Some countries guarantee compensation to foreign investors in their constitutions, statutes, or treaties. Others (such as the United States) provide some insurance for their citizens' investments abroad.

3.   Under the principle of comity, a U.S court would defer and give effect to foreign laws and judicial decrees that are consistent with U.S. law and public policy.

4.   A U.S. firm—or any domestic firm—can license its formula, product, or process to a foreign concern to avoid its theft.   The foreign firm obtains the right to make and market the product according to the formula (or the right to use the process) and agrees to keep the necessary information secret and to pay royalties to the licensor.

5.   The practice described in this problem is known as dumping.   Seen as an unfair international trade practice, dumping is the sale of imported goods at "less than fair value."   Based on the price of those goods in the exporting country, an extra tariff can be imposed on the imports.   This is known as an antidumping duty.

Chapter 53

True-False Questions

1.   F.   Important considerations in selecting a lawyer include the attorney's knowledge as to what a client needs, the attorney's willingness to investigate the relevant law, the attorney's ability to communicate with the client, and the attorney's perception of what issues are of foremost concern.

2.   T

3.   F.   A business's name must be different from those of other businesses, to avoid, among other things, misleading consumers.   A corporation's name should also include the word *corporation, company,* or *incorporated.* To protect a corporate name as a trade name within a state in which the firm does business, the name should be filed with the appropriate state office.

4. T

5. F. Through what is termed a private offering, a limited amount of money can be raised from a limited number of investors without first registering the shares with the Securities and Exchange Commission. The requirements include a limit on how much money can be raised, how many investors are asked to buy, and how sophisticated (knowledgeable about investments) the investors are.

6. T

7. F. A contract *should* be in writing in case of a dispute, and in some cases, a contract *must* be in writing to be enforced. The requirement of a writing comes under the Statute of Frauds, which is part of the basic contract law principles that apply to be business.

8. T

9. F. An employer is bound to its promises of employment. Such promises may even be implied from statements in employment manuals. For this reason—and for the reason that other disputes may arise—all terms of employment should be put in writing, including grounds for termination.

10. T

Fill-in Questions

employees; employees; employees

Multiple-Choice Questions

1. D. The benefits of retaining an attorney at any point in a business relationship, but particularly during the start-up of a business, include the responses to this question. Besides providing *legal* advice, a lawyer may be able to direct a new business to potential investors, provide *business* advice, and act as a sounding board for business ideas. Another benefit is the flexibility of payment plans.

2. D. Sole proprietorships and general partnerships avoid the formalities of incorporating or of creating a limited partnership, but there is no business form that avoids all legal requirements. All businesses must meet such requirements as business name registration, occupational licensing, state tax regis-

tration, health and environmental permits, zoning and building codes, import/export regulations, and laws governing the workplace.

3. B. At the initial meeting of a corporation's board of directors, the directors adopt bylaws, appoint corporate officers, and take other necessary steps. Those steps do not include the "adoption" of articles of incorporation, which must be drafted and filed before a corporation exists, or the selection of a corporate name, which is also done before a corporation exists (of course, the name can be changed later).

4. C. Registering a trademark with the U.S. Patent and Trademark Office gives the mark national protection if it is in use or will be within six months. Of course, there are other requirements—the mark must be distinctive, for example, so as not to mislead customers, and must remain in use. The owner must protest others' use of the mark, and the registration must be renewed after five years (and every ten thereafter).

5. A. When an entrepreneur (or any business) wants to exchange an interest in an enterprise for capital and the interest consists of shares of stock, it is subject to securities laws. A limited amount of money can be raised from a limited number of investors without registering the shares with the Securities and Exchange Commission. Offering shares to the public, however, requires that the securities be registered. (There is a simplified registration form for small businesses, known as the Small Corporate Offering Registration, or SCOR.

6. C. The Fair Labor Standards Act (FSLA) requires the payment of the minimum wage, as well as time-and-a-half for overtime. The FLSA also requires employers to keep wage and hour records. (The FLSA applies to businesses with $500,000 or more in sales or those engaged in interstate commerce. In this problem, the firm is engaged in interstate commerce, although the dollar amount of the firm's sales is not stated.) State law, not the FLSA, may require a meal break. This question and answer are based on a question that was included in the November 1994 CPA exam.

Notes

Notes

Notes

Notes

Notes

Notes

Notes

Notes

Notes

Notes

Notes

Notes

Notes

Notes